W9-BLB-850

DEUTSCH - NA KLAR!

DEUTSCH

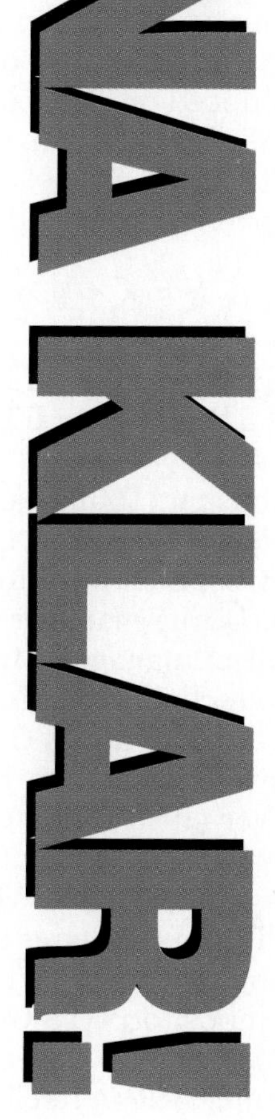

An Introductory German Course

Third Edition

Robert Di Donato
Miami University
Oxford, Ohio

Monica D. Clyde
St. Mary's College of California
Moraga, California

Jacqueline Vansant
University of Michigan, Dearborn

Contributing Writer
Lida Daves-Schneider

Boston Burr Ridge, IL Dubuque, IA Madison, WI New York San Francisco St. Louis
Bangkok Bogotá Caracas Lisbon London Madrid
Mexico City Milan New Delhi Seoul Singapore Sydney Taipei Toronto

McGraw-Hill College
A Division of The McGraw-Hill Companies

This is an  book.

Deutsch: Na klar!
An Introductory German Course

Copyright © 1999, 1995, 1991 by The McGraw-Hill Companies, Inc. All rights reserved. Printed in the United States of America. Except as permitted under the United States Copyright Act of 1976, no part of this publication may be reproduced or distributed in any form or by any means, or stored in a data base or retrieval system, without the prior written permission of the publisher.

This book is printed on acid-free paper.

1 2 3 4 5 6 7 8 9 0 DOR DOR 3 2 1 0 9 8

ISBN 0-07-013705-6 (Student's Edition)
ISBN 0-07-013706-4 (Instructor's Edition)

Publisher: Thalia Dorwick
Sponsoring editor: Leslie Hines
Developmental editor: Gregory Trauth, Paul H. Listen
Marketing manager: Cristene Burr
Project manager: Michelle Munn
Production supervisor: Pam Augspurger
Designer: Francis Owens
Cover designer: Vargas/Williams Design
Cover illustration: *(front cover)* Manuela Hofer/Tony Stone Images, R. Bossu/Sygma; *(back cover)* Foster and Partners, Architects and Designers
Art editor: Nicole Widmyer
Editorial assistant: Beatrice Wikander
Supplement coordinator: Louis Swaim, Florence Fong
Compositor: GTS Graphics
Typeface: New Aster
Printer: RR Donnelly & Sons Company

Because this page cannot legibly accommodate all the copyright notices, page A-88 constitutes an extension of the copyright page.

Library of Congress Cataloging-in-Publication Data

Di Donato, Robert.
Deutsch, na klar! : an introductory German course / Robert Di Donato, Monica D. Clyde, Jacqueline Vansant. — 3rd ed.
p. cm.
Includes index.
ISBN 0–07–013705–6 (student ed.). — ISBN 0–07–013706–4 (teacher ed.)
1. German language—Grammar. 2. German language—Textbooks for foreign speakers—English. I. Clyde, Monica. II. Vansant, Jacqueline, 1954- . III. Title.
PF3112.D48 1998
438.2'421—dc21 98–12953
CIP

http://www.mhhe.com

Contents

Einführung

Sprachtipps	Kulturtipps	Sprache im Kontext

Sprachtipps	Kulturtipps	Sprache im Kontext
Comparing People, Places, and Things: The Comparative of Adjectives and Adverbs 284 Talking About a Vacation 285 Saying How Long Something Lasts: Compound Adjectives with **-ständig, -tägig, -wöchig,** and **-monatig** 286	Deutsche Urlaubszeit 284 Wissenswertes über Deutschland 297	Zuschauen 306 Lesen 307 „Julia: Globetrotterin des Jahres" 309 Sprechen und Schreiben 310
	Stellenanzeigen 322 Der Lebenslauf 325 Das deutsche Schulsystem 326	Zuschauen 337 Lesen 338 „So kriegen Sie den Job" 340 Sprechen und Schreiben 341

Übergang: Gestern und heute 428

Preface

Deutsch: Na klar! offers a versatile, comprehensive, and colorful program for introductory German courses. The new Third Edition provides an innovative package designed to suit a wide variety of approaches, methodologies, and classrooms. Although designed especially for German instructors who want a text that responds to current pedagogical theory and technologies, ***Deutsch: Na klar!*** preserves many standard pedagogical features that instructors have come to trust. Original and standard features offered by ***Deutsch: Na klar!*** include the following.

- A rich array of authentic materials.
- Clear and succinct grammar explanations.
- Strategies that develop receptive skills (listening and reading) as well as productive skills (speaking and writing).
- Abundant communicative activities, together with many form-focused exercises.
- The promotion of meaningful acquisition of vocabulary and structures with considerable regard to accuracy.

One hallmark of ***Deutsch: Na klar!*** is its unique approach to using authentic materials to illustrate vocabulary in context, communicative functions of grammatical structures, and cultural points. Authentic materials motivate students and stimulate interest in the culture and language. Moreover, realia-based activities help students develop receptive skills. The Third Edition integrates both authentic video and computer-based realia into the program. A new video section **(Zuschauen)** appears in each chapter. The new Web feature **(Hier klicken!)** appears at various points throughout the text and offers additional cultural activities. A new CD-ROM helps students practice vocabulary, grammar, and revisit cultural themes in new contexts.

Vocabulary and grammar are presented in a functional framework so that students begin to associate forms with functions. Vocabulary is introduced in context through the use of visuals, dialogues, short narratives, or "built-in" activities to stimulate meaningful learning. Wherever useful, grammatical structures are contrasted with parallel structures in English. Vocabulary and grammar activities progress from controlled and form-focused to open-ended and interactive, and from receptive to productive.

A Listening Comprehension Program is tied to several activities in every chapter. Some listening comprehension activities are designed for global comprehension, whereas others have been designed to give students practice in noting specific details. In a similar fashion, students learn to skim for general information and scan for specific details when reading. In both listening and reading, students are encouraged to use background knowledge and context to aid comprehension.

Through its authentic materials, culture notes, readings, listening passages, and activities, ***Deutsch: Na klar!*** teaches skills that will help students communicate successfully in the German-speaking world.

Organization of the Text

Deutsch: Na klar! consists of a preliminary chapter **(Einführung)**, fourteen regular chapters, and a closing chapter **(Übergang)**. Each of the fourteen regular chapters is developed around a major theme and has the following organization.

Alles klar?
- WÖRTER IM KONTEXT
  Themen 1, 2, 3
- GRAMMATIK IM KONTEXT
- SPRACHE IM KONTEXT
  Zuschauen
  Lesen
  Sprechen und Schreiben

Cultural collages **(Zwischenspiele)**, containing visuals and activities, appear after **Kapitel 3, 6, 9,** and **12**, and give students a chance to review and consolidate what they have learned in previous chapters by applying it to cultural topics pertinent to the German-speaking countries.

A GUIDED TOUR THROUGH DEUTSCH: NA KLAR!

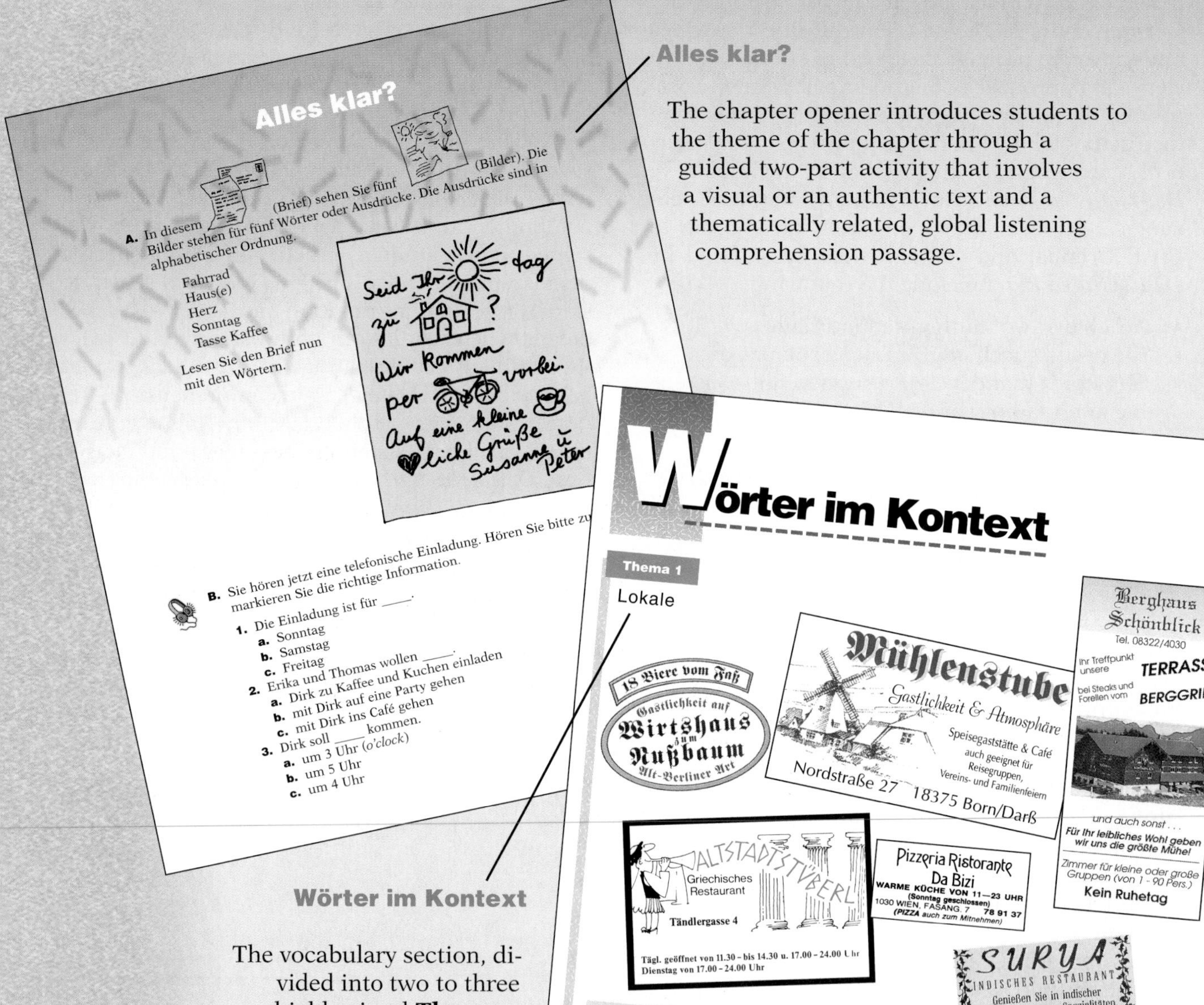

Alles klar?

A. In diesem (Brief) sehen Sie fünf (Bilder). Die Bilder stehen für fünf Wörter oder Ausdrücke. Die Ausdrücke sind in alphabetischer Ordnung.

Fahrrad
Haus(e)
Herz
Sonntag
Tasse Kaffee

Lesen Sie den Brief nun mit den Wörtern.

B. Sie hören jetzt eine telefonische Einladung. Hören Sie bitte zu markieren Sie die richtige Information.

1. Die Einladung ist für ____.
   a. Sonntag
   b. Samstag
   c. Freitag
2. Erika und Thomas wollen ____.
   a. Dirk zu Kaffee und Kuchen einladen
   b. mit Dirk auf eine Party gehen
   c. mit Dirk ins Café gehen
3. Dirk soll ____ kommen.
   a. um 3 Uhr (*o'clock*)
   b. um 5 Uhr
   c. um 4 Uhr

Wörter im Kontext

Thema 1

Lokale

Neue Wörter

- Bier vom Fass
- der Biergarten
- die Küche
- das Restaurant
- der Ruhetag
- geöffnet
- geschlossen
- täglich
- zum Mitnehmen

Alles klar?

The chapter opener introduces students to the theme of the chapter through a guided two-part activity that involves a visual or an authentic text and a thematically related, global listening comprehension passage.

Wörter im Kontext

The vocabulary section, divided into two to three highly visual **Themen,** presents various aspects of the chapter theme. Each **Thema** is followed by various activities **(Aktivitäten)** that encourage vocabulary learning in context.

Grammatik im Kontext

Grammar is presented in succinct explanations with abundant charts and examples and, whenever possible, via authentic materials. Some grammar explanations expand on points that are previewed in **Sprachtipps.**

Grammatik im Kontext

Nouns, Gender, and Definite Articles°

Nomen, Genus und bestimmte Artikel

Nouns in German can be easily recognized because they are capitalized.

German nouns are classified by grammatical gender as either masculine, feminine, or neuter. The definite articles **der, die,** and **das** (all meaning *the* in German) signal the gender of nouns.

MASCULINE: **der**	FEMININE: **die**	NEUTER: **das**
der Mann	die Frau	das Kind (*child*)
hnort	die Straße	das Haus
f	die Adresse	das Geld (*money*)

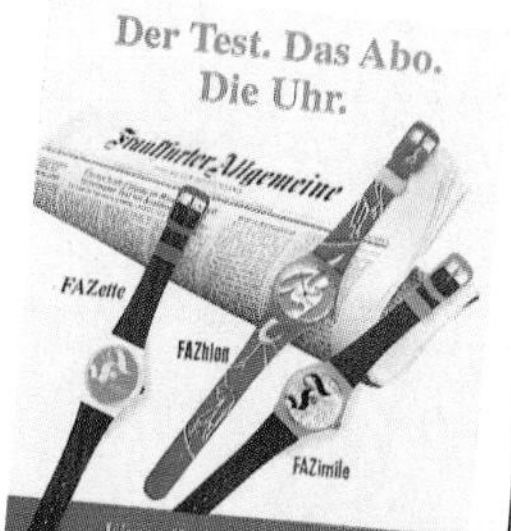

Sprache im Kontext

Zuschauen

Vorschau

Sehen Sie sich den Wetterbericht ohne Ton an, und beantworten Sie die folgenden Fragen.

1. Wie ist das Wetter in Deutschland?
2. Für welche Jahreszeit ist der Wetterbericht wohl? Sommer? Winter? Herbst? Frühling?
3. Woher weiß man, welche Jahreszeit es ist?
4. In welcher Region Deutschlands wird es am Nachmittag am wärmsten?
5. In welcher Region Deutschlands ist es am Nachmittag heiter?
6. In welcher Region Deutschlands wird es schneien?

Arbeit mit dem Videotext

A. Sehen Sie sich den Wetterbericht jetzt mit Ton an, und beantworten Sie die folgenden Fragen.

Sprache im Kontext

This culminating four-skills section is divided into three parts: **Zuschauen,** a new video section with pre- and post-viewing activities; **Lesen,** an authentic reading passage with pre- and post-reading activities; and **Sprechen und Schreiben,** interactive, task-oriented activities that provide open-ended oral and written practice on the chapter theme.

The *Deutsch: Na klar!* vocabulary system

Vocabulary displays may include one or more of the following: authentic materials, line art, descriptive texts, dialogues, and built-in activities. Using contextual guessing, students "discover" the meaning of the new vocabulary, which is highlighted in bold type or, for authentic materials, via **Neue Wörter** lists.

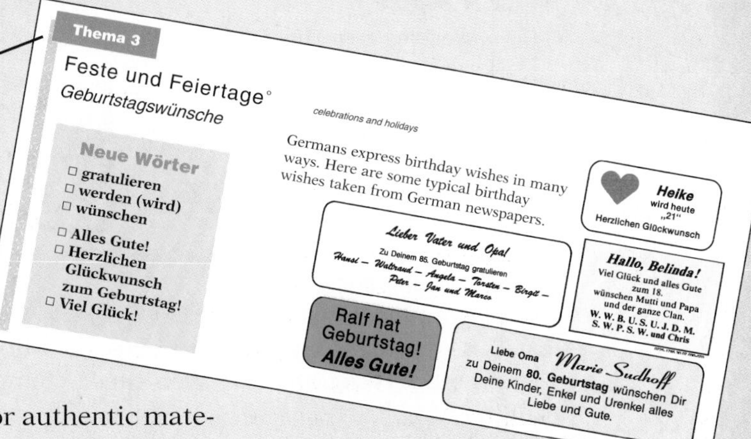

Thema 3

Feste und Feiertage°

Geburtstagswünsche

celebrations and holidays

Neue Wörter

- ☐ gratulieren
- ☐ werden (wird)
- ☐ wünschen
- ☐ Alles Gute!
- ☐ Herzlichen Glückwunsch zum Geburtstag!
- ☐ Viel Glück!

Germans express birthday wishes in many ways. Here are some typical birthday wishes taken from German newspapers.

Analyse

- Identify all personal pronouns in the ads and announcements and determine whether they are in the nominative or in the accusative case.
- Provide the English meaning of each phrase.

Wir sind da, wo Sie uns brauchen.

1. mein . . . *my dear*

Analyse

Before doing **Aktivitäten** or **Übungen,** students develop receptive skills by examining authentic texts for specific vocabulary or grammatical structures.

Übung 4 Uwes Zimmer

This is Uwe's dorm room. What pieces of furniture are there? What other objects do you see? What does Uwe need?

Das Zimmer hat _____.
Ich sehe auch noch _____.
Uwe braucht noch _____.

Aktivitäten und Übungen

A broad range of activities and exercises allows for structured communicative practice of vocabulary and grammatical structures. Whereas some activities and exercises are tied to the in-class tape and provide receptive vocabulary and grammar practice, others develop productive skills.

Icons

Icons identify listening comprehension, information gap, partner- pair or small-group activities, as well as activities requiring an extra sheet of paper.

Hier klicken!

Weiteres zum Thema Dresden finden Sie bei ***Deutsch: Na klar!*** im World-Wide-Web unter www.mhhe.com/german.

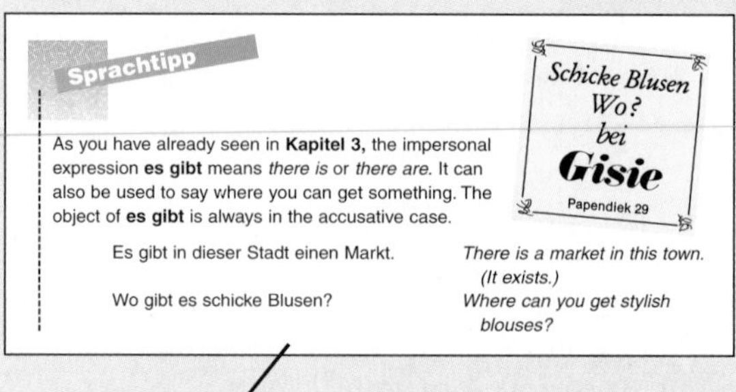
Sprachtipp

As you have already seen in **Kapitel 3,** the impersonal expression **es gibt** means *there is* or *there are.* It can also be used to say where you can get something. The object of **es gibt** is always in the accusative case.

Es gibt in dieser Stadt einen Markt.	*There is a market in this town. (It exists.)*
Wo gibt es schicke Blusen?	*Where can you get stylish blouses?*

Hier klicken!

At relevant locations throughout the text, this new feature directs students to the ***Deutsch: Na klar!*** Web site (http://www.mhhe.com/german), which contains additional cultural activities with links to on-line Internet realia.

Sprachtipp

Expressions and "grammar for communication" are provided to assist students in carrying out a given activity. Grammar points may be elaborated on in the same or a later chapter.

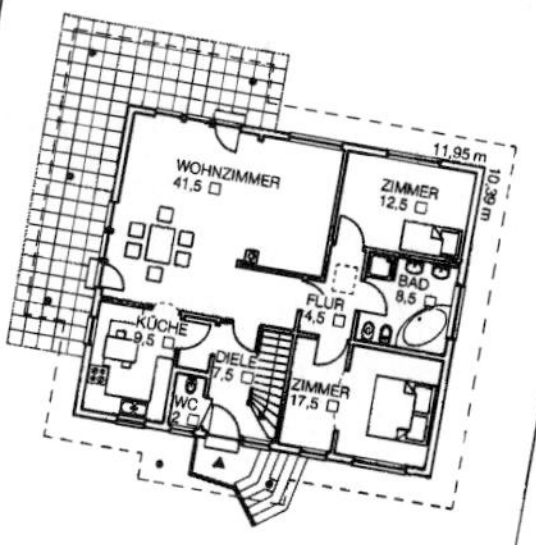

Kulturtipp

Enhanced with photos or other visuals, this feature expands on the cultural information presented in the **Themen,** activities and exercises, and readings.

Kulturtipp

In German-speaking countries, the kitchen and bathroom are not counted as "rooms," when describing the number of rooms in an apartment. Thus, a **Zweizimmerwohnung** has one bedroom and a living room, while a **Dreizimmerwohnung** has two bedrooms and a living room. An **Appartement** is a studio, or efficiency apartment.

WOHNZIMMER 41,5 □
ZIMMER 12,5 □
BAD 8,5 □
FLUR 4,5 □
KÜCHE 9,5 □
DIELE 7,5 □
WC
ZIMMER 17,5 □
11,95 m

Lesen

Zum Thema

A. Vorteile (*advantages*) **und Nachteile** (*disadvantages*) **des Stadtlebens.** Arbeiten Sie mit einem Partner / einer Partnerin. Machen Sie eine Liste von den Vorteilen und Nachteilen des Stadtlebens.

B. Zusammenwohnen. Interviewen Sie zwei Studenten/Studentinnen, und berichten Sie danach im Plenum.

1. Worüber ärgerst du dich (*do you get irritated*), wenn du zu Hause bist? Was stört (*disturbs*) dich?
2. Was machst du, wenn deine Mitbewohner/Mitbewohnerinnen/Nachbarn/Nachbarinnen zu laut sind?
   ... für ein friedliches (*peaceful*) Zusammenleben in

Zum Thema

This section contains activities that prepare students to read the text. Students use their background knowledge or brainstorm about the topic to predict what will happen in the reading passage.

Auf den ersten Blick

A. The following text on cafés in Vienna contains many cognates and other words that look similar in English and German. Scan the text and make a list of such words.

BEISPIEL: traditionell

B. Now scan the text for compound words. Say the words aloud and try to identify their components. Can you guess their meaning from the components?

BEISPIEL: das Kaffeehaus = Kaffee + Haus = *coffeehouse, café*

Auf den ersten Blick

In this activity, students skim the reading to get the gist or scan it for specific pieces of information in order to achieve a global understanding.

Zum Text

1. Wer erzählt die Geschichte, ein Mann oder eine Frau? Welchen Beweis (*evidence*) können Sie dafür bringen?
2. Suchen Sie nach Wörtern und Äußerungen, die weitere Informationen über die Hauptpersonen geben. Was können Sie aus diesen Details schließen (*conclude*)? Es steht z. B. im Text, dass der junge Mann „eine geschwollene Lippe" hat.
3. Wann erfahren die Leser, dass eine der Hauptpersonen ein großes Problem hat? Wie würden Sie in dieser Situation handeln (*act*)? Welche Rolle spielt die Fahrkarte?
4. Sie hören nur eine Seite des Telefongesprächs. Was könnte die Person am anderen Ende sagen?
5. Sie sind Detektiv / Detektivin. Lesen Sie die Geschichte ein zweites Mal. Glauben Sie dieser Frau? Wenn nicht, was für Beweise haben Sie, dass sie lügt?
6. Die Geschichte endet mit einem Brief. Was sagt uns der Brief über die Erzählerin? Ist Charlotte eventuell (*possibly*) dieselbe Person, mit der die Erzählerin am Telefon gesprochen hat? Welchen Beweis haben Sie dafür oder dagegen?

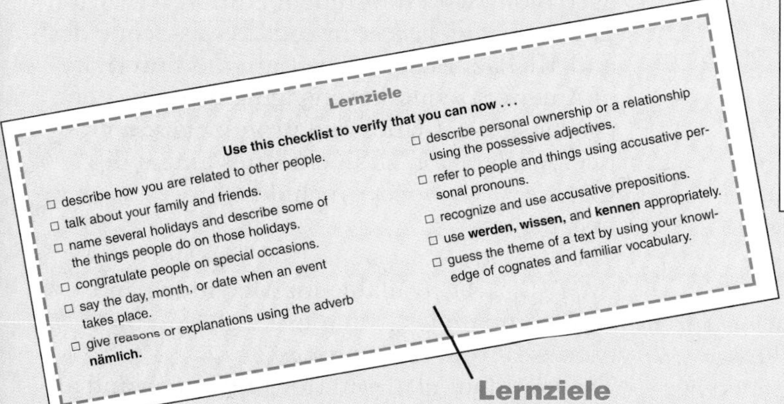

Lernziele

Use this checklist to verify that you can now . . .

- □ describe how you are related to other people.
- □ talk about your family and friends.
- □ name several holidays and describe some of the things people do on those holidays.
- □ congratulate people on special occasions.
- □ say the day, month, or date when an event takes place.
- □ give reasons or explanations using the adverb **nämlich.**
- □ describe personal ownership or a relationship using the possessive adjectives.
- □ refer to people and things using accusative personal pronouns.
- □ recognize and use accusative prepositions.
- □ use **werden, wissen,** and **kennen** appropriately.
- □ guess the theme of a text by using your knowledge of cognates and familiar vocabulary.

Zum Text

Here students read intensively, focusing on content, vocabulary, structures, and finally, implications and interpretation.

Lernziele

Appearing at the end of every chapter, **Lernziele** function as a study aid for students to verify that they have reached the learning goals of the chapter.

WHAT'S NEW IN THE THIRD EDITION?

Throughout the revision process, our goal has been to retain the features that reviewers have praised and that set ***Deutsch: Na klar!*** apart from other first-year German books. In response to instructors' feedback on the previous edition, we have reduced the number of readings in the **Lesen** section to one per chapter, reduced the overall quantity of active vocabulary, and endeavored to offer cultural perspectives from the three principal German-speaking countries.

Major features appear in the visual *Guided Tour Through* ***Deutsch: Na klar!***. Enhancements to the Third Edition include the following.

- The orthography reflects the German spelling reform. The vocabulary lists indicate all new spellings with an asterisk. Pre-reform spellings of these words can be found in Appendix E.
- We have updated many pieces of realia, choosing pieces for their cultural content and illustrative value.
- The directed conversation activities have been simplified and are now easier to follow.
- The presentation of adjective endings has been both streamlined and simplified.
- The **Sprache im Kontext** section now opens with a section entitled **Zuschauen** that utilizes authentic video material found on the *Video to accompany* ***Deutsch: Na klar!***.
- Four new readings appear: in **Kapitel 3** ("Vatertag"), **5** ("Einkaufsbummel im World Wide Web"), **8** ("Erholungstypologie"), and **10** ("Julia: Globetrotterin des Jahres").
- The thematic content of the final chapter, **Übergang,** has been revised to reflect recent developments in Germany.
- Austria and Switzerland are now highlighted in many of the contextualized communicative activities and culture topics.
- The sequencing of **Kapitel 13** and **Kapitel 14** has been reversed so that the more abstract concepts of **Die öffentliche Meinung** follow the chapter on **Medien und Technik.**
- A new Web feature, entitled **Hier klicken!**, allows students to explore interesting links by connecting to the ***Deutsch: Na klar!*** Web site at **http://www.mhhe.com/german**. This site, available in Spring 1999, also includes engaging Web-based activities.
- The *Listening Comprehension Program* (which accompanies the main text) and the *Audio Program* (which accompanies the *Laboratory Manual*) are now available on audiocassettes and audio CDs.
- A new interactive CD-ROM provides students with additional form-focused practice. It also contains cultural and video features and an on-line dictionary, among others.

SUPPLEMENTS

The following components of ***Deutsch: Na klar!*** Third Edition are designed to complement your instruction and to enhance your students' learning experience. Please contact your local McGraw-Hill sales representative for details concerning policies, prices, and availability of the supplementary materials, as some restrictions may apply. Available to students and instructors:

- The ***Student Text*** includes a grammar appendix and German-English/ English-German end vocabularies.
- The ***Workbook***, by Jeanine Briggs, now includes additional form-focused vocabulary and grammar exercises as well as abundant guided writing practice.
- The ***Listening Comprehension Program*** contains material tied to the listening activities in the main text. The audiotapes or CDs, provided free to instructors for in-class use, are packaged along with the student edition.
- The ***Laboratory Manual***, by Lida Daves-Schneider and Michael Büsges (The Catholic University of America), contains engaging listening comprehension activities and pronunciation practice. Available on audiocassettes and audio CD, the ***Audio Program*** includes ***Tapescript*** for instructors.
- The ***McGraw-Hill Electronic Language Tutor*** (MHELT 2.1), available for Macintosh and IBM compatibles, contains single-response exercises from the main text.
- The new dual-platform (for Macintosh and all IBM compatibles) ***CD-ROM to accompany Deutsch: Na klar!*** contains additional form-focused vocabulary and grammar practice,

along with other features designed to make learning German with ***Deutsch: Na klar!*** easier and more engaging.

- The new *Web site to accompany* ***Deutsch: Na klar!***, located at http://www.mhhe.com/german, contains multiple links to culturally informative Web sites in Germany, Austria, and Switzerland as well as accompanying Web-based activities.
- *A Practical Guide to Language Learning: A Fifteen-Week Program of Strategies for Success*, by H. Douglas Brown (San Francisco State University), is a brief introduction to the language-learning process for beginning language students. It is available for student purchase.

Available to instructors only:

- The *Annotated Instructor's Edition* of the main text includes marginal notes, answers, and a tapescript to the in-text listening comprehension activities.
- The combined *Instructor's Manual* and *Testing Program* provides theoretical background, practical guidance, and ideas for using ***Deutsch: Na klar!***. It also contains tests and exams written by Jennifer Redmann (Ripon College) and Pennylyn Dykstra-Pruim (Michigan State University).
- The *Tapescript* contains the material found on the *Audio Program*.
- The revised *Video to accompany* ***Deutsch: Na klar!*** contains 30 minutes of award-winning commercials and non-commercial footage. Additional video activities can be found in the *Instructor's Manual*.
- The *McGraw-Hill Video Library of Authentic Materials: A German TV Journal* includes authentic segments from German television (ZDF) and a *User's Guide*. Topics relate directly to the main themes in the text. The *User's Guide* contains a variety of activities that can be duplicated for students.
- *Color Slides* include a manual of commentary and questions.
- A *Training/Orientation Manual* by James F. Lee (Indiana University) offers practical advice for beginning language instructors and coordinators.

ACKNOWLEDGMENTS

The publisher would like to thank those instructors who participated in surveys and reviews that were indispensable in the development of ***Deutsch: Na klar!*** Third Edition. The appearance of their names does not necessarily constitute their endorsement of the text or its methodology.

Ruth Barney, Caldwell College
Elizabeth Bernhardt, Stanford University
Konstanze A. Brown, University of Texas-El Paso
Siegrun Bubser-Wildner, University of Northern Iowa
Jeanette R. Clausen, Indiana University, Purdue University-Fort Wayne
J. Harvey Cole, Grove City College
Lauren Levine Enzie, University of Massachusetts-Amherst
Vic Freund, Centralia College
Charlotte L. Goedsche, University of North Carolina-Asheville
Roman Graf, Middlebury College
Christina E. Guenther, Bowling Green State University
John E. Harrington, North Carolina Central University
Mark W. Himmelein, Mount Union College
Gisela Hoecherl-Alden, University of Pittsburgh
Laura M. Jackson, Washington University
Achim Kopp, Susquehanna University
Judy Laing, Anoka Ramsey Community College
Caralinda Lee, Saint Mary's College of California
Ruediger Lehnardt, Utoch Valley State College
Katherine Maloof, Shoreline Community College
Carl Niekerk, University of Illinois at Urbana-Champaign
John C. Pisoni, Eastern Michigan University
Richard M. Reiten, Virginia State University
Lana Rings, University of Texas-Arlington
Erika Streuer, Miracosta College
Friedrun Sullivan, Anne Arundel Community College
Rodney Swensoa, Pacific Lutheran University
Cynthia Trocchio, Kent State University
Eric W. Tschuy, Mount Hood Community College
William Van Grit, Pacific Union College

Leon G. Van Poelvoorde, Macomb Community College
Marilya Veteto-Conrad, Northern Arizona University
Ingebord C. Walther, Duke University
Hannelore Weber, University of Notre Dame
Larry D. Wells, Binghamton University
Erlis Wickersham, Rosemont College
Doris C. Wicks, University of Tulsa
Ingrid Widenhorn-Smith, Indiana University, Purdue University-Fort Wayne
Wilma Wierenga, Rochester Institute of Technology

We would also like to thank the many people who worked on this book behind the scenes: Our development editor, Paul Listen, who expertly commented on all aspects of the manuscript; Stephen Newton (University of California, Berkeley) and Bettina Pohle (University of California, Berkeley), for their contributions to the **Zuschauen** section; Claudia Becker (Loyola University of Chicago), who, as the native reader, edited the language for authenticity, style, and consistency; Daniela Dosch, who painstakingly compiled the German-English / English-German vocabularies; and David Sweet, who secured reprint permissions for the realia and texts.

The look of this Third Edition owes much to the creative talents of Juan Vargas, who designed the interior of the book as well as the cover. We would also like to acknowledge Wolfgang Horsch for his engaging line drawings, many of which are new in this edition.

The authors also wish to acknowledge the editing, production, and design teams at McGraw-Hill: Diane Renda, Sharla Volkersz, and Michelle Munn, whose editorial expertise helped transform manuscript into book and who saw the book through the complex manufacturing stages; Francis Owens and Nicole Widmyer, who oversaw the book and cover design and illustration programs; and Cristene Burr and the rest of the McGraw-Hill marketing and sales staff, who have so actively promoted this book over the past two editions. Finally, we would like to express our gratitude to the McGraw-Hill foreign language editorial staff: Gregory Trauth, who made significant contributions to the development of the program; Thalia Dorwick, whose belief in the project made it a reality, and whose constant support helped bring it to completion; and, finally, Eirik Børve, whose vision made this book happen in the first place.

EXCITING NEW TECHNOLOGIES FOR *DEUTSCH: NA KLAR!* THIRD EDITION

- An integrated *Video Program*: This 30-minute video contains award-winning commercial and non-commercial authentic footage taken from German television. Each chapter of the main text contains a new feature, entitled **Zuschauen,** which contains a video-based activity for listening and viewing practice. Additional commercial footage can be found on this video, many pieces of which have accompanying activities in the *Instructor's Manual*.
- New *Audio CDs:* The *Listening Comprehension Program*, packaged with the Student Edition, and the *Audio Program* that accompanies the *Laboratory Manual*, are now available on audio CD as well as traditional audiocassettes. The digital format of the audio CDs offers students a crisper, clearer listening experience. The CDs for the *Audio Program* are available for student purchase.
- An integrated *Web site* brings the German-speaking world directly to your students. The **Hier klicken!** feature in the main text directs students to the *Web site to accompany* ***Deutsch: Na klar!***, where they will find an abundance of links to culturally authentic Web sites, along with accompanying Web-based activities.
- A new *CD-ROM*: Available in Spring 1999, this dual platform CD-ROM (for Macintosh and IBM compatibles), offers students additional meaningful practice in German, with innovative and visually appealing form-focused vocabulary and grammar exercises, cultural activities (many with critical thinking questions), integrated video, a link to the *Web site to accompany* ***Deutsch: Na klar!***, and many other features.

Deutschland und Luxemburg
Einwohner
Deutschland (1998): 82,0 Mio
Luxemburg (1998): 418 000
Maßstab 2,0 cm = 100 km
DÄNEMARK
OSTSEE
NORDSEE
POLEN
DIE NIEDERLANDE
BELGIEN
TSCHECHIEN
FRANKREICH
DIE SCHWEIZ
ÖSTERREICH
LUXEMBURG
SCHLESWIG-HOLSTEIN
MECKLENBURG-VORPOMMERN
HAMBURG
BREMEN
NIEDERSACHSEN
BRANDENBURG
BERLIN
SACHSEN-ANHALT
NORDRHEIN-WESTFALEN
THÜRINGEN
SACHSEN
HESSEN
RHEINLAND-PFALZ
SAARLAND
BADEN-WÜRTTEMBERG
BAYERN
Kiel
Schwerin
Hamburg
Bremen
Hannover
Berlin
Potsdam
Magdeburg
Düsseldorf
Bonn
Erfurt
Dresden
Wiesbaden
Mainz
Saarbrücken
Stuttgart
München
Luxemburg
Flensburg
Helgoland
Hiddensee
Rügen
Stralsund
Rostock
Greifswald
Lübeck
Güstrow
Neubrandenburg
Cuxhaven
Bremerhaven
Emden
Leer
Oldenburg
Lüneburg
Prenzlau
Ostfriesische Inseln
LÜNEBURGER HEIDE
Elbe
Havel
Oder
Ems
Weser
Osnabrück
Wolfsburg
Brandenburg
Frankfurt
Eisenhüttenstadt
Bielefeld
Hameln
Braunschweig
Bad Harzburg
Münster
TEUTOBURGER WALD
Brocken
Wernigerode
Dessau
Wittenberg
Cottbus
HARZ
Dortmund
Paderborn
Essen
Göttingen
Eisleben
Halle
Ruhr
Kassel
Leipzig
Görlitz
Neiße
Krefeld
Saale
Meißen
Weimar
Köln
Rhein
Aachen
Eisenach
Jena
Gera
Chemnitz
Marburg
Zwickau
THÜRINGER WALD
Gießen
Fulda
Suhl
ERZGEBIRGE
Limburg
RHÖN
Koblenz
Mosel
Frankfurt
EIFEL
Main
Bayreuth
HUNSRÜCK
Würzburg
Trier
Worms
Nürnberg
Ludwigshafen
Mannheim
FRÄNKISCHE ALB
Kaiserslautern
Heidelberg
Rothenburg ob der Tauber
BÖHMER WALD
Regensburg
BAYERISCHER WALD
Karlsruhe
Straubing
Passau
Donau
Isar
SCHWÄBISCHE ALB
VOGESEN
SCHWARZWALD
Neckar
Tübingen
Ulm
Augsburg
Inn
Rottweil
Chiemsee
Freiburg
BAYERISCHE ALPEN
Friedrichshafen
Berchtesgaden
Garmisch-Partenkirchen
Konstanz
Lindau
Bodensee
Zugspitze

Reykjavik
ISLAND
NORWEGEN
SCHWEDEN
FINNLAND
Oslo
Helsinki
Tallinn
ESTLAND
Stockholm
LETTLAND
Riga
Schottland
Nordirland
NORDSEE
Kopenhagen
OSTSEE
LITAUEN
Wilna
DÄNEMARK
ATLANTISCHER OZEAN
IRLAND
Dublin
England
Minsk
DIE NIEDERLANDE
(ZU RUSSLAND)
WEISSRUSSL
Wales
Berlin
Warschau
GROSSBRITANNIEN
Den Haag
London
POLEN
Brüssel
DEUTSCHLAND
Kie
Der Ärmelkanal
BELGIEN
Prag
Luxemburg
TSCHECHIEN
Paris
LUXEMBURG
DIE SLOWAKEI
MOLDAW
LIECHTENSTEIN
Wien
Budapest
Kischi
Bern
ÖSTERREICH
UNGARN
FRANKREICH
DIE SCHWEIZ
Ljubljana
RUMÄNIEN
SLOWENIEN
Zagreb
Mailand
Venedig
Bukarest
Belgrad
KROATIEN
SERBIEN UND MONTENEGRO
BOSNIEN UND HERZEGOWINA
Sarajevo
BULGARIEN
ANDORRA
MONACO
ADRIATISCHES MEER
Skopje
Sofia
VATIKANSTADT
Korsika
Rom
Tirana
PORTUGAL
Madrid
ITALIEN
ALBANIEN
MAKEDONIEN
Lissabon
Sardinien
SPANIEN
TYRRHENISCHES MEER
Mallorca
GRIECHENLAND
IONISCHES MEER
Athen
Straße von Gibraltar
Sizilien
Algier
Tunis
MALTA
KRE
Rabat
TUNESIEN
MITTELMEER
MAROKKO
ALGERIEN
Tripolis
LIBYEN

Europa, Nordafrika und der Mittlere Osten

Maßstab 2,0 cm = 500 km

EU-LÄNDER (1998)	EINWOHNER (1998)
Belgien	10,2 Mio.
Dänemark	5,3 Mio.
Deutschland	82,0 Mio.
Finnland	5,1 Mio.
Frankreich	58,5 Mio.
Griechenland	10,5 Mio.
Großbritannien	58,9 Mio.
Irland	3,6 Mio.
Italien	57,5 Mio.
Luxemburg	0,4 Mio.
Niederlande	15,6 Mio.
Österreich	8,0 Mio.
Portugal	9,9 Mio.
Schweden	8,9 Mio.
Spanien	39,3 Mio.
Gesamtbevölkerungszahl	373,7 Mio.

Österreich

Einwohner (1998): 8 Mio

Maßstab 1,5 cm = 50 km

TSCHECHIEN
DEUTSCHLAND
UNGARN
SLOWENIEN
ITALIEN
DIE SCHWEIZ
OBERÖSTERREICH
NIEDERÖSTERREICH
WIEN
BURGENLAND
STEIERMARK
SALZBURG
KÄRNTEN
TIROL
VORARLBERG
SÜDTIROL
Osttirol (zu Tirol)
Gmünd
Horn
Krems
Donau
Linz
Sankt Pölten
Wien
Melk
Amstetten
Baden
Eisenstadt
Neusiedler See
Gmunden
Salzburg
Bad Ischl
Salzkammergut
Wiener Neustadt
Mariazell
Liezen
Hallstatt
Enns
Bruck an der Mur
Oberwart
Güssing
Graz
Mur
Sankt Georgen
Radstadt
Mauterndorf
Bischofshofen
Zell am See
Bruck
Salzach
Kufstein
Wörgl
Sankt Johann in Tirol
Kitzbühel
Inn
Innsbruck
Bodensee
Bregenz
Reutte
Feldkirch
Arlberg
Landeck
Vintschgau
Meran
Bozen
Lienz
Spittal an der Drau
Feldkirchen
Drau
Klagenfurt
Villach
Wörther See

Die Schweiz und Liechtenstein

Einwohner

Schweiz (1998): 7,1 Mio

Liechtenstein (1998): 30 000

Maßstab 2,0 cm = 50 km

NIDW = NIDWALDEN
OBW = OBWALDEN

DEUTSCHLAND
FRANKREICH
ÖSTERREICH
LIECHTENSTEIN
ITALIEN
SCHAFFHAUSEN
Schaffhausen
Rhein
Kreuzlingen
BASEL (STADT)
Basel
THURGAU
Frauenfeld
Thur
Winterthur
Bodensee
Liestal
BASEL (LAND)
Baden
ZÜRICH
Zürich
Zürichsee
St. Gallen
St. Margrethen
AUSSER-RHODEN
APPENZELL
Herisau
Appenzell
INNER-RHODEN
Delemont
JURA
AARGAU
Aarau
SOLOTHURN
Solothurn
Aare
Reuss
Biel
LUZERN
Luzern
Zug
ZUG
Einsiedeln
SANKT GALLEN
Vaduz
JURA
Neuchâtel
NEUENBURG
Neuenburger See
Bern
BERNER OBERLAND
Vierwaldstätter See
Stans
SCHWYZ
Schwyz
Glarus
GLARUS
Braunwald
Sarnen
NIDW.
UNTERWALDEN
OBW.
Altdorf
Engelberg
Chur
Klosters
Davos
Rhein
BERN
Thun
Brienz
Brienzer See
Thuner See
Interlaken
URI
Fribourg
Andermatt
Disentis
GRAUBÜNDEN
Inn
WAADT
FREIBURG
Jungfrau
Grindelwald
Jungfraujoch
A L P E N
St. Moritz
Lausanne
Genfer See
Montreux
Gstaad
Tessin
Rotten
Brig
TESSIN
Bellinzona
GENF
Genf
Sion
Rhône
WALLIS
Locarno
Zermatt
Matterhorn
Lugano
Langensee

Einführung

Begegnungen

Einführung. Note: The **Einführung** aims to familiarize students with the range of activities in the book. Students will use German in simple communicative situations which focus mainly on sharing basic personal information. They will also see authentic texts throughout the book. In some cases the texts and pictures illustrate a particular point, in others they provide the reading and listening material.

Dialogue 1. Suggestion: Use the vocabulary in the dialogue to introduce yourself to the class and to ask students what their names are. Move from student to student, saying: *Guten Tag! Mein Name ist ______. Herzlich willkommen! Und wie ist Ihr Name?* Shake hands with students during the interaction and point out that this is usual when greeting someone outside the classroom. Read the dialogue through, ensuring that you are clearly playing the roles of different people (i.e., draw figures on the board, use different voices, stand in different positions), have students practice dialogues in pairs.

Hallo! Guten Tag! Herzlich willkommen!*

TENNISTRAINER: **Guten Tag! Herzlich willkommen! Mein Name ist** Pohle, Norbert Pohle. **Und wie ist Ihr Name?**

SABINE: Sabine Zimmermann.

TENNISTRAINER: Und Sie? **Wie heißen Sie?**

ANTONIO: **Ich heiße** Antonio Coletti.

ARI: Und **ich bin** Ari Pappas.

Hallo! Suggestion: Ask students if they already know any German greetings. Write them on the board.

Im Tennisklub in Offenbach

PETER: **Grüß dich.** Ich heiße Peter Sedlmeier.

KATARINA: Mein Name ist Katarina Steinmetz.

PETER: **Woher kommst du?**

KATARINA: **Aus** Dresden. Und du?

PETER: Aus Rosenheim.

Dialogue 2. Suggestion: Set the scene of two students meeting each other. Explain that the language is more informal. Model the dialogue, and have students take roles to practice. Follow up with similar dialogues, where students introduce themselves to each other.

Auf einem Studentenball in Bonn

*New, active vocabulary is shown in bold print.

HERR GROTE: **Frau** Kühne, **das ist Herr** Michels aus Berlin. Frau Kühne kommt aus Potsdam.
HERR MICHELS: **Freut mich.**
FRAU KÜHNE: **Gleichfalls.**

Ein Treffen (*meeting*) in Berlin

Kulturtipp. Note: This recurring feature introduces cultural information that relates to the topics of activities or readings in the chapter. In the early chapters they are in English to ensure that the students understand them. In later chapters they are in German.

Kulturtipp

German speakers express formality and informality by the way they address each other. **Sie** (*You*) is used for strangers and acquaintances. Family members and friends address each other with **du** (*you*), as do children and, generally, students among each other. Otherwise, only very close, personal, and long-time friends (**Freunde**) will address each other with **du** and first names. Most people whom we refer to as friends in America or Canada would be considered acquaintances (**Bekannte**) by German speakers and would be addressed as **Herr (Pohle)** or **Frau (Kühne)** and **Sie.**

The word **Frau** is becoming the standard way of addressing all women, particularly in a professional setting and at universities. The word **Fräulein** is still used by some speakers, according to personal preference, or in some areas such as southern Germany, to address young females under the age of 18.

1. *user ID*
2. bei . . . *please bring along at every visit*

Aktivität 1 Wie ist der Name? 

Introduce yourself to several people in your class and ask them where they are from.

S1: Mein Name ist _____.
S2: Ich heiße _____.
S1: Woher kommst du?
S2: Aus _____. Und du?
S1: Aus _____.

Aktivität 1. Suggestion: Before beginning the activity, write the necessary phrases on the board, so that students can work without their books. Students should stand up and walk around the room and talk to as many different people as possible within the time limit you have set. Make sure that you monitor the students' interactions.

Aktivität 2 Darf ich vorstellen?° 

May I introduce?

Choose a partner from the people you have just met in **Aktivität 1** and introduce him/her to another classmate.

BEISPIEL: GINA: Paul, das ist Chris aus Lexington.
PAUL: Freut mich.
CHRIS: Gleichfalls.

Aktivität 2. Suggestion: Model the interaction by introducing a couple of students to each other. To make the activity as authentic as possible, remind students to introduce people to each other whom they think might not yet have met.

Wie schreibt man das?°

How is that spelled?

When you introduce yourself, or give information about yourself, you often have to spell out words for clarification. In contrast to English, German follows fairly predictable spelling and pronunciation rules. You will gradually learn these rules throughout the course. Native speakers of German are learning new spelling rules, too, since a spelling reform has been recently instituted. All but the most recent texts you might read will still have the old spelling, so you will see the old spelling as well as the new in your chapter vocabulary lists.

The German alphabet has the same twenty-six letters as the English alphabet, plus four other letters of its own. The four special German letters are written as follows. Note that the letter **ß** has no capital.

Ä ä a-Umlaut: **Bär, Käse**
Ö ö o-Umlaut: **böse, hören**
Ü ü u-Umlaut: **müde, Süden**
ß sz („ess tsett"): **süß, Straße** (*used after long vowels and diphthongs*)

Wie schreibt man das? Point Out: While we refer to letters with an umlaut as a-, o-, or u-umlaut, these are distinct letters and sounds in German. German speakers refer to them as *ä*, *ö*, and *ü*. Model these sounds carefully.

An example of spelling reform changes is displayed with the word *nass*, formerly spelled *naß*.

You'll find more about the German spelling reform in ***Deutsch: Na klar!*** on the World Wide Web at www.mhhe.com/german.

The following alphabet house (**Buchstabenhaus**) shows how German schoolchildren learn to write the letters of the alphabet. In addition to the individual letter, the **Buchstabenhaus** also practices such frequently used combinations as **ch, sch** and the diphthongs.

Wie schreibt man das? Suggestion: Have students discover which letters are different from the way they learned to write when they were in school.

Have students look at the children's handwriting in the letters to President Hoover in the **Übergang** chapter at the end of the book.

Aktivität 3. Suggestion: Have students repeat in groups of three letters. It is best to write out and point to letters on the board as they are spoken.

Follow-up: Pass out a set of cards with a letter of the alphabet on each card. Say the letters at random. As each is said, the student with the corresponding card holds it up.

Aktivität 3 Wir lernen das Abc.°

Repeat the letters of the German alphabet after your instructor.

° *We're learning the ABC's.*

Follow-up. Typewriter: Assign each student to play a letter of the alphabet; include the umlaut letters. Then call out a familiar word in German, e.g., *Name.* Students become a living typewriter. The student who is *N* stands up, says *N,* and remains standing. Then *A, M,* and *E* do the same. After the word is spelled, the whole class repeats the word.

Aktivität 4 B-E-R-L-I-N: So schreibt man das!°

Listen as your instructor spells some common German words. Write the words as you hear them.

° *That's how you spell it!*

Aktivität 4. Suggestion: Say, then spell, each word. Then say the word again. You may wish to repeat the spelling. This should be a playful and low-anxiety activity. 1. *Musik* 2. *Herz* 3. *Bücher* 4. *schön* 5. *groß*

Aktivität 5 Wie bitte?°

I beg your pardon?

Aktivität 5. Suggestion: Demonstrate this activity by referring to the accompanying drawing first. Students turn to each other to do the activity. Have them reverse roles.

Introduce yourself to another student and spell your name.

BEISPIEL: S1: Mein Name ist _____.
S2: Wie bitte?
S1: *(repeat your name; then spell it in German)*
S2: Ah, so!

Aktivität 6 Buchstabieren Sie!°

Spell!

Think of a common German word, name, product, or company name. Without saying the word, spell it in German (**auf Deutsch**) for a classmate, who writes it down and reads the word back to you.

Aktivität 6. Suggestion: Spot-check students' words by having several students spell the words they have written. Encourage them to come up with words other than the ones listed here.

Frankfurt
Autobahn
Delikatessen
Gesundheit
Einstein
Volkswagen
Kindergarten

Hallo!—Mach's gut!°

Take care!

Hallo! Mach's gut! Point Out: Greetings differ from region to region; e.g., Austrians who know each other will say *Servus. Hallo* and *Hi* are very popular among young people.

How do people in German-speaking countries greet one another and say good-bye? Look at the following expressions and illustrations, and see whether you can guess which ones are greetings and which are good-byes.

Suggestion: Model the greetings using various kinds of intonation and emotional states, e.g., enthusiastic and glad to see someone, sad, displeased to see someone. Have students repeat what you say and how you say it.

Hallo, Musikfreunde!

Realia. *Zur Trennung:* This is from a greeting card. *Grüß Gott!* is the first frame of a cartoon series by Eva Haue from her book *Vielleicht sind wir doch zu verschieden. Gute Nacht* is a segment of an ad for environmentally safe mattresses. The ad appeared in the *Harzburger Zeitung* of the small German town of Bad Harzburg, a well-known health resort in north central Germany.

German speakers use various formal and informal hellos and good-byes, depending on the situation and the person with whom they are speaking.

Saying hello:

FORMAL	CASUAL	USE
guten Morgen	Morgen	*until about 10:00* A.M.
guten Tag	Tag	*generally between 10:00* A.M. *and early evening*
guten Abend	'n Abend*	*from about 5:00* P.M. *on*
grüß Gott†	grüß Gott	*southern German and Austrian for* **guten Tag**
	grüß dich	*greeting among young people*
	hallo	*any time (emphatic)*
	grüezi	*standard Swiss greeting*

Saying good-bye and good night:

FORMAL	CASUAL	USE
auf Wiedersehen	Wiederseh'n	*any time*
	mach's gut	*among young people, friends, and family*
	tschüs	*among young people, family*
gute Nacht	Nacht	*only when someone is going to bed at night*

Note: The word **tschüs,** sometimes spelled **tschüss,** is related to the French word **adieu.**

*The **'n** before **Abend** is short for **guten.**

†*Lit.* Greetings in the name of God.

Aktivität 7 Was sagt man?°

What do you say?

What would people say in the following circumstances?

1. _____ your German instructor entering the the classroom
2. _____ two students saying good-bye
3. _____ a person from Vienna greeting an acquaintance
4. _____ two students meeting at a café
5. _____ a mother as she turns off the lights in her child's room at night
6. _____ a student leaving a professor's office
7. _____ family members greeting each other in the morning
8. _____ a hostess and her guests saying good-bye in the evening

a. Gute Nacht!
b. Grüß dich!
c. Tschüs!
d. Mach's gut!
e. Guten Tag!
f. (Auf) Wiedersehen!
g. (Guten) Morgen!
h. Grüß Gott!
i. Hallo!
j. Guten Abend!

Aktivität 7. Suggestion: Have students look over the possible responses before answering the questions. Remind them to think about the intonation and tone of voice that they would use in each situation.

Na, wie geht's?°

So, how's it going?

German has several ways of asking *How are you?*

(Na,) wie geht's?
Wie geht es dir? } *a family member or friend*

Wie geht es Ihnen, Herr Lindemann? } *an acquaintance*

You can respond in a number of different ways.

+++
ausgezeichnet

++
sehr gut

+
danke, gut

+/−
so lala

−
nicht besonders gut

−−
schlecht

Analyse

Realia. *Na, wie geht's* is taken from a brochure advertising a health product made from ginseng root.

Analyse. Note: This type of analytical exercise involving brief authentic materials will appear frequently throughout the book. Use one of the following approaches to these materials: 1. Have students do the exercise with a partner in class. 2. Do the exercise yourself with the whole group. Model the new vocabulary introduced here. 3. Have students prepare such exercises ahead of time.

Look at the two illustrations and answer the questions.

- What types of texts are shown?
- What expression do both illustrations have in common?
- What expression does the postcard writer use to express how she's doing?

Na, wie geht's?

Sicherlich bald besser![1]

Hallo!
Na wie geht's?
Hier ist's ewig Super. Bloß das Geld geht weg wie sonst was, in 1 Woche komme ich schon wieder heim!
Tschüß
Deine Birgit

An
Melissa Weber
Kolpingstr. 9
53121 Bonn

KARTEN 60 Jahre Werbung für Bayern

KUNSTVERLAG MAXIMILIAN LIEBL, 93051 Regensburg, Cranachweg 10

1250 Jahre Fulda Deutsche Bundespost 80

MÜNCHEN 11.-4.94-18 81477

1. Sicherlich . . . *Surely better soon!*

Cartoon. The cartoon in the **Kulturtipp** box appeared in the German TV magazine *Funk Uhr.*

Kulturtipp

German speakers will ask someone **Na, wie geht's?** or **Wie geht es Ihnen?** only if they already know the person well. When you meet a native speaker of German for the first time, do not ask this question. When you do ask a friend, be prepared for a detailed answer, particularly if the person is not feeling well. Unlike the English expression *How are you?,* **Wie geht's?** or **Wie geht es Ihnen?** is not used as a general greeting.

1. Ich . . . *I don't know! I feel so beat this morning!*

Realia. Note: Reading strategies will be the focus of the **Lesen** section of **Sprache im Kontext** in each chapter. However, students should be encouraged to practice techniques such as contextual guessing when working with the realia wherever it occurs. For this reason, only a minimal amount of glossing will be provided for most of the realia.

Aktivität 8 Wie geht's?

Listen as three pairs of people greet each other and conduct brief conversations. Indicate whether the statements below match what you hear.

	JA	NEIN
DIALOG 1		
a. The conversation takes place in the morning.	☐	☒
b. The greetings are informal.	☒	☐
c. The man and the woman are both doing fine.	☐	☒
DIALOG 2		
a. The two speakers must be from southern Germany or Austria.	☒	☐
b. The speakers are close friends.	☐	☒
c. Both of them are doing fine.	☒	☐
DIALOG 3		
a. The two speakers know each other well.	☒	☐
b. The man is feeling great.	☒	☐
c. They use a formal expression to say good-bye.	☐	☒

Aktivität 8. Note: Listening comprehension exercises will appear throughout the book. In the **Themen** section of each chapter, the focus will be on new vocabulary.

Pre-listening Suggestion: Give students time to read through the information in the activity before you play the tape. Encourage them to make a habit of this, as it provides clues about what they will hear.

Post-listening Suggestion: After you have gone over the correct answers, focus on the words and expressions in each dialogue that provide the correct answers. Then play each dialogue again, so that the students can listen to them fully aware of what they are hearing.

Aktivität 9 Und wie geht es dir?

Start a conversation chain by asking one classmate how he/she is.

BEISPIEL: S1: Na, Peter, wie geht's?
S2: So lala. Wie geht es dir, Kathy?
S3: Ausgezeichnet! Und wie geht's dir, . . . ?

Aktivität 9. Note: Make sure that questions are directed to those across the room as well as to those next to the questioner.

So zählt man auf Deutsch.°

°This is how you count in German.

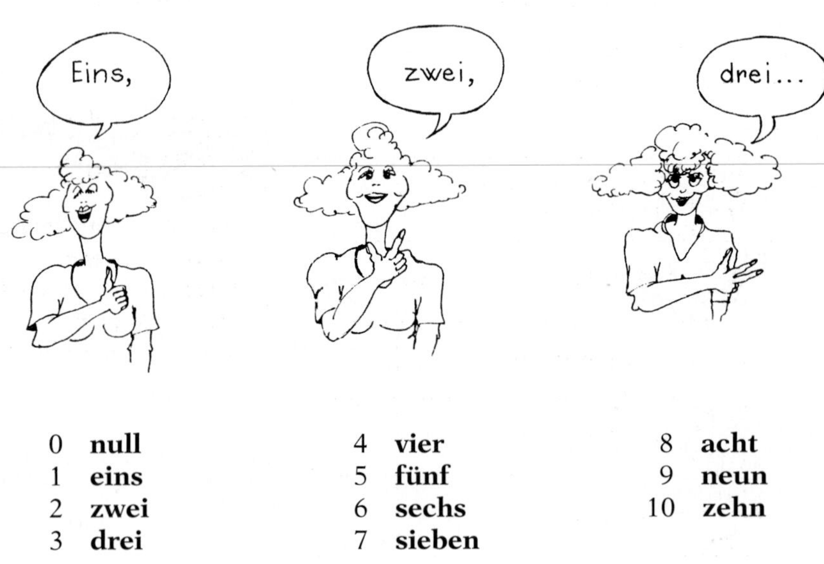

0 **null**
1 **eins**
2 **zwei**
3 **drei**
4 **vier**
5 **fünf**
6 **sechs**
7 **sieben**
8 **acht**
9 **neun**
10 **zehn**

So zählt man auf Deutsch. Suggestion: Model the numbers from 0 to 20 and have students repeat them. Introduce new numbers two or three at a time, and begin from 1 each time to reinforce the lower numbers. Use your fingers to count from 0 to 10, but make sure you use your fingers as a German speaker would (as illustrated in the drawing). For numbers over 10 and for review, write numbers on the board or hold up flash cards as you say the numbers.

Follow-up: Pass out flash cards with numbers on them. Say numbers at random; the student with the number holds up the card.

Point Out: You might want to mention to students the two different German terms for "number." *Zahl* refers to numbers used by themselves, whereas *Nummer* refers to numbers in context. For example: *Sieben und elf sind Zahlen,* but *Heikes Nummer ist 0651-0001.*

11	**elf**	20	**zwanzig**	100	**(ein)hundert**
12	**zwölf**	30	**dreißig**	200	**zweihundert**
13	**dreizehn**	40	**vierzig**	300	**dreihundert**
14	**vierzehn**	50	**fünfzig**	1 000	**(ein)tausend**
15	**fünfzehn**	60	**sechzig**	2 000	**zweitausend**
16	**sechzehn**	70	**siebzig**	3 000	**dreitausend**
17	**siebzehn**	80	**achtzig**		
18	**achtzehn**	90	**neunzig**		
19	**neunzehn**				

Follow-up: Play bingo. Students draw up own cards of nine numbers between 0 and 20, or 0 and 30, and cross off numbers as you call them. The first person to cross out all numbers calls "bingo" and must then call out the crossed-out numbers so you can verify them. Have a small prize for the first three or four winners.

The numbers 21 through 99 are formed by combining the numbers 1–9 with 20–90.

21	einundzwanzig	24	vierundzwanzig	27	siebenundzwanzig
22	zweiundzwanzig	25	fünfundzwanzig	28	achtundzwanzig
23	dreiundzwanzig	26	sechsundzwanzig	29	neunundzwanzig

The numbers *one* and *seven* are written as follows:

1 7

German uses a period or a space where English uses a comma.

1.000 7 000

In German-speaking countries, telephone numbers generally have a varying number of digits and may be spoken as follows:

24 36 71 zwei, vier – drei, sechs – sieben, eins
or vierundzwanzig – sechsunddreißig – einundsiebzig

Point Out: In spoken German, especially on the phone, people often say **zwo** for **zwei** to avoid confusion with **drei.**

Suggestion: Remember that it takes a long time to become proficient with numbers. Students should use single digits to practice telephone numbers and zip codes. Double-digit numbers should be considered passive vocabulary and only used if necessary for house numbers. Students will have an opportunity to begin using double-digit numbers actively in **Kapitel 1.**

1. Telefonische . . . *Submit your ad by phone*

Aktivität 10 Wichtige Telefonnummern°

important phone numbers

Imagine that you are calling for some important telephone numbers. Write the phone numbers you hear in the appropriate space.

Wie sind die Telefonnummern?

Telefon-Ansagen	☎		
Fernsehprogramme	1 15 03	Theater-und Konzert-veranstaltungen	1 15 17
Kinoprogramme	1 15 11	Verbraucher- und Einkauftipps	1 16 06
Küchenrezepte	11 67	Wettervorhersage	38 53
Sportnachrichten	11 63	Zahlenlotto	11 62
		Zeitansage	1 19 94

You'll find more about telephone numbers in ***Deutsch: Na klar!*** on the World Wide Web at www.mhhe.com/german.

Aktivität 10. Suggestion: For this activity, you may wish to play the tape or simply read the script aloud. It is important to read it at normal speed. Students may ask you to repeat by saying *Wie bitte?*

Analyse

Look over the three examples of addresses (**Adressen**) from German-speaking countries. How do they differ from the way addresses are written in your country?

- What is the name of the street (**Straße**)? the town (**Stadt**)?
- Where is the house number (**Hausnummer**) placed? Where is the zip code (**Postleitzahl**) placed?
- Can you guess what the **A** before **9020 Klagenfurt** and the **CH** before **8050 Zürich-Oerlikon** represent?

UNIVERSITÄT FÜR BILDUNGSWISSENSCHAFTEN KLAGENFURT
Universitätsstraße 65–67
A-9020 Klagenfurt

Filiale Oerlikon
CH-8050 Zürich-Oerlikon, Ohmstrasse 14
Telefon 01-312 10 14
Telex 823 221
Telegramm: Travellerag Zürich

Deutsche Welle
50588 Köln
Deutschland
DW

Point Out: **CH** stands for Confoederatio Helvetica (= Switzerland) and **A** for Austria.

Kulturtipp

As in the United States, zip codes in Germany consist of five digits. Zip codes in Austria, Liechtenstein, and Switzerland have four digits. When mail is sent between countries in Europe, international abbreviations are used for the country names. Can you match the following country names with the correct abbreviations?

Belgien (B)
Dänemark (DK)
Deutschland (D)
Frankreich (F)
Griechenland (GR)
Großbritannien (GB)
Irland (IRL)
Italien (I)
Liechtenstein (FL)
Luxemburg (L)
die Niederlande (NL)
Österreich (A)
Polen (PL)
Portugal (P)
Rumänien (RO)
Russland (RUS)
die Schweiz (CH)
die Slowakei (SK)
Spanien (E)
Tschechien (CZ)
Ungarn (H)

RO	DK	GR
F	CZ	A
IRL	D	PL
SK	B	GB
CH	I	L
E	NL	RUS
FL	H	P

Aktivität 11 Adressen

Identify the addresses in the following illustrations and read them aloud.

Aktivität 11. Suggestion: Read each of the addresses to the students. Have them identify each one in the illustrations.

Mathias Fritz
Walserstraße 29 · D-87569 Mittelberg
Telefon 0 83 29/67 50
oder auf der Piste
06 63/5 03 15
SNOWBOARDSCHULE AHORN

Wir machen alles......
wenn es um Urlaub geht!
SunMade Touristik i.Gr.
Hamburger Str. 132
22083 Hamburg
Tel.: 040-29 19 56
Fax.: 299 16 80

Hier klicken!

You'll find more about the postal and country codes in ***Deutsch: Na klar!*** on the World Wide Web at www.mhhe.com/german.

Realia. The information on *Snowboardschule Ahorn* appeared in one of their brochures. The ad for *SunMade Touristik* appeared in the newspaper *Szene Hamburg.*

Aktivität 12 Die Adresse und Telefonnummer, bitte! 

You will hear three brief requests for addresses and telephone numbers. As you listen, mark the correct street numbers and jot down the zip codes and telephone numbers.

1. Professor Hausers Adresse ist . . .

   Gartenstraße 9 12 19

   82067 Ebenhausen/Isartal

   Die Telefonnummer ist 41 34 76.

2. Die Adresse von Margas Fitnessstudio ist . . .

   Bautzner Straße 5 15 14

   01093 Dresden

   Die Telefonnummer ist 20 86 73.

3. Die Adresse von Autohaus Becker ist . . .

   Landstuhler Straße 54 44 45

   66482 Zweibrücken-Ixheim

   Die Telefonnummer ist 1 88 42.

Aktivität 13 Hin und her°: Wie ist die Postleitzahl? 

This is the first of many activities in which you will exchange information with a partner. Here, one of you uses the chart below; the other turns to the corresponding chart in Appendix A. Take turns asking each other for the zip codes missing from your charts.

BEISPIEL: S1: Wie ist die Postleitzahl von Eisenach?
S2: Die Postleitzahl von Eisenach ist D-99817. Wie ist die Postleitzahl von Bitburg?
S1: Die Postleitzahl von Bitburg ist D-54634.

D-99817	Eisenach
D-54634	Bitburg
A-5020	Salzburg
CH-3800	Interlaken
D-94315	Straubing
D-06217	Merseburg
D-21614	Buxtehude
FL-9490	Vaduz

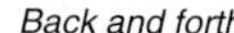

Back and forth

Aktivität 13. This is the first of many information-gap activities designed to create a genuine exchange of information in a controlled context. One student uses the chart here, the other must turn to Appendix A. Each student has only half the information in the chart and must ask his/her partner questions to fill in the missing pieces. Model questions and answers are given. Since this is the first information-gap activity, be sure your students understand how the activity works by demonstrating the model with one student and then having the class observe two paired students performing an exchange.

Note: Point out to students that the international country abbreviations are treated as part of the zip code when mail is sent between countries.

Aktivität 14. Sugggestion: Review with students the information sought.

Note: Some students may be reluctant to share personal information with their classmates. Be sure to let them know that they may make up fictional personal information about themselves.

Aktivität 14 Ein Interview 

A. Interview a partner using the questions provided in the **Sprachtipp.** Note the information your partner gives you.

Name	
Wohnort (*place of residence*)	
Straße und Hausnummer	
Postleitzahl	
Telefonnummer	

To get personal information from someone you would address with **du,** ask:

Wie heißt du?
Wo wohnst du?
Wie ist deine Adresse?
Wie ist die Postleitzahl?
Wie ist deine Telefonnummer?

B. Now tell the class about the person you interviewed.

BEISPIEL: Das ist Kerstin aus Superior. Die Adresse ist 678 Maple Street. Die Postleitzahl ist 54880. Die Telefonnummer ist 392-4797.

Realia. This ad for the mail order company *Quelle* was taken from the 1993 *Postleitzahlenbuch.*

1. Ich . . . *I don't know*
2. ne = eine

Nützliche Ausdrücke im Sprachkurs°

useful expressions for the language course

Nützliche Ausdrücke im Sprachkurs. Suggestion: Go over the teacher's expressions using mime and demonstration where possible. Have students respond to your commands, so that it is clear they understand them. Make sure that students can say the students' expressions properly.

IHR DEUTSCH**LEHRER** / IHRE DEUTSCH**LEHRERIN** SAGT

Bitte, hören Sie zu!	*Please listen.*
Bitte, nehmen Sie ein Blatt Papier!	*Please take out a sheet of paper.*
Bitte, machen Sie die Bücher auf Seite _____ auf!	*Please open your books to page _____.*
Bitte, lesen Sie!	*Please read.*
Bitte, machen Sie die Bücher zu!	*Please close your books.*
Bitte, gehen Sie an die Tafel!	*Please go to the board.*
Bitte, setzen Sie sich!	*Please be seated.*
Haben Sie Fragen?	*Do you have any questions?*
Ist alles klar?	*Is everything clear?*
Noch einmal, bitte.	*One more, please; could you say that again, please?*
Wiederholen Sie, bitte!	*Please repeat.*

SIE SAGEN

Langsamer, bitte!	*Slower, please.*
Wie, bitte?	*Pardon? What did you say?*
Wie schreibt man _____?	*How do you write _____?*
Ich habe eine Frage.	*I have a question.*
Wie sagt man _____ auf Deutsch?	*How do you say _____ in German?*
Was bedeutet _____?	*What does _____ mean?*
Das weiß ich nicht.	*I don't know.*
Ich verstehe das nicht.	*I don't understand.*
Ja.	*Yes.*
Nein.	*No.*

Realia. The picture of Hamburg's *Gelbe Seiten* is taken from the newspaper *Szene Hamburg.*

Sie können schon etwas Deutsch!°

You already know some German!

Even if you have never studied German before, you will soon find that you know more German than you think. For example, look at the following ad taken from a German phone book's yellow pages (**gelbe Seiten**).

Analyse

- What is this ad for?
- Which words are *identical* in English?
- Which words in the ad look *similar* to words you use in English?

Words like **Motel, Hotel, Restaurant,** and **Sauna** are borrowed from other languages: **Motel** from American English, **Restaurant** and **Hotel** from French, and **Sauna** from Finnish. These words are used internationally.

Some words in the ad look similar to English words. Look more closely at one of those words: **Biergarten.** You may already have seen the word **Biergarten** in an English-language text. This word has been borrowed from German along with some other German words commonly used in English, such as **Kindergarten** or **Delikatessen.** You recognize the words *beer* and *garden* in **Biergarten. Bier** and *beer,* **Garten** and *garden* look similar, are pronounced similarly, and have the same meaning in both languages. These words are cognates. Cognates are related words; that is, they are descended from the same word or form. Since English and German are both Germanic languages, they share many cognates. This common linguistic ancestry will help you a great deal in understanding German. Recognizing cognates is an important skill stressed throughout this textbook.

Cognates like **Bier** and **Garten** are easy to recognize. Understanding other words takes more imaginative guessing: for instance, what do you think **Hallenbad** means? Other words in the ad probably look completely unfamiliar; they are not cognates or words that are used internationally. The word **Ruf,** for instance, is not easily recognizable when the word is by itself. The meaning can be guessed from the context, however, and you already know a synonym for this word. What is it?

Now that you have analyzed in some detail what kind of place "Zum Dorfkrug" is, summarize what you have found out. Add any additional information you were able to extract from the ad by guessing.

Analyse. Note: It may be necessary to "walk students through" a piece of realia to accustom them to dealing with authentic texts. **Point Out:** Cognates are clues to meaning in most texts. Also encourage students to draw on their background knowledge when approaching these texts.

Realia. This ad was taken from Göttingen's yellow pages.

Aktivität 15 Informationen finden

An important first step in reading is identifying the type of text you have in front of you. Look for verbal as well as visual clues. Look at the excerpts on the next page. Write the letter of each excerpt in front of the appropriate category in the list below (some categories will remain empty).

Aktivität 15. Suggestion: This activity familiarizes students with various types of texts in German. Students can work in pairs. After students complete the exercise, ask them how they were able to recognize the various categories.

1. __e__ an ad for a movie
2. _____ a list of the week's bestsellers
3. __b__ a concert announcement
4. __d__ a headline
5. _____ a short news item about crime in Germany
6. __a__ an ad for a restaurant
7. __c__ a section from a TV guide

(a)

(b)

(c) (d) (e)

Aktivitäten 15 und 16. Throughout the course, students will be confronted with texts which are above their productive ability. If students are tempted to look up words they don't recognize, encourage them to refrain. Emphasize that it is more productive to work from context and cognates as much as possible at first. When adult readers can identify the type of text they are looking at, their background knowledge of the world and the subject will help them to decipher meaning, particularly when cognates are present. The object of using authentic readings is to aid the students in reading real texts written for German speakers rather than simplified ones devised specifically for foreign language learners. It is important that students develop productive reading strategies in German, strategies which they probably use automatically in English, but which may not come naturally in dealing with a foreign language text.

Realia. The cafe/restaurant ad (a) is from *Charakter: Göttingens City-Magazin.* Ads (b) and (e) appeared in the *Berliner Morgenpost.* The TV guide excerpt (c) is from *TV-Media,* from Austria. The headline (d) is from the *Berliner Zeitung.*

Aktivität 16 Freizeitspaß

Working with a partner, find out as much information as possible about the ad **Freizeitspaß.** You don't have to understand every word or sentence to get the gist.

1. What is advertised here?
2. Which words do you recognize immediately?
3. What two cognates do you see in the word **Tanzschule**?
4. In which city is the **Tanzschule** located?
5. Which words look familiar in the last sentence of the ad?
6. What could this sentence mean?

Aktivität 17 Sie verstehen schon etwas Deutsch!°

You already understand some German!

You have learned that you can use visual and verbal cues to understand a considerable amount of written and spoken German. Now you will hear some short radio announcements and news headlines. Listen for cognates and other verbal clues, as you try to understand the gist of what is being said. As you hear each item, write its number in front of the topic(s) to which it corresponds. Not all the topics below will be mentioned.

Aktivität 17. Suggestion: Play the tape twice, once for students to complete the exercise and the second time to check responses.

1	Automobil	____	Musik	3	Sport
____	Bank	____	Politik	____	Tanz
____	Film	4	Restaurant	2	Theater
5	Kinder				

Wo spricht man Deutsch?°

Where is German spoken?

Naturally, German is spoken in Germany, but it is also spoken in many other countries. Which of the following countries have relatively large German-speaking populations?

- □ Polen
- □ Österreich
- □ Tschechien
- □ die Schweiz
- □ Ungarn
- □ Argentinien
- □ Bosnien
- □ Liechtenstein
- □ Luxemburg
- □ Brasilien
- □ Rumänien
- □ Italien

German is the official language of Germany (**Deutschland**), Austria (**Österreich**), and Liechtenstein. It is one of four official languages of Switzerland (**die Schweiz**) and one of three official languages of Luxemburg and Belgium. German is also spoken in regions of France, Denmark, Italy, Czechia, Poland, Rumania, Bosnia and Herzegovina, Hungary, Latvia, Lithuania, Estonia, Russia, and the Ukraine. Altogether, between 120 and 140 million Europeans speak German as their first language—more than the number of people in Europe who speak English as their first language.

German is also spoken by many people as a first language in other countries such as Brazil, Argentina, Canada, and the United States (Pennsylvania Dutch). In Namibia, German is spoken by a sizable minority. It is estimated that outside of Europe an additional 20 million people speak German as their first language.

Note: Namibia was a former German colony.

Maps: For more detail of Europe and the principal German-speaking countries, refer students to the maps in the front of this book.

According to U.S. Department of Commerce figures, over 50 million U.S. citizens claim German descent.

At present, approximately 20 million people worldwide are learning German in formal courses. Two-thirds of these people live in eastern Europe.

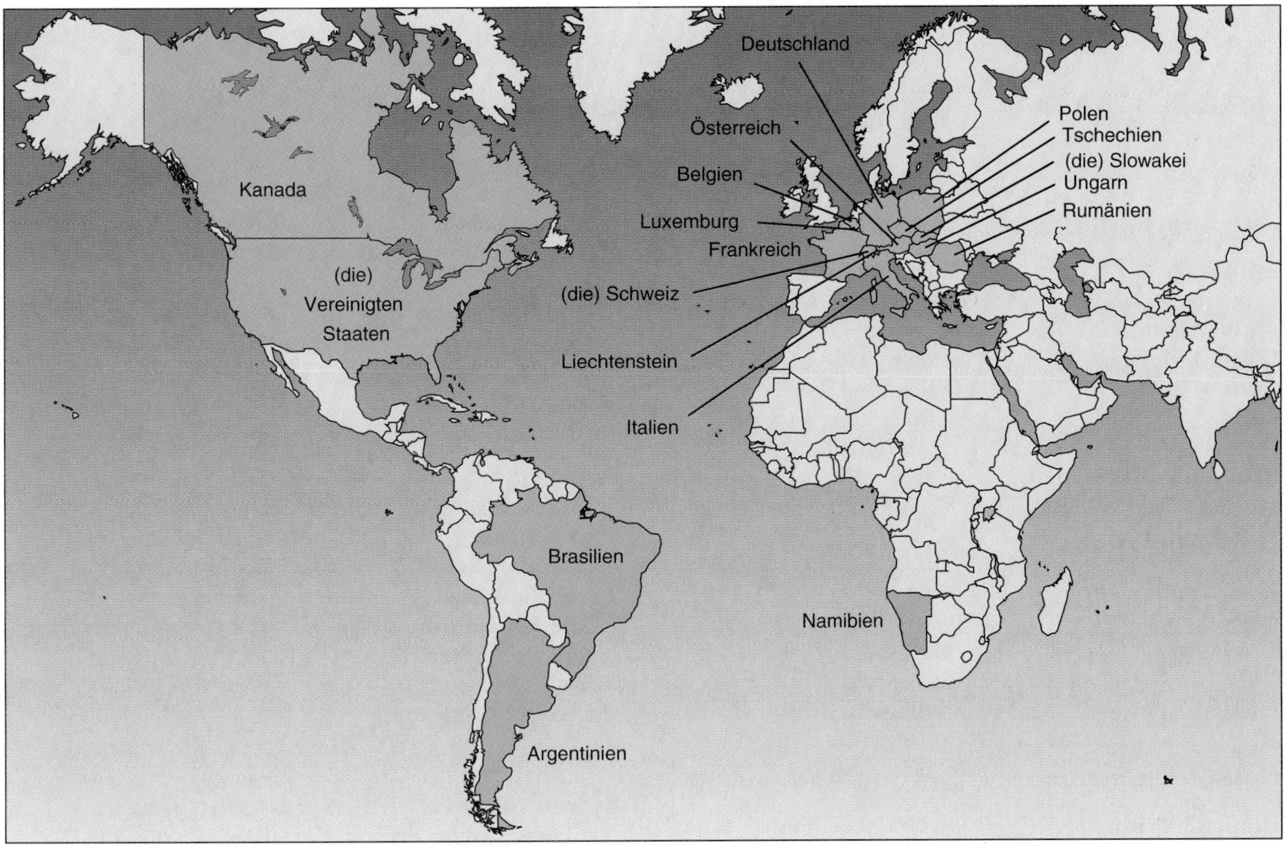

Deutschland
Österreich
Belgien
Luxemburg
Frankreich
(die) Schweiz
Liechtenstein
Italien
Polen
Tschechien
(die) Slowakei
Ungarn
Rumänien
Kanada
(die) Vereinigten Staaten
Brasilien
Argentinien
Namibien

Aktivität 18 Eine Fernsehwerbung°

TV commercial

Vorschau

Watch the video of the **Quelle-Katalog** commercial without the sound.

- Who is the man?
- Who is the woman?
- What is this advertisement for?

Arbeit mit dem Videotext

A. Watch the advertisement again. Concentrate only on the picture. Imagine what these two people might say to each other at the end. Write a short, simple dialogue with the German words and phrases that you already know.

B. The commercial ends with the phrase: **„Die Herrenmode** (*men's fashion*). **Der neue Quelle-Katalog.“** Do you find this ad effective? Why (not)?

C. Could this ad be used in your country for a different mail-order catalogue company? Why (not)?

Wortschatz: Vocabulary lists are organized into conceptual groups, where possible, or into grammatical categories. Students should use these lists as a study checklist.

Wortschatz

Zur Begrüßung	Greetings
grüß dich	hello, hi (*among friends and family*)
guten Abend	good evening
(guten) Morgen	good morning
(guten) Tag	hello, good day
hallo	hello (*among friends and family*)
herzlich willkommen	welcome

Beim Abschied	Saying Good-bye
(auf) Wiedersehen	good-bye
gute Nacht	good night
Mach's gut.	take care, so long (*informal*)
tschüs*	so long, bye (*informal*)

Bekannt werden	Getting Acquainted
Frau; die **Frau**	Mrs., Ms.; woman
Fräulein; das **Fräulein**	Miss; young lady
Herr; der **Herr**	Mr.; gentleman
der **Lehrer /** die **Lehrerin**	teacher
Das ist . . .	This is . . .
Wie heißt du?	What's your name? (*informal*)
Wie ist dein Name?	What's your name? (*informal*)
Woher kommst du?	Where are you from? (*informal*)
Wie heißen Sie?	What's your name? (*formal*)
Wie ist Ihr Name?	What's your name? (*formal*)
Woher kommen Sie?	Where are you from? (*formal*)
Ich bin . . .	I'm . . .
Ich heiße . . .	My name is . . .
Ich komme aus . . .	I'm from . . .
Mein Name ist . . .	My name is . . .
bitte	please; you're welcome
bitte schön	please; you're very welcome
bitte sehr	please; you're very welcome
danke	thanks
danke schön	thank you very much
danke sehr	thank you very much
freut mich	pleased to meet you
gleichfalls	likewise
und	and

Auskunft erfragen	Asking for Information
Wie heißt . . .	What is the name of . . .
die Stadt?	the town; city?
die Straße?	the street?
Wie ist . . .	What is . . .
die Adresse?	the address?
die Hausnummer?	the street address?
die Postleitzahl?	the zip code?
deine/Ihre Telefonnummer?	your (*informal*) / *formal*) telephone number?

Nach dem Befinden fragen	Asking About Someone's Well-being
Wie geht's?	How are you (*informal*)?
Wie geht's dir?	How are you (*informal*)?
Wie geht es Ihnen?	How are you (*formal*)?
ausgezeichnet	excellent
sehr gut	very well; fine; good
danke, gut	fine, thanks
so lala	OK, so-so
nicht besonders gut	not particularly well
schlecht	bad(ly), poor(ly)

Im Deutschunterricht	In German Class
Das weiß es nicht.	I don't know.
Ich habe eine Frage.	I have a question.
Ich verstehe das nicht.	I don't understand.
Ja.	Yes.
Langsamer, bitte.	Slower, please.
Nein.	No.
Was bedeutet _____?	What does _____ mean?
Wie bitte?	Pardon? What did you say?
Wie sagt man _____ auf Deutsch?*	How do you say _____ in German?
Wie schreibt man _____?	How do you write _____?

*See Appendix E for alternate spelling.

Zahlen (*Numbers*)

0	**null**	17	**siebzehn**
1	**eins**	18	**achtzehn**
2	**zwei**	19	**neunzehn**
3	**drei**	20	**zwanzig**
4	**vier**	30	**dreißig**
5	**fünf**	40	**vierzig**
6	**sechs**	50	**fünfzig**
7	**sieben**	60	**sechzig**
8	**acht**	70	**siebzig**
9	**neun**	80	**achtzig**
10	**zehn**	90	**neunzig**
11	**elf**	100	**(ein)hundert**
12	**zwölf**	200	**zweihundert**
13	**dreizehn**	300	**dreihundert**
14	**vierzehn**	1 000	**(ein)tausend**
15	**fünfzehn**	2 000	**zweitausend**
16	**sechzehn**	3 000	**dreitausend**

Deutschsprachige Länder und ihre Nachbarn	German-speaking Countries and their Neighbors
Belgien	Belgium
Dänemark	Denmark
Deutschland	Germany
Frankreich	France
Italien	Italy
Liechtenstein	Liechtenstein
Luxemburg	Luxembourg
die **Niederlande** *(pl.)*	Netherlands
Österreich	Austria
Polen	Poland
die **Schweiz**	Switzerland
Slowenien	Slovenia
Tschechien	Czech Republic
Ungarn	Hungary

Lernziele°

°*learning goals*

Use this checklist to verify that you can now . . .

- ☐ introduce yourself and others.
- ☐ say the alphabet and spell.
- ☐ use common greetings.
- ☐ ask about someone's well-being and respond to inquiries about your own well-being.
- ☐ read numbers and count.
- ☐ give your telephone number and address, and ask others for theirs.
- ☐ understand and use some basic classroom expressions.
- ☐ recognize cognates and use them to understand the gist of simple texts.
- ☐ name some European countries and identify the countries where German is spoken.

Lernziele: Learning goals are at the end of every chapter. Show students how the goals relate to information and activities in the chapter. You may wish to have your students look at this list before they begin work in the chapter. Encourage them to use this checklist to monitor their progress and to assist them during review.

Kapitel 1

Über mich und andere

Studenten in der Mittagspause

Kapitel 1. Suggestion: You may preview the theme of this chapter by describing yourself and sharing some personal information (where you are from, where you live, etc.). Some of this will be review from the **Einführung.** Other information can be introduced using mime and pictures.

Alles klar?

A. One of the things you will learn to do in German is to give information about people in different contexts and situations. People give information about themselves in personal documents—documents they use in everyday life—as, for example, in personal IDs. Let's take a close look at one.

Alles klar? Note: Beginning with this chapter, the **Alles klar?** section introduces the major chapter topic through illustrations and other visuals that set the tone for the chapter. Students will be asked to react to them and to express their own opinions.

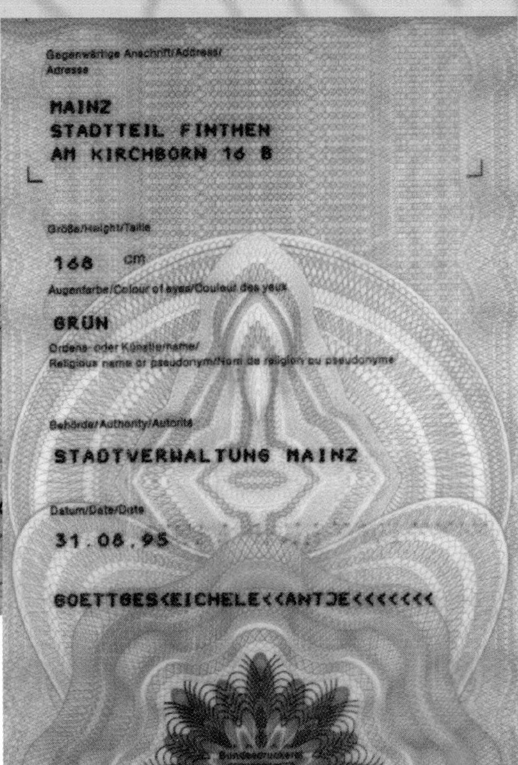

Try to find the following information in the personal ID:

- What is the full name of the ID holder?
- Why does she have two last names?
- Where was she born?
- When was she born?
- Where does she live?
- What information is provided after the word **Größe**?
- What color are her eyes?
- What does the word **Unterschrift** refer to?

Vokabelsuche (*word search*). Find the German word for:

1. birthdate
2. birthplace
3. color of eyes
4. height

If this activity is done in class, give students time to scan the information requested as well as the documents. Then call on individuals for responses. Or have them work in pairs, allowing three to four minutes to complete the activity. Otherwise, have students do the activity as homework.

Tell students that they will be learning more about Antje Göttges-Eichele and her family throughout the book.

B. You will now hear five speakers introduce themselves. As you listen, see whether you can hear what cities they are from.

1. Berlin Leipzig München
2. Rostock Köln Luzern
3. Wien Jena Mainz
4. Düsseldorf Graz Leipzig
5. Erfurt Zürich Frankfurt

Alles klar! Part B. Suggestion: You may wish to have your students look at the color maps of Germany, Austria, and Switzerland at the front of the book as they listen.

Wörter im Kontext. Note: Each chapter is divided into three sections: **Wörter im Kontext, Grammatik im Kontext,** and **Sprache im Kontext.** The first section provides opportunities to acquire new vocabulary and expressions by exploring authentic materials, dialogues, and visuals. Students are asked to analyze the materials and figure out the meaning of words on their own. The activities of this section practice and recycle the vocabulary. Some grammar is previewed in short notes titled **Sprachtipp.** Activities are targeted at getting students to interact.

Thema 1

Persönliche Angaben°

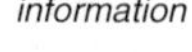
°*information*

Wer sind diese Leute? Scan the information, then read the summary about each person. Mark what is correct (**das stimmt**) and what is incorrect (**das stimmt nicht**) in each summary.

Vorname: Harald
Nachname: Lohmann
Geburtsdatum: 23.5.56
Geburtsort: Dessau
Beruf: Hochschullehrer
Wohnort: Magdeburg
Straße und Hausnummer: Bahnhofstraße 20
Land: Deutschland

Vorname: Daniela
Nachname: Lercher
Geburtsdatum: 7.1.1974
Geburtsort: Graz
Beruf: Studentin
Wohnort: Wien
Straße und Hausnummer: Mozartstraße 36
Land: Österreich

Vorname: Anton
Nachname: Rütli
Geburtsdatum: 14.10.53
Geburtsort: Luzern
Beruf: Architekt
Wohnort: Luzern
Straße und Hausnummer: Schulstrasse 8
Land: Schweiz

	DAS STIMMT	DAS STIMMT NICHT
1. Haralds **Nachname** ist Lohmann.	☒	☐
Er ist **Journalist.**	☐	☒
Er **kommt** aus Deutschland.	☒	☐
Er **wohnt** in Regensburg.	☐	☒
Seine Adresse ist Bahnhofstraße 20.	☒	☐
2. Die Frau heißt Daniela Lercher.	☒	☐
Sie wohnt in Salzburg.	☐	☒
Sie kommt aus Österreich.	☒	☐
Sie ist **Studentin.**	☒	☐
3. Herr Rütli ist Architekt **von Beruf.**	☒	☐
Er heißt Anton mit Vornamen.	☒	☐
Er kommt aus Luzern in der Schweiz.	☒	☐
Seine Adresse ist Kirchplatz 76.	☐	☒

Exercise. Note: Let students work in pairs to check information. As for all such exercises, give them a moment to scan the information as well as the requests for information. Spot-check responses. **Suggestion:** Three pairs of students, one for each item, can work at the board.

Kulturtipp

Everyone who lives in Germany must register with the **Einwohnermeldeamt** (residents' registration office) within two weeks of moving to a new community. This applies to everyone, even students living in a community only temporarily. The **Einwohnermeldeamt** must also be notified when one moves out of a community.

You'll find more about the **Einwohnermeldeamt** in ***Deutsch: Na klar!*** on the World Wide Web at www.mhhe.com/german.

Aktivität 1 Eine neue Studentin

Julie, who recently arrived in Berlin, is registering at the **Einwohnermeldeamt.** Listen to the interview between the official and Julie. What information does the official ask her for? Check **ja** if the information is asked for, **nein** if it is not.

	JA	NEIN
BEISPIEL: Vor und Nachname	☒	☐
1. Wohnort in den USA	☒	☐
2. Beruf	☒	☐
3. Geburtsort	☐	☒
4. Geburtsdatum	☒	☐
5. Telefonnummer	☐	☒
6. Straße und Hausnummer	☒	☐
7. Postleitzahl	☐	☒

Aktivität 2 Fragen Sie!°  

°*Ask!*

A. Find out some personal information from one or two people in your class by asking the following questions. Jot down the answers and then report the information to the class.

1. Wie ist dein Name, bitte?
2. Wie ist deine Adresse?
3. Wie ist deine Telefonnummer?
4. Und was ist dein Geburtsort?

B. Tell the class what you've found out. Say:

- Das ist _____.
- (Tims/Marys) Adresse ist _____.
- Seine/Ihre Telefonnummer ist _____.
- Sein/Ihr Geburtsort ist _____.

Aktivität 2. Follow-up suggestion: Wrap up with a poll of who lives where and who was born where, based on the information that students have gathered.

Suggestion. Point out the meaning of **sein** and **ihr** and that the ending **e** reflects a feminine noun.

Aktivität 2. Note: Some students may be reluctant to share personal information with their classmates, especially at the beginning of the semester. Be sensitive to this and let them know that they may provide made-up personal information.

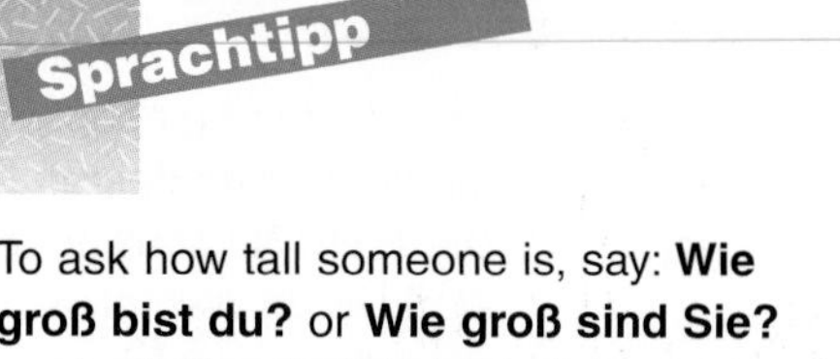

To ask how tall someone is, say: **Wie groß bist du?** or **Wie groß sind Sie?**

In stating their height, German speakers use the metric system. If you are 1.63 m (163 cm) tall, you can express it as follows: **Ich bin eins dreiundsechzig (groß).** In German, it's written **1,63 m.**

1 cm (Zentimeter)	= 0.39 in. (inch)
1 in. (inch)	= **2.54 cm (Zentimeter)**

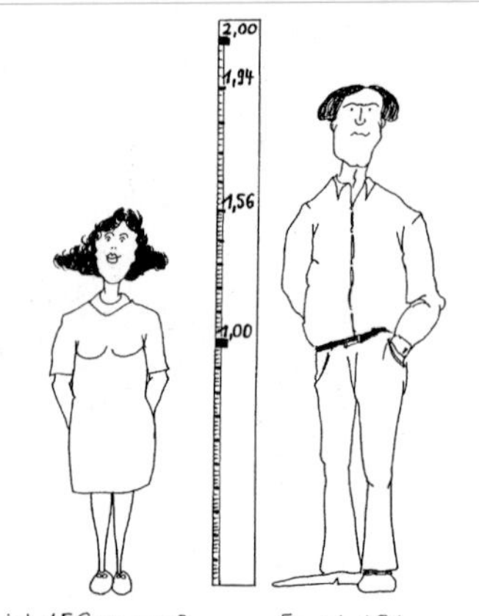

Sprachtipp. Note: This recurring feature focuses on an item of idiomatic usage of the language, or it briefly previews a grammar point that is explained in detail in the grammar section of the same or of a later chapter.

Aktivität 3 Wie groß bist du? Wie alt bist du?

Figure out your height in meters with the help of the conversion chart. Then exchange this information with one or two people in the class.

BEISPIEL: S1: Wie groß bist du?
S2: Ich bin 1,64 (eins vierundsechzig) groß.
S1: Wie alt bist du?
S2: Ich bin dreiundzwanzig.

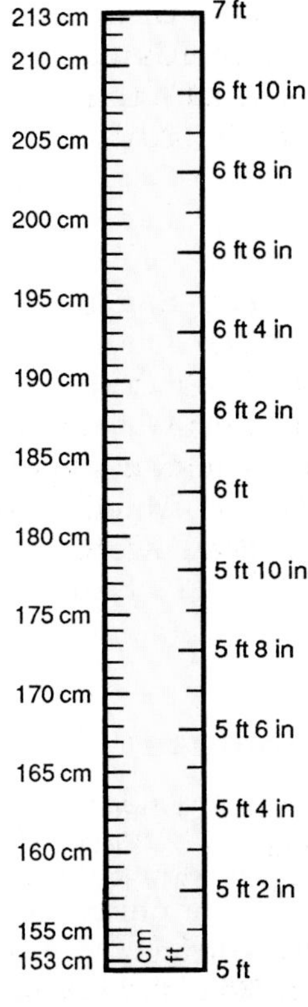

Thema 2. Note: To introduce the new vocabulary, play or read the dialogues to the class. Remind students that they do not need to understand every word at first; rather they should use the context to arrive at the meaning of words they do not know. The **Analyse** that follows will also aid comprehension.

Thema 2

Sich erkundigen°

° *inquiring*

„Glücksrad Fortuna"

QUIZMASTER: Guten Abend, meine Damen und Herren. Willkommen im Studio bei Glücksrad Fortuna. Mein Name ist Dieter Sielinsky. Wer gewinnt **heute Abend**—und was? Das ist die große Frage! Und nun zu unserem ersten Kandidaten. Wie ist Ihr Name, bitte?
KANDIDAT: Lentz, Gertraud Lentz.
QUIZMASTER: Woher kommen Sie, Frau Lentz?
KANDIDAT: Aus München.
QUIZMASTER: Frau Lentz, was sind Sie von Beruf?
KANDIDAT: Ich bin Hausfrau.
QUIZMASTER: Haben Sie Hobbys, Frau Lentz?
KANDIDAT: Ja, natürlich! **Lesen, Reisen, Kochen, Wandern,** und ich mache gern **Kreuzworträtsel.**
QUIZMASTER: Wie **finden** Sie Berlin?
KANDIDAT: **Sehr interessant, wirklich** faszinierend.
QUIZMASTER: So, danke sehr, Frau Lentz.
KANDIDAT: Bitte schön.
QUIZMASTER: Na dann, **viel Spaß** und **viel Glück.**

Ein ***Gespräch an der Uni***

HELMUT: Grüß Gott! Helmut Sachs.
JULIE: Guten Tag! Ich heiße Julie Harrison.
HELMUT: Woher kommst du, Julie?
JULIE: Ich komme aus Cincinnati.
HELMUT: Cincinnati, wo ist denn das?
JULIE: In den USA, im Mittelwesten, im Bundesstaat Ohio.
HELMUT: **Sag** mal, was **machst** du **jetzt** hier?
JULIE: Ich **lerne Deutsch** am Sprachinstitut. Und du?
HELMUT: Ich **studiere** Physik an der T. U.
JULIE: Was ist die T. U. **denn?**
HELMUT: Die Technische **Universität.** Und wie lange **bleibst** du **hier** in München?
JULIE: Zwei **Semester. Nächstes Jahr** bin ich wieder in Ohio.
HELMUT: Ach so.

Analyse

Look again at the dialogues and find the following information:

- How does the quizmaster ask his guest what her name is?
- What phrase does the quizmaster use to ask Frau Lentz where she is from?
- What does the quizmaster ask to find out Frau Lentz's profession?
- What question does the quizmaster ask to find out about Frau Lentz's hobbies?
- How do Helmut and Julie greet each other?
- How does Helmut ask Julie where she is from?
- What phrase does Helmut use to ask Julie what she is doing in Munich?
- Helmut doesn't know where Cincinnati is. What does he ask Julie to get that information?

Sprachtipp

To say that you are studying at a university or to state your major, use the verb **studieren.**

Ich **studiere** Physik in München.

To say you are studying, such as for a test, use **arbeiten** or **lernen.**

Ich **lerne** heute für Chemie.

To say that you are learning or taking a language, use the verb **lernen.**

Ich **lerne** Deutsch.

Aktivität 4 Steht das im Dialog?

Mark whether the statements below are correct or incorrect, based on the information found in the dialogues in Thema 2.

	DAS STIMMT	DAS STIMMT NICHT
1. Der Quizmaster heißt Dieter Sielinsky.	☒	☐
2. Der Kandidat kommt aus Augsburg.	☐	☒
3. Frau Lentz ist Professorin von Beruf.	☐	☒
4. Tanzen ist ein Hobby von Frau Lentz.	☐	☒
5. Frau Lentz findet Berlin zu groß.	☐	☒
6. Julie lernt Deutsch in München.	☒	☐
7. Helmut studiert Mathematik.	☐	☒
8. Julie bleibt zwei Jahre in München.	☐	☒

Sprachtipp

You may have already noticed that people address each other in different ways. In German, people are addressed either formally, with **Sie,** or informally, with **du.**

du (*you*): informal, one person
Sie (*you*): formal, one or more people, always capitalized

Another form, **ihr,** is used to address more than one person informally. It is the plural of **du.**

Use **du** (or **ihr** in plural) for	Use **Sie** for
a family member	a stranger
a close friend	an acquaintance
a fellow student	anyone you would address with a title, such as **Herr** or **Frau**
a child	
an animal	

Aktivität 5 Fragen und Antworten°

°questions and answers

Match each question in the left-hand column with a possible answer from the right-hand column.

Aktivität 5. Suggestion: Students can work in pairs. Call on individuals to supply responses. After the exercise has been completed, students can act out the dialogue.

1. _____ Wie heißen Sie?
2. _____ Woher kommst du?
3. _____ Was machen Sie hier?
4. _____ Wo ist das?

a. Ich studiere hier.
b. Das ist im Mittelwesten.
c. Mein Name ist Meier.
d. Ich heiße Keller.
e. Ich lerne Deutsch.
f. Ich komme aus Deutschland.
g. Ich bin aus Kalifornien.

Aktivität 6 Was sagen diese Leute zueinander°?

to each other

Determine whether the following phrases and questions would be used by two students addressing each other, by a professor and a student, or by both pairs of speakers.

Aktivität 6. Suggestion: Have students work in pairs, taking turns saying a sentence and marking an X in the appropriate column. Check responses to several items or to all, keeping in mind that some of the expressions might fall into both categories.

		ZWEI STUDENTEN	PROFESSOR UND STUDENT
1.	Was studierst du?	☒	☐
2.	Grüß dich!	☒	☐
3.	Auf Wiedersehen.	☐	☒
4.	Wie heißt du?	☒	☐
5.	Guten Tag!	☒	☒
6.	Wie heißen Sie?	☐	☒
7.	Was machst du hier?	☒	☐
8.	Was studieren Sie?	☐	☒
9.	Tschüs!	☒	☐
10.	Mach's gut!	☒	☐

Aktivität 7 Eine Konversation

Aktivität 7. Suggestion: Write this or a similar dialogue out on a transparency and cut it up so that each utterance is on a separate piece. Have students arrange the sentences correctly, on the overhead. These pieces can function as cues when they act out the dialogue.

When rearranged, the following sentences will form a short conversation between Herr Brinkmann and Frau Garcia who are just getting acquainted. Create the conversation. Then perform it with a partner.

_____ Ich finde Hamburg interessant.
_____ Und was machen Sie hier?
_____ Wie bitte?
_____ Guten Tag. Mein Name ist Brinkmann.
_____ Ich komme aus Florida.
_____ Brinkmann.

__1__ Guten Tag. Ich heiße Garcia.
_____ Ach so!
_____ Wie finden Sie Hamburg?
_____ Ich besuche Freunde.
_____ Woher kommen Sie?

Aktivität 8 Kurzdialoge°

brief dialogues

Aktivität 8. Suggestion: Play the tape twice or say each item twice. When checking responses, replay each item on tape or read it aloud. Then ask students to give the correct response to all items marked "illogical."

Listen to the brief conversational exchanges and indicate in each case whether the response to the first question or statement is logical (**logisch**) or illogical (**unlogisch**).

	LOGISCH	UNLOGISCH
1.	☒	☐
2.	☐	☒
3.	☒	☐
4.	☒	☐
5.	☐	☒
6.	☒	☐
7.	☐	☒
8.	☒	☐
9.	☐	☒
10.	☒	☐

Aktivität 9 Was studierst du?

A. Find your major in the following list. Then, by asking questions, try to find at least one other classmate who has the same major as you.

Note: Provide students with majors not listed if the need arises. Note also the list in Appendix B.

BEISPIEL: S1: Was studierst du?
S2: Ich studiere Geschichte. Und du?
S1: Ich studiere Informatik.

Astronomie	Geschichte (*history*)	Philosophie
Betriebswirtschaft (*management*)	Informatik (*computer science*)	Physik
Biologie	Kunst (*art*)	Politologie
Chemie	Literatur	Psychologie
Deutsch/Germanistik	Maschinenbau (*engineering*)	Russisch
Englisch/Anglistik	Mathematik	Soziologie
Französisch/Romanistik	Musik	Spanisch/Romanistik
Geographie	Pädagogik	Volkswirtschaft (*economics*)

B. Now report back to the class. Does anyone have the same major as you?

BEISPIEL: Ich studiere Informatik. Candice und Ben studieren auch Informatik.

Thema 3

Meine Eigenschaften°

°*characteristics*

Ich bin freundlich, tolerant und—so finden meine Freunde—sympathisch. Ich habe zwei Hobbys: Bücher lesen und Filme sehen.

Ich bin etwas exzentrisch aber nie langweilig. Ich diskutiere gern.

Ich bin ernst und ruhig. Meine Hobbys? Ich koche gern und höre gern Musik.

Ich bin sportlich. Wandern macht mir Spaß.

So bin ich! Check off characteristics that apply to you.

□ chaotisch	□ **langweilig**
□ dynamisch	□ liberal
□ **ernst**	□ **lustig**
□ exzentrisch	□ **nett**
□ **faul**	□ **praktisch**
□ **fleißig**	□ **romantisch**
□ **freundlich**	□ **ruhig**
□ **hübsch**	□ **sympathisch**
□ interessant	□ tolerant
□ **konservativ**	□ **treu**

Das macht mir Spaß! Check off your interests and hobbies.

□ **Bücher** lesen	□ **Kochen**
□ ins Café **gehen**	□ Musik
□ **Computerspiele spielen**	□ Natur
	□ **Reisen**
□ **Diskutieren**	□ Sport
□ **Essen**	□ **Tanzen**
□ Fernsehen	□ Videos machen
□ Fotografieren	□ **Wandern**
□ im Internet surfen	□ **Zeitung** lesen
□ **Karten spielen**	

Meine Eigenschaften. Suggestion: Point out to students that the opposite meaning of some adjectives can be expressed by adding the prefix **un-** or **in-**, e.g. **unfreundlich** and **intolerant.**

One way to say that you like (doing) something is by using the expression **Spaß machen.**

Fotografieren **macht mir Spaß.**
I like photography.

Was macht dir Spaß?
What do you like (to do)?

Aktivität 10 Wie bin ich? Was macht mir Spaß?

Write down two adjectives that describe you and one interest of yours. Your instructor will collect and redistribute everyone's list. Then each class member will read a description out loud, while the others try to guess who the writer is.

BEISPIEL: Ich bin dynamisch und exzentrisch. Im Internet surfen macht mir Spaß.

Aktivität 10. Note: This activity allows students to link pieces of information together. It prepares them for constructing longer sentences later on.

Related Activity. Brainstorm with the class for names of famous people (*der Präsident, die Königin von England, der Bundeskanzler, die Frau des Präsidenten,* singers, actors, etc.). Which qualities do students associate with these people?

Aktivität 11 Wichtig° oder nicht?

°*important*

1. Make a list of three characteristics and three interests that you consider important in a friend.
2. Tally the results on the board.
   Which characteristic is most important for the class?
   Which interest is most frequently mentioned?

Grammatik im Kontext. Note: This section aims to give students a concise explanation of basic grammar. Specific points brought up previously in a **Sprachtipp** are elaborated. Exercises reinforce grammar points and incorporate them into meaningful contexts that parallel the chapter themes. Listening exercises focus on grammar points as well. Whenever possible, grammar points are illustrated by authentic materials. Make sure to integrate these visuals into the discussion of a grammar point by asking students to analyze them. Grammar sections should be previewed in class and then assigned for homework.

Grammatik im Kontext

Nouns, Gender, and Definite Articles°

°Nomen, Genus und bestimmte Artikel

Nouns in German can be easily recognized because they are capitalized.

German nouns are classified by grammatical gender as either masculine, feminine, or neuter. The definite articles **der, die,** and **das** (all meaning *the* in German) signal the gender of nouns.

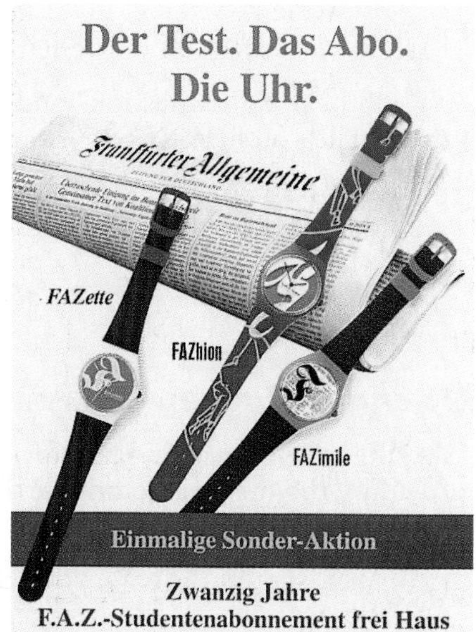

MASCULINE: **der**	FEMININE: **die**	NEUTER: **das**
der Mann	die Frau	das Kind (*child*)
der Wohnort	die Straße	das Haus
der Beruf	die Adresse	das Geld (*money*)

Realia. The ad for watches is taken from the *Studentenpresse* in Heidelberg.

The grammatical gender of a noun that refers to a human being generally matches biological gender; that is, most words for males are masculine and words for females are feminine. Aside from this, though, the grammatical gender of German nouns is largely unpredictable.

Even words borrowed from other languages have a grammatical gender in German, as you can see from the following newspaper headline.

Fußball ist der Hit

Since the gender of nouns is generally unpredictable, you should make it a habit to learn the definite article with each noun.

Sometimes gender is signaled by the ending of the noun. The suffix **in,** for instance, signals a feminine noun.

Suggestion: Point out to students other endings associated with particular genders.

der Student, die Student**in**
der Freund, die Freund**in**
der Amerikaner, die Amerikaner**in**
der Professor, die Professor**in**

When added to a noun, the suffix **lein** or **chen** alters the meaning of the noun, changing it to a diminutive. Such nouns are always neuter.

der Mann → das Männlein, das Männchen (*little man*)
das Buch → das Büchlein (*booklet*)
die Stadt → das Städtchen (*small town*)

Note that the vowels **a, o, u,** and **au** take umlaut when the diminutive suffixes are added: **a → ä, o → ö, u → ü, au → äu.**

Compound nouns (**Komposita**) always take the gender of the last noun.

der Biergarten = das Bier + der Garten
das Telefonbuch = das Telefon + das Buch
die Telefonnummer = das Telefon + die Nummer

Übung 1 Was hören Sie? 

Übung 1. Suggestion: Play the tape for students twice: once to do the exercise and again to check responses.

You will hear eight questions and statements. For each one, circle the definite article you hear.

1.	der	die	das	**5.**	der	die	das
2.	der	die	das	**6.**	der	die	das
3.	der	die	das	**7.**	der	die	das
4.	der	die	das	**8.**	der	die	das

Übung 2 Fragen und Antworten 

Working with a partner, take turns asking and answering questions while providing the missing definite articles. Choose answers from the expressions provided.

1. Wie ist _____ Adresse vom Hotel Adlon?	in Deutschland
2. Wo wohnt _____ Professor?	23 47 99
3. Woher kommt _____ Kind?	aus Österreich
4. _____ Telefonnummer vom Theater, bitte!	Hauptstraße 7
5. Wo ist _____ Biergarten?	keine Ahnung (*no idea*)
6. Wie heißt _____ Film im Roxie?	in Köln

Personal Pronouns°

°Personalpronomen

A personal pronoun stands for a person or a noun.

Ich bin praktisch.	*I am practical.*
Du bist nett, Ilse.	*You are nice, Ilse.*
Der Mercedes—ist **er** neu?	*That Mercedes—is it new?*

Realia. This saying is printed on a bumper sticker (*Aufkleber*).

1. Ich . . . *I am really sharp. (I am great in every way.)*

The following personal pronouns function as subjects in a sentence.

	SINGULAR		PLURAL	
1st Person	ich	*I*	wir	*we*
2nd Person	du	*you (informal)*	ihr	*you (informal)*
	Sie	*you (formal)*	Sie	*you (formal)*
3rd Person	er	*he; it*	sie	*they*
	sie	*she; it*		
	es	*it*		

The first-person pronoun **ich** is not capitalized unless it is the first word in the sentence.

German has three second-person pronouns to express *you*: **du, ihr,** and **Sie. Du** is used to address a family member, a close friend, or a child. **Ihr** is used to address two or more people whom you would address individually with **du.** The formal second-person pronoun **Sie** is used for any other person or persons. Note that **Sie** is always capitalized.

The third-person singular pronouns **er, sie,** and **es** reflect the grammatical gender of the person or the noun for which they stand (the so-called "antecedent"). Thus, the pronoun **er** may mean *he* or *it* in English and **sie** may mean *she* or *it.*

Mark und **Anja** sind Studenten. **Er** kommt aus Bonn. **Sie** kommt aus Wien.	*Mark and Anja are students. He comes from Bonn. She comes from Vienna.*
—Wie ist **der Film?** —**Er** ist wirklich lustig.	*How is the film?* *It is really funny.*
—Wo ist **die Zeitung?** —**Sie** ist hier.	*Where is the newspaper?* *It is here.*

Übung 3 *du, ihr* oder *Sie*?

How would you address the following people? Complete each question with the appropriate pronoun: **du, ihr,** or **Sie.**

1. Herr Professor Rauschenbach:
   Woher kommen _____?
2. Drei Freunde:
   Was macht _____ heute?
3. Eine Freundin:
   Wann arbeitest _____ heute?
4. Eine Touristin aus Amerika:
   Wie finden _____ Dresden?
5. Zehn Touristen aus Kanada:
   Wie finden _____ Wien?
6. Zwei Kinder:
   Woher kommt _____?
7. Ihre Mutter:
   Was machst _____ da?

Übung 4 Hin und her: Wer sind diese Personen? 

Übung 4. One student works with the chart here, the other uses the chart in Appendix A.

Working with a partner, take turns asking and answering questions. Use the pronouns **er, sie,** or **es** in your answers.

BEISPIEL: S1: Wie ist Herr Eichele?
S2: Er ist tolerant.

FRAGEN	ANTWORTEN
Wie ist Herr Eichele?	tolerant
Woher kommen Herr und Frau Eichele?	aus Koblenz
Was ist Frau Eichele von Beruf?	Sozialarbeiterin
Wie heißt Frau Eichele mit Vornamen?	Regina
Wo studiert Hans?	in Berlin
Wie heißt unser Deutschbuch?	*Deutsch: Na klar!*

Übung 4. Note: Tell students they will be learning more about the Eichele family in **Kapitel 3.**

Übung 5 Was meinst du?° 

What do you think?

Ask a partner for his/her opinion. Create questions with the words in column A, completing each blank with information of your choice. Then have your partner answer your question by choosing an appropriate adjective from column B. Follow the model.

BEISPIEL: S1: Sag mal, wie ist der Film „Titanic"?
S2: Er ist ausgezeichnet.

A	B
der Film _____	ausgezeichnet
das Buch _____	langweilig
das Wetter (*weather*) in _____	gut
die Studentenzeitung _____	nicht besonders gut
das Essen im Studentenwohnheim _____	lustig
der _____kurs* (z. B. Deutschkurs)	interessant
	schlecht

The Verb: Infinitive and Present Tense°

Das Verb: der Infinitiv und das Präsens

In German, the basic form of the verb, the infinitive, consists of the verb stem plus the ending **en** or, sometimes, just **n.**

VERB STEM	ENDING	INFINITIVE
komm	**en**	kommen
wander	**n**	wandern

*Refer to the list of subjects in **Aktivität 9, Was studierst du?,** earlier in this chapter.

The present tense is formed by adding different endings to the infinitive stem. These endings vary according to the subject of the sentence.

Here are the present-tense forms of three common verbs.

kommen			
ich	komm**e**	wir	komm**en**
du	komm**st**	ihr	komm**t**
er / sie / es	komm**t**	sie	komm**en**
Sie komm**en**			

arbeiten			
ich	arbeit**e**	wir	arbeit**en**
du	arbeit**est**	ihr	arbeit**et**
er / sie / es	arbeit**et**	sie	arbeit**en**
Sie arbeit**en**			

tanzen			
ich	tanz**e**	wir	tanz**en**
du	tanz**t**	ihr	tanz**t**
er / sie / es	tanz**t**	sie	tanz**en**
Sie tanz**en**			

In German, four different personal endings can be added to the infinitive stem to form the present tense: **e, (e)st, (e)t,** and **(e)n.** In contrast, English has only one ending, *(e)s,* for the third-person singular form (*comes, goes*).

Other verbs conjugated like **kommen** are **besuchen** (*to visit*), **bleiben** (*to stay*), **fragen, gehen, lernen, machen, sagen, spielen, studieren, wandern,** and **wohnen.**

Verbs with stems ending in **d, t** or a consonant cluster add an **e** before the **st** or **t** endings. This makes them easier to pronounce. Another verb conjugated like **arbeiten** is **finden.**

When a verb stem ends in **ß, s,** or **z,** the **du-**form is identical with the **er/sie/es-**form. Two other verbs conjugated like **tanzen** are **heißen** and **reisen**.

When the infinitive is used as a noun, it is capitalized.

Mein Hobby ist **Kochen**. *My hobby is **cooking.***

Analyse

Analyse. Note: The purpose of this type of exercise is to take a closer look at the grammatical structure or usage of a grammar point just introduced.

- Identify the different verb endings in the illustrations.
- What are the subjects in each of the sentences? Are they in the singular or in the plural?
- What is the infinitive form of the verbs?

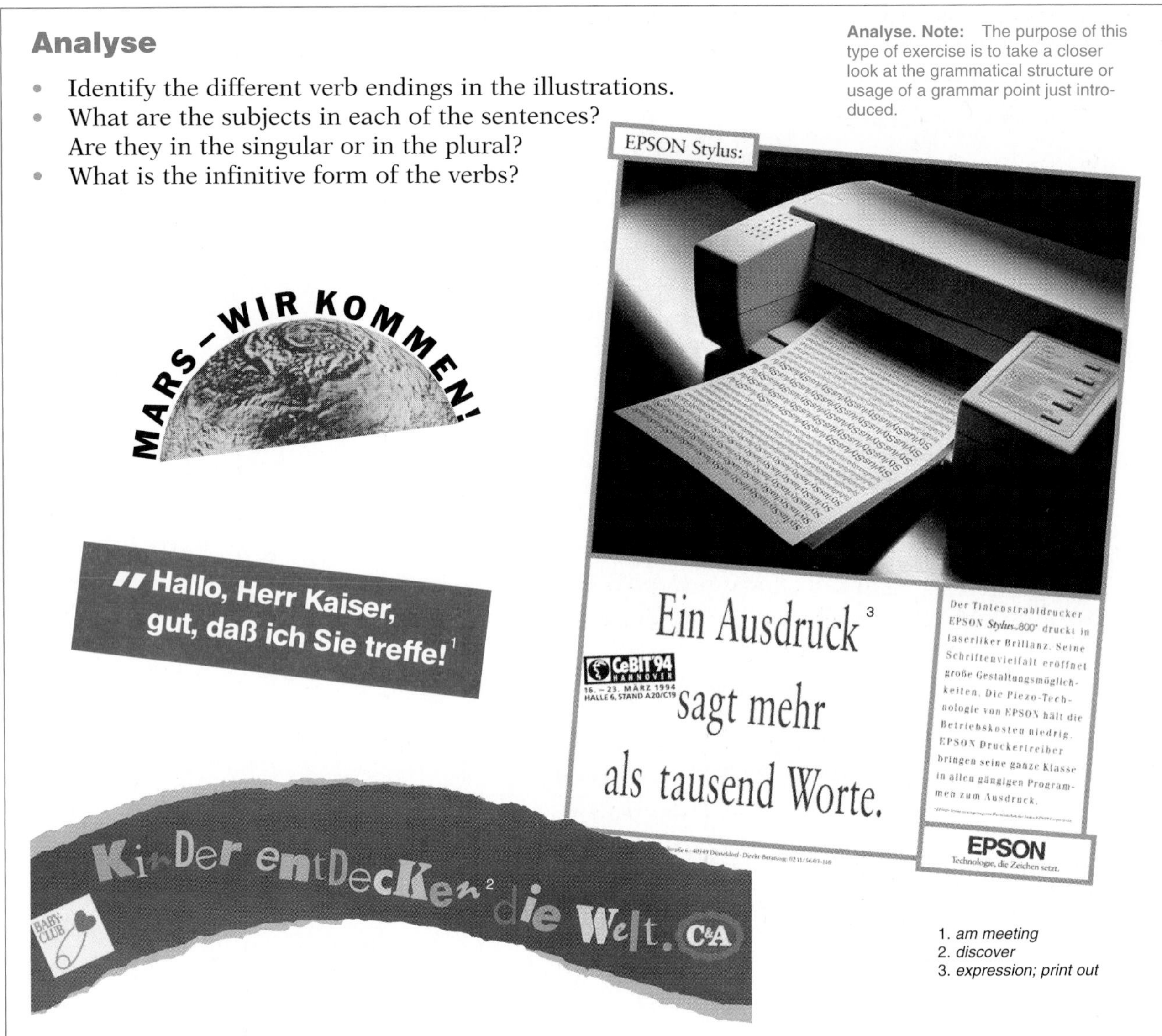

1. *am meeting*
2. *discover*
3. *expression; print out*

Realia. *Mars:* This is from an advertisement in the *Frankfurter Allgemeine Zeitung* for a book by the British author Frank Miles, *Aufbruch zum Mars.* *Epson:* This appeared in the news magazine *Stern.* *Hallo:* These words appeared in an ad for the Hamburg-Mannheimer health insurance company. *Kinder:* This ad is taken from the women's magazine *Freundin.*

Use of the Present Tense

The present tense in German may express either something happening at the moment or a recurring or habitual action.

Wolfgang spielt Karten.	*Wolfgang is playing cards.*
Antje arbeitet abends.	*Antje works in the evening.*

It can also express a future action or occurrence, particularly with an expression of time.

Nächstes Jahr lerne ich Spanisch.	*Next year I'm going to learn Spanish.*

German has only one form of the present tense, whereas English has three different forms.

Hans **tanzt** wirklich gut. { *Hans* ***dances*** *really well.* / *Hans* ***is dancing*** *really well.* / *Hans* ***does dance*** *really well.* }

Übung 6 Was Sie nicht sagen!°

°You don't say!

Übung 6. Suggestion: Have students work in pairs on this. Then follow up by personalizing some of the short dialogues, asking students to supply information about themselves.

Complete these short dialogues with the appropriate verb endings.

1. A: Herr Meier, ich höre, Sie komm_____ aus Wien?
   B: Nein, ich komm_____ aus München.
2. C: Sag mal, was mach_____ Mark denn jetzt in New York?
   D: Er studier_____ Musik dort.
   C: Und wie find_____ er die Stadt?
   D: Ganz fantastisch. Ja, und er spiel_____ schon am Broadway.
   C: Echt (*really*)?
3. E: Was studier_____ du hier in Göttingen, Kerstin?
   F: Ich studier_____ Geschichte und Psychologie.
4. G: Guten Morgen, meine Damen und Herren. Ich heiß_____ Andreas Siebert. Wir besuch_____ heute das Museum in Berlin-Dahlem.
   H: Und wann geh_____ wir ins Kabarett?
5. I: Grüß dich, Peter! Was mach_____ du denn? Arbeit _____ du hier?
   J: Ja, ich arbeit_____ hier.
6. K: Tag, Claudia. Grüß dich, Uwe. Was mach_____ ihr zwei denn hier in Bonn?
   L: Wir studier_____ hier.
   K: Seit wann (*since when*) studier_____ ihr nicht mehr in Regensburg?
   L: Seit Oktober. Claudia studier_____ Jura, und ich studier_____ Betriebswirtschaft.

Übung 7 Wer sind sie? Was machen sie?

You read and heard about the following people earlier in this chapter. What do you remember about them? Tell a partner what you recall. Also, include some information about yourself and your friends.

Gertraud Lentz	arbeiten (in)	Deutsch
Dieter Sielinsky	besuchen	Berlin
Helmut Sachs	kommen (aus)	München
Julie Harrison	lernen	Physik
Meine Freunde und ich	wohnen (in)	Amerika
Ich	studieren	Freunde
?*	?	?

* ? is used throughout for open option, personalized expansion.

The Verbs *sein* and *heißen*

The irregular verb **sein** is used to describe or identify someone or something.

> Marion **ist** Studentin.
> Sie **ist** sehr sympathisch.

sein			
ich	**bin**	wir	**sind**
du	**bist**	ihr	**seid**
er / sie / es	**ist**	sie	**sind**
	Sie **sind**		

The verb **heißen** is used to identify a person or object.

Die Professorin **heißt** Baumann.	*The professor's name is Baumann.*
Wie **heißt** du?	*What is your name?*
Wie **heißt** das auf Deutsch?	*What is that called in German?*

Realia. *Ich bin ein Adler:* This drawing appears on a greeting card.

Realia. These two ads came from the personals section of a German newspaper, the *Klever Wochenblatt.* Kleve is a small town near the Dutch border.

Übung 8 Zwei Menschen

Read the two ads and answer the questions.

Ich heiße Petra, bin 28 Jahre alt, 168 cm groß und arbeite in einem Ingenieurbüro.

Jürgen ist 25 Jahre alt, 185 cm groß, blond, sportlich-schlank, gut aussehend und sympathisch.

1. Wie heißt der Mann?
2. Wie heißt die Frau?
3. Wie alt ist die Frau?
4. Wie alt ist der Mann?
5. Wie groß ist der Mann?
6. Wie groß ist die Frau?
7. Wie ist Jürgen? (drei Adjektive)
8. Was macht Petra?

Übung 9 So ist er.°

°*That's the way he is.*

Everyone is picking on Thomas. Complete the sentences with the appropriate form of **sein.**

1. Die Freundin von Thomas sagt: „Du _____ so konservativ, Thomas."
2. Thomas sagt: „Wie bitte? Ich _____ sehr liberal."
3. Der Vater von Thomas sagt: „Thomas _____ nicht sehr praktisch."
4. Die Mutter von Thomas sagt: „Wir _____ zu kritisch. Thomas _____ noch sehr jung."
5. Der Chef von Thomas sagt zu Thomas: „Herr Berger, Sie _____ nicht besonders fleißig."
6. Thomas denkt: „Ihr _____ alle unfair. Ich _____ ein Genie!"

Word Order° in Sentences

°Wortstellung

As in English, the subject of a German sentence frequently stands at the beginning of the sentence and is followed by the conjugated verb (the verb with the personal ending).

Meine Familie wohnt in Österreich. *My family lives in Austria.*
Ich studiere in Deutschland. *I am studying in Germany.*

If another sentence element, such as an adverb, stands at the beginning of the sentence, the conjugated verb stays in the second position. The subject follows the verb in the third position. This kind of word order, with the subject following the verb, is referred to as *inverted word order.*

The fixed position of the conjugated verb as the second sentence element is one of the most important characteristics of a German sentence.

FIRST ELEMENT	VERB	SUBJECT	OTHER ELEMENTS
1	*2*	*3*	*4*
Morgen	besuche	ich	Freunde.
Heute	spielen	wir	Karten.
Nächstes Jahr	studiert	Wendy	in Deutschland.

Übung 10 Wann machen Sie das?

Choose an item from each of the four columns and create declarative sentences.

BEISPIEL: Jetzt studiert mein Freund Medizin.

Heute	besuchen	wir	(in) Deutschland
Morgen (*tomorrow*)	studieren	ich	Karten
Nächstes Jahr	spielen	mein Freund	Freunde
Jetzt	lernen	meine Freundin	Deutsch
Heute Abend	?	?	Tennis
?			Informatik
			Medizin
			?

Übung 10. Suggestion: Students can do this type of exercise in small groups.

Variation: Write out the words on separate pieces of paper. Distribute one word to each student. Students consult each other to formulate sentences.

Follow-up: Reinforce the distinction between **studieren** and **lernen** by adding questions: *Wer lernt tanzen/ Deutsch/Spanisch/kochen/schwimmen? Wer studiert Physik/Literatur/*etc.*?*

Übung 11 Wer macht was und wann?

For each group of words create several sentences, using different word order in each.

BEISPIEL: besuchen / das Museum / heute / wir →
Wir besuchen heute das Museum.
Heute besuchen wir das Museum.
Das Museum besuchen wir heute.

1. Karten / wir / spielen / heute Abend
2. bei McDonald's / Peter / arbeitet / jetzt

3. ich / sehr interessant / finde / Berlin
4. spielen / wir / morgen / Tennis mit Boris
5. das Museum / Herr Schaller / nächtes Jahr / besucht / in Dresden

Übung 12 Meine Pläne°

°plans

Tell a partner some of the things you will do today, tomorrow, and next year. Then make a list of your partner's plans and be prepared to tell the class about them.

BEISPIEL: Heute spiele ich Karten. Morgen arbeite ich. Nächstes Jahr studiere ich in Deutschland.

Asking Questions°

°Fragen stellen

There are two types of questions. One, the information question, asks for specific information and always begins with an interrogative pronoun. In this type of question, the conjugated verb appears in the second position.

1. am . . . *on the weekend*

Note: You may wish to point out to students that an alternative to the term "interrogative pronoun" is "question word."

Realia. . . . und was machst du am Wochenende? This is from a greeting card.

INTERROGATIVE PRONOUN	CONJUGATED VERB	SUBJECT	OTHER ELEMENTS
1	*2*	*3*	*4*
Woher	kommen	Sie?	
Was	machen	wir	heute?
Wie	heißt	der Professor?	

Some common interrogative pronouns are:

wann	when	**wie lange**	how long
warum	why	**wie viel**	how much
was	what	**wie viele**	how many
wer	who	**wo**	where
wie	how	**woher**	from where

Another type of question requires "yes" or "no" for an answer. Such yes/no questions begin with a conjugated verb. The subject immediately follows the verb. German has no equivalent for the English progressive present tense or for the verb *to do* used as an auxiliary in questions.

Realia. Kommst du bald? This is from a greeting card.

CONJUGATED VERB	SUBJECT	OTHER ELEMENTS	
1	*2*	*3*	
Kommst	du	bald?	*Are you coming soon?*
Haben	Sie	Hobbys?	*Do you have hobbies?*
Studiert	Ulrike	Biologie?	*Does Ulrike study biology?* / *Is Ulrike studying biology?*

denn, doch, and ja

To convey strong interest or surprise, add the particle **denn** to the question.

Was machst du **denn?** — *What are you doing?* (strong interest)

Arbeitest du **denn** heute? — *Are you working today?* (surprise)

To give an affirmative answer to a yes/no question phrased in the negative, use the particle **doch.**

—Lernst du **nicht** Chinesisch? — *Aren't you learning Chinese?*
—**Doch.** — *Yes (I am).*

To give an affirmative answer to all other yes/no questions, use **ja.**

Übung 13 Fragen und Antworten

Übung 13. Additional Exercise: Have students rephrase each question using **denn.** Be sure to have them practice correct question intonation as well.

First, complete each question with an interrogative pronoun. Then take turns with a partner asking and answering these questions. More than one interrogative pronoun may be possible.

1. _____ heißt du?
2. _____ kommst du?
3. _____ studierst du?
4. _____ findest du die Uni?
5. _____ machst du am Wochenende?
6. _____ gehst du nach Hause?
7. _____ ist deine Telefonnummer?
8. _____ kostet (*costs*) dein Deutschbuch?

Übung 14 Zur Information

Take a survey. Formulate five questions. Use them to find someone who does these, or similar things.

BEISPIEL: S1: Wer wohnt im Studentenwohnheim?
S2: Ich wohne im Studentenwohnheim.
oder Matt wohnt im Studentenwohnheim.

Wer	gehen	heute	Tennis
	spielen	jetzt	tanzen
	wohnen	morgen	Karten
	kommen	manchmal	schwimmen
	lernen	nie	aus _____
			im Studentenheim

Übung 15 Wie bitte?

Imagine that you did not entirely catch what someone said to you. Working with a partner, take turns making a statement by filling in the blanks with information of your own choice, and asking the other person to repeat the information.

Übung 15. Suggestion: Have students fill in the blanks with information of their choice. Then have them do a role play, making statements and asking questions to repeat the information.

BEISPIEL: S1: Ich heiße Karl-Heinz Rüschenbaum.
S2: Wie bitte? Wie heißt du?
S1: Karl-Heinz Rüschenbaum.
S2: Ach so!
S1: Ich komme aus . . . (usw. [*and so on*])

1. Ich heiße _____.
2. Ich komme aus _____.
3. Das ist in _____.
4. Ich studiere _____.
5. _____ ist sehr interessant.
6. Nächstes Jahr studiere ich in _____.

Übung 16 Das Studentenleben°

°*student life*

A. You will hear some information about a German university student. Compare what you hear with the statements below. If a statement is incorrect, find the correct answer from among the choices in parentheses.

	DAS STIMMT	DAS STIMMT NICHT
1. Die Studentin heißt Claudia. (_____ Katrin, __x__ Karin)	☐	☒
2. Sie kommt aus Göttingen. (__x__ Dresden, _____ Bremen)	☐	☒
3. Der Familienname ist Renner. (_____ Reuter, _____ Reiser)	☒	☐
4. Sie studiert jetzt in Tübingen. (__x__ Göttingen, _____ Dresden)	☐	☒
5. Sie studiert Mathematik. (_____ Jura, __x__ Informatik)	☐	☒
6. Sie wohnt bei einer Familie. (__x__ im Studentenwohnheim, _____ allein)	☐	☒
7. Sie geht oft schwimmen. (_____ wandern, _____ Tennis spielen)	☒	☐
8. Sie geht oft ins Café. (_____ in die Disko, _____ ins Museum)	☒	☐

B. Now formulate yes/no questions based on the statements in Part A. Ask another student in your class to verify the information.

BEISPIEL: S1: Heißt die Studentin Claudia?
S2: Nein, sie heißt Karin.

Sprache im Kontext. Note: The goal of this section is to activate the four skills through a variety of activities. The section opens with a video activity, includes a reading with accompanying exercises, and culminates in writing and speaking assignments. In the video and reading sections, students are not expected to understand everything. Particularly in the initial chapters, global comprehension is the goal.

Sprache im Kontext

Zuschauen

Vorschau

Watch the commercial without sound. What product is advertised here?

Nippon

Arbeit mit dem Videotext

A. Read the following questions before you watch the commercial again. As you have seen, this commercial is very quick, so you should watch it several times before you answer the questions.

1. We see twenty-one different people in the commercial. Whom would you like to meet?
2. Describe in German what you think this person is like.
3. Write three German questions you would like to ask this person.
4. Choose one of the people in the commercial and create a **Steckbrief** (*wanted poster*) for him/her. Include the following information: ***Vorname, Name, Geburtsdatum, Beruf, Wohnort, Straße und Hausnummer, Land, Hobbys und Interessen.***

B. Reflect on the Nippon commercial and answer the following questions.

1. How is Nippon trying to sell its product?
2. Do you think that this is an effective commercial for the product? Would you be inclined to try Nippon? Why (not)?

Lesen

Lesen. Note: These sections focus on developing effective reading strategies. Here, basic techniques such as skimming, scanning, and reading for specific information are introduced. You should stress recognizing cognates and guessing from context. Although the texts are not meant to be read aloud in class, it may be useful to deal with certain parts of the readings as a class activity, especially at the beginning of the course. Prereading activities, called **Auf den ersten Blick,** will require students to brainstorm and speculate about the text. We recommend doing **Auf den ersten Blick** in class the day before the reading is assigned. Such an approach will provide you with an opportunity to clear up any potential misunderstandings or false assumptions about the main topic of the text. In the section titled **Zum Text,** students work with the text to acquire vocabulary and gather more detailed information.

Zum Thema°

about the topic

Where do the students in your German class come from? Were all students in the class born in the same country? What nationalities and ethnic groups are represented? How many students can speak more than one language? How many students have bilingual parents?

Auf den ersten Blick°

at first glance

1. Look at the title and the text itself. What type of text do you think this is? What led you to your conclusions?
2. Label the exchanges in the dialogue with *S1* (*Speaker 1*) and *S2* (*Speaker 2*).
3. Now read the dialogue aloud with a partner, each taking one of the two roles.
4. Skim the text for references to geographical locations and references to a person's appearance.
5. From the context, what do you think **reden** and **aussehen** (**siehst . . . aus, sehe aus**) mean?

Auf den ersten Blick. Students will need a lot of reassurance and encouragement to develop a positive attitude toward reading authentic material. The texts will seem daunting if approached word for word, but with proper application of the strategies suggested here, students will learn to enjoy taking risks when exploring an unknown text. The readings have been left largely unglossed so that students are compelled to guess meanings. Emphasize to students that they should avoid using the dictionary. In going over the text with them in class you may wish to point out the meaning of certain words, after students have tried to guess their meanings.

Dialog

von Nasrin Siege

„Du redest so gut deutsch. Wo kommst du denn her?“
„Aus Hamburg.“
„Wieso? Du siehst aber nicht so aus!“
„Wie sehe ich denn aus?“
„Na ja, so schwarzhaarig und dunkel . . . “
„Na und?“
„Wo bist du denn geboren?“
„In Hamburg.“
„Und dein Vater?“
„In Hamburg.“
„Deine Mutter?“
„Im Iran.“
„Da haben wir's!“
„Was denn?“
„Daß du keine[1] Deutsche bist!“
„Wer sagt das?“
„Na ich!“
„Warum?“

1. *no*

Reading. “Dialog” by Nasrin Siege appeared in *Texte dagegen,* a volume of fiction against xenophobia and racism. Note the use of colloquialisms such as splitting the interrogative **woher** and the sentence “Weiß ich auch nicht,” which is short for “Das weiß ich auch nicht.”

Even if students don't know the exact meaning of a word, they may be able to categorize it. This is a skill which will help them to use a dictionary judiciously. Depending on one's purpose in reading, knowing the general category of something may be sufficient for a general understanding of a text.

Zum Text°

°about the text

1. What can you find out about the birthplace, place of residence, citizenship of Speaker 2? What else can you find out about him or her?
2. Consider what you've learned about different forms of "you" in German. Speculate: How old are the two speakers? How well do they know each other? Where might this dialogue take place? How do you think it started?
3. Why is the nationality of Speaker 2 an issue for Speaker 1?

You'll find more about the topic of foreigners in Germany in ***Deutsch: Na klar!*** on the World Wide Web at www.mhhe.com/german

Kulturtipp

More than seven million foreigners make up roughly 9% of Germany's population and contribute to the country's economic growth. Most Germans and foreigners live in peaceful coexistence; however, incidents of discrimination and even violence against foreigners have occurred, especially following the economic difficulties in the wake of the unification of Germany in 1990. The German government strives to integrate children of foreigners into the German school system and to promote tolerance toward foreigners through media campaigns.

Dein Christus ein Jude
Dein Auto ein Japaner
Deine Pizza italienisch
Deine Demokratie griechisch
Dein Kaffee brasilianisch
Dein Urlaub türkisch
Deine Zahlen arabisch
Deine Schrift lateinisch
Und Dein Nachbar nur ein Ausländer?

Plakat gegen Rassismus und Ausländerfeindlichkeit (*anti-foreigner sentiments*), gesehen in einer Hamburger U-Bahn Station

Sprechen und Schreiben°

°speaking and writing

Aktivität 1 Ein Interview

Interview a classmate you have not already met to find out

- his/her name
- where he/she comes from
- where he/she was born
- where his/her father/mother is from
- what he/she is studying

1. As a class, formulate the questions in German for the interview, using the appropriate form of *you.*
2. Interview your partner.
3. Report your findings to the class.

Aktivität 2 Ein Bericht°

°report

Using the answers to your questions in **Aktivität 1,** write a summary of your interview.

Wortschatz

Eigenschaften	**Characteristics**
alt	old
ernst	serious
faul	lazy
fleißig	industrious, diligent
freundlich	friendly
groß	tall; big, large
hübsch	pretty, cute
interessant	interesting
konservativ	conservative
langweilig	boring
lustig	cheerful; fun
nett	nice
praktisch	practical
romantisch	romantic
ruhig	quiet
sympathisch	likable
treu	loyal

Substantive	**Nouns**
der **Amerikaner** / die **Amerikanerin**	American
der **Beruf**	profession
Was sind Sie von Beruf?	What do you do for a living?
das **Buch**	book
(das) **Deutsch**	German (language)
das **Essen**	food
der **Freund** / die **Freundin**	friend
das **Geburtsdatum**	birthdate
der **Geburtsort**	birthplace
das **Geld**	money
das **Interesse**	interest
das **Jahr**	year
nächstes Jahr	next year
das **Kind**	child
der **Mann**	man
der **Name**	name
der **Nachname**	family name, surname
der **Vorname**	first name, given name
der **Professor** / die **Professorin**	professor
das **Semester**	semester
der **Student** / die **Studentin**	student
die **Universität**	university
der **Wohnort**	place of residence
die **Zeitung**	newspaper

Verben	**Verbs**
arbeiten	to work
besuchen	to visit
bleiben	to stay, remain
diskutieren	to discuss
finden	to find
fragen	to ask
gehen	to go
heißen	to be called, be named
kochen	to cook
kommen	to come
lernen	to learn, study
machen	to do, make
Kreuzworträtsel machen	to do crossword puzzles
reisen	to travel
sagen	to say, tell
sein	to be
spielen	to play
Computerspiele spielen	to play computer games
Karten spielen	to play cards
studieren	to study
tanzen	to dance
wandern	to hike
wohnen	to reside, live

Personalpronomen	**Personal Pronouns**
ich	I
du	you (*informal sg.*)
er	he; it
sie	she; it; they
es	it
wir	we
ihr	you (*informal pl.*)
Sie	you (*formal sg. / pl.*)

Fragewörter	**Interrogative Words**
wann	when
warum	why
was	what

wer	who
wie	how
wie lange	how long
wie viel*	how much
wie viele	how many
wo	where
woher	from where

Sonstiges — Other

Das macht mir Spaß.	That's fun.
denn	(*particle used in questions to express interest*)
doch	yes (*positive answer to a negative question*)
heute	today
heute Abend*	this evening
hier	here
jetzt	now
sag mal	tell me
sehr	very
viel	a lot, much
Viel Glück!	Good luck!
Viel Spaß!	Have fun!
viele	many
wirklich	really

Lernziele

Use this checklist to verify that you can now . . .

- ☐ give personal information about yourself (and others) such as your name, address, telephone number, home town, height, and place of birth.
- ☐ mention a few subjects you are studying.
- ☐ describe your personal characteristics and those of others.
- ☐ name some of your hobbies and interests.
- ☐ conjugate regular verbs in the present tense.
- ☐ use simple declarative sentences to make statements.
- ☐ ask "information" and "yes/no" questions.
- ☐ answer questions using **ja** and **doch.**
- ☐ apply basic reading strategies in order to identify types of texts, recognize cognates, and understand the gist of some types of texts through contextual guessing.

*See Appendix E for alternate spelling.

Kapitel 2

Wie ich wohne

Zettel am „schwarzen Brett" (*bulletin board*) an der Uni

Kapitel 2. Suggestion: Introduce the theme of this chapter by focusing on the students' concern for housing. Is housing also a problem in your community? State in simple German where you live, and briefly describe your home. Ask students where they live. Be tolerant if their answers are only partially in German and grammatically incorrect, and be prepared to help them with their answers.

Alles klar?

A. Just as in North America, flyers (**Anschlagzettel**) are a popular way to make announcements, advertise, or disseminate information in German-speaking countries. What, do you think, is the purpose of the flyer shown here? Once you've determined the purpose, answer the multiple-choice questions.

- Wo findet man (*one*) so einen Anschlagzettel?
  - **a.** in einer Klinik
  - **b.** an der Uni
  - **c.** in einem Garten
- Die vier Studentinnen suchen _____.
  - **a.** einen Regenschirm
  - **b.** eine Wohnung
  - **c.** ein Dach

- Sie brauchen _____ Zimmer.
  - **a.** zwei bis (*to*) drei
  - **b.** sechs bis sieben
  - **c.** vier bis fünf
- Sie möchten (*would like*) eine Wohnung _____.
  - **a.** im Stadtzentrum
  - **b.** in einem Vorort (*suburb*)
  - **c.** auf dem Lande (*in the country*)

Vokabelsuche. Find the German word for:

1. kitchen
2. bath
3. central location
4. reward

B. Listen to the following short conversations. Mark the kind of apartment the speakers are looking for.

1. **a.** eine Zweizimmerwohnung
b. eine Dreizimmerwohnung

2. **a.** eine Zweizimmerwohnung mit Küche und Bad
b. eine Dreizimmerwohnung in zentraler Lage

3. **a.** ein Zimmer bei einer Familie
b. ein Zimmer in einem Studentenheim

Alles klar? Suggestion: Give students several minutes to scan both the questions and the flyer from a university bulletin board, *das Schwarze Brett,* before responding.

Follow-up: You may "narrate" the flyer to the students. Or, with the help of the questions, individual students can explain sections of the flyer.

Realia. This flyer was distributed at the university in Göttingen and demonstrates the imagination required to obtain student housing. The reward of 100 Marks reflects how keen competition for housing is.

Kulturtipp

In German-speaking countries, the kitchen and bathroom are not counted as "rooms," when describing the number of rooms in an apartment. Thus, a **Zweizimmerwohnung** has one bedroom and a living room, while a **Dreizimmerwohnung** has two bedrooms and a living room. An **Appartement** is a studio, or efficiency apartment.

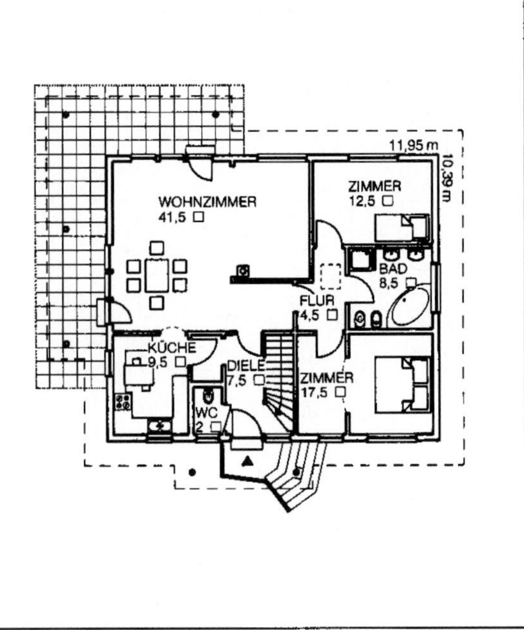

Realia. The floor plan is taken from the publication *Pro Fertighaus.*

Suggestion: After students read the Kulturtipp, have them determine what size apartment is depicted in the floor plan.

Wörter im Kontext

Thema 1. Suggestion: Once students have worked with the dialogue, ask them questions such as the following: *Was sucht Ulla? Wo gibt es ein Zimmer? Wie sieht das Zimmer aus? Wie hoch ist die Miete? Wo liegt die Wohnung?*

Thema 1

Auf Wohnungssuche°

° in search of an apartment

Ulla und Stefan treffen sich (meet) *vor der* ***Mensa*** *der Uni Freiburg. Ulla hat ein großes* ***Problem.***

STEFAN: Tag, Ulla! Wie geht's?
ULLA: Ach, nicht besonders.
STEFAN: **Was ist denn los?**
ULLA: Ich **suche dringend** eine **Wohnung** oder ein **Zimmer.** Wohnungen sind aber alle **so teuer.**
STEFAN: Ist denn **nichts frei** im **Studentenheim?**
ULLA: Hier in Freiburg? **Bestimmt** nicht!
STEFAN: Hier ist die Zeitung von heute. **Vielleicht** gibt es (*there is*) doch **etwas.** Ah, hier, Wohnungsanzeigen. **Da,** schau mal: **schönes, möbliertes** Zimmer.
ULLA: Wie **hoch** ist die **Miete?**
STEFAN: **Nur** 200 Mark.
ULLA: Das ist **recht preiswert.** Wo ist das Zimmer?
STEFAN: In Zußdorf.
ULLA: In Zußdorf?! Kommt nicht in Frage! Das ist viel zu weit weg.
STEFAN: Na, da **hast** du **Recht.** Preiswert ist es, **aber** Zußdorf ist nicht **gerade** zentral gelegen.

Mark whether the following statements are correct (**das stimmt**) or incorrect (**das stimmt nicht**) based on the information in the dialogue.

	DAS STIMMT	DAS STIMMT NICHT
1. Stefan sucht ein Zimmer.	☐	☒
2. Im Studentenheim ist nichts frei.	☒	☐
3. Stefan findet eine Wohnungsanzeige in der Zeitung.	☒	☐
4. Das Zimmer ist nicht möbliert.	☐	☒
5. Die Miete ist nicht sehr preiswert.	☐	☒
6. Zußdorf ist nicht zentral gelegen.	☒	☐

Wo und wie wohnen Sie? Note: Expressions using the dative case should be treated as lexical items. Dative prepositions will be covered in **Kapitel 5,** prepositions that take either the dative or accusative in **Kapitel 6.**

Wo und wie wohnen Sie?

- ☐ allein in einem Zimmer / einer Wohnung
- ☐ bei (*with*) den Eltern (*parents*)
- ☐ bei einer Familie
- ☐ im **Studentenwohnheim**
- ☐ in einem **Haus**
- ☐ in einer **Wohngemeinschaft (WG)**
- ☐ mit einem **Mitbewohner** / einer **Mitbewohnerin** zusammen (*together*)

Beschreiben Sie Ihre Wohnung / Ihr Zimmer! / Ihr Haus!

Suggestion: Remind students that *sie* is used to refer to *Wohnung* and *es* to *Zimmer* or *Haus.*

Sie/Es hat . . .

- ☐ ein **Arbeitszimmer**
- ☐ eine schöne Aussicht (*view*)
- ☐ ein **Badezimmer** / **Bad**
- ☐ einen **Balkon**
- ☐ ein **Esszimmer**
- ☐ ein (zwei/drei) **Fenster**
- ☐ eine **Garage**
- ☐ einen **Garten**
- ☐ eine **Küche**
- ☐ ein (zwei/drei) **Schlafzimmer**
- ☐ ein **Wohnzimmer**
- ☐ ein **Terrasse**

Sie/Es ist . . .

- ☐ **groß**
- ☐ **klein**
- ☐ **dunkel**
- ☐ **hell**
- ☐ **möbliert**
- ☐ **unmöbliert**
- ☐ **preiswert**
- ☐ **teuer**
- ☐ **ruhig**
- ☐ **laut**

Die Miete ist . . .

- ☐ **hoch**
- ☐ **niedrig**

The indefinite articles **ein/eine** are used with the subject of a sentence.

Das ist **ein** Balkon. Das ist **ein** Badezimmer. Das ist **eine** Küche.

When a masculine noun is used as the direct object of a verb, **ein** changes to **einen.**

Mein Haus hat ein Badezimmer, eine Küche und **einen** Balkon.

Aktivität 1. Suggestion: Go over the ads with students before starting the listening comprehension. Focus on those details that are most pertinent to the exercise.

Aktivität 1 Wir brauchen eine Wohnung / ein Zimmer.

Scan the five ads from people looking for housing. Label the ads from 1 to 5 in the order in which you hear them.

4 — **Freundl. junger 37-jähriger Englischlehrer su. 1 Zi. in WG um mit Euch Deutsch zu sprechen und es besser zu lernen. ☎ 570 56 39**

2 — **Freundlicher Schauspieler[5] aus Hamburg sucht Zi in WG vom 1. Mai bis 1. August in München. ☎ 637 88 78, ♂ Manfred**

5 — **Musiker (24) sucht Zimmer oder Raum in WG o.ä.[1] zum 1.6. oder etwas früher. ☎ 040/439 84 20 Markus (rufe zurück[2]) PS.: Zahle[3] bis 500 DM incl.[4]**

1 — **Fotodesigner, 22, sucht preiswertes Zimmer in junger WG, mögl.[6] zentral zum 1.7.87. Kischel Benno, Westendstr. 237, 8 Mü 21 (telefonisch schlecht erreichbar[7])**

3 — **Architekturstudentin (25) sucht zum 1. od. 15.5. ruhiges Zim. bis 400,— incl. in WG ☎ 857 63 90 (evtl.[8] 50 72 58)**

1. o. ä. = oder ähnliches *or something similar* 2. rufe . . . *call back* 3. *pay* 4. incl. = inclusive *including utilities* 5. *actor* 6. mögl. = möglich *possible* 7. schlecht . . . *difficult to reach* 8. evtl. = eventuell *maybe*

Realia. These ads are from the *Münchner Stadt-Zeitung,* which attracts a young and fairly unconventional readership.

Sprachtipp

The abbreviation **DM** stands for **Deutsche Mark** and may be found before or after the price.

DM 200, –
200, – DM

In either case, the price would be read as **zweihundert Mark.** A single mark is **eine Mark.**

Sprachtipp. Suggestion: Write a few prices on the board and have students practice saying them.

Sprachtipp

In German, attributive adjectives—that is, adjectives in front of nouns—take endings.

Ich suche ein möbliert**es** Zimmer.

I'm looking for a furnished room.

Predicate adjectives—that is, adjectives used after the verb **sein**—do not take endings.

Das Zimmer ist möbliert.

The room is furnished.

You will learn more about attributive adjective endings in **Kapitel 9.**

Aktivität 2 Wer braucht eine Wohnung?

Look over the five ads from **Aktivität 1** and say as much as you can about each.

BEISPIEL: Ein Englischlehrer sucht ein Zimmer in einer WG.
Er ist 37.
Er ist freundlich und nett.

Aktivität 3 Eine Anzeige° schreiben

° ad

Using the newspaper ads on this page and the previous pages as models, create a simple ad in the following format. Trade ads with another person, who will read yours to the class.

{Student / Studentin / ?} sucht {großes / kleines / ruhiges / helles / möbliertes / unmöbliertes / ?} Zimmer mit {Telefon / Bad / Küche / Garten / ?} in {einer WG / einem Haus / zentraler Lage / ?} bis zu DM __.

Auf Möbelsuche im Kaufhaus

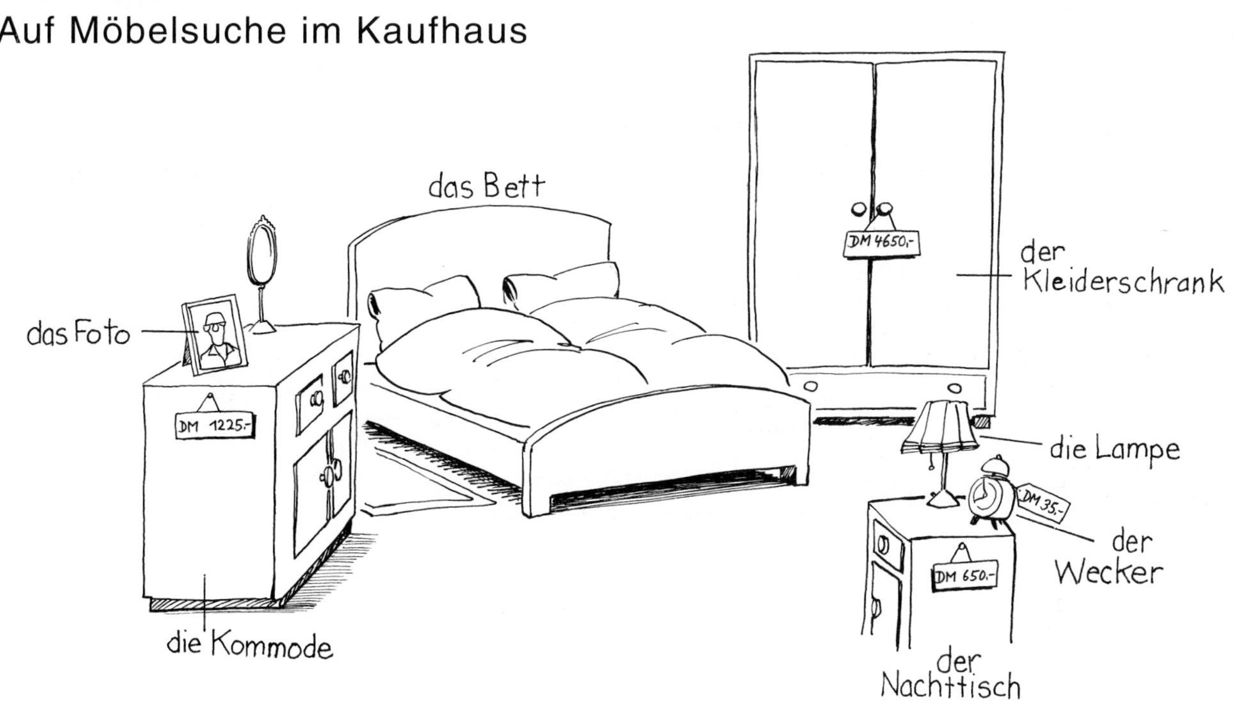

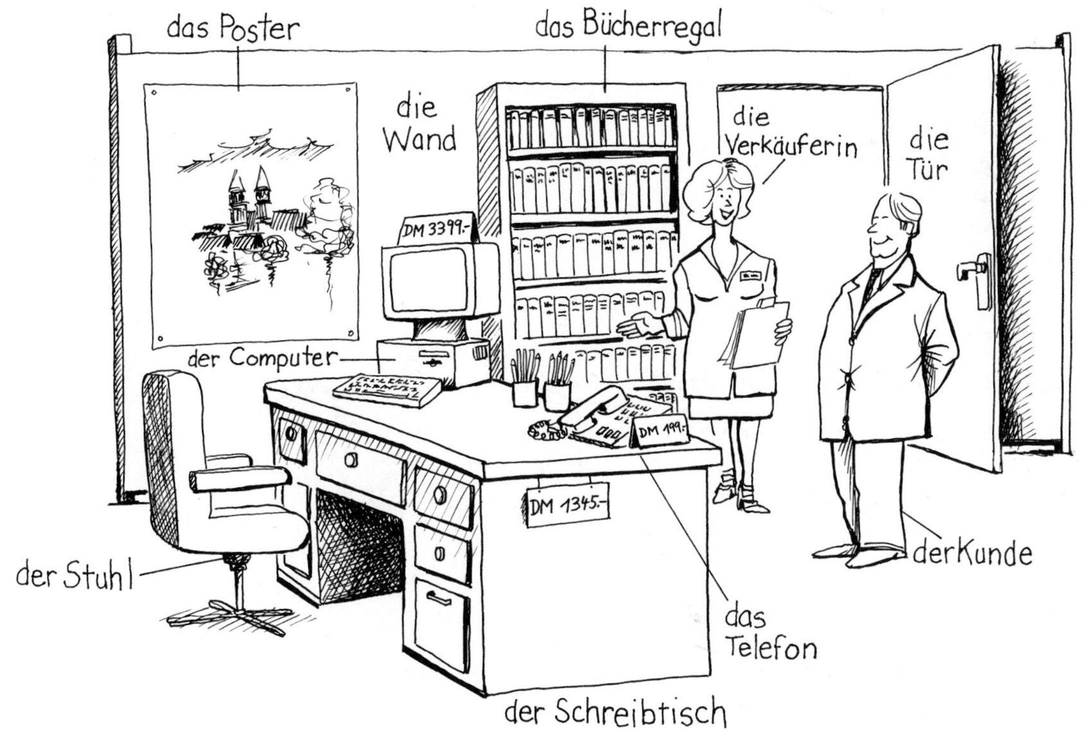

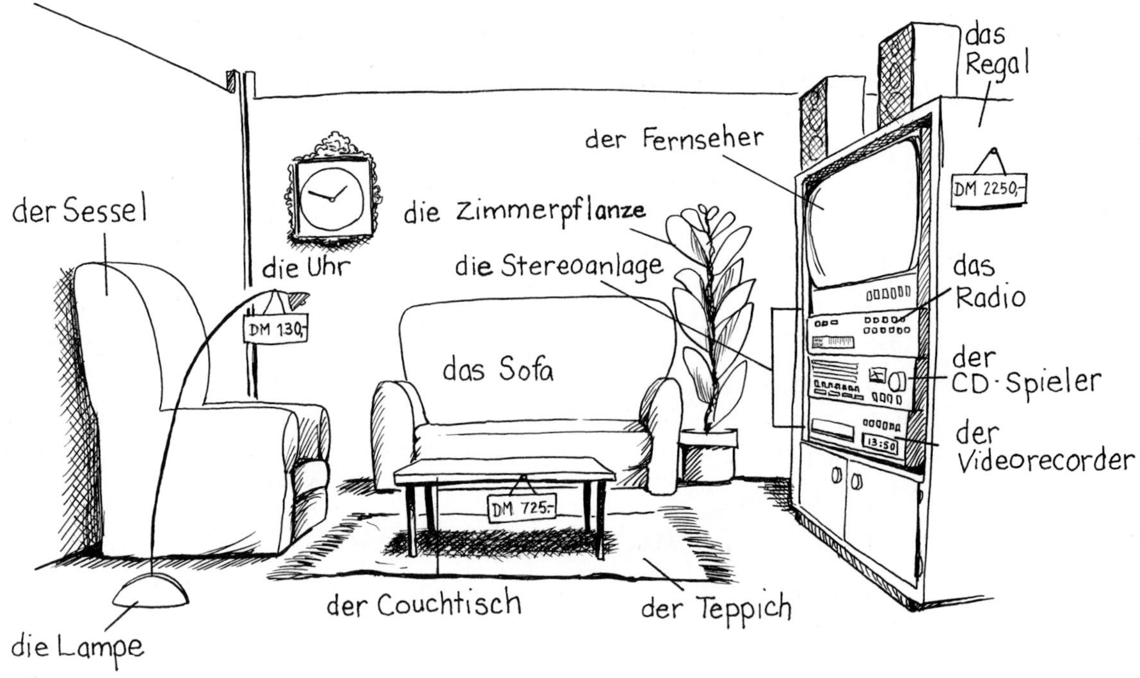

Was haben Sie **schon** in Ihrem Zimmer / in Ihrer Wohnung?

Haben Sie . . .

- □ einen **Fernseher?**
- □ eine **Lampe?**
- □ einen **CD-Spieler?**
- □ ein **Radio?**
- □ ?

Was brauchen Sie **noch?**

Brauchen Sie . . .

- □ einen **Computer?**
- □ ein **Bücherregal?**
- □ ?

Was **kostet** er/sie/es?

- □ der Computer kostet 3399 Mark.
- □ ?

Aktivität 4 Ulla hat jetzt endlich° ein Zimmer. 

°*finally*

Listen as Ulla tells her friend Karin about the room she just found. As you listen, jot down at least three items that Ulla has and identify the three items she still needs.

WAS ULLA IM ZIMMER HAT	WAS ULLA NOCH BRAUCHT
ein Bett	eine Lampe
einen Schreibtisch, einen Stuhl	ein Bücherregal
einen Tisch, einen Sessel	Telefon

Aktivität 5 Einkäufe°

°*purchases*

Look at the department store displays at the beginning of **Thema 2** and give your opinion of the furniture and other items shown.

BEISPIEL: S1: Wie findest du den Computer?
das Bett?
die Lampe?
S2: Sehr schön. Und wie findest du _____?

Aktivität 5. Variation: Bring in pictures of furniture and ask students for their opinions.

REAKTIONEN

zu	teuer	praktisch
sehr	hässlich (*ugly*)	(un)bequem
nicht	schön	billig (*cheap*)
	preiswert	toll (*neat*)

Sprachtipp

When a masculine noun is used as the direct object of a verb, **der** changes to **den.** The neuter and feminine articles **das** and **die** remain unchanged.

Wie findest du **den** Computer?
but Wie findest du **das** Bett und **die** Lampe?

Aktivität 6 Ein Gespräch im Kaufhaus

Listen as Ulla talks with a salesperson. Then answer the true/false questions and correct any false statements.

	DAS STIMMT	DAS STIMMT NICHT
1. Ulla braucht nur eine Lampe.	☐	☒
2. Ulla findet die italienische Lampe schön.	☒	☐
3. Die Lampe aus Italien ist nicht teuer.	☐	☒
4. Ulla kauft eine Lampe für DM 50, –.	☒	☐
5. Das Kaufhaus führt keine (*no*) Bücherregale.	☒	☐

Hier klicken!

You'll find more about home furnishings in German speaking countries in ***Deutsch: Na klar!*** on the World Wide Web at www.mhhe.com/german.

Thema 3

Was wir gern machen

Was machen diese Leute gern? Match the captions with the corresponding drawing.

1. _____ Herr Wurm **liest** gern **Bücher.**
2. _____ Frau Schlemmer **isst** gern.
3. _____ Ernst Immermüd **schläft** gern.
4. _____ Uschi Schnell **fährt** gern **Motorrad.**
5. _____ Gerhard Glotze **sieht** gern **Videos.**
6. _____ Frau Renner **läuft** gern.

a.

b.

c.

d. **e.**

f.

Was machen Sie gern?

	JA	NEIN
Hören Sie gern Musik?	☐	☐
Tanzen Sie gern Tango?	☐	☐
Essen Sie gern Fisch?	☐	☐
Fahren Sie gern **Auto?**	☐	☐
Kochen Sie gern?	☐	☐
Schreiben Sie gern **Briefe?**	☐	☐
Schwimmen Sie gern?	☐	☐
Telefonieren Sie gern mit einem **Handy**?	☐	☐

Suggestion: Have students check off two or three things they like to do and then have them say what they enjoy doing.

In **Kapitel 1** you learned to express what you like to do, using the expression **Spaß machen** (*to be fun*).

Another common way to say you like to do something is to use the adverb **gern** with a conjugated verb.

Ich esse **gern** Fisch.	*I like to eat fish.*
Ich schwimme **gern.**	*I like to swim.*

If you want to say you dislike doing something, use **nicht gern.**

Ich esse **nicht gern** Fisch.	*I don't like to eat fish.*
Ich schwimme **nicht gern.**	*I don't like to swim.*

Note that **(nicht) gern** usually precedes direct objects.

Ich spiele **gern** Tennis.	*I like to play tennis.*
Karin trinkt **nicht gern** Kaffee.	*Karin doesn't like to drink coffee.*
Georg isst **gern** Vanilleeis.	*Georg likes to eat vanilla ice cream.*
Frau Spitz hört **nicht gern** laute Musik.	*Ms. Spitz does not like to listen to loud music.*

Realia. *Goldmann* is a German publishing company.

GOLDMANN
LESEN MACHT SPASS

Analyse

- What activities are described in the ad and headline?
- Can you rephrase the following sentences using **(nicht) gern?**

1. Wandern macht mir Spaß.
2. Arbeiten macht mir keinen (*no*) Spaß.

Warum ich so gern in Hamburg arbeite
Von WOLFGANG JOOP, Hamburg
Ich lebe und arbeite in Hamburg.

Realia. **"Warum ich so gern in Hamburg arbeite"** is the title of an article that appeared in the newspaper *Welt am Sonntag.*

Point out. gerne is a variant of gern

Aktivität 7 Zwei Leipziger°

°two people from Leipzig

Answer the questions about the Knobels, based on the information given in their personal biographies.

Aktivität 7. Suggestion: Make up a chart like the biographies shown. Then have students interview one or two other people. This can be followed by a class discussion of what students like.

1. Was trinkt Frau Knobel gern? Und ihr Mann?
2. Was essen die Knobels gern?
3. Was trägt Frau Knobel gern? Und ihr Mann?
4. Was für (*what kind of*) Musik hören sie gern?
5. Was für ein Auto fährt Frau Knobel gern? Und ihr Mann?
6. Was für Hobbys hat Frau Knobel? Und ihr Mann?

Name: Marianne Knobel
Alter: 54
Lieblingsgetränk: Rotwein
Lieblingsessen: Nudelgerichte[1]
Lieblingskleidung: Jeans, Röcke[2]
Lieblingskomponist: Gustav Mahler
Lieblingsauto: Nissan Sunny
Hobbys: Bücher lesen, Kochen, Sport[3]

Name: Martin Knobel
Alter: 58
Lieblingsgetränk: Bier
Lieblingsessen: Hackbraten[4]
Lieblingskleidung: Jeans, Pullover
Lieblingskomponist: Ludwig van Beethoven
Lieblingsauto: BMW M5
Hobbys: Zeitung lesen, ins Kino gehen

1. *pasta dishes*
2. *skirts*
3. *doing sports*
4. *meatloaf*

Aktivität 8 Hin und her: Machen sie das gern?

Find out what the following people like to do or don't like to do by asking your partner.

BEISPIEL: S1: Was macht Denise gern?
S2: Sie reist gern. Was macht Thomas nicht gern?
S1: Er fährt nicht gern Auto.

	GERN	NICHT GERN
Thomas	arbeiten	Auto fahren
Denise	reisen	kochen
Niko	Eis essen	Karten spielen
Anja	laufen	Bier trinken

Aktivität 9 Machst du das gern oder nicht gern?

Ask three people in your class: **„Was machst du gern, und was machst du nicht gern?"** Report your findings to the class.

BEISPIEL: Jeff reist gern, aber er tanzt nicht gern.
Sharon spielt gern Karten, aber sie kocht nicht gern.
Dave hört gern Musik, aber er arbeitet nicht gern.

Grammatik im Kontext

The Plural of Nouns°

°Substantive im Plural

German forms the plural of nouns in several different ways. Some plurals have the same form as the singular, others add special plural endings and may even umlaut the stem vowels. The following chart shows the most common plural patterns and the notation of those patterns in the vocabulary lists of this book.

The Plural of Nouns. Suggestion: Introduce plurals by mentioning in the plural several items that you have recently purchased. Let students hear plural nouns in a natural context. This can be accompanied by visuals, or you can write items on the board or use an overhead projector. **Point out:** Noun plurals cannot be acquired overnight. At this point students need to familiarize themselves with the different possibilities of plural formation rather than to memorize long lists.

SINGULAR	PLURAL	TYPE OF CHANGE	NOTATION
das Zimmer	die Zimmer	*no change*	-
die Mutter	die Mütter	*stem vowel is umlauted*	¨
der Tag	die Tage	*ending* **e** *is added*	**-e**
der Stuhl	die Stühle	*stem vowel is sometimes umlauted*	**¨e**
das Haus	die Häuser	*ending* **er** *is added and stem vowel is umlauted*	**¨er**
die Lampe	die Lampen	*ending* **n** *is added*	**-n**
die Frau	die Frauen	*ending* **en** *is added*	**-en**
die Studentin	die Studentinnen	*ending* **nen** *is added*	**-nen**
das Radio	die Radios	*ending* **s** *is added*	**-s**

A few simple rules will help you form the plurals of some nouns.

1. The plural of masculine nouns denoting nationality or profession and ending in **er** is identical to the singular.

SINGULAR	PLURAL
der Amerikaner	die Amerikaner
der Wecker	die Wecker

2. Feminine nouns ending in **in** form the plural by adding **nen** to the singular.

SINGULAR	PLURAL
die Amerikanerin	die Amerikanerinnen
die Mitbewohnerin	die Mitbewohnerinnen

3. Feminine nouns ending in **e** form the plural by adding **n** to the singular.

SINGULAR	PLURAL
die Küche	die Küchen
die Miete	die Mieten

4. Nouns ending in vowels other than **e** usually form the plural by adding **s.**

SINGULAR	PLURAL
das Kino	die Kinos
die Party	die Partys*
das Sofa	die Sofas

Sprachtipp

In order to use gender-inclusive language, some writers use a masculine form followed by a slash and the feminine ending: **Student/in, Amerikaner/in.** One frequently encounters **-Innen** for the gender-inclusive plural of such nouns (as in **StudentInnen** and **AmerikanerInnen**), a convention which has gained some degree of acceptance as a substitute for the more cumbersome **Studenten und Studentinnen** or **Amerikaner und Amerikanerinnen.**

Übung 1 Wie viele

List items in your classroom, students in your class, and things that you and your friends have.

BEISPIEL: Das Klassenzimmer hat 27 Stühle und 25 Studenten.

das Klassenzimmer	Fenster (-)	Student (-en)	Freundin (-nen)
ich	Tür (-en)	Studentin (-nen)	Uhr (-en)
mein Freund / meine Freundin	Stuhl (¨-e)	Buch (¨-er)	Problem (-e)
?	Tisch (-e)	Freund (-e)	?

The Nominative and Accusative Cases°

°Kasus: der Nominativ und der Akkusativ

In English, the subject and direct object in a sentence are distinguished by their placement. The subject usually precedes the verb, whereas the direct object usually follows the verb.

In German, however, either the subject or the direct object may precede the verb. Subjects are in the nominative case, while direct objects are in the accusative case. You can always identify subjects and direct objects by context and, in the case of masculine nouns, by the **en** ending of the article (**den**, **einen**). In **Kapitel 5** and **Kapitel 9**, you will learn about two other cases, the dative and the genitive.

*Note that the plural of nouns ending in **y** is **ys,** not **ies: Party, Partys; Hobby, Hobbys.**

The Definite Article°: Nominative and Accusative

der bestimmte Artikel

You are already familiar with the nominative case. Those are the forms you have used in **Kapitel 1.** Here are the nominative and accusative case forms of the definite articles (*the*).

	SINGULAR			PLURAL
	Masculine	*Neuter*	*Feminine*	*All Genders*
Nominative (subject)	der } Sessel	das } Sofa	die } Lampe	die } Stühle
Accusative (direct object)	**den** } Sessel	das } Sofa	die } Lampe	die } Stühle

Note that only the masculine definite article has a distinct accusative form: **den.** In the plural, there is only one article for all three genders: **die.**

The Indefinite Article°: Nominative and Accusative

der unbestimmte Artikel

As you have already seen in **Kapitel 1,** masculine and neuter nouns both use **ein** in the nominative case. Here are the nominative and accusative forms of the indefinite articles (*a/an*).

	SINGULAR			PLURAL
	Masculine	*Neuter*	*Feminine*	*All Genders*
Nominative	ein } Sessel	ein } Sofa	eine } Lampe	– Stühle
Accusative	**einen** } Sessel	ein } Sofa	eine } Lampe	– Stühle

Note that only the masculine indefinite article has a distinct accusative form: **einen.**

Analyse

Read the following ad for IKEA stores and answer the questions.

- What is the subject of all of the sentences?
- Find the direct objects preceded by definite articles. What is the gender of each of these nouns?
- Find the one direct object that is preceded by an indefinite article. What is the nominative form of this noun?
- Several accusative objects are in the plural; only one of these is preceded by a definite article. Identify this noun and its article.
- Which direct objects are not preceded by definite articles? What is the gender of each of these nouns?

Analyse. Suggestion: Preview in class, then assign for homework. Discuss the **Analyse** in class the following day. Use the excerpt from this IKEA ad by personalizing it: *Was brauchen Sie? Brauchen Sie das? (z.B. Geld, Gesundheit, Liebe usw.)*

Realia. This is a portion of an ad for IKEA stores, a chain carrying inexpensive but stylish Scandinavian furniture and household items. Typically, IKEA furniture has to be assembled by the customer. The text of the entire ad is much longer and reads almost like a story, making readers forget it is an advertisement.

1. *everything*
2. *nothing*
3. *light*
4. *love*
5. *health*
6. *happiness, luck*
7. *sun*
8. das Buch . . . *the book of books*
9. *egg timer*
10. sich . . . *himself/herself*
11. *beloved*

Weak Masculine Nouns°

° schwache Maskulina

A few masculine nouns have special accusative singular forms. Five nouns of this type are:

NOMINATIVE	ACCUSATIVE
der/ein **Mensch**	den/einen Mensch**en**
der/ein **Student**	den/einen Student**en**
der/ein **Herr**	den/einen Herr**n**
der/ein **Name**	den/einen Name**n**

Weak masculine nouns, as they are called, are indicated in the vocabulary lists of this book by the notation (**-en** *masc.*) or (**-n** *masc.*).

Nominative and Accusative Interrogative Pronouns°

Interrogativpronomen im Nominativ und Akkusativ

To ask about the subject of a sentence, use **wer** (*who*) or **was** (*what*). To ask about the direct object, use **wen** (*whom*) or **was** (*what*).

Wer braucht Geld?	*Who needs money?*
Was ist ein Gnu?	*What is a gnu?*
Wen besucht Frau Martin?	*Whom is Mrs. Martin visiting?*
Was braucht der Mensch?	*What does a person need?*

Was ist das?

ein Fussballspieler

Realia. This riddle is from the Swiss magazine *Brückenbauer*, published by the *Migros* department store chain.

Übung 2 Neu in Göttingen

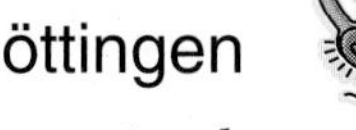

You will now hear a conversation between Stefan and his friend Birgit. As you listen, check off what Stefan already has and what he still needs for his new apartment. Not all items are mentioned; leave them blank.

	DAS HAT STEFAN	DAS BRAUCHT STEFAN
1. eine Stereoanlage	☐	☐
2. eine Zimmerpflanze	☐	☐
3. eine Uhr	☐	☐
4. einen Couchtisch	☐	☐
5. einen Computer	☐	☐
6. einen Schreibtisch	☐	☒
7. ein Bücherregal	☐	☒
8. eine Kaffeemaschine	☐	☒
9. einen Schlafsack (*sleeping bag*)	☒	☐
10. ein Bett	☐	☒
11. einen Sessel	☐	☐

Übung 3 Was brauchen Sie noch?

You are shopping for several items. Referring to the items and prices under **Thema 2: Auf Möbelsuche im Kaufhaus** in this chapter, create short conversational exchanges with a partner.

BEISPIEL: S1: Ich brauche eine Lampe.
S2: Hier haben wir Lampen.
S1: Was kosten die Lampen?
S2: 130 Mark.
S1: Das ist aber teuer.

Here are some additional noun plurals:

Betten	Sessel	Uhren
Kaffeemaschinen	Sofas	Videorecorder
schnurlose Telefone	Stereoanlagen	Wecker

Übung 4 Uwes Zimmer

This is Uwe's dorm room. What pieces of furniture are there? What other objects do you see? What does Uwe need?

Das Zimmer hat _____.
Ich sehe auch noch _____.
Uwe braucht noch _____.

Übung 5 Was brauchen Sie dringend?

A. Look at the following advertisement. Indicate several items that you could use.

B. Now look at the advertisement and prices below. You have 500 marks. What will you buy?

BEISPIEL: Ich kaufe den Tisch für _____ Mark und das Bett für _____ Mark.

Übung 5. Suggestion: Give students several minutes to scan the ad in order to think of several items. Have students compare lists. One student can report what another has on his or her list. This activity also works well in pairs, with each student asking alternately *Was kaufst du?* If the activity is done in pairs, encourage students to comment on the items to be bought by adding such information as *Das finde ich praktisch.*

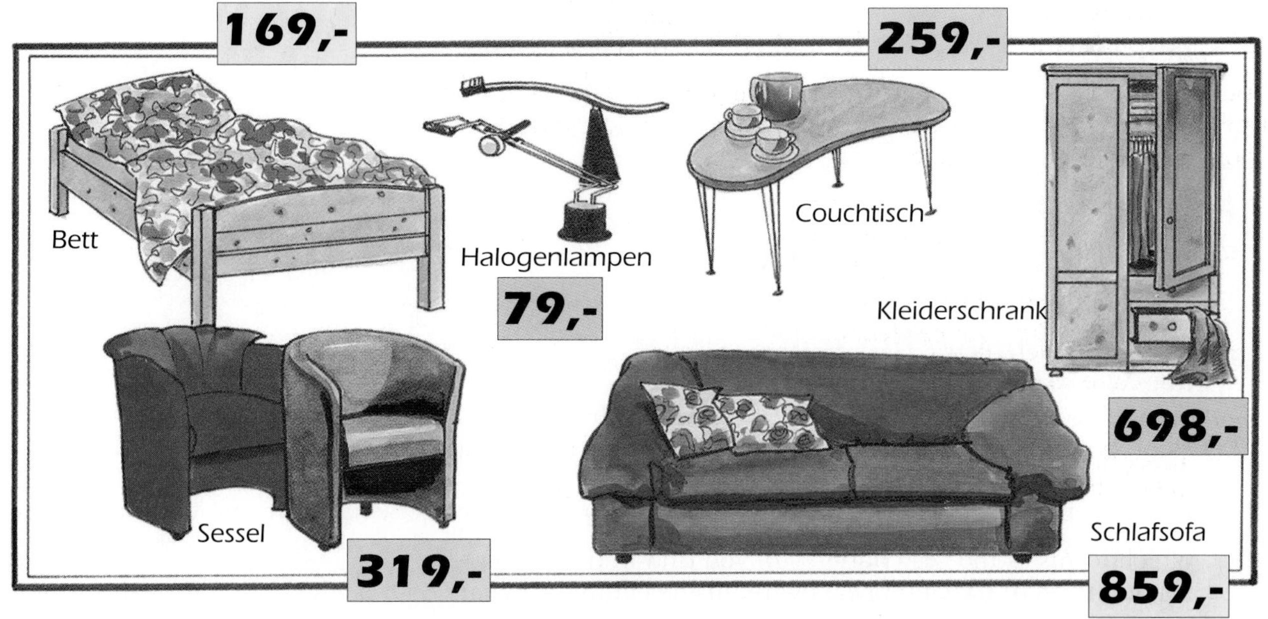

The Verb *haben*

The present tense of **haben** is irregular in the **du-** and **er/sie/es-**forms.

haben			
ich	habe	wir	haben
du	**hast**	ihr	habt
er / sie / es	**hat**	sie	haben
Sie haben			

The verb **haben,** like many other verbs, needs an accusative object (a direct object) to form a complete sentence.

Wir haben **eine Vorlesung** um zwei Uhr.	*We have a lecture at two o'clock.*
Anja hat **einen Schreibtisch.**	*Anja has a desk.*

Some other verbs like this are **brauchen, finden, kaufen,** and **suchen.**

Other verbs need no accusative (direct) object. Besides **sein** and **heißen,** some other such verbs you already know are **bleiben, kommen, wandern,** and **wohnen.**

The verb **haben** is used in a number of common expressions:

Durst haben	*to be thirsty*
gern haben	*to like a person or thing*
Hunger haben	*to be hungry*
Lust haben	*to feel like doing something*
Recht haben	*to be correct, to be right*
Zeit haben	*to have time*

Analyse

Analyse. Explain to students that in casual spoken German the *e* of the *ich*-form is usually dropped. The full form with *e* is standard for written and formal spoken German,

Read the dialogue and answer the questions.

Ein Gespräch zwischen zwei Studenten. Es ist 12 Uhr mittags.

JÜRGEN: Grüß dich, Petra. Hast du Hunger?
PETRA: Warum fragst du?
JÜRGEN: Ich geh' jetzt essen. Ich hab' Hunger. Kommst du mit?
PETRA: Na gut. Da kommt übrigens Hans. Der hat bestimmt auch Hunger.
HANS: Habt ihr zwei vielleicht Hunger?
PETRA: Ja, und wie! Aber ich hab' nicht viel Zeit. Um zwei haben wir nämlich eine Vorlesung.

- Which forms of the verb **haben** can you find in the dialogue?
- The **ich**-form of **haben** appears without the ending **e.** What could be the reason for this?

Übung 6 Hast du Hunger?

Complete the sentences with **haben** or **sein.**

Jürgen, Petra und Hans _____ Studenten.[1] Es _____ gerade Mittagszeit.[2] Jürgen _____ Hunger.[3] Er fragt Petra: „_____ du Hunger?"[4] Hans _____ Petras Freund.[5] Hans und Petra _____ um zwei eine Vorlesung.[6] Sie _____ nicht viel Zeit.[7] Und Jürgen _____ nicht viel Geld.[8] Er fragt Hans „_____ du etwas Geld?"[9]

Note: Throughout *Deutsch: Na klar!,* sentences within paragraphs are numbered at the end of the sentence.

Negation with *nicht,* and the Negative Article *kein*°

Verneinung

In **Kapitel 1** you learned to negate a simple statement by adding the word **nicht** (*not*) before a predicate adjective.

You will learn more about the placement of **nicht** in **Kapitel 11** and **Kapitel 12.**

Die Lampe ist **nicht** billig. — *The lamp is not cheap.*

You can also use **nicht** to negate an entire statement, or just an adverb.

Karin kauft die Lampe **nicht.** — *Karin is not buying the lamp.*
Ralf schreibt **nicht** besonders gut. — *Ralf doesn't write particularly well.*

One other important way to express negation is by using the negative article **kein.**

The forms of **kein** (*no, not a, not any*), the negative article, parallel the forms of **ein.**

	SINGULAR						PLURAL	
	Masculine		*Neuter*		*Feminine*		*All Genders*	
Nominative	kein	Sessel	kein	Sofa	keine	Lampe	keine	Stühle
Accusative	keinen	Sessel	kein	Sofa	keine	Lampe	keine	Stühle

Use **kein** to negate a noun that would normally be preceded by an indefinite article or no article at all.

—Hast du einen Computer? — *Do you have a computer?*
—Nein, ich habe **keinen** Computer. — *No, I don't have a computer.*
—Hast du Geld? — *Do you have any money?*
—Nein, ich habe **kein** Geld. — *No, I do not have any money.*
—Hast du Zeit, Uschi? — *Do you have any time, Uschi?*
—Nein, ich habe **keine** Zeit. — *No, I have no time.*

Übung 7 Immer diese Ausreden!°

Excuses, excuses!

Everyone has a different excuse for turning down an invitation. Listen and check off the excuse given by each person.

1. Reinhard
   ☐ hat keine Zeit.
   ☐ hat keine Lust.
   ☒ hat kein Geld.
2. Erika
   ☐ hat keinen Freund.
   ☐ hat keine Zeit.
   ☒ hat keine Lust.
3. Frau Becker
   ☒ trinkt keinen Kaffee.
   ☐ hat keine Lust.
   ☐ hat keine Zeit.
4. Jens und Ulla
   ☐ haben kein Examen.
   ☒ haben keine Zeit.
   ☐ haben keinen Hunger.
5. Peter
   ☒ hat keine Lust.
   ☐ hat kein Geld.
   ☐ hat kein Auto.

Zwei Störche und ein Frosch

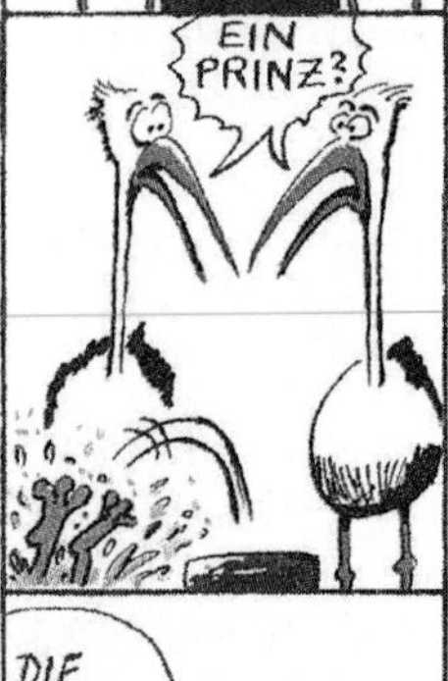

1. Die . . . *That line never fails.*

Übung 8 Das Frühstück°

breakfast

Look at the cartoon to the right. What seems to be the problem? Underline the correct option for each sentence.

1. Die zwei Störche (*storks*) suchen **ein/kein** Frühstück.
2. Störche essen **fern/nicht gern** Frösche (*frogs*) zum Frühstück.
3. Der Frosch hat **ein/kein** Problem.
4. Der Frosch ist in Wirklichkeit (*in reality*) **ein/kein** Prinz.
5. Ich finde diesen Cartoon **lustig/nicht lustig**!

Übung 9 Ein Interview: Was hast du alles in deiner Wohnung oder in deinem Zimmer?

Find out what your partner has in his/her room.

BEISPIEL: S1: Hast du eine Stereoanlage?
S2: Ja. Und du, hast du eine Stereoanlage?
S1: Nein, ich habe keine Stereoanlage.

Hast du . . . ?

Computer	Kommode
Stereoanlage	Teppich
Schreibtisch	Regal
Lampe	Stuhl
Telefon	Wecker
Sessel	Nachttisch
Fernseher	Telefon
Sofa	Videorecorder
Bett	Couchtisch
Zimmerpflanze	Computertisch

Übung 9. Suggestion: Have students furnish a fantasy room with a certain number of objects. They draw a picture of the room and furnishings. Then, in pairs, each person tries to find out what is in the partner's room.

Verbs with Stem-vowel Changes

A number of verbs have vowel changes in the second-person singular (**du**) and third-person singular (**er/sie/es**) of the present tense.

1. a → ä	fahren: du **fährst,** er/sie/es **fährt**
	schlafen: du **schläfst,** er/sie/es **schläft**
2. au → äu	laufen: du **läufst,** er/sie/es **läuft**
3. e → i	essen: du **isst,** er/sie/es **isst**
	geben: du **gibst,** er/sie/es **gibt**
	nehmen: du **nimmst,** er/sie/es **nimmt**
	sprechen: du **sprichst,** er/sie/es **spricht**
4. e → ie	lesen: du **liest,** er/sie/es **liest**
	sehen: du **siehst,** er/sie/es **sieht**

Here are the present-tense forms of **nehmen** and **fahren.** Note that **nehmen** also has consonant changes.

nehmen			
ich	nehme	wir	nehmen
du	**nimmst**	ihr	nehmt
er / sie / es	**nimmt**	sie	nehmen
	Sie nehmen		

fahren			
ich	fahre	wir	fahren
du	**fährst**	ihr	fahrt
er / sie / es	**fährt**	sie	fahren
	Sie fahren		

Note that the vowel changes occur in the **du-** and **er/sie/es-**forms only. All the other verb forms are based on the stem of the infinitive. Verbs with vowel changes will be indicated as such in the vocabulary sections of each chapter: **schlafen** (**schläft**).

Übung 10 Was machen sie gern?

1. Ich _____ gern italienisch, Karin _____ gern chinesisch. (essen)
2. Klaus und Petra _____ heute im Restaurant. (essen) Petra _____ Fisch, und Klaus _____ ein Wiener Schnitzel. (nehmen)
3. Hans braucht eine Lampe. Er _____ eine supermoderne Lampe im Kaufhaus. (sehen)
4. Ilse _____ gern Auto. Morgen _____ wir nach Berlin. (fahren)
5. Herr Renner _____ jeden Tag im Park. Dort _____ viele Jogger. (laufen)
6. Was _____ du gern? Ich _____ gern Zeitung. (lesen)

Übung 11 Was machen Sie gern, manchmal, nie, oft, selten, viel?

Tell a partner several things you do or don't like to do and how often: **gern, manchmal** (*sometimes*), **nie** (*never*), **oft, selten, viel.** Report to the class what you've learned.

BEISPIEL: S1: Ich esse gern, ich tanze manchmal, ich laufe nie.
S2: John isst gern, tanzt manchmal und läuft nie.

arbeiten	Karten/Tennis/Fußball spielen	reisen	tanzen
Auto/Motorrad fahren	laufen	schlafen	trinken
deutsch sprechen	esen	schwimmen	wandern
essen			

Demonstrative Pronouns°

°Demonstrativpronomen

ROBERT: Was kostet der Schreibtisch hier?
VERKÄUFERIN: **Der** kostet 1.000 Mark.

ULLA: Wie findest du meine neue Lampe?
ROBERT: **Die** finde ich prima.

HERR HOLZ: Was kostet der Sessel hier?
VERKÄUFER: **Der** kostet nur 250 Mark.
FRAU HOLZ: Gut, **den** nehmen wir.

In conversational German, demonstrative pronouns may be used instead of personal pronouns to talk about someone or something previously mentioned. In the nominative and accusative cases, the demonstrative pronouns are identical to the corresponding definite articles. Since demonstratives are more emphatic than regular pronouns, they are usually placed at the beginning of a sentence.

Übung 12 Was machen diese Leute schon wieder°?

°*yet again*

Refamiliarize yourself with the characters and drawings oin **Thema 3** in the **Wörter im Kontext** section of this chapter. What are these people doing again? In your answer, replace the names with demonstrative pronouns.

BEISPIEL: Was macht Frau Schlemmer schon wieder? →
Die isst schon wieder.

1. Was macht Ernst Immermüd schon wieder?
2. Was macht Herr Wurm schon wieder?
3. Was macht Gerhard Glotze schon wieder?

4. Was macht Uschi Schnell schon wieder?
5. Was macht Frau Renner schon wieder?

Sprache im Kontext

Zuschauen

Vorschau

Fanfare

1. Watch the ad without sound. What is this commerial about?
2. Watch the ad again, this time with sound. Mark the words that you hear.
   - □ Fahrrad
   - □ Kreuzworträtsel
   - □ Fanfare
   - □ Waffelröllchen
   - □ tanzen
   - □ Wien
   - □ Tradition
   - □ vier

Arbeit mit dem Videotext

A. Watch the ad again, then answer the following questions.

1. Was machen die Personen gern?
2. Was essen die Personen gern?
3. Aus welcher Stadt kommt „Fanfare“ Schokolade?
4. Was bedeuten diese Wörter?

a.	knusprig	□ soft	□ stale	□ crisp
b.	umhüllt	□ wrapped in	□ hilly	□ picked from
c.	zart	□ hard	□ delicate	□ dark

B. Now answer the following questions relating to you personally.

1. Tanzen Sie gern?
2. Was machen Sie sonst noch gern?
3. Essen Sie gern Schokolade? Wenn ja, welche Sorte? Wenn nein, warum nicht?
4. Was essen Sie sonst noch gern?

Lesen

Wie und wo wohnen junge Leute in Deutschland? In this section you will look at texts in which young people in Germany tell how they live.

Wie wohnen Sie? Suggestions: This may be done as a partner activity, with students jotting down the answers on a separate sheet.

Follow-up: The first four answers can be linked in a third-person report. Call on several students to do this. Record answers to the first four questions on the board to develop a class profile, e.g., *Drei Studenten wohnen bei ihren Eltern. Zwölf Studenten wohnen in einer Wohnung. Vier Studenten wohnen in einem Studentenheim.*

Zum Thema

Wie wohnen Sie?  

A. Take a few moments to complete the questionnaire, then interview a partner to see how he/she answered the questions.

1. Ich wohne ____.
   - **a.** in einem Studentenheim
   - **b.** in einer Wohnung
   - **c.** bei meinen Eltern
   - **d.** in meinem eigenen (*own*) Haus
   - **e.** privat in einem Zimmer
   - **f.** ?
2. Ich teile (*share*) mein Zimmer / meine Wohnung / mein Haus mit ____.
   - **a.** einer anderen Person
   - **b.** zwei, drei, vier, . . . Personen
   - **c.** niemand anderem. Ich wohne allein.
3. Ich habe ____.
   - **a.** eine Katze
   - **b.** einen Hund (*dog*)
   - **c.** einen Goldfisch
   - **d.** andere Haustiere (eine Kobra, einen Kanarienvogel, . . .)
   - **e.** keine Haustiere
4. Ich wohne gern / nicht gern ____.
   - **a.** in einer Großstadt
   - **b.** in einer Kleinstadt
   - **c.** auf dem Land
5. Als Student hat man hier ____ Probleme, eine Wohnung zu finden.
   - **a.** keine
   - **b.** manchmal
   - **c.** große
6. Die Mieten sind hier ____.
   - **a.** niedrig
   - **b.** hoch

B. Report to the class what you found out about your partner.

Auf den ersten Blick

In the following passages students in Bonn, the capital of former West Germany, and Rostock, a city in northeastern Germany, tell about their living arrangements. Skim through the texts and for each one organize the vocabulary you recognize into the following categories.

	PERSON	HOUSING	OBJECTS FOUND IN ROOM
BEISPIEL:	Katja	Studentenwohnheim	Betten, Schreibtisch, Esstisch, Regale . . .

So wohne ich

Name: *Katja Meierhans*
Wohnort: *Rostock*
Hauptfächer: *Mathematik, Chemie*

Während des Studiums wohne ich im Studentenwohnheim mit noch einer[1] Studentin auf einem Zimmer; Gemeinschaftswaschräume[2] und WCs[3] für den ganzen Flur[4] (22 Zimmer); im Raum sind Betten, Schreibtisch, Esstisch, viele Regale, viele Schränke. Ich bin zufrieden[5]. Zu Hause (300 km von Rostock) wohne ich bei meinen Eltern. Wir haben mein Zimmer zusammen ausgebaut[6], deshalb[7] ist es natürlich mehr nach meinen Wünschen. Ich fahre gern nach Hause, aber in Rostock bin ich unabhängiger[8].

Name: *Christina Stiegen*
Wohnort: *Niederkassel (Rheidt)*
Hauptfächer: *Politologie, Italienisch*

Ich wohne in einer Wohnung etwas außerhalb von[9] Bonn. Die Wohnung hat $52m^2$, zwei Zimmer, Küche, Diele[10], Bad. Ich teile mir[11] die Wohnung mit meinem Freund, der auch in Bonn studiert. Es handelt sich um[12] eine Dachwohnung[13].

Name: *Jennifer Wolcott*
Wohnort: *Mönchengladbach*
Hauptfächer: *Englisch, Politische Wissenschaften*

Ich wohne in einem Zimmer ($12m^2$) in einem Studentenwohnheim. In dem Zimmer sind ein großer Schreibtisch mit Schubladen[14], ein Bett, ein Regal, ein Kleiderschrank und ein Waschbecken[15] mit Spiegel[16]. Ich habe einen Teppich[17] hingelegt, Pflanzen auf die große Fensterbank[18] gestellt, noch ein Regal (für meine vielen Bücher und meine Stereoanlage). Außerdem habe ich Bilder, Poster und Erinnerungen[19] an die weißen Wände gehängt. Ich teile Bad/Toiletten und eine große Küche mit zwanzig Studenten.

Name: *Peter Kesternich*
Wohnort: *Euskirchen*
Hauptfächer: *Englisch, Geschichte*

Ich wohne in einem Zimmer bei meinen Eltern. Ich fahre jeden Morgen mit dem Zug[20] zur Uni (ca. 50 Min.). Das ist für mich praktischer (und billiger), als in Bonn ein Zimmer zu suchen.

1. noch . . . *one other* 2. *common washrooms* 3. *toilets* 4. *floor* 5. *content, satisfied* 6. *renovated* 7. *for that reason* 8. *more independent* 9. etwas . . . *just outside of* 10. *front hall* 11. teile . . . *share* 12. Es . . . *It is* 13. *attic apartment* 14. *drawers* 15. *sink* 16. *mirror* 17. *carpet* 18. *windowsill* 19. *mementos, souvenirs* 20. *train*

Zum Text

Zum Text. Note: The goal is not to have students understand every word but to read the text to complete the task.

A. Read the texts more thoroughly and look at the drawings on page 74. Which description most closely matches which drawing?

You'll find more about housing in German-speaking countries in ***Deutsch: Na klar!*** on the World Wide Web at www.mhhe.com/german.

1.

2.

3.

4.

B. Look at the following chart and then scan the texts for specific information in order to complete it. If there is no information given for a particular category, leave that space blank.

NAME	WOHNORT	WIE DIE PERSON WOHNT	WAS SIE IM ZIMMER HAT	WEITERE INFORMATIONEN

1. Using the information in the chart, construct sentences about the students. Have the rest of the class guess which person you are describing.
2. Using the information in the chart, describe one of the people by creating true and false statements. The rest of the class has to say whether your statements are true or false.

Sprechen und Schreiben

Aktivität 1 Mitbewohner(in) gesucht!°

° *sought*

Imagine that you live in an apartment with two or three other roommates and that one of the roommates has just moved out. Working with one or two other students and using the housing ads in the **Wörter im Kontext** section as a guide, create an ad about your apartment. Begin your ad as follows:

> **Mitbewohner(in) gesucht! Zimmer in ____ zimmerwohnung/Haus frei.**

Aktivität 2 Zusammenwohnen, aber mit wem?°

° *living together, but with whom?*

Aktivität 2. Suggestion: Students formulate questions as a group; the instructor or a student can put them on the board or overhead. The questions can also be assigned as homework that you can quickly check before students interview one another.

A. Now pair up with someone who was not in your group in **Aktivität A** and interview him/her to see whether you are compatible. Use the questions below as a point of departure, and add your own questions to reflect your personal needs. Then switch roles. Repeat the interview with at least one other person.

S1 asks:

- how large the room is
- if the room is furnished
- how much the rent is
- if they have a telephone, garden, garage

S2 asks the other person whether he/she:

- smokes (**rauchen**)
- has a pet (**ein Haustier**)
- has a car
- uses the telephone (**telefonieren**) a lot
- often has friends over (**Besuch haben**)
- plays loud music (**laute Musik**)

B. After you've interviewed a couple of prospective roommates or housemates, meet with your original group, compare notes, then report to the class about whom you chose.

BEISPIEL: Wir vermieten das Zimmer an Jeanine. Sie ist sehr nett und sympathisch. Sie spielt keine laute Musik. . . .

Wortschatz

Im Kaufhaus	At the Department Store
das **Bett, -en**	bed
der **CD-Spieler, -**	CD player
der **Computer, -**	computer
der **Fernseher, -**	TV set
das **Foto, -s**	photograph
der **Kleiderschrank, ¨e**	clothes closet
die **Kommode, -n**	dresser
die **Lampe, -n**	lamp
das **Poster, -**	poster
das **Radio, -s**	radio
das **Regal, -e**	shelf
das **Bücherregal, -e**	bookcase, bookshelf
der **Sessel, -**	armchair
das **Sofa, -s**	sofa
die **Stereoanlage, -n**	stereo
der **Stuhl, ¨e**	chair
das **Telefon, -e**	telephone
der **Teppich, -e**	rug, carpet
der **Tisch, -e**	table
der **Couchtisch, -e**	coffee table
der **Nachttisch, -e**	nightstand
der **Schreibtisch, -e**	desk
die **Uhr, -en**	clock
der **Videorecorder, -**	video recorder, VCR
der **Wecker, -**	alarm clock

Das Haus	The House
das **Bad, ¨er**	bathroom
der **Balkon, -s**	balcony
das **Fenster, -**	window
die **Garage, -n**	garage
der **Garten, ¨**	garden, yard
das **Haus, ¨er**	house
die **Küche, -n**	kitchen
die **Terrasse, -n**	terrace, patio
die **Tür, -en**	door
die **Wand, ¨e**	wall
das **Zimmer, -**	room
das **Arbeitszimmer, -**	workroom, study
das **Badezimmer, -**	bathroom
das **Esszimmer, -***	dining room
das **Wohnzimmer, -**	living room

Sonstige Substantive	Other Nouns
das **Auto, -s**	car
das **Handy, -s**	cellular telephone
der **Herr, -en** (**-n** *masc.*	gentleman
das **Kaufhaus, ¨er**	department store
der **Kunde, -n** (**-n** *masc.*)	(male) customer
die **Kundin, -nen**	(female) customer
die **Mark** (*sg. and pl.*)	mark
DM (Deutsche Mark)	DM (German marks)
die **Mensa,** *pl.* **Mensen**	student cafeteria
der **Mensch, -en** (**-en** *masc.*)	person, human being
die **Miete**	rent
der **Mitbewohner, -** / die **Mitbewohnerin, -nen**	roommate
das **Motorrad, ¨er**	motorcycle
das **Problem, -e**	problem
das **Studenten(wohn)heim, -e**	dormitory
der **Tag, -e**	day
der **Verkäufer, -** / die **Verkäuferin, -nen**	salesperson
das **Video, -s**	video(tape)
die **Wohngemeinschaft, -en (WG)**	shared housing
die **Wohnung, -en**	apartment
die **Zeit, -en**	time
die **Zimmerpflanze, -n**	houseplant

Verben	Verbs
brauchen	to need
essen (isst)*	to eat
fahren (fährt)	to drive, ride
Auto fahren	to drive a car
Motorrad fahren	to ride a motorcycle
geben (gibt)	to give
haben (hat)	to have
Durst haben	to be thirsty
gern haben	to like (*a person or thing*)
Hunger haben	to be hungry

* See Appendix E for alternate spellings.

Lust haben	to feel like (*doing something*)
Recht haben	to be correct
Zeit haben	to have time
hören	to hear, listen
kaufen	to buy
kosten	to cost
laufen (läuft)	to run, jog
lesen (liest)	to read
nehmen (nimmt)	to take
schlafen (schläft)	to sleep
schreiben	to write
schwimmen	to swim
sehen (sieht)	to see
sprechen (spricht)	to speak
suchen	to look for
trinken	to drink

Adjektive und Adverbien — Adjectives and Adverbs

aber	but, however
bequem	comfortable, comfortably
bestimmt	definite(ly), certain(ly)
billig	inexpensive(ly), cheap(ly)
da	there
dringend	urgent(ly)
dunkel	dark
frei	free(ly)
gerade	just, exactly
gern	gladly
gern + *verb*	to like to do something
hell	bright(ly), light
hoch	high(ly)
klein	small
möbliert	furnished
niedrig	low
noch	still; yet
nur	only
preiswert	a bargain, inexpensive(ly)
recht	quite, rather
recht preiswert	quite inexpensive
schön	nice(ly), beautiful(ly)
schon	already
selten	rare(ly)
so	so
teuer	expensive(ly)
vielleicht	maybe, perhaps
wieder	again

Sonstiges — Other

etwas	something; somewhat, a little (*adverb*)
Ich habe keine Lust.	I don't feel like it.
kein	no, none, not any
nichts	nothing
Was ist denn los?	What's the matter?
wen (*acc.*)	whom (*accusative*)

Lernziele

Use this checklist to verify that you can now . . .

- ☐ read and understand German housing ads.
- ☐ describe the way you (and others) live.
- ☐ talk about prices in German.
- ☐ describe some of the furnishings and other items you (and others) have and need.
- ☐ give your opinions about types of housing, furnishings, and other objects.
- ☐ describe some activities you (and others) like or don't like to do.
- ☐ form the plural of nouns you have learned in this and previous chapters.
- ☐ form sentences and questions using (accusative) direct objects.
- ☐ recognize and use special masculine nouns.
- ☐ use common expressions with **haben.**
- ☐ form negative sentences and questions, using **kein** and **nicht.**
- ☐ recognize and use verbs with stem-vowel changes in the present tense.
- ☐ recognize and use demonstrative pronouns in the nominative and accusative cases.
- ☐ scan texts for specific information.

Kapitel 3

Familie und Freunde

Familienfeier bei Kaffee und Kuchen

Kapitel 3. Introduce the chapter theme (family, days and dates, special events) by talking about your own experiences: How large is your family? Are certain dates, months, times of the year important in your family?

Alles klar?

Families are important in every culture. We define ourselves most often in terms of our family background. Even with the fast pace of modern life, family members take time to come together for important celebrations such as weddings, birthdays, and holidays.

A. Below you see a picture of Ulrike Eichele's family. Your knowledge of cognates and contextual guessing will help you identify Ulrike's relatives. Can you guess at what family celebration the picture was taken? Who do you think the unlabeled people are?

Photo. After students have looked at and discussed the photo of Ulrike's family, tell them that the photo was taken after her brother's civil marriage ceremony. A separate civil ceremony is required under German law, but many couples have a religious ceremony as well.

B. Now listen as Ulrike describes her family. As you listen, indicate whether the following statements are correct or incorrect.

	DAS STIMMT	DAS STIMMT NICHT
1. Auf dem Foto steht Familie Eichele vorm Kaufhaus.	☐	☒
2. Familie Eichele wohnt in Koblenz.	☒	☐
3. Ulrikes Bruder Wolfgang heiratet.	☐	☒
4. Ulrike ist 21 Jahre alt.	☐	☒
5. Sie findet ihren Bruder Hans nett.	☒	☐
6. Ein Sohn ist 25 Jahre alt und heißt Wolfgang.	☒	☐
7. Wolfgang studiert Physik in Berlin.	☐	☒

Wörter im Kontext

Thema 1

Ein Familienstammbaum°

° family tree

Ulrike Eicheles Familie

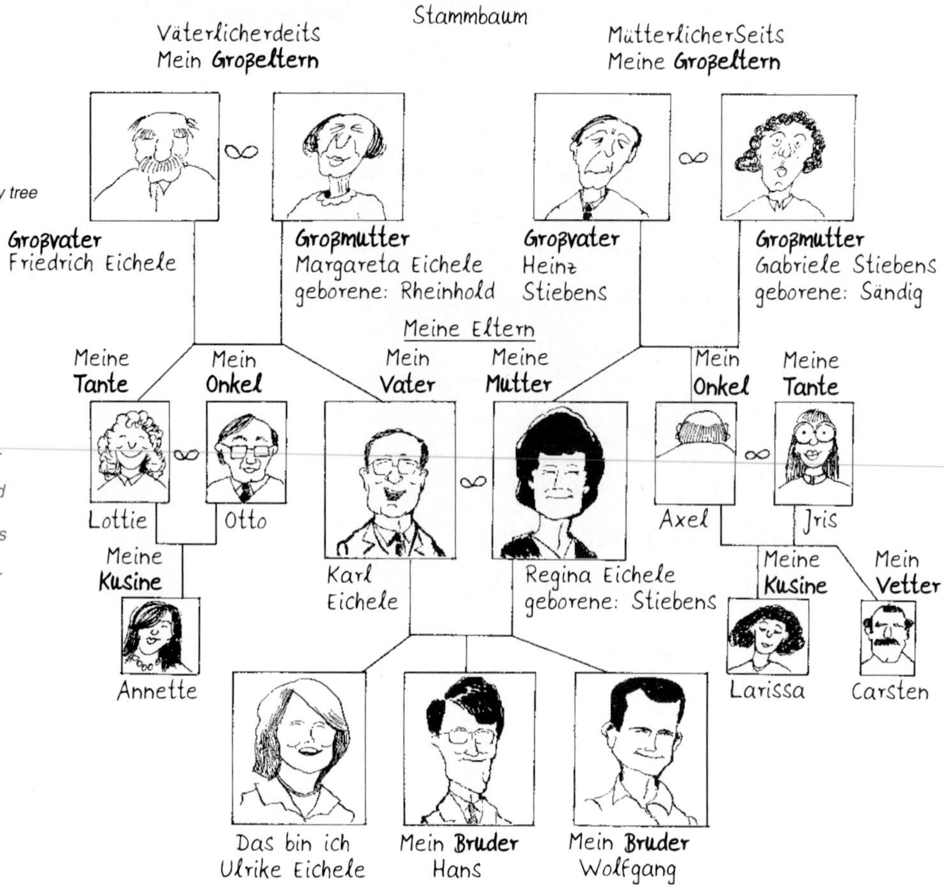

Stammbaum

Väterlicherdeits
Mein **Großeltern**

Mütterlicherseits
Meine **Großeltern**

Großvater
Friedrich Eichele

Großmutter
Margareta Eichele
geborene: Rheinhold

Großvater
Heinz
Stiebens

Großmutter
Gabriele Stiebens
geborene: Sändig

Meine Eltern

Meine **Tante**
Lottie

Mein **Onkel**
Otto

Mein **Vater**
Karl
Eichele

Meine **Mutter**
Regina Eichele
geborene: Stiebens

Mein **Onkel**
Axel

Meine **Tante**
Iris

Meine **Kusine**
Annette

Meine **Kusine**
Larissa

Mein **Vetter**
Carsten

Das bin ich
Ulrike Eichele

Mein **Bruder**
Hans

Mein **Bruder**
Wolfgang

Ein Familienstammbaum.
Suggestion: Introduce vocabulary using the family tree of Ulrike Eichele. Ask questions such as the following: 1. *Ulrike hat vier Großeltern. Wer sind sie? Was heißt mütterlicherseits und väterlicherseits?* 2. *Wie heißt Ulrikes Großmutter mütterlicherseits? Und väterlicherseits?* 3. *Wie viele Kinder haben ihre Großeltern väterlicherseits?* 4. *Ulrikes Mutter hat einen Bruder. Er ist Ulrikes ______.* 5. *Ulrikes Vater hat eine Schwester. Sie ist Ulrikes ______.* 6. *Tante Lottie und ihr Mann haben nur eine Tochter. Sie heißt Annette und ist Ulrikes ______.* 7. *Ulrikes Onkel Axel und seine Frau Iris haben zwei Kinder. Carsten ist Ulrikes ______, und Larissa ist ihre ______.*

Wer ist wer? How is each relative related to you?

1. _____ der **Bruder**
2. _____ der **Enkel**
3. _____ die **Enkelin**
4. _____ die **Geschwister** (*pl.*)
5. _____ die **Großeltern** (*pl.*)
6. _____ die **Großmutter (Oma)**
7. _____ der **Großvater (Opa)**
8. _____ die **Kusine (Cousine)**
9. _____ der **Neffe**
10. _____ die **Nichte**
11. _____ der **Onkel**
12. _____ der **Schwager**
13. _____ die **Schwägerin**
14. _____ die **Schwester**
15. _____ die **Tante**
16. _____ der **Vetter (Cousin)**

a. Das ist der **Sohn** Ihres (*of your*) Bruders oder Ihrer (*of your*) Schwester.
b. Das ist die **Tochter** Ihrer Eltern.
c. Das ist die Tochter Ihres Bruders oder Ihrer Schwester.
d. Das ist die Schwester Ihres Vaters oder Ihrer Mutter.
e. Das ist der Sohn Ihrer **Kinder.**
f. Das ist die Tochter Ihres Onkels und Ihrer Tante.
g. Das ist der **Mann** Ihrer Schwester.
h. Das sind die Söhne und Töchter Ihrer Eltern.
i. Das ist die Mutter Ihres Vaters oder Ihrer Mutter.
j. Das ist der Bruder Ihres Vaters oder Ihrer Mutter.
k. Das ist der Sohn Ihrer Eltern.
l. Das ist der Vater Ihres Vaters oder Ihrer Mutter.
m. Das ist der Sohn Ihres Onkels und Ihrer Tante.
n. Das ist die Tochter Ihrer Kinder.
o. Das ist die **Frau** Ihres Bruders.
p. Das sind die Eltern Ihrer Eltern.

As in English, to indicate that somebody is related to another person, add an **s** to the person's name—though without an apostrophe.

Das ist Ulrike **Eicheles** Familie.
Ulrikes Eltern heißen Karl und Regina.

Another way to indicate relationships is with the preposition **von** (*of*).

Das ist die Familie **von** Ulrike Eichele.
Die Eltern **von** Ulrike heißen Karl und Regina.

The **von** construction is preferred if a name ends in an **s** or **z.**

Die Frau **von** Hans heißt Antje.
Das Haus **von** Familie Stiebens ist sehr modern.

Aktivität 1 Ein Interview

A. Ask a person in your class about his/her family.

1. Wo wohnt deine Familie?
2. Wie viele Geschwister hast du?
3. Wie heißen deine Geschwister?
4. Wie heißen deine Eltern?
5. Wie alt sind deine Geschwister?
6. ?

Aktivität 1. Suggestion: Before doing this activity, brainstorm possible questions with students for number 6. Then have students work in pairs to interview each other, taking notes. Ask several students to report their findings.

B. Report back to the class about your partner's family.

BEISPIEL: Jennys Familie wohnt in Salt Lake City. Jenny hat fünf Brüder und drei Schwestern. Ihre Brüder heißen Mark und Stephen . . .

Aktivität 2 Generationen: Wer ist wer?

Aktivität 2. Suggestion: Students can work in pairs to ask and answer the questions.

Look closely at the family portrait and answer the questions.

Landkinder: Tochter Susanne, 18; Großmutter Alma, 63; Tochter Nicole, 19; Urgroßmutter Pauline, 87; Mutter Frauke, 40

1. Wie viele Generationen sind auf diesem Bild?
2. Wie heißen die Frauen mit Vornamen?
3. Wie heißen die zwei jüngsten (*youngest*) Frauen? Wie alt sind sie?
4. Wer ist die älteste (*oldest*) Frau? Wie alt ist sie?
5. Wer ist die Mutter von Susanne und Nicole?
6. Wer ist die Großmutter von Frauke?
7. Wer ist die Tochter von Pauline?

To indicate that someone is related only through one parent, compounds can be formed using **Stief-** (*step*) and **Halb-** (*half*). The German equivalent to English *great* is the prefix **Ur-**.

Maria ist meine **Stiefschwester.**
Maria is my stepsister.

Mein **Halbbruder** heißt Jens.
My half-brother is named Jens.

Wilhelmine ist meine **Urgroßmutter.**
Wilhelmine is my great-grandmother.

Aktivität 3 Eine Familie

Aktivität 3. Suggestion: This activity is a summary of **Aktivität 2.** To reinforce new vocabulary, do as a whole-group activity or as homework.

Fill in the missing information.

1. Susanne und Nicole sind Fraukes ____ .
2. Pauline ist Susannes und Nicoles ____ und Fraukes ____ .
3. Alma ist Paulines ____ und Susannes und Nicoles ____ .
4. ____ spielt gern Fußball. Sie ist Paulines Enkelin.
5. Alma hat zwei Enkelinnen, ____ und ____ . Und wer ist das in der Mitte? Sie gehört (*belongs*) auch zur Familie.

Aktivität 4 Ein merkwürdiger° Stammbaum

°curious

Answer the questions based on the "family tree."

1. Eine ganze Familie feiert Geburtstag. Wie heißt diese Familie?
2. Wen gibt es, und wen gibt es nicht in diesem Stammbaum?
   BEISPIEL: Es gibt einen Großvater, aber es gibt keine Großmutter.
3. Wie alt ist der Großvater? Was meinen Sie?
   a. ca. 80 Jahre alt **b.** ca. 100 Jahre alt
   c. ca. 50 Jahre alt
4. Welche Namen dieser Familie kennen Sie? Welche Namen kennen Sie nicht?
5. Wie heißt der **Käfer** auf Englisch?

Aktivität 4. Suggestion: Students should first scan the realia and the accompanying questions. Then ask them to complete the activity in pairs or threes, asking each other the questions. Afterward, elicit responses from the students as a whole group. Ask students what the family's last name is (*Volkswagen*).

Realia. This was part of a congratulatory ad placed in the *Süddeutsche Zeitung* of Munich by *DSM,* a large chemical concern. It congratulates *Volkswagen,* on the occasion of its 50th birthday.

Wir gratulieren der ganzen Familie.

Der Kalender. Suggestion: Introduce days of the week and have students repeat them. On which days do you have German class?

Introduce months by mentioning events that occur in each month, e.g., *Das zweite Semester beginnt im Januar. Der Valentinstag ist im Februar.* Write only the name of the month on the board as you do this. Students will become accustomed to hearing *im Januar, im Juni,* etc. **Point out:** All months are masculine, but the definite article is not usually used with the month.

Thema 2

Der Kalender: Die Wochentage und die Monate

Oktober

Montag	Dienstag	Mittwoch	Donnerstag	Freitag	Samstag	Sonntag
				1	2	3
4	5	6	7	8	9	10
11	12	13	14	15	16	17
18	19	20	21	22	23	24
25	26	27	28	29	30	31

die Monate	
Januar	Juli
Februar	August
März	September
April	Oktober
Mai	November
Juni	Dezember

Use the following phrases to say the day or month when something takes place.

—Wann wirst du 21?
—Ich werde **am Samstag** 21.

—Wann hast du Geburtstag?
—Ich habe **im Dezember** Geburtstag.

Aktivität 5 Wie alt bist du?

Aktivität 5. Suggestion: Who is the oldest in the class? the youngest? Do any students share a birthday?

Interview several classmates to learn their ages and birthdates.

BEISPIEL: S1: Wie alt bist du?
S2: Ich bin 23.
S1: Wann wirst du 24?
S2: Ich werde im August 24. Und du?

Aktivität 6 Eine Einladung° zum Geburtstag 

invitation

Listen and take notes as Tom and Heike talk about an upcoming birthday party. Read the questions first before listening to the conversation.

1. Wer hat Geburtstag? Heike
2. Wann ist der Geburtstag? Samstag
3. Wo ist die Party? bei Heike zu Hause
4. Wer kommt sonst noch (*else*)? Gabi, Jürgen, Heikes Eltern und Geschwister
5. Kommt die Person am Telefon, oder nicht? Ja, er kommt.

Aktivität 6. Suggestion: Students should scan the questions before listening to the dialogue. Play the tape once; students answer as many questions as they can, based on one listening. Play the tape a second time and have students complete any unfinished questions.

Aktivität 7 Hin und her: Verwandtschaften

Additional activity: Have students create a similar chart with real family members, keeping kinship terms but changing names and ages.

Ask a partner questions about Ulrike's family.

BEISPIEL: S1: Wie ist Axel mit Ulrike verwandt?
S2: Axel ist Ulrikes Onkel.
S1: Wie alt ist er denn?
S2: Er ist 51.

PERSON	VERWANDTSCHAFT	ALTER
Axel	Onkel	51
Antje	Schwägerin	29
Annette	Kusine	20
Hans	Bruder	30
Friedrich	Großvater	75

Thema 3

Feste und Feiertage°

celebrations and holidays

Geburtstagswünsche

Realia. These birthday greetings are from two German newspapers, the *Harzburger Zeitung* and the *Neue Osnabrücker Zeitung.*

Neue Wörter

- ☐ gratulieren
- ☐ werden (wird)
- ☐ wünschen
- ☐ Alles Gute!
- ☐ Herzlichen Glückwunsch zum Geburtstag!
- ☐ Viel Glück!

Germans express birthday wishes in many ways. Here are some typical birthday wishes taken from German newspapers.

Heike
wird heute
„21"
Herzlichen Glückwunsch

Lieber Vater und Opa!
Zu Deinem 85. Geburtstag gratulieren
Hansi – Waltraud – Angela – Torsten – Birgit – Peter – Jan und Marco

Hallo, Belinda!
Viel Glück und alles Gute zum 18.
wünschen Mutti und Papa und der ganze Clan.
W. W. B. U. S. U. J. D. M. S. W. P. S. W. und Chris

Ralf hat Geburtstag!
Alles Gute!

Liebe Oma *Marie Sudhoff*
zu Deinem **80. Geburtstag** wünschen Dir Deine Kinder, Enkel und Urenkel alles Liebe und Gute.

Neue Wörter. These checklists appear in the **Themen** along with authentic materials such as ads, graphs, and menus. As your students work with the authentic materials, they should try to figure out the meaning of the words by identifying cognates and by contextual guessing. Once they have figured out the meaning of a vocabulary item, they should place a check mark beside the word. They can confirm their understanding of the words by looking for them in the vocabulary list at the end of the chapter.

Feiertage in der Familie Eichele

Valentinstag kennen Hans und Wolfgang aus den USA. Nicht viele Deutsche **feiern** diesen Tag. **Muttertag** ist für Frau Eichele nicht so **wichtig,** aber ihre Familie gibt ihr **oft** Blumen.

Dieses Jahr gibt es eine **Hochzeit** in ihrer Familie. Ulrikes Kusine Larissa **heiratet** nämlich im Juni. Die Familie **plant** ein großes **Familienfest** mit einem Abendessen in der Marxburg am Rhein. Ulrikes Großeltern feiern dieses Jahr ihre goldene Hochzeit.

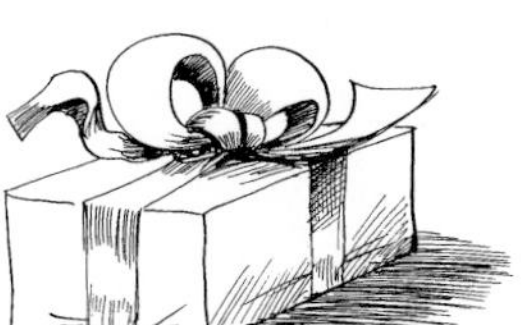

Ulrike hat im Oktober **Geburtstag.** Dieses Jahr feiert sie bei ihrer Kusine Julia in den USA. **Natürlich** schicken ihre Eltern **Geschenke** aus Deutschland, und **es gibt** eine kleine **Party.**

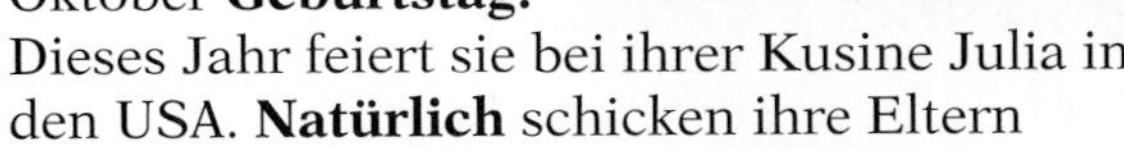

Weihnachten hat eine lange **Tradition.** Die Familie isst abends sehr spät, und es gibt **immer** schöne Geschenke.

Silvester fahren Eicheles oft zu Freunden. Manchmal bleiben sie aber zu Hause und haben ein kleines Feuerwerk **um Mitternacht** im Garten.

To form most ordinal numbers (*first, second, third,* and so on) in German, add the suffix **te** or **ste** to the cardinal number. Note that the words for *first, third, seventh* and *eighth* are exceptions to the rule.

eins	**erste**
zwei	zwei**te**
drei	**dritte**
vier	vier**te**
fünf	fünf**te**
sechs	sechs**te**
sieben	**sieb(en)te**
acht	**achte**
neun	neun**te**
zehn	zehn**te**
elf	elf**te**
zwölf	zwölf**te**
dreizehn	dreizehn**te**
. . .	. . .
zwanzig	zwanzig**ste**
hundert	hundert**ste**
tausend	tausend**ste**

Analyse

Answer these questions about the birthday greetings in **Thema 3.**

- Find at least two different expressions of good wishes in the ads.
- Who are the family members who are sending birthday greetings to Belinda? to Marie Sudhoff?
- Marie Sudhoff is being addressed as "liebe Oma." To which family member does the term of endearment **Oma** refer?
- One birthday greeting gives no name but says only "lieber Vater und Opa." To which family member does the term of endearment **Opa** probably refer? Do you think this ad is directed to one or two people? What clue(s) helped you arrive at your answers?

To talk about the date, you can say:

—**Welches Datum ist heute?**
—Heute ist **der erste** Dezember.

—**Welches Datum ist morgen?**
—Morgen ist **der zweite** Dezember.

To talk about dates for special occasions, you can say:

—**Wann hast du Geburtstag?**
—**Am 18.** (achtzehn**ten**) September.

—Wann feiern deine Eltern ihren Hochzeitstag?
—**Am 26.** (sechsundzwanzig**sten**) März.

Note the addition of a final **n** in the expression **am _____ (s)ten.** Note also that ordinal numbers are written with a period: **18.**

Kulturtipp

Legal holidays in German-speaking countries are largely religious holidays. The most important ones are Christmas (**Weihnachten**), New Year (**Neujahr**) and Easter (**Ostern**) and are celebrated for two days each. An important non-religious holiday in Germany is the Day of German Unity (**Tag der deutschen Einheit**) on October 3.

There are a number of regional holidays as well. Mardi Gras (**Karneval** in the Rhineland and **Fasching** in southern Germany) is celebrated before Lent in early spring. People get one day off work to participate in the merriment in and out of doors. Germans in northern and eastern regions do not celebrate Mardi Gras.

Germans go all out for family celebrations such as weddings, silver and golden wedding anniversaries, and birthdays with a round number, such as 40, 50, or 60.

Karnevalsumgang (*Mardi Gras parade*), Köln

Aktivität 8 Geburtstagsgrüße 

Choose several of the following words and phrases to create birthday greetings for someone.

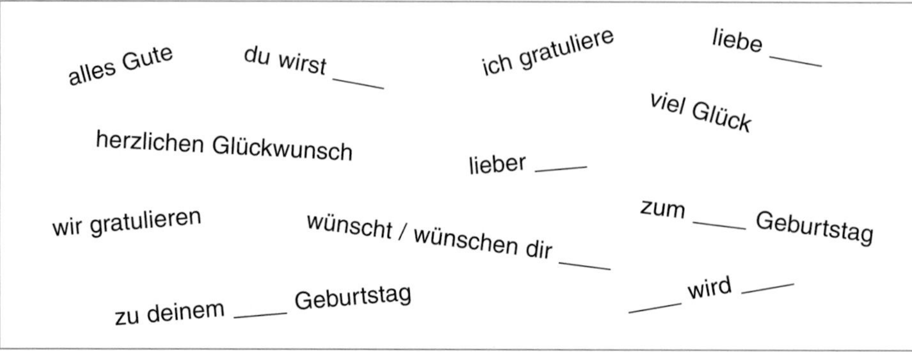

You'll find more about holidays and festivals in German speaking countries in ***Deutsch: Na klar!*** on the World Wide Web at www.mhhe.com/german.

Aktivität 9 Eine Einladung zu einer Party

Invite someone to a party, using the expressions provided.

BEISPIEL: S1: Ich mache am Sonntag eine Party. Ich möchte dich einladen.
S2: Am Sonntag? Vielen Dank. Ich komme gern.
oder Vielen Dank. Leider kann ich nicht kommen. Ich muss nämlich arbeiten.

OTHER EXCUSES
Es tut mir leid.
Ich bin leider nicht zu Hause.
Ich fahre nämlich nach ____ .
Mein Vater / Meine Mutter u.s.w. (*and so on*) hat nämlich auch Geburtstag.

Aktivität 9. Suggestion: Have students circulate and do this activity with a number of different students. Encourage them to give other reasons for not being able to go. Stress that they may either accept or decline the invitation.

When stating your reason for an action, use the adverb **nämlich** in the explanation.

Ich kann nicht kommen. Ich fahre **nämlich** nach Hamburg.
I cannot come. The reason is, I am going to Hamburg.

Note that there is no exact equivalent of **nämlich** in English.

Grammatik im Kontext

Possessive Adjectives°

°Possessivpronomen

Possessive adjectives (*my, your, his, our*) indicate ownership or belonging. You have already seen and used possessive adjectives.

—Wie ist **Ihr** Name? *What is your name?*
—**Mein** Name ist Schiller. *My name is Schiller.*

Wie heißt **deine** Schwester. *What's your sister's name?*

Each possessive adjective corresponds to a personal pronoun.

PERSONAL PRONOUN	POSSESSIVE ADJECTIVE		PERSONAL PRONOUN	POSSESSIVE ADJECTIVE	
ich	**mein**	*my*	wir	**unser**	*our*
du	**dein**	*your (informal)*	ihr	**euer**	*your (informal)*
Sie	**Ihr**	*your (formal)*	Sie	**Ihr**	*your (formal)*
er	**sein**	*his; its*			
sie	**ihr**	*her; its*	sie	**ihr**	*their*
es	**sein**	*its*			

The formal possessive adjective **Ihr** (*your*) is capitalized, just like the formal personal pronoun **Sie** (*you*). Note that the possessive adjective **ihr** (not capitalized) can mean either *her* or *their*; context makes the meaning clear.

Possessives—short for possessive adjectives—take the same endings as the indefinite article **ein.** Unlike **ein,** however, they also have plural forms. They agree in gender, case, and number with the nouns they modify.

The nominative and accusative forms of **mein** and **unser** will illustrate the pattern for all possessives. Note that the accusative form differs from the nominative form only in the masculine singular.

Possessive Adjectives. Note: Students have already been exposed to a number of possessive adjectives in every chapter. Relate a personal anecdote containing possessive adjectives; have students clap their hands every time they hear one.

Note: Point out to students that they will frequently see **du** and **ihr** forms capitalized in letters; however, this convention has become obsolete with the new spelling reform.

	SINGULAR			PLURAL
	Masculine	*Neuter*	*Feminine*	*All Genders*
Nominative	mein Freund unser Freund	mein Buch unser Buch	mein**e** Oma unser**e** Oma	mein**e** Eltern unser**e** Eltern
Accusative	mein**en** Freund unser**en** Freund	mein Buch unser Buch	mein**e** Oma unser**e** Oma	mein**e** Eltern unser**e** Eltern

The pronoun **euer** drops the **e** of the stem when an ending is added; for example **euere** → **eure, eueren** → **euren.**

Note: You may want to point out that the **e** of **unser** is frequently dropped when an ending is added.

Ruth Brandt,

Unsere Omi ist das Liebste, was[1] wir haben, das wollen wir ihr heute einmal[2] sagen: WIR LIEBEN DICH

Deine Kinder
Deine Enkelkinder

1. das . . . *the dearest thing that*
2. *just*

Analyse

- Scan the Valentine's Day greetings on the next page taken from a German newspaper and identify all possessive adjectives.
- Determine whether the possessives refer to a male or female individual or to several people. What is the gender of each name or noun?

Analyse. Suggestion: Have students create their own valentine messages, using expressions found in the ads and possessive adjectives.

Herzliche Grüße zum Valentinstag

Realia. These Valentine's Day messages were part of an entire newspaper page of valentines that appeared in the *Rheinische Post* of Düsseldorf on *Valentinstag. Valentinstag* has only recently begun to catch on in some areas of Germany.

Liebe Beate, ich liebe Dich **Dein Rainer** GF100037	*Für meine Lieben Helmut und Sandra* einen lieben Gruß und ein dickes Küßchen[2] **Eure Doris Ma** GF100081	*Hallo Maus!* Nun ist es doch schon das 4. Jahr! **In Liebe Deine Katze** GE90558
Guten Morgen, mein Tiger Die Welt[1] ist wieder schön durch Dich. **Dein Stern von Rio** GD81183	*Lieber Andre!* Alles Liebe zum Valentinstag. **Dein Häschen** GF100036	*Liebe Christina* Zum Valentinstag herzliche Grüße und alles Liebe und Gute wünscht **Dir Dein Vater** GC114748

1. *world*
2. ein . . . *a big fat kiss*

Übung 1 Herzlichen Glückwunsch!

You will hear eight congratulatory messages taken from a radio program. Write down who receives the greetings (**der Empfänger**) and who sends them (**der Absender**). Include the possessive adjectives you hear, if any. Follow the example.

Übung 1. Note: It is a common practice on local radio stations to have a program for reading congratulatory messages.

	EMPFÄNGER	ABSENDER
1.	*unsere Mutter*	*deine Kinder*
2.	unser Opa	deine Enkel
3.	Uwe	deine Freundin
4.	unser Vater	deine Söhne
5.	unsere Tochter	deine Eltern
6.	Eltern	eure Kinder
7.	meine Kinder	eure Mutter
8.	Gabi	dein Tiger

Übung 2. Suggestion: Have students work in pairs, assigning one conversation per pair. Then have each pair act out its conversation. As students listen to the conversations being acted out, have them fill in the possessives as they hear them.

Übung 2 Kleine Gespräche im Alltag°

everyday life

Complete the minidialogues with the appropriate possessive adjectives.

1. CLAUDIA: Hast du ____ Telefonnummer?
STEFAN: Ja, und wie ist ____ neue Adresse?
CLAUDIA: ____ neue Adresse ist Rosenbachweg 2.

2. LILO: Und dies hier ist ____ Freund.
HELGA: Wie heißt er denn?
LILO: ____ Name ist Max.
HELGA: Max? Na, so was! So heißt nämlich ____ Hund.

3. HERR WEIDNER: Und was sind Sie von Beruf, Frau Rudolf?
FRAU RUDOLF: Ich bin Automechanikerin.
HERR WEIDNER: Und was ist ____ Mann von Beruf?
FRAU RUDOLF: ____ Mann ist Hausmann.
HERR WEIDNER: Wie bitte? Hausmann?

4. FRAU SANDERS: Ach, wie niedlich! Ist das ____ Tochter?
FRAU KARSTEN: Ja, das ist ____ Tochter.
FRAU SANDERS: Und ist das ____ Hund?
FRAU KARSTEN: Ja, das ist ____ Hund. Das ist der Caesar.

5. INGE: Kennst du ____ Freund Klaus?
ERNST: Ich kenne Klaus nicht, aber ich kenne ____ Schwester.
INGE: Morgen besuchen wir ____ Eltern in Stuttgart.

6. KLAUS: Morgen fahren Inge und ich nach Stuttgart.
KURT: Wie fahrt ihr denn?
KLAUS: Wir nehmen ____ Wagen.
KURT: ____ Wagen?
KLAUS: Na, klar. Warum denn nicht?
KURT: ____ Wagen gehört ins Museum, nicht auf die Autobahn.

7. POLIZIST: Ist das ____ Wagen?
FRAU KUNZE: Ja, leider ist das ____ Wagen.
POLIZIST: Hier ist Parkverbot.

Übung 3 Persönliche Angaben

A. Complete a personal profile of yourself. Add one or two items of your own choice.

____ Name ist ____ .
____ Adresse ist ____ .
____ Telefonnummer ist ____ .
____ Familie wohnt in ____ .
____ Mutter heißt ____ .
____ Vater heißt ____ .
____ Geschwister heißen ____ .
____ Wagen/Motorrad ist ein ____ .
____ Geburtstag ist im ____ . (z.B. Juli)
____ Lieblings-____ ist ____ .

B. Exchange personal profiles with someone in your class and report about him/her to the class.

BEISPIEL: Das ist Sam Lee. Seine Telefonnummer ist 354–8762. Sein Lieblingsessen ist Pizza.

Personal Pronouns in the Accusative Case°

°Personalpronomen im Akkusativ

You have already learned the personal pronouns for the nominative case. Here are the corresponding accusative forms.

NOMINATIVE	ACCUSATIVE		NOMINATIVE	ACCUSATIVE	
ich	**mich**	*me*	wir	**uns**	*us*
du	**dich**	*you (informal)*	ihr	**euch**	*you (informal)*
Sie	**Sie**	*you (formal)*	Sie	**Sie**	*you (formal)*
er	**ihn**	*him; it*			
sie	**sie**	*her; it*	sie	**sie**	*them*
es	**es**	*it*			

The third-person singular pronouns **ihn, sie,** and **es** must agree in gender with the noun to which they refer. Note also that in the accusative case **ihn** can mean *him* or *it* and **sie** can mean *her* or *it* depending on the gender of the noun to which they refer.

—Kennst du **meinen Freund?**	*Do you know my friend?*
—Ja, ich kenne **ihn.**	*Yes, I know him.*
—Brauchst du **deinen Wagen** heute?	*Do you need your car today?*
—Na klar brauche ich **ihn.**	*But of course I need it.*
—Hast du **meine Telefonnummer?**	*Do you have my phone number?*
—Ich glaube, ich habe **sie.**	*I think I have it.*

Personal Pronouns in the Accusative Case. Suggestion: Provide some quick drills to practice the third person pronouns, particularly with inanimate objects. *Kennen Sie die Stadt (die Straße, den Film, den Professor, das Buch, den Hund)?* Have students respond only with accusative pronouns.

Analyse

- Identify all personal pronouns in the ads and announcements and determine whether they are in the nominative or in the accusative case.
- Provide the English meaning of each phrase.

Analyse. Suggestion: Go over the items, reading them aloud and brainstorming with the class what they refer to.

Mein Schatz,[1]
Ich liebe Dich.
Deine Jutta
GA140650

1. mein . . . *my dear*

Übung 4 Im Café Kadenz

Übung 4. Suggestion: Assign individual conversations to pairs of students. Have each pair act out its conversation. Also suitable as homework.

Several students are conversing at different tables at the Café Kadenz. Complete the blanks with appropriate personal pronouns in the nominative or the accusative case.

1. A: Wie findest ____ den Professor Klinger?
   B: Also, ich finde ____ einfach unmöglich. ____ kommt nie pünktlich. Wir warten (*wait*) und warten, dann kommt ____ endlich und hält seine Vorlesung, keine Diskussion, keine Fragen, nichts. ____ ist echt langweilig.
   A: Ich verstehe ____ nicht, Karin. Warum gehst du dann hin?
2. C: Nimmst du jetzt das Linguistik-Seminar?
   D: Ja, ich brauche ____ für mein Grundstudium.
3. E: Und wie findest du deine Mitbewohner im Wohnheim?
   F: Ich mag (*like*) ____ nicht besonders. Ich finde ____ unfreundlich. Aber da sind zwei Italienerinnen aus Venedig. ____ sind wirklich nett. Ich verstehe ____ allerdings nicht immer, besonders wenn ____ italienisch sprechen.
4. G: Im Lumière läuft „Der englische Patient."
   H: Stimmt! Die Filmkritiker finden ____ ausgezeichnet.
5. I: Da kommt endlich unser Kaffee. Wie trinkst du ____?
   J: Gewöhnlich trinke ich ____ schwarz.
6. K: Nächste Woche bekommen wir Besuch. Meine Eltern besuchen ____ für drei Tage. Das wird ganz schön anstrengend (*taxing*).
   L: Ich verstehe ____ nicht. Ich finde ____ sehr nett.

Übung 5 Wie findest du das?

Übung 5. Note: Have students first figure out which questions they would like to ask; allow for variations and additional items not on the list. Then have students ask each other questions while mingling. Have several students present their questions and the answers they received.

With a partner, create five questions regarding student life. Then interview several people in your class.

BEISPIEL: S1: Wie findest du die Vorlesungen von Professor Ziegler?
S2: Ich finde sie anstrengend. Und du?
S1: Ich finde sie viel zu abstrakt.

Essen in der Mensa	anstrengend
Kaffee in der Mensa	faul
Leben an der Uni	sympathisch
Uni-Zeitung	langweilig
Studenten an der Uni	schlecht
Mitbewohner im Studentenheim	gut
Professor ____	konservativ
Film ____	interessant
____ -Vorlesung	arrogant
?	?

Prepositions with the Accusative Case°

°Präpositionen mit dem Akkusativ

You have already seen and used a number of German prepositions.

Ich studiere Architektur **in** Berlin.
Meine Schwester wohnt **bei** einer Familie.
Ich brauche eine Lampe **für** meinen Schreibtisch.

The use of prepositions, in English as well as in German, is highly idiomatic. An important difference, however, is that German prepositions require certain cases; that is, some prepositions are followed by nouns or pronouns in the accusative case, others by nouns or pronouns in the dative or genitive case. In this chapter, we will focus on prepositions that always require the accusative case.

Wir sind für Sie da!

Der freundliche Kunden-Service

ACCUSATIVE PREPOSITIONS

durch	through, across
für	for
gegen	against; around (*with time*)
ohne	without
um	at (*with time*)
um (. . . herum)	around (*a place*)

Accusative Prepositions. Note: Telling time is formally presented in Kapitel 4. In this chapter students will work only lexically with expressions of time such as **um 4.**

Es ist **gegen** fünf Uhr.	*It's around five o'clock.*
Herr Krause fährt **durch** die Stadt.	*Mr. Krause drives through town.*
Er braucht ein Geschenk **für** seine Tochter.	*He needs a gift for his daughter.*
Er geht **ohne** seine Frau einkaufen.	*He goes shopping without his wife.*
Die Geburtstagsfeier beginnt **um** sechs.	*The birthday party begins at six.*
Er sucht einen Parkplatz und fährt dreimal **um** den Marktplatz (**herum**).	*He looks for a parking space and drives around the marketplace three times.*

When the preposition **um** is used to indicate movement around something, the word **herum** is often added.

Um . . . herum. Suggestion: Practice **um . . . herum** by demonstrating it and having students say what you are doing, e.g., *Sie gehen* **um** *den Tisch* **herum, um** *den Stuhl* **herum.**

um die Stadt (**herum**)
um den Tisch (**herum**)

Three of the accusative prepositions contract with the article **das.**

durch das → **durchs** Zimmer
für das → **fürs** Auto
um das → **ums** Haus

Übung 6 Max braucht ein Geschenk.

Complete the text with appropriate prepositions.

Max braucht dringend ein Geschenk ____ seinen Freund Tim.[1] Tim hat alles und braucht nichts, aber morgen ist sein Geburtstag. ____ sechs Uhr gibt Tim eine kleine Party ____ ein paar Freunde.[2] Max hat nicht viel Geld; außerdem ist er ____ (*against*) teure Geschenke.[3] Aber ganz ____ (*without*) Geschenk geht es auch nicht.[4]

Also geht er in eine Buchhandlung (*bookstore*). Ein Buch ist immer gut. Er geht ____ einen Tisch mit Sonderangeboten (*sale items*) herum.[5] Fünfzig Mark ____ die Autobiographie von Madonna?[6] Er hat nichts ____ Madonna, aber nein, danke.[7] Max hat aber nicht viel Zeit. ____ vier Uhr hat er ein Seminar.[8] Was tun?

Übung 7 Geschenke

Geschenke. Suggestion: Personalize this exercise by having students say for whom they need a gift. Students respond by making suggestions: e.g., S1: *Ich brauche ein Geschenk für meine Mutter.* S2: *Ein Buch ist immer gut.*

Horst Fischer needs Christmas presents for his friends and relatives. Who will get what gift?

BEISPIEL: Sein Bruder hat keine Uhr. →
Die Armbanduhr ist für seinen Bruder.

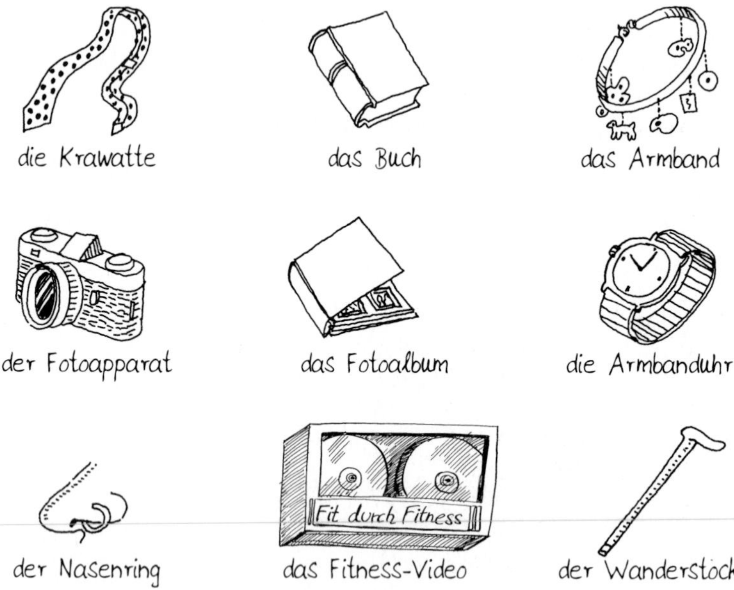

1. Sein Freund Marco ist etwas exzentrisch.
2. Seine Tante Elfriede liest gern.
3. Seine Eltern reisen und fotografieren viel.
4. Sein Großvater wandert gern.
5. Sein Onkel Hubert hat schon alles.
6. Seine Schwester Heike fährt oft nach Spanien.
7. Seine Freundin Gabi trägt gern Schmuck (*jewelry*).
8. Seine Kusine Anneliese ist ein Fitnessfan.

The Verb *werden*

The verb **werden** means *to become.* Here are its present-tense forms.

werden			
ich	werde	wir	werden
du	**wirst**	ihr	werdet
er / sie / es	**wird**	sie	werden
Sie werden			

Realia. „Heidewitzka, Herr Kapitän!" is the beginning of a popular song.

Übung 8 Kennen Sie eigentlich meine Familie?

Complete the sentences using the form of **werden.**

1. Das bin ich ganz links im Bild. Ich ____ im September 16 Jahre alt.
2. Meine zwei Kusinen ____ am Samstag 13.
3. Mein kleiner Bruder Bernd ____ im November 11.
4. Meine kleine Schwester Sara ____ dieses Jahr 3 Jahre alt.
5. Mein Vater hat im Dezember Geburtstag. Er ____ 38 Jahre alt.
6. Mein Großvater fragt immer: „Wann ____ du fünfzehn?" Er vergisst (*forgets*), dass ich schon fünfzehn bin!

Meine Familie

Übung 9. Suggestion: Have students ask a variation of questions 1 and 3 of a number of classmates and write down their answers. (*Wie alt wirst du dieses Jahr? Wann wirst du 50/100?*) Then ask the whole class the questions in the exercise. Students answer with information gathered about a classmate (e.g., *Barbara wird dieses Jahr 22; in 78 Jahren wird sie 100.*)

Übung 9 Eine Umfrage: Wer wird wann wie alt?

Do a class poll:

1. Wer ____ dieses Jahr ____ Jahre alt?
2. Wie viele Leute ____ dieses Jahr 18?
3. Wann ____ du 50? 100? (Ich werde in 30 Jahren 50.)
4. Wann ____ dein Freund oder deine Freundin ____ ?

The Verbs *wissen* and *kennen*

ZEITUNGSLESER WISSEN MEHR!

1832-1982
Wer kennt Goethe?

Wissen/Kennen. **Suggestion:** Practice **kennen** first by asking a number of simple questions that students answer simply with **nein/ja.** *(Kennen Sie . . . Professor/Film/Buch/das Spiel . . . ?)* Then practice **wissen** with simple questions *(Wie viele Studenten studieren Deutsch?)* that allow students to answer: *Das weiß ich nicht.* Finally, add the idea of an indirect question: *Wissen Sie, wo ich wohne?* Keep questions brief to avoid complications with the end position of the verb.

1. *nobody*

The verbs **wissen** and **kennen** both mean *to know.* **Wissen** means *to know facts,* while **kennen** means *to know or be acquainted/familiar with a person or thing.*

Ich **weiß** deine Telefonnummer nicht.	*I don't know your phone number.*
Ich **kenne** Herrn Meyer nicht persönlich, aber ich **weiß,** wer er ist.	*I don't know Mr. Meyer personally, but I know who he is.*

wissen			
ich	**weiß**	wir	wissen
du	**weißt**	ihr	wisst
er / sie / es	**weiß**	sie	wissen
Sie wissen			

kennen			
ich	kenne	wir	kennen
du	kennst	ihr	kennt
er / sie / es	kennt	sie	kennen
Sie kennen			

Johann Wolfgang von Goethe, 1749–1832

Übung 10 Die neue Mitbewohnerin

Wendy, an exchange student from San Diego, is new in Göttingen and lives in a dorm. Listen to Wendy's questions and check off the appropriate negative responses.

	WEISS ICH NICHT.°	NEIN, KENNE ICH NICHT.°
1.	☒	☐
2.	☐	☒
3.	☒	☐
4.	☒	☐
5.	☒	☐

Übung 10. Suggestion: Make sure students understand the distinction between the two phrases. The ones used here represent a more casual way of speaking, typical for everyday conversation among young people. Allow a first listening where everyone notes their answers; a second time around, compare answers.

Don't know. (casual)

	WEISS ICH NICHT.	NEIN, KENNE ICH NICHT.
6.	☒	☐
7.	☐	☒
8.	☒	☐

Übung 11. Suggestion: Do the first example with the whole class to make sure students know Goethe and *Die Leiden des jungen Werther.* Then have pairs read each segment of the exercise.

Übung 11 Wissen oder kennen?

Complete the minidialogues with the correct form of **wissen** or **kennen.**

1. A: ____ du Goethe?
   B: Nein, aber ich ____ , wer er ist.
   A: ____ du seinen Roman, „Die Leiden (*sufferings*) des jungen Werther"?
   B: Nein, den ____ ich nicht. Aber mein Professor ____ ihn bestimmt.
2. C: ____ du, welcher Film heute im Odeon läuft?
   D: Das ____ ich nicht. Aber der Toni, der ____ das bestimmt. Der ____ alles.
3. E: Wo wohnt ihr eigentlich jetzt?
   F: In der Schillerstraße. ____ du die?
   E: Nein, ich ____ aber, wo die Goethestraße ist.
4. G: ____ ihr schon, wo ihr nächstes Semester studiert?
   H: Nein, wir ____ nur, dass wir nicht hier bleiben.
5. I: Ich ____ , wo eine Wohnung frei wird.
   J: Wo denn?
   I: In der Weenderstraße.
   J: Die ____ ich nicht. Wo ist die denn?
6. K: Ihr ____ doch den Peter?
   L: Peter Schnitzler?
   K: Nein, Peter Sudhoff.
   L: Tut mir leid, den ____ wir nicht.

Sprachtipp

Wissen, like the verb *to know* in English, is often used with indirect questions.

Wissen Sie, wie der Mann da **heißt?**
Do you know what that man's name is?

Ich weiß nicht, wo Heike **wohnt.**
I don't know where Heike lives.

In indirect questions, the conjugated verb comes at the end of the clause. Note that a comma separates the introductory phrase from the indirect question.

Übung 12 Ein neugieriger° Mensch

°*inquisitive*

Find out what your partner knows by taking turns asking each other questions.

BEISPIEL: S1: Kennst du den neuen Film von Steven Spielberg?
S2: Nein, den kenne ich nicht. Kennst du den neuen Film von Sönke Wortmann?
S1: Ja, den kenne ich.

Kennst du . . .
- das neue Buch von ____ ?
- den neuen Film von ____ ?
- die Mutter / den Vater von ____ ?
- Herrn Professor ____ ?
- Frau Professor ____ ?
- die Rockgruppe ____ ?
- die Stadt ____ ?

Weißt du . . .
- die Telefonnummer von ____ ?
- die Adresse von ____ ?
- den Vornamen von Herrn / Frau ____ ?
- wie alt ____ ist?
- wann ____ Geburtstag hat?
- wann das nächste Semester beginnt?

Sprache im Kontext

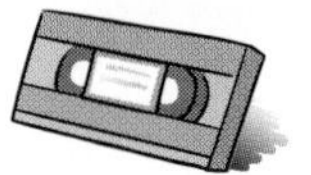

Zuschauen

Merci

Vorschau

Watch the commercial several times and concentrate on what you see. There is no spoken language. What do you think this commercial is for?

Arbeit mit dem Videotext

A. Watch the commercial again several times with sound.

1. Choose five scenes and describe the relationship between the people you see, using the family terms you have learned.

2. Describe the mood of the people in each of the five scenes you chose, using the following adjectives: **lustig, romantisch, traurig, glücklich, unglücklich, ernst, gut, schlecht, langweilig, deprimiert, aggressiv, müde**

B. Pick one of the five scenes you chose and imagine that you are one of the two people in that scene. Which person are you and what would you say to the other person (in German)?

Lesen

Zum Thema

Eine Umfrage (*survey*). Fill out the questionnaire and compare answers in class.

A. What holidays are important in your own family?

	WICHTIG	UNWICHTIG
1. Geburtstage	☐	☐
2. Hochzeitstage	☐	☐
3. religiöse Feiertage	☐	☐
4. nationale Feiertage	☐	☐
5. Muttertag	☐	☐
6. Vatertag	☐	☐

Zum Thema. Suggestion. Give students several minutes to complete the questionnaire. Then turn it into a listening activity, recording the number of student responses on the board; e.g., *Wie viele finden Geburtstage wichtig? Familienfest zum Muttertag? Zum Vatertag?* In this way a class profile will emerge.

B. How do you celebrate Mother's Day and Father's Day?

	ZUM MUTTERTAG JA	ZUM MUTTERTAG NEIN	ZUM VATERTAG JA	ZUM VATERTAG NEIN
1. Wir haben ein großes Familienfest.	□	□	□	□
2. Wir gehen ins Restaurant.	□	□	□	□
3. Ich kaufe ein Geschenk für meine Mutter / meinen Vater.	□	□	□	□
4. Ich mache an diesem Tag nichts Besonderes.	□	□	□	□
5. ?	□	□	□	□

Auf den ersten Blick

A. Skim the text and guess the theme. Look at the pictures, the bold-faced print, and familiar words. These texts are probably:

1. fathers talking about the importance of Father's Day.
2. young people telling about their fathers on Father's Day.
3. young people talking about how they celebrate Father's Day.

Explain your answer.

B. Scan the text for the vocabulary that fits under the following rubrics:

- □ words related to family
- □ types of presents

Zum Text

A. **Guessing from context.** The verb **feiern** and the noun **Feier** are key words in this text. If you don't know what they mean, which clues can you use to help you guess?

Wolfgang Fellier in Innsbruck

fragt junge Leute:

Feierst du den Vatertag?

Radislav Jovic, 13:

Ja, ich feiere den Vatertag schon. Ich finde, er ist genauso wichtig wie[1] der Muttertag. Man soll schließlich beide Elternteile gleich behandeln.[2] Ein Geschenk bekommt mein Vater auch, dafür gebe ich gerne mein Taschengeld aus. Ich werde ihm ein Rasierwasser[3] oder ein Parfüm kaufen.

Werner Klicova, 15:

Wir feiern heute, obwohl gar nicht Vatertag ist. Ich werde meinen Vater nämlich zu einem Konzert einladen. Eigentlich feiere ich das ganze Jahr über Vatertag, weil ich einfach super mit ihm auskomme.[4] Er hat eine ähnliche Frisur[5] wie ich und ist viel mehr ein cooler Kollege als ein autoritärer Elternteil.

Tanja Pescosta, 16:

Wir werden alle zusammen essen gehen, und der Vater bekommt auch ein Geschenk, aber eine Feier, so intensiv wie beim Muttertag, gibt es bei uns nicht. Das liegt wohl daran,[6] daß man die Arbeit der Mutter besser mitbekommt. Mein Vater freut sich[7] allerdings sehr über die Anerkennung am Vatertag.

1. genau . . . *just as important as*
2. gleich . . . *treat the same*
3. *aftershave*
4. *get along*
5. ähnliche . . . *similar hairstyle*
6. Das . . . *That's probably because*
7. freut . . . *is glad*

Zum Text. Note: It is important to do contextual guessing exercises in class. When students' guesses are off the mark, you can guide them to make better guesses by having them articulate what led them to their guess and teaching them to look for evidence to confirm their guesses. Reassure your students that we all make false assumptions about texts. The goal is to learn how to move on until they can confirm their assumptions.

B. Now read the statements by the three young people in order to answer the following questions. As you work through the text, note which words you have to look up, if any, in order to find the information.

1. Who finds Father's Day important?
2. Who is going out to eat for Father's Day?
3. Who is buying something for his/her father?
4. Who is taking his/her father to a concert?
5. Who celebrates Mother's Day more than Father's Day?

C. Close reading

1. Some of the opinions in the text are cued by these phrases:
   - **Ich finde . . .**
   - **Man soll . . .**

Recognizing such phrases will improve your understanding when reading. Locate these phrases in the text. Do you agree with the opinions expressed?

2. Reread the text and locate evidence for the following.
   - Indication that Mother's Day and Father's Day have different importance.
   - Speculation on reasons for the difference.
   - Evidence that some of the speakers have traditional expectations of men and women.

Sprechen und Schreiben

Aktivität 1 Eine Person vorstellen

Work in small groups. Bring in a picture of your family, a family member, or a friend and describe the person or people in the picture to your group.

BEISPIEL: Das ist meine Mutter. Sie heißt Barbara. Sie ist 44 Jahre alt. Sie hat im April Geburtstag. Sie ist sehr aktiv. Sie kocht gern und läuft gern.

Aktivität 1. Suggestion: As each student describes his or her picture, the others take notes. One student in each group should be called on to report on one of the photos described.

Aktivität 2 Ein Bericht

Write a short report about yourself and your family or write about a friend and his/her family. Include in your report:

- wie groß die Familie ist und wo sie wohnt
- wann Sie Geburtstag haben
- was Sie und andere Familienmitglieder (*family members*) gern machen (kochen, tanzen usw.)
- Lieblings . . . (-sport, -komponist, -musiker)
- Probleme (kein Geld, zu viel Geld . . .)

Aktivität 2. Suggestion: Have students form groups of five. One narrates the report he or she wrote to the group; the others take notes, and one of them reports to the whole class.

Additional activity. Hand out Uwe Timm's poem "Erziehung" and read it aloud in the class. Have students guess what it is about. Have them guess the meaning of the word *Erziehung*.

Wortschatz

Der Stammbaum	Family Tree
der **Bruder, ¨**	brother
die **Eltern** (*pl.*)	parents
der **Enkel, -**	grandson
die **Enkelin, -nen**	granddaughter
die **Familie, -n**	family
die **Frau, -en**	wife
die **Geschwister** (*pl.*)	siblings
die **Großeltern** (*pl.*)	grandparents
die **Großmutter, ¨**	grandmother
der **Großvater, ¨**	grandfather
die **Kusine, -n** / die **Cousine, -n**	(female) cousin
der **Mann, ¨er**	husband
die **Mutter, ¨**	mother
der **Neffe, -n** (**-n** *masc.*)	nephew
die **Nichte, -n**	niece
die **Oma, -s**	grandma
der **Onkel, -**	uncle
der **Opa, -s**	grandpa
der **Schwager, ¨**	brother-in-law
die **Schwägerin, -nen**	sister-in-law
die **Schwester, -n**	sister
der **Sohn, ¨e**	son
die **Tante, -n**	aunt
die **Tochter, ¨**	daughter
der **Vater, ¨**	father
der **Vetter, -n** / der **Cousin, -s**	(male) cousin

Die Wochentage	Days of the Week
der **Montag**	Monday
am Montag	on Monday
der **Dienstag**	Tuesday
der **Mittwoch**	Wednesday
der **Donnerstag**	Thursday
der **Freitag**	Friday
der **Samstag** / der **Sonnabend**	Saturday
der **Sonntag**	Sunday

Die Monate	The Months
der **Januar***	January
im Januar	in January
der **Februar**	February
der **März**	March
der **April**	April
der **Mai**	May
der **Juni**	June
der **Juli**	July
der **August**	August
der **September**	September
der **Oktober**	October
der **November**	November
der **Dezember**	December

Feste und Feiertage	Holidays
das **Familienfest, -e**	family gathering
(der) **Fasching**	Mardi Gras (*southern Germany*)
der **Geburtstag, -e**	birthday
das **Geschenk, -e**	gift, present
die **Hochzeit, -en**	wedding
der **Kalender, -**	calendar
(der) **Karneval**	Mardi Gras (*Rhineland*)
der **Muttertag**	Mother's Day
das **Neujahr**	New Year's Day
(das) **Ostern**	Easter
die **Party, -s**	party
(das) **Silvester**	New Year's Eve
die **Tradition, -en**	tradition
der **Valentinstag**	Valentine's Day
das **Weihnachten**	Christmas
der **Weihnachtsbaum, ¨e**	Christmas tree

Verben	Verbs
feiern	to celebrate
gratulieren	to congratulate
heiraten	to marry
kennen	to know (*be acquainted with a person or thing*)

*__Jänner__ is used in Austria.

planen	to plan
werden (wird)	to become, be
wissen (weiß)	to know (*something as a fact*)
wünschen	to wish

Adjektive und Adverbien — Adjectives and Adverbs

immer	always
morgen	tomorrow
nämlich	namely, that is to say
natürlich	natural(ly)
oft	often
wichtig	important

Ordinalzahlen — Ordinal Numbers

erste	first
der erste Mai	May first
am ersten Mai	on May first
zweite	second
dritte	third
vierte	fourth
fünfte	fifth
sechste	sixth
sieb(en)te	seventh
achte	eighth
neunte	ninth
zehnte	tenth
elfte	eleventh
zwölfte	twelfth
dreizehnte	thirteenth
zwanzigste	twentieth
hundertste	hundredth
tausendste	thousandth

Possessivpronomen — Possessive Adjectives

mein	my
dein	your (*informal sg.*)
sein	his; its
ihr	her; its; their
unser	our
euer	your (*informal pl.*)
Ihr	your (*formal*)

Akkusativpräpositionen — Accusative Prepositions

durch	through
für	for
gegen	against; around (+ *time*)
ohne	without
um	at (+ *time*)
um (. . . herum)	around (*spatial*)

Akkusativpronomen — Accusative Pronouns

mich	me
dich	you (*informal sg.*)
ihn	him; it
sie	her; it; them
es	it
uns	us
euch	you (*informal pl.*)
Sie	you (*formal*)

Sonstige Ausdrücke — Other Expressions

Alles Gute!	All the best!
Herzlichen Glückwunsch zum Geburtstag!	Happy birthday!
um Mitternacht	at midnight
Wann hast du Geburtstag?	When is your birthday?
Welches Datum ist heute/morgen?	What is today's/tomorrow's date?
es gibt	there is / there are

Lernziele

Use this checklist to verify that you can now . . .

- ☐ describe how you are related to other people.
- ☐ talk about your family and friends.
- ☐ name several holidays and describe some of the things people do on those holidays.
- ☐ congratulate people on special occasions.
- ☐ say the day, month, or date when an event takes place.
- ☐ give reasons or explanations using the adverb **nämlich.**
- ☐ describe personal ownership or a relationship using the possessive adjectives.
- ☐ refer to people and things using accusative personal pronouns.
- ☐ recognize and use accusative prepositions.
- ☐ use **werden, wissen,** and **kennen** appropriately.
- ☐ guess the theme of a text by using your knowledge of cognates and familiar vocabulary.

Erstes Zwischenspiel

Persönlichkeiten: Drei Kurzbiographien

Wolfgang Amadeus Mozart

(*1756–1791*)

Geburtsort: Salzburg
Geburtsdatum: 27. Januar 1756
Sternzeichen: Wassermann[1]
Vater: Leopold
Mutter: Maria Anna
Geschwister: Marianne, genannt „Nannerl"
verheiratet[2] mit: Constance geb. Weber
Kinder: Karl und Wolfgang
Wohnort: Wien
Beruf: Kapellmeister und Komponist
Hauptwerke: Opern (z.B. „Don Giovanni", „Die Zauberflöte"); 41 Symphonien; Kirchenmusik (z.B. „Krönungsmesse",[3] „Requiem"); Konzerte und Kammermusik (z.B. „Eine kleine Nachtmusik")
Hobbys: Musik, Tanzen, Geselligkeit,[4] Reisen
Lieblingskomponist: Joseph Haydn

Wolfgang Amadeus Mozart, ca. 1783

Leopold Mozart und seine Kinder Wolfgang und „Nannerl", 1763

Paula Modersohn-Becker (*1876–1909*)

Geburtsort: Dresden
Geburtsdatum: 8. Februar 1876
Sternzeichen: Wassermann
Vater: Woldemar
Mutter: Mathilde
Geschwister: sechs; vier jüngere, zwei ältere
verheiratet mit: Otto Modersohn
Kinder: Mathilde
Wohnort: zuletzt in Worpswede*

Paula Modersohn-Becker: Worpsweder Landschaft, um 1900

Beruf: Malerin
Hauptwerke: Landschaftsmalerei,[5] Porträts, Stilleben
Hobbys: Musik, Tanzen, Kochen, Lesen, Zeichnen
Lieblingsdichter: Rainer Maria Rilke

Paula Modersohn-Becker, Selbstbildnis

[1]*Aquarius* [2]*married* [3]*Coronation Mass* [4]*conviviality* [5]*landscape painting*

*Worpswede ist ein Künstlerdorf in der Nähe von Bremen.

Albert Einstein (*1879–1955*)

Geburtsort: Ulm
Geburtsdatum: 14. März 1879
Sternzeichen: Fisch
Vater: Hermann
Mutter: Pauline
Geschwister: Maria („Maja")
verheiratet mit: zuerst Mileva, dann Elsa
Kinder: Hans und Eduard
Wohnort: zuletzt in Princeton, New Jersey
Beruf: Physiker (Nobelpreis, 1921)
Hauptwerk: Relativitätstheorie
Hobbys: Musik, Geige[1] spielen, Segeln[2]
Lieblingskomponist: Mozart
Lieblingsphilosoph: Immanuel Kant

(*links*) **Albert Einstein als Kind, mit seiner Schwester Maja**

(*rechts*) **Albert Einstein beim Segeln**

Aktivität 1 Darf ich vorstellen?

Suppose you had to introduce Mozart, Einstein, or Modersohn-Becker to someone at a party. Make three statements about eachthat characterize who they are.

BEISPIEL: Darf ich vorstellen, das ist Herr/Frau . . .
Er/Sie ist . . .
Er/Sie schreibt/malt/wohnt in . . .

Aktivität 2 Rollenspiel

Imagine that you could interview the people you just read about. With a partner, select one of the three, then create the interview. You could begin as follows:

BEISPIEL: S1: Wo sind Sie geboren, Frau Modersohn-Becker?
S2: In Dresden.
S1: Sind Sie verheiratet? . . .

Aktivität 3 Ein Steckbrief[3]

Choose a well-known historical person and gather information to write a **Steckbrief** about her or him. Present the information in class without revealing who the person is. Let the members of the class guess her or his identity.

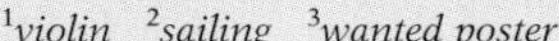

[1]*violin* [2]*sailing* [3]*wanted poster*

Kapitel 4

Mein Tag

Morgens in einer Kleinstadt

Kapitel 4. Suggestion: Introduce this chapter by talking about your daily routine, i.e., what you do at different times of the day, when you get up, go to bed, eat, etc. Ask students yes/no questions about the same topics. Incorporate adverbs of time and modals.

Alles klar?

Realia. This re-creation of an ad for the German postal system encourages people to communicate with each other by writing more often.

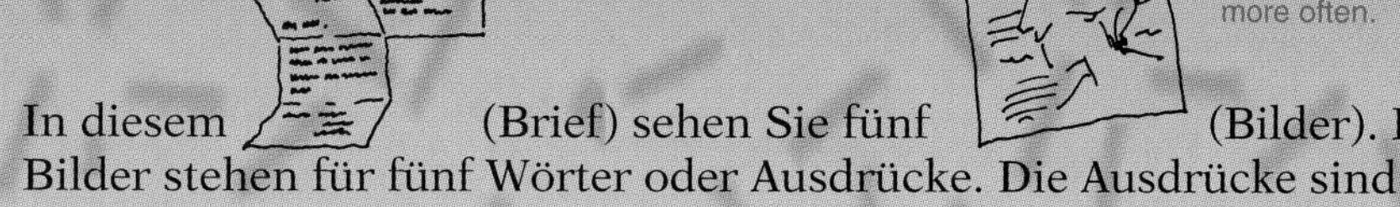

A. In diesem (Brief) sehen Sie fünf (Bilder). Die Bilder stehen für fünf Wörter oder Ausdrücke. Die Ausdrücke sind in alphabetischer Ordnung.

Fahrrad
Haus(e)
Herz
Sonntag
Tasse Kaffee

Lesen Sie den Brief nun mit den Wörtern.

B. Sie hören jetzt eine telefonische Einladung. Hören Sie bitte zu, und markieren Sie die richtige Information.

Realia. Suggestion: Have students scan the note to determine (1) what kind of text it is and (2) what it might be about.

1. Die Einladung ist für _____.
- **a.** Sonntag
- **b.** Samstag
- **c.** Freitag

2. Erika und Thomas wollen _____.
- **a.** Dirk zu Kaffee und Kuchen einladen
- **b.** mit Dirk auf eine Party gehen
- **c.** mit Dirk ins Café gehen

3. Dirk soll _____ kommen.
- **a.** um 3 Uhr (*o'clock*)
- **b.** um 5 Uhr
- **c.** um 4 Uhr

Wörter im Kontext

Thema 1

Der Tagesablauf°

Dies ist Wolfgang Eicheles Wochenplan für die nächsten drei Tage.

daily schedule

Note: Remind students of Wolfgang's relationship to the family introduced in **Kapitel 3.** Wolfgang studies at the FU in Berlin. You can point out where the places in the *Wochenplan* are located.

WOCHENPLAN

	Zeit	Tagesplan	✓
15 Donnerstag	8:00	einkaufen gehen	
	:	(KaDeWe)	
	12:00	mit Thomas essen	
	14:00	im Tierpark	
	:	spazieren gehen	
	21:00	fernsehen	
	:		
16 Freitag	7:00	„Die Zeit" lesen	
	10:00	Wohnung aufräumen	
	:		
	15:00	Erika + Thomas auf eine	
	:	Tasse Kaffee einladen	
	20:00	ins Kino gehen	
	:	(Zoo)	
17 Samstag	:	lange schlafen	
	10:00	gemütlich frühstücken	
	21:00	mit Freunden ausgehen	
18 Sonntag	:		
	:		
	:		

Was möchte Wolfgang machen—und wann? Sehen Sie sich Wolfgangs Wochenplan an, und ergänzen Sie Wolfgangs Pläne.

Thema 1: Have students complete the sentences following Wolfgang's *Wochenplan*.

heute 15.Okt

heute Morgen 8.00 Uhr
heute Vormittag 10.00 Uhr
heute Mittag 12.00 Uhr
heute Nachmittag 15.00 Uhr
heute Abend 20.00 Uhr

- ☐ **Heute Morgen** möchte Wolfgang einkaufen gehen.
- ☐ **Heute Mittag** möchte er ______________.
- ☐ **Heute Nachmittag** möchte er ______________.
- ☐ **Heute Abend** möchte er ______________.

morgen 16.Okt

Morgen früh 8.00 Uhr
morgen Vormittag 10.00 Uhr
morgen Mittag 12.00 Uhr
morgen Nachmittag 15.00 Uhr
morgen Abend 20.00 Uhr

- ☐ **Morgen früh** möchte Wolfgang *Die Zeit* lesen.
- ☐ **Morgen Vormittag** möchte er ______________.
- ☐ **Morgen Nachmittag** möchte er______________.
- ☐ **Morgen Abend** möchte er ______________.

am Samstag 17.Okt

Samstagmorgen 8.00 Uhr
Samstagvormittag 10.00 Uhr
Samstagmittag 12.00 Uhr
Samstagnachmittag 15.00 Uhr
Samstagabend 20.00 Uhr

- ☐ **Samstagmorgen** möchte Wolfgang lange schlafen.
- ☐ **Samstagvormittag** möchte er ______________.
- ☐ **Samstagabend** möchte er ______________.

Und Sie? Was möchten Sie tun—und wann?

Further practice: Write the following on the board: ______ *möchte ich* ______. Have the class stand up. Each student completes the sentence using words of his or her own choice. As they complete their sentences, students sit down.

Note: Point out to students that in combination with *heute* and *morgen* (tomorrow), the words *Morgen* (morning), *Vormittag, Mittag* and *Nachmittag* are capitalized, but that in combination with days of the week they form compounds.

Sprachtipp

To find out at what time something takes place, ask:

Um wie viel Uhr _____?

To say at what time something takes place, use the following expressions:

um ein Uhr (1.00 Uhr)	**um ein Uhr dreißig** (1.30 Uhr)
um ein Uhr zehn (1.10 Uhr)	**um ein Uhr vierzig** (1.40 Uhr)
um ein Uhr fünfzehn (1.15 Uhr)	**um ein Uhr fünfundvierzig** (1.45 Uhr)

Aktivität 1 Was macht Wolfgang am Wochenende?

Sehen Sie sich die Bilder an, und ergänzen Sie Wolfgangs Pläne für das Wochenende.

1. Um _____ schläft Wolfgang noch. Dann klingelt der Wecker.
2. Um _____ **steht** er endlich **auf.**
3. Von _____ bis _____ geht er joggen.

4. Um _____ **frühstückt** er und liest die Zeitung.
5. Um _____ **ruft** er einen Freund **an.**
6. Um _____ trifft er eine Freundin im Café.

7. Um _____ geht er einkaufen.
8. Um _____ spielt Wolfgang Fußball auf dem Sportplatz.
9. Um _____ ist er mit Freunden im Kino.

When you do something on a regular basis, use the following adverbs to express the day or the time.

montags	**morgens**
dienstags	**vormittags**
mittwochs	**mittags**
donnerstags	**nachmittags**
freitags	**abends**
samstags/sonnabends	**nachts**
sonntags	

In German, general time precedes specific time.

GENERAL *SPECIFIC*

Ich habe donnerstags um 13.00 Uhr Chemie.

GENERAL *SPECIFIC*

Ich komme heute Abend um 7 Uhr vorbei.

Aktivität 2 Hin und her: Zwei Stundenpläne

Aktivität 2. Sven's schedule appears here; Frank's appears in Appendix A.

A. Sven und Frank sind 18 Jahre alt und gehen aufs Gymnasium (*secondary school*). Vergleichen Sie ihre Stundenpläne. Welche Kurse haben sie zusammen (*together*)?

BEISPIEL: S1: Welchen Kurs hat Sven dienstags um acht?
S2: Dienstags um acht hat Sven Informatik. Welchen Kurs hat Frank dienstags um acht?
S1: Dienstags um acht hat Frank Physik.

Svens Stundenplan

Zeit	Montag	Dienstag	Mittwoch	Donnerstag	Freitag	Samstag
$8-8^{45}$	Englisch	Informatik	Chemie	Physik	frei	Deutsch
$8^{45}-9^{30}$	Englisch	Informatik	Chemie	Physik	Kunst	Deutsch
$9^{35}-10^{20}$	Religion	Deutsch	Erdkunde	Deutsch	Sozialkunde	
$10^{40}-11^{25}$	Religion	Mathematik	Mathematik	Mathematik	Deutsch	
$11^{30}-12^{15}$	Erdkunde	Kunst	Sozialkunde	Geschichte	Geschichte	
$12^{15}-13^{00}$	Mathematik	Physik	Informatik	Englisch	Chemie	
$13^{15}-14^{00}$				Sport		
$14^{00}-14^{45}$				Sport		

Langenscheidt L

Note: This schedule is based on the schedule at the *Burgstraße Gymnasium* in Kaiserslautern. Tell students that most schools have a recess or break (*Pause*), usually in the morning. See if they can determine when the *große Pause* takes place. Both Sven and Frank have classes on Saturday morning, but only on the 2nd and 4th Saturday of the month. A growing trend in Germany is to do away with Saturday classes altogether.

B. Sven und Frank möchten Tennis spielen. Wann ist die beste Zeit? Wann haben sie beide frei?

Aktivität 3 Wie sieht Ihr Stundenplan aus?°

°How does your schedule look?

Vergleichen Sie Ihren Stundenplan mit dem von den anderen Studenten/Studentinnen in Ihrem Kurs. Hat jemand Kurse mit Ihnen zusammen?

BEISPIEL: S1: Was hast du donnerstags um 10?
S2: Donnerstags um 10 habe ich _____. Und du?
S1: Ich habe _____.

Aktivität 3. Point Out: Refer students to the list of academic subjects in Appendix B.

Aktivität 4 Bist du heute Abend zu Hause?

Laden Sie sich (*yourself*) zu einem Freund / einer Freundin (*friend's house*) ein. Sagen Sie, wann Sie vorbeikommen und wie lange Sie bleiben möchten. Benutzen Sie Ausdrücke wie **heute Abend und morgen Abend.** Geben Sie auch die genaue Uhrzeit an. Benutzen Sie dieses Sprechschema.

Aktivität 4. Suggestion: Follow up with questions such as *Wann kommt _____ vorbei?* to elicit responses such as _____ *kommt Samstagnachmittag um vier vorbei.*

S1	S2
1. Bist du _____ zu Hause?	**2a.** Ja, ich bin zu Hause. **2b.** Nein, ich bin leider nicht zu Hause.
3a. Kann ich dann _____ vorbeikommen? **3b.** Schade. Wann kann ich denn mal vorbeikommen?	**4a.** Ja, gern. Ich sehe dich also _____. **4b.** Kannst du _____ kommen?
5a. Schön. **5b.** Ja, gern.	**6.** Wie lange kannst du denn bleiben?
7. _____ Stunde(n).	

Thema 2

Die Uhrzeit

Wie spät ist es?
Wie viel Uhr ist es?

Es ist eins.

Es ist **ein Uhr.**
Es ist dreizehn Uhr.

Es ist zehn (Minuten) **nach** eins.

Es ist ein Uhr zehn.
Es ist dreizehn Uhr zehn.

Thema 2. Point Out: Both *Wie viel Uhr ist es?* and *Wie spät ist es?* are used to ask "What time is it?" *Wie viel Uhr . . .* is somewhat more formal than *Wie spät . . .* The examples on the left are considered informal; those on the right are considered more formal. **Suggestion:** Present times using an actual clock (or one made from a paper plate), moving the hands to correspond to the times in the examples. Students repeat the times. Check students' comprehension by reviewing the examples in random order, using the clock, and asking students to say what time it is.

Es ist **Viertel nach** eins.

Es ist ein Uhr fünfzehn.
Es ist dreizehn Uhr fünfzehn.

Es ist **halb** zwei.

Es ist ein Uhr dreißig.
Es ist dreizehn Uhr dreißig.

Es ist zwanzig (Minuten) **vor** zwei.

Es ist ein Uhr vierzig.
Es ist dreizehn Uhr vierzig.

Es ist **Viertel vor** zwei.

Es ist ein Uhr fünfundvierzig.
Es ist dreizehn Uhr fünfundvierzig.

Es ist zehn (Minuten) vor zwei.

Es ist ein Uhr fünfzig.
Es ist dreizehn Uhr fünfzig.

Eine **Minute** hat sechzig **Sekunden,** eine **Stunde** sechzig Minuten und ein Tag vierundzwanzig Stunden.

Aktivität 5 Zeitansagen°

° *time announcement*

Markieren Sie die Uhrzeiten, die Sie hören.

	a.	b.	c.
1.	7.38	17.35	17.30
2.	3.06	2.06	20.16
3.	14.00	14.15	14.05
4.	12.25	10.24	11.25
5.	19.45	9.45	19.40
6.	13.00	3.40	13.40
7.	0.15	0.05	0.45
8.	20.05	20.50	21.50

In official timetables—for instance, in radio, television, movie, and theater guides—time is expressed according to the twenty-four-hour system.

1.00–12.00 Uhr	*1:00 A.M. to 12:00 noon*
13.00–24.00 Uhr	*1:00 P.M. to 12:00 midnight*

Midnight may also be referred to as **0 (null) Uhr.**

When writing time in numbers, German speakers usually separate hours and minutes with a period, instead of a colon as in English.

Analyse

Sehen Sie sich die Zeichnung an, und beantworten Sie die Fragen.

Analyse. Suggestion: Have students give time in both the twelve- and twenty-four-hour systems.

- Wie spät ist es in New York?
- Wie spät ist es in Tokio?
- Wie spät ist es in Bombay?
- Die vierte Uhr zeigt (*shows*) die „gute alte Zeit". Warum hat der Mann wohl (*probably*) diese Uhr gern?
    - **a.** Er hat Kuckucksuhren gern.
    - **b.** Heute ist alles so hektisch.
    - **c.** Die Kuckucksuhr geht langsamer als die anderen Uhren.
    - **d.** ?

Realia. This cartoon appeared in *P.M.* magazine.

Aktivität 6 Wie viel Uhr ist es? Wie spät ist es?

BEISPIEL: Wie viel Uhr ist es? (Wie spät ist es?) → Es ist Viertel nach sieben.

1. **2.** **3.**

4. 

5.

6. 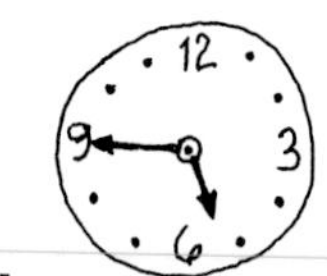

7. 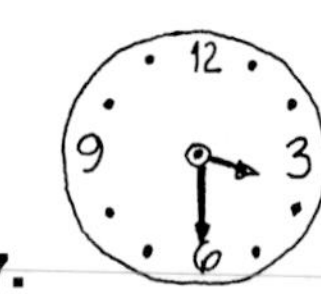

Aktivität 7 Mein Zeitbudget

A. Wie viel Zeit verbringen (*spend*) Sie mit diesen Dingen? Tragen Sie in die Tabelle ein, wie viel Zeit Sie pro Woche mit jeder Tätigkeit verbringen. Fragen Sie dann einen Partner / eine Partnerin:

1. Wie viel Zeit verbringst du mit _____ (Lesen, Essen, Arbeiten usw.)?
2. Wie viel Zeit hast du für dich?

Tätigkeit	Montag bis Freitag	Wochenende	insgesamt
Vorlesungen Labor Lesen Schreiben			
Nebenarbeit			
Essen Frühstück Mittagessen Abendessen			
Einkaufen Sport Schlafen			
Zeit für mich Fernsehen Zeitung/Bücher lesen Freunde besuchen			

B. Berichten Sie, wie Ihr Partner / Ihre Partnerin seine/ihre Zeit verbringt.

BEISPIEL: Laura verbringt drei Stunden/Minuten pro Woche mit Fernsehen.

Thema 3

Kino, Musik und Theater

JAN: Ich **gehe** heute abend **ins Theater.** Willst du mit?
ULLA: Nein, danke. Ich bin kein Theaterfan. Ich möchte **lieber** ins Kino.
JAN: So. Du bist ein Kinofan. Was für (*what kind of*) **Filme** siehst du denn gern?
ULLA: **Am liebsten** Horrorfilme und Psychothriller—die sind so **spannend.**

Was für Filme sehen Sie gern?

- □ Horrorfilme
- □ **Komödien**
- □ Psychothriller
- □ Liebesfilme
- □ **Krimis**
- □ Science-fiction-Filme
- □ Abenteuerfilme
- □ Wild-West-Filme

Was sehen Sie gern auf der Bühne (*on stage*)?

- □ **Tragödien**
- □ Lustspiele (*comedies*)
- □ Musicals
- □ **Theaterstücke**
- □ **Opern**
- □ **Ballette**

Was für **Musik** hören Sie gern?

- □ klassische Musik
- □ Heavy Metal
- □ Rockmusik
- □ Techno
- □ alternative Musik
- □ Jazz
- □ Soul
- □ Western-Musik
- □ Rap

Aktivität 8 Zwei Einladungen°

°invitations

Sie hören zwei Dialoge. Wer spricht? Wohin möchten die Sprecher gehen? Warum ist es nicht möglich (*possible*)? Markieren Sie die richtige Information.

DIALOG 1

1. Die Sprecher sind
   - a. ein Professor und ein Student.
   - b. zwei Studentinnen.
   - c. eine Studentin und ein Freund.
2. Der eine Sprecher möchte
   - a. zu Hause arbeiten.
   - b. ins Kino.
   - c. ins Konzert.
3. Die Sprecherin muss leider
   - a. arbeiten.
   - b. in eine Vorlesung.
   - c. einen Brief schreiben.

DIALOG 2

1. Die Sprecher sind
   - a. zwei Studenten.
   - b. zwei Professoren.
   - c. ein Student und eine Freundin.
2. Die eine Sprecherin möchte
   - a. ins Kino.
   - b. in eine Vorlesung.
   - c. Karten spielen.
3. Der andere Sprecher
   - a. hat eine Vorlesung.
   - b. hat Labor.
   - c. muss in die Bibliothek.

Aktivität 9 Was machst du so° am Wochenende?

°generally

Interviewen Sie einen Partner / eine Partnerin. Was tut er/sie gern am Wochenende? Nennen Sie mindestens vier Dinge. Berichten Sie dann darüber.

BEISPIEL: S1: Was machst du am Wochenende?
S2: Ich gehe schwimmen.

MÖGLICHE ANTWORTEN

Ich **gehe** (tanzen, **spazieren,** einkaufen, laufen, schwimmen, wandern, ?).
Ich stehe (früh, **spät,** ?) auf.
Ich spiele (Karten, Tennis, ?).
Ich rufe (+ *person*) an.
Ich **räume** (mein Zimmer, meine Wohnung, meinen Kleiderschrank, ?) **auf.**
Ich gehe (ins Kino, ins Theater, ins Konzert, in die Oper, in die Disko).
Ich lade (Freunde, ?) ein.
Ich sehe fern.
?

Sprachtipp

To say where you are going, use the following expressions.

Ich gehe { **ins Kino.** / **ins Theater.** / **ins Konzert.** / **in die Oper.** / **in die Disko.** }

Aktivität 10 Was hast du vor?°

What are you planning to do?

Schauen Sie sich die Programme für Kino, Theater und Musik an. Sagen Sie, wohin Sie gehen wollen.

Realia. The ads for *Phantom der Oper, Deutsche Oper Berlin, Berliner Kammerspiele,* and *Theater in Berlin* are from the *BZ* newspaper. The ads for the *Kulturhaus Spandau*, the *Schiller Theater* and *Cafétheater Schalotte* are from the magazine *Tip-Berlin*.

THEATER	Montag, 10. 3. 1997	Dienstag, 11. 3. 1997
Deutsche Oper Berlin 341 02 49	20.00 Kammermusik im Foyer: **Ensemble „das neue Werk" Berlin**	17.00 Foyer: **„Klein-Siegfried"**
Berliner Kammerspiele 391 55 43	**Biedermann und die Brandstifter** von Max Frisch Freitag und Sonnabend 18.00 Uhr	

19.6.
Theaterwerkstatt Charlottenburg
Neil Simon
Brooklyn Memoiren
Cafétheater Schalotte, 1000 Berlin 10
Behaimstr. 22, 20 Uhr

Schiller Theater
Heute 20.00 Uhr
Frauen. Krieg. Lustspiel
von Thomas Brasch
Mit A. Domröse. U. Höpfner u. H. Thate
Regie: George Tabori
Karten Tel. 319 52 36

Weiteres zum Thema Konzert und Theater finden Sie bei ***Deutsch: Na klar!*** im World-Wide-Web unter www.mhhe.com/german.

S1	S2
1. Was hast du am Samstag vor?	**2.** Ich gehe ins Theater / in die Oper / ?. Willst du mit?
3. Was gibt es denn?	**4.** Ein Musical / eine Oper / ? von (+ *name*).
5a. So? Wann fängt er/es/sie denn an? **5b.** Ach, ich bleibe lieber zu Hause.	**6a.** _____. **6b.** Schade.

Kulturtipp

In Deutschland gibt es in den Groß- und Kleinstädten über 400 öffentliche und private Theater. Der deutsche Staat subventioniert (*subsidizes*) die meisten von ihnen mit insgesamt über zwei Milliarden Mark pro Jahr, damit die Preise für die Theaterkarten nicht zu teuer werden. Viele Deutsche haben ein Theaterabonnement. Die deutschen Theater spielen gerne klassische Stücke, die oft modernisiert oder politisiert werden, um sie aktuell und interessant zu machen.

Stadttheater Göttingen

Grammatik im Kontext

Separable-Prefix Verbs°

°Verben mit trennbaren Präfixen

You are already familiar with sentences like the following:

Susanne und Peter **kommen** per Fahrrad **vorbei.**	*Susanne and Peter **are coming by** on their bikes.*
Ich gehe heute tanzen. **Kommst** du **mit?**	*I am going dancing today. Will you **come along**?*

German, like English, has many two-part verbs that consist of a verb and a short complement that alters or in some way affects the meaning of the main verb. Examples of such two-part verbs in English are:

to come by, to come along, to call up, to get up

Wüstenrot-Rendite[1]-Programm mit 936 Mark pro anno.

Jede Million fängt klein an.

1. *yield on investment*
2. *simple*

Realia. *Jede Million fängt klein an* is a well-known ad slogan for *Wüstenrot,* a German investment house. The text of the ad, which is omitted, encourages savers to begin with a small amount—*78 Marks* a month—to start out on the road to becoming millionaires.

Realia. *Ich rufe an* is from an ad for the *Deutsche Bundespost.*

Kommen . . . vorbei and **kommst . . . mit** are examples of such two-part verbs in German. They are also called separable-prefix verbs. In the infinitive, the separable part of these verbs forms the verb's prefix. The prefixes are always stressed.

ánrufen   ánfangen   vorbéikommen   mítkommen

In a declarative sentence or in a question, the prefix is separated from the conjugated verb and placed at the end of the sentence.

—**Kommst** du heute Abend **vorbei?**	*Are you coming by tonight?*
—Ja, aber ich **rufe** vorher **an.**	*Yes, but I'll call first.*

Here are examples of some commonly used separable-prefix verbs.

VERB	BEISPIEL
abholen (holt . . . ab) to pick up	Ich **hole** dich um 6 Uhr **ab.**
anfangen (fängt . . . an) to begin	Wann **fängt** die Vorlesung **an?**
anrufen (ruft . . . an) to call up	Ich **rufe** dich morgen **an.**
aufhören (hört . . . auf) to end, quit	Der Regen **hört** nicht **auf.**
aufräumen (räumt . . . auf) to clean up	Er **räumt** sein Zimmer **auf.**
aufstehen (steht . . . auf) to get up	Er **steht** um 9 Uhr **auf.**
aufwachen (wacht . . . auf) to wake up	Wann **wachst** du gewöhnlich **auf?**
einkaufen (kauft . . . ein) to shop	Herr Lerche **kauft** immer morgens **ein.**
einladen (lädt . . . ein) to invite	Ich **lade** dich zum Essen **ein.**

einschlafen (schläft . . . ein) to fall asleep	Ich **schlafe** gewöhnlich nicht vor Mitternacht **ein.**
mitkommen (kommt . . . mit) to come along	**Kommst** du **mit?**
mitnehmen (nimmt . . . mit) to take along	**Nimmst** du einen Regenschirm **mit?**
vorbeikommen (kommt . . . vorbei) to come by	Wir **kommen** Sonntag **vorbei.**
vorhaben (hat . . . vor) to plan to do	Was **hast** du heute **vor?**
zurückkommen (kommt . . . zurück) to come back	Wann **kommst** du **zurück?**

Separable-prefix verbs are listed in the vocabulary of this book as follows:

auf•hören
vor•haben (hat vor)

When the verb stem shows stem-vowel changes or other irregularities in the present tense, the separable-prefix verb will also have these changes.

anfangen	Der Film **fängt** um 20.00 Uhr **an.**
mitnehmen	**Nimmst** du einen Schirm **mit?**

So geben Sie Ihre Anzeige[1] auf:[2]

01 30/81 80 10

07 11/1 82-13 49
Faxaufträge am Anzeigenschluß nur bis 16 Uhr!

★34200#

Coupon ausfüllen, und einsenden

1. *ad*
2. geben . . . auf *place*

The Sentence Bracket°

Die Satzklammer

Separable-prefix verbs show a sentence structure that is characteristic for German: The finite verb and its complement form a bracket around the core of the sentence. The conjugated verb is the second element of the sentence, and the separable prefix is the last element.

Ich **fange** jetzt ein neues Leben **an.**

Another example of the sentence bracket can be seen in such sentences as:

Klaus and Erika **gehen** Sonntag mit Freunden **tanzen.**

The conjugated verb **gehen** and the infinitive **tanzen** form a bracket around: **Sonntag mit Freunden. Tanzen** is a necessary verbal complement; without it, the idea of the sentence is incomplete.

Übung 1 Daniels Tagesablauf

Daniel ist Künstler (*artist*), aber die Kunst (*art*) allein bringt nicht genug Geld ein. Sie hören jetzt eine Beschreibung von Daniels Tagesablauf. Markieren Sie alle passenden Antworten auf jede Frage.

Übung 1. Suggestion: Have students scan the questions and possible answers before listening to the passage for the first time. Allow students time to answer the questions. Let students listen a second time in order to complete the exercise before going over the answers together.

1. Wann wacht Daniel gewöhnlich (*usually*) auf?
   a. sehr früh
   b. sehr spät
   c. um 5 Uhr
2. Wohnt Daniel allein oder mit jemandem zusammen?
   a. allein
   b. mit seinem Bruder
   c. mit seiner Freundin
3. Was tut Daniel für die Familie Schröder?
   a. Er geht einkaufen.
   b. Er geht mit dem Hund (*dog*) spazieren.
   c. Er macht Reparaturen.
4. Wann fängt Daniels Arbeit im Hotel an?
   a. um 6 Uhr
   b. um 7 Uhr
   c. um 5 Uhr
5. Wann kommt Daniel nach Hause zurück?
   a. um 12 Uhr nachts
   b. um 6 Uhr abends
   c. so gegen 3 Uhr nachmittags
6. Was macht Daniel dann zuerst?
   a. Er geht schlafen.
   b. Er geht einkaufen.
   c. Er räumt das Zimmer auf.
7. Wann fängt Daniels Leben für die Kunst an?
   a. spät nachmittags
   b. am Wochenende
   c. so gegen Mitternacht
8. Wie verbringt Daniel manchmal seinen Abend?
   a. Er sieht fern.
   b. Er lädt Freunde ein.
   c. Er ruft Freunde an.
9. Wann schläft Daniel gewöhnlich ein?
   a. um 12 Uhr nachts
   b. nicht vor 1 Uhr nachts
   c. so gegen halb eins

Übung 2 Was Daniel macht

Erzählen Sie mit Hilfe der Fragen und Antworten in Übung 1, was Daniel jeden Tag macht.

BEISPIEL: Daniel wacht gewöhnlich sehr früh auf.

Übung 2. Suggestion: Do as a whole- class activity. Allow students to add as much detail as possible. **Additional Activity:** Copy the tapescript and white-out the prefixes of all separable-prefix verbs appearing in the text. Make copies for the entire class. This can also be done as additional homework or to reinforce new vocabulary and practice narrating a series of events.

Übung 3 Eine Verabredung°

°*date*

Die folgenden Sätze stellen eine Konversation zwischen zwei Bekannten, Hans und Petra, dar. Ergänzen Sie zuerst die Verben mit den fehlenden (*missing*) Präfixen. Arrangieren Sie dann die Sätze als Dialog, und üben Sie den Dialog mit einem Partner / einer Partnerin.

Übung 3. Suggestion: Have students work alone to fill in the prefixes. Then have them work in pairs to rearrange the sentences and practice "making a date" in German.

_____ Um acht. Ich komme um halb acht _____ und hole dich _____.
_____ Ja, ich gehe ins Kino. Im Olympia läuft ein neuer Film mit Keanu Reeves. Kommst du _____?
_____ Schön. Hinterher lade ich dich zu einem Bier _____.
_____ Gerne. Wann fängt der Film denn _____?
__1__ Hast du für heute Abend schon etwas _____?

Übung 4 Was ich so mache

Übung 4. Suggestion: Have students work in pairs, taking turns reading a statement and then commenting. Have them jot down their partner's answers. A few students will be asked to report back to the class what their partner does.

Was machen Sie immer, manchmal, selten, nie, oft, gewöhnlich? Vergleichen Sie sich (*compare yourself*) mit den Personen in den folgenden Sätzen.

BEISPIEL: Hans schläft gewöhnlich in der Vorlesung ein. →
Ich schlafe nie in der Vorlesung ein.

1. Daniel steht gewöhnlich sehr früh auf.
2. Er geht am Wochenende einkaufen.
3. Lilo geht oft mit ihrem Hund spazieren.
4. Hans räumt selten sein Zimmer auf.
5. Lilo schläft gewöhnlich beim Fernsehen ein.
6. Daniel lädt manchmal abends Freunde ein.
7. Daniel schläft selten vor 1 Uhr nachts ein.
8. Lilo ruft ihre Eltern selten an.
9. Daniel geht selten mit Freunden aus.

Übung 5 Mein Tag

Wie sieht Ihr typischer Tagesablauf aus? Fragen Sie einen Partner / eine Partnerin, was er/sie macht. Machen Sie sich Notizen und berichten Sie.

BEISPIEL: S1: Wann stehst du gewöhnlich auf?
S2: Ich stehe so um sechs Uhr auf. Und du?

Modal Auxiliary Verbs°

Modalverben

Modal auxiliary verbs (for example, *must, can, may*) express an attitude toward an action.

Morgen **möchten** wir Tennis spielen.	*Tomorrow we* ***would like to*** *play tennis.*
Am Wochenende **wollen** wir Freunde besuchen.	*On the weekend we* ***want to*** *visit friends.*
Kannst du morgen vorbeikommen?	***Can*** *you come by tomorrow?*

The examples show:

- The modal auxiliary verb is in the second position in a statement or at the beginning of the sentence in a yes/no question.
- Its complement, the verb that expresses the action, is in the infinitive form and stands at the end of the sentence.
- The modal verb and infinitive form a sentence bracket like other verbs with fixed verbal complements.

Am Wochenende **wollen** wir Freunde **besuchen.**

German has the following modal verbs.

dürfen	to be allowed to, may	**Dürfen** wir hier rauchen? *May we smoke here?*
können	to be able to, can	Ich **kann** dich gut verstehen. *I can understand you well.*
mögen	to like, care for	**Mögen** Sie Bücher? *Do you like books?*
müssen	to have to, must	Er **muss** heute arbeiten. *He has to work today.*
sollen	to be supposed to, shall	Wann **sollen** wir vorbeikommen? *When are we supposed to come by?*
wollen	to want to, plan to do	**Willst** du mitgehen? *Do you want to go along?*

1. *novels*

Realia. This ad is for two novels by the contemporary German novelist Johannes Mario Simmel, one of the most widely read authors of popular literature.

The Present Tense of Modals

Modals are irregular verbs. With the exception of **sollen,** they have stem-vowel changes in the singular. Note also that the first- and third-person singular forms are identical and have no personal ending.

Note: Point out to students the older spelling *muß, mußt, müßt.*

	dürfen	können	mögen	müssen	sollen	wollen
ich	**darf**	**kann**	**mag**	**muss**	**soll**	**will**
du	d**a**rfst	k**a**nnst	m**a**gst	m**u**sst	sollst	w**i**llst
er / sie / es	**darf**	**kann**	**mag**	**muss**	**soll**	**will**
wir	dürfen	können	mögen	müssen	sollen	wollen
ihr	dürft	könnt	mögt	müsst	sollt	wollt
sie	dürfen	können	mögen	müssen	sollen	wollen
Sie	dürfen	können	mögen	müssen	sollen	wollen

Möchte (*would like to*), one of the most common modal verbs, is the subjunctive of **mögen.** Note that the first- and third-person singular forms are identical.

Wir **möchten** morgen Tennis spielen. *We would like to play tennis tomorrow.*

möchte			
ich	**möchte**	wir	möchten
du	möchtest	ihr	möchtet
er / sie / es	**möchte**	sie	möchten
	Sie möchten		

Realia. This cartoon appeared in the *Westdeutsche Zeitung*, published in Düsseldorf. It is not uncommon to be asked to show one's ticket on a bus, streetcar, or subway. Either the conductor or, more often, a *Kontrolleur* comes around asking all passengers to prove they have paid their fare by showing their tickets.

„Darf ich einmal Ihren Fahrschein sehen!"

Modals Without a Dependent Infinitive

The modal **mögen** is frequently used without a dependent infinitive.

Er **mag** seine Arbeit im Hotel. — *He likes his work in the hotel.*

The verb **gehen** is frequently omitted in a sentence with any modal verb.

Ich **muss** jetzt in die Vorlesung (**gehen**). — *I have to go to the lecture now.*

Ich **möchte** jetzt nach Hause (**gehen**). — *I would like to go home now.*

Er **will** heute Abend ins Theater (**gehen**). — *He wants to go to the theater this evening.*

Analyse

Analyse. Suggestion: Include realia illustrating modals from the previous page. Encourage students to guess the meaning whenever possible.

Scan the headlines and visuals.

- Identify all modal auxiliary verbs in the headlines and visuals. Give the English equivalents of the sentences.
- What verbs express the action in those sentences?
- Mark the two parts of each sentence bracket.

Ich möchte mehr Informationen über Greenpeace!

So schön (spannend, aufregend)[1] kann Fernsehen sein

Die Studenten wollen streiken
Protest gegen Studienbedingungen[4] / Heute Vollversammlungen[5]

1. *exciting*
2. *slip*
3. *keep lying there*
4. *requirements for academic study*
5. *plenary meetings*

Übung 6 Was kann man da machen?

BEISPIEL: in der Bibliothek →
S1: Was kann man in der Bibliothek machen?
S2: Da kann man Bücher lesen!

1. im Restaurant
2. im Kino
3. im Café
4. im Bett
5. im Kaufhaus
6. im Park
7. in der Bibliothek

a. Filme sehen
b. einkaufen
c. schlafen
d. Kaffee trinken
e. Bücher lesen
f. essen
g. spazieren gehen

Sprachtipp

The indefinite pronoun **man** (*one, people, you, they*) is used to talk about a general activity.

Hier darf **man** nicht parken.

You may not park here. (Parking is not allowed here.)

Übung 7 Was darf man hier (nicht) machen?

BEISPIEL: Hier darf man nicht parken.

1. 

2. 

3. 

4.

5. 

6. 

campen
schnell fahren
schwimmen
spielen
rauchen
von 8 bis 14 Uhr parken

Übung 7. Suggestion: Personalize this exercise by asking students to state what is allowed where they live: *Darf man hier (auf dem Unigelände) rauchen? Darf man hier parken?*

Übung 8 Was möchtest du lieber° machen?

Fragen Sie Ihren Partner / Ihre Partnerin, was er/sie lieber machen möchte.

°*rather*

BEISPIEL: lange schlafen oder Tennis spielen? →
S1: Was möchtest du lieber machen: lange schlafen oder Tennis spielen?
S2: Ich möchte lieber Tennis spielen.

1. Zeitung lesen oder fernsehen?
2. lange schlafen oder einkaufen gehen?
3. ins Café oder ins Kino gehen?
4. deine Familie anrufen oder einen Brief schreiben?
5. ein Picknick machen oder spazieren gehen?
6. eine Party zu Hause machen oder ausgehen?
7. zu Hause bleiben oder Freunde besuchen?

Übung 8. Suggestion: Model the example with a student to convey the meaning of **lieber.** Point out that **lieber** is the comparative form of **gern.** Do the exercise as a whole-class activity and have the student who has just answered initiate the next set of questions.

Übung 9 Im Deutschen Haus 

Übung 9. **Point Out:** Is there a German house on your campus? If so, provide students with some information about it.

Chris und Jeff wohnen im Deutschen Haus an einer amerikanischen Universität. Sie sollen so oft wie möglich deutsch miteinander sprechen. Hören Sie zu, und kreuzen Sie die richtige Information an.

	DAS STIMMT	DAS STIMMT NICHT
1. Chris muss für einen Test arbeiten.	☒	☐
2. Chris stört (*disturbs*) seinen Mitbewohner Jeff.	☒	☐
3. Jeff wird jetzt auch müde (*tired*).	☒	☐
4. Chris kann nur laut lernen.	☒	☐
5. Chris geht in die Bibliothek.	☐	☒

Übung 10 Was sind die Tatsachen?

Was wissen Sie über die beiden Bewohner des Deutschen Hauses? Bilden Sie Sätze.

Chris	sollen	ins Badezimmer gehen
Jeff	müssen	deutsche Grammatik lernen
	können	ein A bekommen
	wollen	nur laut Deutsch lernen
	möchte	Jeff nicht stören
		auch arbeiten
		jetzt auch schlafen
		nicht arbeiten
		lesen

Übung 11 Pläne für eine Party

Brigitte, Lisa und Anja haben endlich ein Dach über dem Kopf: eine Wohnung auf einem alten Bauernhof (*farm*) in der Nähe (*vicinity*) von Münster. Jetzt planen sie eine Party. Setzen Sie passende Modalverben in die Lücken ein.

BRIGITTE: Also wen _____ (*want to*) wir denn einladen?[1]
LISA: Die Frage ist: Wie viele Leute _____ (*can*) wir denn einladen?[2] Wir haben ja nicht so viel Platz.
ANJA: Im Wohnzimmer _____ (*can*) bestimmt zwanzig Leute sitzen.[3]
LISA: Und tanzen _____ (*can*) wir in der Diele (*hallway*).[4]
ANJA: Und wer _____ (*is supposed to*) für so viele Leute kochen?[5]
LISA: Ich _____ (*want*) lieber nur ein paar Leute einladen.[6]
ANJA: Wir sagen allen, jeder _____ (*is supposed to*) was zum Essen mitbringen.[7]
BRIGITTE: Ich _____ (*would like to*) Kartoffelsalat (*potato salad*) mit Würstchen machen.[8]
LISA: Gute Idee. Das ist einfach, und das _____ (*like*) auch alle.[9]
ANJA: Tut mir leid, aber ich _____ (*like*) Kartoffelsalat nicht.[10]
BRIGITTE: Ich _____ (*can*) auch was Italienisches machen, Pizza oder Lasagne.[11]
LISA: Wir _____ (*may*) aber nicht nur Bier servieren, wir _____ (*have to*) auch Mineralwasser oder Cola servieren, für die Autofahrer.[12]

Übung 12 Ein Picknick im Grünen

Einige Mitbewohner im internationalen Studentenwohnheim planen ein Picknick. Wer bringt was mit?

BEISPIEL: Andreas will ein Frisbee mitbringen. Er soll auch Mineralwasser besorgen.

Jürgen aus München	wollen	Brot und Käse (*cheese*)	kaufen
Stephanie aus den USA	müssen	Mineralwasser	besorgen (*get*)
die Zwillinge aus Italien:	möchte	Bier	mitbringen
Paola und Maria	sollen	eine Decke (*blanket*) zum Sitzen	machen
Nagako aus Tokio		ein Radio	
Michel aus Frankreich		ein Frisbee	
ich		eine Pizza	
		Kartoffelsalat	
		Sushi	

Übung 13 Kommst du mit?

Übung 13. Suggestion: This activity is best done with students circulating in class. Assign several students to act as observers who jot down the different excuses they hear and report them to the class afterward.

Arbeiten Sie mit einem Partner / einer Partnerin zusammen. Laden Sie ihn/sie ein, etwas mit Ihnen zu unternehmen (*do*). Er/Sie soll die Einladung ablehnen (*decline*) und einen Grund (*reason*) dafür angeben.

BEISPIEL: S1: Ich will heute Tennis spielen. Möchtest du mitkommen?
S2: Nein, leider kann ich nicht. Ich muss nämlich arbeiten.

heute Abend ins Rockkonzert gehen
in die Disko gehen
nach (+ *place*) fahren
ins Grüne fahren
Tennis spielen
Karten spielen
eine Party machen
?

The Imperative°

° der Imperativ

The Imperative. Suggestion: Introduce imperatives through Total Physical Response (TPR) techniques. Have students carry out several typical classroom actions: *Stehen Sie auf! Machen Sie die Tür auf! Gehen Sie an die Tafel! Öffnen Sie Ihr Buch!*

The imperative is the verb form used to make requests and recommendations, to give instructions, advice, or commands.

Formal Imperative

You are already familiar with the form of the imperative used in common classroom instructions.

Wiederholen Sie bitte!	*Repeat, please.*
Hören Sie zu!	*Listen!*
Sagen Sie das auf Deutsch!	*Say that in German.*

These are examples of formal imperatives, used for anyone you would address as **Sie.**

The formal imperative is formed by inverting the subject (**Sie**) and the verb. Note that the formal imperative has the same word order as a yes/no question; only punctuation or intonation identifies it as an imperative. Imperatives in written German often end in an exclamation point.

Particles and *bitte* with the Imperative

Requests or commands are often softened by adding the word **bitte** and particles such as **doch** and **mal. Bitte** can stand at the beginning, in the middle, or at the end of the sentence. The particles **doch** and **mal** follow the imperative form. They have no English equivalent.

Hören Sie **bitte** zu!	*Listen, please.*
Bitte, nehmen Sie Platz.	*Please have a seat.*
Kommen Sie **doch** heute vorbei.	*Why don't you come by today?*
Rufen Sie mich **mal** an!	*Give me a call (some time).*

Übung 14 In der Sprechstunde°

° office hour

Mary Lerner geht zum Professor in die Sprechstunde. Kreuzen Sie an, ob es um eine Frage oder eine Aufforderung (*command*) geht.

	FRAGE	AUFFORDERUNG		FRAGE	AUFFORDERUNG
1.	☐	☒	**8.**	☒	☐
2.	☐	☒	**9.**	☐	☒
3.	☐	☒	**10.**	☒	☐
4.	☒	☐	**11.**	☒	☐
5.	☐	☒	**12.**	☐	☒
6.	☒	☐	**13.**	☒	☐
7.	☐	☒	**14.**	☐	☒

Übung 14. Note: The listening text focuses on distinguishing a yes/no question (rising intonation) from a formal request (falling intonation). **Suggestion:** Once students have completed the listening part and marked their answers, go over each sentence once more and illustrate the differences in intonation. Have students repeat questions and then turn them into requests by changing their intonation and vice versa. In the case of questions, have students provide possible answers as well.

Singular Informal Imperative

The singular informal imperative is used for anyone you address with **du.** It is formed for most verbs simply by dropping the **st** ending from the present tense.

du kommst → **Komm!**
du sprichst → **Sprich!**
du rufst . . . an → **Ruf . . . an!**

Verbs that show a vowel change from **a** to **ä** (or **au** to **äu**) in the present tense have no umlaut in the imperative.

du fährst → **Fahr!**
du läufst → **Lauf!**

1. *fly*
2. Die . . . *the world at your feet*
3. Eine . . . *distinctive gift idea*

Realia. *Flieg mit mir* is from an advertising agency in Hamburg. *Schreib mal wieder* is from the German postal service.

The singular informal imperative will end in **e** if the stem ends in **d, t,** or a cluster of consonants. In all other regular verbs the **e** is optional.

du arbeitest → **Arbeite!**
du lädst . . . ein → **Lade . . . ein!**

but du lernst → **Lern(e)!**

1. *enjoy*

Mach' Dir ein paar
schöne Stunden...
geh' ins **Kino**

Realia. *Sag Ja zu Yes* appeared on the back of a form for train connections (*Reiseverbindungen*) used by the travel agency (*DER*) of German *Bundesbahn.* Note the apostrophe after **mach'** and **geh'** used to indicate the dropped **e** ending.

Übung 15 Wir duzen einander unter Studenten.°

We students say **du** *to each other.*

Übung 15. Suggestion: This exercise lends itself to variations; do a quick oral drill of reversing the exercise by providing a **du**-imperative and asking students to express it in a formal imperative.

Stellen Sie sich vor, Sie sind neu im Studentenwohnheim und reden alle Ihre Mitbewohner zuerst mit „Sie" an. Jetzt müssen Sie „du" lernen, denn alle Studenten duzen einander. Setzen Sie die Imperativsätze in die du-Form.

BEISPIEL: Bitte, kommen Sie herein! → Bitte, komm herein!

1. Bitte, sprechen Sie etwas langsamer!
2. Laden Sie mich bitte auch zur Party ein!
3. Arbeiten Sie nicht so viel!
4. Fahren Sie doch am Wochenende mit mir nach Heidelberg!
5. Bleiben Sie doch noch ein bisschen.
6. Besuchen Sie mich mal.
7. Rufen Sie mich morgen um 10 Uhr an!
8. Gehen Sie doch mit ins Kino!
9. Kommen Sie doch morgen vorbei!
10. Nehmen Sie die Zeitung mit!
11. Sehen Sie mal, hier ist ein Foto von meiner Familie!

Plural Informal Imperative

The plural informal imperative is used to request something from several persons whom you individually address with **du.**

Kommt zu uns!	*Come see us.* (*lit., Come to us.*)
Fahrt jetzt nach Hause!	*Drive home now.*
Gebt mir bitte etwas zu essen!	*Give me something to eat, please.*

This imperative form is identical to the **ihr**-form of the present tense, but without the pronoun **ihr.**

Übung 16 Pläne unter Freunden

Sie möchten Ihren Freunden sagen, was sie alles tun sollen. Machen Sie aus den Fragen Imperativsätze. Benutzen Sie dabei auch **doch, mal** oder **bitte.**

BEISPIEL: Kommt ihr heute Abend vorbei? →
Kommt doch heute Abend vorbei!

1. Ladet ihr mich ein?
2. Ruft ihr mich morgen an?
3. Holt ihr mich ab?
4. Sprecht ihr immer deutsch?
5. Hört ihr zu?
6. Geht ihr mit ins Kino?
7. Kommt ihr morgen vorbei?

Übung 16. Suggestion: Stress the distinction in the intonation of a question and a request when doing this exercise. **Point Out:** In the colloquial phrase *Geht ihr mit ins Kino?*, the separable prefix (**mit**) does not stand at the end of the sentence but rather precedes the location.

Imperative of *sein*

The imperative forms of the verb **sein** are irregular.

Formal:	
Seien Sie bitte um 10 Uhr hier!	*Please be here at ten o'clock.*
Informal Singular:	
Bitte, **sei** doch so nett und komm vorbei!	*Please be so kind as to come by!*
Informal Plural:	
Seid doch bitte freundlich!	*Please be friendly!*

Übung 17 Situationen im Alltag

Ergänzen Sie die passende Form des Imperativs von **sein.**

1. Ich muss Sie warnen: Autofahren in Deutschland ist ein Abenteuer. _____ bitte vorsichtig!
2. Sie gehen mit zwei Freunden ins Konzert. Die Freunde sind nie pünktlich und das irritiert Sie. Sie sagen zu ihnen: „_____ aber bitte pünktlich!"
3. Ihr Mitbewohner / Ihre Mitbewohnerin im Studentenwohnheim ist sehr unordentlich. Sie erwarten Ihre Eltern zu Besuch und bitten ihn/sie: „_____ so nett und räum deine Sachen auf!"
4. Drei Mitbewohner im Studentenwohnheim haben um drei Uhr morgens immer noch laute Musik an. Sie klopfen irritiert gegen die Wand und rufen: „_____ endlich ruhig und macht die Musik aus!
5. Frau Kümmel zu Frau Honig: „_____ bitte so nett und kommen Sie morgen vorbei!"

Übung 17. Point Out: The phrase *Sei so gut/nett und . . .* and its variations are used in polite conversation in connection with a request. Have students add the appropriate forms of *Sei / Seid / Seien Sie so gut/nett* to *Ruf mich morgen an! Komm morgen vorbei! Öffnen Sie bitte das Fenster! Geht jetzt! Mach die Tür zu!*

Sprache im Kontext

Zuschauen

Vorschau

Schwartau Extra

Sehen Sie sich die Werbung ohne Ton (*sound*) an. Wofür ist das vielleicht eine Werbung?

- □ eine Rakete (*rocket*)
- □ ein Bett
- □ eine Hotelkette (*hotel chain*)
- □ eine Marmelade

Arbeit mit dem Videotext

A. Sehen Sie sich die Werbung mit Ton an. Beantworten Sie dann die folgenden Fragen.

1. Was macht die Frau zuerst?
□ Sie schläft. □ Sie arbeitet. □ Sie steht auf.

2. Was bringt der Mann?
□ das Abendessen □ das Frühstück □ das Mittagessen

3. Was ist Schwartau Extra?
□ ein Saft □ eine Marmelade □ eine Kaffeesorte

4. Welche Tageszeit ist es vielleicht?
□ 17.00 Uhr □ 22.45 Uhr □ 7.30 Uhr

5. Was sagt der Mann, als er die Frau weckt?
□ „Ich liebe Schwartau zum Frühstück." □ „Wo ist mein Frühstück?" □ „Liebling, Frühstück!"

B. Beschreiben Sie jetzt in vier Sätzen, was die Frau *nach* dem Frühstück macht.

Lesen

The reading here describes daily routines and everyday pleasures.

Zum Thema

Immer das Gleiche (*the same thing*)?

A. Ergänzen Sie die Tabelle!

MEIN ALLTAG		MEIN GEBURTSTAG	
Uhrzeit	*Aktivität*	*Uhrzeit*	*Aktivität*
	aufstehen		
	ins Bett gehen		

B. Machen Sie etwas Besonderes (*something special*) an Ihrem Geburtstag, oder ist er wie jeder andere Tag? Berichten Sie mit Hilfe der Tabelle!

BEISPIEL: Gewöhnlich stehe ich um 7 Uhr auf. Aber an meinem Geburtstag schlafe ich lange.

Auf den ersten Blick 

Überfliegen Sie (*skim*) den Text, „Immer das gleiche"! Suchen Sie Wörter, die in die folgenden Kategorien passen!

BEISPIEL: SCHULE:
lernen

ZU HAUSE:
kleine Geschwister

UNTERWEGS:
viele Menschen

Immer das Gleiche: Straßenverkehr in der Großstadt, München

Immer das gleiche

von Christine Wuttke

Jeden Tag das gleiche.
Ich geh' in die Schule,
lern was—oder auch nicht.
Sehe immer die vielen Menschen,
die unterwegs sind,
entweder mit der Straßenbahn[1]
oder zu Fuß
oder auch mit dem Auto.
Und ich fahr lächelnd[2] an den
Autoschlangen[3] vorbei.
Auch wenn[4] man als Radfahrer
Mühe[5] hat, vorwärtszukommen,
ist man doch oft schneller.
In der Schule sind es dann überall
dieselben Erzählungen[6] der Lehrer:
Ihr lernt für euch, nicht für mich.
Und was sonst noch so typisch ist.
In den Arbeiten frage ich mich,
was das Klima[7] ist, was der Transformator ist,
oder was ist der Satz aus der Wassermusik.
Und ich kann mal wieder nur abgucken.[8]
Endlich wieder zu Hause,
haben die kleineren Geschwister sogar
mal das Fernsehen abgestellt[9] und spielen
im Kinderzimmer.
Dann geh' ich zum Klavierunterricht,[10]
zu Freunden oder in die Stadt,
und zähle die Werbeplakate[11]
an den Schaufenstern.
Abends im Bett denke ich dann,
wie „friedlich"[12] der Tag doch wieder war.
Immer das gleiche.

Oder ist es nicht jeden Tag was Besonderes,[13]
was man erlebt[14]?
Aber doch das gleiche?
Sehe ich nicht jeden Tag andere Leute
auf den Straßen?
Reden die Lehrer nicht doch immer
was anderes?
Schreiben sie nicht jedesmal andere Arbeiten,
in denen[15] man auch mal was weiß?
Aber es ist jeden Tag das gleiche.

Reading. Note: You may want to point out to students that the spelling reform rules require capitalization of *Gleiche,* whereas it is not capitalized in the poem.

Point out: *Wassermusik* refers to Handel's famous instrumental music suite *Water Music.*

1. *street car* 2. *smiling* 3. *rows of cars* 4. Auch . . . *even if* 5. *difficulty* 6. *stories* 7. *climate* 8. *to copy from someone* 9. haben . . . abgestellt *turned off* 10. *piano lesson* 11. *billboards* 12. *peaceful* 13. was . . . *something special* 14. *experiences* 15. *which*

Using a dictionary. Suggestion: Assign students the task of finding the titles, call numbers, and locations of the German-English dictionaries in your library.

Using a Dictionary

As you read a text, you may be tempted to look up most of the words you do not know. Before reaching for the dictionary, however, try to guess the meaning of words from the context. If you find you really must use a dictionary, consider the following:

- Many compound words are not listed in dictionaries. To discover their meaning, look up the components and determine the meaning of the compound from the definitions of its components.
- Some forms found in texts differ from those listed in dictionaries. For example, nouns and pronouns are listed in the nominative singular; verbs are listed under their infinitive forms.
- Some words have multiple meanings. You will need to choose the correct meaning of the word based on its use in the text.

For practice in using a dictionary, do the following exercise:

- Can you figure out what **Autoschlange** means by looking up its components?
- Under which entry would you find **jeden?** the phrase **ich fahr . . . vorbei?**
- How many different meanings can you find for **Satz?** Which of those meanings most closely fits the context of the word as it is used in the poem **Immer das gleiche**?
- Cross-check your definition by looking the assumed English equivalent up in the English-German section of your dictionary.
- Underline all words in the text that you do not understand. Choose five and look them up. In what form do they appear in the dictionary? How many meanings are given? Which meaning best fits the context?

Zum Text

A. Lesen Sie den Text, und beantworten Sie die Fragen.

1. Wie alt mag die Autorin sein?
2. Ist sie eine Schülerin, eine Universitätsstudentin oder eine Lehrerin? Woher wissen Sie das?
3. Wo lebt die Autorin? in einer Stadt oder auf dem Land? Wie beweist (*shows*) der Text das?
4. Wie groß ist ihre Familie?

B. In most of the text the author uses declarative sentences stating what she does every day. In the last verse she uses words such as **aber** and **oder** and asks herself whether each day really is the same. What does she say about each day that might make it different even if she still has the same routine?

Sprechen und Schreiben

Aktivität 1 Nicht immer das Gleiche!

A. Imagine that you find yourself transported to a desert island. Make two lists. The first should outline your usual routine. The second will include those things that you can or can't do, you want or don't want to do, or you need or don't need to do, now that you are on the island.

B. Compare your list with those of your classmates. Working in small groups, prepare a letter which you might put in a bottle telling of your life on the island.

Aktivität 1. Suggestion: Write on the board the two categories *Zu Hause* and *Auf der Insel.* Have students brainstorm possible activities for each category.

Additional Activity. Have students write a composition about their daily routine.

Aktivität 2 Ein Gedicht°

Schreiben Sie ein Gedicht mit dem Titel „Immer das Gleiche". Tauschen Sie (*trade*) Ihr Gedicht mit dem von einem Partner / einer Partnerin aus. Lesen Sie das Gedicht vor.

°*poem*

Wortschatz

Tageszeiten	**Times of Day**
heute Morgen*	this morning
heute Vormittag*	today before noon
heute Mittag*	this noon
heute Nachmittag*	this afternoon
heute Abend*	this evening; tonight
morgen früh	tomorrow morning
morgen Vormittag*	tomorrow before noon
morgen Mittag*	tomorrow noon
morgen Nachmittag*	tomorrow afternoon
morgen Abend*	tomorrow evening; tomorrow night
Samstagmorgen*	Saturday morning
Samstagvormittag*	Saturday before noon
Samstagmittag*	Saturday noon
Samstagnachmittag*	Saturday afternoon
Samstagabend*	Saturday evening; Saturday night

morgens	in the morning, mornings
vormittags	before noon
mittags	at noon
nachmittags	in the afternoon, afternoons
abends	in the evening, evenings
nachts	at night, nights
montags	Mondays, on Monday(s)
dienstags	Tuesdays, on Tuesday(s)
mittwochs	Wednesdays, on Wednesday(s)
donnerstags	Thursdays, on Thursday(s)
freitags	Fridays, on Friday(s)
samstags; sonnabends	Saturdays, on Saturday(s)
sonntags	Sundays, on Sunday(s)

* See Appendix E for alternate spelling.

Unterhaltung	Entertainment
das **Ballett, -e**	ballet
die **Disko, -s**	disco
in die Disko gehen	to go to a disco
der **Film, -e**	film
das **Kino, -s**	cinema, (movie) theater
ins Kino gehen	to go to the movies
die **Komödie, -n**	comedy
das **Konzert, -e**	concert
ins Konzert gehen	to go to a concert
der **Krimi, -s**	crime, detective, mystery film or book
die **Musik**	music
die **Oper, -n**	opera
in die Oper gehen	to go to the opera
das **Theaterstück, -e**	play (stage) drama
das **Theater, -**	(stage) theater
ins Theater gehen	to go to the theater
die **Tragödie, -n**	tragedy

Verben mit trennbaren Präfixen	Verbs with Separable Prefixes
ab•holen	to pick up (*from a place*)
an•fangen (fängt an)	to begin
an•rufen	to call up
auf•hören (mit)	to stop (*doing something*)
auf•räumen	to clean up, straighten up
auf•stehen	to get up; to stand up
auf•wachen	to wake up
aus•gehen	to go out
ein•kaufen (gehen)	to (go) shop(ping)
ein•laden (lädt ein)	to invite
ein•schlafen (schläft ein)	to fall asleep
fern•sehen (sieht fern)	to watch television
mit•kommen	to come along
mit•nehmen (nimmt mit)	to take along
vorbei•kommen	to come by
vor•haben (hat vor)	to plan (*to do*)
zurück•kommen	to return, come back

Modalverben	Modal Verbs
dürfen (darf)	to be permitted to; may
können (kann)	to be able to; can
mögen (mag)	to care for; to like
möchte	would like to
müssen (muss)*	to have to; must
sollen	to be supposed to; ought, should
wollen (will)	to want to; to plan to

Uhrzeiten	Time
die **Minute, -n**	minute
die **Sekunde, -n**	second
die **Stunde, -n**	hour
Wie spät ist es?/Wie viel Uhr ist es?	What time is it?
Um wie viel Uhr?	At what time?
Es ist eins./Es ist ein Uhr.	It's one o'clock.
halb: halb zwei	half: half past one, one-thirty
Viertel: Es ist Viertel nach/vor zwei.	quarter: It's a quarter after/to two.
nach: fünf nach zwei	after: five after two
vor: fünf vor zwei	to, of: five to/of two
um: um zwei	at: at two

Sonstiges	Other
frühstücken	to eat breakfast
die Tasse, -n	cup
eine Tasse Kaffee	a cup of coffee
früh	early
gemütlich	cozy, cozily
gewöhnlich	usual(ly)
spannend	suspenseful
spät	late
spazieren gehen	to go for a walk
Ich gehe spazieren.	I'm going for a walk.
doch	(*intensifying particle used with imperatives*)
mal	(*softening particle used with imperatives*)
lieber: möchte lieber	would rather
am liebsten: möchte am liebsten	would like to (do) most
man	one, people, you, they
Hier darf man nicht parken.	You may not park here.

*See Appendix E for alternate spelling.

Lernziele

Use this checklist to verify that you can now . . .

- ☐ describe your daily routine.
- ☐ tell the time.
- ☐ state at what time something takes place.
- ☐ describe and talk about the kinds of entertainment you like.
- ☐ invite someone to go out with you.
- ☐ use verbs with separable prefixes in the present tense.
- ☐ use the modal verbs in the present tense.
- ☐ make general statements, using **man.**
- ☐ make requests and recommendations, give instructions, advice, or commands using imperative forms.
- ☐ soften requests and commands, using **bitte, doch,** and **mal**.
- ☐ make guesses about the meanings of unfamiliar vocabulary by using the context of the text and your knowledge of cognates, and by breaking compounds down into smaller elements.
- ☐ use a German-English dictionary.

Kapitel 5

Einkaufen

Auf dem Markt

Kapitel 5. Suggestion: Approach the material in this chapter by talking about things you need and where you would buy them. Talk about what you are wearing and where you buy your clothes. Recycle vocabulary from previous chapters, e.g., **Kapitel 2,** in which shopping was first introduced. You could also talk about what you eat for certain meals and review time by mentioning when you eat. Be sure to involve students by asking questions.

Alles klar?

A. Hertie ist eine Kaufhauskette (*department store chain*) in Deutschland. Was kann man alles bei Hertie kaufen? Wo findet man es?

BEISPIELE: Man kann da Computer kaufen. Computer findet man im vierten Stock.

Man kann da Bücher kaufen. Bücher findet man im Erdgeschoss.

4 HERTIE 4. Die 4. Dimension moderner Technik
- Computer/HIFI/TV/Video/CD-Center
- Foto – Optik/Filme/Fotoannahme
- Elektro Groß- und Kleingeräte
- Beleuchtung/Lampen
- Telefon-Shop/Braun-Shop

Kundendienst/Bankschalter/Kartenvorverkauf

3
Bettwaren/Bettwäsche/Frottierwaren
Gardinen/Dekostoffe/Tischwäsche
Teppiche/Orientteppiche/Bodenbeläge
Geschenkartikel/Seidenblumen
Glas/Porzellan
Haushaltswaren/Heimwerker/Autozubehör
Kurzwaren/Handarbeiten/Stoffe

2 TREND COMPANY HERTIE
Esprit-Shop
Jeans-Wear
Mode-Boutiquen
Cafe „Trend"
Kinderkonfektion/Baby-Wäsche
Schuhe/Sport/Fahrräder/Camping
Friseursalon

1
Damenkonfektion/Damenhüte
Damenwäsche/Miederwaren/Bademoden
Lederbekleidung/Pelze/Trachten
Herrenkonfektion/Herrenartikel/Wäsche
Herren-Strickwaren HERTIE-Reisebüro

E[1]
Christ-Juweliere und Uhrmacher
Lederwaren/Reisegepäck
Lotto/Toto/Tabak – Zeitschriften
Modewaren/Schirme/Handschuhe
Parfümerie/Kosmetik/Drogerie/Parfümerie „ORLY"
Schreibwaren/Bücher
Strümpfe/Strumpfboutique „Hot-Socks"
Uhren/Schmuck

	JA	NEIN	IN WELCHEM STOCK?
Autos	☐	☒	
Haustiere	☐	☒	
Lebensmittel	☒	☐	U
Pullover	☒	☐	1, 2
Schreibwaren	☒	☐	E
Schuhe	☒	☐	2
Sofas	☐	☒	
Sportartikel	☒	☐	2
Telefonapparate	☒	☐	4
Teppiche	☒	☐	3

Realia. Suggestion: Give students several minutes to skim the information in class, or else assign the text for homework. Have students formulate statements similar to the ones in the examples. Be sure to personalize the material by asking students what they need or would like to buy at *Hertie*. Explain that *Hertie* is a typical large department store. Ask students what differences they notice in the goods and services offered at a department store like *Hertie* and those with which they are familiar. For example, most department stores like *Hertie* do not sell furniture, but they do include a supermarket.

1. E = Erdgeschoss (*ground floor*)
2. U = Untergeschoss (*basement*)

B. Sie hören nun vier Ansagen (*announcements*) im Kaufhaus. Markieren Sie, was die Sprecher beschreiben.

1. Kosmetik Kameras Fahrräder
2. Schmuck Betten Schuhe
3. Bücher Kaffeemaschinen Lederjacken
4. Jeans Lampen Videorecorder

Realia (p. 141). *Koffermemo* appeared in the *Frankfurter Rundschau* as an advertisement for the clothing chain *C&A. Erholungspreise:* Note that in some instances, compound formation requires a linking *-s-* between word elements.

Wörter im Kontext

Thema 1

Kleidungsstücke

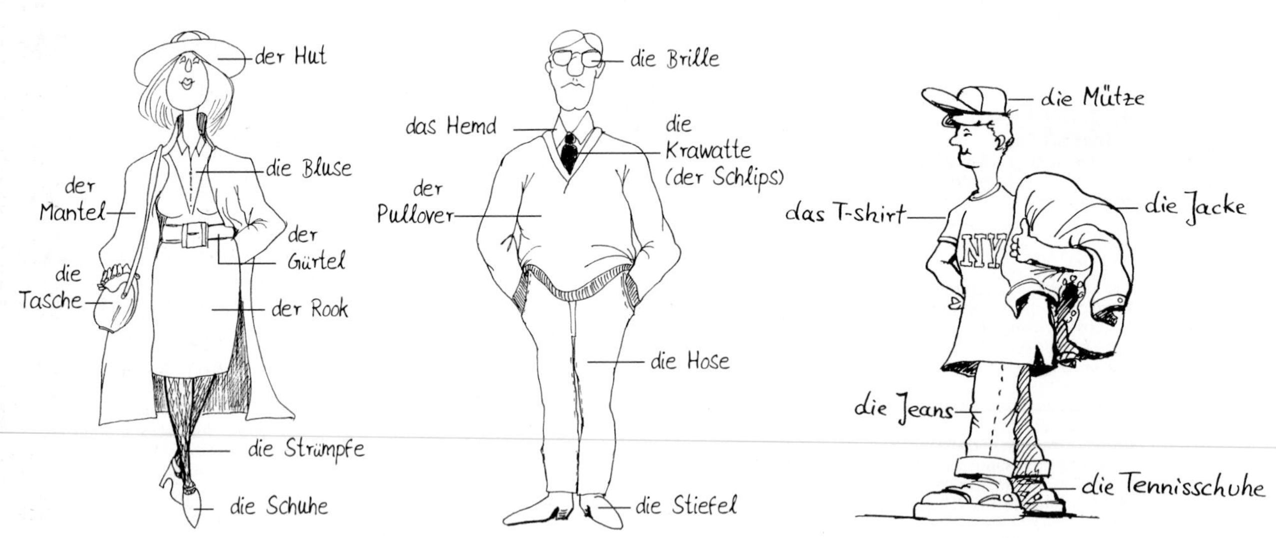

Was haben Sie alles zu Hause in Ihrem Kleiderschrank (*closet*)?

- □ einen **Anzug**
- □ einen **Badeanzug**
- □ **Hausschuhe**
- □ einen Jeansrock
- □ ein **Kleid**
- □ einen Parka
- □ ein **Sakko**
- □ einen **Schal**
- □ eine Skihose
- □ **Socken**
- □ einen Wintermantel

Analyse

Das Koffer-Memo zeigt eine Liste von Kleidungsstücken für den Urlaub.

- Welche Kleidungsstücke sind nur für Mädchen (*girls*)? Welche sind für Mädchen und für Jungen (*boys*)?
- Welche Sachen auf dieser Liste tragen Sie besonders gern?
- Suchen Sie auf der Liste vier zusammengesetzte Wörter (*compounds*). Nennen Sie die einzelnen Wortelemente.
- Bilden Sie nun Ihre eigenen Wörter.

BEISPIEL: Bade- + Hose = Badehose

Bade-		Anzug
Leder-		Mantel
Baumwoll-	+	Hose
Trainings-		Hemd
Regen-		Schuhe

Analyse. Point Out: *Trainings- und Jogginganzüge = Trainingsanzüge und Jogginganzüge.* The hyphen after *Trainings-* stands for the word shared with the following compound (*Anzüge*).

Koffer-Memo
Alles zu Erholungspreisen

Für Kleinkinder

T-Shirts	4.-
Shorts	6.-
Boxer-Shorts	6.50
Cordhosen	12.-
Kleidchen[1]	15.-
Lack-Regenmäntel	9.-
Leder-Sandalen	18.-

Für Schüler und Teener

Badeanzüge und Bikinis	12.-
Shorts	8.-
Blusen	14.-
Röcke	16.-
Kleider	20.-
Hemden	10.-
Sweatshirts	10.-
Baumwollhosen	17.-
Trainings- und Jogginganzüge	27.-
Sportschuhe	12.-
Wäsche-Garnituren[2]	6.-
Shorty-Schlafanzüge	10.-

C&A

...wo Mode so wenig kostet

1. *child's dress*
2. *sets of underwear*

Aktivität 1 Was tragen Sie gewöhnlich?

Aktivität 1. Suggestion: Discuss what students are wearing in class that day.

Sagen Sie, was Sie in den folgenden Situationen tragen.

BEISPIEL: Ich trage gewöhnlich Jeans und ein T-Shirt zur Uni. Zur Arbeit trage ich ein Sporthemd, eine Hose und ein Sakko.

zur Arbeit	einen Anzug
zur Uni	einen Badeanzug
im Winter	ein Kleid
im Urlaub auf Hawaii	ein Abendkleid
zu einem Rockkonzert	einen Wintermantel
zu Hause	Jeans
auf einer Fete	ein T-Shirt
zu einer Hochzeit	ein Sporthemd
?	eine Hose
	ein Sakko
	?

As you have already seen in **Kapitel 3,** the impersonal expression **es gibt** means *there is* or *there are.* It can also be used to say where you can get something. The object of **es gibt** is always in the accusative case.

Es gibt in dieser Stadt einen Markt.	*There is a market in this town. (It exists.)*
Wo gibt es schicke Blusen?	*Where can you get stylish blouses?*

Use the preposition **bei** and the name of the place to say where you can get something.

Blusen gibt es **bei** Gisie.	*You can get blouses at Gisie's (shop).*
—Wo gibt es Handtaschen?	*Where can you get purses?*
—**Bei** Hertie.	*At Hertie's.*

Aktivität 2 Ich brauche neue Bekleidung.°

° *clothing*

Aktivität 2. Note: Bekleidung is a collective noun. It is not generally found in the plural or with the indefinite article. To indicate one or more particular items of clothing, German uses the term **Kleidungsstück.**

Was brauchen Sie, und wo gibt es das? Was kostet das?

BEISPIEL: S1: Ich brauche dringend einen Anzug. Wo gibt es hier Anzüge?
S2: Anzüge gibt es bei Straub.
S1: Weißt du, wie viel ein Anzug da kostet?
S2: Es gibt Anzüge für 350 Mark.

Pullover (Pulli)
Stiefel
Jacke
Hose
Bluse
Sakko
Rock
Anzug
?

Realia. 1. *Das neue Jahr . . .* is from an ad for a store (*Straub*) in Oberursel. 2. *Sonderangebot* is from the *Klever Wochenblatt*.

Aktivität 3 Koffer packen!°

° *Let's pack our bags!*

Spielen Sie in Gruppen von vier bis fünf Personen. So spielt man es:

BEISPIEL: S1: Ich packe fünf Bikinis in meinen Koffer.
S2: Ich packe fünf Bikinis und Sportschuhe in meinen Koffer.
S3: Ich packe fünf Bikinis, Sportschuhe und Ledersandalen in meinen Koffer.

Wer etwas vergisst (*forgets*) oder falsch sagt, scheidet aus (*drops out*).

Thema 2

Beim Einkaufen im Kaufhaus 

Beim Einkaufen im Kaufhaus. Suggestion: Begin by looking at the picture. What is happening? Where can you buy a shirt? Introduce new words using pictures, mime, and classroom situations. After students have heard the dialogue and then read it, assign pairs to role-play it.

weiß
rot
orange
gelb
grün
blau
lila
beige
braun
grau
schwarz

Antjes Vater geht einkaufen, denn er braucht ein paar neue Hemden.

VERKÄUFER: Bitte schön. Kann ich Ihnen helfen?
HERR GÖTTGES: Ich brauche ein paar **neue** Sporthemden.
VERKÄUFER: Welche **Größe** brauchen Sie?
HERR GÖTTGES: Größe 42.
VERKÄUFER: Und welche **Farbe?**
HERR GÖTTGES: Grün oder blau.
VERKÄUFER: **Wie gefällt Ihnen dieses gestreifte Hemd** in Marineblau? Sehr dezent (*tasteful*) und **modisch.**

HERR GÖTTGES: Ich finde, **die Farbe steht mir** nicht. Haben Sie das in Hellblau?
VERKÄUFER: Ja, hier ist ein Hemd in Hellblau.
HERR GÖTTGES: Ist das aus Baumwolle oder Synthetik?
VERKÄUFER: Das ist 100 Prozent Baumwolle. Möchten Sie es **anprobieren?**
HERR GÖTTGES: Nein, das ist nicht **nötig.** Größe 42 **passt mir** bestimmt. Wie viel kostet dieses Hemd?
VERKÄUFER: 80 Mark.
HERR GÖTTGES: Gut. Ich nehme drei Hemden.
VERKÄUFER: Alle in Hellblau?
HERR GÖTTGES: Nein, geben Sie mir bitte zwei in Blau und ein Hemd in Weiß.
VERKÄUFER: Das macht zusammen 240 Mark. Bitte **zahlen** Sie vorne an der **Kasse!**
HERR GÖTTGES: Danke schön.
VERKÄUFER: Bitte sehr.

kariert
gestreift

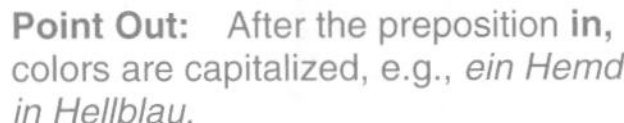

Point Out: After the preposition **in**, colors are capitalized, e.g., *ein Hemd in Hellblau.*

Aktivität 4 Im Kaufhaus

Ergänzen Sie die fehlenden Informationen aus dem Dialog im Thema 2.

1. Der Kunde braucht _____.
2. Der Verkäufer möchte _____ und _____ wissen.
3. Der Kunde braucht _____ 42.
4. Größe 42 _____ ihm.
5. Das Hemd in Marineblau _____ ihm nicht.
6. Das Hemd ist aus _____.
7. Der Kunde _____ 240 Mark für drei Hemden.

To talk about how clothing fits, how it looks, and whether you like it, you can use the following expressions.

—**Gefällt Ihnen** dieses Hemd?
Do you like this shirt?

—Ja, es **gefällt mir.**
Yes, I like it.

—Größe 42 **passt ihr** bestimmt.
Size 42 will fit her for sure.

—Das Hemd **steht dir** gut.
The shirt looks good on you.

European sizes vary greatly from American sizes.

Für Damen: Kleider, Mäntel, Jacken, Blusen						
in USA	6	8	10	12	14	16
in Deutschland	34	36	38	40	42	44

Für Herren: Mäntel, Anzüge, Sakkos					
in USA	36	38	40	42	44
in Deutschland	46	48	50	52	54

Herrenhemden						
in USA	14	14½	15	15½	16	16½
in Deutschland	36	37	38	39	40	42

Schuhgrößen (Damen und Herren)								
in USA	5½	6½	7½	8½	9½	10½	11½	12½
in Deutschland	37	38	39/40	41	42	43	44	45

In many stores you will also find the sizes S, M, L, and XL (small, medium, large, and extra-large) for clothing. In addition, shoes are sometimes labeled with American sizes.

1. Tolle . . . *great deals*

Realia. This is from the *Süddeutsche Zeitung* of Munich, advertising the *Hirmer* department store.

Kulturtipp. Suggestion: Have students figure out their German clothing and shoe sizes. Use the information in a brief listening activity by asking questions such as *Wer hat Schuhgröße 42?* or *Wer hat Kleidergröße 36?* Students raise their hands to respond when an item applies to them.

Aktivität 5 Gespräche im Geschäft

Was brauchen die Leute? In welcher Größe und in welcher Farbe? Ergänzen Sie die Tabelle.

Aktivität 5. Suggestion: Play each dialogue once so students get the gist of it. Then play each one a second time while students complete the chart. Check students' responses by calling on individuals to report.

	WAS?	IN WELCHER GRÖSSE?	IN WELCHER FARBE?
Dialog 1	Schuhe	44	Schwarz
Dialog 2	Hose	38	Blauweiß
Dialog 3	Bluse	38	Rot
Dialog 4	Wintermantel	44	Dunkelblau

Aktivität 6 Farben und Größen

Fragen Sie andere im Deutschkurs.

1. Welche Farbe ist deine Lieblingsfarbe?
2. Welche Farben stehen dir gut?
3. Trägst du gern bunte (*colorful*) Sachen?
4. Trägst du gern gestreifte oder karierte Sachen?
5. Welche Größe trägst du in Blusen oder in Hemden?
6. Welche Schuhgröße brauchst du?

Aktivität 6. Suggestion: Have students answer the questions at home and be prepared to discuss their answers in class the next day, or have students pick out three questions to ask two other students in class. Have them report their findings.

Weiteres zum Thema Einkaufen finden Sie bei ***Deutsch: Na klar!*** im World-Wide-Web unter www.mhhe.com/german.

Aktivität 7. Suggestion: The day before you plan on doing this activity, tell students to come to class the next day wearing something unusual.

Aktivität 7 Wer trägt was?

Beschreiben Sie, was und welche Farben jemand in Ihrem Deutschkurs trägt. Sagen Sie den Namen der Person nicht. Die anderen im Kurs müssen erraten (*guess*), wer das ist.

BEISPIEL: Diese Person trägt eine Bluse. Die Bluse ist rotweiß gestreift. Sie trägt auch Jeans; die sind natürlich blau. Und ihre Schuhe sind, hm, lila. Wer ist das?—Das ist Winona.

Aktivität 8 Ein Gespräch im Geschäft

Spielen Sie ein Gespräch zwischen einem Verkäufer / einer Verkäuferin und einem Kunden / einer Kundin. Benutzen Sie dabei die folgenden Wörter und Ausdrücke.

Farbe
Ich möchte gern ____.
kosten
Größe
zu groß
____ Mark
passt mir (nicht)
Wie gefällt Ihnen ____?
preiswert
anprobieren
Bitte sehr.
zu klein
zu teuer
Ich brauche ____.
Ich nehme ____.
steht mir (nicht)
Das macht zusammen ____.
Danke schön.

Thema 3

Lebensmittel

Lebensmittel. Suggestion: Use pictures to help introduce the vocabulary, or lead students through the ad, and have them guess the meaning of the new vocabulary.

Suggestion: Tell your students the current exchange rate. Are the prices higher or lower than they expect?

Realia. This ad is from the Multi-Center store in Kaiserslautern.

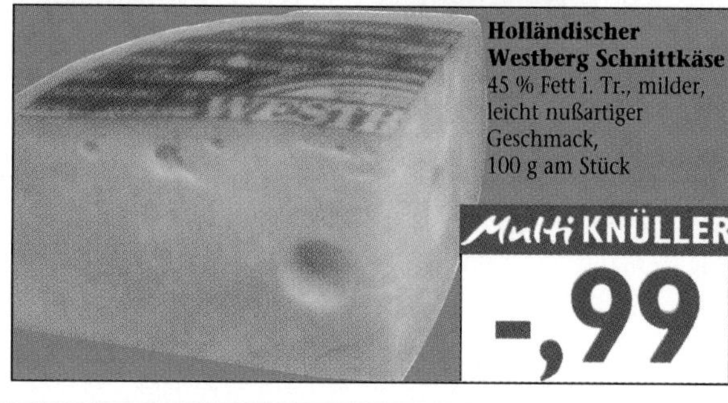

Neue Wörter

GETRÄNKE
- ☐ das **Mineralwasser**
- ☐ der **Apfelsaft**

ADJEKTIVE
- ☐ **frisch**
- ☐ **gefroren**
- ☐ **zart**

OBST
- ☐ die **Weintraube**

GEMÜSE
- ☐ die **Kartoffel**

FLEISCHWAREN
- ☐ der **Aufschnitt**
- ☐ das **Hähnchen**
- ☐ der **Schinken**
- ☐ das **Rindfleisch**
- ☐ das **Schweinefleisch**
- ☐ der **Truthahn**

MILCHPRODUKTE
- ☐ der **Joghurt**
- ☐ der **Käse**

GETREIDEPRODUKTE
- ☐ das **Müsli**

A. In welche Kategorie gehört das? Ordnen Sie die Wörter einer passenden untenstehenden Kategorie zu.

Äpfel	**Eis**	Mineralwasser	**Steak**
Apfelstrudel	**Erdbeeren**	Müsli	**Tee**
Aufschnitt	**Gurken**	**Pfeffer**	**Toilettenpapier**
Bananen	**Hähnchen**	**Rasiercreme**	Tomaten
Bier	**Karotten**	Rindfleisch	Truthahn
Blumenkohl	Kartoffeln	Rohmilch	Vollkornbrot
Brokkoli	**Kekse**	**Saft**	Weintrauben
Brot	Knäckebrot	**Salz**	**Wurst**
Brötchen	Kräutertee	**Schnitzel**	**Zahnpasta**
Butter	**Kuchen**	**Shampoo**	**Zucker**
Cola	**Make-up**		
Eier	**Milch**		

Thema 3. Suggestion: Interview different students. Ask them
- what kinds of fruits and vegetables they like to eat.
- what kinds of meat products they like to eat (or whether they are vegetarians).
- what kinds of beverages they usually buy.

BACKWAREN: Brot, . . .	Apfelstrudel, Brötchen, Kekse, Knäckebrot, Kuchen
OBST UND GEMÜSE: Kartoffeln, . . .	Äpfel, Bananen, Blumenkohl, Brokkoli, Erdbeeren, Gurken, Karotten, Tomaten, Weintrauben
BIOKOST: Vollkornbrot, . . .	Kräutertee, Müsli, Rohmilch
FLEISCHWAREN: Steak, . . .	Aufschnitt, Hähnchen, Rindfleisch, Schnitzel, Truthahn, Wurst
GETRÄNKE: Cola, . . .	Apfelsaft, Bier, Mineralwasser, Saft
ANDERE LEBENSMITTEL: Pfeffer, . . .	Butter, Eier, Eis, Milch, Salz, Tee, Zucker
TOILETTENARTIKEL: Shampoo, . . .	Make-up, Rasiercreme, Toilettenpapier, Zahnpasta

B. Mini-Umfrage: Was essen Sie gewöhnlich zum **Frühstück?** Zum **Mittagessen?** Zum **Abendessen?**

Note: Point out the differences between traditional American meals and traditional German meals.

Viele Deutsche kaufen heute in großen, modernen **Supermärkten** ein. Es gibt aber immer noch viele Spezialgeschäfte, besonders in kleinen Städten, wie die **Metzgerei,** die **Bäckerei,** die **Konditorei,** den **Getränkeladen** und den **Obst- und Gemüsestand. Medikamente** auf Rezept kann man in Deutschland nicht in einer **Drogerie** kaufen, sondern nur in einer **Apotheke.** Im **Bioladen** gibt es Produkte, die nicht mit chemischen Mitteln behandelt (*treated*) sind.

Analyse

Sehen Sie sich die Supermarktanzeige im Thema 3 an.

- Welche Milchprodukte bietet der Supermarkt an? Welche Getränke? Welche Fleischwaren?
- Aus welchem Land kommen das Gemüse und das Obst? Der Käse?
- Nennen Sie drei Marken (*brand names*).
- Wie spät hat der Supermarkt geöffnet (*open*)?

Sprachtipp. Point Out: The American pound is 454 grams, whereas the metric pound is 500 grams. One liter is slightly more than a quart. One U.S. gallon = 3,78 liter. Normally prices are written with a comma separating *Mark* and *Pfennige*.

Suggestion: Practice the metric system and reading prices by asking students how much the items in the ads in *Thema 3* cost in various quantities.

The metric system is used in German-speaking countries. The following abbreviations for weights and measures are commonly used:

1 kg = 1 Kilogramm = 1000 Gramm = 2 Pfund
500 g = 500 Gramm = 1 Pfund
1000 ml = 1000 Milliliter
0,75 l = 0,75 Liter
1 l = 1 Liter

Other abbreviations used are:

Kl. I = Klasse I *top quality*
Stck. = Stück *piece*

To read prices out loud:

DM 11,99 = elf Mark neunundneunzig *or* elf neunundneunzig
DM 1,49 = eine Mark neunundvierzig *or* eins neunundvierzig
DM 0,75 = fünfundsiebzig Pfennig

Aktivität 9 Wo? Was? Wie viel?

Sie hören drei Dialoge: in einer Bäckerei, auf dem Markt und in einer Metzgerei. Kreuzen Sie das richtige Geschäft an. Ergänzen Sie die Tabelle.

Aktivität 9. Suggestion: Make sure students understand how to work with the chart: Place check marks under correct store and write in what the item is and its price. Play each dialogue once. Then let students listen a second time, pausing after each dialogue to let them write down the information.

	MARKT	BÄCKEREI	METZGEREI	WAS?	PREIS?
Dialog 1			X	Würstchen Aufschnitt	DM 17,50
Dialog 2		X		Brötchen Schwarzbrot	DM 6,50
Dialog 3	X			Erdbeeren Tomaten	DM 8,-

Aktivität 10 Einkaufstag für Jutta 

Jutta gibt eine Party. Deshalb (*For that reason*) muss sie einkaufen. Schreiben Sie einen Text für die Bilder. Benutzen Sie Elemente aus beiden Spalten (*columns*) unten.

So beginnt die Geschichte: Jutta gibt am Wochenende eine Party. Deshalb geht sie heute einkaufen.

Aktivität 10. Suggestion: Have students work in pairs. They should first scan the pictures to see where Jutta is going. Review the meaning of vocabulary: *zuerst*, *zuletzt*, *deshalb*, *jetzt*. Students match up sentence halves and then match sentences and pictures. Call on pairs to supply a description for each picture, thereby creating a *Bildgeschichte*. **Follow-up:** Have students supply a description for each picture without referring to a written text.

Dort kauft sie	Obst und Gemüse—alles ganz frisch.
Zuletzt geht sie	Brot, Brötchen und Käsekuchen.
Zuerst geht sie	und geht nach Hause.
Da gibt es	zur Bäckerei.
Dann geht sie	zum Lebensmittelgeschäft.
Jutta braucht auch	zur Metzgerei.
Deshalb geht sie auch	Würstchen zum Grillen.
Jetzt hat sie alles	Kaffee, Zucker, Milch und Käse.
In der Bäckerei kauft sie	zum Markt.
Am Obst- und Gemüsestand kauft sie	Blumenkohl und Kartoffeln.
	Äpfel, Bananen und Weintrauben—alles ganz frisch.

Aktivität 11 Preiswert einkaufen! 

Stellen Sie sich vor, Sie haben nur 20 Mark für Essen und Trinken übrig und müssen damit ein ganzes Wochenende auskommen. Wählen Sie Waren aus den Anzeigen (*ads*) aus. Vergleichen Sie (*compare*) Ihre Listen im Plenum.

BEISPIEL: Wir kaufen ein Bauernbrot für DM 1,79; 200 g Kalbsleberwurst für DM 2,56; 1 Kilo Tomaten für DM 2,98 und eine Schwarzwälder Kirschtorte für DM 9,95.

Realia. The ad for *Mühlbacher Bauernbrot,* offered by the German grocery chain *Tengelmann,* is from the *Süddeutsche Zeitung.*

NeuKauf

Unser Metzgermeister empfiehlt:
vm vinzenzmurr

1a Rinderrouladen 100 g 1.39
Delik. Kalbsleberwurst extra i. Fettdarm, DLG-präm. 100 g 1.28

Aus den Obst- und Gemüsegärten der Welt

Spanische Navel-Orangen HKL II 3 kg 3.98
Spanische Satsumas HKL II 1 kg 1.58
Italienische Kiwi Stück -.48
Spanische Tomaten HKL. I 1 kg 2.98
Griechische Gurken HKL. I 350-450-g-Stück -.98
Holländischer Kopfsalat HKL. I Stück -.98

1. *farmer's bread*
2. *pumpernickel*
3. *whole food three-grain*
4. Schwarzwälder . . . *Black Forest cherry torte*

Aktivität 11. Suggestion: Have students work in pairs. They should first scan the ads and then preview vocabulary with the whole group. Set a time limit of about five minutes to draw up the lists. Spot-check several pairs by asking *Was kaufen Sie mit Ihren 20 Mark?*

Aktivität 12 Ein Menü für eine Party

A. Sie planen mit einem Freund / einer Freundin ein Menü für eine Party. Was wollen Sie servieren? Hier sind einige Vorschläge (*suggestions*). Wählen Sie Dinge aus jeder Gruppe aus.

zum Essen: Würstchen, Steaks, Hamburger, Kartoffelsalat, Kartoffelchips, Pommes frites, Salat, Gemüse, ?
zum Nachtisch: Eis, Pudding, frische Erdbeeren, Käsekuchen, ?
zum Trinken: Mineralwasser (Sprudel), Bier, Wein, Limonade, ?

Aktivität 12. Note: This interactive activity allows for personal choices. Review the vocabulary first, then have students do the activity. Call on several pairs to role-play a dialogue for the whole class, using the outline on p. 151.

S1	S2
1. Wollen wir _____ grillen?	**2a.** Gut. Machen wir _____ mit _____ und _____. **2b.** Nein, ich möchte lieber _____ mit _____ und _____.
3a. Und zum Nachtisch? **3b.** Na gut, und _____?	**4.** Was sollen wir dazu trinken?
5. _____.	**6a.** Na, gut. **6b.** Also, _____ schmeckt doch nicht dazu. Ich schlage vor (*suggest*), wir trinken _____.

B. Tragen Sie Ihre Partypläne im Plenum vor.

Grammatik im Kontext

The Dative Case°

der Dativ

As you have learned, the nominative case is the case of the subject; the accusative case is used for direct objects and with a number of prepositions. These cases are signalled by special endings of articles and possessive adjectives, as well as by different forms for personal pronouns.

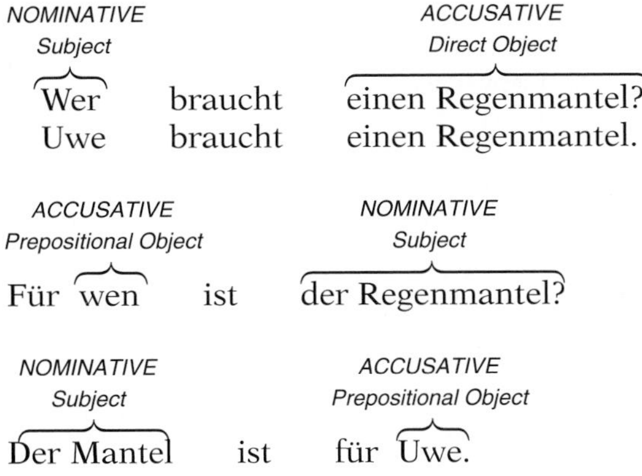

The dative case, like the accusative, serves several distinct functions; it is used primarily:

- for indirect objects (indicating the person to/for whom something is done)
- with certain verbs
- with specific prepositions

As with the other cases, special forms of pronouns and endings for articles and possessive adjectives signal the dative case.

The dative object answers the question **wem**? (*whom?, to/for whom?*)

Wem zeigt der Verkäufer drei Ringe?	*To whom is the salesman showing three rings?*
Er zeigt sie **Herrn Ebert.**	*He's showing them to Mr. Ebert.*
Wem kauft Herr Ebert einen Ring?	*For whom is Mr. Ebert buying a ring?*
Er kauft ihn **seiner Frau.**	*He's buying it for his wife.*
Wem hilft der Verkäufer?	*Whom is the salesman helping?*
Er hilft **dem Kunden.**	*He's helping the customer.*

Personal Pronouns

The following chart shows the personal pronouns in the dative case next to their corresponding nominative forms.

NOMINATIVE	DATIVE		NOMINATIVE	DATIVE	
ich	**mir**	*to/for me*	wir	**uns**	*to/for us*
du	**dir**	*to/for you (informal)*	ihr	**euch**	*to/for you (informal)*
Sie	**Ihnen**	*to/for you (formal)*	Sie	**Ihnen**	*to/for you (formal)*
er	**ihm**	*to/for him; to/for it*			
sie	**ihr**	*to/for her; to/for it*	sie	**ihnen**	*to/for them*
es	**ihm**	*to/for it*			

Articles and Possessive Adjectives

The following chart shows the dative endings for articles and possessive adjectives. Note that the masculine and neuter endings are identical.

MASCULINE	NEUTER	FEMININE	PLURAL
d**em** / (k)ein**em** / mein**em** } Mann	d**em** / (k)ein**em** / mein**em** } Kind	d**er** / (k)ein**er** / mein**er** } Frau	d**en** / kein**en** / mein**en** } Kunden

Weak Masculine Nouns

Nouns in the dative singular do not normally take an ending. However, weak special masculine nouns that take **n** or **en** in the accusative (**Kapitel 2**) take these same endings in the dative.

NOMINATIVE	ACCUSATIVE	DATIVE
der Herr	den Herr**n**	dem Herr**n**
der Kunde	den Kunde**n**	dem Kunde**n**
der Mensch	den Mensch**en**	dem Mensch**en**
der Name	den Name**n**	dem Name**n**
der Student	den Student**en**	dem Student**en**

In the dative plural, nouns add **n** to the plural ending, unless the plural already ends in **n.** Nouns whose plural ends in **s,** however, remain unchanged in the dative plural.

SINGULAR	PLURAL	
	Nominative	*Dative*
der Verkäufer	die Verkäufer	den Verkäufer**n**
der Mann	die Männer	den Männer**n**
die Verkäuferin	die Verkäuferinnen	den Verkäuferinnen
but das Auto	die Autos	den Autos

The Dative Case for Indirect Objects

As in English, many German verbs take both a direct object and an indirect object. The direct object, in the accusative, will usually be a thing; the indirect object, in the dative, will normally be a person. Examples of verbs that take two objects in German are:

empfehlen (empfiehlt)	to recommend
geben (gibt)	to give
glauben	to believe
kaufen	to buy
leihen	to lend, borrow
sagen	to tell, say
schenken	to give as a gift
schicken	to send
schreiben	to write
wünschen	to wish
zeigen	to show

The Dative Case for Indirect Objects. Note: German does not distinguish between "lend" and "borrow." Both English verbs are rendered into German by **leihen.** Thus, *Ich leihe dir Geld.* I'll lend you some money. *Ich leihe mir Geld.* I'm borrowing some money (for myself).

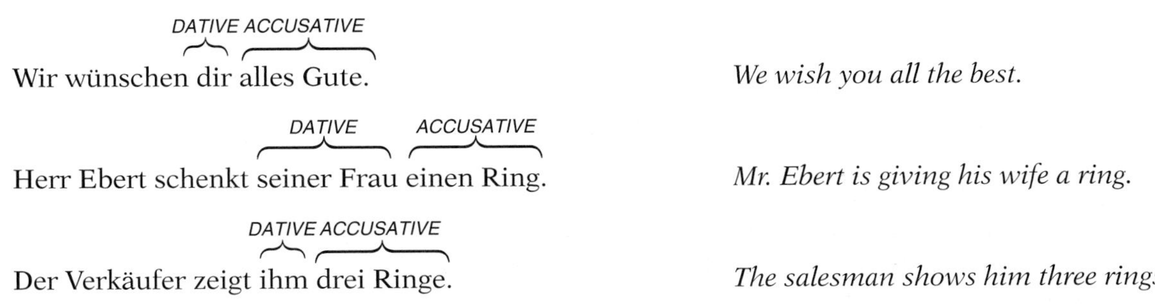

Note: The dative object generally precedes the accusative object. If, however, the accusative object is a pronoun, it will precede the dative object.

Ich gebe meiner Freundin (DATIVE) Blumen (ACCUSATIVE). *I'm giving my friend flowers.*

Ich gebe sie (ACCUSATIVE) meiner Freundin (DATIVE). *I'm giving them to my friend.*

Realia. 1. The ad for *Restaurant Haus Kuckuck* appeared in the weekly *Klever Wochenblatt.* 2. *Da schaut* . . . This ad for financial advisers appeared in *München* 8/93. 3. *Geben Sie* . . . This headline is taken from an ad for hair care products. It appeared in *Brigitte.* 4. *Wenn Sie* . . . This appeared in *Journal für Deutschland* in a little section on how to write to them.

Analyse

Analyse. Suggestion: Review accusative case endings and personal pronouns before approaching dative objects through the **Analyse.** Do this as a whole group.

Scan the following ads.

- Find a dative (noun) object. What is the verb that requires this dative object to be used?
- Find several personal pronouns in the dative. What is the nominative form of each of these pronouns? What verbs in the ads require these dative pronouns to be used?

Wir wünschen unseren Gästen und Bekannten[1] *ein gesundes Neues Jahr.*

Ab Januar 1995 möchten wir Ihnen unsere neue Speiseauswahl[2] *anbieten.*[3]

Restaurant Haus Kuckuck
Bedburg-Hau

Horst und Christine Schmidt

DA SCHAUT JEMAND AUF IHR GELD! WOLLEN SIE ES IHM GEBEN?

Sicher nicht. Schenken Sie dem Mann nicht weiter Ihr Geld.

Liebe Mutti,

Zum Geburtstag wünschen wir dir alles, alles Gute

Vati und die ganze Bande[4]

Geben Sie Ihrem Haar einen modischen Kick...

HENNA PLUS

Wenn Sie uns schreiben wollen ...

1. *acquaintances*
2. *menu*
3. *offer*
4. die . . . *the whole gang*

Übung 1 Situationen im Alltag

Sie hören fünf Dialoge. Kreuzen Sie für jeden Dialog den Satz an, der zu dem Thema passt.

1. Hans braucht unbedingt etwas Geld.
   ☒ Sein Freund kann ihm nichts leihen.
   ☐ Sein Freund schreibt ihm einen Scheck.
2. Zwei Studentinnen brauchen Hilfe.
   ☐ Ein Herr auf der Straße gibt ihnen etwas Geld.
   ☒ Ein Herr zeigt ihnen den Weg zum Café.
3. Helmut hat Geburtstag.
   ☒ Marianne schreibt ihm eine Karte.
   ☐ Marianne kauft ihm eine CD.
4. Eine Studentin erzählt einem Bekannten über ihren Tagesablauf.
   ☒ Sie empfiehlt ihm Yoga.
   ☐ Sie hat keine Zeit für Yoga.
5. Achim sagt, er lebt nur von Brot und Wasser.
   ☐ Er sagt, er gibt viel Geld für Brot aus.
   ☒ Man kann ihm nicht alles glauben.

Übung 1. Suggestion: Have students listen to each mini-dialogue in succession. Expand the questions about each situation. Incorporate the dative verbs in as many questions as possible. Ask students to summarize each dialogue orally.

Übung 2 Hin und her: Geschenke, Geschenke!

In der Familie Eichele gibt es viele Feste, z.B. Geburtstage, Hochzeitstage, Weihnachten. Wer kauft wem was und wann? Fragen Sie Ihren Partner / Ihre Partnerin.

BEISPIEL: S1: Was kauft Ulrike ihrem Bruder Hans zum Geburtstag?
S2: Ulrike kauft ihrem Bruder Hans eine Jacke zum Geburtstag.
oder: S1: Wem kauft Hans win Video zu Weihnachten?
S2: Hans kauft seiner Schwester Ulrike ein Video zu Weihnachten.

WER	WEM	WAS	ZU WELCHEM ANLASS°
Ulrike	ihr Bruder Hans	eine Jacke	zum Geburtstag
Hans	seine Schwester	ein Video	zu Weihnachten
Herr Eichele	sein Sohn Wolfgang	ein Fahrrad	zum Geburtstag
Frau Eichele	ihr Mann	drei Krawatten	zu Weihnachten
die Eichele Kinder	ihre Eltern	Konzertkarten	zum Hochzeitstag
Ulrike	ihre Kusine Annette	Ohrringe	zum Geburtstag

°*occasion*

Übung 3 Wem schenkst du das?

BEISPIEL: S1: Wem schenkst du den Hut?
S2: Den schenke ich meiner Oma.

der Hut

ein Aquarium mit zwei Goldfischen

das Handy

die Krawatte

die Flasche Wein

das Buch

die Inline-Skates

der Rucksack

Verbs with a Dative Object Only

A number of common German verbs always take an object in the dative case. Note that these dative objects usually refer to people.

danken	Ich **danke** dir für die Karte.	*I thank you for the card.*
gefallen	Wie **gefällt** Ihnen dieses Hemd?	*How do you like this shirt?**
gehören	Der Mercedes **gehört** meinem Bruder.	*The Mercedes belongs to my brother.*
helfen	Der Verkäufer **hilft** dem Kunden.	*The salesperson is helping the customer.*
passen	Größe 48 **passt** mir bestimmt.	*Size 48 will surely fit me.*
schmecken	Der Kuchen **schmeckt** mir gut.	*The cake tastes good (to me).*
stehen	Das Kleid **steht** dir gut.	*The dress looks good on you.*

A number of frequently used idiomatic expressions also require dative objects. Some of these you have already seen.

Wie geht es **dir?**	*How are you?*
Es geht **mir** nicht gut.	*I am not well.*
Das tut **mir** leid.	*I'm sorry.*

Verbs that take only a dative object are indicated in the vocabulary lists of this book as follows: (*dat.*)

Adjectives with the Dative Case

The dative case is also used with several adjectives, often in conjunction with the adverb **zu** (*too*).

Tausend Mark für dieses Kleid? Das ist **mir** zu teuer.	*A thousand marks for this dress? That's too expensive (for me).*
Das ist **mir** egal.	*I don't care.*
Es ist **mir** kalt.	*I'm cold.*

Übung 4 Wem gehört das denn?

Sagen Sie, wem diese Dinge gehören.

BEISPIEL: S1: Wem gehört die Uhr?
S2: Ich glaube, die gehört meinem Freund.

* *Lit.: How does this shirt please you?*

der tolle BMW	Touristen aus Deutschland, Kanada . . .
das Fotoalbum	meine Schwester . . .
die Schuhe	unser Deutschlehrer / unsere Deutschlehrerin
die Kamera	ich
die vielen Koffer	mein Freund
die Tasche	deine Freundin
die modischen Ohrringe	?
der Strohhut	
das karierte Hemd	
der gestreifte Pullover	
?	

Übung 5 Hallo, wie geht's?

Ergänzen Sie die fehlenden Personalpronomen.

1. A: Hallo, Brigitte, wie geht es _____?
   B: Danke, _____ geht's gut. Und wie geht's deinem Bruder?
   A: Ach, es geht _____ nicht besonders im Moment. Er hat zu viel Arbeit.
2. C: Hallo, Petra und Christoph. Wie geht es _____ beiden denn?
   D: Danke, es geht _____ gut.
3. E: Guten Tag, Herr Sanders. Ich hoffe, es geht _____ gut.
   F: Danke, es geht.
   E: Und wie geht es Ihrer Frau?
   F: Ach, es geht _____ immer gut.

Übung 6 Ein schwieriger° Kunde

°difficult

Übung 6. Suggestion: Review the meanings of the verbs first. Then let students work in pairs to complete the dialogue. Have several pairs role-play the completed dialogue for the class.

Ergänzen Sie den Dialog mit passenden Verben und Pronomen im Dativ.

VERKÄUFER: Kann ich _____ _____?[1] (*help you*)
KUNDE: Ja. Ich brauche ein Geschenk für meine Freundin. Können Sie _____ vielleicht etwas _____?[2] (*recommend to me*)
VERKÄUFER: Eine Bluse vielleicht?
KUNDE: _____ Sie _____ bitte eine Bluse in Größe 50.[3] (*Show me*)
VERKÄUFER: Größe 50?
KUNDE: Ich glaube, Größe 50 _____ _____ bestimmt.[4] (*fits her*)
VERKÄUFER: Hier habe ich eine elegante Seidenbluse. In Schwarz.
KUNDE: Nein, Schwarz _____ _____ nicht.[5] (*look good on her*)
VERKÄUFER: Wie _____ _____ diese Bluse in Lila?[6] (*do you like*)
KUNDE: Schrecklich. Diese Farbe _____ _____ überhaupt nicht.[7] (*I like*)
VERKÄUFER: Hier habe ich ein Modell aus Paris für 1250 Mark. Ich garantiere, diese Bluse _____ _____ bestimmt.[8] (*she will like*)
KUNDE: Sie machen wohl Spaß. Das ist _____ _____.[9] (*too expensive for me*)
VERKÄUFER: Kann ich _____ etwas anderes _____?[10] (*show you*)
KUNDE: Können Sie _____ vielleicht ein T-Shirt _____?[11] (*show me*)
VERKÄUFER: Ja, natürlich. Hier habe ich ein ganz . . .
KUNDE: Oh, je. Es ist schon halb sechs. Es tut _____ _____.[12] (*I'm sorry.*) Ich muss sofort gehen. Ich _____ _____ für Ihre Hilfe.[13] (*thank you*) Auf Wiedersehen.

Übung 7 Sei ehrlich°!

honest

Wie gefällt dir das?

BEISPIEL: S1: Wie gefällt dir Juttas Hut?
S2: Nicht schlecht. Der gefällt mir.
S1: Ich finde ihn etwas bizarr.

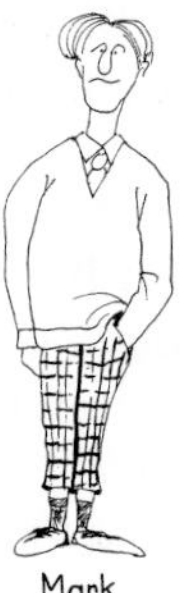

Ich finde ihn/es/sie . . .	sehr schick	überhaupt nicht
. . . gefällt mir . . .	sehr gut	unmöglich
. . . steht ihm/ihr	nicht schlecht	zu kurz/eng
. . . passt ihm/ihr	etwas bizarr	?
. . . ist ihm/ihr		

Übung 7. Follow-up: Expand this activity by bringing a number of clothing items that students describe and express their opinion about.

Prepositions with the Dative Case

Prepositions that require the dative case of nouns and pronouns include:

aus	from, out of	Richard kommt gerade **aus** dem Haus.
		Alexandra kommt **aus** Jena.
	(made) of	Das Hemd ist **aus** Baumwolle.
bei	near	Die Bäckerei ist **beim** Marktplatz.
	at (the place of)	Schicke Blusen gibt es **bei** Gisie.
	for, at (a company)	Manfred arbeitet **bei** VW.
	with	Sybille wohnt **bei** ihrer Großmutter.
mit	with	Herr Schweiger geht **mit** seiner Frau einkaufen.
		Katja wohnt **mit** ihrer Freundin Beate zusammen.
	by (means of)	Wir fahren **mit** dem Bus.
nach	to	Der Bus fährt **nach** Frankfurt.
		Ich fahre jetzt **nach** Hause.
	after	**Nach** dem Essen gehen wir einkaufen.
seit	since	**Seit** gestern haben wir schönes Wetter.
	for (time)	**Seit** einem Monat kauft sie nur noch Bio-Brot.
von	from	Das Brot ist frisch **vom** Bäcker.
		Frank kommt gerade **vom** Markt.
	by (origin)	Dieses Buch ist **von** Peter Handke.
zu	to	Wir gehen heute **zum** Supermarkt.
		Dirk muss schon um fünf Uhr **zur** Arbeit.
	at	Er ist jetzt wieder **zu** Hause.
	for	**Zum** Frühstück gibt es Müsli.

Note that **nach Hause** and **zu Hause** are set expressions. **Nach Hause** is used to say that someone is *going* home, while **zu Hause** means someone is *at* home.

The following contractions are common:

bei dem → **beim**	Jürgen kauft sein Brot nur **beim** Bäcker.
von dem → **vom**	Er kommt gerade **vom** Markt.
zu dem → **zum**	Er muss jetzt noch **zum** Bäcker.
zu der → **zur**	Dann geht er **zur** Bank.

Vom Korn[1] zum Brot

Mühlenbäckerei
BORGMANN
Mühlenstraße 11 • Kranenburg
Inh. Ralf Borgmann
Telefon 0 28 26 / 2 65

1. Vom . . . *From grain to bread*

Realia. This ad for *Mühlenbäckerei Borgmann* shows a windmill, a typical sight in this area of the German Niederrhein close to the Dutch border.

Übung 8 Ein typischer Tag

Sie hören eine Beschreibung von Maxis Tagesablauf. Was stimmt? Was stimmt nicht? Geben Sie die richtige Information an.

	DAS STIMMT	DAS STIMMT NICHT
1. Maxi wohnt seit einem Monat in Göttingen.	☒	☐
2. Maxi wohnt allein in einer Wohnung.	☐	☒
3. Sie kann zu Fuß zur Universität gehen.	☒	☐
4. Maxi kommt gerade aus der Bibliothek.	☐	☒
5. Dann geht sie in die Mensa.	☐	☒
6. Maxi und Inge gehen zum Supermarkt.	☒	☐
7. Beim Bäcker kaufen sie ein Brot.	☐	☒
8. Maxi muss noch zur Bank.	☒	☐

Übung 9 Auskunft° geben

°information

Ergänzen Sie die fehlenden Präpositionen.

1. Sag mal, wo gibt es hier denn schicke Blusen? —_____ Gisie.
2. Die Bluse steht dir gut. Ist sie _____ Leinen oder Synthetik?
3. Ist diese Bluse neu? —Ja, sie ist ein Geschenk _____ meiner Mutter.
4. Das Brot schmeckt ausgezeichnet. Woher hast du es? —Es ist _____ der Bäckerei.
5. Gehst du zu Fuß einkaufen? —Nein, ich fahre _____ dem Wagen zum Supermarkt.
6. Bitte, komm _____ dem Einkaufen sofort _____ Hause.
7. Ich plane schon _____ drei Monaten eine Grillparty.
8. Wollen wir die Party _____ dir oder _____ mir _____ Hause machen?

Übung 10 Ein typischer Tag für Michael

Setzen Sie die fehlenden Präpositionen, Artikel und Endungen ein.

1. Michael wohnt _____ sein_____ Bruder zusammen in einer alten Villa in Berlin.
2. Er geht schon _____ 6 Uhr _____ _____ Haus.

3. Er fährt _____ sein_____ Moped _____ Arbeit.
4. Er arbeitet _____ _____ Hotel Zentral.
5. Er arbeitet da schon _____ ein_____ Jahr. Die Arbeit gefällt ihm sehr.
6. Er arbeitet _____ Leute_____ _____ vielen Länder_____ zusammen, z. B. _____ Jugoslawien, Spanien, Afghanistan und Amerika.
7. Abends _____ d_____ Arbeit trifft er oft ein paar Freunde.
8. Dann geht er _____ sein_____ Freunde _____ in eine Kneipe.
9. Michael kocht gern. _____ Frühstück gibt es oft so etwas wie Rührei _____ Zwiebeln und Zucchini.
10. Das ist ein Rezept _____ Mexiko.
11. Er hat das Rezept _____ sein_____ Freundin Marlene.

Übung 11 Seit wann ist das so?

Arbeiten Sie mit einem Partner / einer Partnerin zusammen. Stellen Sie Fragen.

BEISPIEL: S1: Seit wann wohnst du hier?
S2: Seit drei Semestern.

1. Deutsch lernen
2. Auto fahren können
3. den Professor / die Professorin kennen
4. hier wohnen
5. an dieser Uni studieren
6. ?

Interrogative Pronouns° *wo, wohin,* and *woher*

Interrogativpronomen

The interrogative pronouns **wo** and **wohin** both mean *where*. **Wo** is used to ask where someone or something is located, **wohin** to ask about the direction in which someone or something is moving. **Woher** is used to ask where someone or something comes from.

Wo bist du denn jetzt?	Zu Hause.
Wo wohnst du?	In Berlin.
Wo kauft Maxi ihr Brot?	Beim Bäcker.
Wohin gehst du? (**Wo** gehst du **hin**?)	Zur Bibliothek.
Wohin fährst du? (**Wo** fährst du **hin**?)	Nach Deutschland.
Woher kommen die Orangen? (**Wo** kommen die Orangen **her**?)	Aus Spanien.
Woher hast du die gute Wurst? (**Wo** hast du die gute Wurst **her**?)	Vom Metzger.

Note that the words **wohin** and **woher** are frequently split (**wo . . . hin, wo . . . her**), especially in casual conversation.

Übung 12 Wo, wohin, woher?

Bilden Sie die Fragen zu den Antworten.

BEISPIEL: Ich muss heute noch *zur Bank.* →
Wohin musst du heute noch?
oder: Wo musst du heute noch hin?

1. Brötchen gibt es *beim Bäcker.*
2. Mark muss heute noch *zur Metzgerei.*
3. Sein Freund kommt gerade *vom Bioladen.*
4. Die Studentinnen trinken einen Kaffee *im Café Kadenz.*
5. Wir gehen später *zum Supermarkt.*
6. Antje ist heute *zu Hause.*
7. Die Leute kommen gerade *aus dem Kino.*
8. Sie gehen jetzt alle *nach Hause.*

der-Words: *dieser, jeder,* and *welcher*

The demonstrative adjectives **dieser** (*this*) and **jeder** (*every*), and the interrogative adjective **welcher** (*which*), have the same endings as the definite article. Like the definite article, they signal the gender, case, and number of the noun that follows them. For this reason they are frequently called **der**-words.

Dieser Mantel passt mir gut.	*This coat fits me well.*
Ich kann nicht **jede** Farbe tragen.	*I cannot wear every color.*
Welches Hemd möchten Sie?	*Which shirt would you like?*
Diese Schuhe sind unbequem.	*These shoes are uncomfortable.*

The plural of **jeder** is **alle.**

Alle Studenten tragen Jeans.	*All students wear jeans.*

All **der**-words follow this pattern of endings:

	MASCULINE	NEUTER	FEMININE	PLURAL
Nominative	dies**er**	dies**es**	dies**e**	dies**e**
Accusative	dies**en**	dies**es**	dies**e**	dies**e**
Dative	dies**em**	dies**em**	dies**er**	dies**en**

Übung 13 Mini-Dialoge im Geschäft

Setzen Sie die passende Form von **dieser, jeder/alle** oder **welcher** ein.

1. A: Was kosten _____ Stiefel hier?
   B: _____ Stiefel meinen Sie?
2. C: Wie finden Sie _____ Mantel?
   D: _____ Mantel meinen Sie?

3. E: Wie viel kostet _____ Hemd?
   F: _____ Hemden kosten 75 Mark.
4. G: Was kostet _____ Anzug?
   H: Wir haben _____ Woche ein Sonderangebot. _____ Anzug im Laden kostet nur 350 Mark.
5. I: Sind _____ Blusen aus Baumwolle?
   J: Ja, _____ Blusen in unserem Laden sind aus Baumwolle. Wir führen nur Bekleidung aus Naturfasern (*natural fibers*).
6. K: Haben Sie _____ Rock in meiner Größe?
   L: _____ Größe brauchen Sie denn?
7. M: Passt die Bluse zu _____ Rock?
   N: _____ Bluse meinen Sie?

Sprache im Kontext

Zuschauen

Vorschau

Beantworten Sie die folgenden Fragen, *bevor* Sie sich die Werbung ansehen.

1. Beschreiben Sie einen typischen Punker. Was für ein Mensch ist er?
2. Beschreiben Sie eine typische Oma. Was für ein Mensch ist sie?

Philadelphia

Arbeit mit dem Videotext

A. Sehen Sie sich jetzt die Werbung ohne Ton an, und beantworten Sie die Fragen.

1. Beschreiben Sie den Punker, den Sie in der Werbung sehen.
2. Beschreiben Sie die Oma, die Sie in der Werbung sehen.

B. „Jemandem aus der Hand fressen" heißt ungefähr „alles machen, was ein anderer Mensch von einem will". Sehen Sie jetzt die Werbung mit Ton an, und beantworten Sie die Fragen.

1. Warum isst der Pinkpunker Omi Kleinhuber aus der Hand?
2. Stellen Sie sich vor, Sie sind Omi Kleinhuber. Was verlangen Sie von dem Pinkpunker?

Lesen

Zum Thema

A. Wo kaufen Sie ein? Kreuzen Sie die Geschäfte oder Geschäftsalternativen an, in denen Sie einkaufen!

- □ auf dem Flohmarkt
- □ auf dem Markt
- □ im Supermarkt
- □ in der Drogerie
- □ in der Apotheke
- □ in einer Boutique
- □ in einem Einkaufszentrum
- □ aus einem Versandkatalog
- □ im Internet

B. Was kann man hier kaufen? Schauen Sie sich die Liste in A an. Sagen Sie, was man dort kaufen kann!

C. Interviewen Sie jemanden im Kurs. Machen Sie eine Umfrage!

1. Kaufst du gern ein?
2. Wie oft gehst du einkaufen? (jeden Tag, einmal/zweimal/dreimal in der Woche, ?)
3. Wo kaufst du am liebsten ein?
4. Hast du jemals etwas im Internet bestellt?

Auf den ersten Blick. Have students work with the cognates. Point out how new German expressions are coined using English words even when English already has a different expression for a given concept; for example, *Shopping City* (German) instead of *shopping mall* (English).

Auf den ersten Blick

A. Schauen Sie sich das Bild, den fett gedruckten Text und den Text in Großbuchstaben an.

1. Was für ein Text ist „Einkaufsbummel im World-Wide-Web"?
   - **a.** ein Artikel
   - **b.** eine Liste
   - **c.** ein Leserbrief (*letter to the editor*)
2. Welches Thema hat der Text?
   - **a.** ein Einkaufszentrum in der Stadt
   - **b.** gute Webseiten zum Einkaufen
   - **c.** Einkaufen im Internet

B. Überfliegen Sie den Text! Suchen Sie Wörter, die in die folgenden Kategorien passen!

EINKAUFEN	COMPUTER
____________________	____________________
____________________	____________________
____________________	____________________

EINKAUFSBUMMEL IM WORLD WIDE WEB

CYBERSHOP.

Die ganze Welt ist Einkaufsstraße: TV-MEDIA auf Shoppingtour.

Das Internet als globaler Kaufladen: „E-Commerce" ist aus dem World Wide Web längst nicht mehr wegzudenken. Die aufwendigste[1] Form, im Internet Geschäfte zu machen,[2] nennt sich „Shopping Mall" und hat viel Ähnlichkeit[3] mit einer realen Shopping City: Unter dem Dach einer einzigen Internet-Adresse sind die verschiedensten[4] „Cybershops" untergebracht.[5] Der Vorteil[6] für den Surfer: Man braucht jeweils nur eine Adresse anzuwählen und erspart sich[7] zeitraubende (und teure) Shoppingfahrten durchs Internet.

Das Einkaufen selbst ist unbürokratisch: Manchmal genügt[8] ein Mausklick aufs Bild der dargebotenen Ware – und schon wandert das gute Stück in den virtuellen Warenkorb. Bestätigt[9] man die Bestellung am Ende des Shopping-Rundgangs, dann nimmt die Order online ihren Lauf.[10]

Auch per Nachnahme.[11] Nicht immer wird beim Web-Shopping mit Kreditkarte bezahlt. Die Alternative für alle, die Angst vor finsteren Hackern haben: Das Online-Bestellformular[12] ausdrucken[13] und ganz konventionell faxen oder per Post schicken.

Apropos Post: Viele Online-Shops versenden ihre Waren mittlerweile auch per Nachnahme. ■

RAINER GRÜNWALD

1. *most involved*
2. Geschäfte . . . *to do business*
3. *similarity*
4. *most diverse*
5. *located*
6. *advantage*
7. erspart . . . *saves oneself*
8. *suffices*
9. *confirms*
10. nimmt . . . *the order takes its course online*
11. per . . . *by C.O.D.*
12. *order form*
13. *print out*

der **Saft, ¨e**	juice
der **Apfelsaft, ¨e**	apple juice
der **Tee**	tea
das **Wasser**	water
das **Mineralwasser**	mineral water

Milchprodukte	Dairy Products
die **Butter**	butter
das **Ei, -er**	egg
das **Eis**	ice-cream; ice
der **Joghurt**	yogurt
der **Käse**	cheese
die **Milch**	milk

Sonstige Lebensmittel	Other Foods
das **Müsli, -**	granola; cereal
der **Pfeffer**	pepper
das **Salz**	salt
der **Zucker**	sugar

Toilettenartikel	**Toiletries**
das **Make-up**	make-up
die **Rasiercreme, -s**	shaving cream
das **Shampoo, -s**	shampoo
das **Toilettenpapier**	toilet paper
die **Zahnpasta**	toothpaste

Geschäfte	**Stores, Shops**
die **Apotheke, -n**	pharmacy
die **Bäckerei, -en**	bakery
die **Drogerie, -n**	toiletries and sundries store
die **Konditorei, -en**	pastry shop
der **Laden, ¨**	store
der **Bioladen, ¨**	natural foods store
der **Getränkeladen,**	beverage store
die **Metzgerei, -en**	butcher shop
der **Obst- und Gemüsestand, ¨e**	fruit and vegetable stand
der **Supermarkt, ¨e**	supermarket

Kleidungsstücke	**Articles of Clothing**
der **Anzug, ¨e**	suit
der **Badeanzug, ¨e**	bathing suit
die **Bluse, -n**	blouse
der **Gürtel, -**	belt
das **Hemd, -en**	shirt
die **Hose, -n**	pants, trousers
der **Hut, ¨e**	hat
die **Jacke, -n**	jacket
die **Jeans**	jeans
das **Kleid, -er**	dress
die **Krawatte, -n**	necktie
der **Mantel, ¨**	coat
die **Mütze, -n**	cap
der **Pullover, -**	pullover sweater
der **Rock, ¨e**	skirt
das **Sakko, -s**	sport coat
der **Schal, -s**	scarf
der **Schlips, -e**	necktie
der **Schuh, -e**	shoe
der **Hausschuh, -e**	slipper
der **Tennisschuh, -e**	tennis shoe
die **Socke, -n**	sock
der **Stiefel, -**	boot
der **Strumpf, ¨e**	stocking; sock
das **T-Shirt, -s**	T-shirt

Sonstige Substantive	**Other Nouns**
das **Abendessen**	evening meal
die **Brille, -n**	(pair of) eyeglasses
die **Farbe, -n**	color
das **Frühstück**	breakfast
die **Größe, -n**	size
die **Kasse, -n**	cash register; check-out
das **Medikament, -e**	medicine
das **Mittagessen**	midday meal; lunch
der **Rucksack, ¨e**	backpack
die **Tasche, -n**	handbag

Farben	**Colors**
beige	beige
blau	blue
braun	brown
gelb	yellow
grau	gray
grün	green
lila	purple
orange	orange
rot	red
schwarz	black
weiß	white

Verben	Verbs
an·probieren	to try on
danken (*dat.*)	to thank
empfehlen (empfiehlt)	to recommend
gefallen (gefällt) (*dat.*)	to be pleasing
gehören (*dat.*)	to belong to (*a person*)
glauben	to believe
helfen (hilft) (*dat.*)	to help
leihen	to lend; borrow
passen (*dat.*)*	to fit
schenken	to give (*as a gift*)
schicken	to send
schmecken (*dat.*)	to taste (good)
stehen (*dat.*)	to look good (*on a person*)
tragen (trägt)	to wear; carry
zahlen	to pay
zeigen	to show

Sonstige Adjektive und Adverbien	Other Adjectives and Adverbs
frisch	fresh(ly)
gefroren	frozen
gestreift	striped
kariert	plaid
modisch	fashionable, fashionably
neu	new
nötig	necessary
zart	tender

der-Wörter	*der*-Words
alle	all
dieser	this
jeder	each, every
welcher	which

Dativpronomen	Dative Pronouns
mir	(to/for) me
dir	(to/for) you (*informal sg.*)
ihm	(to/for) him/it
ihr	(to/for) her/it
uns	(to/for) us
euch	(to/for) you (*informal pl.*)
ihnen	(to/for) them
Ihnen	(to/for) you (*formal*)

Dativpräpositionen	Dative Prepositions
aus	from; out of, (made) of
bei	at; near; with
mit	with; by means of
nach	after; to
seit	since; for (+ *time*)
von	of; from; by
zu	to; at; for

Fragewörter	Question Words
wem	(to/for) whom
wohin	(to) where

Sonstiges	Other
nach Hause	(to) home
zu Hause	at home
egal: Das ist mir egal.	I don't care.

*See Appendix E for alternate spelling.

Lernziele

Use this checklist to verify that you can now . . .

- ☐ identify articles of clothing.
- ☐ describe where you can buy articles of clothing.
- ☐ name colors and patterns.
- ☐ identify your clothing sizes using the German sizing system.
- ☐ offer opinions about clothing using verbs like **gefallen, passen,** and **stehen.**
- ☐ identify some basic foods and the shops where you would purchase them in Germany.
- ☐ express weights and measures using the metric system.
- ☐ read German prices.
- ☐ use **der-**words.
- ☐ understand the dative case and its use.
- ☐ identify direct and indirect objects and verbs, prepositions, and adjectives that require the dative case.
- ☐ differentiate between **wo, wohin,** and **woher.**

Kapitel 6

Wir gehen aus

Familienessen in einem Restaurant

Kapitel 6. Suggestion: Describe a recent visit to a restaurant. Discuss with the class which kinds of restaurants are in town, and which ones they like.

Alles klar?

A. Die Offenbach-Stuben ist ein Restaurant in Berlin.

- Was kann man in den Offenbach-Stuben essen?
- Wie viele Plätze gibt es im Restaurant?
- Wie kann man dort zahlen?
- Wann kann man dort essen?
- Wer hat schon einmal dort gegessen?
- In welcher Straße befindet sich das Restaurant?

B. Doris, eine Freundin von Antje Göttges-Eichele, hat die Uni gewechselt und studiert jetzt in Berlin. Sie ist beim Info-Büro des Astas an der FU. Hören Sie jetzt ihr Gespräch mit der Asta-Referentin (*adviser*), und ordnen Sie die Charakterisierungen dem richtigen Restaurant zu.

RESTAURANT	CHARAKTERISIERUNG
1. _____ Brazil	**a.** gemütlich
2. _____ Kartoffelkeller	**b.** in der Oranienburger Straße
3. _____ Kellerrestaurant	**c.** macht viel Spaß
4. _____ Ristorante Italiano	**d.** nicht so teuer
	e. österreichische Küche
	f. rappelvoll
	g. Rezepte von Helene Weigel
	h. vegetarisch

Note: *FU* stands for *Freie Universität.* In general, *Asta* stands for *Allgemeiner Studierender Ausschuss.* The FU in Berlin uses the designation *Allgemeiner StudentInnen Ausschuss.* This organization helps students with academic problems, financial aid (BAföG), and housing. In Berlin, Asta holds itself responsible for raising the political awareness of students and cultivating relationships among international students.

Wörter im Kontext

Restaurant Ads. Suggestion: Focus students' attention on one piece of realia at a time, asking questions such as *Was für Gerichte bietet das Restaurant an? Was kann man dort trinken? Möchten Sie dort essen?*

Thema 1

Lokale

Realia. These restaurant and café ads represent the cities of Berlin, Bonn, Regensburg, Vienna and the villages of Born and Oberstdorf.

Berghaus Schönblick

Tel. 08322/4030

Ihr Treffpunkt unsere **TERRASSE**

bei Steaks und Forellen vom **BERGGRILL**

und auch sonst . . .

Für Ihr leibliches Wohl geben wir uns die größte Mühe!

Zimmer für kleine oder große Gruppen (von 1 - 90 Pers.)

Kein Ruhetag

Pizzeria Ristorante
Da Bizi
WARME KÜCHE VON 11—23 UHR
(Sonntag geschlossen)
1030 WIEN, FASANG. 7 **78 91 37**
***(PIZZA** auch zum Mitnehmen)*

SURYA
INDISCHES RESTAURANT
Genießen Sie in indischer Atmosphäre unsere Spezialitäten, Huhn, Lamm, vegetarische Speisen zu kleinen Preisen.
Grolmanstraße 22 · 10623 Berlin-Charlbg.
(am Savignyplatz)
☎ **312 91 23 - täglich 12.00 - 1.00 Uhr**

Neue Wörter

- □ **Bier vom Fass**
- □ der **Biergarten**
- □ die **Küche**
- □ das **Restaurant**
- □ der **Ruhetag**
- □ **geöffnet**
- □ **geschlossen**
- □ **täglich**
- □ **zum Mitnehmen**

Kaiser von China
China Restaurant
- In der Kaiserpassage 18 / Eingang Wesselstraße 53113 Bonn · Telefon (02 28) 65 88 30
- **Restaurant Hong Kong** Brassertufer 1 · 53111 Bonn · Tel. (02 28) 65 17 06
- **Restaurant Hongdi / Siegburg** mit schönem Biergarten am Mühlenbach · Auf der Kälke 1-3, beim Kreishaus · 53721 Siegburg · Tel. (0 22 41) 5 69 94

German has many different words for places where one can eat or drink something.

das **Café**	café serving mainly desserts—**Kaffee und Kuchen**—but also offering a limited menu
der **Gasthof / ** das **Gasthaus**	small inn with pub or restaurant
die **Gaststätte**	full-service restaurant
der **Imbiss**	fast-food stand; snack counter
die **Kneipe**	small, simple pub or bar; typical place where students gather (**Studentenkneipe**)
das **Lokal**	general word for an establishment that serves food and drinks
das **Restaurant**	generic word for *restaurant*
das **Wirtshaus**	pub serving mainly alcoholic beverages and some food

Often the words **Stube** or **Stüberl** will appear as a part of the name, as in „Altstadtstüberl" or „Mühlenstube". **Stube** is an older word for *room* and suggests a cozy atmosphere.

To call or address your waiter (**der Kellner, der Ober**) or waitress (**die Kellnerin**), say: **Herr Ober** or **Bedienung, bitte.**

The generic term **Bedienung** is often used in place of **Kellner, Kellnerin,** and **Ober.**

Eine Wirtshaustür in München

Analyse Wo gibt es das?

Schauen Sie sich die Anzeigen im **Thema 1** an. In welches Lokal können Leute gehen, die

- gern griechisch essen?
- gern im Biergarten sitzen?
- gern Bier vom Fass trinken?
- etwas zum Mitnehmen möchten?
- Vegetarier sind?
- ein großes Familienfest feiern möchten?
- gern auf der Terrasse sitzen?

Und Sie? In welches Lokal möchten Sie gehen? Warum?

Aktivität 1 Umfrage

Beantworten Sie die Fragen.

1. Gehen Sie oft essen? Wie oft? Einmal die Woche, einmal im Monat?
2. Essen Sie gern griechisch, chinesisch, italienisch . . . ?
3. Wie heißt Ihr Lieblingsrestaurant? Welche Spezialitäten gibt es dort?
4. Wann hat Ihr Lieblingsrestaurant Ruhetag? Ist es an allen Tagen der Woche geöffnet?
5. Was trinken Sie normalerweise, wenn Sie ausgehen?
6. Gibt es Cafés in Ihrer Stadt? Was kann man dort essen und trinken?

Aktivität 1. Suggestion: 1. Have students answer the questions at home. 2. Have students work in small groups to answer these questions. Ensure that they change the questions from the **Sie-**form to the **du-**form. In each case, follow up with a class discussion of students' preferences.

Aktivität 2 Ich habe Hunger. Ich habe Durst.

Wo gibt es was zu essen und zu trinken in Ihrer Stadt?

Vorschläge (*recommendations*) für Essen und Trinken: Pizza, Bier (vom Fass), griechische Küche, indische Spezialitäten (z.B. Lamm), internationale Küche (z.B. chinesische oder italienische Spezialitäten), ein Eis, eine Tasse Kaffee.

S1	S2
1. Ich habe Hunger. Ich habe Durst.	**2.** Magst du _____? Isst du gern _____? Möchtest du _____?
3. Ja. Wo kann man das bekommen?	**4.** Im _____.
5. Wann ist es geöffnet? Ist es heute geöffnet?	**6a.** Ich weiß es nicht genau. **6b.** Täglich von _____ bis _____.

Aktivität 2. Suggestion: You could use ads from restaurants in another city. These need not necessarily be from Europe. If you have a German language paper in your area, use that.

Geselligkeit in einer Kneipe

Die Speisekarte, bitte!

Die Speisekarte, bitte! Suggestion: Bring in copies of real menus from different types of restaurants.

Frisch vom Grill und aus der Pfanne

1. **Schweinshaxen** (1000 g) mit Sauerkraut und Kartoffelpüree	DM 17,50
2. **Spanferkel auf Biersauce** mit Bratkartoffeln und Krautsalat	DM 18,50
3. **Bayrischer Leberkäs'** mit Spiegelei und Bratkartoffeln	DM 13,50
4. **Nürnberger Rostbratwürst'l** mit Sauerkraut und Kartoffelpüree	DM 12,50
5. Argentinisches **Rumpsteak** (200 g) mit Zwiebeln, Champignons und Bratkartoffeln	DM 24,50
6. **Rumpsteak** nach Art des Hauses (200 g, scharf) mit Zwiebeln, Paprika, Pepperoni, Knoblauchbutter und Pommes frites	DM 24,50
7. **Roastbeef** (kalt) auf Salatkranz mit Remouladensauce und Bratkartoffeln	DM 18,50
8. Geschnetzeltes **«Züricher Art»** mit Reis oder Butterspätzle	DM 19,50
9. **Matjes** nach **«Hausfrauenart»** mit Apfelsahne, Zwiebelringe und Bratkartoffeln	DM 13,50
10. Bayrischer **Käseteller** mit Brot und Butter	DM 13,00
11. **Vegetarischer Teller** Gemüserosti auf Käsesauce	DM 10,50

Alle Gerichte wahlweise auch mit Pommes frites.

Unsere Salatbar

12. Salat **«Niçoise»** mit Gurken, Tomaten, grünem Salat, Paprika, Ei, Thunfisch und Oliven	DM 12,50
13. Kleiner **Salat** mit Gurken, Tomaten, grünem Salat und Paprika	DM 5,50
14. **Bauernsalat** mit Schafskäse, Tomaten, grünem Salat, Zwiebeln, Oliven, Kräutervinaigrette	DM 12,50
15. **«Joh. Matz»** mit frischen, knackigen Blattsalaten der Saison, Streifen vom Schweizer Käse, gekochtem Schinken, Tomaten, Gurken, Ei u. Island-Dressing	DM 12,50

Biere

Matz Pilsener naturtrüb	0,2 l	DM	2,40
Matz Pilsener naturtrüb	0,4 l	DM	4,80
Matz Pilsener naturtrüb **herb**	0,2 l	DM	2,40
Matz Pilsener naturtrüb **herb**	0,4 l	DM	4,80

Für den kleinen Hunger

16. **2 Münchener Weißwürste** mit süßem Senf und Brot	DM 7,50
17. **Sauerfleisch** mit Salatbeilage u. Bratkartoffeln	DM 10,50
18. Hausgebeizter **Graved Lachs** auf Kartoffelpuffer mit einer Senf-Dill-Honigsauce	DM 11,50
19. **Ofenkartoffel** mit Sour-Creme	DM 4,00
20. **Gulaschsuppe**	DM 5,50
21. **Chili «Con Carne»** dazu Baguette	DM 8,50

Dessert

22. **Rote Grütze** mit Vanillesauce	DM 6,50
23. **Kaiserschmarren** mit Kompott	DM 7,50
24. Kleiner **«Eiweißschock»** Magerquark mit frischen Früchten, Nüssen und Honig	DM 6,50
25. **Vanilleeis** mit heißen Himbeeren und Sahnehaube	DM 7,50
26. **Eisbecher «Matz Brauhaus»** Sahneeis mit Früchten	DM 6,50

Alkoholfreies

Coca Cola, Fanta, Sprite	0,2 l	DM	3,00
Tönissteiner Sprudel	0,25 l	DM	3,00
Apfelsaft	0,2 l	DM	3,50
Orangensaft	0,2 l	DM	3,50
Schweppes **Soda**	0,2 l	DM	3,50
Schweppes **Bitter Lemon**	0,2 l	DM	3,50
Schweppes **Tonic Water**	0,2 l	DM	3,50
Spezi	0,4 l	DM	6,00

JOH. MATZ · Gasthaus-Brauerei
Eppendorf
Robert-Koch-Straße 36 / Ecke Kümmellstraße
(gleich hinter C&A) · 20249 Hamburg
Tel. (040) 46 50 33 · Fax (040) 46 50 34
Geöffnet ab 17.00 Uhr
Warme Speisen 17.00–24.00 Uhr

Suchen Sie die Wörter auf der Speisekarte auf Seite 175. Können Sie vom Kontext erraten (*guess*), wie die Wörter auf Englisch heißen?

Suggestion: Have students prepare this for homework. Discuss in class.

1. __h__ die **Bratkartoffeln**
2. __k__ der **Champignon**
3. __e__ der **Eisbecher**
4. __d__ das **Gericht**
5. __i__ der **Grill**
6. __j__ der **Leberkäs**
7. __m__ die **Olive**
8. __b__ die **Paprika**
9. __o__ die **Pfanne**
10. __f__ die **Pommes frites**
11. __q__ der **Reis**
12. __c__ die **Sahne**
13. __r__ der **Salat**
14. __s__ das **Sauerkraut**
15. __l__ der **Senf**
16. __g__ das **Spiegelei**
17. __p__ der **Teller**
18. __t__ die **Tomate**
19. __a__ die **Weißwurst**
20. __n__ die **Zwiebel**

a. Bavarian white sausage
b. bell pepper
c. cream; whipped cream
d. dish (*a prepared item of food*)
e. dish of ice cream
f. french fries
g. fried egg
h. fried potatoes
i. grill; barbecue
j. meat loaf Bavarian style
k. mushroom
l. mustard
m. olive
n. onion
o. pan, skillet
p. plate
q. rice
r. salad; lettuce
s. sauerkraut
t. tomato

Eine Mahlzeit (*meal*) besteht oft aus mehreren Gängen (*courses*): Vorspeise, Hauptgericht, Beilage und Nachspeise. Ordnen Sie die Speisen in die richtige Kategorie ein!

alkoholfreies Bier	**Hühnerbrust**	**Pilsener**	**Schweinebraten**
Apfelstrudel	Kartoffelpüree	Pommes frites	**Suppe**
Brezeln	**Käsekuchen**	Reis	**Wein**
Eis	Krabbencocktail	Sauerkraut	**Wiener Schnitzel**
gemischter Salat	Lachs		

VORSPEISEN	HAUPTGERICHTE	BEILAGEN
Suppe	Hühnerbrust	Kartoffelpüree
Krabbencocktail	Lachs	Reis
Brezeln	Schweinebraten	Pommes frites
gemischter Salat	Wiener Schnitzel	Sauerkraut

NACHSPEISEN	GETRÄNKE
Apfelstrudel	Pilsener
Käsekuchen	alkoholfreies Bier
Eis	Wein

Every area of Germany has its own regional specialties. The menu shown in **Thema 2** features some typical Bavarian dishes. Favorites are **Schweinshaxen** (*pig's feet*), **Spanferkel** (*suckling pig*), **Leberkäs** (*a type of meat loaf*), and **Weißwurst** (*a type of veal sausage*). Meat is frequently pork (**Schweinefleisch**). Beef (**Rindfleisch**) is also found on menus but is much more expensive. Germans are becoming more diet-conscious; therefore, many restaurants are introducing lighter fare such as chicken breast (**Hühnerbrust**) and turkey (**Truthahn** or **Pute**). Favorite dessert items include **Rote Grütze**, a compote made from crushed strawberries, currants, and cherries, and—in Bavaria—**Kaiserschmarren**, a sweet crepe-like omelet.

Ein stolzer (*proud*) Wirt mit köstlichen (*delicious*) Gerichten aus seinem Restaurant

Aktivität 3 So viele Speisen!

Welche Speisen gehören nicht in die Kategorie?

BEISPIEL: Rumpsteak, Münchner Weißwürste, (Vegetarischer Teller)

1. Kleiner Salat, Käsekuchen, Bauernsalat
2. Weißwürste, Schweinshaxen, Pommes frites
3. Rote Grütze, Rumpsteak, Vanilleeis
4. Kartoffelpüree, Gulaschsuppe, Sauerkraut
5. Bier, Apfelsaft, Spiegelei

Aktivität 3. Suggestion: Have students work in pairs, taking turns saying the items in each line aloud and deciding on the correct answer. When the activity is completed, check it by calling on individuals for responses.

Aktivität 4 Was bestellen° Norbert und Dagmar?

° *are ordering*

Hören Sie zu, und ergänzen Sie die Tabelle.

	NORBERT	DAGMAR
Vorspeise	Gulaschsuppe	Gulaschsuppe
Hauptgericht	Spanferkel mit Bratkartoffeln	Nürnberger Rostbratwürst'l mit Kraut und Kartoffelpüree
Getränk	Bier	alkoholfreies Bier

Weiteres zum Thema Restaurant und Gerichte finden Sie bei ***Deutsch: Na klar!*** im World-Wide-Web unter www.mhhe.com/german.

Aktivität 5 Was sollen wir bestellen? 

Schauen Sie sich die Speisekarte im Thema 2 an, und besprechen Sie zu zweit oder zu dritt, was Sie bestellen möchten. Pro Person können Sie nur DM 35,– ausgeben.

BEISPIEL: Ich nehme Gulaschsuppe als Vorspeise. Als Hauptgericht nehme ich Weißwürste mit Senf und Brot. Und als Nachspeise nehme ich Kaiserschmarren mit Kompott.

Notieren Sie Ihre Bestellung:

Vorspeise: Summe:
Hauptgericht:
Nachspeise:

Aktivität 5. Suggestion: First have students scan the menu given earlier, or one that you have brought in. Have them jot down what they would order without spending more than 35 Marks. Then ask them to tell each other what they would like and how much it would cost. Have students report back to the class on what others have ordered. Challenge them to come up with the most interesting meal for the least amount of money.

Aktivität 6 Im Restaurant 

Bilden Sie kleine Gruppen. Eine Person spielt den Ober oder die Kellnerin und nimmt die Bestellungen der Gäste an.

S1		S2	
KELLNER/IN		GAST	
1.	Bitte schön. Was darf's sein?	**2.**	Ich möchte gern _____.
3.	Und zu trinken?	**4.**	Bringen Sie mir bitte _____.
5.	Sonst noch was? (*Anything else?*)	**6a.** **6b.**	Ja, _____. Nein, das ist alles.

Aktivität 6. Suggestion: Group students in fours. Have them choose one to be the server. They could use their food selections from the previous activity, so that they concentrate on their language rather than choosing the food. Discuss the **Sprachtipp** earlier in the chapter about addressing the server in a restaurant.

Thema 3

Im Restaurant

Welches Bild passt zu welchem Mini-Dialog?

Im Restaurant. Suggestion: You may need to point out certain clues to the students. For example, in A the woman is handing the waiter some money. The man in B has nothing but flowers on the table. The man standing in F is pointing to the chair in front of him. Have students act out the mini-dialogues after they have matched them with the pictures.

a.

b.

c.

1. b —Herr **Ober,** die **Speisekarte,** bitte!

2. d —Wir möchten **bestellen.**
—Ja, bitte, was **bekommen** Sie?
—Ich **nehme** die gegrillte Hühnerbrust.

3. a —Zahlen bitte!
—**Das macht zusammen** 58,40 Mark.
—60,– Mark.
—**Vielen Dank.**

4. f —**Entschuldigen Sie,** bitte! **Ist hier noch frei?**
—Nein, **hier ist besetzt,** aber **da drüben** ist **Platz.**

5. c —Herr Ober, ich habe **Messer, Löffel** und **Serviette,** aber keine **Gabel.**
—Und ich habe keine Serviette.

6. e —Hier ist es aber **ziemlich voll. Hoffentlich** müssen wir nicht lange auf einen Platz **warten.**

d.

e.

f.

Kulturtipp

In all but the most exclusive restaurants in German-speaking countries, it is acceptable for people to ask to share a table if it is very crowded. Simply ask: **Ist hier noch frei?** The answer might be: **Ja, hier ist noch frei.** Or: **Nein, hier ist besetzt.**

Aktivität 7 Im Brauhaus Matz

Zwei Freunde, Jens und Stefanie, sind im Brauhaus Matz. Hören Sie zu, und ergänzen Sie den Text mit Informationen aus dem Dialog.

Stefanie und Jens suchen einen Platz in einem Restaurant.[1] Es ist ziemlich voll.[2] Jens sieht zwei Leute an einem Tisch.[3] Da ist noch Platz für zwei Leute.[4] Er geht an den Tisch und fragt: „Ist hier noch frei?"[5] Die Antwort am ersten Tisch ist: „Nein".[6] Die Antwort am zweiten Tisch ist: „Ja".[7]

Aktivität 8 Ist hier noch frei? 

Bilden Sie mehrere Gruppen. Einige Personen suchen Platz.

S1	S2
1. Entschuldigen Sie. Ist hier noch frei?	**2a.** Ja, hier ist noch ______. **2b.** Nein, hier ist leider ______. Aber da drüben ist noch ______.
3a. Danke schön. **3b.** (*geht zu einem anderen Tisch*)	

Aktivität 8. Suggestion: Set up the classroom so that half the class is sitting in groups of two or three. The other students individually approach a group and initiate a conversation.

Kulturtipp

When adding up your restaurant bill (**Rechnung**), your waiter or waitress will often ask whether you want to pay separately (**getrennt**) or together (**zusammen**). When paying, you do not have to add a tip, as it is always included in your bill. The menu sometimes indicates this by stating:

Bedienungsgeld und Mehrwertsteuer enthalten.	*Tip (service fee) and value-added tax (federal sales tax) included.*

It is customary to round up the figures on your bill to the next mark or two, but this practice is entirely up to the individual.

HOTEL VIER JAHRESZEITEN
RESTAURANT HAERLIN
HAMBURG

Herr/Frau/Firma

GRILL

T63/1 13.04.92
RECHNUNG 3 03 193
SEITE 1 GÄSTEZAHL 2

2 KL. SALAT	7,00	14,00
1 KALBSSTEAK	64,00	64,00
1 HECHTSOUFFLE	56,00	56,00
1 DP. ESPRESSO	9,00	9,00
1 CAPPUCCINO	6,50	6,50
1 IPHÖFER BURG	13,50	13,50
2 TONIC WATER	6,00	12,00
1 CINZANO	11,00	11,00
SUMME:		186,00

INCL. 14,0% MWST: 22,84 DM

ES BEDIENTE SIE HERR SÖHLBRANDT

Aktivität 9 Wir möchten zahlen, bitte. 

Was haben diese Leute bestellt? Wie viel kostet es? Kreuzen Sie an, was Sie hören.

Aktivität 9. Follow-up: Put the activity and the dialogues in context by telling students about paying the bill in a German restaurant.

		GETRÄNKE		ESSEN		BETRAG
Dialog 1		2 Bier	x	Knackwürste*		DM 14,50
		3 Cola		Weißwürste		20,40
	X	3 Bier		Bockwürste†	x	24,50
			x	Sauerkraut		
				Brot		

* saveloy, a type of German sausage
† a type of German sausage similar to a hot dog in its flavor and consistency

		GETRÄNKE		ESSEN		BETRAG
Dialog 2		2 Tassen Tee		2 Stück Käsekuchen		DM 12,75
	X	2 Tassen Kaffee	X	1 Stück Käsekuchen		7,25
		1 Tasse Kaffee	X	1 Stück Obsttorte	X	17,45
Dialog 3		2 Bier	X	Leberknödlsuppe*		DM 70,40
	X	5 Bier	X	Schweinskotelett	X	78,40
		3 Bier	X	Brezeln		87,40
			X	Weißwürste		
				Sauerkraut		

Two-Way Prepositions. Suggestion: Review prepositions that take accusative only and dative only first. **Note:** The two-way prepositions refer primarily to location. Model the difference between using the dative or accusative and utilizing typical classroom situations, e.g., stand next to a table and say *Ich stehe am Tisch.* Move to the door . . . *Ich gehe an die Tür.*

Grammatik im Kontext

Two-Way Prepositions°

°Wechselpräpositionen

So far you have learned two kinds of prepositions: prepositions that must always be used with the accusative case and others that must always be used with the dative case.

In addition, a number of prepositions take either the dative or the accusative, depending on whether they describe a location or direction. The most common of these prepositions are:

an	at, near
auf	on, on top of, at
hinter	behind, in back of
in	in
neben	next to
über	above, over
unter	under, beneath, below; among
vor	in front of; before
zwischen	between

Auf dem Bauernhof kann man gut frisches Obst und Gemüse kaufen.

*liver dumpling soup

When answering the question **wo,** these prepositions take the dative case. When answering the question **wohin,** they take the accusative case.

WO?	STATIONARY LOCATION (DATIVE)
Wo kauft man Brot?	In **der** Bäckerei.
Wo zahlt der Kunde?	An **der** Kasse.
Wo kauft man frisches Gemüse?	Auf **dem** Bauernhof.
Wo soll ich warten?	Vor **dem** Geschäft.

WOHIN?	DIRECTION (ACCUSATIVE)
Wohin geht Frau Glättli?	In **die** Bäckerei.
Wohin geht der Kunde?	An **die** Kasse.
Wo gehst du hin?	Auf **den** Markt.
Wo geht Herr Sauer hin?	In **das Geschäft**.

The following contractions are common:

an dem → **am**	Das Kaufhaus steht **am** Markt.
an das → **ans**	Geh doch **ans** Fenster!
in dem → **im**	Frau Kraus isst **im** Restaurant.
in das → **ins**	Nikola geht gleich **ins** Geschäft.

Realia. *Café Derks* is located in Kleve. The ad is from the *Klever Wochenblatt.*

1. *specialty store*

Analyse

Suchen Sie in den folgenden Anzeigen Präpositionen mit Dativ- oder Akkusativobjekten. Ordnen Sie sie ein!

	WO? (DATIV)	WOHIN? (AKKUSATIV)
BEISPIEL:	im alten Forsthaus	

Analyse. Suggestion: Let students skim the ads first. The exercise can be done as homework or as class activity. Once all prepositional phrases have been identified, ask students to form simple content questions that would be answered by a phrase, like *Was kann man im alten Forsthaus machen?*

Restaurant
Schubert-Stüberln
Küchenchef
Franz Zimmer
hinter dem Burgtheater, vis-à-vis der Universität,
beim Dreimäderlhaus
Schreyvogelgasse 4, 1010 Wien
Telefon für Tischreservierung 63 71 87

Mach' Dir ein paar schöne Stunden...
geh' ins Kino

Kulinarische Notizen
Ein Brevier für Genießer.
Biergartenromantik im alten Forsthaus

Realia. *Kulinarische Notizen* is a regular newspaper section in the *Bonner Generalanzeiger.* It features an article describing what *Forsthaus Telegraph,* a restaurant near Bonn, has to offer in the way of scenic beauty as well as gastronomic delicacies. The *Olympia Einkaufszentrum* is located in Munich. *Schubert-Stüberln* is located in Vienna.

Übung 1 Am Feierabend°

Was machst du gern/oft/manchmal/nie am Feierabend?

BEISPIEL: S1: Gehst du gern ins Café?
S2: Ja, ich gehe gern ins Café.
oder Nein, ich gehe nicht gern ins Café.

der Biergarten
das Café
das Fitnesszentrum
das Kino
die Kneipe
das Restaurant
der Sportclub
die Stadt
der Supermarkt
das Theater
?

after work

Übung 1. Suggestion: Have students working in pairs ask each other questions and note their partner's answers. Have several students report back about what their partners like or do not like to do.

Übung 2 Wo kauft Mark ein?

Mark muss heute einkaufen. Hier ist sein Einkaufszettel. Wo gibt es das?

BEISPIEL: Käsekuchen → Käsekuchen gibt es in der Konditorei.

der Supermarkt
die Metzgerei
die Buchhandlung
der Markt
das Schuhgeschäft
die Bäckerei
die Konditorei

Einkaufszettel
250 g Aufschnitt
Käsekuchen
150 g Emmentaler Käse
6 Brötchen
12 Würstchen zum Grillen
1 Pfund Kaffee
Schwarzbrot
2 Flaschen Sprudel[1]
4 Tomaten
nicht vergessen:
Wörterbuch
Tennisschuhe

1. *mineral water*

Übung 3 Ein Einkaufszentrum

Wie kommt man dahin, und was kann man dort machen? Schauen Sie sich die Werbung an, und beantworten Sie die Fragen.

BEISPIEL: Wie kommt man zum Einkaufszentrum Spahn? → Man kommt mit dem Bus dahin.

Realia. This ad is from the *Frankfurter Rundschau.*

Suggestion: Have students work in pairs, taking turns asking and answering the questions.

1. Mit welcher Buslinie kann man dahin fahren?
2. Wo gibt es etwas zu essen?
3. Wo kann man Lampen kaufen?
4. Wo kann man parken?
5. Wo gibt es Geschenke zu kaufen?
6. Wohin kann man seine Kinder bringen?

NÜTZLICHE WÖRTER
die Boutique
der Bus
die Buslinie
die Cafeteria
der Parkplatz
die Spielecke
das Studio

To suggest to a friend that you do something together, you can use the expression **Lass uns (doch) . . . :**

Lass uns doch ins Restaurant gehen!	*Let's go to a restaurant!*
Lass uns türkisch essen!	*Let's eat Turkish food!*

Sprachtipp. Point Out: **Lass** is the informal imperative form of **lassen.** Point out the alternative spelling *laß* in the realia.

Realia. *Der Magen knurrt mir* translates "My stomach is growling." Use the "*Knurr! Knuurr!*" realia, a faxable invitation and response form, to practice *Lass uns . . .* in preparation for **Übung 4.** One student proposes, "Lass uns essen. Sag mir, wie." Another student responds, "Lass uns vegetarisch essen." Several expressions (*Ohne misch = ohne mich; Wenisch = wenig; Köstlisch = köstlich; Gar nisch = gar nicht*); are deliberately misspelled in order to rhyme with words like *Griechisch, Hektisch,* and *Fisch.*

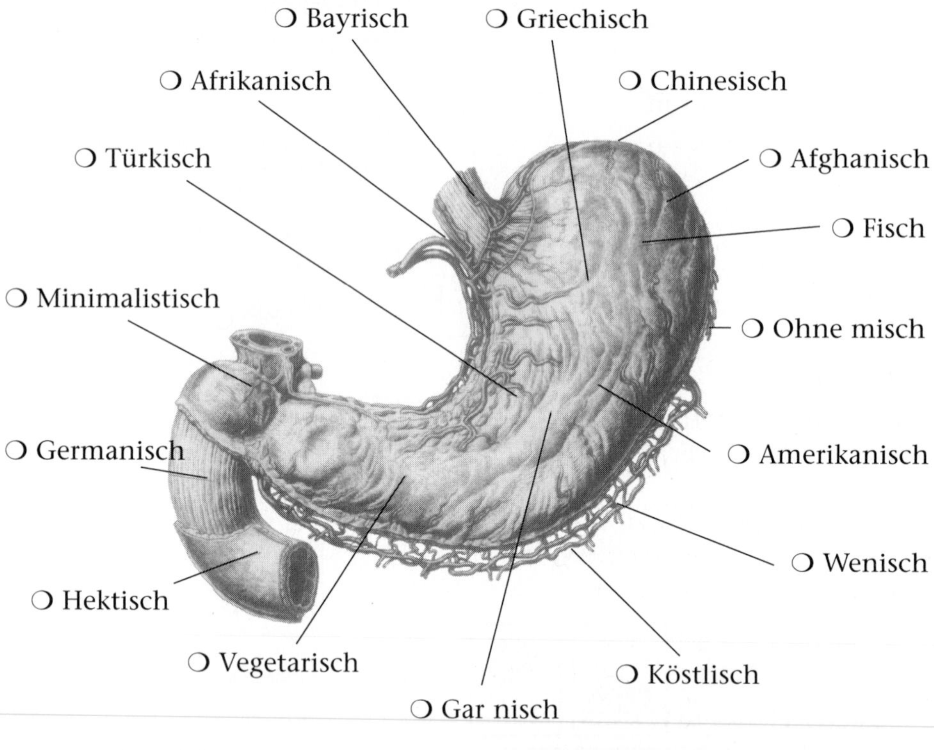

Übung 4 Wo sollen wir nur parken?

Sie und ein Freund / eine Freundin haben heute Nachmittag viel vor. Sie wollen mit dem Wagen in die Stadt. Wo können Sie parken?

BEISPIEL: Sie wollen ins Kino. →
Lass uns hinter dem Kino parken.

1. Sie wollen ins Kino.
2. Sie müssen zum Bahnhof (*train station*).
3. Sie gehen ins Theater.
4. Sie wollen im Kaufhaus und auf dem Markt einkaufen.
5. Sie wollen im Stadtpark spazieren gehen.
6. Sie wollen ins Museum.
7. Sie wollen in den Bierkeller im Rathaus (*town hall*).

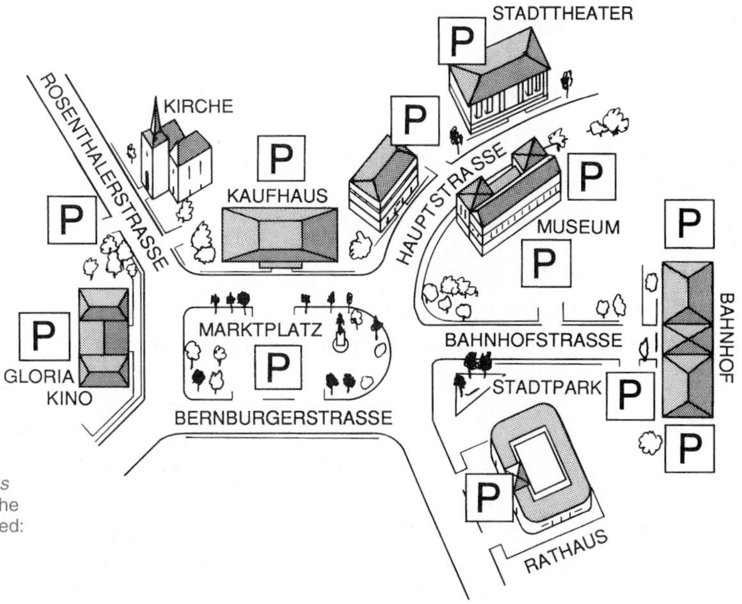

Übung 4. Suggestion: The exercise will elicit a variety of answers. Encourage students to make counterproposals: *Lass uns hinter dem Kino parken. Nein, lass uns vor dem Kino parken.* The drawing also lends itself to describing where something is located: *Wo liegt der Bahnhof?*

Describing Location

Describing Location. Suggestion: These verbs can be practiced first by using simple classroom situations: *Wo liegt Jeffs Buch? (unter dem Tisch); Wo steht der Stuhl? (neben der Tur).*

The verbs **hängen, liegen, sitzen, stecken,** and **stehen** can indicate where someone or something is located.

hängen	to be (hanging)
liegen	to be (lying)
sitzen	to be (sitting)
stecken	to be (inserted)
stehen	to be (standing)

When a two-way preposition is used with one of these verbs indicating location, the object of the preposition is in the dative case. Remember to use the interrogative pronoun **wo** to ask where someone or something is located.

—**Wo hängt** das Bild? —Es hängt **im** Museum.	*Where is the picture hanging?* *It's hanging in the museum.*
—**Wo liegt** die Rechnung? —Sie liegt **neben** der Serviette.	*Where is the bill?* *It's next to the napkin.*
—**Wo sitzen** die Studenten? —Sie sitzen **auf einer** Bank **im** Park.	*Where are the students sitting?* *They're sitting on a bench in the park.*
—**Wo steckt** der Schlüssel? —Er steckt **im** Wagen.	*Where is the key?* *It's in the car.*
—**Wo steht** der Wagen? —Er steht **auf dem** Parkplatz **beim** Markt.	*Where is the car?* *It's in the parking lot by the market.*

Übung 5 Idylle im Park

Claudia und Jürgen verbringen (*are spending*) einen Samstagnachmittag im Park. Beantworten Sie die Fragen zum Bild.

Übung 5. Follow-up: Have students write a paragraph describing the *Idylle im Park.*

Additional activity: Bring in pictures from your picture file and have students describe where things are located.

1. Wo liegt Jürgen?
2. Wo sitzt Claudia?
3. Wo hängt eine Spinne?
4. Wo sitzt der Hund?
5. Wo sitzt der Vogel?
6. Wo steht der Picknickkorb?
7. Wo steckt die Weinflasche?
8. Wo liegt das Buch?

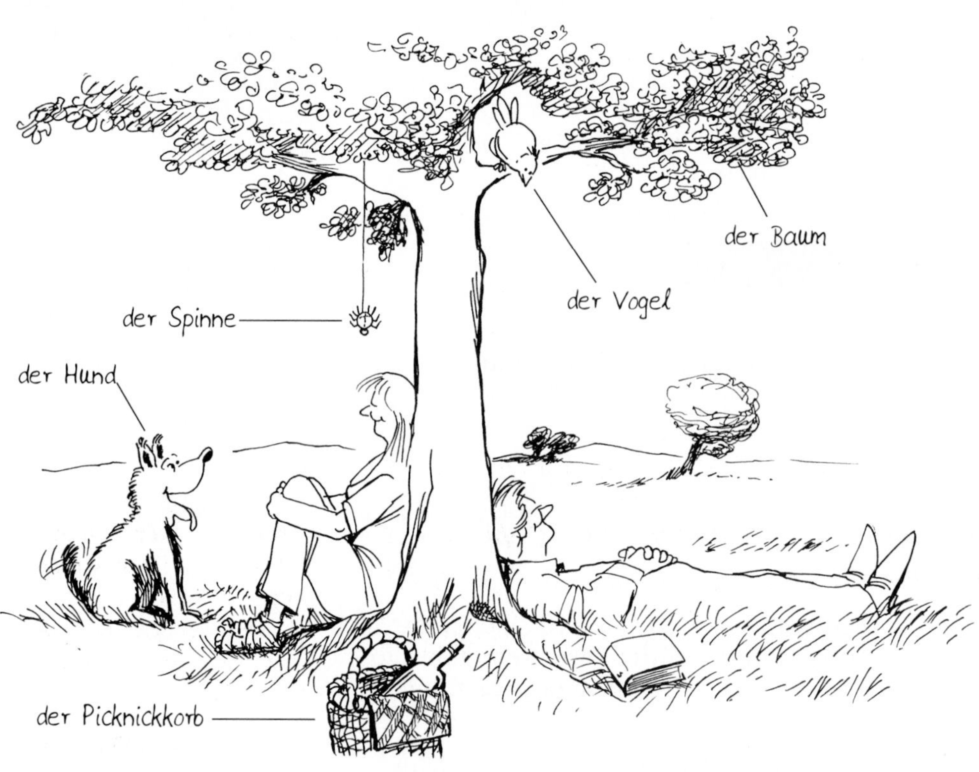

Übung 6 In einem Gartenlokal°

pub with a beer garden

Ergänzen Sie das passende Verb: **hängen, liegen, sitzen, stecken** oder **stehen.**

Andreas und Thomas _____ in einem Gartenlokal.[1] Das Lokal heißt „Im Forsthaus". Es _____ sehr schön im Grünen nicht weit von Bonn.[2] Vor dem Lokal _____ viele Autos.[3] Im Biergarten _____ Papierlaternen.[4] Auf dem Tisch vor Andreas und Thomas _____ zwei Gläser Bier.[5] Unter dem Tisch direkt neben ihnen _____ ein Dackel (*dachshund*).[6] Er gehört zu den Gästen am Nebentisch. Um den Tisch _____ vier Leute.[7] Der Ober _____ jetzt neben Andreas.[8] Ein Bleistift (*pencil*) _____ in seiner Tasche.[9] Die Rechnung _____ schon auf dem Tisch.[10]

Describing Placement

The verbs **legen, setzen,** and **stellen,** as well as **hängen** and **stecken,** can indicate where someone or something is being put or placed.

hängen	to hang, to put/place	**stecken**	to insert, to put/place
legen	to lay, to put/place	**stellen**	to stand, to put/place
setzen	to set, to put/place		

When a two-way preposition is used with one of these verbs indicating placement, the object of the preposition is in the accusative case. Remember to use the interrogative pronoun **wohin** to ask where someone or something is being put or placed.

—**Wohin hängt** der Mann den Mantel?	*Where is the man hanging the coat?*
—Er hängt ihn **an den** Haken.	*He's hanging it on the hook.*
—**Wo legt** der Kellner die Rechnung **hin?**	*Where is the waiter putting the bill?*
—Er legt sie **auf den** Tisch.	*He's laying it on the table.*
—**Wohin setzt** die Frau das Kind?	*Where is the woman putting the child?*
—Sie setzt es **auf den** Stuhl.	*She's putting him/her on the chair.*
—**Wo steckt** die Kellnerin das Geld **hin**?	*Where is the waitress putting the money?*
—Sie steckt es **in die** Tasche.	*She's putting it in the purse.*
—**Wohin stellt** der Kellner den Stuhl?	*Where is the waiter putting the chair?*
—Er stellt ihn **an den** Tisch.	*He's placing it at the table.*

Sprachtipp

The verb **setzen** is frequently used with a personal pronoun that reflects the subject of the sentence. Used in this reflexive way, the verb means *to sit down.*

Ich setze **mich** an den Tisch.
I sit down at the table.
Wir setzen **uns.**
We sit down.

In the third-person singular and plural this reflexive pronoun is always **sich.**

Die Studenten setzen **sich** auf die Bank.
The students sit down on the bench.

Übung 7 Im Lokal

Andreas trifft ein paar Freunde im „Kartoffelkeller". Ergänzen Sie die Sätze mit **hängen, legen, setzen, stecken** oder **stellen.**

1. Andreas und drei Studienfreunde _____ sich an einen Tisch beim Fenster.
2. Andreas _____ seinen Rucksack unter den Stuhl.
3. Michael _____ seinen Rucksack an seinen Stuhl.
4. Der Kellner kommt nach langem Warten und _____ die Speisekarte auf den Tisch.
5. Die vier bestellen zuerst etwas zu trinken. Der Kellner _____ vier Colas auf den Tisch.
6. Da kommt noch ein Freund, Phillipp, an den Tisch zu ihnen. Andreas _____ noch einen Stuhl an den Tisch.
7. Phillipp _____ sich neben Andreas.
8. Er _____seine Bücher auf den Tisch.
9. Seine Handschuhe (*gloves*) _____ er in seinen Rucksack.

Übung 8 Ein Abend im Kartoffelkeller!

Ergänzen Sie die Sätze mit einem passenden Verb: **liegen, sitzen, stehen, legen, setzen** oder **stellen.**

1. Im Zentrum von Berlin _____ das Restaurant „Kartoffelkeller".
2. Im Restaurant ist es heute sehr voll. An allen Tischen _____ schon Leute, und einige suchen noch Platz.
3. Ein paar Leute _____ draußen vor dem Lokal und warten, dass jemand geht.
4. Man _____ hier auch sehr gemütlich. Und die Preise sind nicht so hoch. Deshalb ist es unter Studenten populär.
5. Endlich kommt eine Kellnerin und _____ die Speisekarte auf den Tisch.
6. Auf der Speisekarte _____: „Spezialität unseres Hauses ist Kartoffelsuppe mit Brot."
7. Die Kellnerin _____ neben dem Tisch und wartet auf die Bestellung.
8. Am Nebentisch _____ einige Studenten und diskutieren laut.
9. Ein Student _____ sich an die Theke (*counter*) und bestellt ein Bier.
10. Der Kellner _____ das Bier vor ihn auf die Theke.

The verb **stehen** is used idiomatically to say that something has been stated (in print).

—Hier gibt es auch vegetarische Kost.
They have vegetarian food here.
—Wo **steht** das?
Where does it say that?

Additional Activity. Have students work in pairs with one student doing what the other student tells him/her to do. Put the following example on the board: *Leg das Buch bitte unter den Tisch!*

Übung 9 Die verlorene Theaterkarte

Michael kann seine Theaterkarte nicht finden. Wo steckt sie wohl? Eine Person denkt sich aus, wo die Karte ist. Die anderen im Kurs müssen raten (*guess*), wo die Karte ist.

BEISPIEL: S1: Steckt die Theaterkarte in seiner Hosentasche?
S2: Nein.
S1: Ist die Theaterkarte auf dem Schreibtisch?
S2: Nein. (usw.)

Übung 9. Suggestion: Have students say how Michael should clean up his room by saying where he should put things.

Expressing Time with Prepositions

The following two-way prepositions, when expressing time, always take the dative case:

vor drei Tagen	*three days ago*
vor dem Theater	*before the play*
in einer Stunde	*in one hour*
zwischen 5 und 7 Uhr	*between 5 and 7 o'clock*

You have learned several other prepositions expressing time—not two-way prepositions—that also take the dative case.

nach dem Theater	*after the play*
seit einem Jahr	*for a year*
von 5 bis 7 Uhr	*from 5 to 7 o'clock*

The prepositions **um** and **gegen** always take the accusative.

bis (um) 5 Uhr	*until 5 o'clock*
(so) gegen 7 Uhr	*around 7 o'clock*

In German, expressions of time always precede expressions of place.

Vor und nach dem Theater an die schönste Bar in der Stadt

TIME PLACE
Wir kommen so gegen zehn Uhr nach Hause.

Übung 10 Was machst du gewöhnlich um diese Zeit?

Arbeiten Sie mit einem Partner / einer Partnerin zusammen.

BEISPIEL: S1: Was machst du nach dem Deutschkurs?
S2: Da gehe ich in die Bibliothek.

von _____ bis _____	vor _____	arbeiten	ausgehen
zwischen _____ und _____	nach _____	schlafen	einkaufen gehen
so gegen _____	?	essen	fernsehen
um _____			?

Expressing Events in the Past

Like English, German has several tenses to express events in the past. The most common are the simple past tense (**das Imperfekt**) and the present perfect tense (**das Perfekt**). The present perfect tense, which will be introduced in **Kapitel 7,** is preferred in conversation, while the simple past is primarily used in writing. In the case of **haben, sein,** and the modal verbs, however, the simple past is more common in conversation. The simple past tense of all other verbs will be introduced in **Kapitel 10.**

The Simple Past Tense of *sein* and *haben*

	sein	**haben**
ich	war	hatte
du	warst	hattest
er/sie/es	war	hatte
wir	waren	hatten
ihr	wart	hattet
sie	waren	hatten
Sie	waren	hatten

Realia. This cartoon appeared in *Bunte* magazine.

Analyse

Read the cartoon.

- What forms of the verbs **haben** and **sein** are used?
- The answer to the friend's question contains no verb or object because they are understood. What would the complete sentence be?
- How would the friend pose her questions if the speakers were adults addressing each other formally?

1. *difficulties*

Übung 11 Ausreden° und Erklärungen°

excuses / explanations

Übung 11. Suggestion: Have students work in pairs.

Ergänzen Sie **haben** oder **sein** im Imperfekt.

1. A: Warum _____ Sie gestern und vorgestern nicht im Deutschkurs, Herr Miller?
   B: Es tut mir leid, Herr Professor, aber meine Großmutter _____ krank (*sick*).
2. C: Rolf, _____ du gestern Abend noch in der Bibliothek?
   D: Nein, die _____ geschlossen. Außerdem _____ ich keine Lust zum Arbeiten. Ich _____ aber im Kino!
3. E: Warum _____ Michael und Peter nicht auf der Party bei Ulla?
   F: Sie _____ keine Zeit.
4. G: Ihr _____ doch gestern im Café Käuzchen, nicht?
   H: Nein, wir _____ im Café Kadenz. Im Käuzchen _____ es zu voll.
   G: Wie _____ es denn?
   H: Die Musik _____ gut, aber der Kaffee _____ schlecht.
5. I: Frau Steinmetz, warum _____ Sie gestern nicht in der Vorlesung?
   J: Ich _____ beim Zahnarzt (*dentist*). Ich _____ Zahnschmerzen (*toothache*).

Übung 12 Wo warst du denn? 

Fragen Sie Ihren Partner / Ihre Partnerin!

BEISPIEL: S1: Wo warst du denn Freitagabend?
S2: Da war ich im Theater.
S1: Wie war's denn?
S2: Sehr langweilig.

WO	WIE
auf einer Party	langweilig
bei Freunden	interessant
im Kino	nicht besonders gut
im Restaurant	schön
zu Hause	?
auf dem Sportplatz	
im Theater	
?	

Übung 12. Suggestion: You may wish to reuse this activity after introducing the simple past tense of modals. Have students expand on their answers: S1: *Wo warst du denn heute Nachmittag?* S2: *Ich war im Kino.* S1: *Wie war's denn?* S2: *Nicht besonders gut. Ich konnte den Film nicht verstehen.*

The Simple Past Tense of Modals

	dürfen	**können**	**mögen**	**müssen**	**sollen**	**wollen**
ich	dur**f**te	ko**n**nte	m**o**chte	mu**ss**te	so**ll**te	w**o**llte
du	dur**f**test	ko**n**ntest	m**o**chtest	mu**ss**test	so**ll**test	w**o**lltest
er, sie, es	dur**f**te	ko**n**nte	m**o**chte	mu**ss**te	so**ll**te	w**o**llte
wir	dur**f**ten	ko**n**nten	m**o**chten	mu**ss**ten	so**ll**ten	w**o**llten
ihr	dur**f**tet	ko**n**ntet	m**o**chtet	mu**ss**tet	so**ll**tet	w**o**lltet
sie	dur**f**ten	ko**n**nten	m**o**chten	mu**ss**ten	so**ll**ten	w**o**llten
Sie	dur**f**ten	ko**n**nten	m**o**chten	mu**ss**ten	so**ll**ten	w**o**llten

As with **haben** and **sein,** the first- and third- persons singular and first- and third- persons plural of the simple past tense of modals are identical. Note also that modals have no umlaut in the simple past tense.

Peter **wollte** gestern in die Disko. Er **musste** aber zu Hause bleiben.	*Peter wanted to go to the disco yesterday. But he had to stay home.*
Wir **konnten** keinen Parkplatz finden.	*We couldn't find a parking place.*

Suggestion: You may want to point out to students the alternate spelling of the preterite of *müssen* with *ß* instead of *ss.*

Übung 13 Kleine Probleme

Ergänzen Sie die fehlenden Modalverben im Imperfekt.

Gestern Abend waren wir im Theater. Wir _____ (wollen) in der Nähe vom Theater parken.[1] Da _____ (dürfen) man aber nicht parken.[2] Wir _____ (können) keinen Parkplatz auf der Straße finden.[3] Deshalb _____ (müssen) wir ins Parkhaus fahren.[4] Katrin _____ (sollen) vor dem Theater auf uns warten.[5] Sie _____ (müssen) lange warten.[6] Nach dem Theater _____ (wollen) wir noch ins Café Kadenz.[7] Da _____ (können) wir keinen Platz bekommen.[8] Wir _____ (müssen) also nach Hause fahren.[9]

Übung 14 Bei mir zu Hause

Wie war das bei Ihnen zu Hause?

BEISPIEL: Als (*as a*) Kind mochte ich keinen Fisch essen.

ich	dürfen	Fisch/Brokkoli/Spinat essen
wir Kinder	können	Gemüse essen
mein Vater	sollen	am Wochenende den Wagen waschen
?	mögen	jeden Tag Hausaufgaben machen
	müssen	abends in Ruhe die Zeitung lesen
	wollen	abends nicht fernsehen
		nur am Wochenende ins Kino gehen
		um zehn im Bett sein
		?

Übung 15 Hin und her: Warum nicht? 

Fragen sie Ihren Partner / Ihre Partnerin, warum die folgenden Leute nicht erschienen sind (*didn't show up*).

BEISPIEL: S1: Warum war Andreas gestern Vormittag nicht in der Vorlesung?
S2: Er hatte keine Lust.

PERSON	WANN	WO	WARUM
Andreas	gestern Vormittag	in der Vorlesung	keine Lust haben
Anke	Montag	zu Hause	arbeiten müssen
Frank	gestern Abend	auf der Party	keine Zeit
Yeliz	heute Morgen	in der Vorlesung	krank sein
Mario	vorgestern	im Café	kein Geld haben
Ihr Partner / Ihre Partnerin			

Sprache im Kontext

Zuschauen

Vorschau

Beantworten Sie diese Frage, bevor Sie die Werbung sehen. Was denken Sie sich, wenn Sie auf der Straße eine junge Frau mit einem älteren Mann zusammen sehen?

- Ich denke mir nichts dabei. Es ist mir ganz egal. □
- Ich meine, dass da ein Vater mit seiner Tochter spazieren geht. □
- Ich denke: „Wie nett! Eine junge Frau hilft einem alten Mann auf der Straße." □
- Ich frage mich: „Was sieht eine so junge Frau in einen so alten Mann?" □
- ? □

Visa

Arbeit mit dem Videotext

Sehen Sie sich jetzt die Werbung an, und beantworten Sie die Fragen.

A. **1.** Wie heißt die Frau?
2. Was sagt der Mann, als er zahlen möchte?
3. Der Mann fragt: „Was machen wir jetzt?" Wie antwortet die Frau auf diese Frage?
4. Warum essen die beiden in einem Restaurant?

B. **1.** In dem Raum sehen Sie ganz kurz zwei Frauen. Die eine Frau kommentiert: „Es könnte glatt (*easily*) der Vater sein." Schreiben Sie den Dialog weiter.
2. Der Slogan für Visa lautet: „Die Freiheit nehme ich mir". In verschiedenen Szenen sieht man eine Art von „Freiheit". Beschreiben Sie eine Art von Freiheit, die Sie in der Werbung sehen.
3. Wie finden Sie diese Werbung? Hat man mehr Freiheit, wenn man eine Kreditkarte hat?

Lesen

Zum Thema

In meiner Freizeit. Beantworten Sie die folgenden Fragen. Vergleichen Sie dann Ihre Antworten im Plenum (*with the whole group*). Gibt es Gemeinsames (*commonalities*)? Was für ein Bild ergibt sich über die Freizeit?

1. Wohin gehen Studenten und Studentinnen, wenn sie etwas Freizeit zwischen Lehrveranstaltungen (*classes*) haben? am Abend? am Wochenende?
2. Wohin gehen Sie, wenn Sie etwas Freizeit haben und etwas trinken möchten?
3. Lesen Sie Zeitungen oder Zeitschriften (*magazines*) in Ihrer Freizeit? Wenn ja, welche? Wo lesen Sie sie?
4. Wie oft schreiben Sie Briefe? Wo schreiben Sie sie?
5. Gibt es ein populäres Lokal in Ihrer Nähe, wo man einen guten Kaffee oder Tee trinken kann?
6. Wo gehen Sie hin, wenn Sie Ruhe haben möchten?
7. Was kann man alles in einem Café machen? Diskutieren Sie im Plenum.

The First Coffeehouse

Legend has it that when the Turkish army fled Vienna in 1683, they left behind sacks of coffee beans. Though no one knows for sure who got the coffee, Georg Franz Kolschitzky is said to have been awarded 500 sacks for his service during the siege of Vienna; the story goes that he opened the first coffeehouse. The earliest official records, however, show that Johannes Diodato was awarded a license to sell coffee on January 17, 1685.

Weiteres zum Thema Kaffeehäuser und Cafés finden Sie bei ***Deutsch: Na klar!*** im World-Wide-Web unter www.mhhe.com/german.

Auf den ersten Blick

Auf den ersten Blick. Suggestion: Have students do this for homework in preparation for discussion of the text. Students compare their lists of cognates and compound words in class with a partner. Alternately, have students complete **Auf den ersten Blick** in class, and do the **Zum Text** section as homework.

A. The following text on cafés in Vienna contains many cognates and other words that look similar in English and German. Scan the text and make a list of such words.

BEISPIEL: traditionell

B. Now scan the text for compound words. Say the words aloud and try to identify their components. Can you guess their meaning from the components?

BEISPIEL: das Kaffeehaus = Kaffee + Haus = *coffeehouse, café*

Kaffeehäuser

Das Kaffeehaus ist für den Wiener der traditionelle Treffpunkt untertags. Hier kannst du stundenlang in Ruhe bei einem Kaffee sitzen, Zeitung lesen (in fast allen „Alt-Wiener-Kaffeehäusern" liegen internationale Zeitungen aus), mit jemandem plaudern,[1] Schach[2] oder—in manchen Kaffeehäusern—auch Billard spielen. Man trinkt natürlich Kaffee. Den großen oder den kleinen Braunen oder Schwarzen oder die Melange (ein Milchkaffee). Kleine Imbisse sind zu haben, aber auch die Kaffeehaus-küche sollte man nicht unterschätzen. Allerdings sind die Preise wegen[3] der kalkulierten langen Aufenthaltszeit[4] des Gastes höher als[5] im Beisl.[6]

Aus *live Wien für junge Leute,* Vienna Tourist Board

1. *chat* or *gossip*
2. *chess*
3. *because of*
4. *stay*
5. höher . . . *higher than*
6. *restaurant (Austrian), similar to a* Kneipe

Zum Text

A. Was kann man in einem Kaffeehaus machen? Steht das im Text?

	STEHT IM TEXT	STEHT NICHT IM TEXT
1. Briefe schreiben	☐	☐
2. Kaffee trinken	☐	☐
3. Musik spielen	☐	☐
4. Zeitung lesen	☐	☐
5. etwas essen	☐	☐
6. Schach oder Billard spielen	☐	☐
7. Klavier (*piano*) spielen	☐	☐
8. stundenlang plaudern	☐	☐

Zum Text A. Suggestion: Various students should formulate the questions for the rest of the class, e.g., *Kann man im Kaffeehaus Briefe schreiben?*

B. Nennen Sie drei Kaffeegetränke.

C. Vokabelübung

1. Bilden Sie Komposita (*compound words*). Wählen Sie Wortteile aus jeder Spalte (*column*).

BEISPIEL: Kaffee + -häuser = Kaffeehäuser

A		B
Kaffee		-punkt
Treff		-lang
Milch	+	-häuser
unter		-kaffee
stunden		-schätzen

2. Ergänzen Sie den Text mit den Komposita.

Lotte und ich treffen uns jeden Dienstag in der Stadt. Unser normaler _____ ist ein Kaffeehaus im ersten Bezirk.[a]* Es gibt sehr viele _____ in Wien.[b] Dort kann man _____ sitzen.[c] Ich trinke immer einen _____.[d] Die Wiener sagen „Melange" dazu. Manchmal esse ich auch dort. Es ist nicht schlecht. Man soll das Essen in den Kaffeehäusern nicht _____.[e] Es kostet allerdings mehr als in einem Restaurant oder Beisl, weil die Aufenthaltszeit normalerweise länger ist.

Zum Text C. Suggestion: Have students work in pairs to complete this exercise. Check responses quickly and have students use the compound nouns in the **Lückentext** that follows.

Sprechen und Schreiben

Aktivität 1 Ein Literatenkaffeehaus in Wien

Es kommen viele berühmte (*famous*) Leute ins Literatenkaffeehaus. Spielen Sie eine Szene in kleinen Gruppen. S1 spielt den Kellner / die Kellnerin. S2, S3 und S4 sind berühmte Personen. Können die anderen erraten (*guess*), wer Sie sind? Sagen Sie den Namen nicht, aber benehmen (*act*) Sie sich wie diese Person.

Aktivität 1. Suggestion: Have students focus on famous people from the German-speaking world. Brainstorm and come up with a list of people and their characteristics: who they are, what they do, what they like and dislike. Assign students the task of finding information about one of the people, reporting briefly during the next class.

Aktivität 2 Ihr Lieblingslokal

Schreiben Sie einen Absatz (*paragraph*) über Ihr Lieblingslokal. Wo liegt es? Was machen Sie dort? Was mögen Sie? Warum? Wie oft gehen Sie dorthin? Wie ist die Atmosphäre? Was machen Sie dort?

*The First District in Vienna is in the center of the city.

Wortschatz

Lokale — Eating and Drinking Establishments

das **Café, -s**	café
die **Gaststätte, -n**	full-service restaurant
der **Imbiss, -e***	fast-food stand
die **Kneipe, -n**	pub, bar
das **Lokal, -e**	restaurant, pub, bar
das **Restaurant, -s**	restaurant

Im Restaurant — In the Restaurant

Gänge — Courses

die **Vorspeise, -n**	appetizer
das **Hauptgericht, -e**	main dish
die **Beilage, -n**	side dish
die **Nachspeise, -n**	dessert
der **Nachtisch, -e**	dessert

Getränke — Beverages

Bier vom Fass*	draft beer
das **Pilsener, -**	Pilsner beer
der **Wein, -e**	wine

Speisen — Foods

die **Bratkartoffeln** (*pl.*)	fried potatoes
die **Brezel, -n**	pretzel
der **Champignon, -s**	mushroom
der **Eisbecher, -**	dish of ice cream
die **Hühnerbrust**	chicken breast
der **Käsekuchen**	cheese cake
der **Leberkäs**	meat loaf (*Bavarian style*)
die **Olive, -n**	olive
die **Paprika**	bell pepper
die **Pommes frites** (*pl.*)	french fries
der **Reis**	rice
die **Sahne**	cream; whipped cream
der **Salat, -e**	salad; lettuce
das **Sauerkraut**	sauerkraut
der **Schweinebraten, -**	pork roast
der **Senf**	mustard
das **Spiegelei, -er**	fried egg (*sunny-side up*)
die **Suppe, -n**	soup
die **Tomate, -n**	tomato
die **Weißwurst, ¨e**	white sausage
das **Wiener Schnitzel, -**	Wiener schnitzel, breaded veal cutlet
die **Zwiebel, -n**	onion

Sonstige Substantive — Other Nouns

die **Bedienung**	service
der **Biergarten, ¨**	beer garden
die **Gabel, -n**	fork
das **Gericht, -e**	dish (*of prepared food*)
der **Grill**	grill, barbeque
der **Kellner, -** / die **Kellnerin, -nen**	waiter / waitress / server
die **Küche**	food, cuisine; kitchen
der **Löffel, -**	spoon
das **Messer, -**	knife
der **Ober, -**	waiter
die **Pfanne, -n**	pan
der **Platz, ¨e**	place, seat
die **Rechnung, -en**	bill
der **Ruhetag, -e**	day that a business is closed
die **Serviette, -n**	napkin
die **Speisekarte, -n**	menu
der **Teller, -**	plate

Verben — Verbs

bekommen	to get
Was bekommen Sie?	What will you have?
bestellen	to order
entschuldigen	to excuse
Entschuldigen Sie!	Excuse me!
hängen	to hang; to be hanging
lassen	to let
Lass uns (doch) . . .*	Let's . . .
legen	to lay, put (*in a lying position*)
liegen	to lie; to be located
setzen	to set; put (*in a sitting position*)
sitzen	to sit
stecken	to insert/put (*inside*); to be (*inside*)
stehen	to stand; to be located

* See Appendix E for alternate spelling.

stellen	to stand up; place, put (*in a standing position*)
warten	to wait

Adjektive und Adverbien — Adjectives and Adverbs

alkoholfrei	nonalcoholic
besetzt	occupied, taken
Hier ist besetzt.	This place is taken.
da drüben	over there
frei	free; available
Ist hier noch frei?	Is this place taken?
geöffnet	open
geschlossen	closed
getrennt	separate(ly)
hoffentlich	I hope
täglich	daily
vegetarisch	vegetarian
voll	full; crowded
ziemlich	somewhat, rather
zusammen	together
Das macht zusammen . . .	The total is . . .

Wechselpräpositionen — Dative/Accusative Prepositions

an	at, on, to, near
auf	on, on top of, at
hinter	behind, in back of
in	in; to (*a place*)
neben	next to, beside
über	over, above
unter	under, below, beneath; among
vor	before, in front of
zwischen	between

Präpositionen (Temporal) — Prepositions (Temporal)

bis (um): bis (um) fünf Uhr	till: till five o'clock
(so) gegen: (so) gegen fünf Uhr	around/about: around five o'clock
in (+ *Dat.*): **in zwei Tagen**	in: in two days
nach: nach Dienstag	after: after Tuesday
seit: seit zwei Jahren	since, for: for two years
von: von zwei bis drei Uhr	from: from two to three o'clock
vor (+ *Dat.*): **vor zwei Tagen**	ago: two days ago
zwischen: zwischen zwei und drei Uhr	between: between two and three o'clock

Sonstiges — Other

Vielen Dank!	Many thanks!
zum Mitnehmen	(food) "to go"; take-out

Lernziele

Use this checklist to verify that you can now . . .

- ☐ identify various types of eating and drinking establishments found in German-speaking countries.
- ☐ say what foods you like or dislike.
- ☐ order food and drink from a menu in a German restaurant.
- ☐ identify various German foods.
- ☐ describe location or direction, using two-way prepositions.
- ☐ ask about location or direction, using **wo** and **wohin.**
- ☐ make suggestions, using **lass uns doch.**
- ☐ describe location using the verbs **hängen, liegen, sitzen, stecken,** and **stehen.**
- ☐ describe placement using the verbs **hängen, legen, setzen, stecken,** and **stellen.**
- ☐ express time using accusative, dative, and two-way prepositions.
- ☐ express events in the past, using the simple past tense of **haben, sein,** and the modal verbs.
- ☐ identify cognates and compound words in order to aid your understanding of texts.

Zweites Zwischenspiel

Die deutsche Regionalküche

Das Essen ist in jeder Kultur wichtig.[1] Mehrere Faktoren (z.B. Geschmack,[2] Klima und geographische Lage) bestimmen die Speisen, die man in einer bestimmten Region isst.

Aktivität 1 Die deutsche Küche[3]

Kennen Sie typische Gerichte aus deutschsprachigen Ländern? Stellen Sie mit einem Partner / einer Partnerin eine Liste zusammen.

Aktivität 2 Kulinarische Geographie

Können Sie die Gegenden oder Orte auf der Landkarte auf S. xxv–xxviii finden, die mit den folgenden Speisen verbunden sind?

Berliner Pfannkuchen[4]
Dresdner Stollen[5]
Emmentaler Käse
Frankfurter Würstchen
Leipziger Allerlei[6]
Limburger Käse
Linzer Torte[7]
Nürnberger Lebkuchen[8]
Salzburger Nockerln[9]
Westfälischer Schinken[10]
Wiener Schnitzel
Wiener Würstchen

Wiener oder Frankfurter?

Manche Speisen haben verschiedene Namen, je nachdem, wo man sie isst.

Weil's Wurst ist
von Gerhard C. Krischker

in wien
heißen die wiener
frankfurter

dafür heißen
in frankfurt die frankfurter
wiener

[1]*important* [2]*taste* [3]*cuisine* [4]*jelly-filled donut* [5]*fruit cake* [6]*mixed vegetables* [7]*jam-filled tart* [8]*gingerbread* [9]*soufflé made of baked egg whites and sugar* [10]*smoked raw ham*

Ein Käsesortiment

Wurstsorten

Aktivität 3 Ein einheimisches[1] Gericht

Gibt es Speisen oder Gerichte, die für Ihre Gegend typisch sind? Schreiben Sie ein Gedicht darüber oder über Ihre Lieblingsspeise!

So isst man . . .

Manche Speisen kann man nicht so leicht essen. Lesen Sie die folgenden Hinweise aus dem Buch *Wenn Sie mich so fragen*.

FRAGE: Wie isst man Spargel[2]* richtig?

ANTWORT: Sie können ihn heutzutage[3] ohne weiteres[4] mit dem Messer schneiden und mit der Gabel essen. Denn die modernen Messer oxydieren nicht, und deshalb kann der Spargel nicht mehr „nach Messer" schmecken. Wenn ich allerdings[5] zu einem richtigen Spargel-essen eingeladen werde, esse ich ihn auch heute noch zünftig nach alter Art, also mit den Fingern.

FRAGE: Zur Hochzeit haben wir Kuchengabeln geschenkt bekommen. Deckt[6] man sie eigentlich zu jedem Kuchen[7]?

ANTWORT: Nein, nur wenn man Torte, Obst oder einen anderen feuchten[8] Kuchen anbietet. Trockenen Kuchen oder Gebäck kann man mit der Hand nehmen und ohne Gabel essen. Größere Kuchenstücke essen sich leichter von Hand gebrochen.

[1]*local* [2]*asparagus* [3]*nowadays* [4]*without concern* [5]*however* [6]*set* [7]zu . . . *whenever cake is served* [8]*moist* [9]*customs*

Aktivität 4 So esse ich das

Zeigen Sie, wie man die folgenden Speisen isst.

Pommes frites	Kartoffelpüree
Schweinebraten	Grüner Salat
Suppe	Bockwurst
Tomaten	Käsekuchen
Eis	

Kuchen und Gebäck

Aktivität 5 Andere Länder, andere Sitten[9]

Suchen Sie sich eine Stadt in einem deutschsprachigen Land aus und suchen Sie im Internet, ob Sie etwas über regionale Küche oder Restaurants in dieser Stadt herausfinden können. Berichten Sie im Plenum, was Sie herausgefunden haben.

Aktivität 5. Note: Guide students in formulating their expressions following patterns in the example, in particular the use of the perfect tense.

BEISPIEL: Ich habe in Bern, in der Schweiz, das Restaurant „Bürgerhaus" gefunden. Es liegt in der Nähe der Neuen Gasse 20, im Herzen der Stadt und nur zwei Minuten vom Bahnhof. Es gibt da traditionelle Küche und türkische Spezialitäten.

*Die „Spargelzeit" fängt traditionell in der Mitte des Sommers an. Man isst frischen, weißen Spargel mit Kartoffeln und Kochschinken.

Kapitel 7

Freizeit und Sport

Nachbarschaftliches Fußballspiel in Köln

Kapitel 7. Suggestion: To introduce the material of this chapter, talk about leisure-time activities that you and other people enjoy. Bring in pictures and discuss them with your class.

Alles klar?

A. Schauen Sie sich das Freizeit-Budget der Deutschen an.

1. *expenditures*
2. *leisure goods*
3. *budgets of working people*
4. mit . . . *with median incomes*

- Wie viel geben die Deutschen für _____ aus?
  a. Auto **b.** Radio, Fernsehen
  c. Computer, Elektronik **d.** ?
- Wie viel Geld geben Sie im Monat ungefähr für die Freizeit aus?
- Wofür (*For what*) geben Sie Geld aus? Wie viel?

BEISPIEL: Ich gebe ungefähr 20 Dollar im Monat fürs Kino aus. Ich gebe nichts für Garten und Haustiere aus.

Realia. Suggestions: 1. Have students scan the graphic and guess the meaning of words they do not know. 2. Ask students to comment on differences between German and American expenditures on leisure activities. *Das Budget für die Freizeit* is published by *Globus Kartendienst*.

B. Sie hören nun drei kurze Dialoge. Wie verbringen Ulrike, Wolfgang und Antje ihre Freizeit?

1. Ulrike
  a. Tanzen **b.** Schwimmen
  c. Kochen **d.** Lesen

2. Wolfgang
  a. Fußball **b.** Fernsehen
  c. Lesen **d.** Rad fahren

3. Antje
  a. ins Kino gehen **b.** Kochen
  c. Musik spielen **d.** im Internet surfen

Wörter im Kontext

Thema 1

Sportarten°

Wo macht man das? Kombinieren Sie!

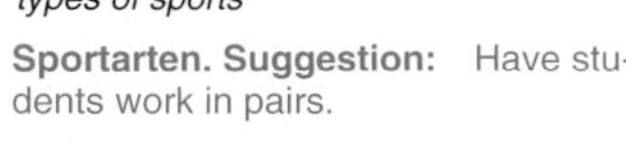

types of sports

Sportarten. Suggestion: Have students work in pairs.

1. Beate wandert gern.

2. Kerstin fährt Rad.

3. Heinz angelt oft im Sommer.

4. Uwe und Erich machen dreimal die Woche Bodybuilding.

BEISPIEL: Man wandert im Wald oder am Fluss.

wandern	im **Fitnesscenter**
Rad fahren	auf der Straße
angeln	auf dem **See**
tauchen	im **Wald**
reiten	am **Fluss**
segeln	im **Meer**
Bodybuilding machen	in der **Turnhalle**
Aerobic machen	auf der **Wiese**

5. Lisa macht jeden zweiten Tag Aerobic.

6. Manfred segelt gern.

7. Renate taucht gern.

8. Eva reitet jeden Tag.

Die Karte „Naherholung" zeigt, welche Sportmöglichkeiten es in und um Göttingen gibt. Schauen Sie sich die Bildsymbole auf der Karte an. Welche Sportarten kann man hier treiben? Wo kann man das machen?

BEISPIELE: Man kann auf dem Kiessee und auf dem Wendebach-Stausee segeln.

Note: Point out that the various sports facilities are often combined with place names, for example, *Freibad Nikolausberg, Sporthalle Geismar* and *Freibad Rosdorf.* Bowling has almost completely replaced the traditional game of ninepins, *Kegeln.*

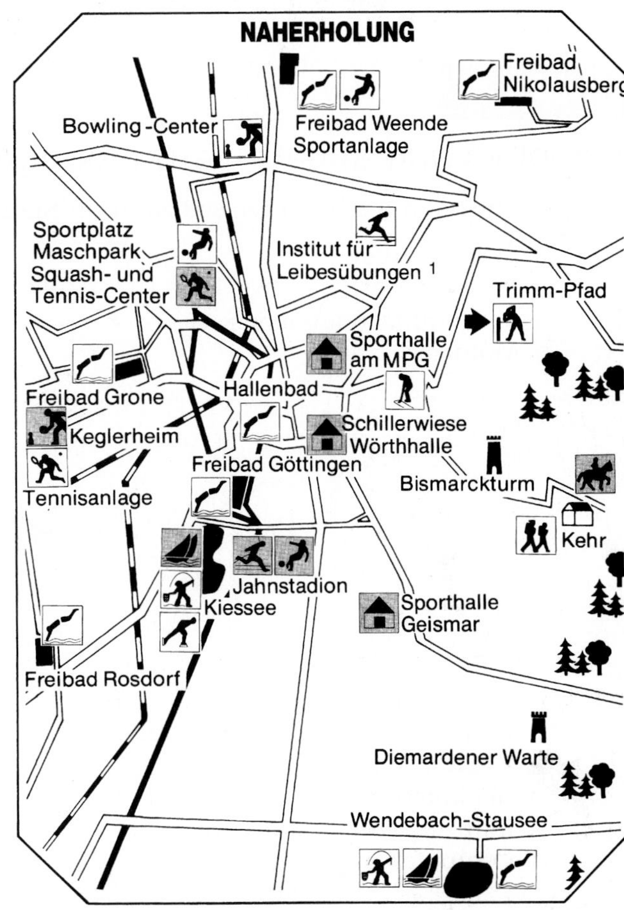

1. *physical education* **Realia.** *Naherholung* appeared in a brochure published by the city of Göttingen (*Jugendamt und Sport- und Bäderamt*) to advise its citizens of local opportunities for leisure-time and sports activities.

Neue Wörter

- □ das **Eisstadion,** *pl.* die **Eisstadien**
- □ das **Freibad, ¨er**
- □ **Fußball spielen**
- □ das **Hallenbad, ¨er**
- □ **joggen**
- □ der **Schlittschuh, -e**
- □ **Schlittschuh laufen**
- □ das **Schwimmbad, ¨er**
- □ **schwimmen gehen**
- □ die **Sporthalle, -n**
- □ der **Sportplatz, ¨e**
- □ das **Stadion,** *pl.* die **Stadien**
- □ die **Tennisanlage, -n**
- □ der **Tennisplatz, ¨e**
- □ **Tennis spielen**
- □ der **Trimm-Pfad, -e**
- □ **turnen**

Aktivität 1 Was braucht man für diese Sportarten?

Bilden Sie Sätze mit Elementen aus beiden Spalten (*columns*).

BEISPIEL: Zum Angeln braucht man eine Angelrute.

zum Angeln	ein Fahrrad (*bicycle*)
zum Reiten	Schwimmflossen (*fins*)
zum Wandern	einen Ball
zum Tauchen	eine Angelrute (*fishing pole*)
zum Fußballspielen	ein Pferd (*horse*)
zum Rad fahren	Wanderschuhe
zum Segeln	ein Segelboot

Aktivität 2 Ein Gespräch über Sport

Bilden Sie kleine Gruppen und diskutieren Sie. Welche Sportarten treiben Sie gern? Wie oft?

To say how often you do something, use the following expressions:

jeden Tag
every day
einmal die Woche
once a week
zweimal die Woche
twice a week
dreimal im Monat
three times a month
einmal im Jahr
once a year

BEISPIEL: S1: Ich jogge gern, und ich wandere auch gern.
S2: Wie oft machst du das?
S1: Ich gehe einmal im Monat wandern, aber ich jogge jeden Tag.

Thema 2

Weiteres zum Thema Freizeit und Sport finden Sie bei ***Deutsch: Na klar!*** im World-Wide-Web unter www.mhhe.com/german

Hobbys und andere Vergnügungen°

° *pleasures*

Wie **verbringen** Sie Ihre Freizeit? Kreuzen Sie an!

□ **Sport treiben**
□ Musik hören
□ mit Freunden ausgehen
□ Motorrad fahren
□ spazieren gehen
□ Briefmarken (*stamps*) sammeln
□ Drachen (*kite*) **fliegen**

□ in Ausstellungen (*exhibits*) gehen
□ **Karten** spielen
□ Ski fahren
□ Münzen (*coins*) **sammeln**
□ Computerspiele spielen

□ **zeichnen**
□ Musik spielen
□ fotografieren
□ Klavier spielen
□ **malen**

□ **Schach spielen**
□ fernsehen
□ **faulenzen**
□ Windsurfing gehen
□ lesen
□ Camping gehen
□ am Wagen arbeiten
□ im Garten arbeiten
□ träumen
?

Vergleichen Sie Ihre Liste mit der einer anderen Person im Kurs. Können Sie drei Dinge finden, die Sie gemeinsam am **Wochenende** machen können?

Aktivität 3 Wie hast du deine Freizeit verbracht?°

° *How did you spend your free time?*

Fragen Sie einen Partner / eine Partnerin: Wie hast du in den letzten acht Tagen deine Freizeit verbracht?

BEISPIEL: Ich habe Musik gehört. Ich bin mit Freunden ausgegangen.
Ich habe jeden Tag ferngesehen.

mit Freunden	bin . . . ausgegangen
mit einem Freund	bin . . . in die Disko / ins Kino gegangen
mit einer Freundin	habe . . . Musik gehört/gespielt
allein	habe . . . ferngesehen
	habe . . . im Garten gearbeitet

Aktivität 3. Suggestion: First have students scan the range of possibilities. This activity can be done with the whole group. Encourage students to link together several pieces of information. Brainstorm other activities with the group, providing new vocabulary as needed.

Kulturtipp

In ihrer Freizeit treiben viele Deutsche gern Sport; besonders beliebt sind Fußball, Radfahren, Schwimmen und Tennis. Andere bleiben lieber zu Hause und machen Gartenarbeit, pflegen (*take care of*) ihren Wagen, spielen mit ihren Haustieren, sammeln Briefmarken, lesen oder sehen fern. Viele Deutsche haben ein Hobby, das sie in einem Verein (*club*) ausüben. In vielen Städten gibt es Gesangs- und Heimatvereine sowie (*as well as*) Vereine für Schützen (*archery*), Amateurfunker (*ham radio operators*) und Kegelklubs.

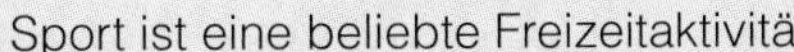
Sport ist eine beliebte Freizeitaktivität

Aktivität 4 Möchtest du mitkommen?

Machen Sie eine Verabredung (*date*).

S1	S2
1. Ich gehe heute Bowling. Möchtest du mitkommen? ins Kino. ins Theater. in ein Rockkonzert. ins Stadtbad.	**2a.** Ja, gern, um wie viel Uhr denn? **2b.** Ich kann nicht.
3a. Um _____ Uhr. Nach dem Abendessen um _____. Nach der Vorlesung um _____. **3b.** Warum denn nicht?	**4a.** Wo wollen wir uns treffen (*meet*)? **4b.** Ich muss arbeiten. Ich habe kein Geld. keine Zeit. keine Lust.
5a. Vor dem Kino. Vor der Bibliothek. Im Studentenheim. Bei mir zu Hause. **5b.** Schade.	**6a.** Gut. Ich treffe dich dann um _____

Aktivität 5 Pläne für einen Ausflug°

° excursion

Verena und Antje machen Pläne fürs Wochenende. Sie wohnen beide in Düsseldorf. Hören Sie sich den Dialog an, und markieren Sie dann die richtigen Antworten.

	DAS STIMMT	DAS STIMMT NICHT	KEINE INFORMATION
1. Verena und Antje planen einen Ausflug.	☒	☐	☐
2. Sie wollen im Neandertal wandern.	☐	☒	☐
3. Es dauert nur eine Stunde bis zum Neandertal.	☐	☒	☐
4. Der Weg führt (*leads*) durch den Wald.	☒	☐	☐
5. Auf dem Wege dahin wollen sie ein Picknick machen.	☐	☐	☒
6. Antje will ihren Freund Stefan einladen.	☒	☐	☐

Thema 3

Jahreszeiten und Wetter

Jahreszeiten und Wetter. Suggestions: 1. Bring in pictures showing different kinds of weather conditions. 2. Talk about the local weather during the different seasons. 3. Talk about the weather in German-speaking countries.

Die ***Jahreszeiten:*** der Frühling, der Sommer, der Herbst, der Winter
Welches Bild passt zu welcher Jahreszeit?

Der Berliner Wannsee im Sommer.

Am Kornmarkt in Heidelberg im Winter.

Der Grundlsee in Österreich im Herbst.

Das Städtchen Creuzburg im Frühling.

Wann **passiert** das? im Winter, im Sommer, im Frühling/Frühjahr, im Herbst?

1. Die Blätter (*leaves*) **fallen** von den Bäumen. Es kann auch **regnerisch** werden.
2. Leute schwimmen im Freibad. An manchen Tagen ist der **Himmel wolkenlos.**
3. Es **regnet** viel, und die Blumen blühen.
4. Die Tage sind kurz. Für viele Menschen **dauert** diese Jahreszeit zu lang.
5. Es wird **kühler,** und **oft** gibt es **Regenschauer.**
6. Es ist sehr **heiß** und manchmal sogar **schwül.**
7. **Drinnen** ist es schön **warm, draußen** aber wirklich **scheußlich.** Es gibt wenig **Sonnenschein,** ein starker **Wind** bläst, und der Himmel ist oft **bewölkt.**

Der Wetterbericht

Welcher **Wetterbericht** passt zu welchem Bild?

1. _____ Im Norden beginnt es zu regnen, und morgen regnet es den ganzen Tag. Am Abend: **Regen,** eventuell auch **Hagel.**
2. _____ Im Moment ist es **wolkig** und **bedeckt.** Die **Temperatur** heute Nachmittag ist kühl, aber heute Abend wird es **kalt.**
3. _____ In der Karibik ist es **sonnig, heiter** und warm. Wir haben den ganzen Tag **angenehme** Temperaturen. Erst morgen (*not until tomorrow*) wird es wieder heiß.
4. _____ Im Süden gibt es **Gewitter.** Es **blitzt** und **donnert.**
5. _____ In den **Bergen schneit** es im Moment. Die Skifahrer sind begeistert über den **Schnee.**
6. _____ Im Rheinland gibt es heute Morgen **Nebel,** nachher **einzelne Wolken.**

a. b. c. d. e. f.

Welche Stadt assoziieren Sie mit welchem Wetter?

1. _____ Die **Sonne scheint**; es ist schön warm.	a. Chikago
2. _____ Man braucht oft einen **Regenschirm.**	b. Athen
3. _____ Es ist **neblig** und kühl.	c. Kairo
4. _____ Es ist tagsüber sehr heiß (35 **Grad**).	d. San Franzisko
5. _____ Es ist **windig.**	e. London

Aktivität 6 Ein Wetterbericht

Realia. This weather report is from the *Berliner Zeitung* of March 10, 1997.

A. Lesen Sie den Text zum Wetterbericht, und beantworten Sie die folgenden Fragen.

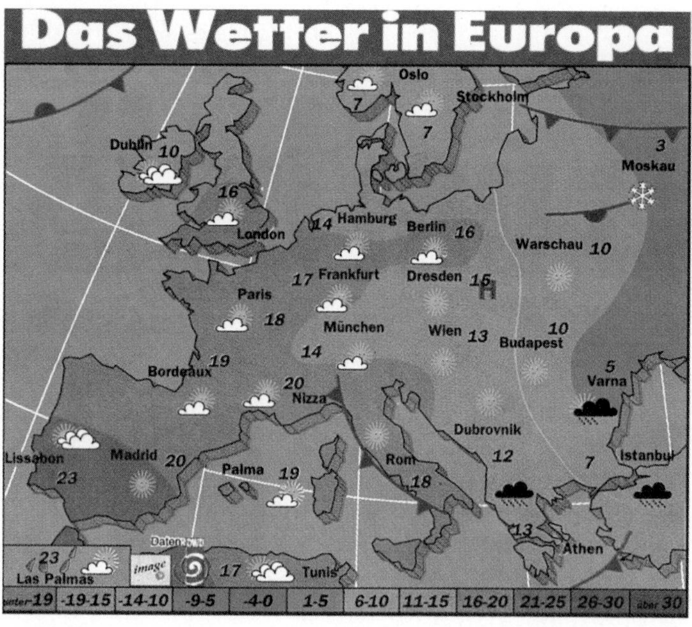

Das Hochdruckgebiet über Polen bestimmt weiterhin das Wetter in Deutschland. Nachts bleibt es noch empfindlich kalt.

In Berlin und Brandenburg überwiegend sonnig und niederschlagsfrei. Höchste Temperaturen am Tage zwischen 13 und 17 Grad, in Berlin um 16 Grad. Schwacher Wind aus Südwest. Nachts meist gering bewölkt und trokken, Temperaturrückgang auf 3 bis -1 Grad, in Berlin auf 2 Grad.

Übriges Deutschland: Im Norden in den Frühstunden vereinzelt noch Nebelfelder, sonst den ganzen Tag über sonniges Wetter. Höchste Temperaturen zwischen 10 Grad an der Küste und bis 20 Grad am Oberrhein. Meist schwacher Wind aus südöstlicher Richtung. Nachts im Norden zeitweise wolkig, aber überwiegend trocken. Sonst gering bewölkt oder aufklarend.

1. Dieser Wetterbericht ist wahrscheinlich für einen Tag im __d__.
   a. Juli **b.** Oktober **c.** Januar **d.** März
2. Nachts soll es __b__.
   a. warm werden **b.** kalt bleiben **c.** Nebel geben **d.** regnen
3. Im Norden soll es tagsüber __c__.
   a. windig sein **b.** bewölkt sein **c.** sonnig sein **d.** kalt werden
4. An der Küste ist die Höchsttemperatur etwa (*about*) __d__.
   a. 20 C **b.** −1 C **c.** zwischen 13 und 17 C **d.** 10 C

Aktivität 6. Suggestion: Begin by having students glance over the map, noting the temperatures in various cities. If they are accustomed to fahrenheit readings, make comparisons with centigrade so that they get a sense of the season. Have them read the short text and work in pairs or groups to answer the four questions under the weather map. Note the significance of the second sentence, *Nachts bleibt es noch empfindlich kalt,* in determining that the month is more likely March than October. Go over the answers as a class. For part B, a quick geography review may be in order. Assign each pair or group a certain city, region, or country. They then describe the weather in that locale using the example as a model.

B. Schauen Sie sich jetzt die Wetterkarte an, und sagen Sie, wie das Wetter in den verschiedenen Gebieten ist.

BEISPIEL: In Skandinavien ist es ziemlich kalt aber heiter. Die Höchsttemperatur ist 7 Grad.

Skandinavien
Berlin
Spanien
Griechenland
Russland
?

Aktivität 7 Wetterberichte im Radio 

Sie hören fünf kurze Wetterberichte für fünf Städte in Europa. Kreuzen Sie die richtigen Informationen an, und notieren Sie die Temperaturen in Grad Celsius.

Aktivität 7. Suggestion: First have students scan the possibilities. Then let them hear the weather reports and fill in the information. Check students' responses by asking *Wie ist das Wetter in ______?* Students use the information on their chart in their responses.

	ZÜRICH	WIEN	BERLIN	PARIS	LONDON
sonnig	☒	☐	☐	☒	☐
warm	☒	☐	☐	☒	☐
wolkig bis heiter	☐	☐	☒	☐	☐
(stark) bewölkt	☐	☒	☐	☐	☒
Nebel	☐	☐	☐	☐	☒
Schauer	☐	☐	☒	☐	☐
Regen	☐	☐	☐	☐	☒
Wind	☐	☐	☐	☒	☐
Gewitter	☐	☒	☐	☐	☐
Grad Celsius	20–25	18	20	29	10

Aktivität 8 So ist das Wetter in . . .

Woher kommen Sie? Wie ist das Wetter dort?

BEISPIEL: Ich komme aus San Franzisko. Dort ist das Wetter im Sommer oft kühl und neblig. Im Frühling ist es meistens sonnig. Und im Winter regnet es.

Aktivität 8. Suggestion: The activity can be done in pairs, with students jotting down what their partner says so they can report back to the whole group afterwards.

Weiteres zum Thema Wetter finden Sie bei ***Deutsch: Na klar!*** im World-Wide-Web unter www.mhhe.com/german.

Aktivität 9 Ihr Wetterbericht

Schreiben Sie einen Wetterbericht für Ihr Gebiet (*area*).

BEISPIEL: Das Wetter für Donnerstag: schwül und heiß. Temperaturen: 30–35 Grad Celsius. Das Wetter für morgen: morgens Nebel, dann sonnig, um 30 Grad.

Grammatik im Kontext

Connecting Ideas: Coordinating Conjunctions°

°koordinierende Konjunktionen

Conjunctions connect words, phrases, and sentences. You already know **und** and **oder,** which are coordinating conjunctions:

Herr **und** Frau Baumann sitzen vor dem Fernseher.
War der Abend langweilig **oder** amüsant?

Other coordinating conjunctions are:

aber but, however **sondern** but, rather **denn** because, for*

* **denn** is also used as an intensifying particle in questions: **Wo wart ihr *denn* gestern?**

Expressing a Contrast: *aber* vs. *sondern*

Das Spiel war kurz, **aber** spannend.	*The game was short but exciting.*
Der Film hat zwar nicht lang gedauert, **aber** er war sehr interessant.	*Admittedly the movie didn't last long, but it is was very interesting.*
Es ist nicht warm, **sondern** kalt draußen.	*It isn't warm but rather cold outside.*
Das ist kein Regen, **sondern** Hagel!	*That's not rain but hail!*

The conjunction **aber** is normally used to juxtapose ideas. The adverb **zwar** may be used with **aber** to accentuate the juxtaposition. If, however, a negative (**nicht** or **kein**) is part of the first contrasted element *and* two mutually exclusive ideas are juxtaposed, **sondern** must be used.

Note: Point out that the combination of *zwar . . . aber* is very common. The contrast becomes clear when expressed as: on the one hand, on the other hand. The position of *zwar* parallels *nicht:*

Es ist draußen zwar kalt, aber sonnig. Es ist draußen nicht kalt, sondern warm.

mutually exclusive:	nicht warm, **sondern** kalt (warm / kalt)
	kein Regen, **sondern** Hagel (Regen / Hagel)
not mutually exclusive:	kurz, **aber** spannend (kurz, spannend)
	nicht lang, **aber** interessant (nicht lang, interessant)

When used to connect sentences, coordinating conjunctions do not affect word order. Each sentence can be stated independently of the other.

Erst muss ich heute arbeiten,	**und**	dann gehe ich Tennis spielen.
Ich spiele gern Tennis,	**aber**	mein Freund spielt lieber Karten.
Willst du mit zum Sportplatz,	**oder**	willst du zu Hause bleiben?
Ich möchte zum Sportplatz,	**denn**	da gibt es ein Fußballspiel.
Ich bleibe nicht zu Hause,	**sondern**	ich gehe zum Sportplatz.

Übung 1 Wie ist das Wetter?

Gebraucht man hier **aber** oder **sondern?** Ergänzen Sie die Sätze.

1. Gestern war es zwar kalt, _____ sonnig.
2. Bei uns gibt es im Winter keinen Schnee, _____ nur viel Regen.
3. Im Frühling wird es hier nie heiß, _____ im Sommer wird es manchmal sehr heiß.
4. Es regnet zwar noch nicht, _____ ich glaube, es gibt bald (*soon*) ein Gewitter.
5. Es gibt heute keinen Regen, _____ Sonnenschein.
6. Es schneit nicht, _____ es regnet.
7. Es regnet zwar nicht, _____ ich nehme doch lieber einen Regenschirm mit.
8. Bei dem Regen gehe ich nicht spazieren, _____ bleibe lieber zu Hause.

Übung 2 Freizeitpläne

Ergänzen Sie: **und, aber, oder, denn, sondern.**

Jörg _____ seine Freundin Karin planen einen Ausflug _____ ein Picknick.[1] Die Frage ist: wohin _____ wann?[2] Heute geht es leider nicht, _____ es regnet, _____ morgen haben beide keine Zeit.[3] Also müssen sie bis zum Wochenende warten. Sie wollen diesmal nicht mit dem Auto ins Grüne fahren, _____ mit ihren Fahrrädern.[4] Das dauert zwar länger (*longer*), _____ macht bestimmt mehr Spaß.[5] Sie wollen an einen See,

_____ da können sie schwimmen gehen.[6] Danach können sie ein Picknick im Wald machen, _____ sie können am See bleiben.[7] Karin ist nicht für die öffentlichen (*public*) Picknickplätze, _____ da sind meistens zu viele Leute, Kinder _____ Hunde, Onkel _____ Tanten.[8] Jörg lädt seinen Freund Andreas ein, _____ der kann leider nicht mit.[9] Es tut ihm leid, _____ er muss arbeiten.[10]

Expressing Events in the Past: The Present Perfect Tense°

°das Perfekt

In German, the present perfect tense is used conversationally to talk about past events, although, as you learned in **Kapitel 6,** a number of common verbs (**sein, haben** and the modals) generally use the simple past tense in conversation. There is essentially no difference in meaning between the two tenses.

—Gestern **habe** ich Fußball **gespielt.**	*I played soccer yesterday.*
—Wer **hat** denn **gewonnen?**	*Who won?*
—Wir **haben** fünf zu null **verloren.** Dann **sind** wir in die Kneipe **gegangen.**	*We lost five to zero. Then we went to the pub.*

As in English, the present perfect tense in German consists of two parts: the present tense of an auxiliary verb (**haben** or **sein**) and a past participle. While in English the auxiliary verb is always a form of *to have,* in German the auxiliary verb is **haben** for some verbs and **sein** for others. The auxiliary verb and the past participle form a sentence bracket (**Satzklammer**), with the participle placed at the end of the sentence.

Unsere Mannschaft **hat** fünf zu null **verloren.**

Dann **sind** wir nach Hause **gegangen.**

Most verbs use the auxiliary **haben** in the present perfect tense. You will learn about the use of **sein** as the auxiliary later in this chapter.

Analyse

Uwe und Klaus reden über ihr Lieblingsthema: Fußballvereine (*soccer teams*).

UWE: Hast du schon gehört? Bayern München hat gestern gegen Dynamo Dresden verloren. Null zu zwei!
KLAUS: Unglaublich! Hast du das in der Zeitung gelesen?
UWE: Ich habe es im Fernsehen gesehen.
KLAUS: Wie lange hat das Spiel gedauert?
UWE: Etwas über zwei Stunden. Dynamo Dresden hat sehr gut gespielt. Letzte Woche haben sie auch gegen Bremen gewonnen; eins zu null.
KLAUS: Ja, aber gegen den FC [Fußballclub] Nürnberg haben sie drei zu null verloren.

- Identify the past participles in the dialogue.
- What endings do these participles have?
- With what syllable do nearly all of the participles begin?
- What are the infinitives of these verbs?

Formation of the Past Participle°

das Partizip Perfekt

German, like English, distinguishes between two types of verbs: weak verbs (**schwache Verben**) and strong verbs (**starke Verben**). They form their past participles differently.

Weak Verbs

Weak verbs form the past participle by combining the verb stem with the prefix **ge** and the ending **(e)t.** The ending **et** is used when the verb stem ends in **t, d,** or a consonant cluster that is difficult to pronounce without the additional **e.**

INFINITIVE	PREFIX	STEM	ENDING	PAST PARTICIPLE
hören	**ge**	hör	**t**	gehört
dauern	**ge**	dauer	**t**	gedauert
warten	**ge**	wart	**et**	gewartet
öffnen	**ge**	öffn	**et**	geöffnet

Ich habe **gehört,** Dynamo Dresden hat sehr gut **gespielt.**	*I heard that Dynamo Dresden played very well.*
Wir haben lange **gewartet.**	*We waited for a long time.*

Übung 3 In meiner Kindheit 

Drei Leute erzählen über ihre Hobbys als Kinder. Was hat ihnen Spaß gemacht? Was stimmt, und was wissen wir nicht?

	DAS STIMMT	KEINE INFORMATION
1. Herr Harter hat		
Trompete gespielt	☒	☐
Insekten gesammelt	☒	☐
viel Fernsehen geschaut	☐	☒
2. Frau Beitz hat		
mit ihrer Katze gespielt	☐	☒
die Tiere (*animals*) im Zoo gefüttert (*fed*)	☒	☐
Comic-Hefte gesammelt	☐	☒
3. Herr Huppert hat		
Bücher von Karl May gelesen	☒	☐
gern Cowboy gespielt	☒	☐
im Schulorchester gespielt	☐	☒
Fußball gespielt	☒	☐

Realia. This is a program cover of the popular *Karl-May-Spiele* performed each year in Bad Segeberg, Schleswig-Holstein.

Übung 4 Haben Sie das als Kind gemacht?

Kreuzen Sie an, was Sie als Kind gern, manchmal oder nie gemacht haben. Bilden Sie dann Sätze aus einigen dieser Aktivitäten.

BEISPIEL: Als Kind habe ich gern gemalt, aber ich habe nie mit Puppen gespielt.

	GERN	MANCHMAL	NIE
Briefmarken sammeln	☐	☐	☐
Insekten sammeln	☐	☐	☐
Comic-Hefte sammeln	☐	☐	☐
sammeln	☐	☐	☐
mit Puppen (*dolls*) spielen	☐	☐	☐
Klavier spielen lernen	☐	☐	☐
Gitarre spielen lernen	☐	☐	☐
lernen	☐	☐	☐
die Tiere im Zoo füttern	☐	☐	☐
Cowboy und Indianer spielen	☐	☐	☐
viel Fernsehen schauen	☐	☐	☐
Kaugummi/Süßigkeiten (*sweets*) kaufen	☐	☐	☐
malen	☐	☐	☐
zeichnen	☐	☐	☐
Musik hören	☐	☐	☐
?	☐	☐	☐

Übung 4. Suggestion: For variation, have students say what they liked particularly well: *Briefmarken Sammeln hat mir Spaß gemacht* (*Ich habe gern Briefmarken gesammelt*), etc. **Point Out:** the expression *Spaß gemacht* requires changing the infinitives to gerunds, which are capitalized.

Realia. This bill is from a restaurant called *Nudelhaus* in Göttingen. The new *Postleitzahl* for this address in Göttingen is 37073. You might take this opportunity to talk about the old system of *Postleitzahlen. Hefeweizen* is a popular wheat beer. The line reading ENTH. MWST. means that the value-added tax (*Mehrwertsteuer*) of DM 3.62 is included (*enthalten*) in the total price of DM 29.50. It is not added to the bill at the end as is customary in countries such as the United States.

Übung 5 Im Nudelhaus

Wie haben Inge und Claudia den Abend verbracht? Setzen Sie das Partizip Perfekt ein.

Inge und Claudia haben ein gemütliches Restaurant in der Stadt _____ (suchen).[1] Im Nudelhaus war es sehr voll. Der Kellner hat sie _____ (fragen): Wollen Sie warten?[2] Sie haben ziemlich lange auf einen Platz _____ (warten).[3] Der Kellner hat die Speisekarte auf den Tisch _____ (legen).[4] Am Nebentisch haben einige Leute Karten _____ (spielen).[5] Sie haben laut _____ (lachen [*to laugh*]).[6] Das Essen hat sehr gut _____ (schmecken).[7] Es hat nur 29.50 Mark _____. (kosten)[8] Auf dem Weg nach Hause hat Claudia am Kiosk eine Zeitung _____ (kaufen).[9] Dann hat sie noch etwas an ihrer Seminararbeit _____ (arbeiten).[10]

1. *wheat beer*
2. *cash total*
3. enth. = enthält *includes*
4. MwSt. = Mehrwertsteuer *value-added tax*

Strong Verbs

Strong verbs form the past participle by placing the prefix **ge** before the stem of the verb and adding the ending **en.** With some verbs the stem of the participle is identical to the infinitive stem, while with many others the stem shows vowel and consonant changes.

INFINITIVE	PREFIX	STEM	ENDING	PAST PARTICIPLE
lesen	**ge**	les	**en**	gelesen
kommen	**ge**	komm	**en**	gekommen
gehen	**ge**	gang	**en**	gegangen
sitzen	**ge**	sess	**en**	gesessen
trinken	**ge**	trunk	**en**	getrunken

Following are other familiar strong verbs and their past participles. A complete list of strong and irregular verbs is in Appendix C.

INFINITIVE	PAST PARTICIPLE	INFINITIVE	PAST PARTICIPLE
bleiben	(ist)*geblieben	reiten	(ist) geritten
essen	gegessen	schlafen	geschlafen
fahren	(ist) gefahren	schreiben	geschrieben
fallen	(ist) gefallen	sehen	gesehen
finden	gefunden	sein	(ist) gewesen
geben	gegeben	sitzen	gesessen
hängen	gehangen	stehen	gestanden
helfen	geholfen	tragen	getragen
laufen	(ist) gelaufen	trinken	getrunken
lesen	gelesen	werden	(ist) geworden
nehmen	genommen		

Note: Point out to students the two different participles for *hängen*. Used without a direct object, the verb *hängen* has the past participle *gehangen;* used with a direct object, it has the past participle *gehängt*.

Übung 6 Fragen und Antworten

Folgen Sie dem Beispiel.

BEISPIEL: Wohin seid ihr gestern Abend gegangen? (ins „Nudelhaus")
→ Wir sind ins „Nudelhaus" gegangen.

1. Wo seid ihr gestern Abend gewesen? (im „Nudelhaus")
2. Was hast du da gegessen? (grüne Schinkennudeln)
3. Und was hast du dazu getrunken? (ein Hefeweizen)
4. Hat es dort auch Unterhaltung gegeben? (Musik)
5. Habt ihr noch andere Freunde da gesehen? (niemand)
6. Wie lange seid ihr im „Nudelhaus" geblieben? (etwa eine Stunde lang)
7. Bist du dann sofort nach Hause gegangen? (noch zur Bibliothek)

Mixed Verbs

A few verbs include features of both weak and strong verbs in the past participle. Like weak verbs, the participles of mixed verbs end in **(e)t**; like many strong verbs, the verb stem undergoes a change.

INFINITIVE	PAST PARTICIPLE
bringen	gebracht
kennen	gekannt
wissen	gewusst

*Indicates a verb that uses **sein** as its auxiliary. See page 218.

Verbs with Inseparable Prefixes°

Verben mit untrennbaren Präfixen

Inseparable prefixes are syllables like **be, er, ge,** and **ver.** A verb with such a prefix forms the past participle without an additional **ge** prefix. Verbs with inseparable prefixes may be weak or strong.

INFINITIVE	PAST PARTICIPLE
bekommen	bekommen
bestellen	bestellt
erzählen	erzählt
gefallen	gefallen
gewinnen	gewonnen
verlieren	verloren
verkaufen	verkauft

Realia. *Reserviert für 5 Personen:* This is a place card reserving a table at the restaurant *Nürnberger Bratwurstglöckl* in Munich.

1. *starting at*

Verbs Ending in *-ieren*

Verbs ending in **ieren** also form the past participle without adding a prefix. These verbs are all weak.

INFINITIVE	PAST PARTICIPLE
diskutieren	diskutiert
fotografieren	fotografiert
gratulieren	gratuliert
passieren	(ist) passiert
reservieren	reserviert
studieren	studiert

Verbs with Separable Prefixes°

Verben mit trennbaren Präfixen

Separable-prefix verbs form the past participle by inserting the **ge** prefix between the separable prefix and the verb stem. These verbs may be weak or strong.

INFINITIVE	PAST PARTICIPLE
anrufen	angerufen
aufgeben	aufgegeben
aufstehen	(ist) aufgestanden
ausgehen	(ist) ausgegangen
einladen	eingeladen
einschlafen	(ist) eingeschlafen
mitbringen	mitgebracht
mitkommen	(ist) mitgekommen
mitnehmen	mitgenommen
vorbeikommen	(ist) vorbeigekommen
zurückkommen	(ist) zurückgekommen

Übung 7 Kleine Situationen

Ergänzen Sie das Partizip Perfekt. Sie finden die starken Partizipien in **Appendix D.**

1. Gestern hat in der Zeitung _____ (stehen): Großer, graugetigerter Kater, rotes Halsband mit Glöckchen _____ (verlieren). Wer hat ihn _____ oder _____ (sehen, finden)? Er hört auf den Namen Charly.
2. In den letzten Tagen ist es recht kalt _____ (werden). Die Wetterexperten prophezeien (*are forecasting*) Schnee.
3. Wir haben gestern Abend noch lange über die Probleme mit dem Studium _____ (diskutieren). Ich bin erst um drei Uhr nachts _____ (einschlafen). Und dann bin ich um sechs Uhr _____ (aufstehen). Kein Wunder, dass ich heute kaputt bin.
4. —Wo hast du deinen Freund kennen _____ (lernen).
   —Jemand hat ihn zu einer Party _____ (einladen).
5. Wir haben für acht Uhr einen Tisch im Nudelhaus _____ (reservieren). Wir haben alle eine Pizza _____ (bestellen).
6. —Wie hat es euch im Nudelhaus _____ (gefallen)?
   —Sehr gut. Warum bist du nicht _____ (mitkommen).

Verloren/Gefunden

Großer, graugetigerter Kater, rotes Halsband mit Glöckchen. Wer hat ihn gesehen oder gefunden? Hört auf den Namen Charly. Finderlohn.

The Use of *sein* in the Present Perfect Tense

Most verbs use **haben** as the auxiliary verb in the present perfect tense. If a verb has a direct object, it must use **haben. Sein** is used with verbs that indicate movement from one place to another (e.g., **gehen** and **kommen**) or a change of condition (e.g., **aufwachen** and **werden**). In addition, such verbs must not have a direct object.

Unsere Mannschaft **hat** das Fußballspiel **gewonnen.**	*Our team won the soccer game.*
Die Fans **haben** auf den Straßen **getanzt.**	*The fans danced in the streets.*

Tanzen expresses movement, but not from one place to another; therefore its present perfect tense is formed with **haben.**

but	Rudi **ist** zum Fußballplatz **gegangen.**	*Rudi went to the soccer field.*
	Nach dem Spiel **ist** er nach Hause **gefahren.**	*After the game he went home.*

Gehen and **fahren** indicate movement from one place to another. Other verbs in this category are **kommen (ist gekommen), laufen (ist gelaufen),** and **fliegen (ist geflogen).**

Gestern **ist** Peter 21 **geworden.**	*Yesterday Peter turned 21.*
Ich **bin** heute spät **aufgewacht.**	*I woke up late today.*

Werden and **aufwachen** express a change of condition, such as a change in age or the transition from sleeping to being awake. Other verbs in this category are **aufstehen (ist aufgestanden)** and **einschlafen (ist eingeschlafen).**

The Use of *sein*. Suggestion: Practice a number of the verbs by asking personalized questions such as *Wie alt sind Sie? Wann sind Sie (21) geworden? Wann sind Sie gestern Abend schlafen gegangen? Sind Sie sofort eingeschlafen? Wann sind Sie aufgewacht? Sind Sie sofort aufgestanden?* (A variation of this will be practiced later in **Übung 12.**)

Several other important verbs using **sein** in the present perfect tense are **sein, bleiben,** and **passieren.**

Wo **ist** Rudi gestern **gewesen?**	*Where was Rudi yesterday?*
Wir **sind** zu Hause **geblieben.**	*We stayed home.*
Unsere Mannschaft hat verloren? Wie **ist** das **passiert?**	*Our team lost? How did that happen?*

Note: Verbs conjugated with **sein** in the present perfect tense will be listed in the vocabulary sections as follows: **einschlafen (schläft ein), ist eingeschlafen.**

Übung 8 Kleine Gespräche im Alltag

Ergänzen Sie **sein** oder **haben.**

1. LINDA: Tag, Hans! _____ ihr gestern Abend noch ins Kino gegangen?
   HANS: Ja, wir _____ einen alten Film mit Charlie Chaplin im Rialto gesehen. Und du, was _____ du gestern Abend gemacht?
   LINDA: Ich _____ zu Hause geblieben und _____ gearbeitet.
   HANS: Wir _____ dann hinterher noch ein Bier getrunken. Ich _____ erst nach eins ins Bett gekommen.
2. KARL: Mein neuer Wagen ist schon kaputt.
   UTE: Wie _____ denn das passiert?
   KARL: Ich _____ gegen einen Baum gefahren.
3. SABINE: Ich _____ gestern mit Gabi telefoniert. Sie _____ gerade aus Hamburg zurückgekommen.
   NINA: Wie _____ es ihr denn dort gefallen?
   SABINE: Gut. Aber es _____ jeden Tag geregnet.
4. MARTIN: Gestern _____ Stefan dreißig geworden.
   GABI: Mein Gott, so alt? Das _____ ich gar nicht gewusst.

Realia: The *Fremdenverkehrsverein* in the community of Jork (near Buxtehude on the Elbe) put out a tourist brochure about their region, *Das Alte Land.* This logo is from the cover.

1. *Tourism Office*
2. = eingetragener Verein) *registered association*

Übung 9 Hin und her: Wochenende und Freizeit

Warum haben sie das gemacht? Stellen Sie Ihrem Partner / Ihrer Partnerin Fragen, um die Gründe (*reasons*) zu erfahren.

BEISPIEL: S1: Warum ist Dagmar ins Alte Land gefahren?
S2: Sie wollte auf einem Bauernhof Obst kaufen.

WER	WAS	WARUM
Dagmar	ins Alte Land fahren	auf einem Bauernhof Obst kaufen wollen
Thomas	in den Sportclub gehen	Fitnesstraining machen wollen
Jürgen	zu Hause bleiben	seine Lieblingssendung im Fernsehen sehen wollen
Stefanie	Hans anrufen	auf die Party nicht kommen dürfen
Susanne	sehr lange schlafen	die ganze Woche schwer arbeiten müssen

Übung 10 Brigitte und Rainer: Ein modernes und fast unglaubliches Märchen

Ergänzen Sie die Verben im Perfekt.

Brigitte _____ Rainer bei einem Musikfest kennen _____ (lernen).[1] Brigitte _____ mit einer Jugendgruppe Trompete _____ (spielen).[2] Rainer _____ unter den Zuhörern _____ (sitzen).[3] Später _____ alle _____ (tanzen).[4] Rainer _____ _____ (aufstehen) und an Brigittes Tisch _____ (kommen).[5] Er _____ sie zum Tanzen _____ (auffordern [*to ask*]).[6] Leider _____ er ihr beim Tanzen mehrmals auf die Füße _____ (treten [*to step*])![7] Brigitte _____ ihm aber trotzdem ihre Telefonnummer _____ (geben).[8] Gleich am nächsten Tag _____ Rainer Brigitte _____ (anrufen).[9] Am Wochenende _____ er sie zu Hause _____ (besuchen).[10] Er _____ ihr Blumen _____ (mitbringen [*to bring along*]).[11] Letzte Woche _____ die beiden _____ (heiraten).[12]

Übung 11 Früher und heute

Achim hat seinen Lebensstil geändert (*changed*). Bilden Sie Sätze nach dem Beispiel.

Übung 11. Suggestion: As a first step, have students do sentences in the left-hand column first, without combining them with the right-hand column. Have them determine first whether a verb is strong or weak and what auxiliary verb it requires. **Follow-up:** Ask students to come up with statements that express what they used to do and what they do now.

BEISPIEL: Früher hat er viel gearbeitet, aber jetzt faulenzt er nur.

	FRÜHER		JETZT
1.	im Studentenheim wohnen	→	in einer WG mit sechs Leuten wohnen
2.	Geschichte studieren	→	den ganzen Tag Gedichte schreiben
3.	nur Bier trinken	→	nur noch Mineralwasser trinken
4.	alles essen	→	Vegetarier sein
5.	jeden Tag in die Kneipe gehen	→	selten in die Kneipe gehen
6.	klassische Musik hören	→	nur laute Rockmusik spielen
7.	viel Sport treiben	→	nur vor dem Fernseher sitzen
8.	seine Mutter immer zum Geburtstag anrufen	→	das immer vergessen (*to forget*)

Übung 12 Ein Bericht über das Wochenende

Sprechen Sie mit einem Partner / einer Partnerin über Ihr Wochenende. Berichten Sie dann im Plenum.

Übung 12. Suggestion: Have students scan the list of expressions first and check those that apply to them. Ask them to add activities that are not listed and pertain to what they did, e.g., **arbeiten.** Then have student pairs create the dialogue. Ask several pairs to report to the class about their partner's weekend.

BEISPIEL: S1: Wann bist du letztes Wochenende aufgestanden?
S2: Um 7 Uhr.
S1: Was hast du dann gemacht?

im Bett bleiben	einen Film sehen	dann
lange schlafen	Karten/Fußball/? spielen	danach (*afterward*)
aufstehen	Freunde besuchen	vorher (*before that*)
die Zeitung lesen	ins Fitnesscenter gehen	zuerst (*first*)
frühstücken		
Freunde/Eltern anrufen		

Sprache im Kontext

Zuschauen

Vorschau

Sehen Sie sich den Wetterbericht ohne Ton an, und beantworten Sie die folgenden Fragen.

1. Wie ist das Wetter in Deutschland?
2. Für welche Jahreszeit ist der Wetterbericht wohl? Sommer? Winter? Herbst? Frühling?
3. Woher weiß man, welche Jahreszeit es ist?
4. In welcher Region Deutschlands wird es am Nachmittag am wärmsten?
5. In welcher Region Deutschlands ist es am Nachmittag heiter?
6. In welcher Region Deutschlands wird es schneien?

Wetterbericht

Arbeit mit dem Videotext

A. Sehen Sie sich den Wetterbericht jetzt mit Ton an, und beantworten Sie die folgenden Fragen.

1. Wie kalt war es heute Morgen östlich von Moskau?
2. In welcher Region ist es am kältesten?
3. Wo bleibt es in der Nacht frostfrei?
4. Welcher Monat ist es?
5. Wird es über das Wochenende weiterhin kalt oder etwas wärmer sein?
6. Wann kommt der nächste Wetterbericht? später am Abend? am nächsten Tag? erst in acht Tagen?

B. Schreiben Sie einen typischen Wetterbericht (1) für den Sommer und (2) für den Winter in Ihrer Heimatstadt.

Lesen. Zum Thema. Note: Although students haven't learned the comparative yet, this is an opportunity for them to be exposed to a limited number of comparative and superlative forms in a structured context. **Suggestion:** Write these structures on the board:

__ hat/haben mehr Feiertage als __
__ hat/haben weniger Feiertage als __
__ hat/haben die meisten Feiertage.
__ hat/haben die wenigsten Feiertage.

You may also need to review the names of the European countries. Remind the students which countries are feminine or plural.

Lesen

Zum Thema

A. Wie viel Freizeit hat man in verschiedenen Ländern? Schauen Sie sich die Tabelle „Ferien im Vergleich" an. Benutzen (*use*) Sie die Tabelle, um die folgenden Fragen zu beantworten.

1. Wie viele Urlaubstage haben die Finnen? Wie viele bezahlte Feiertage?
2. Welche Länder haben mehr bezahlte Feiertage als (*than*) Deutschland?
3. Welche Länder haben weniger (*fewer*) Urlaubstage als Deutschland?
4. Wie viele bezahlte Feiertage haben die US-Amerikaner?
5. Welche Länder in dieser Tabelle haben weniger Urlaubstage als die USA? Überrascht das Sie?

B. Was machen die Deutschen in ihrer Freizeit? Schauen Sie sich die Entspannungshitliste an. Vergleichen Sie Ihre Freizeitbeschäftigungen mit denen der Deutschen.

- Was machen Sie gern in Ihrer Freizeit?
- Stehen Ihre Freizeitaktivitäten auf der Liste?

C. Machen Sie eine Liste der sechs (6) beliebtesten Freizeitaktivitäten in Ihrer Klasse. Vergleichen Sie Ihre Klasse mit den Deutschen.

1. Was ist die beliebteste Freizeitbeschäftigung in Ihrer Klasse?
2. Was steht an zweiter Stelle (*place*) für die Klasse?
3. Steht diese Aktivität auf der Liste der Deutschen?
4. Welche Unterschiede (*differences*) und Ähnlichkeiten (*similarities*) gibt es?

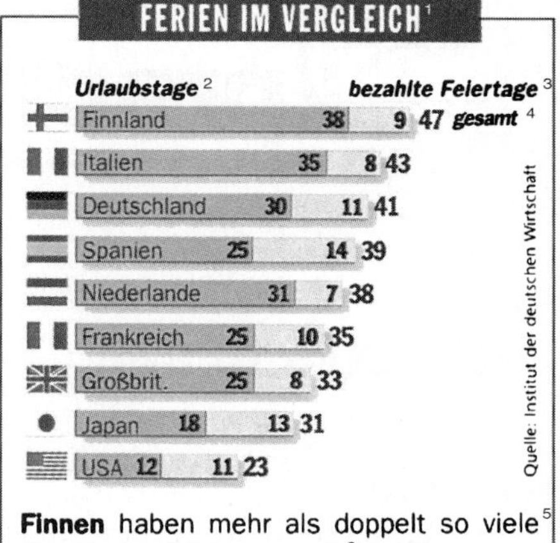

FERIEN IM VERGLEICH[1]

	Urlaubstage[2]	bezahlte Feiertage[3]	gesamt[4]
Finnland	38	9	47
Italien	35	8	43
Deutschland	30	11	41
Spanien	25	14	39
Niederlande	31	7	38
Frankreich	25	10	35
Großbrit.	25	8	33
Japan	18	13	31
USA	12	11	23

Quelle: Institut der deutschen Wirtschaft

Finnen haben mehr als doppelt so viele[5] Urlaubs- und Feiertage wie[6] US-Bürger

FOCUS-Magazin

ENTSPANNUNGSHITLISTE[7]

Die beliebtesten Freizeitbeschäftigungen[8] der Deutschen

	in Prozent
Musik hören	41
fernsehen	35
Zeitung lesen	35
gut Essen gehen	29
feiern, Freunde treffen	24
Auto fahren	21

Quelle: Verbraucheranalyse '96

Medien beherrschen[9] den größten Teil der Freizeit am Feierabend[10] und am Wochenende

FOCUS-Magazin

1. Ferien . . . *comparing time off* 2. *vacation days* 3. bezahlte . . . *paid holidays* 4. *total* 5. mehr . . . *more than twice as many* 6. *as* 7. *most popular ways to relax* 8. beliebtesten . . . *favorite leisure pursuits* 9. *dominate* 10. *after work*

Auf den ersten Blick

A. Schauen Sie sich den Text an. Um was für einen (*what kind of*) Text handelt es sich? Woher wissen Sie das? Welche Erwartungen (*expectations*) tragen Sie an einen solchen Text?

B. Assoziationen: Was fällt Ihnen zu den folgenden „Vergnügungen" ein? (*What comes to your mind with respect to the following "pleasures"?*)

BEISPIEL: Schnee → Winter, Spaß, Schneemann, kalt

1. Reisen
2. Schwimmen
3. freundlich sein
4. bequeme Schuhe
5. Hund
6. Schokolade
7. gute Musik
8. Kinder

Realia: *Ferien im Vergleich* and *Entspannungshitliste* are from FOCUS magazine.
Note: These two tables lend themselves well to discussion of cultural contrasts.

Assoziationen. Suggestion: Do these associations with the whole group. Write the associations on the board as students give them.

Vergnügungen

von Bertolt Brecht

Der erste Blick[1] aus dem Fenster am Morgen
Das wiedergefundene alte Buch
Begeisterte Gesichter[2]
Schnee, der Wechsel der Jahreszeiten
Die Zeitung
Der Hund
Die Dialektik
Duschen, Schwimmen
Alte Musik
Bequeme Schuhe
Begreifen[3]
Neue Musik
Schreiben, Pflanzen
Reisen
Singen
Freundlich sein.

Bertolt Brecht
1898–1956

1. *glance* 2. Begeisierte . . . *enthusiastic faces*
3. *understanding*

Vergnügungen. Suggestion: Bring in additional information about Bertolt Brecht.

Zum Text

A. Die Wörter **Duschen, Pflanzen, Reisen** können die Pluralformen sein von: **Dusche** (*shower*), **Pflanze** (*plant*), **Reise** (*trip*); oder sie können auch Verbalformen sein: **Duschen** = *taking a shower;* **Pflanzen** = *planting;* **Reisen** = *traveling.* Wie versteht Brecht diese Wörter wahrscheinlich? Als Dinge (Objekte) oder als Aktivitäten? Warum ist das wichtig?

B. Sind Brechts Vergnügungen ungewöhnliche oder ganz normale Vergnügungen? Welche finden Sie ungewöhnlich? Warum?

Weiteres über Bertolt Brecht finden Sie bei ***Deutsch: Na klar!*** im World-Wide-Web unter www.mhhe.com/german.

Sprechen und Schreiben

Aktivität 1 Ihr Gedicht

Schreiben Sie ein Gedicht mit dem Titel „Vergnügungen". Tauschen Sie Ihr Gedicht mit dem von einem Partner / einer Partnerin aus. Lesen Sie das Gedicht Ihres Partners / Ihrer Partnerin vor.

Aktivität 2 Eine Ferienreise

Viele Leute reisen gern in ihrer Freizeit. Schreiben Sie einen Absatz über eine Reise, die Sie einmal gemacht haben. Was haben Sie alles getan und gesehen? Wo und was haben Sie gegessen? Wie lange waren Sie unterwegs? Wie war das Wetter?

Wortschatz

Sport und Vergnügen	Sports and Leisure
das **Aerobic**	aerobics
Aerobic machen	to do aerobics
angeln	to fish
das **Bodybuilding**	body-building, weight training
Bodybuilding machen	to do body-building
faulenzen	to be lazy, lie around
der **Fußball, ⸚e**	soccer; soccer ball
Fußball spielen	to play soccer
joggen	to jog
die **Karte, -n**	card
malen	to paint
Rad fahren (fährt Rad), ist Rad gefahren*	to bicycle, ride a bike
reiten, ist geritten	to ride (horseback)
sammeln	to collect
das **Schach**	chess
Schach spielen	to play chess
der **Schlittschuh, -e**	ice skate
Schlittschuh laufen (läuft), ist gelaufen	to ice skate
schwimmen gehen, ist schwimmen gegangen	to go swimming
segeln	to sail
der **Sport,** *pl.* **Sportarten**	sports, sport
Sport treiben, getrieben	to play sports
tauchen	to dive
das **Tennis**	tennis
Tennis spielen	to play tennis
turnen	to do gymnastics
zeichnen	to draw

Orte	Locations
der **Berg, -e**	mountain
das **Eisstadion,** *pl.* **Eisstadien**	ice-skating rink
das **Fitnesscenter,-***	fitness center, gym
der **Fluss, ⸚e***	river
das **Freibad, ⸚er**	outdoor swimming pool
das **Hallenbad, ⸚er**	indoor swimming pool
das **Meer, -e**	sea, ocean
das **Schwimmbad, ⸚er**	swimming pool
der **See, -n**	lake
die **Sporthalle, -n**	sports arena
der **Sportplatz, ⸚e**	athletic field
das **Stadion,** *pl.* **Stadien**	stadium
die **Tennisanlage, -n**	tennis court
der **Tennisplatz, ⸚e**	tennis court
der **Trimm-Pfad, -e**	jogging path
die **Turnhalle, -n**	gymnasium
der **Wald, ⸚er**	forest
die **Wiese, -n**	meadow

Die Jahreszeiten	Seasons
das **Frühjahr**	spring
der **Frühling**	spring
der **Herbst**	autumn, fall
der **Sommer**	summer
der **Winter**	winter

Das Wetter	Weather
das **Gewitter, -**	thunderstorm
der **Grad**	degree(s)
35 Grad	35 degrees
der **Hagel**	hail
der **Himmel**	sky
der **Nebel**	fog
der **Regen**	rain
der **Regenschauer, -**	rain shower
der **Schnee**	snow
die **Sonne**	sun
Die Sonne scheint.	The sun is shining.
der **Sonnenschein**	sunshine
die **Temperatur, -en**	temperature
der **Wetterbericht, -e**	weather report
der **Wind, -e**	wind
die **Wolke, -n**	cloud
blitzen	to flash
Es blitzt.	There's lightning.
donnern	to thunder
Es donnert.	It's thundering.
regnen	to rain
Es regnet.	It's raining.
schneien	to snow
Es schneit.	It's snowing.

*See Appendix E for alternate spelling.

angenehm	pleasant(ly)
bedeckt	overcast
bewölkt	overcast, cloudy
einzeln	scattered; intermittent
heiß	hot
heiter	fair, bright
kalt	cold(ly)
kühl	cool(ly)
neblig	foggy
regnerisch	rainy
scheußlich	terrible, terribly
schwül	muggy, humid
sonnig	sunny
warm	warm(ly)
windig	windy
wolkenlos	cloudless
wolkig	cloudy

Sonstige Substantive — Other Nouns

der **Regenschirm, -e**	umbrella
die **Woche, -n**	week
das **Wochenende, -n**	weekend

Verben — Verbs

bringen, gebracht	to bring
dauern	to last; to take
fallen (fällt), ist gefallen	to fall
fliegen, ist geflogen	to fly
passieren, ist passiert	to happen
reservieren	to reserve
verbringen, verbracht	to spend (*time*)
verlieren, verloren	to lose

Sonstiges — Other

aber	but, however
denn	because, for
draußen	outside
drinnen	inside
einmal	once
einmal die Woche	once a week
einmal im Monat	once a month
einmal im Jahr	once a year
zweimal	twice
dreimal	three times
früher	earlier, once, used to (*do, be, etc.*)
gestern	yesterday
jeden Tag	every day
oder	or
sondern	but, rather

Lernziele

Use this checklist to verify that you can now . . .

- ☐ discuss typical leisure-time activities in German-speaking countries.
- ☐ talk about different types of sports and leisure-time activities you engage in.
- ☐ talk about the weather in various seasons and places.
- ☐ form compound sentences using the coordinating conjunctions.
- ☐ distinguish and use appropriately **aber** and **sondern.**
- ☐ talk about events in the past, using the present perfect tense.

Kapitel 8

Wie man fit und gesund bleibt

Der bekannte Kurort Baden-Baden

Kapitel 8. Introduce the chapter by talking about the things people do to stay fit and healthy. Recycle vocabulary on sport and food during this introduction. Personalize the discussion to include what students in the class do.

Alles klar?

A. Schauen Sie sich die Anzeige für Baden-Baden an, einen Kurort in Deutschland. Was kann man in Baden-Baden unternehmen (*do*)? Machen Sie eine Liste.

BEISPIEL:	SPORT	UNTERHALTUNG	GESUNDHEIT
	schwimmen	ins Theater gehen	in die Sauna gehen

B. Was machen diese Leute in Baden-Baden? Kreuzen Sie an.

	HERR/FRAU LOHMANN	HERR KRANZLER	FRAU DIETMOLD
Golf	☐	☒	☐
Karten spielen	☒	☐	☐
Massage	☒	☐	☒
Mini-Golf	☐	☐	☒
Sauna	☐	☒	☐
Schwimmen	☐	☒	☐
Spazierengehen	☒	☐	☐
Tanzen	☐	☐	☒
Theater	☐	☐	☒
Thermalbad	☒	☒	☒
Tischtennis	☐	☐	☒
Trinkkur	☐	☒	☒
Wandern	☐	☒	☐

Realia. Suggestion: Take a few minutes to introduce the idea of the *Kurort*. Have students look at the map to see if they can find towns with the word **Bad** in the name. *Baden-Baden:* This is a segment of an ad by the *Bäder- und Kurverwaltung* of the city of Baden-Baden, which is world famous for its spas and gambling casinos. Note the word **Casino** in one of the ad's activities squares.

Kulturtipp

Germans often spend several weeks at a health resort after an illness or when they are run down from the strains and stresses of work. There are many health spas (**Heilbäder und Kurorte**) throughout Germany. The national health care system (**Krankenkasse**) pays for such a stay if rest and recuperation (**Kur und Erholung**) are recommended by a physician. At some health spas people go on a **Trinkkur:** at prescribed intervals they drink a glass of the healthful mineral waters for which some spas are famous.

Hier klicken

Weiteres zum Thema Kurorte finden Sie bei ***Deutsch: Na klar!*** im World-Wide-Web unter www.mhhe.com/german.

Wörter im Kontext

Thema 1

Fit und gesund 

Was machen diese Leute, um **fit** zu bleiben?

TINA: Für meine **Gesundheit tue** ich viel. Ich esse vegetarisch, **versuche** so gut es geht, den **Stress** in meinem Leben zu reduzieren. Zur **Arbeit gehe** ich **meistens zu Fuß.** Ich trinke viel **Kräutertee** und nur selten Alkohol, **höchstens ab und zu** ein Glas Wein zum Essen.

WALTER: **Fitness** ist mir sehr wichtig. **Deshalb** rauche ich **nie** und esse **gesund, d.h.** (das heißt) **wenig** Fleisch und viel Gemüse. Ich treibe **regelmäßig** Sport, **besonders** an der frischen **Luft.** Ich möchte **mich fit halten.**

ANITA: **Mindestens** zweimal im Jahr **mache** ich **Urlaub,** denn meine Arbeit ist sehr **anstrengend.** Ich bin nämlich **Krankenschwester.** Ich **achte auf** meine Gesundheit und esse nur **Ökolebensmittel, entweder** direkt vom Bauernhof oder vom **Naturkostladen**. Ich mache jede Woche Yoga. Da kann ich **mich** richtig **entspannen.**

Realia. The organic growers' insignias are from a consumer brochure.

Aktivität 1 Meine Fitnessroutine

A. Was machen Sie, um fit und gesund zu bleiben? Kreuzen Sie an!

Aktivität 1. Follow-up: Poll the class to see who does what. Is this class health conscious?

1. □ joggen
2. □ ins Fitnesscenter gehen
3. □ vegetarisch essen
4. □ meditieren
5. □ Urlaub machen
6. □ wenig Alkohol trinken
7. □ Stress reduzieren
8. □ nicht rauchen
9. □ viel Gemüse/Obst essen
10. □ viel an die frische Luft gehen
11. □ viel zu Fuß gehen
12. □ Yoga machen
13. □ viel Wasser trinken
14. □ ?

B. Sagen Sie nun, wie oft Sie das tun.

BEISPIEL: Ich mache zweimal im Jahr Urlaub.

nie	mindestens/höchstens einmal/ zweimal die Woche
selten	einmal/zweimal/dreimal im Jahr
ab und zu	?
manchmal	
regelmäßig	
jeden Tag	

C. Sagen Sie nun, warum Sie das tun oder nicht tun.

BEISPIELE: Ich jogge nicht. Das ist mir zu langweilig.
Ich esse vegetarisch. Das ist gut für die Gesundheit.

macht mir (keinen) Spaß
ist gut/schlecht für die Gesundheit
macht krank
kostet zu viel Geld
habe keine Zeit/Lust dazu (*for that*)
ist zu anstrengend
ist (un)gesund
reduziert Stress
ist mir zu langweilig
?

Aktivität 2 Beim Fitnessberater°

° fitness adviser

Aktivität 2. Suggestion: Encourage students to be as creative as possible. Follow-up by selecting one or two pairs to perform their conversation in front of the class.

Spielen Sie zusammen mit einem Partner / einer Partnerin ein Gespräch zwischen einem Fitnessberater / einer Fitnessberaterin und einem Klienten / einer Klientin. Was darf man tun? Was nicht? Was sollte (*should*) man tun? Was nicht?

BEISPIEL: S1: Darf ich Wein trinken?
S2: Ja, aber nicht zu viel. Trinken Sie lieber viel Wasser.
S1: Wie viele Stunden sollte man pro Nacht schlafen?
S2: Mindestens sieben Stunden.

Fleisch essen
Vitamintabletten einnehmen
Urlaub machen
Sport treiben
Kräutertee trinken
Kaffee trinken
?

Thema 2

Der menschliche Körper° *body*

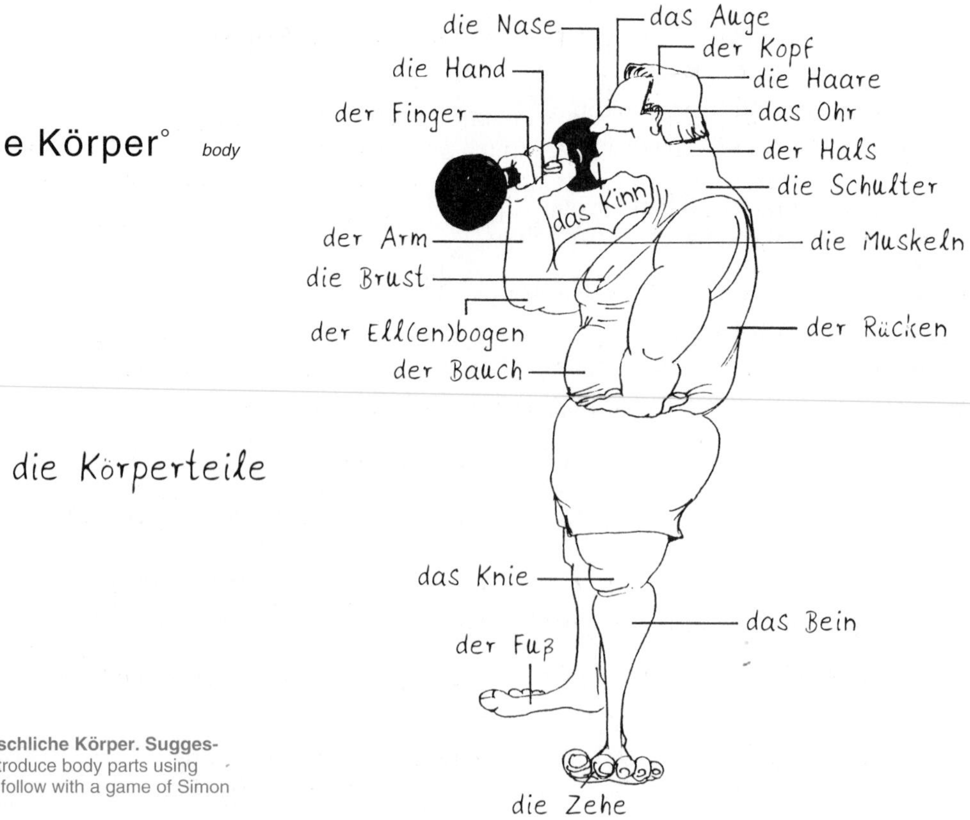

die Körperteile

die Nase
die Hand
der Finger
der Arm
die Brust
der Ell(en)bogen
der Bauch
das Knie
der Fuß
die Zehe
das Auge
der Kopf
die Haare
das Ohr
der Hals
die Schulter
das Kinn
die Muskeln
der Rücken
das Bein

Der menschliche Körper. Suggestion: Introduce body parts using TPR and follow with a game of Simon says.

Ein Telefongespräch

CHRISTOPH: Schmidt.
UTA: Hallo, Christoph? Hier ist Uta.
CHRISTOPH: Ja, grüß dich, Uta.
UTA: Nanu! Was ist denn los? Du **klingst** ja so **deprimiert.**
CHRISTOPH: Ich liege im Bett. Ich **fühle mich hundsmiserabel.**
UTA: **Was fehlt dir** denn?
CHRISTOPH: Ich habe eine **Erkältung,** vielleicht **sogar** die **Grippe.** Der Hals **tut mir weh,** ich kann **kaum schlucken, mir ist schlecht.** Ich habe **Fieber, Halsschmerzen, Husten** und **Schnupfen.** Ich habe **auch Kopfschmerzen** und bin so **müde** und **schlapp.** Und morgen muss ich eine Arbeit bei Professor Höhn **abgeben.**
UTA: **So ein Pech.** Warst du schon beim **Arzt?**
CHRISTOPH: Nein.
UTA: Wie lange bist du denn schon **krank?**
CHRISTOPH: Seit fast zwei Wochen schon.
UTA: Du bist **verrückt!** Geh doch **gleich** zum **Arzt.** Er kann dir sicher was* **verschreiben.**
CHRISTOPH: Aber ich kriege (*get*) bestimmt keinen **Termin.**
UTA: **Das macht nichts.** Geh einfach in die **Sprechstunde.**
CHRISTOPH: Na gut. Ich danke dir für den **Rat.**
UTA: **Nichts zu danken** . . . Ich wünsche dir **gute Besserung!**

Dialogue. Suggestion: Introduce the new words before students listen to the dialogue. Then ask them to describe briefly what is wrong with Christoph and how long he has been sick. Utilize the drawing to describe Christoph's illness. Have students role-play the dialogue.

Aktivität 3 Das Telefongespräch

Ergänzen Sie den Lückentext. Die Information finden Sie in dem Telefongespräch im **Thema 2.**

Christoph klingt sehr _____ am Telefon, denn er fühlt sich _____.[1] Der _____ tut ihm weh, und er kann kaum _____.[2] Er hat auch _____.[3] Seit zwei Wochen ist er _____.[4] Er war noch nicht beim _____.[5] Uta empfiehlt (*recommends*) ihm, in die _____ zu gehen.[6] Uta wünscht ihm _____ _____.[7]

Aktivität 4 Im Aerobic-Kurs

Sie hören einen Aerobic-Lehrer beim Training im Aerobic-Kurs. Numerieren Sie alle Körperteile in der Reihenfolge von 1–10, so wie Sie sie hören. Einige Wörter auf der Liste kommen nicht im Hörtext vor.

1 Arme	5 Füße	3 Knie	10 Muskeln
_____ Bauch	7 Hals	6 Kopf	2 Rücken
_____ Beine	_____ Hände	9 Ohren	8 Schultern
4 Finger			

Aktivität 5. Suggestion: Students should look over all possibilities before listening to each dialogue. After each dialogue is played, pause to let students respond.

Aktivität 5 Beschwerden°

°*complaints*

Was fehlt diesen Leuten? Was sollten sie dagegen tun? Markieren Sie Ihre Antworten.

track 6

DIALOG 1

Leni hat:	Rückenschmerzen	eine Erkältung	Kopfschmerzen
Doris empfiehlt:	Geh zum Arzt.	Leg dicf ins Bett.	Nimm Aspirin.

* **Was,** as used here, is a shortened form of the pronoun **etwas.** It occurs often in colloquial German.

DIALOG 2

Doris hat:	Kopfschmerzen	Bauchschmerzen	Rückenschmerzen
Leni empfiehlt:	Geh zum Arzt.	Trink Kamillentee.	Leg dich ins Bett.

DIALOG 3

Patient hat:	keine Energie	Kopfschmerzen	kann nicht schlafen
Arzt empfiehlt:	mehr Schlaf	Kur im Schwarzwald	Tabletten gegen Streß

Use the following phrase to talk about how you feel:

Ich **fühle mich** nicht wohl.	*I am not well.*

The person with the symptoms refers to himself or herself with a pronoun in the dative case.

Mir ist schlecht.	*I feel sick to my stomach.*
Mir ist warm/kalt.	*I feel warm/cold.*

The verb **fehlen** with the dative case is frequently used to ask "What is the matter?"

Was fehlt dir denn?	*What's the matter with you?*
Was fehlt ihm denn?	*What's the matter with him?*

Use the verb **wehtun** with the dative case to say that something hurts.

Die Füße **tun** { **mir** / **ihm** / **ihr** } **weh.** — { *My* / *His* / *Her* } *feet hurt.*

Aktivität 6. Follow-up: Each student writes a complaint on a slip of paper (no names). Slips are collected and redistributed. As slips are read by individuals, other students give advice.

Aktivität 6 Was fehlt dir denn?

Fragen Sie Ihren Partner / Ihre Partnerin: „Was fehlt dir denn?" Antworten Sie auf seine/ihre Beschwerden mit einem guten Rat.

BEISPIEL: S1: Ich fühle mich so schlapp.
S2: Geh nach Hause und leg dich ins Bett.

BESCHWERDEN	RATSCHLÄGE
Ich fühle mich so schlapp.	Nimm ein paar Aspirin.
Der Hals tut mir weh.	Geh . . .
Ich kann kaum schlucken.	in die Sauna.
Ich habe . . .	nach Hause.
Kopfschmerzen.	zum Arzt.
Rückenschmerzen.	Leg dich ins Bett.
Halsschmerzen.	Nimm mal Vitamin C.
Husten.	Trink heißen Tee mit Rum.
Schnupfen.	?
eine Erkältung.	
Fieber.	
Ich kann nicht schlafen.	
Mir ist schlecht.	
Ich habe zu viel gegessen.	

Realia. These ads for common ailments and complaints appear often in various papers and magazines.

1. *lozenges*
2. *natural remedy*
3. *valerian content*

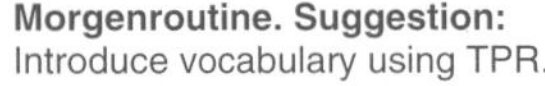

Morgenroutine

a.

b.

c.

d.

e.

f.

g.

Was machen diese Leute morgens? Was passt zu welchem Bild?

1. _____ Er **rasiert sich.**
2. _____ Sie **streckt sich.**
3. _____ Sie **kämmt sich.**
4. _____ Sie **putzt sich die Zähne.**
5. _____ Er **duscht sich.**
6. _____ Er **setzt sich** an den Tisch.
7. _____ Sie **wäscht sich** das **Gesicht.**
8. _____ Er **zieht sich an.**

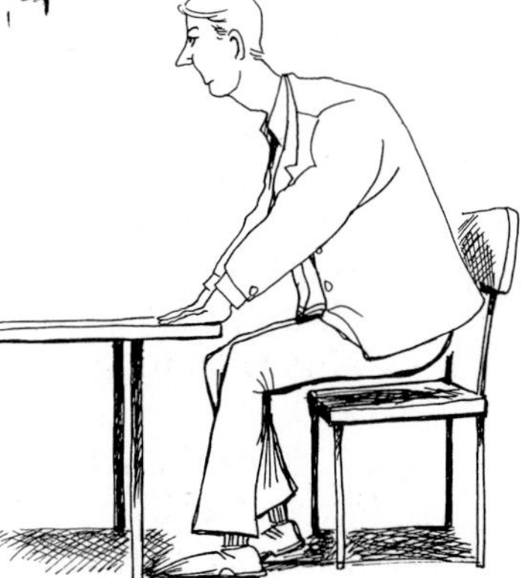

h.

Aktivität 7 Meine Routine am Morgen

Aktivität 7. Follow-up: Have a few students act out their morning routine. Other students have to say what each activity is.

Was machen Sie jeden Morgen? Hier sind einige Dinge, die man morgens oft macht. In welcher Reihenfolge machen Sie alles jeden Morgen? Nummerieren Sie die Aktivitäten unten von 1 bis 8.

_____ Ich ziehe mich an.
_____ Ich dusche mich.
_____ Ich wasche mir das Gesicht.
_____ Ich kämme mich.
_____ Ich strecke mich.
_____ Ich rasiere mich.
_____ Ich setze mich an den Frühstückstisch.
_____ Ich putze mir die Zähne.

Aktivität 8 Hin und her: Meine Routine—deine Routine

Jeder hat eine andere Routine. Was machen diese Leute und in welcher Reihenfolge? Machen Sie es auch so?

BEISPIEL: S1: Was macht Alexander morgens?
S2: Zuerst rasiert er sich und putzt sich die Zähne. Dann kämmt er sich. Danach setzt er sich an den Tisch und frühstückt.

WER	WAS ER/SIE MORGENS MACHT
Alexander	zuerst / sich rasieren / sich die Zähne putzen dann / sich kämmen danach / sich an den Tisch setzen / frühstücken
Elke	zuerst / sich anziehen dann / sich die Zähne putzen danach / sich kämmen
Tilo	zuerst / sich duschen / sich rasieren dann / sich an den Tisch setzen / frühstücken danach / sich die Zähne putzen
Kamal	zuerst / sich das Gesicht waschen dann / frühstücken danach / sich rasieren / sich anziehen
Sie	zuerst / ? dann / ? danach / ?
Ihr Partner / Ihre Partnerin	zuerst / ? dann / ? danach / ?

Grammatik im Kontext

Connecting Sentences: Subordinating Conjunctions°

°unterordnende Konjunktionen

Subordinating conjunctions are used to connect a main (independent) clause and a dependent (subordinate) clause. Four frequently used subordinating conjunctions are **dass** (*that*), **ob** (*whether, if*), **weil** (*because*), and **wenn** (*whenever, if*).

Note that subordinating conjunctions affect the position of the verb in the dependent clause in which they are placed.

Ich hoffe, **dass** du bald gesund wirst.	*I hope that you'll get well soon.*
Ich glaube, **dass** er mitkommt.	*I think he'll come along.*
Weißt du, **ob** Mark krank ist?	*Do you know whether Mark is ill?*
Mark bleibt zu Hause, **weil** er eine Erkältung hat.	*Mark is staying at home because he has a cold.*
Ich bekomme Kopfschmerzen, **wenn** ich zu lange lese.	*I get a headache if I read too long.*
Ich gehe ins Fitnesszentrum, **wenn** ich Zeit habe.	*I go to the fitness center, whenever I have time.*

In dependent clauses the conjugated verb is placed at the end. In the case of a separable-prefix verb, the prefix is joined with the rest of the verb. A comma always separates the main clause from the dependent clause.

MAIN CLAUSE	DEPENDENT CLAUSE
Er bleibt zu Hause,	weil er eine Erkältung **hat.**
Ich weiß nicht,	ob er schon beim Arzt gewesen **ist.**
Ich bin sicher,	dass er **mitkommt.**

If the dependent clause precedes the main clause, the main clause begins with the conjugated verb, followed by the subject.

DEPENDENT CLAUSE	MAIN CLAUSE
Wenn wir Zeit haben,	**gehen** wir am Wochenende ins Fitnesscenter.
Ob Hans Zeit hat,	**weiß** ich nicht.
Weil Mark krank ist,	**bleibt** er zu Hause.

Indirect Questions

An indirect question consists of an introductory clause and a following question. Interrogative pronouns function like subordinating conjunctions when they are in indirect questions, and the conjugated verb is placed at the end.

DIRECT QUESTION	INDIRECT QUESTION
Warum kauft Herr Stierli so viel Vitamin B?	Ich weiß nicht, **warum** Herr Stierli so viel Vitamin B **kauft.**
Was hat er vor?	Ich möchte wissen, **was** er **vorhat.**

A yes/no question is introduced by the conjunction **ob** in the indirect question.

Geht er zu einer Party?	Ich möchte wissen, **ob** er zu einer Party **geht.**

Übung 1 Ein großer Erfolg°

°success

Schauen Sie sich den Cartoon „Herr Stierli" an. Beantworten Sie die Fragen, indem Sie die Konjunktion **weil** benutzen.

Herr Stierli von René Fehr

Realia. The cartoon *Herr Stierli* appeared in the Swiss magazine *Brückenbauer*, published by *Migros-Genossenschaft. Migros* is a large department store chain selling everything from food to clothing. The cartoon makes fun of society at an international party. Herr Stierli is greeted in English, German, and French (*Comment allez-vous?* = "How are you?"). The German phrase *Ich habe die Ehre* ("I am honored") is a formal way of acknowledging someone socially, especially in southern Germany and Austria.

1. Warum ist Herr Stierli zur Apotheke gegangen? (Er wollte Vitamin B kaufen.)
2. Warum hat er fünf Packungen Vitamin B eingenommen (*took*)? (Er brauchte mehr Energie.)
3. Warum war Herr Stierli sehr stolz (*proud*)? (Er war sehr beliebt bei den Gästen.)
4. Warum hatte er so großen Erfolg? (Er hatte vor der Party viel Vitamin B eingenommen.)

Übung 1. Note: Explain that the expression "Vitamin B" is sometimes used figuratively as it is here: "B" stands for *Beziehungen* = connections. Thus a dose of vitamin B means you need connections. Herr Stierli, by ingesting large amounts of vitamin B, is able to make lots of connections at the party and is the most popular guest.

Übung 2 Wie stehen Sie dazu?°

°*What's your opinion?*

Nehmen Sie Stellung (*express an opinion*).

BEISPIEL: S1: Obst ist die beste Nahrung (*food*).
S2: Ich bezweifle (*doubt*), dass Obst die beste Nahrung ist.
oder Ich glaube auch, dass Obst die beste Nahrung ist.

Übung 2. This exercise can be done in pairs, students taking turns expressing their opinions about the statements. Follow-up with a survey in class: *Wer glaubt, dass (Bier dick macht)? Wer bezweifelt, dass; Wer behauptet dass, . . . ?*

REDEMITTEL

Ich bezweifle, dass . . .

Ich glaube, dass . . .

1. Vitamin C ist gut gegen Erkältungen.
2. Klassische Musik ist gut gegen Stress.
3. Rauchen gefährdet (*endangers*) die Gesundheit.
4. Gesundheit ist essbar. (Wer gesund isst, bleibt gesund.)
5. Gesund ist, was gut schmeckt.
6. Hühnersuppe ist gut gegen Erkältungen.
7. Bier macht dick.
8. Vegetarisches Essen ist ideal.
9. Zu viel Zucker macht aggressiv.
10. Knoblauch (*garlic*) hilft gegen Vampire!

Übung 3 Wie gesundheitsbewusst° sind Sie

°*health conscious*

Übung 3. Note: Ensure that students use the **weil** construction. Review use of *denn* and *nämlich* to express reasons.

Fragen Sie Ihren Partner / Ihre Partnerin, was er/sie für die Gesundheit tut und warum.

BEISPIEL: S1: Gehst du regelmäßig zum Arzt?
S2: Nein.
S1: Warum nicht?
S2: Weil ich das unnötig (*unnecessary*) finde.

S1

Gehst du regelmäßig . . .
- zum Arzt?
- zum Zahnarzt (*dentist*)?
- ins Fitnesscenter?
- in die Sauna?
- in Urlaub?
- zur Massage
- ?

Isst du . . .
- vegetarisch?
- Fleisch?
- ?

Rauchst du . . .
- Zigaretten?
- Zigarren?
- Pfeife?
- ?

Trinkst du gern . . .
- Bier/Wein?
- Kräutertee?
- Karottensaft?
- viel Mineralwasser?
- ?

S2

Ich finde das . . .
- nötig/unnötig.
- gesund/ungesund.

Ich habe einfach keine . . .
- Zeit dazu.
- Lust dazu.

Mir macht das (keinen) Spaß.

Das schmeckt mir (nicht).

Das kostet zu viel.

?

Kulturtipp

To purchase prescription drugs in Germany, you have to go to an **Apotheke.** Nonprescription drugs must also be purchased at an **Apotheke.** Nonprescription drugs are not as common in Germany as in the United States or Canada. Toiletries, vitamins, and personal care items are carried by **Drogerien**.

Medikamente gibt es in der Apotheke.

Übung 4 Das mache ich, wenn . . .

Unter welchen Umständen (*circumstances*) machen Sie das?

BEISPIEL: Ich gehe zum Arzt, wenn ich krank bin.

Ich gehe zum Arzt, . . .	Ich brauche Zahnpasta.
zum Zahnarzt, . . .	Ich habe zu viel gegessen.
in die Sauna, . . .	Ich brauche Aspirin.
in die Drogerie, . . .	Ich fühle mich hunds-miserabel.
in die Apotheke, . . .	Ich habe die Grippe.
Ich bleibe im Bett, . . .	Ich fühle mich schlapp.
Ich nehme viel Vitamin C ein, . . .	Ich habe eine Erkältung.
Ich esse Hühnersuppe, . . .	Ich bin krank.
Ich trinke Kräutertee, . . .	Ich habe Zahnschmerzen.
	?

Übung 5 Was tun Sie gewöhnlich?

Sagen Sie, was Sie in diesen Situationen machen.

Übung 5. Suggestion: Have students scan the possibilities before making four statements about themselves. Then have students work in pairs, taking turns asking questions and responding. Have them begin each question by asking, for example, *Was tust du, wenn du eine Erkältung hast?* etc. **Follow-up:** Ask the class questions like *Wer isst Hühnersuppe, wenn er/sie eine Erkältung hat?* You may want to point out that chicken soup for a cold is not a widely-known folk remedy in Germany.

BEISPIEL: Wenn ich eine Erkältung habe, trinke ich viel Kräutertee.

Wenn ich eine Erkältung habe,	im Bett bleiben
Wenn ich nicht einschlafen kann,	Kräutertee trinken
Wenn ich gestresst bin,	heiße Milch mit Honig trinken
Wenn ich mich schlapp fühle,	Rotwein mit Rum trinken
Wenn ich schlecht gelaunt (*in a bad mood*) bin,	in die Sauna gehen
	viel Vitamin C einnehmen
	Hühnersuppe essen
	ein Buch lesen
	meditieren
	?

Übung 6 Ich muss es mir überlegen.°

°think it over

Stefans Freunde wollen Bungee-jumping gehen, und er soll mitmachen. Stefan ist aber sehr skeptisch. Was will er genau wissen?

BEISPIEL: Wo kann man das lernen? →
Er will wissen, wo man das lernen kann.

Er will wissen, . . .

1. Wie gefährlich (*dangerous*) ist das eigentlich?
2. Wie viel kostet das?
3. Was für Kleidung muss man dabei tragen?
4. Muss man zuerst ein Training machen?
5. Wer macht sonst noch mit?
6. Warum muss es ausgerechnet Bungee-jumping sein?
7. Wer hat diese verrückte Idee gehabt?

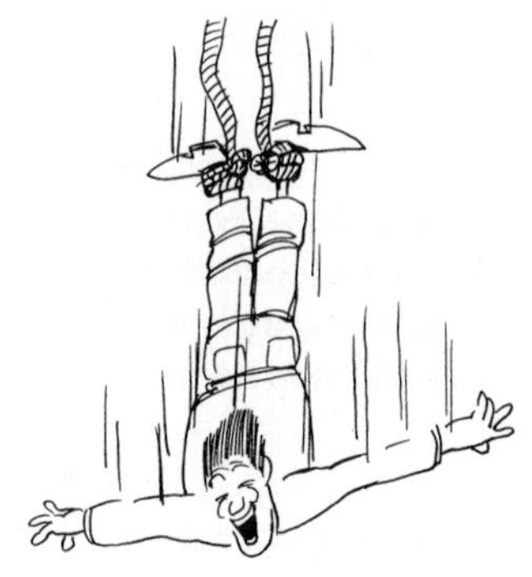

Reflexive Pronouns and Verbs°

°Reflexivpronomen und reflexive Verben

When the subject and pronominal object of a sentence refer to the same person, the object is called a reflexive pronoun.

Wir informieren **uns** über Fitnesscenter.	*We're informing ourselves about fitness centers.*
Die Studenten informieren **sich** über die Kosten.	*The students inform themselves about the costs.*
Informieren **Sie sich** bitte zuerst über die Kosten!	*Inform yourself first about the costs.*

Reflexive Pronouns. Suggestion: Introduce reflexive pronouns and verbs by recycling some of the verbs used in the **WiK:** *Ich halte mich mit Tennis fit. Wie halten Sie sich fit?* **Point out:** The reflexive pronoun is not always expressed in English: "Mr. Stierli keeps fit" (*Herr Stierli hält sich fit*).

Reflexive pronouns are identical to personal pronouns except for the third-person singular and plural and the formal **Sie**-form, all of which are **sich.** The reflexive pronoun may be in the accusative or the dative case, depending on the verb. You will need to remember this distinction only for the **mich/mir**- and **dich/dir**-forms, the only reflexive pronouns with different forms in the dative and accusative. The reflexive pronoun comes after the conjugated verb or, in inverted word order, after the pronoun subject.

Reflexive Pronouns

ACCUSATIVE		DATIVE	ACCUSATIVE		DATIVE
mich	*myself*	**mir**	**uns**	*ourselves*	**uns**
dich	*yourself (informal)*	**dir**	**euch**	*yourselves (informal)*	**euch**
sich	*yourself (formal)*	**sich**	**sich**	*yourselves (formal)*	**sich**
sich	*himself/herself/itself*	**sich**	**sich**	*themselves*	**sich**

Verbs with Accusative Reflexive Pronouns

German uses reflexive pronouns much more extensively than English. Some verbs are always used with a reflexive pronoun.

Entspannen Sie **sich!**	*Relax.*
Beeil(e) dich!	*Hurry up.*
Wie **fühlst** du **dich?**	*How are you feeling?*

Verbs that are always used with a reflexive pronoun in the accusative include the following:

sich aufregen	to get upset
sich beeilen	to hurry
sich entspannen	to relax
sich erholen	to recuperate
sich erkälten	to catch cold
sich fit halten	to keep fit
sich (wohl)fühlen	to feel (well)
sich interessieren (für)	to be interested (in)

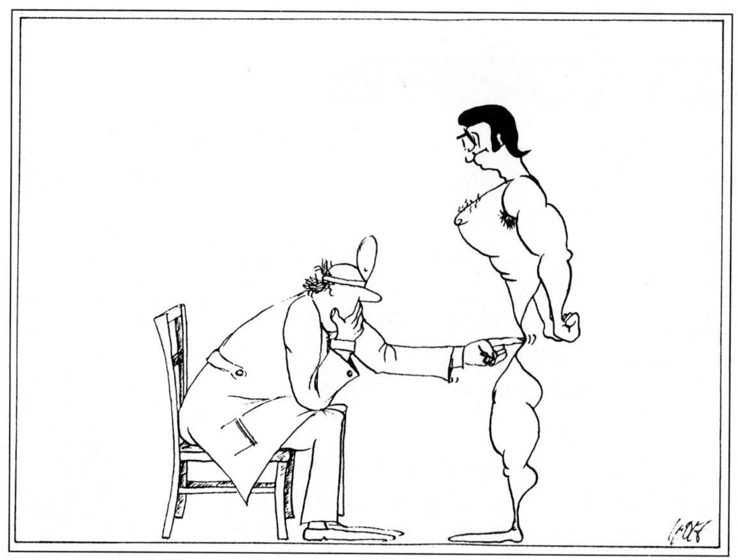

„Bitte entspannen Sie sich!"

Many verbs that require an accusative object can be used both reflexively and nonreflexively, although in many instances there is some change in meaning.

NONREFLEXIVE	REFLEXIVE
Anja **legt** ihre Brille auf den Tisch. *Anja puts her glasses on the table.*	Anja **legt sich** auf das Sofa. (hin). *Anja lies down on the sofa.*
Der Arzt **setzt** das Kind auf den Stuhl. *The doctor puts the child on the chair.*	Er **setzt sich** (hin). *He sits down.*
Das **regt** ihn auf. *That annoys him.*	Ich **rege mich** auf. *I'm getting upset.*

Other verbs that are used both reflexively and nonreflexively include:

	REFLEXIVE	NONREFLEXIVE
(sich) anziehen	to get dressed	to dress (someone else)
(sich) kämmen	to comb one's hair	to comb
(sich) (hin)legen	to lie (down)	to place, lay (down)
(sich) (hin)setzen	to sit (down)	to seat (someone); to set (something down)
(sich) treffen	to meet (one another)	to meet (someone else)
(sich) verletzen	to injure oneself	to hurt, injure
(sich) waschen	to wash oneself	to wash

Analyse

Analyse. Suggestion: Use the cartoon as a point of departure to ask students: *Wie fühlen Sie sich heute?*

Schauen Sie sich den Cartoon an.

- Lesen Sie, was Wurzel denkt, und identifizieren Sie die Sätze mit reflexiven Verben.
- Wie fühlt sich Wurzel heute?
- Fühlt er sich gewöhnlich so gut? Wie oft hat er sich schon so gefühlt?
- Warum fühlt er sich am Ende ganz deprimiert?

Realia. *Wurzel* is the German name for the cartoon dog Fred Basset.

1. *unusual*
2. *sign*

Übung 7 Beim Arzt 

Sie hören eine Besprechung zwischen Herrn Schneider und seinem Arzt. Markieren Sie die richtigen Antworten auf die Fragen.

1. Warum hat Herr Schneider einen Termin beim Arzt?
   - **a.** Er hat einen chronischen Schluckauf (*hiccups*).
   - **b.** Er hat sich beim Fitnesstraining verletzt.
   - **c.** Er fühlt sich so schlapp.
2. Was ist die Ursache (*cause*) seines Problems?
   - **a.** Seine Arbeit bringt viel Stress mit sich.
   - **b.** Er sitzt den ganzen Tag am Schreibtisch.
   - **c.** Seine Arbeit ist so langweilig.
3. Was empfiehlt ihm der Arzt?
   - **a.** Er soll sich eine andere Arbeit suchen.
   - **b.** Er soll sich im Schwarzwald vom Stress erholen.
   - **c.** Er soll Sport treiben.
4. Wie reagiert Herr Schneider auf diese Vorschläge?
   - **a.** Er ist sehr enthusiastisch.
   - **b.** Er hat keine Zeit für eine Kur im Schwarzwald.
   - **c.** Er interessiert sich nicht für Sport.

5. Was verschreibt ihm der Arzt?
   a. Einen täglichen Spaziergang.
   b. Regelmäßig meditieren.
   c. Vitamintabletten.
6. Warum meint der Arzt, dass Herr Schneider mit seinen Nerven am Ende ist?
   a. Er hat einen Schluckauf und weiß es nicht.
   b. Er hat einen nervösen Tick.
   c. Er redet zu viel und zu schnell.

Übung 8 Morgenroutine

Morgens geht es bei der Familie Kunze immer recht hektisch zu. Ergänzen Sie die fehlenden Reflexivpronomen.

Zuerst duscht _____ Herr Kunze.[1] Dann rasiert er _____.[2] Seine Frau ruft: „Bitte, beeil _____, ich muss _____ auch noch duschen."[3]

Cornelia, die siebzehnjährige Tochter, erklärt: „Ich glaube, ich habe _____ erkältet.[4] Ich fühle _____ so schlapp.[5] Ich lege _____ wieder hin."[6] Frau Kunze zu Cornelia: „Zieh _____ bitte sofort an![7] Du fühlst _____ so schlapp, weil du so spät ins Bett gegangen bist."[8] Cornelia: „Reg _____ nicht auf, ich ziehe _____ ja schon an."[9]

Frau Kunze zu Thomas, dem siebenjährigen Sohn: „Es ist schon halb acht, und du musst _____ noch kämmen.[10] Hast du _____ überhaupt schon gewaschen?"[11]

Sabine, die zwölfjährige Tochter, duscht _____ schon seit fünfzehn Minuten.[12]

Herr und Frau Kunze setzen _____ an den Frühstückstisch.[13] Herr Kunze zu seiner Frau: „Wir müssen _____ beeilen.[14] Wo sind die Kinder?" Er ruft ungeduldig: „Könnt ihr _____ nicht ein bisschen beeilen? Es ist schon acht Uhr."[15]

So ist es jeden Morgen: Alle müssen _____ beeilen.[16]

Übung 9 Ratschläge°

° advice

Was kann man Ihnen in diesen Situationen raten?

BEISPIEL: S1: Ich habe die Grippe.
S2: Dann leg dich ins Bett.

1. Sie haben die Grippe.
2. Sie haben sich erkältet.
3. Sie fahren vier Wochen in Urlaub.
4. Sie fühlen sich hundsmiserabel.
5. Sie haben den ganzen Tag in der Bibliothek verbracht.
6. Sie müssen in einer Minute an der Bushaltestelle sein.
7. Sie haben eine schlechte Note (*grade*) in einer Prüfung (*test*) bekommen.

sich beeilen
sich gut erholen
sich ins Bett legen
sich mehr anstrengen
sich hinlegen
sich entspannen
sich ins Café setzen
sich (nicht) aufregen
?

Verbs with Dative Reflexive Pronouns

Many verbs that have indirect objects in the dative case can also be used with reflexive pronouns.

NONREFLEXIVE	REFLEXIVE
Ich kaufe **ihr** einen neuen Wagen.	Ich kaufe **mir** einen neuen Wagen.
I'm buying her a new car.	*I'm buying myself a new car.*

A dative reflexive pronoun is also used with verbs such as **anziehen** (*to dress*), **kämmen** (*to comb*), **putzen** (*to clean*), and **waschen** (*to wash*) when the direct object is a part of the body or a piece of clothing.

Ich **ziehe mir** ein Hemd an.	*I am putting on a shirt.*
Ich **kämme mir** die Haare.	*I am combing my hair.*
Ich **wasche mir** die Hände.	*I am washing my hands.*
Ich **putze mir** die Zähne.	*I am brushing my teeth.*

If a part of the body or a piece of clothing is not mentioned, an accusative reflexive pronoun is used.

Ich **ziehe mich** an.	*I am getting dressed.*
Ich **kämme mich.**	*I am combing my hair.*
Ich **wasche mich.**	*I am getting washed.*

Übung 10 Wie oft machen Sie das?

Fragen Sie Ihren Partner / Ihre Partnerin, wie oft er/sie die folgenden Dinge macht.

Übung 10. Suggestion: Point out that some of the pronouns will be dative, others accusative. Go over the verbs first to determine this. Then have students work in pairs.

BEISPIEL: sich die Zähne putzen →
S1: Putzt du dir jeden Tag die Zähne?
S2: Natürlich putze ich mir jeden Tag die Zähne.

sich die Zähne putzen	nie	jeden Tag
sich die Haare kämmen	ab und zu	jeden Morgen
sich rasieren	oft	jeden Abend
sich einen Kaffee kochen		
sich einen Film ansehen		

Übung 11 Situationen und Lösungen°

°*solutions*

Was machen Sie in diesen Situationen? Bilden Sie Sätze.

BEISPIEL: sich erkälten →
S1: Was machst du, wenn du dich erkältet hast?
S2: Wenn ich mich erkältet habe, mache ich mir einen Tee.

SITUATIONEN	LÖSUNGEN
sich erkälten	sich auf das Sofa legen
Appetit auf etwas Süßes haben	zum Arzt gehen
Kopfschmerzen haben	sich einen Tee kochen
müde sein	sich ausruhen (*rest*)
sich verletzen	sich einen Kuchen backen
sich nicht konzentrieren können	sich etwas Geld leihen (*borrow*)
sich nicht wohl fühlen	sich eine Tasse Kaffee machen
sich über etwas aufregen	meditieren
	?

Sprache im Kontext

Zuschauen

Wick Medi-Nait

Vorschau

Sehen Sie sich die Werbung zuerst ohne Ton an. Beschreiben Sie die Szene.

1. Wo ist der Mann?
2. Mit wem spricht der Mann wohl?
3. Wie ist das Wetter?
4. Welche Jahreszeit ist es wahrscheinlich?
5. Wie heißt das Produkt, das man dem Mann gibt?

Arbeit mit dem Videotext

A. Der Mann beschreibt seine Krankheitssymptome. Welche nennt er?

□ Das Bein tut ihm weh	□ Fieber	□ Halsschmerzen	□ Husten
□ Ihm ist übel	□ Kopfschmerzen	□ Magenschmerzen	□ Die Nase läuft
□ Ohrenschmerzen	□ Rückenschmerzen	□ Schnupfen	□ Zahnschmerzen

B. Der Mann spricht mit seinem Apotheker / seiner Apothekerin. Wir können die Worte des Apothekers / der Apothekerin aber nicht hören. Welche Fragen stellt wohl der Apotheker / die Apothekerin? Was würden Sie dem Mann raten?

Lesen

Zum Thema

A. Wie gesund essen Sie? Wie zufrieden sind Sie mit Ihren Essgewohnheiten? Der folgende Fragebogen ist aus einer deutschen Zeitschrift für Studenten und Studentinnen. Füllen Sie ihn aus, so gut wie Sie können. Vergleichen Sie Ihre Antworten in kleinen Gruppen. Was haben Sie über die Essgewohnheiten der anderen erfahren? Berichten Sie kurz darüber.

BEISPIEL: Die meisten Studenten in unserer Gruppe sind mit sich zufrieden. Drei essen täglich in der Mensa. Eine isst nie in der Mensa. Zwei wohnen bei den Eltern. Einer wohnt allein, und eine in einer Wohngemeinschaft. Alle bereiten eine Hauptmahlzeit am Tag für sich selbst zu. Alle jobben in den Semesterferien.

ERNÄHRUNGSAKTION FÜR STUDENTEN

Keine Zeit zum Essen oder keine Kohle?[1] Essen Nebensache? Zwischendurch mal Pommes mit Mayo, Hamburger oder ein Schokoriegel?[2] Oder ernährungsbewußt nach Vollwertart?[3] Reicht die Mensa? So ganz egal ist das alles nicht. Aber: gelten die alten Vorstellungen[4] über richtiges Essen und richtiges Gewicht[5] tatsächlich noch? Oder ist das alles ein alter Hut?

Sind Sie mit Ihrem Gewicht zufrieden?[6]

☐ nein, ich möchte ______ kg abnehmen

☐ nein, ich möchte ______ kg zunehmen

☐ ja, ich bin zufrieden

Haben Sie schon einmal versucht, Gewicht abzunehmen?

☐ ja, 1 bis 3 mal
☐ ja, 3 bis 10 mal
☐ ja, öfter als 10 mal
☐ nein, noch nie

Wie oft essen Sie in der Mensa?

☐ täglich
☐ mehrmals die Woche
☐ mehrmals im Monat
☐ seltener / nie

Leben Sie allein oder mit anderen zusammen?

☐ allein
☐ mit Partner
☐ mit Eltern
☐ in einer Wohngemeinschaft

Wieviele Hauptmahlzeiten am Tag bereiten Sie selbst für sich zu?

☐ eine
☐ zwei
☐ drei

Wie finanzieren Sie Lebensunterhalt und Studium?

☐ BaföG*/ Eltern / Rente u.ä. :

____ Prozent

☐ Jobben während des Studiums:

____ Prozent

☐ Jobben in den Semesterferien:

____ Prozent

Wieviel Geld haben Sie im Monat für Essen und Trinken zur Verfügung?[7]

☐ bis DM 200,-
☐ DM 200,- bis DM 400,-
☐ mehr als DM 400,-

Wie oft essen, bzw. trinken Sie folgende Lebensmittel? (bitte ankreuzen)
(1) täglich, (2) mehrmals pro Woche, (3) mehrmals pro Monat, (4) selten/nie

1	2	3	4	
☐	☐	☐	☐	Vollkornbrot
☐	☐	☐	☐	Milch/Quark/Joghurt
☐	☐	☐	☐	Käse
☐	☐	☐	☐	Wurst/Schinken
☐	☐	☐	☐	Fleisch
☐	☐	☐	☐	Innereien
☐	☐	☐	☐	Gemüse
☐	☐	☐	☐	Salate
☐	☐	☐	☐	Obst
☐	☐	☐	☐	Süßigkeiten
☐	☐	☐	☐	Fruchtsaft ohne Zucker
☐	☐	☐	☐	Cola/Limonade
☐	☐	☐	☐	Mineralwasser

Vorname: ______________

Name: ______________

Straße, Nr.: ______________

PLZ (neu) ______________

Wohnort: ______________

Geschlecht:
☐ weiblich ☐ männlich

Alter: ____ Jahre

Bisherige Studiendauer: ____ Semester

Fachrichtung:
☐ Naturwissenschaften / Medizin
☐ Rechts- / Wirtschafts- / Sozialwissenschaften
☐ andere Geisteswissenschaften
☐ andere Fachrichtungen:

____

Ihr Körpergewicht: ______ Kilogramm

Ihre Körpergröße: ______ cm

1. *money* (*slang*) 2. *chocolate bar* 3. ernährungsbewusst . . . *nutrition-conscious using natural foods* 4. gelten . . . *do the old notions apply* 5. *weight* 6. *satisfied* 7. zur . . . *at your disposal*

* The **Bundesausbildungsförderungsgesetz** is a governmental financial aid (loan) program to assist university students with expenses.

B. Machen Sie eine Umfrage in der Klasse.

1. Was sind Stressfaktoren in Ihrem Leben.

- □ Arbeit
- □ Universität
- □ Familie
- □ Geld
- □ Leben in der Stadt
- □ Fahren auf der Autobahn
- □ ?
- □ Mein Leben ist stressfrei.

2. Was machen Sie, um sich vom Stress zu erholen?

- □ ein Buch lesen
- □ faulenzen
- □ mit Freunden plaudern
- □ Sport treiben
- □ fernsehen
- □ Musik hören oder spielen
- □ meditieren
- □ ?

Note: You may want to point out to students the alternate spelling **Streß**.

Auf den ersten Blick

A. Der Text „Erholungstypologie" zeigt vier verschiedene Typen von Menschen. Schauen Sie sich die Bilder an.

Wie lebt . . .

1. der Jahresurlauber?
2. der Erholungsverweigerer?
3. der tägliche Genießer?
4. der aktive Besessene?

a. Er arbeitet Tag und Nacht.
b. Er muss immer sportlich aktiv sein.
c. Nur einmal im Jahr fährt er in Urlaub.
d. Jeden Tag erholt er sich.

B. Mit welchem „Typ" können Sie sich identifizieren?

Erholungstypologie

Schuftet elf Monate durch und will im Jahresurlaub sein Erholungsdefizit aufholen. Wird häufig wegen des abrupten Wechsels zwischen Hektik und Ruhe in den Ferien krank, weil er zu ***schnell „umschaltet"*** und seinen Körper dadurch belastet. Ist zudem in Gefahr, Herz, Kreislauf und Immunsystem durch Erholungsmangel ***auf Dauer zu schädigen***

Fühlt sich unersetzlich. Befürchtet immer, im Beruf etwas zu verpassen und hat verlernt, sich mit sich selbst zu beschäftigen. Kann Urlaub nicht aushalten, weil er ***Nichtstun als Belastung*** empfindet. Läßt bei sich selbst und bei anderen kein Durchhängen zu. Ignoriert Warnsignale seines Körpers und ist in Gefahr, ***chronisch krank*** zu werden

Note: If students don't notice it on their own, point out that only men are portrayed in this text. Let them talk about whether they think the four types would be portrayed differently if they were women.

Realia. The *Erholungstypologie* is from the magazine *Focus.*

Reading: This text is unglossed so that students can work on contextual guessing and learn to judge which words are essential for general understanding. Because of this, it is very important to do **Auf den ersten Blick** as a classroom activity.

Additional group activity: Have students list the words they don't know. See how many they can guess from context and which words can be considered unimportant for a general understanding of the text. Coach them on their guesses and act as a dictionary for any essential words that they don't know.

Gönnt sich Abwechslung vom Alltag. Macht kleine Pausen. Erholt sich vom täglichen Streß durch Entspannung (gutes Essen, Musikhören, Fernsehen, Sport). ***Bleibt gesund,*** weil er immer wieder zwischen Tätigkeit und Muße sowie zwischen Aktion und Ruhe wechselt und damit für die Belastungen von Körper und Psyche ***Ausgleich schafft.***

Ist süchtig nach Aktivität. Will immer besser sein als andere und setzt sich auch in der Freizeit unentwegt ***selbst unter Druck.*** Kehrt damit die erholsame Wirkung von sportlichen Betätigungen ins Gegenteil. Quält seinen Körper, statt ihm die notwendige Ruhe zu verschaffen und wird dadurch immer ***weniger leistungsfähig***

Additional activities: The text has many examples of words from the same word family, e.g. wechseln, Wechsel, Abwechslung; belasten, Belastung; Betätigung, Tätigkeit. Have students find the words in the text. Then, rather than looking up each word in a dictionary, ask them to figure out the meanings of related words after looking up just one word in the family. Encourage them to use what they know about suffixes, prefixes and capitalization in German to help determine whether the word is a noun, verb or adjective/adverb. Remind them to draw from the context in which these words appear to help come up with a possible meaning.

Zum Text

A. Der Text „Erholungstypologie" beschreibt vier Typen (Typ 1, 2, 3 und 4) und gibt für jeden Typus eine Beschreibung des Verhaltens (*behavior*) und dessen Auswirking (*effect*) auf die Gesundheit. Dazu gibt der Text auch den Grund (*reason*) dafür an. Lesen Sie den Text durch, und suchen Sie die notwendigen Informationen, um folgende Tabelle auszufüllen.

	VERHALTEN	AUSWIRKING AUF DIE GESUNDHEIT	GRUND
Typ 1:	schuftet elf Monate durch	ist in Gefahr, Herz zu schädigen	weil er zu schnell umschaltet
Typ 2:			
Typ 3:			
Typ 4:			

B. **Intensiver lesen.** Find in the text all examples of the structure **zwischen _____ und _____.** Note the words which appear in these constructions. What is the relationship between the two nouns in each instance?

Sprechen und Schreiben

Aktivität 1 Ihre Erholungstypologie

Welche Erholungstypologie trifft auf Sie zu? Beschreiben Sie sich. Die Klasse soll dann versuchen, Ihre Typologie aufzustellen (*to establish*). Die Klasse soll Ihnen Vorschläge geben, wenn Ihre Erholungstypologie ungesund ist.

Aktivität 2 Was haben Sie letzte Woche für Ihre Gesundheit getan?

Führen Sie eine Woche lang Tagebuch (*diary*) über Ihre Aktivitäten. Haben Sie etwas für Ihre Gesundheit getan? Haben Sie Sport getrieben? Haben Sie zu viel gearbeitet? Haben Sie gesund gegessen? Machen Sie eine Liste mit positiven und negativen Dingen.

BEISPIEL:

DATUM	POSITIV	NEGATIV
am 12.11.	Ich habe Tennis gespielt.	Ich habe nicht lange genug geschlafen.

Weiteres zum Thema Gesundheit finden Sie bei ***Deutsch: Na klar!*** im World-Wide-Web unter www.mhhe.com/german.

Wortschatz

Körperteile / Parts of the Body

der **Arm, -e**	arm
das **Auge, -n**	eye
der **Bauch, ⸚e**	stomach, belly
das **Bein, -e**	leg
die **Brust, ⸚e**	chest; breast
der **Ell(en)bogen, -**	elbow
der **Finger, -**	finger
der **Fuß, ⸚e**	foot
das **Gesicht, -er**	face
das **Haar, -e**	hair
der **Hals, ⸚e**	throat, neck
die **Hand, ⸚e**	hand
das **Kinn, -e**	chin
das **Knie, -**	knee
der **Kopf, ⸚e**	head
der **Muskel, -n**	muscle
die **Nase, -n**	nose
das **Ohr, -en**	ear
der **Rücken, -**	back
die **Schulter, -n**	shoulder
die **Zehe, -n**	toe

Gesundheit und Fitness / Health and Fitness

die **Arbeit, -en**	work; assignment; paper
der **Arzt, ⸚e** / die **Ärztin, -nen**	physician, doctor
die **Erkältung, -en**	cold
das **Fieber**	fever
die **Fitness***	fitness
die **Gesundheit**	health
die **Grippe**	flu
der **Husten**	coughing, cough
der **Krankenpfleger, -** / die **Krankenschwester, -n**	nurse
die **Luft, ⸚e**	air
der **Naturkostladen, ⸚**	organic food store
der **Ökolebensmittel** (*pl.*)	organic food
der **Rat**	advice
die **Schmerzen** (*pl.*)	pains
die **Halsschmerzen**	sore throat
die **Kopfschmerzen**	headache
der **Schnupfen**	nasal congestion; head cold
die **Sprechstunde, -n**	office hours
der **Stress***	stress
der **Termin, -e**	appointment

Reflexive Verben / Reflexive Verbs

sich an•strengen	to exert oneself
sich an•ziehen, angezogen	to get dressed
sich auf•regen	to get upset
sich aus•ziehen, ausgezogen	to get undressed
sich beeilen	to hurry up
sich duschen	to shower
sich entspannen	to relax
sich erholen	to get well, recover
sich erkälten	to catch a cold
sich fit halten (hält), gehalten	to keep fit, in shape
sich fühlen	to feel

* See Appendix E for alternate spelling.

sich (hin•)legen	to lie down
sich (hin•)setzen	to sit down
sich informieren (über)	to inform oneself (about)
sich interessieren (für)	to be interested (in)
sich kämmen	to comb (one's hair)
sich (die Zähne) putzen	to clean, brush (one's teeth)
sich rasieren	to shave
sich strecken	to stretch
sich treffen (mit)	to meet (with)
sich verletzen	to injure oneself
sich waschen (wäscht) gewaschen	to wash oneself

Sonstige Verben / Other Verbs

ab•geben (gibt ab), abgegeben	to turn in, hand in
achten (auf)	to pay attention (to), watch
klingen, geklungen	to sound
Du klingst so deprimiert.	You sound so depressed.
rauchen	to smoke
schlucken	to swallow
tun, getan	to do
verschreiben, verschrieben	to prescribe
versuchen	to try, attempt
weh•tun, wehgetan	to hurt
zu Fuß gehen	to go on foot, to walk

Adjektive und Adverbien / Adjectives and Adverbs

ab und zu	now and then, occasionally
anstrengend	tiring, strenuous
auch	also
besonders	especially
deprimiert	depressed
deshalb	for that reason
d.h. (= das heißt)	that is, i.e.
entweder . . . oder	either . . . or
fast	almost
fit	fit, in shape
gesund	healthy, healthful, well
gleich	immediately
höchstens	at most
hundsmiserabel (*coll.*)	sick as a dog
kaum	scarcely
krank	sick, ill
manchmal	sometimes
meistens	mostly
mindestens	at least
müde	tired
nie	never
regelmäßig	regular(ly)
schlapp	weak, worn out
sogar	even
verrückt	crazy
wenig	little, few

Unterordnende Konjunktionen / Subordinating Conjunctions

dass*	that
ob	whether
weil	because
wenn	if, when

Sonstiges / Other

Das macht nichts.	That doesn't matter.
Gute Besserung!	Get well soon!
Mir ist schlecht.	I'm sick to my stomach.
Nichts zu danken.	No thanks necessary; Don't mention it.
So ein Pech!	What a shame! (What bad luck!)
Urlaub machen	to go on vacation
Was fehlt Ihnen/dir?	What's the matter?

Lernziele

Use this checklist to verify that you can now . . .

- ☐ talk about fitness and describe the things you do to stay healthy and fit.
- ☐ name the parts of the human body.
- ☐ name some common illnesses and describe how you feel when you are sick.
- ☐ describe common grooming habits.
- ☐ form compound sentences using subordinating conjunctions.
- ☐ distinguish **wenn** and **ob** and use them appropriately.
- ☐ use accusative and dative reflexive pronouns and verbs in the present and present perfect tense.

*See Appendix E for alternate spelling.

Kapitel 9

In der Stadt

Promenade am Elbufer in Dresden

Kapitel 9. Suggestion: Introduce the chapter by telling students where you spent your last vacation or where you are planning to go on your next one. Ask students *Wo waren Sie letztes Jahr in den Ferien? Wo verbringen Sie Ihre Ferien am liebsten? In den Bergen? Am Meer? Zu Hause? Wohin würden Sie gern reisen?*

Alles klar?

A. Die alte Residenzstadt Dresden liegt im Bundesland Sachsen südlich von Berlin an der Elbe. Es gibt viele Sehenswürdigkeiten (*tourist attractions*) in und um die Stadt. Man kann z.B. den Zoologischen Garten besuchen oder zum Schloss (*castle*) Weesenstein fahren.

Realia. The ads and map are from brochures published by Dresden-Werbung und Tourismus GmbH.

SCHLOSS WEESENSTEIN

– ein königliches[4] Schloß –

Mittelalterliche Burg,[5] barocker Park, Schloß als Wohnsitz sächsischer Könige[6] im 19. Jahrhundert

Museum • Konzerte • Erlebnisgastronomie • Vermietung von Sälen[7]

Sommer: 9-18 Uhr · Winter: 9-17 Uhr

20 km von der Dresdner Residenz entfernt[8]

B 172 bis Heidenau/Abzweig Altenberg

Schloß Weesenstein • Am Schloßberg 1, Weesenstein

01809 Müglitztal • Tel./Fax: 035027-5426

1. *species* 2. *animal watching* 3. *petting zoo* 4. *royal*
5. *fortress* 6. sächsischer . . . *of Saxon kings*
7. *halls, large rooms*
8. von . . . *away from the Dresden residence*

Suchen Sie in den Werbungen (*advertisements*) die fehlenden Informationen.

1. Schloss Weesenstein ist 20 km von der Dresdner Residenz entfernt.
2. Das Schloss hat einen barocken Park.
3. Wer gern Musik hört, kann dort Konzerte besuchen.
4. Wer Kunst (*art*) gern hat, kann ins Museum gehen.
5. Früher war das Schloss der Wohnsitz sächsischer Könige.
6. Der Zoo Dresden ist attraktiv für Familien.
7. Man erreicht den Zoo mit Bus und Straßenbahn.
8. Für Autos gibt es einen Parkplatz am Haupteingang.

Was würden Sie lieber besuchen, den Zoo oder das Schloss? Warum?

B. Sie machen eine Stadtführung (*guided tour*) durch Dresden. Der Fremdenführer (*tour guide*) erzählt einige Tatsachen über die Stadt. Hören Sie zu und kreuzen Sie an, was stimmt und was nicht stimmt.

	DAS STIMMT	DAS STIMMT NICHT
1. Heute leben etwa 470 000 Einwohner in Dresden.	☒	☐
2. Die erste deutsche Lokomotive kommt aus Dresden.	☒	☐
3. Bierdeckel, Kaffeefilter und Shampoo hat man in Dresden entwickelt.	☐	☒
4. In Dresden hat Richard Wagner die erste deutsche Oper geschrieben.	☐	☒
5. Die Stadt hat viel Kultur anzubieten: Musik, Museen und Theater.	☒	☐
6. Dresden gilt als die europäische Hauptstadt des Films.	☐	☒

Auf der Suche nach Unterkunft. Suggestion: Have students work in groups. Each group chooses a type of lodging and then decides what factors are most important.

Thema 1

Auf der Suche nach Unterkunft°

° *accommodations*

HOTEL VISA

CHIPPENDALE'S GASTRONOMIE SERVICE GmbH
Breitscheidstraße 47
01462 Cossebaude/Dresden
Telefon: (0351) 439 61 61
Telefax: (0351) 439 91 39

- ca. 3 Min. von der Autobahn DD-Altstadt unmittelbar[4] an der Stadtgrenze[5] Dresdens gelegen
- zentrale Lage für viele Ausflugsziele[6]
- 25 modern eingerichtete Zimmer mit Dusche, WC, SAT-TV, Radiowecker
- EZ 108 DM / DZ 138 DM
- reichhaltiges Frühstücksbuffet (inkl.)
- Gruppenpreise auf Anfrage[7]
- Pensionsverpflegung[8] für Reisegruppen

HOTEL & RESTAURANT

An der Rennbahn
★ ★ ★

- zwischen Großen Garten und Rennbahn[10] gelegen
- 10 Autominuten bis zum Zentrum der Stadt
- 22 komfortabel eingerichtete Zimmer mit Dusche, WC, Fön, Farb-TV, Telefon und Minibar
- EZ 130,- bis 165,- DM
- DZ 180,- bis 210,- DM
- incl. reichhaltiges Frühstück
- Gruppenpreise 85,- DM pro Person und Nacht
- Küche mit sächsischen und internationalen Spezialitäten
- Gartenrestaurant

Mit freundlicher Empfehlung[9]
FAMILIE BOLZ

Winterbergstraße 96 · 01237 Dresden - Reick
Telefon (0351) 2 54 00 30 · Telefax (0351) 2 52 27 85

1. *direct-dial telephone*
2. *in the center of*
3. freuen . . . *we look forward to*
4. *directly* 5. *city limit*
6. *excursion destinations*
7. auf . . . *on request*
8. *full room and board provisions*
9. Mit . . . *with kindest regards*
10. *racetrack*

Was ist wichtig für Sie, wenn Sie in einem **Hotel,** einer **Pension** oder einer **Jugendherberge** übernachten? Was ist relevant für Sie, wenn Sie eine **Unterkunft** suchen? Die Unterkunft sollte . . .

- □ **in der Nähe** des Bahnhofs liegen.
- □ in der **Innenstadt** (im Zentrum) liegen.
- □ ein Restaurant im Haus haben.
- □ Kabelfernsehen oder Radio haben.
- □ in ruhiger **Lage** sein.
- □ **Sauna** im Haus haben.
- □ **Bad/Dusche/WC** im Zimmer haben.
- □ **für** Familien mit Kindern **geeignet** sein.
- □ Frühstück **im Preis enthalten.**
- □ einen **Parkplatz** in der Nähe haben.
- □ Tiere **erlauben.**
- □ **günstige** Lage haben.
- □ Telefon im Zimmer haben.
- □ im Bad einen **Fön** haben.

Sprachtipp

Die folgenden Abkürzungen sind typisch:

EZ = das Einzelzimmer *single room*
DZ = das Doppelzimmer *double room*
DU = die Dusche *shower*
WC = die Toilette (Engl. *water closet) toilet*
inkl. = inklusive *included, including*

Aktivität 1 Zwei telefonische Zimmerbestellungen

Was stimmt? Markieren Sie die richtigen Antworten.

ERSTES TELEFONGESPRÄCH

1. Der Gast braucht ein
   - a. Einzelzimmer.
   - b. Doppelzimmer.
2. Er braucht das Zimmer für
   - a. eine Nacht.
   - b. mehrere *(several)* Nächte).
3. Das Hotel hat ein Zimmer frei
   - a. mit Bad.
   - b. ohne Bad.
4. Frühstück ist im Preis
   - a. nicht enthalten.
   - b. enthalten.
5. Der Gast
   - a. nimmt das Zimmer.
   - b. muss ein anderes Hotel finden.

ZWEITES TELEFONGESPRÄCH

1. Das Jugendgästehaus hat
   - a. nur Doppelzimmer.
   - b. nur Mehrbettzimmer.
2. Das Haus ist
   - a. ganz neu.
   - b. sehr alt.
3. Die Übernachtung kostet
   - a. mehr als 20 Mark.
   - b. weniger als 20 Mark.
4. Jedes Zimmer hat
   - a. WC und Dusche.
   - b. fünf Betten.
5. Das Gästehaus liegt
   - a. auf dem Lande.
   - b. in der Nähe der Innenstadt.

Aktivität 1. Suggestion: Have students first scan the information requested in the first telephone conversation. Then let them listen to it on the tape. Students can work in pairs, taking turns responding to each item. Repeat this procedure with the second conversation. **Follow-up:** Exploit both conversations further through questions eliciting more detail, e.g., *Warum muss der Gast im ersten Gespräch ein anderes Hotel suchen? Wie alt ist das Jugendgästehaus genau?* **Point Out: Auf Wiederhören**—the final words of the first telephone conversation—is used only to end a telephone conversation.

Aktivität 2 Wo wollen wir übernachten?°

°*spend the night*

Sie reisen mit Freunden und suchen eine Unterkunft in Dresden. Schauen Sie sich die drei Anzeigen in **Thema 1** genau an, und überlegen Sie sich, in welchem Hotel Sie übernachten wollen. Gebrauchen Sie die folgenden Ausdrücke, um eine Unterkunft vorzuschlagen *(to suggest),* und geben Sie den Grund *(reason)* dafür an.

BEISPIEL: Ich schlage vor, wir übernachten im Hotelschiff „Florentina." Es liegt zentral und hat ein Terrassencafé.

Ich schlage vor, . . .
Mir gefällt das Hotel . . . besser.
Ich brauche . . . im Zimmer / im Hotel.
Das Hotel liegt . . .
Das Hotel . . . ist mir zu teuer.

Weiteres zum Thema Dresden finden Sie bei ***Deutsch: Na klar!*** im World-Wide-Web unter www.mhhe.com/german.

Das Fremdenverkehrsamt (*tourist information bureau*) ist für viele Besucher in deutschen Städten die erste Anlaufstelle (*place they go to*); meist liegt es am Hauptbahnhof oder anderen zentralen Orten. Hier können Touristen viel Wissenswertes über die neue Stadt erfahren. Sie können zum Beispiel Empfehlungen für Restaurants bekommen, eine Stadtrundfahrt buchen und Prospekte (*brochures*) von der Stadt erhalten. Hier gibt es auch eine Zimmervermittlung, bei der Besucher sich nach einem freien Zimmer in einem Hotel oder einer Pension erkundigen (*inquire*) können.

Thema 2

Im Hotel

Teil A: Herr Thompson ***kommt*** *im Hotel „Mecklenheide"* ***an. Zuerst*** *muss er* ***sich anmelden.***

REZEPTION: Guten Abend.
GAST: Guten Abend. Ich habe ein Zimmer für zwei Nächte bestellt.
REZEPTION: **Auf welchen Namen,** bitte?
GAST: Thompson.
REZEPTION: Ah, ja. Herr Thompson. Ein **Einzelzimmer** mit Bad. **Würden Sie bitte** das **Anmeldeformular ausfüllen?**
GAST: Möchten Sie auch meinen **Reisepass** sehen?
REZEPTION: Nein, das ist nicht nötig. Ihr Zimmer liegt im ersten **Stock,** Zimmer 21. Hier ist **der Schlüssel.** Der **Aufzug** ist hier **rechts.**
GAST: Danke.
REZEPTION: Wir bringen Ihr **Gepäck** aufs Zimmer. Haben Sie nur den einen **Koffer?**
GAST: Ja . . . **Übrigens,** wann gibt es morgens Frühstück?
REZEPTION: Zwischen 7 und 10 Uhr im **Frühstücksraum** hier gleich **links** im **Erdgeschoss.**

Dialogue. Note: This dialogue presents a typical situation that a visitor might encounter at a hotel. It recycles vocabulary from previous chapters and vocabulary already introduced in this chapter. New vocabulary and expressions can easily be guessed from the context. **Suggestion:** Play the dialogue once, for students to get the gist. Ask a few basic questions: *Wer sind die Sprecher? Wie heißt der Gast? Wie lange möchte er bleiben?* Then ask students to scan the text once. Help them figure out the meaning of *Würden Sie bitte das Anmeldeformular ausfüllen?* by asking *Was muss ein Gast im Hotel machen, bevor er sein Zimmer bekommt?* To figure out the meaning of **im ersten Stock** and **Erdgeschoss,** refer to the realia showing the *Hotel Mecklenheide.* **Point out:** *Würden Sie . . . ausfüllen* corresponds to the English "Would you fill out . . . ," used for polite requests. **Erster Stock** corresponds to second floor; **zweiter Stock** is the third floor; **Erdgeschoss** is either the ground floor or the first floor.

Realia. This is from a pamphlet advertising the *Hotel Mecklenheide* in Hannover.

GAST: Danke sehr.
REZEPTION: Bitte sehr. Ich wünsche Ihnen einen angenehmen **Aufenthalt.**

Teil B: Herr Thompson ruft die ***Rezeption*** *an und* ***beschwert sich,*** *weil der Fernseher nicht* ***funktioniert.***

REZEPTION: **Rezeption.**
THOMPSON: Guten Abend. Der Fernseher in meinem Zimmer ist **kaputt.** Es gibt kein Bild, keinen Ton, nichts.
REZEPTION: **Das tut mir leid,** Herr Thompson. Ich schicke **sofort jemand** auf Ihr Zimmer. Wenn er den **Apparat** nicht gleich **reparieren** kann, bringen wir Ihnen einen anderen.
THOMPSON: Vielen Dank. **Auf Wiederhören.**
REZEPTION: Auf Wiederhören.

Teil C: Herr Thompson ***reist*** *heute* ***ab.*** *Er geht an die Rezeption.*

THOMPSON: Guten Morgen. Ich reise heute ab.
REZEPTION: Jawohl . . . Zwei **Übernachtungen** und ein **Telefonanruf** nach Wien. Das macht zusammen DM 315,60.
THOMPSON: Nehmen Sie **Kreditkarten** oder **Reiseschecks?**
REZEPTION: Sie können mit Eurokarte, Euroscheck oder in **bar bezahlen.**
THOMPSON: Keine Reiseschecks?
REZEPTION: Doch. Ein Reisescheck **geht auch.**
THOMPSON: Gut.
REZEPTION: Ich brauche nur noch Ihre **Unterschrift** da oben.
THOMPSON: Ach ja, natürlich.
REZEPTION: Hoffentlich hat es Ihnen bei uns gefallen.
THOMPSON: Ja, sehr.

Weiteres zum Thema Hotel und Unterkunft finden Sie bei ***Deutsch: Na klar!*** im World-Wide-Web unter www.mhhe.com/german.

Aktivität 3 Im Hotel

Bilden Sie Sätze!

1. __e__ Ich habe ein Einzelzimmer
2. _____ Würden Sie bitte
3. _____ Ihr Zimmer liegt
4. _____ Wir bringen Ihr Gepäck
5. _____ Ich wünsche Ihnen
6. _____ Der Fernseher in meinem Zimmer
7. _____ Ich möchte heute
8. _____ Kann ich mit Reisescheck
9. _____ Ein Reisescheck
10. _____ Hoffentlich hat es Ihnen bei uns

a. abreisen.
b. ist kaputt.
c. geht auch.
d. bezahlen?
e. bestellt.
f. gefallen.
g. einen angenehmen Aufenthalt.
h. das Anmeldeformular ausfüllen?
i. aufs Zimmer.
j. im ersten Stock.

Aktivität 4 Ein Aufenthalt im Hotel Mecklenheide

Sehen Sie sich die Bilder an, und erzählen Sie die Geschichte von Herrn Thompson im Hotel Mecklenheide.

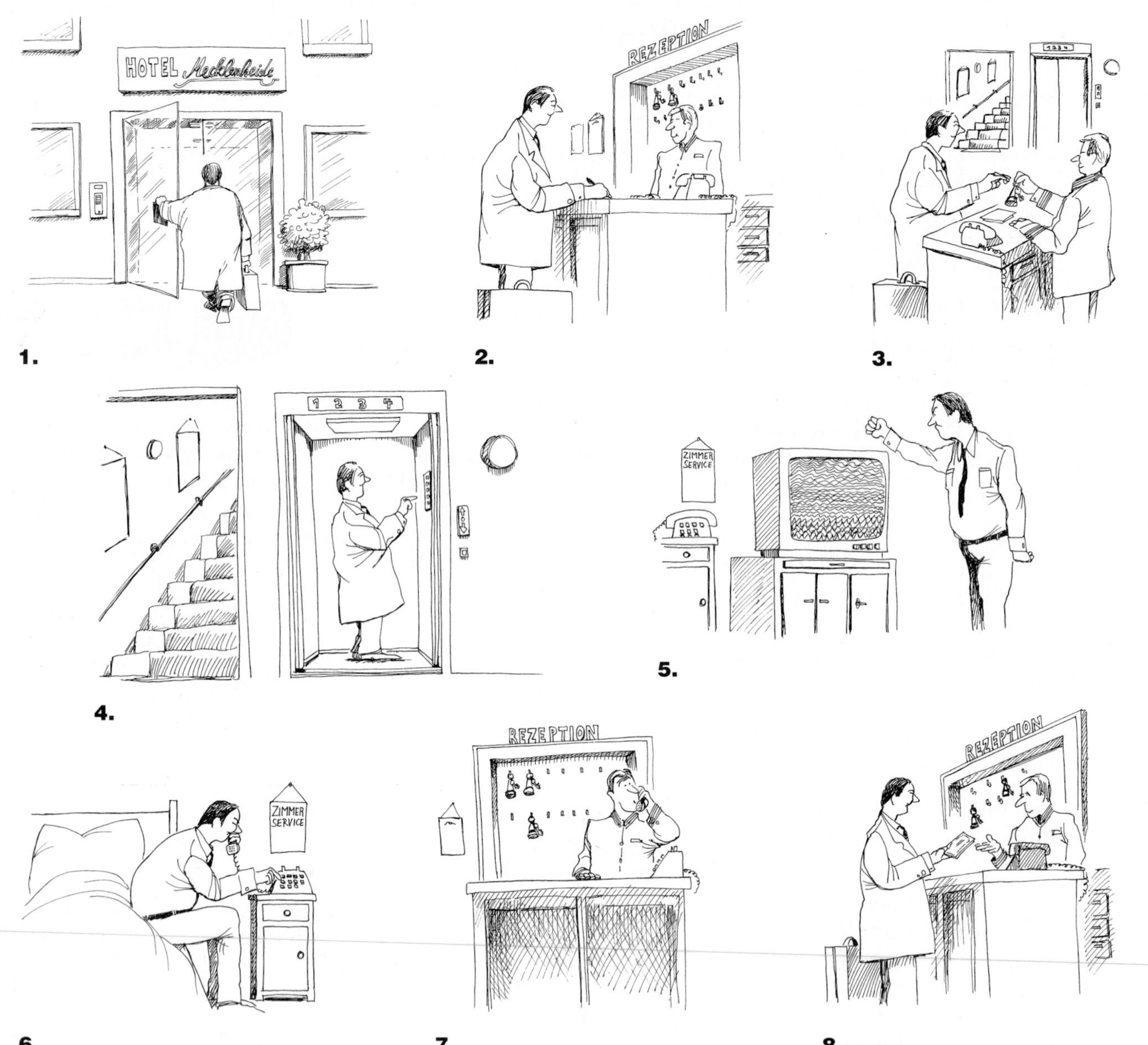

Thema 3

Ringsum° die Stadt

°*all around*

A. Schauen Sie auf den Stadtplan (*city map*) von Warnemünde, um die folgenden angegebenen Orte (*places indicated below*) zu finden.

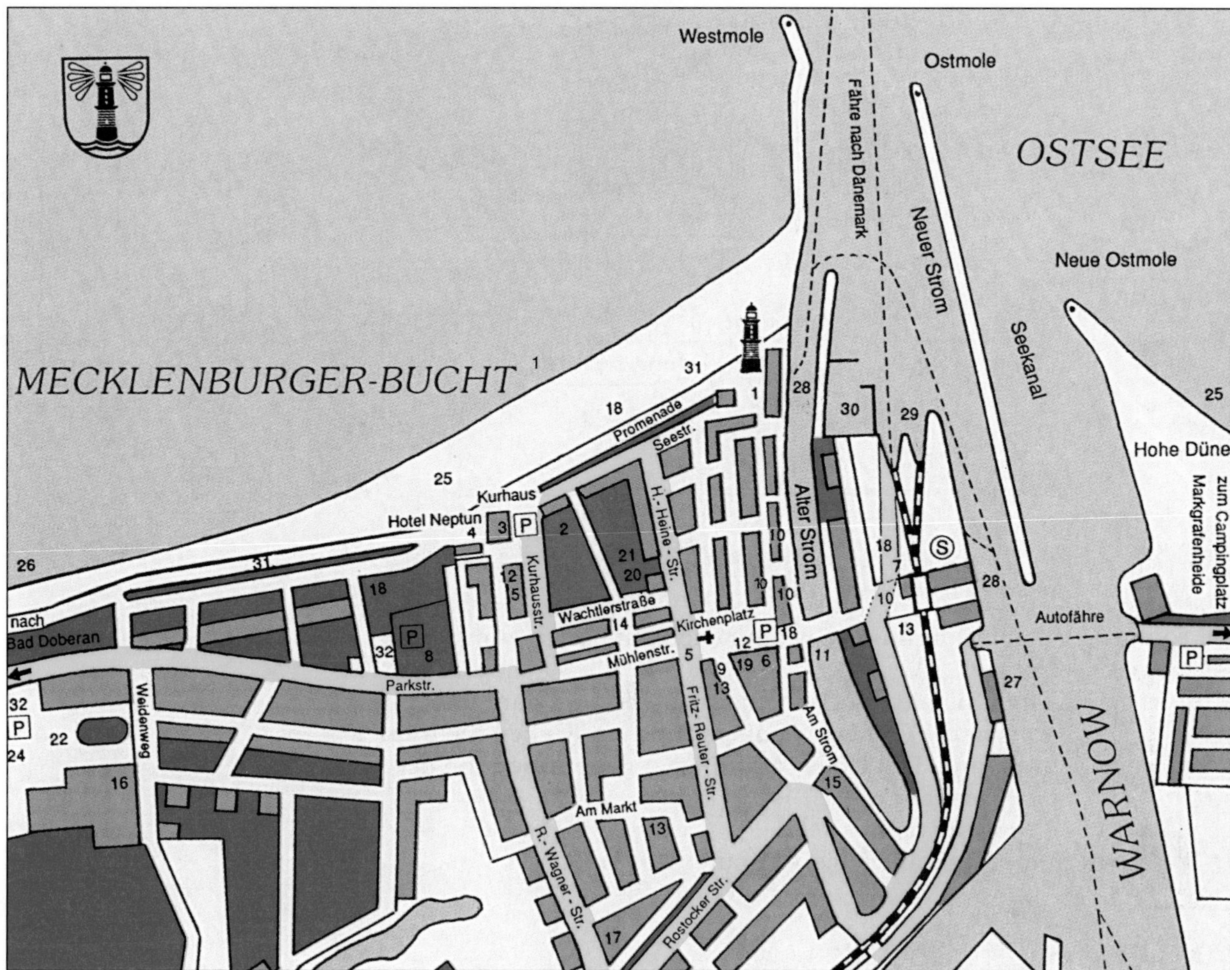

Realia. Ringsum die Stadt. This map is from the *Kuramt Warnemünde.*

B. Welche deutschen Wörter passen zu den englischen Wörtern?

1. __18__ restrooms
2. __9__ post office
3. __17__ gas station
4. __7__ light rail line
5. __4__ swimming facility
6. __29__ (ferry) harbor, dock
7. __10__ bank
8. __14__ movie house/theater
9. __5__ church
10. __8__ cemetery
11. __6__ museum
12. __24__ police (station)
13. __25__ beach

1 Leuchtturm	16 Kuramt[3]
2 Kurhaus	17 **Tankstelle**
3 Hotel Neptun	18 **Toiletten**
4 **Schwimmhalle**	19 Taxi
5 **Kirche**	20 Gäste Service
6 **Museum**	21 Ärzteinformation (üb. Gästeservice)
7 Bahnhof/S-Bahn	22 Sportplatz
8 Alter Friedhof	24 **Polizei**
9 **Post**	25 **Strand**
10 **Bank**	26 Surfen
11 Senatsaußenstelle (Vogtei)[2]	27 Passagierkai
12 Apotheke	28 Weiße Flotte
13 Telefon	29 Fähr-**Hafen**
14 Kino	30 Yacht-Hafen
15 Theater	31 Promenade

1. *bay*
2. *regional Senate office*
3. *resort office*

*Wie komme ich am besten **dahin?***

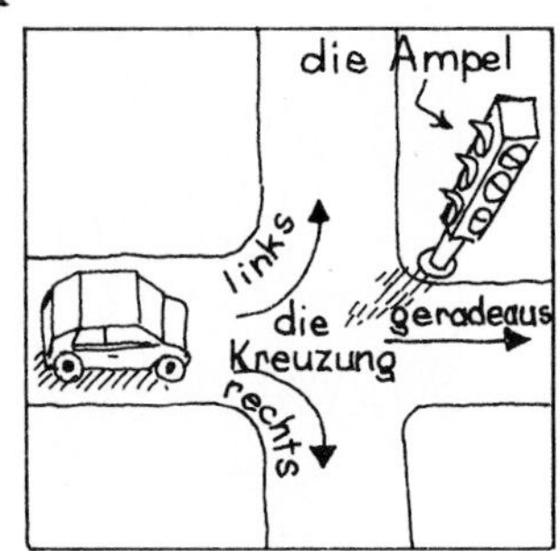

*Ein Tourist steht in Warnemünde vor der Kirche und fragt einen **Passanten nach dem Weg.***

TOURIST: **Entschuldigung,** wie komme ich am besten zum Hotel Neptun?
PASSANT: **Gehen** Sie hier die Mühlenstraße **entlang,** dann **biegen** Sie rechts in die Richard-Wagnerstraße **ein.** Gehen Sie **immer geradeaus.** Das Hotel Neptun liegt **gegenüber** von der Schwimmhalle.
TOURIST: Ist es **weit** von hier?
PASSANT: Nein. **Ungefähr** 5 bis 7 Minuten zu Fuß.

Aktivität 5 Drei Touristen

Drei Leute fragen nach dem Weg. Wohin wollen sie? Wie kommen sie dahin?

	DIALOG 1	DIALOG 2	DIALOG 3
Wohin man gehen will	Markt	Hotel	Post
Wie man dahin kommt	geradeaus, dann links	2 Straßen geradeaus, dann rechts	keine Auskunft

Aktivität 6 Hin und her: In einer fremden° Stadt

°unfamiliar

Sie sind in einer fremden Stadt. Fragen Sie nach dem Weg. Benutzen Sie die Tabelle.

BEISPIEL: S1: Ist das Landesmuseum weit von hier?
S2: Es ist sechs Kilometer von hier, bei der Universität.
S1: Wie komme ich am besten dahin?
S2: Nehmen Sie die Buslinie 7, am Rathaus.

WOHIN?	WIE WEIT?	WO?	WIE?
Landesmuseum	6 km	bei der Universität	Buslinie 7, am Rathaus
Bahnhof	15 Minuten	im Zentrum	mit dem Taxi
Post	nicht weit	in der Nähe vom Bahnhof	zu Fuß
Schloss	15 km	außerhalb der Stadt	mit dem Auto
Opernhaus	ganz in der Nähe	rechts um die Ecke	zu Fuß, die Poststraße entlang

Aktivität 7 In Warnemünde

Schauen Sie sich den Stadtplan von Warnemünde im **Thema 3** an, und fragen Sie einige Studenten/Studentinnen im Kurs, wie Sie am besten an einen bestimmten Ort kommen. Sie stehen vor der Kirche (Nummer 5).

BEISPIEL: S1: Entschuldigung, wie kommt man am besten zum Museum?
S2: Gehen Sie hier geradeaus bis zum Parkplatz. Das Museum ist dann gleich an der Ecke (*corner*).

REDEMITTEL

Entschuldigung, wie komme ich am besten zum/zur _____?
Wie weit ist es bis zum/zur _____?
Wie kommt man zum/zur _____?

Immer geradeaus.
Gehen Sie die _____ Straße entlang.
Gehen Sie links/rechts auf die _____ Straße.
Gleich an der Ecke / um die Ecke.
Es ist zehn Minuten zu Fuß.

Weiteres zum Thema Wegbeschreibung finden Sie bei ***Deutsch: Na klar!*** im World-Wide-Web unter www.mhhe.com/german.

Aktivität 8 Wie kommt man dahin?

Fragen Sie nach dem Weg in Ihrer Stadt oder auf Ihrem Campus. Wählen Sie passende Fragen und Antworten aus jeder Spalte.

BEISPIEL: S1: Entschuldigung, wo ist hier die Post?
S2: Da nehmen Sie am besten den Bus.
S1: Wo ist die Haltestelle (*bus stop*)?
S2: Gleich da drüben.

FRAGEN	ANTWORTEN
Wie kommt man am besten zum Supermarkt / zur Bibliothek / zur Sporthalle?	Immer geradeaus.
Wie weit ist es bis ins Zentrum?	Nächste Kreuzung rechts/links.
Entschuldigung, wo ist hier die Post (Bank, Mensa)?	Da nehmen Sie am besten ____ (den Bus, z.B. Linie 8)
Wo ist die Haltestelle?	Gleich da drüben / Gleich an der Ecke.
?	Fünf Minuten zu Fuß.
	?

Grammatik im Kontext

The Genitive Case°

° der Genitiv

The Genitive Case. Suggestion: Remind students that they have used the genitive case with proper names since Kapitel 3, e.g., *Das ist Franks Schwester. Das ist Familie Schneiders Haus.*

Nouns in the Genitive Case. Suggestion: For quick practice of genitive forms, do a substitution exercise. *Wo liegt deine Wohnung? In der Nähe . . . (Universität, Bahnhof, Park, Theater, Post, Einkaufszentrum, Innenstadt). Wie ist die Telefonnummer . . . (Freund, Freundin, Eltern, Familie, Polizei, Auskunft, Hotel, Reisebüro, Fremdenverkehrsverein)?*

The genitive case is typically used to indicate ownership or a familial or personal relationship, or to define the characteristics of a person, object, or idea.

1. Indicating ownership or a relationship

Der Wagen **meines Vaters** ist in der Werkstatt.	*My father's car is at the repair shop.*
Das Geschäft **unserer Familie** liegt in der Innenstadt.	*Our family's business is located downtown.*
Das Gepäck **der Gäste** steht beim Empfang.	*The guests' luggage is at the reception desk.*
Wo ist die Mutter **des Kindes?**	*Where is the child's mother?*
Der Freund **meiner Schwester** heißt Stefan.	*My sister's boyfriend is named Stefan.*

2. Defining the characteristics of a person, object, or idea

Die Bank liegt im Zentrum **der Stadt.**	*The bank is located in the center of town.*
Mir gefällt die Farbe **deines Wagens.**	*I like the color of your car.*
Das Ende **des Films** war ganz ungewöhnlich.	*The end of the movie was quite unusual.*

As with the other cases, the genitive is signaled by special endings of **der-** and **ein-**words.

SINGULAR			PLURAL
Masculine	*Neuter*	*Feminine*	*All Genders*
des / dies**es** / ein**es** / unser**es** } Gast**es**	**des** / dies**es** / ein**es** / unser**es** } Hotel**s**	**der** / dies**er** / ein**er** / unser**er** } Stadt	**der** / dies**er** / unser**er** } Gäste

Most masculine and neuter nouns in the singular add **s** in the genitive case. Masculine and neuter nouns of one syllable often add **es.**

die Lage dieses Hotel**s**	*the location of this hotel*
die Unterschrift des Gast**es**	*the guest's signature*

Masculine nouns that add **n** or **en** in the dative and accusative also add **n** or **en** in the genitive case.

das Gepäck des Student**en**	*the student's luggage*
der Koffer des Herr**n** aus Hannover	*the suitcase of the gentleman from Hanover*

Note that the noun in the genitive follows the noun it modifies.

In colloquial German, the genitive case is often replaced by the preposition **von** and the dative case.

das Haus **von meinen Eltern**	*the house of my parents*
in der Nähe **vom Bahnhof**	*in the vicinity of the railroad station.*

To ask for the owner of something, use the interrogative pronoun **wessen** (*whose*).

Wessen Koffer ist das?	*Whose suitcase is that?*
Wessen Unterschrift ist das?	*Whose signature is that?*

Masculine Nouns Ending in *-n* or *-en*. Suggestion: Review other nouns that fall into this category: *der Kunde, der Tourist, der Mensch.* For instance, *die Unterschrift des Kunden, des Touristen.*

Proper Names in the Genitive

A proper name normally precedes the noun it modifies. As you learned in **Kapitel 3,** proper names in the genitive add **s** without an apostrophe, in contrast to English.

Martinas Koffer	*Martina's suitcase*
Herrn Kramers Reisepass	*Mr. Kramer's passport*
Frau Kruses Hund	*Mrs. Kruse's dog*

The name of a country or a region in the genitive case may precede or follow the noun it modifies.

Hessen: das Herz **Deutschlands**	*Hesse: the heart of Germany*
München, **Deutschlands** heimliche Hauptstadt	*Munich, Germany's secret capital*

Proper Names in the Genitive: Point Out: A genitive **s** is added to names regardless of the gender of the person. If a name ends in **s,** you will see an apostrophe following the **s** to indicate that a genitive **s** is implied. In modern German this is sometimes avoided by using the preposition **von** with names ending in **z** or **ss** (*das Haus von Familie Schmitz, der Wagen von Hans*). Genitive endings are also added to both parts of a masculine proper name: *Herrn Kramers Koffer,* but *Frau Kramers Tasche.*

Analyse

- Identify the genitive expressions in the illustrations.
- What nouns are modified by the genitive attributes?
- Give appropriate English translations of these phrases.

Realia. *Kaufhaus des Westens* is the largest department store on the European continent, located in Berlin.

Übung 1 Was für eine Stadt ist Wien°?

°Vienna

Beschreiben Sie Wien. Benutzen Sie dabei Genitivattribute.

BEISPIEL: Wien ist eine Stadt der Tradition.

Wien ist eine Stadt . . .	die Kaffeehäuser	der Jugendstil (*art nouveau*)
	das Theater	das Vergnügen (*pleasure*)
	die Musik	die Architektur
	die Museen	die Kirchen
	die Gärten	?

Übung 2 Wo lag Ihr Hotel?

Sie waren gerade in Wien. Beschreiben Sie die Lage des Hotels.

BEISPIEL: Unser Hotel lag in der Nähe eines Cafés.

Unser Hotel lag in der Nähe . . .	ein Park	die Ringstraße
	ein Schloss	das Fremdenverkehrsamt
	ein Kino	die Post
	eine Bank	der Dom (*cathedral*)
	die Donau (*Danube*)	das Rathaus
	die Universität	die U-Bahn
	der Bahnhof	

Übung 3 Wem gehört das? 

Wessen Sachen sind das? Arbeiten Sie mit einem Partner / einer Partnerin.

BEISPIEL: S1: Wessen Gepäck ist das?
S2: Das ist das Gepäck des Gastes.

1. der Wagen → meine Schwester
2. der Rucksack → der Student
3. der Reisepass → der Herr auf Zimmer 33
4. die Unterschrift → meine Freundin
5. der Schlüssel → das Mädchen aus Kanada
6. der Koffer → Martina

Note: **Übung 3** also lends itself to a review of the dative with *gehören:*
—*Wessen Wagen ist das?*
—*Der gehört meinem Bruder.* Or to practice the more colloquial version:
—*Das ist der Wagen von meinem Bruder.*

Übung 4 Zuerst will sie das wissen 

Frau Schimmelpfennig will alles genau wissen, bevor sie ein Zimmer reserviert. Arbeiten Sie mit einem Partner / einer Partnerin. Benutzen Sie in Ihren Antworten den Genitiv.

Suggestion: Have students convert all compound nouns into genitive constructions before beginning the exercise.

BEISPIEL: Wie ist die Hotellage? → (sehr ruhig)
S1: Wie ist die Hotellage?
S2: Die Lage des Hotels ist sehr ruhig.

1. Wo ist der Hoteleingang? → (gleich um die Ecke)
2. Wer ist der Hotelbesitzer? → (ein Herr Schlüter aus Hannover)
3. Wo ist der Hotelparkplatz? → (in der Tiefgarage unter dem Hotel)
4. Wie ist die Hoteladresse? → (Weimarerstraße 137)
5. Wie weit weg ist das Stadtzentrum? → (etwa fünf Minuten mit dem Wagen)
6. Wie hoch ist der Zimmerpreis? → (DM 90 pro Übernachtung)

Prepositions with the Genitive

A number of prepositions are used with the genitive case. Several common ones are:

außerhalb	*outside of*	außerhalb der Stadt
innerhalb	*inside of*	innerhalb einer Stunde
trotz	*in spite of*	trotz des Regens
während	*during*	während des Sommers
wegen	*because of*	wegen der hohen Kosten

In colloquial German, **trotz, während,** and **wegen** may also be used with the dative case.

Prepositions with the Genitive. Suggestion: Practice the preposition **wegen** individually, contrasting it with **weil**; students tend to mix up these words. Do a quick substitution exercise: *Warum studieren Sie hier? Wegen . . . (die Lage, das Wetter, der Ruf der Uni / des Colleges, der Preis, die Studenten, meine Freundin, meine Eltern, mein Vater,* etc.) Now ask students to rephrase their sentences using **weil.** Repeat the question *Warum studieren Sie hier?* Provide cues using the substitution nouns: *Der Ruf der Universität (das Wetter, die Lage, etc.) ist sehr gut.* Or: *Meine Freundin studiert hier; meine Eltern haben die Universität empfohlen.* Students say . . . *weil der Ruf der Universität (das Wetter, die Lage,* etc.) *gut ist,* or *weil meine Freundin hier studiert,* etc.

Note: The prepositions listed here are high-frequency words. You may want to add **(an)statt** (instead). Note that **innerhalb** is generally used with time: *innerhalb eines Tages* (within a day). **Außerhalb** is always used with location.

Übung 5 Notizen von einer Reise nach Wien

Setzen Sie passende Präpositionen mit dem Genitiv ein.

1. _____ unserer Reise nach Wien haben wir viel gesehen.
2. _____ der hohen Hotelpreise haben wir in einer kleinen Pension übernachtet.
3. Die Pension hat _____ der Stadt gelegen.
4. _____ der vielen Touristen war es in Wien schön.
5. _____ der vielen Besucher konnten wir keine Karten für die Spanische Reitschule bekommen.

Übung 6 Erkundigungen°

inquiries

Sie sind fremd in der Stadt, und Sie erkundigen sich auf der Straße. Arbeiten Sie mit einem Partner / einer Partnerin. Gebrauchen Sie Redemittel aus der folgenden Liste.

FÜR DIE FRAGEN

Bitte schön, . . .
Entschuldigung, . . .
Bitte, können Sie mir sagen, . . .

FÜR DIE ANTWORTEN

in der Nähe
in der Mitte
auf der anderen Seite
innerhalb/außerhalb
gegenüber (von)
neben

Richtung Naturpark
Fluss
Konsulat
Rathaus
Ratskeller
Poststraße
Bank
Post
Information
Hauptstraße
Universität
Museumsstraße
Marktplatz
Bahnhofsstraße
Bahnhof
Kunstmuseum
Stadtpark
Weimarerstraße
P
Hotel Zentral
Parkhaus

Stadtplan

BEISPIEL: S1: Bitte schön, wo liegt das Konsulat?
S2: Es liegt in der Nähe des Marktplatzes.

1. das Informationszentrum
2. das Hotel Zentral
3. der Parkplatz des Hotels
4. der Naturpark (innerhalb oder außerhalb)
5. das Kunstmuseum
6. die Post
7. die Universität
8. der Ratskeller

Note: While you want to encourage students to use genitive expressions, a variety of answers is possible, including prepositional phrases in the dative or accusative.

Attributive Adjectives°

attributive Adjektive

Attributive Adjectives. Point out: Students have seen adjectives with endings in the many texts throughout this book. Adjective endings do not interfere with understanding a text, yet they are difficult to master. However, in scanning almost any German text, students will quickly discover that only two adjective endings are used with great frequency: **e** and **en**.

Predicate adjectives—adjectives used after the verbs **sein** and **werden**—take no endings. Attributive adjectives—adjectives preceding nouns—always take endings.

PREDICATE ADJECTIVE: Die Pension Hubertus ist **preiswert.**
ATTRIBUTIVE ADJECTIVE: Diese **preiswerte** Pension liegt außerhalb der Stadt.

Adjectives after a Definite Article or Other *der*-Word

The two most common adjective endings are **e** and **en**. They are used whenever an adjective follows a definite article or other **der**-word like **dieser** or **jeder.***

*This type of adjective ending is traditionally referred to as a *weak* adjective ending.

	SINGULAR			PLURAL
	Masculine	*Neuter*	*Feminine*	*All Genders*
Nom.	der groß**e** Park	das schön**e** Wetter	die lang**e** Straße	die alt**en** Häuser
Acc.	den groß**en** Park	das schön**e** Wetter	die lang**e** Straße	die alt**en** Häuser
Dat.	dem groß**en** Park	dem schön**en** Wetter	der lang**en** Straße	den alt**en** Häusern
Gen.	des groß**en** Parks	des schön**en** Wetters	der lang**en** Straße	der alt**en** Häuser

SUMMARY OF ENDINGS

	SINGULAR			PLURAL
	Masculine	*Neuter*	*Feminine*	*All Genders*
Nom.	e	e	e	en
Acc.	en	e	e	en
Dat.	en	en	en	en
Gen.	en	en	en	en

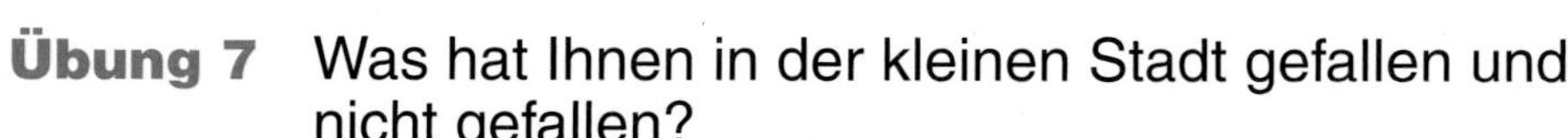

Übung 7 Was hat Ihnen in der kleinen Stadt gefallen und nicht gefallen?

Bilden Sie Sätze mit den Ausdrücken aus den beiden Spalten.

BEISPIEL: Die vielen netten Leute haben mir gefallen.

die Atmosphäre der Stadt	günstig
der Markt	klein
die Kathedrale	gemütlich
die Straßen	(un)freundlich
die Bedienung im Café am Markt	historisch
die Restaurants	alt
die Hotels	schön
das Theater	modern
der Stadtpark	viel
das Landesmuseum	teuer
das Essen im Ratskeller	interessant
	?

Übung 8 Was hast du mir mitgebracht?

Sie sind von einer Reise nach Deutschland zurückgekommen. Was haben Sie allen mitgebracht? Führen Sie kurze Gespräche mit Hilfe der Zeichnungen. Wählen Sie Adjektive aus der Liste.

BEISPIEL: S1: Was hast du mir mitgebracht?
S2: Ich habe dir einen Kalender mitgebracht.
S1: Oh! Vielen Dank für diesen schönen Kalender.

originell	schick	lecker	fabelhaft
schön	bunt	toll	?

Adjectives after an Indefinite Article or Other *ein*-Word

Adjectives preceded by indefinite articles (or other **ein**-words) follow the same pattern as adjectives preceded by **der**-words, except in the masculine nominative and in the neuter nominative and accusative.

	MASCULINE	NEUTER
Nom.	ein groß**er** Park	ein schön**es** Haus
Acc.		ein schön**es** Haus

Heute war **ein** schön**er** Tag.	*Today was a nice day.*
Das ist **unser** neu**es** Haus.	*This is our new house.*
Ich suche **ein** preiswert**es** Hotel.	*I am looking for a reasonably-priced hotel.*
Wo ist **Ihr** neu**er** Wagen?	*Where is your new car?*

When two or more adjectives are used consecutively they will have the same ending.

Ein klein**es,** historisch**es** Hotel liegt in der Altstadt.	*A small, historical hotel is located in the old part of town.*

When used as attributive adjectives, **teuer** and **hoch** drop a letter: **teuer** drops the **e; hoch** drops the **c.**

Das Hotel ist **teuer.** → Das ist ein **teures** Hotel.
Der Preis ist **hoch.** → Das ist ein **hoher** Preis!

Übung 9 Gibt es das in Ihrem Heimatort? 

Stellen Sie einem Partner / einer Partnerin Fragen.

BEISPIEL: ein deutsch_____ Restaurant →
S1: Gibt es in deinem Heimatort ein deutsches Restaurant?
S2: Ja, das gibt es.
oder Nein, das gibt es nicht.

1. ein französisch_____ Restaurant
2. eine bekannt_____ Universität
3. ein alt_____ Rathaus
4. eine modern_____ Untergrundbahn
5. eng_____ Straßen
6. historisch_____ Sehenswürdigkeiten
7. einen groß_____ Flughafen
8. ein berühmt_____ Kunstmuseum
9. einen gemütlich_____ Biergarten
10. ein historisch_____ Hotel

Adjectives without a Preceding Article

An attributive adjective that is not preceded by a **der-** or **ein-**word must take an ending that signals the case, gender, and number of the noun that follows.* With the exception of the genitive singular masculine and neuter, these endings are identical to those of the **der**-words.

	SINGULAR			PLURAL
	Masculine	*Neuter*	*Feminine*	*All Genders*
Nom.	schön**er** Urlaub	gut**es** Wetter	zentral**e** Lage	alt**e** Häuser
Acc.	schön**en** Urlaub	gut**es** Wetter	zentral**e** Lage	alt**e** Häuser
Dat.	schön**em** Urlaub	gut**em** Wetter	zentral**er** Lage	alt**en** Häuser**n**
Gen.	schön**en** Urlaub**s**	gut**en** Wetter**s**	zentral**er** Lage	alt**er** Häuser

SUMMARY OF ENDINGS

	SINGULAR			PLURAL
	Masculine	*Neuter*	*Feminine*	*All Genders*
Nom.	er	es	e	e
Acc.	en	es	e	e
Dat.	em	em	er	en
Gen.	en	en	er	er

Note that an adjective in the genitive singular masculine and neuter always takes the **en** ending.

Wo bekommt man frisch**es** Obst?	*Where can you get fresh fruit?*
Wo bekommt man hier frisch**e** Brötchen?	*Where can one get fresh rolls?*
Bei schlecht**em** Wetter bleibe ich zu Hause.	*In bad weather I'll stay home.*

---

*This type of adjective ending is traditionally referred to as a *strong* adjective ending.

In each of the example sentences on the preceding page, the adjective ending signals the gender, case, and number of the noun.

Two or more attributive adjectives preceding the same noun will have the same ending.

Im Restaurant Mecklenheide versorgt man Sie mit gut**er** deutsch**er** Küche.	*Restaurant Mecklenheide offers good German cuisine.*
Klein**e**, schwarz**e** Katze gefunden, Nähe Universität.	*Found: small, black cat, near university.*

Analyse

Circle all adjectival phrases in the illustrations. Then determine:

- the gender, case, and number of the noun
- why a particular adjective ending is used

HOTEL

ARCADE

member of PULLMAN INTERNATIONAL HOTELS

Das A ARCADE und O OPTIMAL für Bonn!

Sie suchen:

- das Hotel im Herzen der Stadt
- maximalen Komfort, moderne Einrichtung[3]
- die gehobene[4] Mittelklasse
- ein Tagungshotel[6]

Wir bieten:[1]

- **zentrale Lage,** unmittelbar[2] in der Nähe der Fußgängerzone
- 147 **gastfreundliche Zimmer** mit Dusche, WC, Telefon, Kabel-TV u. Radio
- **preiswerte Übernachtung** mit reichhaltigem[5] Frühstücksbuffet, **Restaurant** mit internationaler Küche
- 3 Konferenzräume für 10—150 Personen
- eigene **Tiefgarage**

gastfreundlich • preiswert • zentral

1. *offer*
2. *direct*
3. *furnishings*
4. *upper*
5. *lavish*
6. *conference hotel*

Ältestes renommiertestes Eiscafé in KL

Eiscafé Dolomiten

Bei uns beginnt die Eiszeit - jetzt!!

★ Heiß- und Kaltspezialitäten
★ Eiskreationen mit frischen Früchten
★ Selbstgebackener Kuchen
★ Italienisches Frühstück

An Wochentagen ab 8.30 Uhr geöffnet

Kaiserslautern · Schillerstr. 2 · Tel. 06 31 / 6 31 05

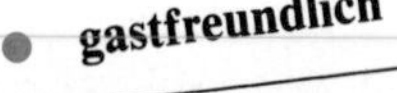

Griechische Aprikosen Klasse 1, 1 kg real spezial 2,98

Spanische Honigmelonen Stück real spezial 1,98

Deutscher Eissalat Klasse 1, Stück real spezial 0,98

Deutsche Möhren Klasse 1, 1 kg real spezial 1,49

Übung 10 Kurze Gespräche

Übung 10. Have your students complete the missing endings before listening, then use the listening phase to check their work.

Sie hören zwei kurze Gespräche. Ergänzen Sie die Adjektivendungen, so wie Sie sie hören.

Dialog 1

GERD: Sag mal, seit wann hast du denn blau_e___ Haare?[1]
GABI: Seit letzt_er___ Woche.[2] Gefallen sie dir?
GERD: Na ja, ich war an deine braun_en___ Haare gewöhnt.[3]
GABI: Ich habe ja auch blau_e___ Augen.[4] Die blau_en___ Haare passen gut zu meinen blau_en___ Augen.[5]
GERD: Ein merkwürdig_er___ Grund (*masc.*). Na ja, meine Oma hat dunkellila Haare.[6]

Dialog 2

PASSANT: Entschuldigung, wo ist das Rathaus?
PASSANTIN: Meinen Sie das alt_e___ oder das neu_e___?[7]
PASSANT: Oh, es gibt zwei? Ein alt_es___ und ein neu_es___?[8] Ich suche das Rathaus mit dem berühmt_en___ Glockenspiel.[9]
PASSANTIN: Also, das ist das alt_e___ Rathaus.[10] Gehen Sie geradeaus, dann die zweit_e___ Straße links.[11] Das Rathaus liegt auf der recht_en___ Seite.[12]

Indefinite Numerals and *alle*

The indefinite numerals **einige** (*some*), **mehrere** (*several*), **viele** (*many*), and **wenige** (*few*) are considered adjectives. They often appear in a series with other adjectives.

Mehrere kleine Hotels bieten Halbpension an.	*Several small hotels offer a two-meal plan.*
In **vielen** kleinen Gasthäusern gibt es nur Frühstück.	*In many small inns, they serve only breakfast.*

The specific numeral **alle** (the plural of **jeder**) is a **der**-word. Thus, adjectives following it take the nonspecific **en** ending.

Alle groß**en** Hotels haben ein Schwimmbad.	*All large hotels have a swimming pool.*

Übung 11 Kleinanzeigen:° Gesucht/Gefunden

° classified ads

Ergänzen Sie die Lücken mit den passenden Adjektivendungen.

1. Studentin sucht schön____ Zimmer in nett_____ Wohngemeinschaft.

2. Freundlich_____ Englischlehrer sucht klein_____ Wohnung in zentral_____ Lage.

3. Italienisch_____ Studentin sucht nett_____ Zimmer im Norden der Stadt.

4. **Gesucht.** Klein_____, schwarz_____ Pudel entlaufen, Nähe Stadtpark. Hört auf den Namen Papageno. Belohnung.

5. **Gefunden.** Groß_____, graugetigert _____ Kater, Nähe Rosenbachstraße und Meisenweg.

6. **Gefunden.** Freundlich_____, klein_____ Katze, schwarz mit weiß_____ Nase, Landeshauptstraße, Ecke Stadtpark.

Übung 12 Hin und her: Was gibt es hier? 

Fragen Sie einen Partner / eine Partnerin nach der fehlenden Information.

BEISPIEL: S1: Was gibt es beim Gasthof zum Bären?
S2: Warme Küche.
S1: Was gibt es sonst noch?
S2: Bayerische Spezialitäten.

WO?	WAS?	WAS SONST NOCH?
Gasthof zum Bären	Küche / warm	Spezialitäten / bayerisch
Gasthof Adlersberg	Biergarten / gemütlich	liegt in Lage / idyllisch
Gasthaus Schneiderwirt	Hausmusik / originell	Gästezimmer / rustikal
Hotel Luitpold	in Lage / idyllisch	Zimmer / rustikal

Adjectives Referring to Cities and Regions

Haben Sie schon einmal im Hotel **Baseler** Hof übernachtet?
Das Hotel liegt in der **Frankfurter** Innenstadt.
Wo trägt man **Tiroler** Hüte?

A city or regional name can be used attributively by adding **er** to the name of the city or region. This is one of the rare instances where an adjective is capitalized in German. No further changes are made. One country name can also be used in this way: **die Schweiz.**

Essen Sie gern **Schweizer** Käse?

Realia. The *Rattenfänger-Reisen* ad is from a brochure of the Hamlin tourist office.

Übung 13 Berichte 

Sie sind gerade von einer Reise nach Hause gekommen. Nun müssen Sie berichten. Beantworten Sie die Fragen: Bist du in . . . gewesen? Hast du . . . gesehen/besucht?

BEISPIEL: Café: viele / nett →
S1: Bist du in einem Café gewesen?
S2: Ich bin in vielen netten Cafés gewesen.

1. Museum: alle / modern
2. Stadt: mehrere / schön
3. Geschäft: einige / teuer
4. Kirche: viele / berühmt
5. Rathaus: alle / historisch
6. Hotel: einige / elegant

Sprache im Kontext

Zuschauen

Vorschau

D1 Telekom

Sehen Sie sich die Werbung ohne Ton an und achten Sie genau auf das, was Sie sehen. Wofür ist das vielleicht eine Werbung?

- Luftballons ☐
- Mundwasser ☐
- Kreditkarte ☐
- Autotelefon-Service ☐
- öffentliche Verkehrsmittel ☐

Arbeit mit dem Videotext

A. Sehen Sie sich die Werbung mit Ton an und spekulieren Sie. Was glauben Sie, was die folgenden Personen sagen?
Was sagt . . .

1. der Mann im Auto zu dem Ballonverkäufer?
2. der Ballonverkäufer zu der Frau im Auto?
3. die Frau zu dem Mann?

B. Stellen Sie sich vor, die Frau und der Mann treffen sich am folgenden Freitagabend. Beschreiben Sie, was die beiden machen.

Lesen

Zum Thema

A. Vorteile (*advantages*) **und Nachteile** (*disadvantages*) **des Stadtlebens.** Arbeiten Sie mit einem Partner / einer Partnerin. Machen Sie eine Liste von den Vorteilen und Nachteilen des Stadtlebens.

B. Zusammenwohnen. Interviewen Sie zwei Studenten/Studentinnen, und berichten Sie danach im Plenum.

1. Worüber ärgerst du dich (*do you get irritated*), wenn du zu Hause bist? Was stört (*disturbs*) dich?
2. Was machst du, wenn deine Mitbewohner/Mitbewohnerinnen/ Nachbarn/Nachbarinnen zu laut sind?
3. Was ist wichtig für ein friedliches (*peaceful*) Zusammenleben in einer Stadt?

C. Was würden Sie machen?

1. Sie müssen für eine Prüfung lernen, und Ihr Mitbewohner / Ihre Mitbewohnerin spielt sehr laute Musik.
2. Sie studieren Musik und müssen jeden Tag üben. Ihre Nachbarn im Haus beschweren sich (*complain*) immer, wenn Sie spielen.
3. Sie wohnen in einer WG. Einer Ihrer Mitbewohner / eine Ihrer Mitbewohnerinnen räumt die Küche nie auf, wenn er/sie gekocht hat.

Zum Thema. C. Suggestion: Have students role-play the various situations.

Auf den ersten Blick

A. In diesem Text stehen die Verben im Imperfekt (*simple past*). Suchen Sie den Infinitiv in der zweiten spalte.

1. _____ spielte	**a.** schlagen (*to hit*)
2. _____ gab	**b.** sprechen
3. _____ stieß	**c.** grüßen
4. _____ losging	**d.** ausziehen (*to move out*)
5. _____ blies	**e.** einziehen (*to move in*)
6. _____ schlug	**f.** losgehen
7. _____ traf	**g.** anfangen
8. _____ grüßte	**h.** stören (*to disturb*)
9. _____ einzog	**i.** stoßen (*to pound*)
10. _____ auszog	**j.** spielen
11. _____ sprach	**k.** blasen (*to blow*)
12. _____ anfing	**l.** treffen
13. _____ störte	**m.** geben

B. Lesen Sie die ersten zwei Absätze (*paragraphs*). Wo findet die Geschichte statt? Wie könnte die Geschichte weitergehen?

Auf den ersten Blick. Suggestion.
A. Read the first two paragraphs of the text aloud, acting out the story, before having students answer these questions.
B. Work on contextual guessing with the students in the first two paragraphs. For example, point out that **Mietshaus** is related to **mieten** and **Haus** and see if they can infer the meaning.

Die Gitarre des Herrn Hatunoglu

von Heinrich Hannover

Frau Amanda Klimpermunter spielte oft und gern Klavier. Aber sie wohnte in einem großen Mietshaus. Und da gab es manchmal Ärger° mit den Mietern der Nachbarwohnungen. Denn die Wände und Decken des Hauses waren dünn.°

In der Wohnung unter Frau Klimpermunter wohnte Herr Maibaum. Wenn oben Klavier gespielt wurde, fühlte sich Herr Maibaum in seiner Ruhe gestört° und schimpfte.° Dann stieß er ein paarmal mit einem Besenstiel an die Decke. Aber Frau Klimpermunter spielte weiter. Und so schaffte sich Herr Maibaum eines Tages eine Trompete an. Und immer, wenn Frau Klimpermunters Klaviermusik losging, trompetete er kräftig° dagegen.

Das störte nun den Nachbarn des Herrn Maibaum, der sich schon über das Klavier genug geärgert hatte. Und jetzt auch noch die Trompete, das war zuviel. Ein paarmal klopfte° er mit einem Holzpantoffel gegen die Wand. Aber Herr Maibaum trompetete weiter. Und so schaffte sich der Nachbar, er hieß Fromme-Weise, eine Posaune an. Und immer, wenn das Klavier und die Trompete im Haus ertönten, blies er laut wie ein Elefant auf der Posaune.

Aber das störte nun Frau Morgenschön, die Wand an Wand mit Herrn Fromme-Weise wohnte. Ein paarmal schlug sie mit dem Kochlöffel gegen die Wand, aber das kümmerte ihren Nachbarn nicht. Und so kaufte sie sich eine Flöte und düdelte dazwischen, wenn die anderen Musikanten im Haus loslegten.

Das störte Herrn Bollermann, der unter Frau Morgenschön wohnte. Er kaufte sich ein Schlagzeug und haute, wenn die anderen herumtönten, kräftig auf die Pauke. Das gab nun alle Tage einen Höllenlärm im Haus, ein fürchterliches Durcheinander—tüdelüdelüt-bumsbums-trärä-trara-bumspeng . . . Wenn man sich auf der Treppe traf, grüßte keiner den anderen, man knallte mit den Türen, es gab immer Krach° im Haus, auch wenn keiner Musik machte.

Aber dann zog Herr Hatunoglu ins Haus ein, ein Ausländer, wie man schon am Namen merkt. Er brachte eine Gitarre mit und freute sich, daß im Haus musiziert wurde. „Da kann ich ja auch ein bißchen Gitarre spielen", sagte er. Aber obwohl man die Gitarre bei dem Lärm, den die anderen Hausbewohner mit ihren Instrumenten machten, gar nicht hören konnte, waren sich plötzlich alle einig: „Die Gitarre ist zu laut." Plötzlich sprachen sie wieder miteinander.

„Finden Sie nicht auch, daß der Herr Hatunoglu mit seiner Gitarre einen unerträglichen Lärm macht?"

„Ja, Sie haben recht, der Mann muß raus."

Sie grüßten sich wieder auf der Treppe und hörten auf, sich gegenseitig zu nerven. Dem Herrn Hatunoglu aber machten sie das Leben schwer. Wenn er anfing, auf der Gitarre zu spielen, klopften sie von oben und von unten und von allen Seiten mit Besenstielen, Kochlöffeln und Holzpantoffeln an Wände und Decken und riefen: „Aufhören! Ruhe im Haus!"

„Was haben die Leute bloß gegen meine Gitarre?" fragte Herr Hatunoglu. Und eines Tages zog er aus.

Kaum war Herr Hatunoglu ausgezogen, ging der Krach im Haus wieder los. Sobald Frau Klimpermunter den ersten Ton auf dem Klavier gespielt hat, packen die anderen Hausbewohner ihre Instrumente aus und legen los: Tüdelüdelüt-bumsbums-trärä-trara-bumspeng . . . Sie sprechen auch nicht mehr miteinander

trouble
thin
disturbed
yelled, swore
powerfully, vigorously
knocked
noise

und grüßen sich nicht mehr auf der Treppe. Und sie knallen° wieder mit den Türen. Aber abends, wenn sie völlig entnervt ins Bett gehen, flüstern sie vor sich hin: „Was war das doch für eine schöne, ruhige Zeit, als noch der Herr Hatunoglu mit seiner Gitarre im Haus wohnte.“

slam

Zum Text

A. Wer wohnt wo? Setzen Sie die Namen der Bewohner in das Bild ein. Welches Instrument gehört zu welcher Person? Welches „Schlagzeug“ gehört zu welcher Person?

Zum Text. A. Homework: Reproduce the house on the board or on a transparency. Have one student go to the board or the overhead projector. The rest of the class tells her or him who lives where, which instrument goes where, and who is using what to bang on the wall.

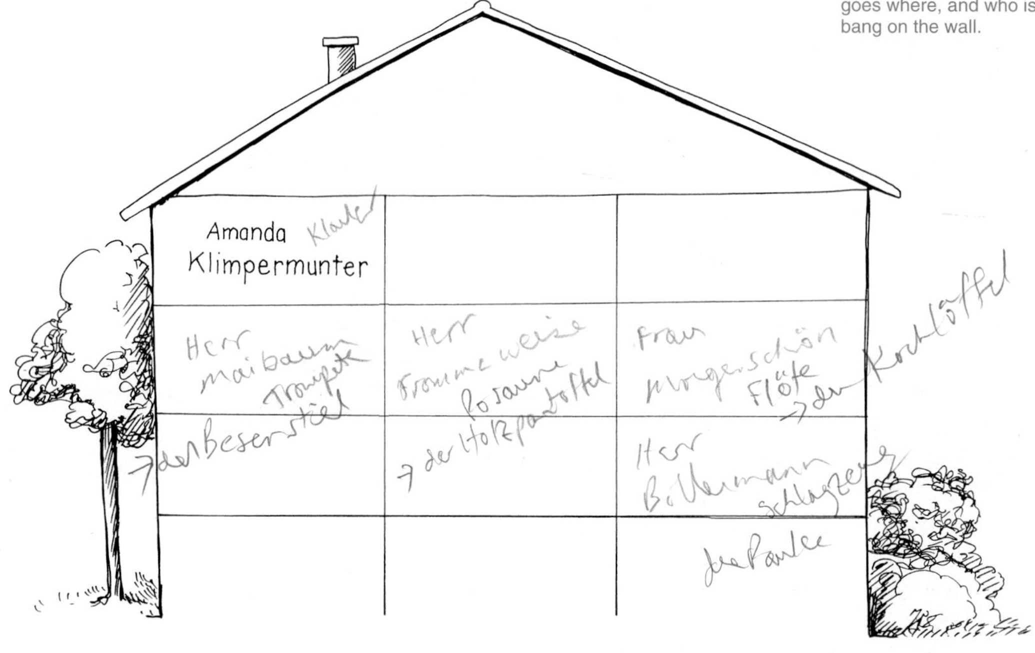

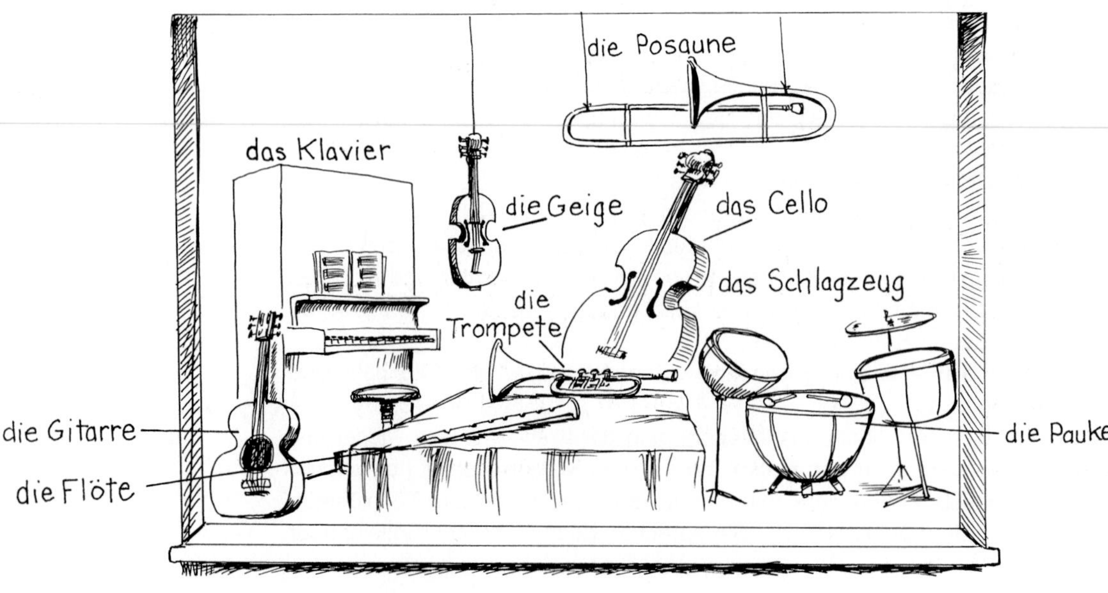

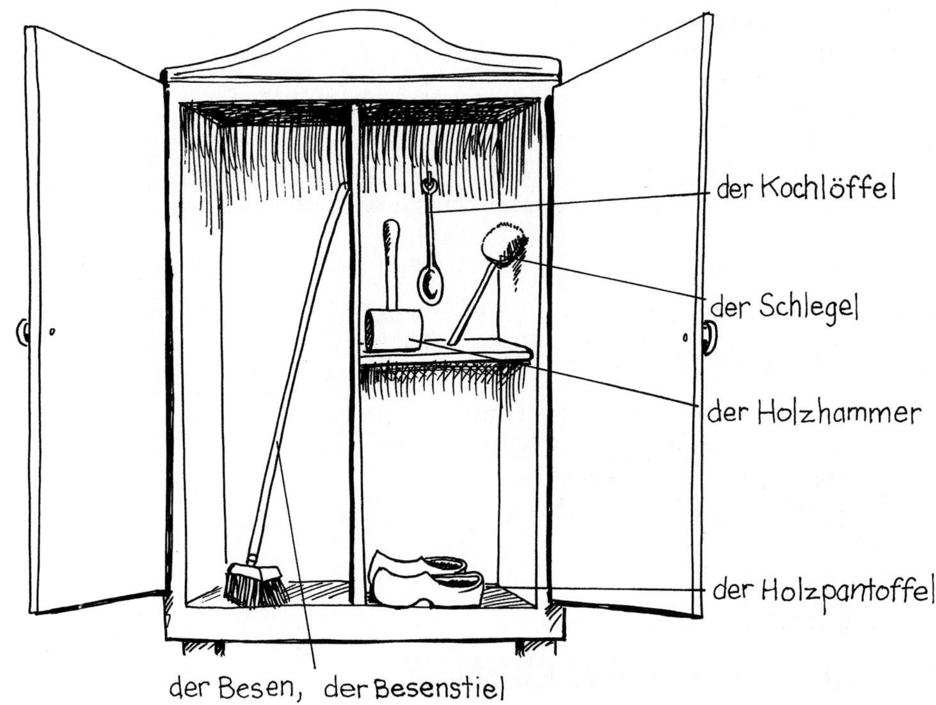

B. Stimmt das? Stimmt das nicht? Oder steht das nicht im Text?

	DAS STIMMT	DAS STIMMT NICHT	DAS STEHT NICHT IM TEXT
1. Herr Hatunoglu ist unfreundlich.	□	□	□
2. Nachdem Herr Hatunoglu einzieht, sprechen die Nachbarn wieder miteinander.	□	□	□
3. Herr Hatunoglu spielt Gitarre und ist sehr froh, dass die anderen Bewohner so viel Musik machen.	□	□	□
4. Die anderen Bewohner mögen Herrn Hatunoglu nicht, weil er so laut ist.	□	□	□
5. Herr Hatunoglu lädt oft Freunde ein, und sie sind sehr laut.	□	□	□
6. Sobald Herr Hatunoglu auszieht, werden die anderen Bewohner miteinander viel freundlicher.	□	□	□

C. Suchen Sie die folgenden Wörter im Text. Welches Wort gehört nach dem Text nicht in die Gruppe?

BEISPIEL: Holzpantoffel Klavier Besen →
Klavier gehört nicht dazu. Frau Klimpermunter spielt Klavier. Die Nachbarn schlagen mit dem Holzpantoffel und Besen gegen die Wand, wenn sie Musik hören.

1. sich etwas anschaffen	düdeln	trompeten
2. schimpfen	die Tür knallen	Krach machen
3. klopfen	schlagen	flüstern
4. anschaffen	aufhören	kaufen

Sprechen und Schreiben

Aktivität 1 Wer bin ich?

Wählen Sie eine Person aus der Geschichte „Die Gitarre des Herrn Hatunoglu". Beschweren Sie sich (*complain*) über die Situation im Haus aus der Perspektive dieser Person. Schreiben Sie Ihre Beschwerde (*complaint*) auf, und lesen Sie sie der Klasse vor. Die anderen müssen raten, wer Sie sind.

Aktivität 1. Suggestion: Collect the complaints and read some aloud or have a student read them. Have students guess which character in the story is complaining.

Aktivität 2 Ein Interview über den Krach im Haus

Interviewen Sie Herrn Hatunoglu und eine weitere Person im Haus. Schreiben Sie mindestens drei Fragen für jede Person auf. Arbeiten Sie in Gruppen zu viert. Zwei Studenten / Studentinnen aus der Klasse übernehmen die Rollen. Die anderen interviewen die beiden.

In der Stadt / In the City

In der Stadt	In the City
die **Ampel, -n**	traffic light
die **Innenstadt, ¨e**	downtown
die **Kreuzung, -en**	intersection
die **Lage, -n**	location
der **Passant, -en (en** *masc.*)	passer-by
die **Polizei**	police, police station
der **Weg, -e**	way

Orte / Places

Orte	Places
die **Bank, -en**	bank
der **Hafen, ¨**	dock, harbor
das **Hotel, -s**	hotel
die **Jugendherberge, -n**	youth hostel
die **Kirche, -n**	church
das **Museum,** *pl.* **Museen**	museum
die **Pension, -en**	bed and breakfast
die **Post,** *pl.* **Postämter**	post office
die **Schwimmhalle, -n**	indoor swimming pool
der **Strand, ¨e**	beach
die **Tankstelle, -n**	gas station

Im Hotel / At the Hotel

Im Hotel	At the Hotel
das **Anmeldeformular, -e**	registration form
der **Apparat, -e**	appliance (*such as television, telephone, camera*)
der **Aufenthalt, -e**	stay
der **Aufzug, ¨e**	elevator
das **Doppelzimmer, -**	room with two beds
die **Dusche, -n**	shower
das **Einzelzimmer, -**	room with one bed
das **Erdgeschoss, -e***	ground floor
der **Frühstücksraum, ¨e**	breakfast room
das **Gepäck**	luggage
der **Koffer, -**	suitcase
die **Kreditkarte, -n**	credit card
der **Parkplatz, ¨e**	parking space; parking lot
der **Preis, -e**	price; cost
im Preis enthalten	included in the cost
der **Reisepass, ¨e***	passport
der **Reisescheck, -s**	traveller's check
die **Rezeption**	reception desk
die **Sauna**	sauna
der **Schlüssel, -**	key
der **Stock,** *pl.* **Stockwerke**	floor, story
der **Telefonanruf, -e**	telephone call
die **Toilette, -n**	restroom
die **Übernachtung, -en**	overnight stay
die **Unterkunft, ¨e**	accommodation
die **Unterschrift, -en**	signature
das **WC, -s**	bathroom, toilet

* See Appendix E for alternate spelling.

Nach dem Weg fragen	Asking Directions
bis: bis zum/zur	to, as far as
gegenüber (+ *dative*)	across from
geradeaus	straight ahead
immer geradeaus	(keep on going) straight ahead
links	left
nach links	(to the) left
rechts	right
nach rechts	(to the) right
weit	far
die **Mitte**	middle
in der Mitte (der Stadt)	in the center (of the city)
die **Nähe**	vicinity
in der Nähe (des Bahnhofs)	near (the train station)

Verben	Verbs
ab•reisen, ist abgereist	to depart
an•kommen, ist angekommen	to arrive
sich an•melden	to check in
aus•füllen	to fill out
sich beschweren über	to complain about
bezahlen	to pay
ein•biegen in (+ *acc.*)	to turn into
entlang•gehen, ist entlanggegangen	to walk along
erlauben	to allow, permit
funktionieren	to work, function
reparieren	to repair

Adjektive und Adverbien	Adjectives and Adverbs
bar	(in) cash
geeignet	suitable
günstig	reasonable (in price)
kaputt	broken
sofort	immediately
übrigens	by the way
ungefähr	about, approximately
zuerst	first

Genitivpräpositionen	Genitive Prepositions
außerhalb	outside of
innerhalb	inside of, within
trotz	in spite of
während	during
wegen	because of, on account of

Sonstige Ausdrücke	Other Expressions
Auf welchen Namen, bitte?	Under what name, please?
Auf Wiederhören!	Good-bye! (*on telephone*)
dahin	there
Wie komme ich am besten dahin?	What's the best way to get there?
Das geht auch.	That'll work too.
Das tut mir leid.	I'm sorry.
Entschuldigung.	Excuse me.
jemand nach dem Weg fragen	to ask someone, somebody for directions
Würden Sie bitte . . . ?	Would you please . . . ?

Lernziele

Use this checklist to verify that you can now . . .

- ☐ describe types of lodging and amenities.
- ☐ book a hotel room, register at, and check out of a hotel.
- ☐ describe cities and various public places found there.
- ☐ ask for / give directions.
- ☐ use the genitive case to describe relationships, ownership, properties, and characteristics.
- ☐ use attributive adjectives in the nominative, accusative, dative, and genitive cases.
- ☐ use the indefinite numerals and **alle** with descriptive adjectives.

Drittes Zwischenspiel

Die Entwicklung der Stadt

Im Laufe der Zeit hat sich das Bild der Stadt sehr verändert.[1] Viele Städte in Deutschland, wie auch anderswo in Europa, haben aber zum Teil ihren ursprünglichen[2] Charakter aus der mittelalterlichen Zeit erhalten.[3] Sie sind stolz auf ihre Vergangenheit, die oft bis ins Mittelalter und manchmal bis in die Römerzeit zurückreicht. Köln wurde zum Beispiel im Jahre 50 gegründet, Erfurt im 9. Jahrhundert. Die Geschichte Goslars reicht in das 10. Jahrhundert zurück. Gelegentlich sind sogar noch Überreste alter Bauten und Denkmäler[4] aus frühen Zeiten zu sehen.

Aktivität 1 Mittelalterliche Städte

Wie sahen Städte im Mittelalter aus? Was gehörte zum typischen Stadtbild? Kreuzen Sie an.

- □ Restaurants
- □ Gefängnis[5]
- □ Burg/Schloss
- □ Universität
- □ Kirche/Dom
- □ Bürgerhäuser[6]
- □ Wachttürme[7]
- □ Krankenhaus
- □ Markt
- □ Geschäfte
- □ Parks
- □ Bibliothek
- □ Schule
- □ Fabrik
- □ Stadtmauer[8]
- □ Rathaus[9]
- □ Museum
- □ Stadttor[10]

Aktivität 2 Nürnberg damals

Schauen Sie sich jetzt diese Stadtansicht von Nürnberg aus dem Jahr 1533 (Seite 289) an. Identifizieren Sie die Hauptmerkmale der Stadt.

1. _____ Burg
2. _____ Kirche
3. _____ Brücke
4. _____ Bürgerhäuser
5. _____ Stadtmauer
6. _____ Wachtturm

- Welche(s) Gebäude[11] bildete(n) den Kern[12] einer mittelalterlichen Stadt? Warum?
- Wer wohnte in der Stadt? Wer wohnte außerhalb der Stadt?

[1]*changed* [2]*original* [3]*preserved* [4]*monuments* [5]*prison* [6]*patrician houses* [7]*watch towers* [8]*city wall* [9]*town hall* [10]*city gate* [11]*buildings* [12]*center*

Erfurt

Köln

Nürnberg heute

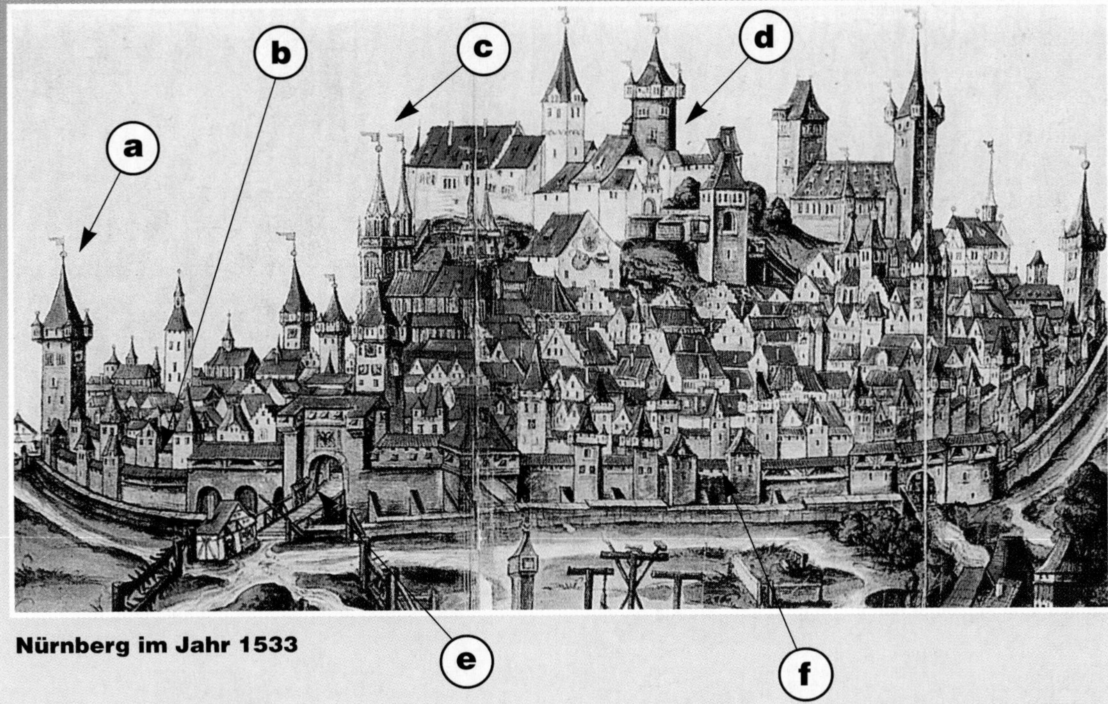

Nürnberg im Jahr 1533

Aktivität 3 Nürnberg heute

Vergleichen Sie die zwei Ansichten von Nürnberg. Obwohl Nürnberg während des Zweiten Weltkriegs fast völlig zerstört[1] wurde, sind noch einige Bauten und Denkmäler aus dem Mittelalter und der Renaissance erhalten. Wie viele der folgenden Bauten und Denkmäler können Sie auf dem Stadtplan finden?

1. St. Sebaldus Kirche (14. Jahrhundert)
2. St. Lorenz Kirche (13.–14. Jahrhundert)
3. das Rathaus (14. Jahrhundert)
4. die Stadtmauer (14.–15. Jahrhundert)
5. der Schöne Brunnen (1389–1396)
6. die Burg (11.–12. Jahrhundert)

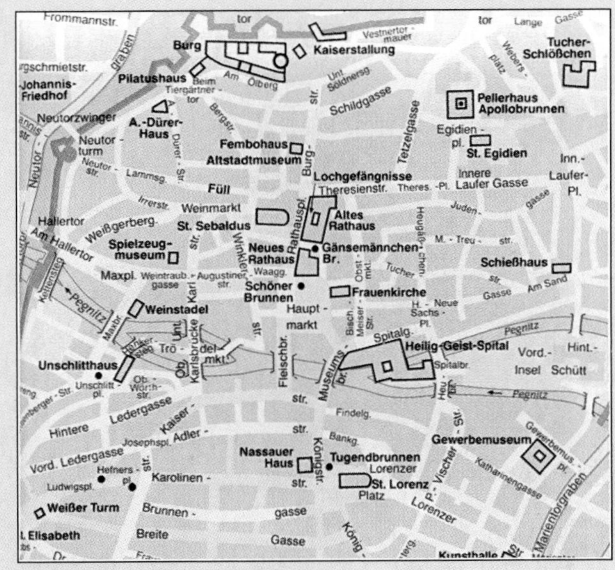

Stadtplan von Nürnberg

Aktivität 4 Auf den Spuren[2] der Stadtentwicklung

Wählen Sie eine Stadt in Ihrem Land aus. Es kann auch Ihre Heimatstadt sein. Beschreiben Sie folgendes:

- Wie sah die Stadt vor 100 Jahren aus?
- Was gehörte damals zum Stadtbild?
- Gab es einen Mittelpunkt der Stadt? Wenn ja, was gehörte dazu? Ein Markt, eine Kirche oder ein anderes Gebäude?
- Welche alten Bauten und Denkmäler sind noch in dieser Stadt erhalten? Welche sind verschwunden[3]? Warum?

[1]*destroyed* [2]*on the track* [3]*disappeared*

Kapitel 10

Auf Reisen

Auf der Blumeninsel Mainau im Bodensee

Kapitel 10. Suggestion: Talk about a trip you took, focusing on your travel preparations, e.g., planning the trip, going to the travel agency. Encourage students to talk about trips they took.

Alles klar?

A. Was planen Sie für Ihren nächsten Urlaub? Was interessiert Sie? Lesen Sie die folgenden Anzeigen!

Realia. *Aktiv-Urlaub* is from the Munich newspaper *Die Süddeutsche.* The other ads are from the newspaper *In München.*

- Auf welcher Reise kann man eine Fremdsprache lernen?
- Welche Reise ist für sportliche Leute am geeignetsten (*most suited*)? Welche Sportarten kann man auf dieser Reise machen?
- Welche Reise verbindet (*connects*) Sport und Kultur?
- Was macht eine Wanderreise attraktiv?
- Was macht Ihnen persönlich in den Ferien Spaß: eine Fremdsprache lernen? Tennisspielen lernen? eine Wanderreise machen? Mountainbiking?

Diesmal Aktiv-Urlaub

BAUMELER Wanderreisen: mehr sehen, mehr erleben.[1] Auf eigenen Füßen unterwegs[2] sein, dort wo wandern sich lohnt.[3] Kleine Gruppen. Kompetente Reiseleitung. Ausgewählte[4] Hotels. Linienflug oder Busreise.

TENNIS & KULTUR IN PRAG

ab DM 345,-

1 Wo inkl.: 5x2(4) Std. **Tennistraining** + HP + Kulturprogramm · Info + Buchung: Tel. (089) 53 94 34 od. 53 64 35 · Fax 532 84 70 **Tamar-Reisen** · Häberlstraße 13 · 8 Mü 2

Sun & Fun • Sport & Spiel • mit Board, Bike, Racket, Badehose und Bikini!

Clubdorf Tortorella • Süditalien • ab 16 Jahre

Beachlife • American Sports • Tennis • Highlife

Termine '93: 5.-19.7./19.7.-2.8./26.7.-8.9./9.8. - 23.8./23.8.-30.8.

1 Woche inkl. Halbpension,[7] Reiseleitung, Aktivprogramm und Bus ab München pro Person DM 735,-

2 Wochen pro Person DM 1198,-

Multi-Sportcamp • Österreich • 14 - 20 Jahre

Snowboard • Tennis • Mountainbike • Fitneß

Piesendorf am Kitzsteinhorn • Termine '93: 31.5.-6.6./25.7.-14.8.

6 Tage inkl. Vollpension,[8] Multisport, Skipaß, Leihmaterial und Betreuung pro Person DM 790,-

Den Geamt-Reisekatalog erhaltet Ihr kostenlos!
Tel.: 089/21 66-243 • Fax: 089/26 04-443

Sport-Scheck REISEN

1. *to experience*
2. *on the road*
3. sich . . . *is worth (it)*
4. *selected*
5. *one-on-one instruction*
6. *day care*
7. *breakfast plus one meal*
8. *three meals*

B. Sie hören drei Gespräche über den Urlaub. Wo haben die Urlauber ihre Ferien verbracht? Was haben sie unternommen?

		WO		WAS
1.	**a.**	an der Nordsee	**a.**	segeln
	b.	an der Ostsee	**b.**	Camping
2.	**a.**	Mexiko	**a.**	Spanisch lernen
	b.	Bolivien	**b.**	tauchen
3.	**a.**	in den Dolomiten	**a.**	Bergsteigen
	b.	im Schwarzwald	**b.**	wandern

Wörter im Kontext

Thema 1

Ich möchte verreisen . . . aber wie?

Wie fahren Sie am liebsten?

- □ mit dem **Wagen**
- □ mit dem **Flugzeug**
- □ mit dem **Fahrrad**
- □ mit dem **Zug** / mit der **Bahn**
- □ mit dem **Bus**
- □ mit dem **Taxi**
- □ mit dem **Motorrad**
- □ mit dem **Heißluftballon**
- □ mit dem **Schiff**
- □ **per Autostop**

Exercises. Suggestion: Have students answer the questions after you have introduced the vocabulary using pictures. Follow up with a class poll to find out the favorite means of transportation and which mode of transport students associate with which adjective.

Und warum das? Welches Verkehrsmittel (*means of transportation*) finden Sie . . .

am **bequem**sten?
am **sicher**sten?
am **schnell**sten?
am praktischsten?
am **unbequem**sten?
am **gefährlich**sten?
am **langsam**sten?
am unpraktischsten?

Fragen Sie einen Partner / eine Partnerin, wie er oder sie verreisen möchte!

BEISPIEL: S1: Also Sven, du möchtest verreisen. Aber wie?
S2: Mit einem Heißluftballon.
S1: Und warum das denn?
S2: Das ist am interessantesten.

Was nehmen Sie **alles** auf Reisen mit?

Realia. *Ihre persönliche Checkliste* is from a brochure of the *Deutsche Bundesbahn.*

Ihre persönliche Checkliste vor der Reise – haben Sie nichts vergessen?

Bekleidung
- ☐ Oberbekleidung und Wäsche
- ☐ Regenbekleidung
- ☐ Handschuhe
- ☐ Badesachen
- ☐ Schlafanzug
- ☐ Kopfbedeckung
- ☐ Schal
- ☐ Sportbekleidung

Schuhwerk
- ☐ Wanderschuhe
- ☐ Hausschuhe
- ☐ Turnschuhe[1]
- ☐ Hüttenschuhe[2]

Toilettensachen
- ☐ Hautcreme
- ☐ Sonnenschutzmittel
- ☐ Erfrischungstücher[4]
- ☐ Haarshampoo
- ☐ Rasierzeug[3]

Für Ihre Aktivitäten im Urlaub
- ☐ Kamera
- ☐ Zubehör (Filter, Wechselobjektive, Blitzgeräte, Belichtungsmesser)
- ☐ Filme
- ☐ Fernglas[5]
- ☐ Stadtpläne
- ☐ Wanderkarten
- ☐ Reiseführer

Achtung! Ist die Lagerzeit der Filme abgelaufen?

Das sollte im Handgepäck nicht fehlen ...
- ☐ Reiseapotheke
- ☐ Reiselektüre

Auch das muß mit – aber nicht im Koffer!
- ☐ Bargeld (auch Fremdwährung)
  Achtung! Höchstgrenzen bei der Deviseneinfuhr nach bestimmten Ländern!
- ☐ Reiseschecks, Euroschecks
  Achtung! Scheckkarte!
- ☐ Reisepaß, Personalausweis
  Achtung! Wann läuft die Geltungsdauer der Pässe ab?
- ☐ Fahrkarten
- ☐ Reiseproviant[7]
- ☐ Platzkarten
- ☐ Bettkarten
- ☐ Liegekarten
- ☐ Familienpaß
- ☐ Senioren-Paß
- ☐ Junior-Paß
- ☐ Fahrplan
- ☐ Reiseversicherungspapiere[6]
- ☐ Kofferschlüssel
- ☐ Wohnungsschlüssel

1. *sneakers*
2. *slippers*
3. *shaving kit*
4. *towelettes*
5. *binoculars*
6. *travel insurance papers*
7. Reiseproviant = Essen und Trinken

Neue Wörter

- ☐ **Achtung!**
- ☐ **das Bargeld**
- ☐ der **Fahrplan**
- ☐ **fehlen**
- ☐ das **Handgepäck**
- ☐ die **Handschuhe**
- ☐ die **Kamera**
- ☐ der **(Personal-) Ausweis**
- ☐ die **Platzkarte**
- ☐ die **Reise**
- ☐ der **Reiseführer**
- ☐ das **Sonnenschutzmittel**
- ☐ der **Urlaub**
- ☐ **vergessen**

Diese Wörter haben alle mit Reisen und Verkehr zu tun. Welches Wort passt nicht in die Reihe?

1.	**Bahnhof**	**Ausweis**	**Flughafen**	**Haltestelle**
2.	**Fahrkarte**	**Platzkarte**	**Flugschein**	**Fahrplan**
3.	**Flugbegleiter**	**Autobahn**	**Buslinie**	**Wanderweg**
4.	**Schaffner**	**Taxifahrer**	**Pilot**	**Passagier**

Aktivität 1 Haben Sie etwas vergessen?

Aktivität 1. Alternative: Have students name from the *Reise-Checkliste* three things they could manage without.

Schauen Sie sich die Reise-Checkliste aus **Thema 1** an, und nennen Sie drei Dinge aus der Liste, die Sie unbedingt (*absolutely*) mitnehmen würden:

BEISPIEL: Ich möchte eine Mountainbike-Tour machen. Ich nehme Sonnenschutzmittel und ein Mountainbike mit.

eine Wanderreise durch Europa
eine Reise nach Hawaii
eine Safari nach Afrika
eine Reise nach _____

Deutsche Arbeitnehmer bekommen im Jahr durchschnittlich (*on average*) sechs Wochen bezahlten Urlaub. Das erklärt, warum der Urlaub ein so wichtiges Thema ist. Wie kann man sechs Wochen freie Zeit sinnvoll planen? Die meisten, vor allem Familien, nehmen den größten Teil des Urlaubs im Sommer, wenn die Kinder Ferien (*school holidays*) haben. Viele Deutsche machen auch im Winter Urlaub: Sie fahren in den Bergen Ski oder suchen ein wärmeres Klima im Süden.

Strandurlaub auf der Nordseeinsel Sylt

Aktivität 2 Hin und her: Was nehmen sie mit? 

Wohin fahren diese Leute im Urlaub? Was nehmen sie mit? Ergänzen Sie die Informationen.

Aktivität 2. Make sure students ask questions on all three categories.

BEISPIEL: S1: Wohin fährt Angelika Meier in Urlaub?
S2: Sie fährt in die Türkei.
S1: Warum fährt sie in die Türkei?
S2: Weil . . .
S1: Was nimmt sie mit?
S2: Sie nimmt . . .

PERSONEN	WOHIN?	WARUM?	WAS NIMMT ER/SIE MIT?
Angelika Meier	in die Türkei	sich am Strand erholen	Buch Sonnenbrille Badesachen
Peter Bayer	auf die Insel Rügen	Windsurfen gehen	Sonnenschutzmittel Badehose
Roland Metz	nach Thüringen	wandern Weimar besichtigen	Stadtpläne Reiseführer Wanderschuhe
Sabine Graf	nach Griechenland	eine Studienreise machen	Reiseführer Wörterbuch Kamera

To form the comparative of an adjective or adverb, add **er** to the basic form.

schnell → schnell**er** (*faster*)
romantisch → romantisch**er** (*more romantic*)

Weiteres zum Thema Reisen finden Sie bei ***Deutsch: Na klar!*** im World-Wide-Web unter www.mhhe.com/german.

Aktivität 3 Vorteile und Nachteile°

° *advantages and disadvantages*

Aktivität 3. Suggestion: Point out the **Sprachtipp** about the comparative form. Then have students scan the possibilities in the sentence builder before they complete the activity, working in pairs. Spot-check the answers by asking several students to state the advantages and disadvantages of various ways of traveling.

Alles hat seine Vorteile und Nachteile. Was meinen Sie?

BEISPIELE: Mit dem Fahrrad erlebt man viel, aber es ist anstrengend.

Mit dem Auto geht es schneller, aber es ist _____.

mit dem/der _____	ist es	nicht	bequem / anstrengend
Bahn (Zug)	sieht man	sehr	billig / teuer
Bus	erlebt man	zu	praktisch / unpraktisch
Fahrrad	kostet es		romantisch / langweilig
Flugzeug	geht es		schnell / langsam
Heißluftballon			sicher / gefährlich
Wagen (Auto)			viel / wenig
per Autostop			
zu Fuß (Wandern)			
?			

A proverb in German says:

Wenn einer eine Reise tut, dann kann er was erleben.
When someone takes a trip, he can experience something.

The verb **erleben** is often used when talking of a vacation. In this context it means to experience, see, and do things that make a lasting impression, whether positive or negative.

Thema 2

Im Reisebüro 

Im Reisebüro. Follow-up: Have students work in pairs and come up with variations on the dialogue. The customer might have different requirements for a vacation, the travel agent different suggestions. You might want to brainstorm various possibilities before the students begin.

Ein Gespräch im Reisebüro zwischen Frau Siemens und Herrn Bittner, einem Angestellten im ***Reisebüro*** (travel agency).

FRAU SIEMENS: Mein Freund und ich möchten dieses Jahr mal einen Aktivurlaub machen. Wir wollen mal was anderes **erleben.** Können Sie etwas **vorschlagen?**

HERR BITTNER: Ja, gern. Wofür interessieren Sie sich denn? Es gibt so viele **Möglichkeiten.** Sind Sie **sportlich aktiv?**

FRAU SIEMENS: Nicht besonders. Manchmal spielen wir Tennis und fahren auch schon mal Rad.

HERR BITTNER: Wie wäre es mit einer Radreise durchs Elsaß—oder mit einem **Segelkurs** an der Ostsee?

FRAU SIEMENS: Ach, ein Segelkurs ist mir zu anstrengend. Ich kann auch nicht gut schwimmen. Und eine Radreise . . . ich weiß nicht. Was können wir **sonst noch unternehmen?**

HERR BITTNER: Wir haben hier ein **Angebot** für eine **viertägige** Wandertour im Naturpark Solling-Vogler in der Nähe von Göttingen. Hier ist ein **Reiseprospekt.** Das kann ich sofort für Sie **buchen.**

FRAU SIEMENS: Hm, klingt gut. Ich sehe hier, die Gruppen sind relativ klein, höchstens zwölf Personen und ein **Reiseleiter.** Wo **übernachtet** man denn?
HERR BITTNER: Im **Zelt** natürlich!
FRAU SIEMENS: Ach, ich weiß nicht, ob mein Freund **damit einverstanden ist.** Er liebt die **Natur** zwar, aber in der Natur übernachten? Das ist etwas anderes. Wo **beginnt** die Wandertour?
HERR BITTNER: In Holzminden. Da treffen sich die Teilnehmer mit dem **Reiseleiter.** Von da aus fährt die Gruppe mit dem Bus zum Park. Die **Fahrt** dauert nicht lange, und **unterwegs** sieht man viel Grünes.
FRAU SIEMENS: Was kostet die Reise **insgesamt?**
HERR BITTNER: **Pro Person** DM 500,-
FRAU SIEMENS: Das ist günstig. Wir werden es uns überlegen. Ich **sage** Ihnen in zwei Tagen **Bescheid.** Den Koffer packe ich noch nicht. Ich **hoffe,** mein Freund ist damit einverstanden.
HERR BITTNER: Ich hoffe es auch. Bis dann. Auf Wiedersehen.
FRAU SIEMENS: Auf Wiedersehen.

Eine Wandertour von vier Tagen ist eine **viertägige** Wandertour. Eine Fahrt von einer Woche ist eine **einwöchige** Fahrt. Ein Aufenthalt von fünf Monaten ist ein **fünfmonatiger** Aufenthalt. So macht man es:

ein		**stündig**		
zwei	+	**tägig**	+	Adjektivendung
drei		**wöchig**		
. . .		**monatig**		

Aktivität 4 Claudia Siemens berichtet

Claudia Siemens berichtet ihrem Freund über ihren Besuch im Reisebüro. Ergänzen Sie die Sätze durch Informationen aus dem Gespräch im **Thema 2.**

CLAUDIA: Ich war heute im Reisebüro. Ich schlage vor, wir machen _____.[1]
MANFRED: Wie lange dauert denn so eine Tour?
CLAUDIA: _____.[2]
MANFRED: Und wo übernachtet man?
CLAUDIA: _____.[3]
MANFRED: Wie viele Leute nehmen (*participate*) an so einer Tour teil?
CLAUDIA: _____.[4]
MANFRED: Was soll das denn kosten?
CLAUDIA: _____.[5]

MANFRED: Ist das nicht ein bisschen teuer?
CLAUDIA: _____.[6]
MANFRED: Was meinst *du?* Sollen wir das machen?
CLAUDIA: Also, ich finde, das ist mal was anderes.
MANFRED: Gut, dann bin ich damit _____.[7]

Weiteres zum Thema Reisebüro finden Sie bei ***Deutsch: Na klar!*** im World-Wide-Web unter www.mhhe.com/german.

Aktivität 5 Pläne für einen interessanten Urlaub

Sie hören vier Gespräche im Reisebüro. Wie, wohin und warum wollen die Leute in Urlaub fahren? Wie lange wollen sie dort bleiben?

Aktivität 5. Follow-up: Have students tell the class **wohin, wie, warum,** and **wie lange** for their own vacation dreams.

PERSONEN	WIE?	WOHIN?	WARUM?	WIE LANGE?
1. *Nicola Dinsing*	mit dem Flugzeug	nach Sizilien	für einen Sprachkurs	vier Wochen
2. *Marianne Koch und Astrid Preuß*	keine Information	nach Korfu	zur Meditation	eine Woche
3. *Herbert und Sabine Lucht*	mit dem Flugzeug, Bus und Schiff	nach Alaska	keine Information	zwei bis drei Wochen
4. *Sebastian Thiel*	keine Information	nach Israel	für eine Studienreise	drei Wochen

Aktivität 6 Überredungskünste°

Versuchen Sie, einen Partner / eine Partnerin zu einem Plan für einen gemeinsamen Urlaub zu überreden (*persuade*). Die Anzeigen auf Seite 281 bieten mögliche Reisen.

°*art of persuasion*

Aktivität 6. Suggestion: Cue students in different pairs to react in different ways, e.g., to be cooperative, to be skeptical, to be uncooperative. Have various pairs role-play their conversations for the class.

S1	S2
1. Ich möchte dieses Jahr nach/in _____. Willst du mit?	**2.** Was kann man denn da unternehmen?
3. Man kann da zum Beispiel _____.	**4.** Ist das alles? Was sonst noch?
5. Nein, man kann auch _____.	**6.** Wo übernachtet man denn?
7. _____.	**8.** Wie viel soll das kosten?
9. _____.	**10.** Wie lange soll die Fahrt dauern?
11. _____.	**12a.** Ich will es mir überlegen. **12b.** Ich weiß nicht, das ist mir zu _____ (teuer, langweilig usw.). **12c.** Klingt in Ordnung. Ich komme mit.

Thema 3

Eine Fahrkarte, bitte! 

Am Fahrkartenschalter im Bahnhof

Wo kann man was machen? Wo passiert was?

1. Am _____ kauft man Fahrkarten für den Zug.
2. Der Zug fährt von _____ 2 ab.
3. Man bekommt Informationen über Züge bei der _____.
4. Auf dem _____ kann man lesen, wann ein Zug ankommt oder abfährt.
5. Die Leute stehen auf dem _____ und warten auf den Zug.

Reiseverbindungen

Deutsche Bahn 

VON *Bad Harzburg*
NACH *Hamburg Hbf*
ÜBER

Gültig[1] *am Montag, dem 09.08.*

BAHNHOF		UHR	ZUG		BEMERKUNGEN[2]
Bad Harzburg	ab	10:46	E	3622	
Hannover Hbf	an	12:25			
	ab	12:43	ICE	794	Zugrestaurant
Hamburg Hbf	an	13:56			

Realia. This information is from a schedule published by *Die Deutschen Bahnen.*

1. *valid*
2. *notes*

MICHAEL: Eine Fahrkarte nach Hamburg, bitte.
BEAMTER: **Hin und zurück?**
MICHAEL: Nein, **einfach, zweiter Klasse**, bitte.
BEAMTER: Das macht DM 89,–. Das ist übrigens der **Sparpreis** für **Jugendliche.** Haben Sie Ihren Ausweis dabei?
MICHAEL: Ja, natürlich. Wann fährt denn der nächste Zug?
BEAMTER: In dreißig Minuten. In Hannover müssen Sie dann **umsteigen.**
MICHAEL: Habe ich da gleich **Anschluss?**
BEAMTER: Sie haben achtzehn Minuten Aufenthalt. Dann können Sie mit dem ICE weiter nach Hamburg fahren. Für den ICE müssen Sie **allerdings** noch einen **Zuschlag** bezahlen und einen Platz reservieren. Möchten Sie im **Großraumwagen** sitzen, oder lieber in einem **Abteil?**
MICHAEL: Lieber in einem Abteil. **Nichtraucher,** bitte. Wann komme ich in Hamburg an?
BEAMTER: Um 13.56 Uhr.
MICHAEL: Danke schön.
BEAMTER: Bitte sehr.

Eine Fahrkarte, bitte! Note: Tell students about the types of trains in Germany. The fastest are the high-speed ICE (*Inter-City Express*) trains, which are equivalent to the *TGV* in France. The IC (*Inter-City*) trains travel quickly and only stop in larger cities. The D-Zug (*Durchgangszug*) travels moderately fast but makes more frequent stops, whereas the *Eilzug* is not really very fast at all and makes frequent stops in small towns.

Aktivität 7 Michaels Pläne

Ergänzen Sie den Text mit Informationen aus dem Dialog im **Thema 3.**

Michael fährt mit dem _____ nach Hamburg.[1] Er kauft seine Fahrkarte am Schalter im _____.[2] Er fährt zweiter _____.[3] Der nächste Zug nach Hannover fährt in _____ ab.[4] Michael muss in Hannover _____.[5] Dort hat er gleich _____ an den ICE nach Hamburg.[6] Für den ICE muss er einen _____ bezahlen und einen _____ reservieren.[7]

Aktivität 8 Am Fahrkartenschalter

Sie hören drei kurze Dialoge am Fahrkartenschalter. Setzen Sie die richtigen Informationen in die Tabelle ein.

INFORMATION	DIALOG 1	DIALOG 2	DIALOG 3
Fahrkarte nach	Hamburg	Salzburg	Bonn
1. oder 2. Klasse	1.	keine Information	keine Information
einfach oder hin und zurück	hin und zurück	hin und zurück	einfach
für wie viele Personen	zwei	fünf	eine
Platzkarten (ja/nein)	ja	nein	nein

Weiteres zum Thema Bahnfahren finden Sie bei ***Deutsch: Na klar!*** im World-Wide-Web unter www.mhhe.com/german.

Grammatik im Kontext

Realia. The prices reflect 1989/1990 fares of the *Deutsche Bundesbahn.*

Fahr & Spar. Die neuen Preise der neuen Bahn.

Günstig fahren Sie zum Fahrpreis. Er beträgt[1] 20 Pfennig pro Kilometer. **–.20**

180.– Günstiger fahren Sie zum Sparpreis von 180 Mark.

Am günstigsten fahren Sie zum Super-Sparpreis von 120 Mark. **120.–**

1. *comes to*

Comparing Things and People

Adjectives and adverbs have three forms.

basic form	Der Fahrpreis ist **günstig.** *The fare is good (in price).*
comparative	Der Sparpreis ist **günstiger.** *The discount fare is better.*
superlative	Der Super-Sparpreis ist **am günstigsten.** *The super-saver fare is the best of all.*

Comparing Two Items

The basic form of an adjective or adverb is used with the expression **so . . . wie** to express that two items are equal, or **nicht so . . . wie** if they are not equal.

Der Bus fährt **so schnell wie** der Zug.	*The bus goes as fast as the train.*
Mit einem Interrail-Pass kann man **so weit** fahren, **wie** man will.	*With an Interrail Pass you can travel as far as you want.*
Der Sparpreis ist **nicht so günstig wie** der Super-Sparpreis.	*The discount fare is not as advantageous as the super-saver fare.*

Übung 1 Vergleiche

Übung 1. Suggestion: Have students work in pairs. This exercise can also be used later for actual comparisons. Ask students to expand the list by making suggestions of their own using phrases such as: *ich meine, ich finde, meiner Meinung nach, . . .*

Was meinen Sie?

BEISPIEL: Segeln / Bungee-jumping →
Ich finde Segeln nicht so gefährlich wie Bungee-jumping.

bequem	romantisch
gefährlich	schön
günstig	sicher
interessant	teuer
praktisch	wichtig

1. eine Wanderreise / eine Busreise
2. eine Zugreise / eine Flugreise

3. eine Fahrt nach Disneyland / eine Reise nach Tahiti
4. eine Fahrt im Heißluftballon / eine Fahrradtour
5. mit der Familie reisen / mit Freunden reisen
6. im eigenen (*one's own*) Land reisen / im Ausland reisen
7. mit dem Motorrad fahren / mit dem Wagen fahren
8. im Zelt schlafen / in der Jugendherberge übernachten
9. mit Bargeld bezahlen / mit einer Kreditkarte bezahlen
10. einen Führerschein auf Reisen mitnehmen / einen Reisepass mitnehmen

Comparison. Suggestion: Point out the similarities between English and German when analyzing comparisons, focusing on the **-er/-est** endings and the fact that German usually expresses the comparative and superlative forms by endings rather than by forms equivalent to "more" and "most" in English.

The Comparative° of Adjectives and Adverbs

°der Komparativ

The comparative form of an adjective or adverb is used to describe things or persons that are dissimilar in quality or quantity.

Die Schaffnerin war **freundlicher als** die Bedienung im Speisewagen.	*The conductor was friendlier than the server in the dining car.*
Mit der Bahn reist man **bequemer als** mit dem Wagen.	*One travels more comfortably by train than by car.*

In German, the comparative is formed by adding **er** to the basic form of the adjective or adverb. The conjunction **als** (*than*) links the two parts of the comparison. Unlike English with its two comparative forms, German has only one form.

freundlich	freundlich**er**	*friendlier*
schnell	schnell**er**	*faster*
bequem	bequem**er**	*more comfortable*
günstig	günstig**er**	*more advantageous*
teuer	teur**er***	*more expensive*

Most adjectives of one syllable with the vowels **a, o,** and **u** have an umlaut in the comparative.

alt	**älter**	*older*
groß	**größer**	*bigger/taller*
kurz	**kürzer**	*smaller/shorter*
lang	**länger**	*longer*
warm	**wärmer**	*warmer*
jung	**jünger**	*younger*
kalt	**kälter**	*colder*
oft	**öfter**	*more often*
stark	**stärker**	*stronger*

Realia. *Die Bayern Cops* is from *Focus* magazine. *Intercity fahren* is from a *Deutsche Bundesbahn* ad.

*Note that **teuer** drops the **e** before the **r** in the stem when the comparative ending is added.

The adverb **immer** used with a comparative form expresses that someone or something is "more and more" so.

Mit der Bahn reisen wird **immer bequemer.**	*Traveling by train is getting more and more convenient.*
Die Züge fahren **immer schneller.**	*Trains are going faster and faster.*

When used attributively, i.e., before the nouns they modify, adjectives in the comparative take adjective endings.

Martina braucht einen größer**en** Koffer.	*Martina needs a bigger suitcase.*
Herr Waldmann braucht ein größer**es** Zelt.	*Mr. Waldmann needs a bigger tent.*

Realia. *Mitfahrzentrale* is from an informational booklet published by the *Verband deutscher Mitfahrzentralen.* The larger German towns, particularly university towns, have a **Mitfahrzentrale** that brings together drivers and passengers to share the cost of car travel. *Billiger zur Arbeit* is from an advertising brochure of the *Deutsche Bundesbahn.*

Analyse

Analyse. Suggestion: Assign this for homework that will be the basis of the next class discussion.

- Identify all adjectives and adverbs in the two ads. Which adjectives or adverbs are in the comparative?
- One comparative form is irregular; however, you can recognize it because it is a cognate. What is this form?
- For whom is the **B & S-Karte** favorably priced? What are the conditions that make commuting cheaper for these people?
- The adjective **sicher** is used in its basic form. What would be the comparative of **sicher?**
- The **Mitfahrzentrale** is a national ride-sharing agency. The ad implies a comparison. How would you complete the comparison? **Mitfahren ist günstiger als . . . und macht mehr Spaß als . . .**

Billiger zur Arbeit. Billiger zur Schule

B & S-Karten: die Fahrkarten für Berufstätige[1] und Schüler

Ist Ihr Weg zwischen Wohnort und Arbeits- oder Schulort weiter als 50 km? Dann fahren Sie mit der B & S-Karte auf dieser Strecke[2] etwa 15 % billiger Bahn.

1. *working people*
2. *route*
3. *ride-sharing*
4. schont . . . *protects the environment*

Übung 2 Alles ändert sich°

° *is changing*

Ergänzen Sie die richtigen Komparativformen.

1. Fliegen wird immer _____. (sicher)
2. Mit dem Zug fahren wird immer _____. (teuer)
3. Die Busse werden immer _____. (bequem)
4. Das Wetter wird immer _____. (schlecht)
5. Die Menschen werden immer _____. (unzufrieden [*dissatisfied*])
6. Das Leben in den Städten wird immer _____. (gefährlich)

7. Die Autos fahren immer _____. (schnell)
8. Das Leben wird immer _____. (kompliziert)
9. Ich werde immer _____. (alt)
10. Die Tage werden immer _____. (kurz)
11. Die Nächte werden immer _____. (lang)

Übung 3 Erzähl mal!

Ein Bekannter / Eine Bekannte von Ihnen ist gerade aus Europa zurückgekommen. Sie wollen wissen, wie es war.

BEISPIEL: schön: Österreich / die Schweiz →
S1: Was ist schöner? Österreich oder die Schweiz?
S2: Österreich ist so schön wie die Schweiz.
oder Ich finde die Schweiz schöner als Österreich.
oder Ich kann nicht sagen, was schöner ist.

1. interessant: Berlin / Wien
2. groß: Wien / Salzburg
3. romantisch: der Rhein / die Donau
4. alt: Köln / Leipzig
5. gemütlich: die Cafés in Wien / die Kneipen in Berlin
6. günstig: ein Hotel / eine Jugendherberge
7. billig: ein Bier / ein Kännchen Kaffee
8. lang: der Rhein / die Elbe
9. schön: Norddeutschland / Süddeutschland
10. praktisch: mit dem Zug / mit dem Bus reisen
11. teuer: ein Essen im Zugrestaurant / ein Essen im Restaurant

Übung 3. Suggestion: Have students work in groups of three to express their opinions. Each group takes turns asking a question, while the other two groups express their opinion. Encourage students to use conversational strategies to express agreement (*Das finde ich auch*) or disagreement (*Im Gegenteil, ich finde . . . schöner*, etc.). **Follow-up:** Have students come up with their own comparisons regarding features of their own lives.

Übung 4 Werners Reisevorbereitungen

Werner erzählt von seinen Reisevorbereitungen. Hören Sie zu, und markieren Sie die beste Ergänzung zu jedem Satz.

1. Werner braucht
   a. mehr Geld. b. mehr Zeit. c. mehr Geduld (*patience*).
2. Er braucht auch
   a. einen kleineren Koffer. b. einen größeren Koffer.
   c. zwei kleinere Koffer.
3. Er nimmt _____ mit.
   a. die kleinere Kamera b. die neuere Kamera
   c. die größere Kamera
4. Dies ist Werners
   a. längster Urlaub. b. teuerster Urlaub. c. kürzester Urlaub.

Übung 5 Probleme im Urlaub

Herr Ignaz Huber aus Oberammergau fährt in Urlaub, aber überall gibt es Probleme. Immer findet er ein Haar in der Suppe.

BEISPIEL: Sein Mietwagen ist zu klein. →
Er wünscht sich einen größeren Wagen.

1. Das Hotel ist zu teuer.
2. Das Hotelzimmer ist ungemütlich.
3. Das Bett ist zu weich.
4. Das Bad ist zu klein.
5. Das Hotelpersonal ist unhöflich.
6. Die Wanderwege sind zu gefährlich.
7. Seine Wanderschuhe sind unbequem.
8. Das Wetter ist zu heiß.
9. Der Urlaub ist zu kurz.

Übung 5. Follow-up: Ask students about vacation problems they have had.

The Superlative° of Adjectives and Adverbs

°der Superlativ

The superlative indicates the highest degree of a quality or quantity.

Die Zugspitze ist der **höchste** Berg Deutschlands.	*The Zugspitze is the highest mountain in Germany.*
Mit dem Flugzeug kommt man **am schnellsten** von Hamburg nach Köln.	*The fastest way to travel from Hamburg to Cologne is by plane.*

The superlative is formed by adding **(e)st-** to the basic form of the adjective or adverb. Unlike English with its two superlative forms, German has only one form.

freundlich	freundlich**st-**	*friendliest*
schnell	schnell**st-**	*fastest*
bequem	bequem**st-**	*most comfortable*
günstig	günstig**st-**	*most advantageous*
teuer	teuer**st-**	*most expensive*

As with the comparative, most adjectives of one syllable with the vowel **a, o,** or **u** have an umlaut in the superlative.

alt	ält**est-**	*oldest*
lang	läng**st**	*longest*
warm	wärm**st**	*warmest*
jung	jüng**st**	*youngest*
kalt	kält**est**	*coldest*
stark	stärk**st**	*strongest*

The form **est** is used to facilitate pronunciation when an adjective or adverb ends in **t, ß, ss,** or **z.**

	interessant	interessant**e**st-	*most interesting*
	kurz	kürz**e**st-	*shortest*
but	groß	größ**t-**	*largest*

When used attributively, adjectives in the superlative take adjective endings.

Arnstadt ist die älteste Stadt Thüringens.	*Arnstadt is the oldest city in Thuringia.*
Das Rathaus ist eines der schönst**en** Rathäuser.	*The town hall is one of the most beautiful town halls.*

Realia. This picture is from an *ADAC* brochure. *ADAC* is somewhat like AAA in the United States.

Point Out: The superlative of **oft (öftest-)** is rarely used; instead, **häufigst-** (most frequently) is used.

The superlative of predicate adjectives or adverbs has the form **am _____ (e)sten.**

Mit dem Zug fährt man **am bequemsten** und **am sichersten.**	*Traveling by train is the most comfortable and the safest (way of traveling).*
Eine Flugreise ist **am teuersten.**	*Flying is the most expensive (way of traveling).*
Ein Mietwagen ist **am praktischsten.**	*A rented car is the most practical (way of traveling).*

Übung 6 Eine Reise nach Österreich

Übung 6. Suggestion: See if your students can answer any of the questions in the exercise. If not, which Austrian towns do they know? Do they know any tourist attractions there?

Sie planen eine Reise nach Österreich und brauchen Information. Was möchten Sie wissen?

1. Wie heißt die _____ (schön) Stadt Österreichs?
2. Wie heißt das _____ (preiswert) Hotel in Wien?
3. Wo liegen die _____ (interessant) Sehenswürdigkeiten?
4. Welches ist das _____ (alt) Schloss?
5. In welchem Café gibt es den _____ (teuer) Kaffee?
6. Wo gibt es die _____ (freundlich) Leute?
7. Wie heißt der _____ (groß) Vergnügungspark in Wien?

Übung 7 Hin und her: Wie war der Urlaub?

Herr Ignaz Huber aus München war drei Wochen im Urlaub in Norddeutschland. Er war zwei Tage in Hamburg, eine Woche in Cuxhaven und nicht ganz zwei Wochen auf der Insel Sylt. Stellen Sie Ihrem Partner / Ihrer Partnerin Fragen über seinen Urlaub. Benutzen Sie den Superlativ.

BEISPIEL: S1: Wo war es am wärmsten?
S2: Am wärmsten war es in Cuxhaven.

	IN HAMBURG	IN CUXHAVEN	AUF DER INSEL SYLT
Wo war es (kalt/warm)?	20° C	25° C	15° C
Wo hat es (häufig/wenig) geregnet?	zwei Tage	einen Tag	fünf Tage
Wo waren die Hotelpreise (günstig/teuer)?	275 Mark	120 Mark mit Vollpension	200 Mark
Wo war das Hotelpersonal (freundlich/unfreundlich)?	freundlich	sehr freundlich	unfreundlich
Wo war der Strand (schön/ unangenehm)?	kein Strand	sauber, gepflegt	zu windig

Irregular Forms of the Comparative and Superlative

A number of adjectives and adverbs have irregular forms for the comparative and/or superlative. The most common ones are:

POSITIVE	COMPARATIVE	SUPERLATIVE
gern	**lieber**	**am liebsten**
gut	**besser**	**am besten**
hoch	**höher**	**am höchsten**
nah	**näher**	**am nächsten**
viel	**mehr**	**am meisten**

1. *advice*
2. sich . . . *earned*

Realia. *Was machen Berliner am liebsten* is excerpted from an ad in the *Berliner Morgenpost* for the TUI travel agency. *Die Plakette für die besten Straßen der Schweiz* is from an ad by the *Deutsche Bundespost.*

When used attributively, the singular adjectives **viel/mehr** and **wenig/weniger** do not take adjective endings.

Ich brauche **mehr** Geld für die Reise.	*I need more money for the trip.*
Ich habe jetzt **weniger** Zeit für Reisen als früher.	*Now I have less time for traveling than (I had) before.*

Übung 8. Suggestion: Brainstorm with your students about other differences among the regions of Germany.

Übung 8 Lokalpatriotismus

Leute aus verschiedenen Gegenden sagen ihre Meinung. Ergänzen Sie die Sätze mit der Komparativform des Adjektivs oder Adverbs in Klammern.

1. Bei euch in Hamburg regnet es _____ als bei uns in Bayern. (viel)
2. Bei uns in Dresden schmeckt das Bier _____ als bei euch in München. (gut)
3. Bei uns in Bayern sind die Bierkrüge _____ als bei euch in Berlin. (groß)
4. Bei uns in Thüringen schmeckt die Wurst _____ als bei euch in Westfalen. (gut)
5. Bei uns in der Schweiz sind die Berge _____ als die bei euch im Harz. (hoch)

Übung 9 Wo mag das sein?

Ergänzen Sie die Fragen mit der Superlativform des Adjektivs oder Adverbs in Klammern.

1. Wo regnet es _____? (viel)
2. Wo sind die Berge _____? (hoch)
3. Wo schmeckt das Bier _____? (gut)
4. Wo sind die Bierkrüge _____? (groß)
5. Wo verbringt man einen Sommerabend _____ in einem Biergarten? (gern)
6. Wo singen die Gäste _____? (laut)
7. Wo kann man die Deutschen _____ verstehen? (gut)
8. Wo feiert man _____? (viel)
9. Wo sind die Burgen _____? (alt)
10. Wo schmeckt das Essen _____? (gut)

Wissenswertes über Deutschland

- Zwei Drittel allen Weins kommt aus Rheinland-Pfalz.
- Mecklenburg-Vorpommern hat 600 Seen.
- Nordrhein-Westfalen hat mehr Industrie als die anderen Bundesländer.
- Die meisten Touristen und Besucher landen auf dem Frankfurter Flughafen.
- Berlin hat über drei Millionen Einwohner.
- Von den neuen Bundesländern ist Sachsen mit 4,9 Millionen Einwohnern am dichtesten besiedelt; am dünnsten besiedelt ist Sachsen-Anhalt mit 3 Millionen Einwohnern.
- Meißen produziert das berühmteste Porzellan.
- Die größte Insel ist Rügen (926 km^2).
- Der längste Fluss ist der Rhein (865 km), der zweitlängste ist die Elbe (700 km).
- Der höchste Berg ist die Zugspitze (2962 m), der zweithöchste ist der Watzmann (2713 m).

Burg Katz am Rhein

Übung 10 Tatsachen° über Deutschland

facts

Suggestion: The preceding **Kulturtipp** contains most of the information needed for **Übung 10.** Have students locate the places indicated in the **Übung** on a map.

Was wissen Sie über die deutschen Bundesländer und Städte? Bilden Sie Sätze.

BEISPIEL: Berlin ist die größte Stadt Deutschlands.

Bayern	ist	das nördlichste Bundesland
Bremen	hat	die meiste Industrie
Berlin	produziert	die höchsten Berge
Frankfurt		das größte Bundesland
Nordrhein-Westfalen		das kleinste Bundesland
München		der größte Flughafen
Mecklenburg-Vorpommern		die größte Stadt Deutschlands
Schleswig-Holstein		der meiste Wein
Rheinland-Pfalz		die meisten Seen
?		?

Übung 11 Was machst du lieber? Was machst du am liebsten?

A. Was machst du lieber im Urlaub?

BEISPIEL: S1: Sharon, was machst du lieber im Urlaub, wandern oder am Strand liegen?
S2: Ich liege lieber am Strand. Und du, Paul?

1. selber fotografieren oder Ansichtskarten kaufen?
2. allein oder mit Freunden reisen?
3. einen Aktivurlaub machen oder faul am Strand liegen?
4. im Zelt schlafen oder in einer Jugendherberge übernachten?
5. Museen besuchen oder schwimmen gehen?
6. eine Stadt besichtigen oder einen Nationalpark besuchen?
7. ?

B. Was machst du am liebsten im Urlaub?

BEISPIEL: S1: Was machst du am liebsten im Urlaub, Nicky?
S2: Am liebsten mache ich eine Reise. Und du, Ben?
S1: Am liebsten bleibe ich zu Hause und faulenze.

eine Reise machen	den ganzen Tag lesen
eine Radtour machen	Sport treiben
eine Wandertour machen	zu Hause bleiben
einen Aktivurlaub machen	nette Leute kennenlernen
interessante Orte besuchen	Museen besuchen
Freunde besuchen	in teuren Hotels wohnen
Abenteuer erleben	?
faulenzen	

Adjectival Nouns°

substantivierte Adjektive

Adjectives can be used as nouns to refer to people and things.

Deutsche und Amerikaner unterscheiden sich deutlich, wenn sie Rechnungen bezahlen: Die meisten **Deutschen** bezahlen ihre Rechnungen in bar; die Amerikaner greifen lieber zur Plastik-Karte. In den USA ist die Kreditkarte nichts **Ungewöhnliches.**

ADJECTIVE	ADJECTIVAL NOUN
deutsch	1. der/die Deutsche (*the German man/woman*) 2. Deutsche/die Deutschen (*[the]Germans*)
bekannt	3. ein Bekannter (*a male acquaintance*) 4. eine Bekannte (*a female acquaintance*)
ungewöhnlich	5. nichts Ungewöhnliches (*nothing unusual*) 6. etwas (was) Ungewöhnliches (*something unusual*)
neu	7. viel Neues (*much [that is] new*) 8. wenig Neues (*little [that is] new*) 9. das Neue (*the new [thing]*)
sonstig	10. Sonstiges (*other [items]*)

Adjectival nouns are capitalized. They follow the rules that apply to attributive adjectives. The gender of adjectival nouns is determined by what they designate: people are masculine or feminine (see examples 1 through 4), abstract concepts are neuter (see examples 5 through 10). After **etwas, nichts, viel,** and **wenig** the adjectival noun is always neuter (see examples 5 through 8).

Übung 12 Wer sind diese Leute?

Ergänzen Sie die Sätze mit einem substantivierten Adjektiv, das mit dem **fettgedruckten** Wort verwandt ist.

BEISPIEL: —Sind Sie aus **Deutschland,** Frau Huber?
—Ja, ich bin Deutsche.

1. Erich ist mir seit Jahren **bekannt.** Er ist ein guter _____ von mir.
2. Seine Mutter ist mir nicht **bekannt.** Sie ist keine _____ von mir.
3. **Reich** und **arm:** Kennen Sie den Spruch: „Die _____ werden reicher, und die _____ werden ärmer"?
4. Wo ist Dieter **angestellt?** Er ist _____ bei der Post.
5. Seine Schwester ist bei der Bank **angestellt.** Sie ist Bank_____.
6. Herr Lindemann ist aus **Deutschland.** Er ist _____.
7. Frau Lindemann ist auch aus **Deutschland.** Sie ist _____.
8. Viele Touristen sind aus **Deutschland.** Die _____ reisen gern.
9. Tina ist mit Timo **verwandt.** Sie ist seine_____.
10. Timos **Verwandt**_____ leben überall in Deutschland.

Übung 13 So etwas! 

Reagieren Sie auf die Aussagen.

BEISPIEL: S1: Die Preise werden immer höher.
S2: Das ist wirklich nichts Neues!

ärgerlich	unglaublich
neu	verrückt
ungewöhnlich	?

1. A: In Kalifornien gibt es oft Erdbeben.
   B: Das ist wirklich nichts _____.
2. C: Gestern hat man mir den Wagen gestohlen.
   D: So etwas _____!
3. E: Zum ersten April bietet das Reisebüro Fröhlich eine Reise zum Mars zum Sparpreis von 2500 Mark hin und zurück.
   F: Und wer wird so etwas _____ glauben?
4. G: Ich besitze zwanzig Kreditkarten.
   H: Das ist doch nichts _____.

Narrating Events in the Past: The Simple Past Tense°

das Imperfekt

German uses the simple past tense to narrate past events in writing or in formal speech. By using this tense, the narrator or writer generally establishes a distance from the events.

The present perfect tense is preferred in conversation when talking about events in the past. In **Kapitel 6,** however, you learned the simple past tense of **haben, sein,** and the modal verbs because these high-frequency verbs are commonly used in the simple past tense in conversation as well as in writing.

Simple Past Tense. Suggestion: Review the past tense of **sein, haben,** and modals first, then do **Übung 14,** which is a pure review exercise.

Weak Verbs°

schwache Verben

Weak verbs form the simple past tense by adding the marker **(e)te** to the stem. The first- and third-person singular do not add a personal ending.

INFINITIVE	STEM	PAST TENSE MARKER	PAST TENS FORM
reisen	reis-	**te**	reiste
warten	wart-	**ete**	wartete
öffnen	öffn-	**ete**	öffnete

Verbs with stems ending in **t** or **d,** as well as verbs with a consonant + **n** in the stem (e.g., **regnen, öffnen**), add **ete** to the stem.

reisen			
ich	reiste	wir	reiste**n**
du	reiste**st**	ihr	reiste**t**
er / sie / es	reiste	sie	reiste**n**
Sie reiste**n**			

warten			
ich	wartete	wir	wartete**n**
du	wartete**st**	ihr	wartete**t**
er / sie / es	wartete	sie	wartete**n**
Sie wartete**n**			

Wir **packten** unsere Sachen in einen Rucksack.	*We packed our things in a backpack.*
Die Fahrt **dauerte** drei Stunden.	*The trip took three hours.*
Wir **warteten** auf den Bus.	*We waited for the bus.*
Wir **übernachteten** in einer Jugendherberge.	*We stayed at a youth hostel.*

Weak verbs with separable and inseparable prefixes have the same past tense stem as the base verb.

Herr Zimmermann **packte** einen Badeanzug **ein.**	*Mr. Zimmermann packed a swimsuit.*
Er **erlebte** viel im Urlaub.	*He saw and did a lot on his vacation.*

Übung 14 Kleine Erlebnisse° im Urlaub

experiences

Ergänzen Sie die Sätze mit passenden Modalverben im Imperfekt: **dürfen, können, müssen, wollen.**

1. Wir _____ per Autostop nach Spanien fahren.
2. Niemand _____ uns mitnehmen.
3. Wir _____ zwei Stunden an der Autobahn warten.
4. Ein Fahrer _____ uns bis nach Freiburg mitnehmen.
5. Wir _____ in der Jugendherberge übernachten, aber dort war kein Platz mehr.
6. Deshalb _____ wir im Park übernachten.
7. Im Park _____ man aber nicht übernachten.
8. Wir _____ aber noch ein Hotel finden.
9. Das _____ wir natürlich nicht, weil es teuer war.

1. auf . . . *on one's own*

Übung 15 Notizen von einer Reise nach Österreich

Familie Seufert schreibt eine „Familienchronik". Bilden Sie Sätze im Imperfekt.

BEISPIEL: die Reise gemeinsam (*together*) planen →
Wir planten unsere Reise gemeinsam.

1. letztes Jahr im Juni eine Reise nach Österreich machen
2. zuerst vom Reisebüro Prospekte holen
3. dann gemeinsam die Reise planen
4. am Wochenende um fünf Uhr morgens starten
5. an der Grenze (*border*) in einer kilometerlangen Autoschlange warten
6. zuerst Salzburg besuchen
7. in einer kleinen, gemütlichen Pension übernachten
8. Donnerstag den ganzen Tag regnen
9. am Wochenende weiter nach Wien reisen
10. ein paar nette Studenten aus den USA kennen lernen
11. halb auf Deutsch und halb auf Englisch mit ihnen reden

Strong Verbs°

starke Verben

Strong verbs change their stem vowel in the simple past tense. Many verbs that are strong in English are also strong in German. The following verbs exemplify different past stems. You will find a complete list of strong verbs in Appendix D.

INFINITIVE	STEM
sehen	sah
stehen	stand
fahren	fuhr
schreiben	schrieb
anfangen	fing an
verlieren	verlor

As with the weak verbs, the first- and third-person singular do not add a personal ending.

Note that a past tense stem ending in a **d, t, s,** or **ß** adds the personal ending **est** to the **du**-form and **et** to the **ihr**-form.

sehen			
ich	sah	wir	sah**en**
du	sah**st**	ihr	sah**t**
er / sie / es	sah	sie	sah**en**
Sie sah**en**			

stehen			
ich	stand	wir	stand**en**
du	stand**est**	ihr	stand**et**
er / sie / es	stand	sie	stand**en**
Sie stand**en**			

As with the weak verbs, strong verbs with separable and inseparable prefixes have the same past tense stem as the base verb.

Frau Becker **stand** heute früh **auf.**	*Ms. Becker got up early today.*
Sie **verstand** aber nicht, warum der Wecker nicht klingelte.	*But she didn't understand why the alarm clock didn't ring.*

Irregular Weak Verbs°

unregelmäßige schwache Verben

Several verbs change their stem vowel *and* add **te** to the changed stem in the simple past, combining aspects of both strong and weak verbs. These verbs include:

bringen → brachte	kennen → kannte
denken → dachte	wissen → wusste

The simple past tense of **werden** (*to become*) is **wurde.**

Beginning with this chapter, the vocabulary section at the end of each chapter will list strong or irregular verbs with their principal parts, as follows:

BEISPIEL: bringen, brachte, gebracht
fahren (fährt), fuhr, ist gefahren
geben (gibt), gab, gegeben
wissen (weiß), wusste, gewusst

The Conjunction *als*

The word **als** has several important functions in German. You have learned to use it in the comparison of adjectives.

Note: Students will tend to confuse the conjunctions **als, wenn,** and **wann.**

Mit dem Zug fährt man bequemer **als** mit dem Bus.

Additionally, **als** can be used as a subordinating conjunction meaning *when,* referring to a one-time event in the past. Sentences with the conjunction **als** are often in the simple past tense, even in conversation.

Als ich in Wien wohnte, bin ich oft in die Oper gegangen.	*When I lived in Vienna I often went to the opera.*
Als er am Bahnhof ankam, war der Zug schon abgefahren.	*When he arrived at the station the train had already departed.*

Analyse Sonderbares° Erlebnis einer Reise

bizarre

Der Baron von Münchhausen lebte im 18. Jahrhundert und hatte einige merkwürdige Abenteuer. Man nannte ihn auch den „Lügenbaron" (*"lying baron"*), weil man ihm seine Geschichten nicht glaubte.

Lesen Sie die folgende Geschichte, und identifizieren Sie alle Verben im Imperfekt. Machen Sie eine Liste der Verben, und geben Sie den Infinitiv an. Welche Verben sind stark? Welche sind schwach?

NEUE VERBEN

absteigen, stieg ab	*to get down*
binden, band	*to tie*
frieren, fror	*to freeze*
schießen, schoss	*to shoot*

Analyse. Suggestion: Introduce this exercise by telling about the Baron von Münchhausen. In a modern film version of his adventures, Münchhausen rides on a cannon ball into the enemy camp and back to his own camp without harm. In another adventure, Münchhausen and his horse are about to drown in a river when he rescues them both by pulling himself up and out of the water by his own long ponytail. **Suggestion:** Preview unknown strong verbs first. Then assign the exercise for homework. **Follow-up:** Have students write a short summary of the Münchhausen story, using the simple past tense.

Münchhausens Reise nach Russland

Meine Reise nach Russland begann im Winter. Ich reiste zu Pferde, weil das am bequemsten war. Leider trug ich nur leichte Kleidung, und ich fror sehr. Da sah ich einen alten Mann im Schnee. Ich gab ihm meinen Reisemantel und ritt weiter. Ich konnte leider kein Dorf° finden. Ich war müde und stieg vom Pferd ab. Dann band ich das Pferd an einen Baumast° im Schnee° und legte mich hin. Ich schlief tief und lange. Als ich am anderen Morgen aufwachte, fand ich mich mitten in einem Dorf auf dem Kirchhof.° Mein Pferd war nicht da, aber ich konnte es über mir hören. Ich schaute in die Höhe° und sah mein Pferd am Wetterhahn des Kirchturms° hängen. Ich verstand sofort, was passiert war. Das Dorf war in der Nacht zugeschneit° gewesen. In der Sonne war der Schnee geschmolzen. Der Baumast, an den ich mein Pferd gebunden hatte, war in Wirklichkeit die Spitze des Kirchturms gewesen. Nun nahm ich meine Pistole und schoss nach dem Halfter.° Mein Pferd landete ohne Schaden° neben mir. Dann reiste ich weiter.

village
branch of a tree / snow
churchyard
in . . . *up* / am . . . *on the weathervane on top of the churchtower*
snowed under
halter
damage

Übung 16 Aus Münchhausens Tagebuch°

daily

Ergänzen Sie die Verben im Imperfekt.

Ich _____ (beginnen) meine Reise nach Russland im Winter.¹ Ich _____ (reisen) zu Pferde, weil das am bequemsten _____. (sein)² Leider _____ (frieren) ich sehr, weil ich nur leichte Kleidung _____. (tragen)³ Plötzlich _____ (sehen) ich einen alten Mann im Schnee.⁴ Ich _____ (geben) ihm meinen Mantel und _____ (reiten) weiter.⁵ Bald war ich müde und _____ vom Pferd _____. (absteigen)⁶ Ich _____ (binden) das Pferd an einen Baumast im Schnee.⁷ Dann _____ ich mich _____ (hinlegen) und _____. (einschlafen)⁸ Als ich am anderen Morgen _____ (aufwachen), _____ (finden) ich mich mitten in einem Dorf.⁹ Ich _____ (wissen) zuerst nicht, wo mein Pferd war.¹⁰ Ich _____ (kennen) keinen Menschen in diesem Dorf.¹¹

Übung 17 Münchhausens Reise  

Sie hören die Geschichte von Münchhausens Reise nach Russland mit sechs Veränderungen (*changes*). Können Sie sie identifizieren?

Übung 17. The six changes are: 1. *Er reiste mit Pferd und Wagen. Richtig: Er reiste zu Pferde.* 2. *Er sah eine alte Frau im Schnee. Richtig: Er sah einen alten Mann.* 3. *Er gab der Frau etwas zu essen. Richtig: Er gab dem Mann seinen Reisemantel.* 4. *Er konnte kein Gasthaus finden. Richtig: Er konnte kein Dorf finden.* 5. *Er wachte mitten auf dem Marktplatz eines Dorfes auf. Richtig: Er wachte auf dem Kirchhof in einem Dorf auf.* 6. *Er sah sein Pferd von der Spitze des Rathauses hängen. Richtig: Er sah sein Pferd am Wetterhahn des Kirchturms hängen.*

Übung 18 Wann war das?

Sagen Sie, wie alt Sie damals waren.

BEISPIEL: den Führerschein machen →
Ich war 17 Jahre alt, als ich den Führerschein machte.

1. in den Kindergarten kommen
2. das erste Geld verdienen (*to earn*)
3. sich zum ersten Mal verlieben (*to fall in love*)
4. den Führerschein machen
5. meine Familie nach _____ umziehen (*to move*)
6. _____ (Freund oder Freundin) kennenlernen
7. meine erste Auslandsreise machen
8. zum ersten Mal tanzen gehen

Übung 18. Suggestion: Start this exercise by reviewing **wann**-questions. Model one question based on the suggestions for this exercise and then ask students to formulate additional questions. Ask for very brief answers only; e.g., to *Wann hast du den Führerschein gemacht?,* the answer could be *Mit 16 Jahren* or simply the year, e.g., *1986.* In a second phase, introduce the conjunction **als,** asking for answers in the form shown in the **Beispiel.** Have students add one item when something special happened in their lives, e.g., *Ich war acht Jahre alt, als ich meinen Hund zum Geburtstag bekam.*

The Past Perfect Tense°

° das Plusquamperfekt

The past perfect describes an event that precedes another event in the past.

Bevor wir in Urlaub fuhren, **hatten** wir alle Rechnungen **bezahlt.**	*Before we went on vacation we had paid all the bills.*
Nachdem wir auf Mallorca **angekommen waren,** gingen wir sofort an den Strand.	*After we had arrived in Mallorca, we immediately went to the beach.*

The conjunctions **bevor** and **nachdem** are commonly used to connect sentences with the simple past and past perfect tenses.

To form the past perfect, combine the simple past of **haben** (*hatte*) or **sein** (*war*) and the past participle of the main verb. Verbs using **sein** in the present perfect tense also use **sein** in the past perfect.

PRESENT PERFECT	PAST PERFECT
Ich **bin** gegangen.	Ich **war** gegangen. (*I had gone.*)
Wir **haben** bezahlt.	Wir **hatten** bezahlt. (*We had paid.*)

Übung 19 Die Fahrt hatte kaum begonnen

Ergänzen Sie die Sätze durch Verben im Plusquamperfekt.

1. Ich _____ schon früh aus dem Haus _____ (gehen), denn mein Flugzeug nach Frankfurt flog um 8 Uhr ab.
2. Ich _____ am Tag zuvor ein Taxi _____ (bestellen).

3. Am Flughafen fiel mir plötzlich ein (*I suddenly remembered*), dass ich die Schlüssel in der Haustür _____ _____ (vergessen).
4. Kein Wunder, denn letzte Nacht _____ ich kaum _____ (schlafen).
5. Sobald ich am Flughafen _____ _____ (ankommen), rief ich eine Nachbarin an.
6. Der Flug nach Frankfurt war verspätet (*late*). Nachdem wir drei Stunden _____ _____ (warten), konnten wir endlich abfliegen.

Übung 20 Nach der Reise

Bilden Sie eine Kettengeschichte (*chain story*).

BEISPIEL: S1: Nachdem ich aus dem Urlaub zurückgekommen war, packte (*unpacked*) ich meinen Koffer aus.
S2: Nachdem ich meinen Koffer ausgepackt hatte, _____.

Nachbarn/Freund/Freundin anrufen	ins Restaurant gehen
Post vom Postamt holen (*to get*)	einkaufen gehen
Katze/Hund aus dem Katzen-/Hundehotel abholen	ein Bad nehmen / duschen
Zeitung lesen	?

Suggestion: Have students begin by working in pairs to compose written sentences before they do the oral activity. During the oral activity, after each response, have the student suggest the name of a fellow classmate to continue the chain.

Sprache im Kontext

Zuschauen

Vorschau

Sehen Sie sich die Werbung ohne Ton an.

1. Was ist eine BahnCard?
2. Warum sollte man eine BahnCard kaufen?
3. Dieser Werbung nach sollte man mit der Bahn fahren. Was sollte man *nicht* machen?

BahnCard

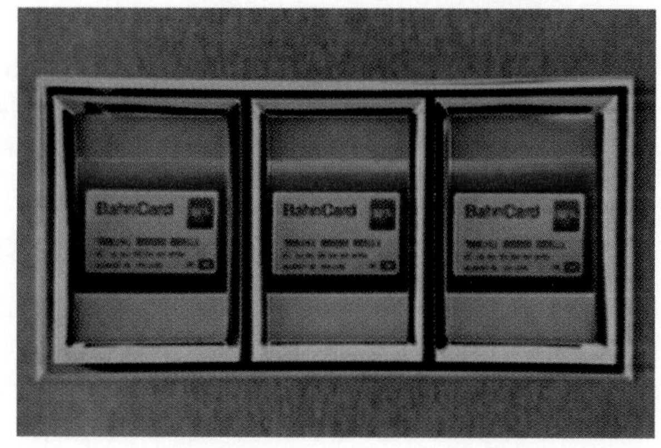

Arbeit mit dem Videotext

A. Sehen Sie sich die Werbung mit Ton mehrmals an. Identifizieren Sie vier der Verkehrsschilder, und zeichnen Sie jedes Verkehrsschild, das Sie identifiziert haben, neben das passende Wort.

Überholverbot	Stop
Stau	Baustelle
Doppelkurve	Umleitung
vorgeschriebene Fahrrichtung links	Bahnübergang mit Schranken oder Halbschranken
Sackgasse	Schneeketten sind vorgeschrieben
30km/h Höchstgeschwindigkeit	Einbahnstraße

B. Beantworten Sie die folgenden Fragen.

1. Fahren Sie gern mit der Bahn? Warum? Warum nicht?
2. Warum fahren die meisten Amerikaner nicht mit der Bahn?
3. Warum ist Bahnfahren populärer in Deutschland als in den USA?

Lesen

Zum Thema

A. Ihr letzter Urlaub. Beantworten Sie die folgenden Fragen, und vergleichen Sie Ihre Antworten mit den Antworten von zwei anderen Studenten oder Studentinnen.

1. Wann haben Sie zum letzten Mal Urlaub gemacht?
2. Wohin sind Sie gefahren?
3. Was haben Sie dort gemacht?
4. Wie war das Wetter dort?
5. Wie lange waren Sie dort?
6. Was hat Ihnen dort (nicht) gefallen?
7. Wer war auch dabei (*present*)?

B. Ein Aktivurlaub. Die Werbung „Sportreisen" zeigt viele Möglichkeiten für einen Aktivurlaub. Schauen Sie sich die Tabelle mit einem Partner / einer Partnerin an.

- Welche Sportarten gibt es?
- Wo finden diese Aktivitäten statt *(take place)?*
- Was macht man alles da?
- Für welche Sportart muss man am fittesten sein?
- Welche Reise möchten Sie machen? Warum?

Sportart	Ort	Leistungen	Reisetermin	Preis	Grad*
Rafting	Colorado/ USA	zwei Übernachtungen im Hotel, Transfer, Raftingtour, Bootsführer, alle Mahlzeiten während der Tour, Campingausrüstung, Anreise in Eigenregie[1]	1., 8., 15.und. 22.9.97	ab 1604 Mark für 7 Tage	●●
Katamaransegeln	Levkada/ Griechenland	Flug, Übernachtungen im Appartement, kostenlose Benutzung der Katamarane und Segelflotte,[2] Teilnahme am Unterricht[3]	1., 8., 15., 22. und 29.9.97	ab 1421 Mark pro Woche	●●●
Tauchen	Villi Varu/ Malediven	Flug ab Düsseldorf, sechs Übernachtungen mit Vollpension, Sechs-Tage-Tauchpaket à 1 Tauchgang[4] täglich und 2 Hausriff-Tauchgänge (inkl. Boot, Flasche, Blei und Bleigurt)[5]	3., 10., 17. und 24.9.97	2360 Mark pro Woche	●
Aktiv-Camp	Berchtesgaden/ Deutschland	Schnupperkurs[6] im Klettergarten,[7] River-Rafting auf der Saalach, Mountainbike-Tour, Bergwanderung, Paragliding-Schnupperkurs, sechs Übernachtungen mit Frühstück, Ausrüstung,[8] Führung[9]	6.–12.9.97	595 Mark	●
Surfen	Bonaire/ Karibik	Flug ab Amsterdam, Übernachtung im Appartement mit Selbstversorgung[10] oder im Hotel mit Frühstück, Surfboard-Miete 335 Mark pro Woche	6., 13., 20. und 27.9.97	ab 2230 Mark pro Woche	●●
Reiten	Costa Blanca/ Spanien	Flug, acht Tage mit sieben Übernachtungen im Appartement mit Selbstversorgung, Reitprogramm, Reitführung, Unterlagen, Qualifikation: sicher in den Grundgangarten,[11] gute Kondition	9.–16.9.97,	ab 2093 Mark	●●

* Zeigt den Grad der körperlichen[12] Fitneß, die der Teilnehmer[13] mitbringen muß: ●●● = sehr gut trainiert, ●● = körperlich fit, ● = auch für Anfänger[14]

1. Anreise . . . *passage excluded* 2. *sailing fleet* 3. Teilnahme . . . *participation in instruction* 4. *dive* 5. Blei . . . *weight and weight belt* 6. *sampler class* 7. *climbing garden* 8. *equipment* 9. *guide* 10. *no meals provided* 11. sicher . . . *secure in all the basic paces* 12. *physical* 13. *participant* 14. *beginners*

Auf den ersten Blick

Auf den ersten Blick. Note: If you do this in class, students can do the **Zum Text** as homework.

A. Schauen Sie sich den Text an! Was für ein Text ist es?

1. ein Interview
2. ein Artikel
3. ein Tagebuch (*diary*)

B. Überfliegen Sie (*skim*) den Text, um das Thema festzustellen (*to establish*)! Wie heißt das Thema dieses Textes?

1. Julias Reise nach Deutschland
2. der Globetrotterin-Preis
3. Julias Reise nach China

C. Suchen Sie Wörter im Text, die unter die folgenden Rubriken passen.

1. Länder: ____________, ____________, . . .
2. Namen: ____________, ____________, ____________, . . .
3. Studium und Beruf: ____________, ____________, . . .
4. Kunst und Kultur: ____________, ____________, . . .

■ Julia Berg, 21, wurde im März von Deutschlands größtem Outdoor-Händler, Globetrotter Ausrüstungen in Hamburg, zur "Globetrotterin des Jahres 1996" gekürt. Zusammen mit ihrem Freund Dov Meguideche reiste sie 1995 auf dem Landweg nach China und wieder zurück nach Deutschland. Nicht die touristischen Höhepunkte, sondern die Auseinandersetzung[1] mit den Menschen bestimmten[2] ihre Reiseroute: Julia lebte in einer mongolischen Familie, beschäftigte sich[3] in China mit Tuschmalerei[4] und lernte in Thailand sowohl das Lederhandwerk als auch die Silberschmiedekunst.[5] ■

★ *Wie ist die Idee zu dieser Reise entstanden?*

1992 war ich mit einem Schüleraustausch[6] in China und zwei Jahre später habe ich an der Uni in Beijing einen Sprachkurs belegt. Damals entstand[7] der Wunsch, auf dem Landweg nach China zu reisen. Beim zweiten Aufenthalt[8] habe ich meinen australischen Freund Dov kennengelernt und wir beschlossen,[9] nach meinem Abitur gemeinsam auf Tour zu gehen.

★ *Was fasziniert Dich so an diesem Land?*

Mit 16 war ich das erste Mal in China. Der Besuch in einem nicht-westlichen Land mit seiner fremden Kultur hat mich sehr beeindruckt.[10] Ich wollte noch mehr darüber erfahren[11] und die Kultur verstehen lernen. Deshalb habe ich mich auch mit Tuschmalerei und der chinesischen Philosophie beschäftigt. Ich habe die Erfahrung gemacht,[12] daß man gerade über die Kunst viele Menschen kennenlernt und einen Einblick[13] in deren Leben erhält.

★ *Waren Deine Erlebnisse in China durchweg[14] positiv?*

Nein, es ist schwierig dort zu reisen. Vor allem die Beamten sind oft sehr unfreundlich. Aber man trifft natürlich auch viele gastfreundliche Menschen und diese Erfahrungen sind es, die mich immer wieder anziehen.

★ *Hat Dich diese Reise verändert?*[15]

Ja. Durch Situationen, in denen ich an einem Tiefpunkt[16] war und sich dann doch alles zum Guten gewendet[17] hat, habe ich mehr Zuversicht[18] bekommen. Wo ich mir früher Sorgen gemacht habe,[19] denke ich jetzt: Das wird schon irgendwie. Ich glaube aber, daß man sich hier engagieren muß. Reiseerfahrungen sollten nicht einfach "weggepackt" werden, wenn man wieder zu Hause ist.

★ *Würdest Du so eine Reise auch alleine machen?*

Es gab viele Momente, in denen ich nicht hätte[20] alleine sein wollen. Zum Beispiel wenn wir völlig verlassen "in the middle of nowhere" festsaßen.[21] Auf der anderen Seite bekommt man alleine mehr Kontakte und ist anderen Menschen gegenüber offener.

★ *Welchen Tip möchtest Du anderen Globetrottern mit auf den Weg geben?*

Auf jeden Fall sollte man ein bißchen von der Sprache des jeweiligen Landes lernen. Das freut die Leute unheimlich[22] und sie merken, daß man Kontakt sucht. Selbst wenn man zu keiner tiefergehenden Unterhaltung fähig ist,[23] es ist eine Geste.

★ *Welche Pläne hast Du für die Zukunft?*[24]

Ich habe mit einem Ethnologiestudium begonnen und möchte am liebsten Korrespondentin im Ausland oder Reiseautorin werden. Außerdem zeichne ich momentan an meinem Kinderbuch über einen kleinen mongolischen Jungen, in dessen Familie wir eine Zeitlang gelebt haben.

Julia, vielen Dank für das Interview.

1. *contact* 2. *determined* 3. beschäftigte . . . *occupied herself* 4. *watercolor painting* 5. *silversmithing* 6. *student exchange* 7. *arose* 8. zweiten . . . *second trip* 9. *decided* 10. *impressed* 11. *learn* 12. Ich . . . *it's been my experience* 13. *insight* 14. *always* 15. *changed* 16. *low point* 17. *turned* 18. *confidence* 19. Sorgen . . . *worried* 20. *would have* 21. *were stuck* 22. *tremendously* 23. zu . . . *is not capable of deep discussions* 24. *future*

Zum Text

A. Die folgenden Aussagen *(statements)* werden im Interview mit Julia *implizit* ausgedrückt. Finden Sie die entsprechenden *(corresponding)* Stellen im Text.

1. Die letzte Reise nach China war Julias dritte Reise nach China.
2. Julia ist diesmal weder *(neither)* mit dem Boot noch *(nor)* mit dem Flugzeug nach China gereist.
3. Julia kann wenigstens ein bisschen Chinesisch.
4. Julia glaubt, dass man ein Land besser verstehen kann, wenn man etwas über die Kunst des Landes weiß.
5. Es gibt vieles an der chinesischen Kultur, was Julia interessiert.
6. Julia sieht Reisen als Teil ihres Lebens und nicht nur Urlaub vom Alltag *(everyday life)*.

B. **Intensiveres Lesen.** Kleine Wörter und Phrasen sind oft wichtige rhetorische Signale, die die Zusammenhänge *(relationships)* zwischen Ideen und Elementen klar machen.

- **Nicht . . . sondern** *(not . . . but)* zeigt einen Gegensatz *(contrast)* auf.
- **Sowohl . . . als auch . . .** *(. . . as well as . . .)* deutet auf Inklusivität.
- **Auf der anderen Seite** *(on the other hand)* findet man da, wo Alternativen berücksichtigt *(considered)* werden.
- **außerdem** *(besides, moreover)* deutet auf zusätzliche *(added)* Informationen.

Finden Sie diese Wörter im Text. Welche Zusammenhänge zeigen diese Wörter im Interview, das Sie gelesen haben?

C. **Arbeit mit dem Wörterbuch.** Suchen Sie die folgenden Wörter im Text. Schlagen Sie diese in einem Wörterbuch nach. Wie viele Bedeutungen finden Sie für jedes Wort? Welche passt am besten?

küren
anziehen
engagieren
verlassen

Sprechen und Schreiben

Aktivität 1 Ein besonderes Interview

Stellen Sie sich vor, Sie arbeiten als Journalist/Journalistin und haben die Gelegenheit (*opportunity*), Julia zu interviewen. Was möchten Sie gern fragen? Notieren Sie drei mögliche Fragen. Eine Studentin / ein Student spielt die Rolle der Julia. Die anderen interviewen sie.

Aktivität 2 Eine Werbung°

Stellen Sie sich vor, Sie arbeiten bei einer Werbeagentur und haben die Aufgabe, einen Prospekt über Ihre Heimatstadt oder eine andere Gegend (*area*) zusammenzustellen. Arbeiten Sie zuerst in Gruppen, um Ideen zu sammeln. Was finden Sie interessant an Ihrer Stadt/Gegend? Was kann man dort unternehmen? Schreiben Sie dann einen Werbetext für Ihre Stadt/Gegend.

° *advertisement*

Sprechen und Schreiben. Additional Activity: Have students bring in a photograph of a trip they took. Divide students into small groups and have them briefly tell about their trip. They can also play Baron von Münchhausen, bringing in any picture and telling a tall tale of a trip they took.

Wortschatz

Verkehrsmittel	Means of Transportation
die **Bahn -en**	railway
der **Bus,** *pl.* **Busse**	bus
das **Fahrrad, ¨er**	bicycle
das **Flugzeug, -e**	airplane
der **Heißluftballon, -s**	hot air baloon
das **Schiff, -e**	ship
das **Taxi, -s**	taxi
der **Wagen, -**	car
der **Zug, ¨e**	train

Im Reisebüro	At the Travel Agency
das **Angebot, -e**	(special) offer
die **Fahrkarte, -n**	ticket
der **Flugschein, -e**	airplane ticket
das **Reisebüro, -s**	travel agency
der **Reiseprospekt, -e**	travel brochure
der **Sparpreis, -e**	discount price
das **Ticket, -s**	ticket

Unterwegs	En Route
die **Abfahrt, -en**	departure
das **Abteil, -e**	compartment
die **Ankunft, ¨e**	arrival
der **Anschluss, ¨e***	connection
die **Auskunft, ¨e**	information
die **Autobahn, -en**	highway
der **Bahnhof, ¨e**	train station
der **Bahnsteig, -e**	train platform
die **Buslinie, -n**	bus line
der **Fahrkartenschalter, -**	ticket window
die **Fahrt, -en**	trip
der **Flugbegleiter, -** / die **Flugbegleiterin, -nen**	flight attendant
der **Flughafen, ¨**	airport
die **Gepäckaufbewahrung**	baggage check
das **Gleis, -e**	track
der **Nichtraucher, -**	nonsmoker
die **Haltestelle, -n**	(bus) stop
der **Großraumwagen, -**	rail car without compartments
der **Passagier, -e** / die **Passagierin, -nen**	passenger
der **Pilot, -en (en** *masc.*) / die **Pilotin, -nen**	pilot
die **Platzkarte, -n**	seat reservation
der **Reiseleiter, -** / die **Reiseleiterin, -nen**	travel guide
der **Schaffner, -** / die **Schaffnerin, -nen**	conductor
der **Taxifahrer, -** / die **Taxifahrerin, -nen**	taxi driver
der **Wanderweg, -e**	hiking trail
der **Zuschlag, ¨e**	surcharge

Zum Mitnehmen auf Reisen	Things to Take Along on a Trip
der **Ausweis, -e**	identification card
das **Bargeld**	cash
der **Fahrplan, ¨e**	schedule

* See Appendix E for alternate spelling.

der **Führerschein, -e**	driver's license
das **Handgepäck**	carry-on luggage
der **Handschuh, -e**	glove
die **Kamera, -s**	camera
der **Personalausweis, -e**	ID card
der **Reiseführer, -**	travel guide
das **Sonnenschutzmittel**	suntan lotion, sunblock
das **Zelt, -e**	tent

Sonstige Substantive	Other Nouns
der/die **Jugendliche, -n**	youth
die **Möglichkeit, -en**	possibility
die **Natur**	nature
die **Reise, -n**	trip, journey
der **Segelkurs, -e**	sailing course
der **Urlaub**	vacation

Verben	Verbs
ab•fahren (fährt ab), fuhr ab, ist abgefahren	to depart
beginnen, begann, begonnen	to begin
Bescheid sagen	to notify
buchen	to book
ein•steigen, stieg ein, ist eingestiegen	to board, get into (*a vehicle*)
erleben	to experience
fehlen	to be missing
hoffen	to hope
übernachten	to stay overnight
um•steigen, stieg um, ist umgestiegen	to transfer
unternehmen (unternimmt), unternahm, unternommen	to undertake
vergessen (vergisst), vergaß, vergessen*	to forget
vor•schlagen (schlägt vor), schlug vor, vorgeschlagen	to suggest, propose

Adjektive und Adverbien	Adjectives and Adverbs
aktiv	active(ly)
alt (älter, ältest-)	old
gefährlich	dangerous(ly)
gern (lieber, liebst-)	gladly (rather, preferably; most preferably)
groß (größer, größt-)	big, large; tall; great
gut (besser, best-)	good (better, best)
hoch (höher, höchst-)	high
insgesamt	altogether, total
jung (jünger, jüngst-)	young
kalt (kälter, kältest-)	cold
kurz (kürzer, kürzest-)	short
lang (länger, längst-)	long
langsam	slow(ly)
nah (näher, nächst-)	near
oft (öfter)	often, frequent
schnell	quick(ly), fast
sicher	safe(ly)
sportlich	athletic
stark (stärker, stärkst-)	strong
viel (mehr, meist-)	much (more, most)
viertägig	four-day
warm (wärmer, wärmst-)	warm

Sonstiges	Other
Achtung!	Attention! Watch out!
allerdings	of course; however
alles	everything
als (*subord. conj.*)	when
bevor (*subord. conj.*)	before
einfach	one-way (ticket); simple
einverstanden sein (mit)	to agree (with), be in agreement (with)
erster/zweiter Klasse fahren	to travel first/second class
hin und zurück	round-trip
nachdem (*subord. conj.*)	after
per Autostop reisen	to hitchhike
pro Person	per person
so . . . wie	as . . . as
Sonst noch etwas?	Anything else?

* See Appendix E for alternate spelling.

Lernziele

Use this checklist to verify that you can now . . .

- ☐ talk about travel plans to express your preferences.
- ☐ book a vacation through a travel agency.
- ☐ buy a ticket at a German railway station.
- ☐ ask for information regarding public transportation.
- ☐ talk about the kinds of things one needs when traveling.
- ☐ use the comparative and superlative forms of adjectives and adverbs when comparing ideas, things, and people.
- ☐ understand and use verbs in the simple past tense and in the past perfect tense.
- ☐ express a more complex series of events by using the conjunctions **als, bevor,** and **nachdem.**
- ☐ identify some important German, Austrian, and Swiss cities and the rivers on which they are located.
- ☐ follow a narrative of a simple legend.

Kapitel 11

Der Start in die Zukunft

In einer Großstadt wie Berlin kann man als Kurier jobben.

Kapitel 11. Suggestion: Introduce the chapter by asking students questions about their career plans, e.g., *Was möchten Sie werden? Warum haben Sie diesen Beruf gewählt? Welche Ausbildung braucht man für diesen Beruf? Was möchten Sie auf keinen Fall werden? Was für Stellen haben Sie schon gehabt?* Write new words for professions and occupations on the board.

Alles klar?

A. Was wollen junge Deutsche vom Beruf? Die Informationen finden Sie im Schaubild.

Realia. The statistic is published by *Globus Kartendienst.*

1. *choice of occupation*
2. *advance*
3. *training position*
4. *dirty work*
5. *qualification*

- Das Wichtigste an einem künftigen Beruf ist _____.
- _____ finden junge Deutsche nicht so wichtig.
- Ungefähr ein Drittel der jungen Leute will _____.
- Ein Viertel der Jugendlichen will keine _____ machen.
- Ein sicherer Arbeitsplatz ist wichtig für _____ der Jugendlichen.

B. Sie hören Gabriele Sommer über ihre Berufspläne sprechen.

- Wie ist sie auf ihre Berufswahl gekommen?
- Wo studiert sie?
- Was studiert sie?
- Was hat sie in ihrem späteren Berufsleben vor?

Wörter im Kontext

Thema 1

Meine Interessen, Wünsche° und Erwartungen°

wishes / expectations

Wie **stellen** Sie **sich** Ihr **Berufsleben vor?** Was wollen Sie vom Beruf? Kreuzen Sie an!

Ich möchte gern. Follow-up: Discuss who would like to do what. Which seem to be the most popular careers in the class?

Ich möchte gern:	JA	NEIN
• **selbständig** arbeiten	☐	☐
• einen sicheren **Arbeitsplatz** haben	☐	☐
• **mich im Freien beschäftigen**	☐	☐
• **Gelegenheit** zum Reisen haben	☐	☐
• **im Ausland** arbeiten	☐	☐
• **möglichst viel** Geld **verdienen** / ein hohes **Gehalt** haben	☐	☐
• eine **abwechslungsreiche Tätigkeit** haben	☐	☐
• bei einer großen **Firma** arbeiten	☐	☐
• einen **Chef** / eine **Chefin** haben, der/die meine Arbeit anerkennt (*appreciates*)	☐	☐
• sympathische **Mitarbeiter/Mitarbeiterinnen** haben	☐	☐
• Menschen **helfen**	☐	☐
• mit Computern arbeiten	☐	☐
• mit Tieren **umgehen**	☐	☐
• großes **Ansehen**/Prestige haben	☐	☐
• im **Büro** arbeiten	☐	☐
• eine leitende Position haben	☐	☐
• **finanziell unabhängig** sein	☐	☐
• keine Schmutzarbeit machen	☐	☐

Vergleichen Sie Ihre Antworten mit denen eines Partners / einer Partnerin. Suchen Sie dann jemanden im Kurs, mit dem Sie mehr als fünf Antworten gemeinsam haben.

Note: Mention to students that seeing a chimney sweep is considered to bring good luck!

Ein Schornsteinfeger arbeitet meistens an der frischen Luft.

Aktivität 1 Drei junge Leute 

Sie hören drei junge Leute über ihre Interessen, Wünsche und Erwartungen sprechen. Was tun sie gern oder nicht gern? Was ist ihnen wichtig oder nicht wichtig?

PERSON	WAS ER/SIE (NICHT) GERN TUT	WAS IHM/IHR (NICHT) WICHTIG IST
Tina	arbeitet gern im Freien, möchte nicht gern im Büro arbeiten	nicht wichtig: großes Ansehen und viel Geld
Markus	reist gern und möchte im Ausland arbeiten	wichtig: mit Menschen zu tun haben
Andrea	arbeitet gern mit ihren Händen; interessiert sich für Maschinen, Computer	keine Information

Hotelkauffrau
Hotelfachfrau
Hotelsekretärin
für abwechslungsreiche Büroarbeit bei sehr guten Weiterbildungs- und Entwicklungsmöglichkeiten gesucht.
Fmp Personalleasing GmbH, Bavariaring 9, München, T. 089/5391 79

Aktivität 2 Hin und her: Wer macht was, und warum? 

Ergänzen Sie die Informationen.

BEISPIEL: S1: Was macht Corinna Eichhorn?
S2: Sie ist Sozialarbeiterin.
S1: Warum macht sie das?
S2: Weil . . .

NAME	BERUF	WARUM?
Corinna Eichhorn	Sozialarbeiterin	Menschen helfen
Karsten Becker	Bibliothekar	sich für Bücher interessieren
Erika Lentz	Filmschauspielerin	mit Menschen zu tun haben
Alex Böhmer	Informatiker	mit Computern arbeiten

Aktivität 3 Berufswünsche

Fragen Sie einen Partner / eine Partnerin: „Was erwartest du von deinem Beruf? Was ist dir nicht so wichtig?" Verwenden Sie einige der folgenden Redemittel.

BEISPIEL: S1: Mir ist ein sicherer Arbeitsplatz wichtig.
S2: Ein sicherer Arbeitsplatz ist mir nicht so wichtig, aber ich erwarte, dass ich Gelegenheit zum Reisen habe.

REDEMITTEL	ERWARTUNGEN
Mir ist ____ (nicht) wichtig.	möglichst viel Geld (verdienen)
Ich erwarte, dass ____	viel Kontakt mit Menschen (haben)
Ich möchte gern ____	anderen Menschen helfen
An erster Stelle kommt ____	Spaß an der Arbeit (haben)
____ interessiert mich (nicht).	nette Mitarbeiter/Mitarbeiterinnen (haben)
	Gelegenheit zum Reisen (haben)
	möglichst viel Freizeit (haben)
	selbständig arbeiten
	im Freien arbeiten
	im Ausland arbeiten
	Ansehen (haben)
	einen sicheren Arbeitsplatz (haben)

Thema 2

Berufe

Realia. *Berufe* is taken from a publication from the *Commerzbank* called *Berufswahl—Tips, Trends, Tests.*

BERUFE

Gesundheitswesen
Arzt/Ärztin
Krankenpfleger/Krankenschwester
Psychologe/Psychologin
Soziarlarbeiter/Sozialarbeiterin
Tierarzt/Tierärztin
Zahnarzt/Zahnärztin

Verwaltung
Rechtsanwalt/Rechtsanwältin
Diplomat/Diplomatin
Finanzbeamter/Finanzbeamtin
Personalchef/Personalchefin

Technischer Bereich
Elektroinstallateur/Elektroinstallateurin
Ingenieur/Ingenieurin
Mechaniker/Mechanikerin
Radio- oder Fernsehtechniker/
Radio- oder Fernsehtechnikerin

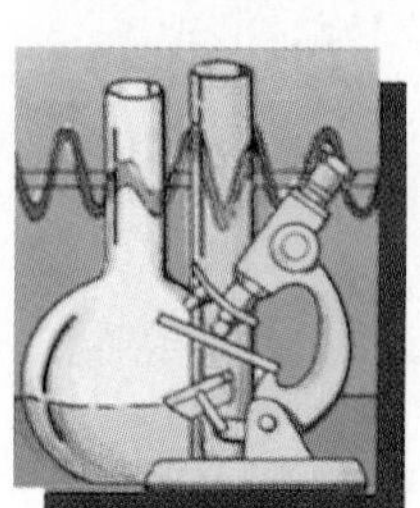

Naturwissenschaften
Biotechnologe/Biotechnologin
Chemiker/Chemikerin
Laborant/Laborantin
Meteorologe/Meteorologin
Physiker/Physikerin

Wirtschaft und Handel

Geschäftsmann/Geschäftsfrau
Informatiker/Informatikerin
Kaufmann/Kauffrau
Sekretär/Sekretärin

Verkehrswesen

Flugbegleiter/Flugbegleiterin
Flugingenieur/Flugingenieurin
Pilot/Pilotin
Reisebüroleiter/Reisebüroleiterin

Kommunikationswesen

Bibliothekar/Bibliothekarin
Dolmetscher/Dolmetscherin
Journalist/Journalistin
Nachrichtensprecher/Nachrichtensprecherin

Kreativer Bereich

Architekt/Architektin
Designer/Designerin
Fotograf/Fotografin
Künstler/Künstlerin
Musiker/Musikerin
Schauspieler/Schauspielerin
Zeichner/Zeichnerin

Aktivität 4 Wer macht was?

Schauen Sie sich die Berufe in Thema 2 an. Welcher Beruf passt zu welcher Beschreibung?

BEISPIEL: Eine Architektin entwirft Häuser.

Wer . . .

1. untersucht Patienten?
2. kennt sich mit Computern aus?
3. spielt im Film oder auf der Bühne (*stage*)?
4. arbeitet in einer Bibliothek?
5. repariert Autos?
6. spielt in einem Orchester?
7. entwirft (*designs*) Gebäude, Häuser und Wohnungen?
8. verkauft für eine Firma Produkte?
9. übersetzt (*translates*) aus einer Sprache in eine andere?
10. malt Bilder?

Aktivität 4. Suggestion: Have students work as quickly as possible in pairs or threes. Give a prize to the first group that finishes with the correct answers.

Aktivität 5 Was meinen Sie?

Suchen Sie Ihre Antworten auf die folgenden Fragen in der Liste von Berufen im **Thema 2.**

1. Wer hat die gefährlichste Arbeit?
2. Welcher Beruf hat das meiste Prestige?
3. Wer befasst sich mit Tieren?
4. Wer arbeitet meistens in einem Büro?

5. Wer verdient das meiste Geld?
6. Für welche Berufe muss man studieren?
7. Welche Arbeit bringt den meisten Stress mit sich?
8. Wer hat die längsten Arbeitsstunden?
9. Wer hat die langweiligste Arbeit?

Aktivität 6 Hin und her: Berühmte° Personen

famous

Diese berühmten Menschen, die alle einen Beruf ausübten, hatten auch andere Interessen. Ergänzen Sie die Informationen.

BEISPIEL: S1: Was war Martin Luther von Beruf?
S2: Er war Priester.
S1: Was für andere Interessen hatte er?
S2: Er interessierte sich für Literatur, Musik und die deutsche Sprache.

Aktivität 6. Bertha von Suttner schrieb *Die Waffen nieder.* 1891 gründete sie die Österreichische Gesellschaft der Friedensfreunde und war Vizepräsidentin des Internationalen Friedenbüreaus in Berlin. 1905 erhielt sie den Nobelpreis.

NAME	BERUF	INTERESSEN
Rainer Werner Fassbinder	Filmregisseur	Literatur, Theater
Bertha von Suttner	Schriftstellerin	die europäische Friedensbewegung
Marlene Dietrich	Schauspielerin	Skifahren
Käthe Kollwitz	Künstlerin	Politik
Martin Luther	Priester	Literatur, Musik, die deutsche Sprache
Willi Brandt	Politiker	Skifahren, Lesen

Aktivität 7 Welcher Beruf ist der richtige?

Machen Sie eine Liste von den Kriterien, die Ihnen im Beruf wichtig sind. Benutzen Sie die Vokabeln im **Thema 1.** Fragen Sie dann jemanden im Kurs, was für einen Beruf er/sie Ihnen empfehlen würde.

BEISPIEL: S1: Ich möchte eine abwechslungsreiche Tätigkeit haben, vielleicht im Büro arbeiten und Kontakt mit Menschen haben. Was empfiehlst du mir?
S2: Ich empfehle dir, Kaufmann/Kauffrau zu werden.

Aktivität 7. Suggestion: Follow up with a class discussion to see if everyone agrees with the advice that was given. If not, what would others advise?

Thema 3

Bewerbungen und Stellenangebote

Ein Stellenangebot

Silvia A., Vertriebs-Repräsentantin

„Klar, ich geh' meinen Weg mit KONICA.

Denn hier finde ich abwechslungsreiche Aufgaben, die mich fordern[1] und fördern. Und Technik, die mir Spaß macht: z.B. erstklassige Kopierer, Telefaxe und digitale Kommunikationssysteme. Abgesehen davon[2] ist Gleichberechtigung kein Fremdwort.[3]

Auch als Frau geh' ich hier meinen Weg."

Vertriebs-Repräsentant/in

Großraum Berlin[4]

Wenn Sie den Erfolg wollen und Verkaufstalent besitzen, sollten Sie über uns nachdenken. Wir haben Spitzenprodukte[5] und ein festes Verkaufsgebiet für Sie. Hier können Sie sich mit Ehrgeiz,[6] Zielstrebigkeit[7] und Ihrer Persönlichkeit eine sichere Existenz aufbauen. Das Rüstzeug[8] bekommen Sie von uns: eine gute Starthilfe und starkes Verkaufstraining. Alles andere bestimmen dann Sie: Ihre weitere Entwicklung bei uns, Ihr Einkommen und Ihre Karrierechancen. Ob als Profi[9] oder als Einsteiger/in.[10] Sie brauchen die Herausforderung.[11]

Deshalb sollten wir uns kennenlernen. Ihr erster Schritt:[12] Schicken Sie Ihre Bewerbung an Herrn Kebsch.

Wir freuen uns auf den Kontakt mit Ihnen.

KONICA BUSINESS MACHINES
INTERNATIONAL GMBH
Vertriebsbüro Berlin
Motzener Straße 12–14
12277 Berlin
Telefon 030/70 78 60

Neue Wörter

- □ die **Aufgabe**
- □ **besitzen**
- □ die **Bewerbung**
- □ der **Erfolg**
- □ **sich freuen (auf)**
- □ die **Gleichberechtigung**
- □ der **Kontakt**
- □ **nachdenken (über)**
- □ die **Technik**

Realia. The *Konica* ad appeared in the *Berliner Morgenpost.*

1. *challenge*
2. abgesehen . . . *apart from that*
3. *foreign word*
4. Großraum . . . *greater Berlin*
5. *top products*
6. *ambition*
7. *determination*
8. *equipment*
9. *professional*
10. *beginner, person coming aboard*
11. *challenge*
12. *step*

- Was für Produkte **stellt** die Firma Konica **her?**
- Warum macht die Arbeit bei dieser Firma Sylvia A. Spaß?
- Was bietet die Firma Vertriebs-Repräsentanten/Repräsentantinnen?
- Was kann man selbst bei dieser Firma bestimmen?
- Was würde Sie an dieser Firma interessieren?
  - □ Verkaufstraining
  - □ festes Verkaufsgebiet *(established sales territory)*
  - □ hohes **Einkommen**
  - □ Gelegenheit zur weiteren **Entwicklung**
  - □ ?

Wie **bewirbt** man **sich** um eine **Stelle?** Bringen Sie folgende Schritte in eine logische Reihenfolge.

> **Suggestion:** Introduce a fictional character and describe the steps he/she went through to apply for a job.

__3__ einen tabellarischen **Lebenslauf** schreiben
__7__ ein **Bewerbungsformular** ausfüllen
__1__ Interessen, Wünsche und Erwartungen mit Familie und Freunden besprechen
__4__ **Unterlagen** (**Abitur** oder anderen Abschluss und **Zeugnisse** von früheren **Arbeitgebern**) sammeln
__8__ **sich** auf das **Vorstellungsgespräch vorbereiten**
__6__ die **Stellenangebote** in der Zeitung durchlesen
__2__ Informationen über verschiedene Karrieren und Berufe sammeln
__5__ zum **Arbeitsamt** an der Uni gehen und mit **Berufsberatern** sprechen

Obwohl immer mehr Firmen ihre Stellenanzeigen an männliche und weibliche Bewerber zugleich richten, gibt es in den deutschsprachigen Ländern kein Gesetz, das einen Arbeitgeber verhindert, eine Stelle nur für Männer oder nur für Frauen auszuschreiben. So findet man zum Beispiel immer noch Anzeigen für „eine Sekretärin" oder für „einen Abteilungsleiter" (*department head*). Auch das Alter (*age*) eines Bewerbers / einer Bewerberin spielt eine Rolle, wie Sie aus der Allianz Anzeige ersehen können.

Die Sprache von Stellenanzeigen hat ihre Besonderheiten (*idiosyncrasies*); so suchen Firmen „Damen und Herren" für eine Stelle als Kaufmann oder Kauffrau, manchmal sogar „eine junge Dame" oder „einen jungen Herrn". „Aussagefähige Unterlagen" (*complete documentation*), die sich z.B. die Firma Allianz (S. 323) für die Bewerbung erbittet, sind Lebenslauf, Zeugnisse und ein Lichtbild (z.B. Passfoto).

Weiteres zum Thema Stellenanzeigen finden Sie bei ***Deutsch: Na klar!*** im World-Wide-Web unter www.mhhe.com/german.

Aktivität 8 Ein Stellenangebot

Lesen Sie das Stellenangebot von der Firma Allianz, und wählen Sie passende Wörter aus der Liste, um die Sätze zu ergänzen.

Lebenslauf	abwechslungsreich
Bewerber/Bewerberinnen	Berufsleben
Zeugnisse	Abitur
Ausbildung	

1. Die Firma Allianz sucht _____ und _____, die ihre Chancen im _____ weiterentwickeln wollen.
2. Eine Qualifikation ist entweder (*either*) das _____ oder die Mittlere Reife.
3. Bei der Firma bekommt man eine _____ zum Versicherungskaufmann oder zur Versicherungskauffrau.
4. Die Aufgaben bei dieser Firma sind interessant und _____.
5. Um sich zu bewerben, muss man Unterlagen, z.B. _____ und _____ an die Firma senden.

Entwicklung zum/zur Versicherungsfachmann/-frau[1]

Sie sind etwa[2] 25 bis 35 Jahre alt, haben mittlere Reife[3] oder Abitur und bereits erste kaufmännische Erfahrungen[4] gesammelt. Ihren bisherigen Weg[5] können, wollen Sie aber nicht weitergehen. Vielmehr[6] würden Sie gerne die Herausforderung[7] annehmen, Ihre Qualifikation noch zu erweitern[8] und dadurch Ihre Chancen im Berufsleben zu verbessern. Von Ihrem Arbeitstag erwarten Sie abwechslungsreiche Aufgaben, Kontakt mit Menschen und sichtbare Erfolge.

Die Allianz sucht Damen und Herren, die denken wie Sie. Sie erhalten[9] bei uns eine einjährige qualifizierte Ausbildung in Theorie und Praxis zum/zur Versicherungsfachmann/-frau,

Wir freuen uns darauf, Sie bald kennenzulernen. Bitte senden Sie Ihre aussagefähigen[10] Unterlagen an die

Allianz Versicherungs-AG
Filialdirektion Ulm
Postfach
89070 Ulm
Telefon (07 31) 15 32-1 21

hoffentlich Allianz versichert

Realia. This ad appeared in the *Südwest Presse.*

1. *insurance specialist*
2. *approximately*
3. mittlere . . . *degree received by students graduating from the* Realschule
4. *experiences*
5. bisherigen . . . *the path you've been taking so far*
6. *rather*
7. *challenge*
8. *expand*
9. *will get*
10. *detailed and informative*

Aktivität 9 Ein Gespräch unter Freunden 

Was stimmt? Was stimmt nicht? Korrigieren Sie die falschen Aussagen.

	DAS STIMMT	DAS STIMMT NICHT
1. Petra sucht einen Ausbildungsplatz.	☒	☐
2. Petra ist noch nicht zum Arbeitsamt gegangen.	☐	☒
3. Petra hat ein interessantes Stellenangebot in der Zeitung gefunden.	☒	☐
4. Petra hat sich um eine Ausbildungsstelle beworben.	☒	☐
5. Petra hat die Firma sofort angerufen.	☐	☒
6. Petra ist sehr enthusiastisch, weil sie die Firma gut kennt.	☐	☒
7. Die Firma verlangt, dass Bewerber Biologie studiert haben.	☐	☒

Analyse

Hier sehen Sie einen typischen tabellarischen Lebenslauf.

- Welche Schulen hat Birgit in Bonn besucht? Mit welchem Abschluss?
- Welche Ausbildung hat sie hinter sich?
- Was ist ihr jetziger Beruf?
- Welche anderen Interessen hat Birgit?

Nun erzählen Sie Birgits Lebenslauf in vollständigen Sätzen. Benutzen Sie folgendes Format.

BEISPIEL: Am 22. Dezember 1959 wurde Birgit in Bonn geboren.

Von _____ bis _____ . . .
Seit _____ . . .
Danach . . .

Grundschule besucht
Realschule besucht
Ausbildung als Bürokauffrau gemacht
als Reisebürokauffrau in Bonn gearbeitet

Lebenslauf

Name	Birgit Hermsen
Geburtsdatum	22. Dezember 1959
Geburtsort	Bonn
Eltern	Friedrich Hermsen Elsbeth Hermsen, geb. Marx
Ausbildungsgang	
1965-1969	Grundschule: Elisabethschule, Bonn
1969-1976	Realschule, Bonn
1974-1975	Austauschschülerin in USA (Experiment in International Living) Redwood City, Kalifornien
1976	Realschulabschluß: Mittlere Reife
1976-1978	Ausbildung als Bürokauffrau, Bonn Reisebüro Wilmers
Seit 1978	Reisebürokauffrau, Bonn Reisebüro am Markt
Familienstand	ledig
Interessen	Reisen (USA, Nepal, Australien und Neuseeland) Sport (Tennis, Reiten) Lesen und Musik

Es ist nicht ungewöhnlich, bei einer Bewerbung einen handschriftlichen Lebenslauf zu verlangen. Die Handschrift ermöglicht einen Einblick in die persönlichen Qualitäten eines Bewerbers oder einer Bewerberin. Oft ist ein Lebenslauf noch in Form eines Berichtes (*narrative*). Ein tabellarischer Lebenslauf nach amerikanischem Muster (*model*) ist auch möglich.

Aktivität 10 Ein Gespräch über eine Stellensuche

Führen Sie mit einem Partner / einer Partnerin ein Gespräch über Stellenangebote. Sie können die Anzeigen in diesem Kapitel oder Anzeigen aus einer Zeitung zur Information benutzen.

S1	S2
1. Was willst du _____ machen? • nach dem Studium • in den Semesterferien • ?	**2.** Ich will mir eine Stelle _____ suchen. • in einem Büro • bei einer Firma • in einer Fabrik • ?
3. Wie findet man _____?	**4.** Man muss mindestens _____ (2/3/4/5/?) Dinge machen: _____. • Informationen über verschiedene Berufe sammeln • Stellenangebote in der Zeitung / im Internet durcharbeiten • zur Arbeitsvermittlung an der Uni gehen • Freunde/Familie/Bekannte fragen • zum Arbeitsamt / zur Berufsberatung gehen • ?
5. Was braucht man für eine Bewerbung?	**6.** Man muss gewöhnlich ein _____ ausfüllen und Arbeitszeugnisse sowie _____ und _____ sammeln.
7. Wie lange dauert es, bis _____?	**8.a.** _____ geht schnell. **b.** Manchmal dauert es _____. **c.** Meistens dauert es _____ Monate.
9. Na, dann drücke ich dir die Daumen!	**10.** Vielen Dank!

Kulturtipp. Note: An excellent illustration of the information in the **Kulturtipp** is in *Transparente Landeskunde,* available from Inter Nationes, 53175 Bonn, Kennedyallee 91–103. **Suggestion:** Ask students to create a chart illustrating the American school system and describe it to a partner playing the role of a German visitor seeking information about American schools.

Mit sechs Jahren beginnt für Kinder in Deutschland die Schule. Alle Kinder gehen zuerst vier bis sechs Jahre lang gemeinsam auf **die Grundschule.** Danach trennen sich die Wege.

Ein Teil der Schüler und Schülerinnen geht dann auf **die Hauptschule,** die nach dem neunten oder zehnten Schuljahr mit dem Hauptschulabschluss endet. Danach suchen sich die meisten Schulabgänger eine Ausbildungsstelle für einen praktischen Beruf. Zweimal die Woche müssen die „Azubis" (Auszubildenden oder Lehrlinge) auf **die Berufsschule** gehen. Dort lernen sie vor allem praktische Fächer, die für den künftigen Beruf wichtig sind.

Ein anderer Teil der Schüler und Schülerinnen geht von der Grundschule auf die **Realschule.** Sie endet nach dem zehnten Schuljahr mit dem **Abschluss** der **mittleren Reife.** Danach geht man auf eine **Fachschule** oder auch auf eine Berufsschule.

Als dritte Möglichkeit gibt es **das Gymnasium.** Das Gymnasium umfasst neun Klassen, vom fünften bis zum dreizehnten Schuljahr. Am Ende von neun Jahren machen Schüler **das Abitur.** Ohne Abitur kann man nicht studieren.

Als Alternative für die drei verschiedenen Schultypen gibt es in Deutschland heutzutage **die Gesamtschule.** Ähnlich wie in amerikanischen Schulen gehen alle Schüler zur selben Schule bis zum Abschluss; daher der Name Gesamtschule.

Wer trifft die Entscheidung, auf welche Schule ein Schüler oder eine Schülerin nach den ersten vier Jahren

Schematische Gliederung des Bildungswesens

Weiterbildung
(allgemeine und berufsbezogene Weiterbildung in vielfältigen Formen)

Berufsqualifizierender Abschluß	Allgemeine Hochschulreife	Berufsqualifizierender Studienabschluß
Fachschule	**Abendgymnasium/ Kolleg**	**Universität/Technische Universität, Pädagogische Hochschule Fachhochschule Verwaltungsfachhochschule Kunsthochschule Gesamthochschule**

Berufsbildender Abschluß — Mittlerer Bildungsabschluß — Fachhochschulreife — Allgemeine Hochschulreife

Schuljahr						Schuljahr
13					**Gymnasiale Oberstufe** (Gymnasium, Berufliches Gymnasium, Fachgymnasium, Gesamtschule)	13
12	**Berufsausbildung in Betrieb u. Berufsschule (Duales System)**	**Berufsaufbau-Schule**	**Berufsfach-Schule**	**Fachober-Schule**		12
11						11
10	Berufsgrundbildungsjahr					10

Abschlüsse an Hauptschulen nach 9 oder 10 Jahren / Realschulabschluß

Schuljahr						Schuljahr
10		**10. Schuljahr**				10
9						9
8	Sonderschule	**Hauptschule**	**Realschule**	**Gymnasium**	**Gesamtschule**	8
7						7
6		*Orientierungs-Stufe* (schulformabhängig oder schulformunabhängig)				6
5						5
4						4
3	Sonderschule	**Grundschule**				3
2						2
1						1
	Sonderkindergarten	**Kindergarten**				

Der erste Schultag: der Ernst des Lebens beginnt.

geht? Gewöhnlich empfiehlt der Klassenlehrer oder die Klassenlehrerin—aufgrund der Leistungen (*achievements*)—auf welche Schule ein Schüler oder eine Schülerin gehen sollte. In einigen Ländern der Bundesrepublik gibt es eine sogenannte Orientierungsstufe (*lit. orientation level*) für das fünfte und sechste Schuljahr. Erst danach entscheidet sich, ob ein Schüler oder eine Schülerin aufs Gymnasium, auf die Realschule oder auf die Hauptschule geht.

Weiteres zum Thema Schule und Bildung finden Sie bei ***Deutsch: Na klar!*** im World-Wide-Web unter www.mhhe.com/german.

Grammatik im Kontext

Future Tense°

das Futur

You may recall that in German the present tense can also refer to future action, particularly when an adverb of time is present.

Nächstes Jahr macht Sabine ein Praktikum in den USA.	*Next year Sabine is going to do an internship in the USA.*
Morgen schickt sie mehrere Bewerbungen ab.	*Tomorrow she will send off several applications.*

In German, the future tense is formed with the auxiliary verb **werden** and the infinitive of the main verb. The infinitive is placed at the end of the sentence. The future tense is used most frequently to express future time when the context provides no other explicit reference to the future.

Eines Tages **werde** ich Erfolg **haben.**	*Someday I will be successful.*
Millionen **werden** meine Bücher **kaufen.**	*Millions will buy my books.*
Wir **werden** mal **sehen.**	*We shall see (if that's the case).*

kaufen	
ich werde kaufen	wir werden kaufen
du wirst kaufen	ihr werdet kaufen
er/sie/es wird kaufen	sie werden kaufen
Sie werden kaufen	

Analyse

Lesen Sie den Cartoon „Poesie".

Realia. Poesie: This cartoon is from *Quick,* a popular German weekly magazine.

- Identify the verbs in each sentence. Which verbs clearly refer to the present?
- Which sentences express the poet's wishful thinking?
- For each sentence expressing the poet's hopes for the future, state the unspoken reality of his present life.

BEISPIEL: Er hat jetzt keinen Erfolg mit seinen Gedichten.

1. *poetry*
2. *poems*
3. *heaven*
4. *lift*
5. mache . . . *continue*
6. wie . . . *as before*
7. *select*
8. *readership*

Expressing Probability

The future tense is frequently used in German to express probability, often with the adverbs **wohl** or **wahrscheinlich** (*probably*).

Consider the following hypothetical scenario concerning the unsuccessful poet of the cartoon ***Poesie.***

> Zehn Jahre später: Der Dichter Anselmus Himmelblau fährt jetzt einen Mercedes 500 SL mit Autotelefon und Minibar und wohnt in einer Villa in Spanien. Auf seiner Luxusjacht in Monte Carlo trifft sich die Prominenz der ganzen Welt . . .

Übung 8 Ein unkonventioneller Klub 

Markieren Sie die richtige(n) Antwort(en).

1. Der eine Sprecher
   a. liest ein Buch. **b.** sieht fern. **c.** schreibt ein Buch.
2. *Das literarische Oktett* ist
   a. ein Gedicht. **b.** der Titel eines Buches. **c.** der Titel einer Erzählung. **d.** der Name eines Klubs.
3. Die Autoren sind
   a. fünf Studentinnen. **b.** acht Studenten. **c.** acht Hausfrauen.
4. Im Buch stehen
   a. nur Geschichten. **b.** nur Gedichte. **c.** hauptsächlich (*mainly*) Geschichten und ein paar Gedichte.
5. Die Themen, über die die Autoren schreiben, beziehen sich auf
   a. Politik. **b.** Sex. **c.** Liebe. **d.** Deutschland.
6. Der Leser des Buches findet das Buch
   a. merkwürdig. **b.** originell. **c.** dumm. **d.** provozierend.

Übung 9 Ein Interview 

Fragen Sie mindestens drei Leute in der Klasse.

BEISPIEL: S1: Was für Filme siehst du am liebsten?
S2: Am liebsten sehe ich Dokumentarfilme.
oder Am liebsten sehe ich Filme, die spannend sind.

1. Was für Filme siehst du am liebsten? (z.B. Abenteuerfilme, Dokumentarfilme, Liebesfilme)
2. Was für einen Wagen fährst du?
3. Was für Musik interessiert dich?
4. Was für Kleidung trägst du am liebsten?
5. Was für Getränke trinkst du am liebsten?
6. Was für Süßigkeiten isst du gern?
7. Was für Leute wohnen auf deiner Etage im Studentenheim?
8. Was für einen Beruf möchtest du haben?
9. Was für . . . ?

Negating Sentences

Summary: The Position of *nicht*

You recall that **nicht** is used when the negative article **kein** cannot be used. The position of **nicht** varies according to the structure of the sentence.

When **nicht** negates a specific sentence element, thereby emphasizing it, it precedes this sentence element.

> Ich komme **nicht heute,** sondern morgen.
> Wir haben **nicht viel Geld.**

When **nicht** negates an entire statement, it generally stands at the end of the sentence.

> Petra kommt morgen leider **nicht.**
> Sie gibt mir das Buch **nicht.**

However, **nicht** precedes:

• *predicate adjectives*	Petras Bewerbungsbrief ist **nicht lang.**
• *predicate nouns*	Das ist **nicht Petras Brief.**
• *verbal complements at the end of the sentence*	
a. *separable prefixes*	Sie schickt den Brief **nicht ab.**
b. *past participles*	Sie hat sich **nicht beworben.**
c. *infinitives*	Sie will sich **nicht bewerben.**
• *prepositional phrases*	Sie hat sich **nicht um die Stelle** beworben.
• *place or direction*	Klaus ist **nicht nach Hause** gegangen.

Übung 10 Das stimmt nicht!

Sagen Sie das Gegenteil (*opposite*).

1. Hans hat die Prüfung bestanden (*passed*).
2. Er kennt den Personalchef der Firma Wüstenrot.
3. Er hat seine Bewerbung zur Post gebracht.
4. Er hat den Personalchef gestern angerufen.
5. Der Personalchef hat ihn zu einem Vorstellungsgespräch eingeladen.
6. Der Personalchef war sehr beeindruckt von (*impressed by*) Hans.
7. Hans hat die Stelle bekommen.
8. Hans war sehr traurig darüber.
9. Er ist wieder zum Arbeitsamt gegangen.
10. Er will weiterstudieren.
11. Er ist sicher, dass er etwas findet.

Negation: *noch nicht, noch kein(e); nicht mehr, kein(e) . . . mehr*

A negative answer to a question that includes the adverb **schon** (*already; yet*) uses either **noch nicht** or **noch kein** (*not . . . yet*). Use the same rules as for **nicht** to place **noch nicht** in the sentence.

—Geht Ute **schon** zur Schule?	*Does Ute go to school yet?*
—Nein, sie geht **noch nicht** zur Schule.	*No, she doesn't go to school yet.*
—Hat Ernst **schon** eine Stelle?	*Does Ernst have a position yet?*
—Nein, er hat **noch keine** Stelle.	*No, he doesn't have a position yet.*

A negative answer to a question with **(immer) noch** uses either **nicht mehr** (*not any longer*) or **kein(e) . . . mehr** (*no more, no longer*).

—Arbeitet Ernst **noch** bei der Bank?	*Does Ernst still work for the bank?*
—Nein, er arbeitet **nicht mehr** da.	*No, he no longer works there.*
—Hat er **immer noch** Arbeit?	*Does he still have a job?*
—Nein, er hat **keine** Arbeit **mehr.**	*No, he doesn't have a job anymore.*

Übung 11 Leider, noch nicht 

Stellen Sie einem Partner / einer Partnerin Fragen.

1. Weißt du schon, was du mal werden willst?
2. Ist dein Bruder / deine Schwester schon mit der Ausbildung fertig?
3. Hast du schon eine Stelle für den Sommer?
4. Hast du schon die Stellenangebote in der Zeitung gelesen?
5. Hast du dich schon um eine Stelle beworben?
6. Hast du den Personalchef der Firma schon angerufen?
7. Hast du schon ein Angebot von der Firma bekommen?

Sprache im Kontext

Zuschauen

Vorschau

A. Beantworten Sie die folgenden Fragen, bevor Sie sich die Werbung ansehen.
- Was trinken Sie normalerweise, wenn Sie Energie brauchen?
- Ist dieses Getränk gut oder schlecht für die Gesundheit?

B. Sehen Sie sich die Werbung jetzt einmal ohne Ton an. Wofür ist das vielleicht ein Werbespot?

Arbeit mit dem Videotext

A. Sehen Sie sich die Werbung mit Ton an, und beantworten Sie die folgenden Fragen.

1. Was ist die Frau von Beruf?
   a. professionelle Body-Builderin
   b. Chirurgin
   c. Krankenschwester
   d. Putzfrau
   e. Tänzerin
2. Warum trinkt sie Nesfit?
3. Was enthält Nesfit?

B. Sehen Sie sich die Werbung noch einmal an!

1. Stellen Sie sich vor, dass Sie die Frau in der Werbung sind und jeden Tag eine Dose Nesfit trinken. Schreiben Sie einen Brief an Nestlé, den Hersteller von Nesfit, und erklären Sie, warum Sie Nesfit so gern trinken.

2. Ihre Meinung.
   - Wie finden Sie diese Werbung? (lustig, doof, interessant, langweilig) Warum?
   - Was würden Sie trinken, wenn Sie „Energie tanken" wollen?

Lesen

Zum Thema

Was sind die beliebtesten Berufe?

Zum Thema. Suggestion: Have students report as a group, while one student records the answers on the board.

1. In Gruppen zu dritt, schreiben Sie drei beliebte Berufe auf. Nennen Sie für jeden Beruf einen Grund, warum so viele Leute sich dafür interessieren. Machen Sie dann eine Umfrage in der Klasse. Welche Berufe wurden am häufigsten genannt? Warum?
2. Die folgenden Kategorien kommen im Artikel „So kriegen Sie den Job" vor. Was sollte man bedenken, wenn man zu einem Vorstellungsgespräch eingeladen ist?

BEISPIEL: Kleidung
Für ein Gespräch bei einer Bank kleidet man sich am besten konservativ.

- Kleidung
- Haltung (*demeanor*)
- Gestik (*gestures*)
- Mimik (Gesichtsausdrücke)
- Sprache
- Make-up

Auf den ersten Blick

1. Schauen Sie sich den Titel und alle Untertitel des Textes auf Seite 340 an. Stellen Sie dabei das Thema des Artikels fest.
2. Welche Informationen erwarten Sie im Text? Lesen Sie den Text, und versuchen Sie dabei, diese Informationen zu finden.
3. Für wen ist der Text geschrieben? Überfliegen Sie kurz den Text, und finden Sie mindestens drei Belege (*clues*).

   BEISPIEL: Im Text steht: „Jetzt müssen Sie nur noch überzeugen, dass Sie genau die Richtige sind."
4. Überfliegen Sie den Text noch einmal, und suchen Sie Wörter, die zu den folgenden Kategorien passen.
   a. Kleidung
   b. Haltung
   c. Gestik
   d. Mimik
   e. Sprache
   f. Make-up

Auf den ersten Blick. Before students read the text, ask them what an article addressed specifically to women who are going for a job interview might talk about.

Zum Text

1. Die Autoren benutzen (sehr oft) den Imperativ, um den Leserinnen zu sagen, was sie während eines Vorstellungsgesprächs machen sollten bzw. nicht machen sollten. Suchen Sie Beispiele im Text, und ordnen Sie diese in die passende Rubrik ein. Unterstreichen Sie die Tipps, die auch auf Männer zutreffen.

WAS SIE MACHEN SOLLTEN	WAS SIE NICHT MACHEN SOLLTEN

2. Sind die folgenden Fragen im Vorstellungsgespräch zulässig (*allowed*) oder unzulässig? Ordnen Sie anhand des Textes die Fragen in die passende Rubrik. Wo steht das im Text?

ZULÄSSIGE FRAGEN	UNZULÄSSIGE FRAGEN

   „Haben Sie vor, Kinder zu bekommen?"
   „Was haben Sie bei der Firma X gemacht?"
   „Warum haben Sie gerade diese Ausbildung gemacht?"
   „Sind Sie verheiratet?"
   „Sind Sie Mitglied (*member*) in einer politischen Partei?"
   „Was sind Ihre beruflichen Ziele (*goals*)?"
   „Sind Sie schwanger?"
   „Was sind Ihre Schwächen (*weaknesses*)?"
   „Warum wollen Sie gerade bei uns arbeiten?"

3. Lesen Sie den Teil „Fragen, die Sie unbedingt stellen sollten" noch einmal. Bilden Sie dann passende Fragen für eine Person, die sich um eine Stelle bewirbt.

BEISPIEL: Was sind die Ziele dieser Firma?

Zum Text. This text uses several useful expressions with a verb + preposition. As a vocabulary building exercise, have students identify the expressions and their meaning. Then have them use the expressions in a sentence.

Bewerbungs-Gespräch

So kriegen Sie den Job

Oft entscheiden 15 Minuten Vorstellungsgespräch in einer Firma über Ihr weiteres Leben. Wir sagen Ihnen, wie Sie sich am besten darauf vorbereiten

Realia. This article is from the magazine *Für Sie.*

ILLUSTRATION: NILS FLIEGNER

Sie haben sich um eine neue Stelle beworben – und halten nun die Einladung zu einem persönlichen Gespräch in Händen. Jetzt müssen Sie „nur" noch überzeugen,[1] daß Sie genau die Richtige sind. Wie Ihnen das gelingt,[2] verraten[3] Ihnen hier gleich zwei Experten: Thomas Briol von der „Baumann Unternehmensberatung", einem der größten Unternehmen dieser Art in Deutschland, und Karriereberaterin Dr. Dagmar Brodersen aus Darmstadt.

Das müssen Sie beachten

Kleidung: Die Kleiderfrage ist abhängig davon,[4] in welcher Branche Sie sich vorstellen. Während Sie in einer Bank oder in einem konventionellen Unternehmen busineßlike in einem Kostüm auftreten sollten, können Sie sich in einer Werbeagentur ruhig flotter und farbiger präsentieren. Wesentlich[5] aber ist, daß Sie sich in Ihrer Kleidung wohl fühlen. Ihr Gegenüber merkt es mit absoluter Sicherheit, wenn Sie sich nur für den Termin „verkleidet"[6] haben.

Haltung: Betreten Sie den Raum, in dem das Vorstellungsgespräch stattfindet, freundlich lächelnd. Kommen Sie nicht mit heruntergezogenen Schultern und vorgebeugt herein, das signalisiert Angst oder Unterwürfigkeit.[7] Wenn Sie Ihren Gesprächspartner begrüßen, dann tun Sie dies mit einem kurzen, kräftigen Händedruck. Seien Sie ungezwungen und natürlich, und blicken Sie Ihrem Gegenüber ruhig und offen ins Gesicht – das gibt Pluspunkte.

Gestik: Auch hier gilt, wie schon beim Betreten des Gesprächsraums, daß Sie Zeichen von Nervosität vermeiden.[8] Besonders häufig[9] ist das verräterische Fingerknipsen[10] oder das Verknoten[11] der Hände.

Mimik: Ihr Gegenüber freut sich, wenn Sie auch in dieser ernsten Gesprächssituation mal lächeln oder lachen. Ein starres Pokerface wirkt ziemlich unsympathisch.

Sprache: Sprechen Sie deutlich, verständlich und langsam. Dadurch verhindern Sie auch, daß Sie sich in der Aufregung verhaspeln.[12] Bleiben Sie trotzdem natürlich, und übertreiben[13] Sie die Selbstdarstellung nicht.

Make-up: Auch hier gilt, daß Sie sich Ihrem Stil entsprechend[14] schminken, jedoch mit Farbe eher zurückhaltend sein sollten.

Fragen, auf die Sie gefaßt sein müssen

Sicherlich werden Sie zu Ihrem Lebensweg gefragt werden. Antworten Sie nicht nur mit den Fakten, die sowieso schon Ihrem Lebenslauf zu entnehmen[15] sind, sondern geben Sie Hintergrundinformation, z.B. warum Sie gerade Ihre Ausbildung, Ihren Beruf gewählt haben. Vorbereitet müssen Sie auch auf die Frage sein, warum Sie sich gerade bei diesem Unternehmen[16] beworben haben. Und gerade als Frau müssen Sie damit rechnen,[17] nach Ihrem Privatleben gefragt zu werden. Wichtig zu wissen: Auf Fragen, ob Sie sich verloben[18] oder heiraten wollen, ob Sie schwanger[19] sind oder einer Partei oder Gewerkschaft angehören, müssen Sie gar nicht bzw. dürfen Sie falsch antworten.

Wenn Sie nach Ihren persönlichen Zielen gefragt werden: Betonen[20] Sie nicht so sehr Ihre privaten Wünsche und Vorstellungen, sondern lassen Sie sich vor allem über Ihre beruflichen Interessen aus.[21]

Gefragt wird gerne auch nach den persönlichen Stärken und Schwächen. Da können Sie durchaus Schwächen zugeben, beispielsweise, daß Sie sich in einer Fremdsprache noch vervollkommnen[22] wollen.

Abschließend wird man oft gefragt, ob man Nebeninteressen hat und in sportlichen, karitativen oder kirchlichen Organisationen tätig ist. Können Sie hier mit „Ja" antworten, haben Sie einen dicken Pluspunkt, weil dies als Zeichen für außergewöhnliches Engagement gewertet wird.

Fragen, die Sie unbedingt stellen sollten

Genauso wichtig wie Ihre Antworten sind aber auch Ihre Fragen: Bleiben Sie nicht stumm, sondern beteiligen Sie sich aktiv am Gespräch: Fragen Sie nach den Zielen des Unternehmens und danach, was gerade Sie dazu beitragen können. Sicherlich interessiert Sie auch alles, was mit Ihrem (künftigen) Tätigkeitsbereich zusammenhängt. Fragen Sie ruhig genau nach. Damit bezeugen[23] Sie Interesse – und machen garantiert einen guten Eindruck.

Wenn Sie das alles beherzigen,[24] könnten Sie Ihren Konkurrenten/innen um eine Nasenlänge voraus sein.

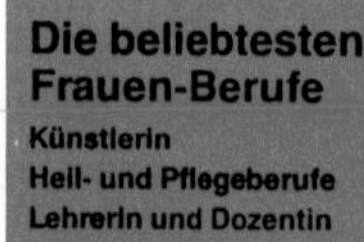

Die beliebtesten Frauen-Berufe

- Künstlerin
- Heil- und Pflegeberufe
- Lehrerin und Dozentin
- Ingenieurin und Architektin
- Ärztin
- Sozialberufe
- Kauffrau
- Psychologin
- Tourismusberufe
- Journalistin

(nach einer Erhebung der Bundesanstalt für Arbeit)

1. *convince*
2. Wie . . . *how to succeed*
3. *reveal*
4. abhängig . . . *depends on*
5. *essential*
6. *dressed up, in costume*
7. *submission*
8. *avoid*
9. *common*
10. *snapping one's fingers*
11. *wringing*
12. sich . . . verhaspeln *get muddled*
13. *exaggerate*
14. *appropriately*
15. *gathered*
16. *company*
17. damit . . . *count on*
18. sich . . . *are getting engaged*
19. *pregnant*
20. *stress*
21. lassen Sie sich . . . aus *express*
22. *to perfect*
23. *demonstrate*
24. *take to heart*

Sprechen und Schreiben

Aktivität 2. Follow-up: 1. Pick the most interesting want ads and photocopy each twice. Divide the class into interviewers and candidates. Then divide each group into smaller groups. Give each group of interviewers one of the want ads from the first set of copies, and have them create a set of questions to ask the candidates. Give each group of candidates one of the want ads from the second set of copies, and have them brainstorm about the kinds of questions they might ask the interviewers and be asked by the interviewers and provide possible answers to the interviewers' questions. 2. Have the interviewers for each group interview the corresponding candidates. Each student should ask at least one question of each candidate. Each candidate should answer and ask the interviewers at least one question. 3. The interviewers should convene for a couple of minutes and select one candidate for the job. Then they should announce their selection to the class and explain why that person was selected.

Additional Activity. *Stellen Sie sich vor, Rotkäppchen oder Aschenputtel (oder eine andere Figur aus einem Märchen oder eine berühmte Person) sucht eine Arbeit. Übernehmen Sie deren Identität. Machen Sie eine Liste von den Eigenschaften dieser Person, ohne die Person zu nennen. Versuchen Sie, Relativsätze zu benutzen. Die anderen müssen raten, wer das ist, und dann der Person eine Arbeit empfehlen.*

Aktivität 1 Ein Blick in die Zukunft

Arbeiten Sie mit einem Partner / einer Partnerin zusammen. Stellen Sie sich vor, Sie sind Hellseher/Hellseherin (*clairvoyant*). Jemand kommt zu Ihnen und möchte gern wissen, was die Zukunft für ihn/sie bereithält (*holds in store*). Werfen Sie einen Blick in die Zukunft.

BEISPIEL: Sie werden eines Tages eine berühmte Dichterin sein. Sie werden jedes Jahr drei neue Bücher schreiben . . .

Aktivität 2 . . . gesucht!

Schreiben Sie eine Stellenanzeige (z.B. Clown gesucht). Welche Qualifikationen muss der Bewerber / die Bewerberin haben (z.B. Sinn für Humor; High-School-Abschluss)? Wie bewirbt man sich um die Stelle (z.B. Senden Sie Ihre Unterlagen an . . .)? Benutzen Sie die Anzeigen in diesem Kapitel als Beispiele.

z.B. Rotkäppchen:
*Ich bin ein Mensch, der lieber im Freien als in einem Büro arbeitet.
Ich gehe gern wandern und habe Blumen gern.
Ich arbeite gern mit älteren Menschen.
Leider werde ich leicht abgelenkt* "distracted". *Also, bin ich nicht immer pünktlich. Ich möchte am liebsten einen Beruf, bei dem ich nicht unter Zeitdruck stehe.
Wer bin ich? Und was wäre eine gute Arbeit für mich?*

Wortschatz

Arbeitswelt	**Work World**
der **Arbeitgeber, -** / die **Arbeitgeberin, -nen**	employer
das **Arbeitsamt, ⸚er**	employment office
der **Arbeitsplatz, ⸚e**	workplace, position
die **Ausbildung**	training
der **Berufsberater, -** / die **Berufsberaterin, -nen**	employment counselor
die **Bewerbung, -en**	application
das **Bewerbungsformular, -e**	application form
das **Büro, -s**	office
der **Chef, -s** / die **Chefin, -nen**	manager, boss, head
das **Einkommen**	income
die **Firma,** *pl.* **Firmen**	firm, company
das **Gehalt, ⸚er**	salary
der **Lebenslauf**	resume
der **Mitarbeiter, -** / die **Mitarbeiterin, -nen**	co-worker, colleague
die **Stelle, -n**	position, job
das **Stellenangebot, -e**	job offer
die **Tätigkeit, -en**	position; activity
das **Vorstellungsgespräch, -e**	job interview

Berufe	**Professions**
der **Architekt** (**-en** *masc.*), **-en** / die **Architektin, -nen** (*R*)	architect
der **Arzt, ⸚e** / die **Ärztin, -nen**	physician, doctor
der **Bibliothekar, -e** / die **Bibliothekarin, -nen**	librarian
der **Chemiker, -** / die **Chemikerin, -nen**	chemist
der **Dolmetscher, -** / die **Dolmetscherin, -nen**	interpreter
der **Fotograf** (**-en** *masc.*), **-en** / die **Fotografin, -nen**	photographer
der **Geschäftsmann,** *pl.* **Geschäftsleute** / die **Geschäftsfrau, -en**	businessman / businesswoman

der **Informatiker, -** / die **Informatikerin, -nen**	computer scientist
der **Ingenieur, -e** / die **Ingenieurin, -nen**	engineer
der **Journalist** (**-en** *masc.*), **-en** / die **Journalistin, -nen**	journalist
der **Kaufmann,** *pl.* **Kaufleute** / die **Kauffrau, -en**	salesman / saleswoman
der **Künstler, -** / die **Künstlerin, -nen**	artist
der **Mechaniker, -** / die **Mechanikerin, -nen**	mechanic
der **Musiker, -** / die **Musikerin, -nen**	musician
der **Physiker, -** / die **Physikerin, -nen**	physicist
der **Psychologe** (**-n** *masc.*), **-n** / die **Psychologin, -nen**	psychologist
der **Rechtsanwalt, ⸚e** / die **Rechtsanwältin, -nen**	attorney
der **Schauspieler, -** / die **Schauspielerin, -nen**	actor
der **Zahnarzt, ⸚e** / die **Zahnärztin, -nen**	dentist

Sonstige Substantive / Other Nouns

das **Abitur, -e**	examination at the end of secondary school (**Gymnasium**)
der **Abschluss, ⸚e***	completion; degree
das **Ansehen**	prestige
die **Aufgabe, -n**	task
das **Ausland** (*no pl.*)	foreign countries
im Ausland	abroad
die **Entwicklung, -en**	development
der **Erfolg, -e**	success
die **Gelegenheit, -en**	opportunity
die **Gleichberechtigung**	equality
die **Grundschule, -n**	primary school
das **Gymnasium, Gymnasien** (*pl.*)	secondary school
der **Kontakt, -e**	contact
das **Leben** (*no pl.*)	life
das **Berufsleben**	professional life
das **Prestige**	prestige
die **Technik, -en**	technique, technology
die **Unterlage, -n**	document (*usu. plural*)
das **Zeugnis, -se**	report card; transcript; evaluation (from a former employer)

Verben / Verbs

sich beschäftigen (mit)	to occupy oneself (with)
besitzen, besaß, besessen	to own
sich bewerben (um)(bewirbt), bewarb, beworben	to apply (for)
sich freuen (auf + *acc.***)**	to look forward to
her•stellen	to produce, manufacture
nach•denken (über + *acc.***), dachte nach, nachgedacht**	to think (about)
um•gehen mit, ging um, ist umgegangen	to deal with
verdienen	to deserve; to earn
Geld verdienen	to earn money
sich vor•bereiten (auf + *acc.***)**	to prepare (for)
sich (*dat.***) vor•stellen**	to imagine
sich (*acc.***) vor•stellen**	to introduce

Adjektive und Adverbien / Adjectives and Adverbs

abwechslungsreich	varied
fest	stable, firm(ly)
finanziell	financial(ly)
möglichst	the most possible
möglichst viel(e)	as much (many) as possible
selbständig	independent(ly)
unabhängig	independent(ly)

Sonstiges / Other

im Freien	outdoors
wahrscheinlich	probably
was für (ein)	what kind of (a)
wohl	probably

* See Appendix E for alternate spelling.

Lernziele

Use this checklist to verify that you can now . . .

- ☐ describe your interests, desires, and expectations with regard to a future occupation.
- ☐ say what you like or dislike about work.
- ☐ identify some common occupations and describe the tasks involved in those occupations.
- ☐ understand German job ads and resumés.
- ☐ ask and answer questions about a potential job.
- ☐ explain the steps involved in applying for a job.
- ☐ describe the main facets of the German school system.
- ☐ use the future tense to talk about future actions or probability.
- ☐ use relative clauses to describe people or things.
- ☐ pose questions about people or things using the expression **was für (ein).**
- ☐ negate sentences properly, using **nicht, kein(e), noch nicht / kein(e),** and **nicht / kein(e) mehr.**

Kapitel 12

Haus und Haushalt

Beim Hausbau. Der Richtkranz (*wreath*) auf dem Dach signalisiert, dass das Haus fast fertig ist.

Kapitel 12. Suggestion: Brainstorm with students (in German) about the different ways they spend their money. Have them talk about what they do to earn money, how much they need, and what their major expenses are. Describe your own housing situation. Have students describe where they live, where their families live, and how and where they would eventually like to live. Will they prefer renting or buying a house? Ask about the availability of affordable housing, a perennial problem in Germany.

Alles klar?

A. Was würden die Personen 1 bis 9 machen, wenn sie viel Geld gewinnen würden? Lesen Sie die Aussagen unter den Bildern. Schreiben Sie dann die passende Nummer der Person neben die Frage.

Was würden Sie machen, wenn Sie 10 MILLIONEN DM gewinnen?

oder 8 Millionen DM oder 6 Millionen DM oder 1 Million DM oder...

1

Mit dem Geld helfe ich armen[1] Menschen.

2

Ich kaufe mir eine Eigentumswohnung.[2]

3

Ich mache[3] mich gleich selbständig.

4

Ich weiß noch nicht, was ich mache.

5

Ich fahre in das Land meiner Träume.[4]

6

Mein Traum ist ein Bauernhof mit Tieren.

7

Wir unterstützen[5] unsere Eltern und Geschwister.

8

Ich beantrage[6] sofort meine Rente.[7]

9

Ich lade alle meine Freunde ein.

Haben Sie schon einmal überlegt, was SIE tun würden, wenn Sie plötzlich so viel Geld gewinnen?

1. *poor*
2. *condominium*
3. *immediately*
4. *dreams*
5. *support*
6. *apply for*
7. *retirement*

Realia. This ad is from the *Staatliche Lotterie-Einnahme der Süddeutschen Klassen-Lotterie Kassel.*

- _____ Wer ist sich noch nicht sicher?
- _____ Wer will eine Wohnung kaufen?
- _____ Wer möchte den Armen helfen?
- _____ Wer will etwas für seine Freunde tun?
- _____ Wer hat Tiere gern?
- _____ Wer interessiert sich für Reisen?
- _____ Wer will der Familie helfen?
- _____ Wer macht sich selbständig?
- _____ Wer möchte sich pensionieren lassen?

B. „Was bedeutet euch Geld?" Diese Frage haben wir Jens, Lucia und Elke gestellt. Hören Sie ihre Antworten. Schreiben Sie J (Jens), L (Lucia) oder E (Elke) neben die zutreffenden Aussagen.

1. __E__ lange Urlaub machen und dann wieder arbeiten
2. __L__ Armen helfen
3. __J__ Geld für medizinische Forschung spenden (*donate*)
4. __L__ ein eigenes Geschäft aufmachen
5. __J__ ein neues Auto oder eine neue Wohnung kaufen
6. __E__ investieren
7. __L__ weiter studieren—vielleicht im Ausland
8. __E__ Geld für Welthungerorganisationen spenden

Weiteres zum Thema Geld und Währung finden Sie bei ***Deutsch: Na klar!*** im World-Wide-Web unter www.mhhe.com/german.

Kulturtipp

Um die Jahrtausendwende führen die EU-Länder eine einheitliche Währung ein: den Euro. Vorher haben sie noch ihre eigene Währung. Die Geldscheine zeigen Menschen, die wegen ihrer wissenschaftlichen, kreativen oder kulturellen Leistungen berühmt sind, z.B. Clara Schumann auf dem deutschen Hundertmarkschein und Sigmund Freud auf der österreichischen Fünfzigschillingnote. Wie gut kennen Sie Ihr Geld? Wer oder was ist auf den verschiedenen Geldscheinen Ihres Landes abgebildet?

Wörter im Kontext

Finanzen der Studenten. Suggestion: How do people in your country spend their money? Brainstorm with the students, and compare this information with that in the graphics.

Thema 1

Finanzen der Studenten

Wie leben deutsche Studenten im Westen und im Osten? Antworten Sie mit Information aus dem Schaubild.

- Wie viel Geld brauchen deutsche Studenten **durchschnittlich** pro Monat?
- Wofür **geben** deutsche Studenten im Westen/Osten das meiste Geld **aus?**
- Wofür geben sie das wenigste Geld aus?
- Was gehört alles in die Rubrik Sonstiges?

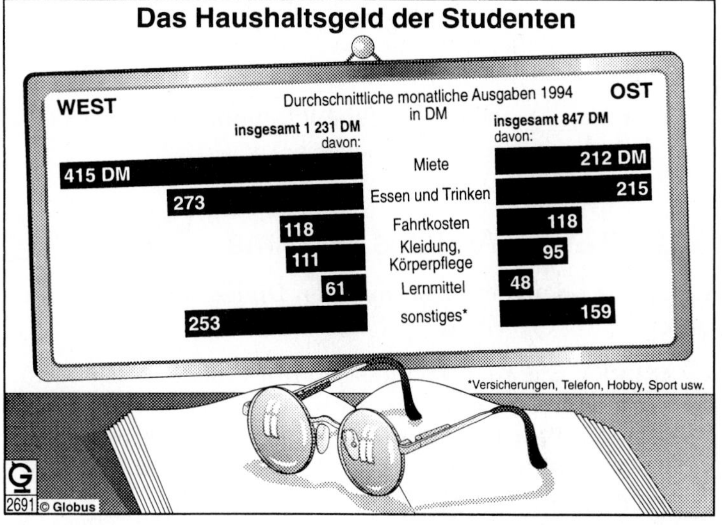

Realia. This information comes from the *Globus Kartendienst*.

Ihr monatliches Budget

- Wofür geben Sie monatlich Geld aus und ungefähr wie viel **im Durchschnitt?** Wofür geben Sie das meiste Geld aus? das wenigste? Wofür geben Sie nur ab und zu oder gar kein Geld aus?

  Prozent Ihrer monatlichen **Einnahmen**

Neue Wörter

- □ die **Ausgabe**
- □ **eigen**
- □ die **Ernährung**
- □ **monatlich**

_____ Miete
_____ **Nebenkosten** (**Strom,** Heizung, eigenes Telefon, Wasser, **Müll**)
_____ Auto (**Benzin, Reparaturen, Versicherung**)
_____ Fahrtkosten (öffentliche Verkehrsmittel, z.B. Bus, Flugzeug, Fahrten nach Hause)
_____ Ernährung (Essen und Trinken, auch Mensa, Restaurants)
_____ **Studiengebühren** (pro Semester, pro **Quartal**)
_____ Lernmittel (Bücher, **Hefte, Bleistifte, Kugelschreiber, Papier, Computerdisketten,** Sonstiges)
_____ Freizeit (Kino, Theater, Partys, Hobbys)
_____ **Sparen** (**Sparkonto,** Sparschwein)
_____ insgesamt (*total*)

Ihr monatliches Budget. Suggestion: To make this activity interactive, have students work in pairs, asking each other how much they spend on the items listed: *Wie viel gibst du für _______ aus?* Students may break down the categories in order to be more precise; e.g., *Lernmittel: Wie viel gibst du für Bücher aus? Hefte?*

- Haben Sie am Ende des Monats etwas Geld **übrig,** oder sind Sie **pleite?** Müssen Sie sich manchmal Geld von Freunden oder Ihrer Familie leihen?
- Schauen Sie sich das Schaubild oben noch einmal an. **Vergleichen** Sie Ihre durchschnittlichen monatlichen Ausgaben mit denen eines deutschen Studenten / einer deutschen Studentin. Wer hat höhere monatliche Ausgaben?

Aktivität 1 Pleite oder nicht? 

Schauen Sie sich Ihr monatliches Budget im **Thema 1** an. Vergleichen Sie jetzt Ihre Ausgaben mit den Ausgaben eines Partners / einer Partnerin, und berichten Sie darüber. Gebrauchen Sie folgende Redemittel.

Ich gebe das meiste Geld für _____ aus.

Das wenigste Geld gebe ich für _____ aus.

Ich gebe nur ab und zu oder gar kein Geld für _____ aus.

Für _____ und _____ gebe ich mehr/weniger Geld aus als mein Partner / meine Partnerin.

Aktivität 2 Andreas Dilemma  

Dialogue. Suggestion: With their books closed, have students listen to the dialogue once. Ask individuals to supply one fact from the dialogue. Encourage students to summarize as much as they can; then have them complete the following activity in pairs. Students read the statements aloud to one another and supply the missing information.

Lesen Sie oder hören Sie sich den Dialog an, und ergänzen Sie die Sätze unten.

ANDREA: Sag mal, könntest du mir einen Gefallen tun?
STEFAN: Was denn?
ANDREA: Würdest du mir bis Ende der Woche 50 Mark leihen? Ich bin total pleite.
STEFAN: Fünfzig Mark? Das ist viel Geld.
ANDREA: Ich musste 150 Mark für Bücher ausgeben. Und jetzt habe ich keinen Pfennig mehr übrig. Ich warte auf Geld von meinen Eltern.
STEFAN: Hm, ich würde es dir gern leihen. Aber 50 Mark habe ich selber nicht mehr. Ich kann dir höchstens 20 Mark leihen.
ANDREA: Ich zahle es dir bis Ende des Monats bestimmt zurück.
STEFAN: Eben hast du gesagt, bis Ende der Woche.
ANDREA: Ja, ja. Das Geld von meinen Eltern kann jeden Tag kommen.
STEFAN: Na gut. Hier ist ein Zwanziger.
ANDREA: Vielen Dank.

Andrea hat kein _____ mehr; sie ist total _____.[1] Sie möchte sich von Stefan _____.[2] Sie hat nämlich ihr ganzes Geld für _____ ausgegeben.[3] Deshalb hat sie jetzt nichts mehr für Essen und Trinken _____.[4] Stefan kann ihr aber _____ leihen.[5] Andrea hofft, dass sie Stefan das Geld bis _____ zurückzahlen kann.[6] Sie wartet auf _____.[7]

BAföG steht für **Bundesausbildungsförderungsgesetz.** Dieses Gesetz (*law*) regelt in Deutschland die staatliche Unterstützung von Schülern und Studenten, die ohne diese Hilfe keine Ausbildung oder Studium finanzieren könnten. BAföG besteht aus Darlehen (*loans*) und Zuschüssen (*stipends*).

Weiteres zum Thema Studium und Finanzen finden Sie bei ***Deutsch: Na klar!*** im World-Wide-Web unter www.mhhe.com/german.

Aktivität 3 Drei Studentenbudgets

Vergleichen Sie die Ausgaben der drei Studenten, und beantworten Sie die Fragen.

	MARION	WOLFGANG	CLAUDIA
Studienfach	Übersetzer (*translator*)/ Dolmetscher	Medizin	Romanistik/Politik
Studiengebühren	keine	keine	keine
Unterhalt (support)	Eltern	BAföG	Eltern
Miete	200 DM (1 Zi, Studentenwohnheim)	300 DM (1 Zi, Küche, Bad außerhalb)	500 DM (1 Zi, Küche, Bad)
Verkehrsmittel	keine (alles mit dem Fahrrad erreichbar)	40 DM	30 DM
Lebensmittel und Mensa	260 DM	350 DM	280 DM
Bücher/Arbeitsmittel	20 DM	100 DM	50 DM
Telefon	10 DM	60 DM (eigenes Telefon)	70 DM (eigenes Telefon)
Freizeit	80 DM	100 DM	100 DM
Fahrt nach Hause	40 DM (Mitfahrgelegenheit) 68 DM (mit der Bahn)	—	20 DM
Sonstiges	40 DM	30 DM	40 DM

1. Wie viel Geld geben Marion, Wolfgang und Claudia insgesamt monatlich aus?
2. Wofür geben sie das meiste Geld aus?
3. Wer bezahlt die höchste Miete? Wo ist die Miete billiger?
4. Warum bezahlt Marion weniger als die zwei anderen fürs Telefon?
5. Wer hat die höchsten Kosten für Bücher und Arbeitsmittel?
6. Was ist—außer (*besides*) Miete—günstig, wenn man im Studentenwohnheim wohnt?
7. Wer unterstützt (*supports*) die drei Studenten finanziell?
8. Warum hat Marion keine Ausgaben für Verkehrsmittel?
9. Wer lebt am sparsamsten (*most thriftily*)?

Aktivität 4 Einnahmen und Ausgaben 

Vier Studenten sprechen über ihre monatlichen Einnahmen und Ausgaben. Kreuzen Sie das Zutreffende (*the items that apply*) an. Notieren Sie unter „Ausgaben", wie viel die Studenten für ihre Miete ausgeben.

	STEFANIE	GERT	SUSANNE	MARTIN
1. Einnahmen von:				
a. Job während des Semesters	☐	☐	☒	☒
b. Job während der Semesterferien	☒	☒	☐	☒
c. Eltern	☒	☐	☒	☒
d. Stipendium/BAföG	☐	☒	☐	☐
2. Ausgaben für:				
a. Zimmer (privat)	______	300 DM	______	______
b. Studentenwohnheim	200 DM	______	______	______
c. eigene Wohnung	______	______	______	400 DM
d. Wohngemeinschaft	______	______	350 DM	______

Unsere eigenen vier Wände (idiomatic for "our own home"). Note: Students must refer to the floor plan to fill in the information. **Follow-up: Lückendiktat.** Ask students to draw two rectangles on a piece of paper to represent the outlines of a floor plan. Have students draw and write the names of the floors and rooms in the blank floor plans as they are described and dictated; they can check the accuracy of their floor plan by comparing it with the one here.

Thema 2

Unsere eigenen vier Wände

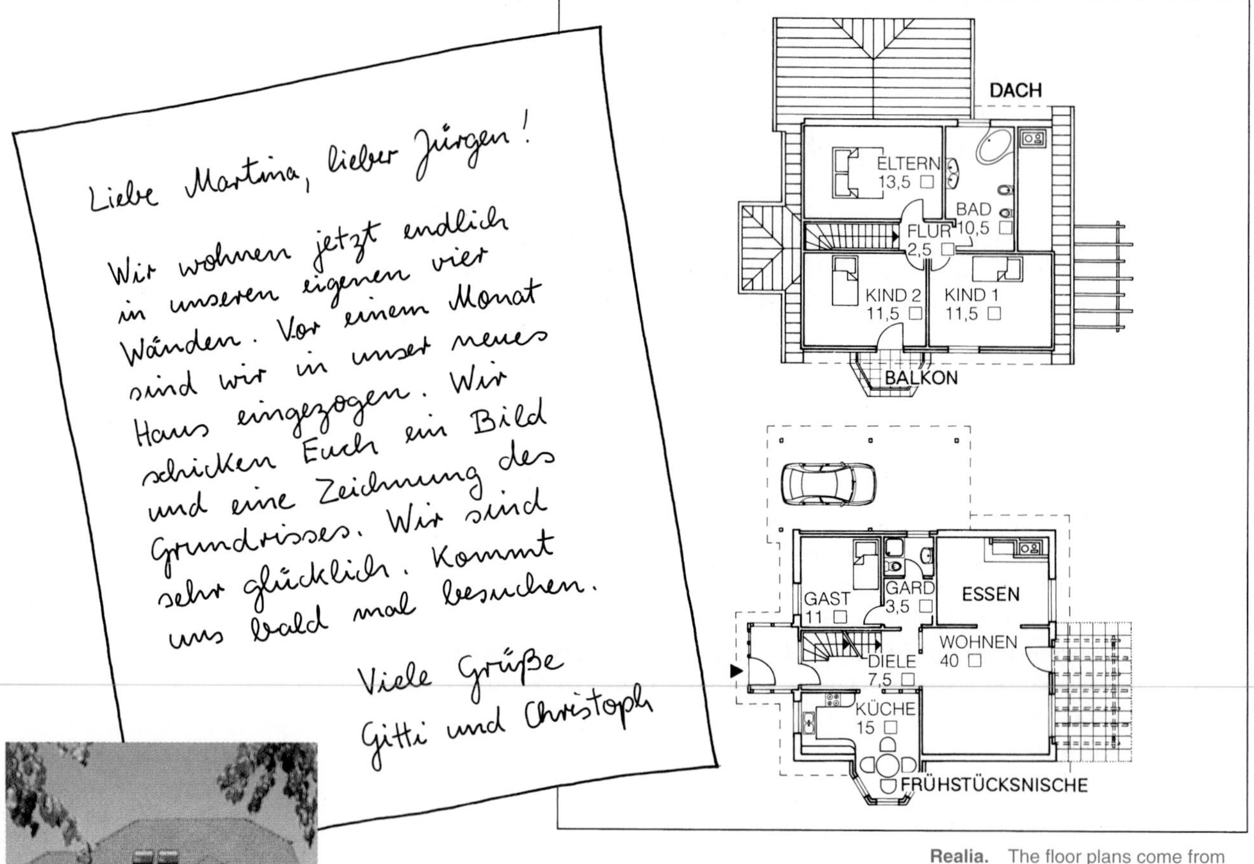

Liebe Martina, lieber Jürgen!

Wir wohnen jetzt endlich in unseren eigenen vier Wänden. Vor einem Monat sind wir in unser neues Haus eingezogen. Wir schicken Euch ein Bild und eine Zeichnung des Grundrisses. Wir sind sehr glücklich. Kommt uns bald mal besuchen.

Viele Grüße
Gitti und Christoph

Realia. The floor plans come from *Pro Fertighaus.*

Hier ist Gittis und Christophs neues Haus. Das Haus hat zwei Stockwerke: _____ und _____.[1] Vom **Eingang** kommt man zuerst in die _____.[2] Links neben der **Diele** ist die _____.[3] Von der Diele geht man rechts in die _____, komplett mit _____.[4] Von der Diele führt auch noch eine Tür ins _____.[5] Von da aus kommt man ins _____.[6] In der Diele führt eine **Treppe nach oben** ins **Dachgeschoss.** Man kommt zuerst in den _____.[7] Im Dachgeschoss sind drei Schlafzimmer, zwei _____ und ein _____.[8] Oben ist auch ein großes _____.[9] Und das Haus hat auch noch einen schönen _____.[10] Von der Diele führt auch eine Treppe **nach unten** in den **Keller** (nicht auf dem Grundriss). Für den Wagen haben Gitti und Christoph nur eine Überdachung. Später wollen sie sich eine Garage **bauen** lassen (*have built*).

Neue Wörter

- □ das **Dach**
- □ das **Dachgeschoss**
- □ **einziehen**
- □ der **Flur**
- □ die **Frühstücksnische**
- □ **Gard.** = die **Garderobe**
- □ **Gast** = das **Gästezimmer**
- □ **viele Grüße**
- □ die **Zeichnung**

Aktivität 5 Die ideale Wohnung

Drei Leute (Frau Heine, Herr Zumwald und Thomas) berichten, was für eine Wohnung sie suchen, und was ihnen in der Wohnung wichtig oder unwichtig ist. Stellen Sie zuerst fest, wer welchen Wohnungstyp sucht. Dann notieren Sie in der Tabelle, was jedem wichtig (w) oder unwichtig (u) ist.

Wer sucht:

ein Zimmer in einer Wohngemeinschaft? _____

eine Neubauwohnung in der Innenstadt? Frau Heine

ein älteres Haus außerhalb der Stadt? Herr Zumwald

eine gemütliche Altbauwohnung in der Stadt? Thomas

WICHTIG/UNWICHTIG	FRAU HEINE	HERR ZUMWALD	THOMAS
Lage	w	w	w
Zentralheizung	w	w	w
Balkon	w		
Garage	u		u
Garten		w	
Teppichboden (carpeting)		u	u
Waschmaschine			w

Aktivität 6 Hin und her: Meine Wohnung—deine Wohnung

Aktivität 6. Suggestion: Make sure students go beyond the Model in asking questions: *Wie groß ist das Wohnzimmer? Hat die Wohnung ein Bad oder mehr als ein Bad?* **Note:** For the personalization phase, students should imagine that they have just bought their dream home.

Diese Leute haben entweder eine neue Wohnung oder ein neues Haus gekauft. Wer hat was gekauft? Wie viele Stockwerke gibt es? Wie groß ist das Wohnzimmer? Wie viele WCs oder Badezimmer gibt es?

BEISPIEL: S1: Was für eine Wohnung hat Bettina Neuendorf gekauft?
S2: Eine Eigentumswohnung.
S1: Wie viele Stockwerke hat die Wohnung?
S2: Eins.
S1: Und wie viele Schlafzimmer?

PERSON	TYP	STOCKWERKE	SCHLAFZIMMER	WOHNZIMMER	WC/BAD
Bettina Neuendorf	Eigentumswohnung	eins	eins, aber auch ein kleines Gästezimmer	mit Esszimmer kombiniert 30 Quadratmeter	eins
Uwe und Marion Baumgärtner	Haus	zwei	drei: Elternschlafzimmer, Kinderschlafzimmer, Gästezimmer	sehr groß mit Balkon 37 Quadratmeter	zwei Badezimmer: eins im Dachgeschoss und eins im Erdgeschoss
Sven Kersten	Eigentumswohnung	zwei	zwei, eins als Gästezimmer benutzt	mit Esszimmer zusammen 35 Quadratmeter, Balkon vom Wohnzimmer	zwei, ein WC und ein Bad
Carola Schubärth	Haus	eins	zwei: ein Schlafzimmer ist Arbeitszimmer	klein 25 Quadratmeter	ein Bad
ich					
mein Partner / meine Partnerin					

Aktivität 7 Der Grundriss

A. Sie sehen auf der nächsten Seite einen Grundriss. Identifizieren Sie, wo das Wohnzimmer, das Esszimmer, die Küche, das Schlafzimmer und andere Räume sind. Beschreiben Sie dann, wo die Zimmer liegen. Diese Wohnung liegt im dritten Stock eines großen Wohnhauses. Man kann die Treppe hinaufgehen oder mit dem Aufzug fahren.

Zuerst kommt man in _____.
Rechts von _____ ist _____.
Von der _____ führt eine Tür ins _____.
Neben der _____ ist ein _____ und daneben ein _____.
Vom Wohnzimmer geht man auf _____.

B. Zeichnen Sie nun den Grundriss Ihrer Wohnung / Ihres Hauses. (Wenn Sie in einem Studentenheim wohnen, zeichnen Sie eine Phantasiewohnung.) Geben Sie Ihrem Partner / Ihrer Partnerin die Zeichung, und beschreiben Sie ihm/ihr, wo die Zimmer liegen. Ihr Partner / Ihre Partnerin setzt die Zimmernamen in den Grundriss. Schauen Sie sich dann die Zeichnung an, um zu sehen, ob Ihr Partner / Ihre Partnerin alles richtig identifiziert hat.

Beginnen Sie so: Zuerst kommt man in _____.

Thema 3

Mieten und Vermieten

Ein Mietgesuch

Realia. This student flyer seeks a housing opportunity in Göttingen. It was found on the university's characteristic bulletin board, the so-called *Schwarzes Brett.*

1. Gö = Göttingen *university town in north central Germany*
2. *community*
3. *since*
4. *lead*

Mietangebote

1\.

Land-WG sucht Mitbewohner(in)!

Wir, Bruno (26) und Britta (21), Hund und Katze, vermieten eine ganze obere Etage in einem älteren Bauernhaus 1 1/2 Zimmer, ca 38 qm. Benutzbar[1] sind Küche, Bad, großer Garten. Die Miete beträgt monatlich 300-DM, plus 30.-DM Nebenkosten. 20 km von Göttingen. Ab 1. Juni.

2\.

Mieter gesucht für große, **helle** 3 Zimmer in Neubau, ab 1. August, ca. 70 qm. Balkon, eingerichtete Küche (Spülmaschine, Kühlschrank), Waschraum mit Maschine, Zentralheizung, Teppichboden, Bad und WC, Garage. Zu Fuß ca. 15 Minuten von der Universität, 5 vom Bahnhof, 10 Minuten vom Zentrum. Tiere nicht erwünscht. Miete DM 680.-Nebenkosten DM 83.-

1\. *available for use*

Lesen Sie zuerst das Mietgesuch auf der vorigen Seite. Wer sucht was und wo?

Lesen Sie dann die zwei Mietangebote. Welches Angebot würden Sie Brigitte und Matthias empfehlen?

Ich finde Angebot Nummer ____ ideal für Brigitte und Matthias, denn es gibt dort ____.

Ich würde Brigitte und Matthias Angebot Nummer ____ empfehlen, denn ____. Es gibt jedoch ein Problem: ____

Neue Wörter

- □ **ab 1. (erstem) Juni =**
- □ **bald**
- □ das **Bauernhaus**
- □ **betragen**
- □ **ca. = circa**
- □ **einrichten**
- □ die **Etage**
- □ **sich freuen über (*acc.*)**
- □ **ganz**
- □ der **Hund**
- □ die **Katze**
- □ der **Kühlschrank**
- □ der **Mikrowellenherd**
- □ **mögl. = möglichst**
- □ der **Neubau**
- □ **qm.** = der **Quadratmeter**
- □ **spätestens**
- □ die **Spülmaschine**
- □ der **Teppichboden**
- □ das **Tier**
- □ die **Umgebung**
- □ **vermieten**

Aktivität 8 Drinnen und draußen

Was passt zusammen?

1. ____ Man stellt sie im Winter an.
2. ____ Die gehören zu den Nebenkosten.
3. ____ Man stellt den Wagen dort hinein.
4. ____ Hier kocht man.
5. ____ Dort wäscht man sich.
6. ____ Der liegt auf dem Boden.
7. ____ Damit wäscht man.
8. ____ So etwas findet man meist auf dem Land.
9. ____ Der hält z.B. Milch, Käse, Fleisch und Gemüse frisch.

a. der Teppich
b. die Waschmaschine
c. Strom, Heizung, Telefon
d. die Zentralheizung
e. der Kühlschrank
f. die Garage
g. das Bauernhaus
h. die Küche
i. das Bad

Aktivität 9 Ist die Wohnung noch frei?

Frau Krenz hat eine große, helle Dreizimmerwohnung zu vermieten. Die Anzeige stand in der Zeitung. Herr Brunner hat auf die Anzeige hin angerufen. Er weiß, wie groß die Wohnung ist und wie hoch die Miete ist. Was will er noch von der Vermieterin wissen? Kreuzen Sie alles Zutreffende an.

1. Herr Brunner will wissen,
   - ☒ ob die Heizung in den Nebenkosten einbegriffen ist
   - ☐ ob die Küche einen Mikrowellenherd hat
   - ☐ wie er vom Haus in die Innenstadt kommt
   - ☒ wo die Wohnung liegt
   - ☒ ob es einen Aufzug gibt
   - ☐ wo man parken kann
2. Frau Krenz will von Herrn Brunner wissen,
   - ☐ wie viele Kinder er hat
   - ☒ ob er verheiratet ist
   - ☐ ob er Arbeit hat
   - ☒ wann er vorbeikommen kann
   - ☐ wann er einziehen möchte

Weiteres zum Thema Wohnungsangebote finden Sie bei ***Deutsch: Na klar!*** im World-Wide-Web unter www.mhhe.com/german.

Aktivität 10 Ein interessantes Angebot

Sie interessieren sich für ein Mietangebot, das Sie in der Zeitung gesehen haben und rufen deshalb den Vermieter / die Vermieterin an. Benutzen Sie die Konversationstips.

S1 VERMIETER/VERMIETERIN	S2 ANRUFER/ANRUFERIN
1. State your last name.	**2.** Greet the person, state your last name, and ask whether the apartment is still available.
3. Say it is still available.	**4.** Ask how much the rent is.
5. State a price.	**6.** Ask whether this price includes all household bills.
7. State that everything is included **(inklusive)** except the heat.	**8.** Tell the landlord/landlady that you have a cat or dog.
9. Say that it's all right.	**10.** Find out where the apartment is located.
11. Give the address and location. Suggest to the caller a time when he/she can come to see it.	**12.** Say that the time is suitable.
13. Say good-bye.	**14.** Say good-bye.

Grammatik im Kontext

Referring to Things and Ideas: *da*-Compounds°

°Adverbialpronomen

In German, a personal pronoun following a preposition generally refers to a person or another living being.

Der Student wartet auf die Professorin.	*The student is waiting for the professor.*
Er wartet schon lange auf **sie.**	*He has been waiting for her for a long time.*

When the object of a preposition refers to a thing or an idea, this is represented by a compound consisting of the demonstrative adverb **da** and the preposition, a word referred to as a **da**-compound. **Da** becomes **dar** when the preposition begins with a vowel.

Marion wartet auf einen Brief von ihrem Freund.	*Marion is waiting for a letter from her boyfriend.*
Sie wartet schon lange **darauf.**	*She has been waiting for it for a long time.*
—Bist du für eine Geschwindigkeitsbegrenzung auf der Autobahn?	*Are you for a speed limit on the freeway?*
—Ich bin **dafür,** aber viele Autofahrer sind **dagegen.**	*I am for it but many drivers are against it.*
Manfred hat ein neues Motorrad.	*Manfred has a new motorcycle.*
Er will **damit** um die Welt fahren.	*He wants to drive around the world with it.*

Da/Dar can combine with most accusative and dative prepositions to form a compound. Some common ones are:

daran	**dahinter**	**darunter**
darauf	**darin**	**davon**
daraus	**damit**	**davor**
dabei	**danach**	**dazu**
dafür	**daneben**	
dagegen	**darüber**	

The preposition **ohne** does not form a **da**-compound; it is always used with an accusative pronoun.

$$\begin{array}{lcl} \text{Ich brauche Erfolg.} \rightarrow & & \\ \text{Geld.} \rightarrow & \text{Ohne} \left\{ \begin{array}{c} \text{ihn} \\ \text{es} \\ \text{sie} \end{array} \right\} & \text{kann ich nicht leben.} \\ \text{Liebe.} \rightarrow & & \end{array}$$

The Adverb *dahin*

The adverbial pronoun **dahin** (there) is commonly used in conjunction with verbs of motion to refer to expressions of location.

Review: Go over **wo . . . hin** in conjunction with **da . . . hin** to emphasize the customary splitting of these pronouns in conversational German.

Gehst du gleich **zu Achims Party?**	—Ich gehe später **dahin.**
Wann fliegt Martina **nach Spanien?**	—Sie fliegt überhaupt nicht **dahin.**
Ich muss heute **zur Bank.**	—Ich muss auch **dahin.**

In spoken German **dahin** is often abbreviated to **hin.**

Hans muss noch zur Bank.	Er will erst später **hin.**

Also in spoken German, **da** may be placed at the beginning of a sentence for emphasis, while **hin** is placed at the end of the sentence.

Gehst du oft ins Museum?	**Da** gehe ich nur selten **hin.**

Analyse

- Identify all **da**-compounds in the following text.
- What nouns do these **da**-compounds refer to?
- Restate all **da**-compounds as prepositional objects using the nouns to which they refer.

Sabines Zimmer im Studentenwohnheim

Sie zahlt nur 300 Mark pro Monat dafür. Links an der Wand ist ein Waschbecken. Darüber hängt ein Spiegel. Daneben hängt ein Haken mit einem Handtuch. Rechts an der Wand steht ein Schreibtisch. Davor steht ein Stuhl. Darauf liegen viele Bücher und Papiere. Hinten an der Wand steht ein Bett. Darunter liegen Sabines Schuhe. Rechts neben dem Bett steht ein kleines Bücherregal. Darüber ist ein Fenster mit einer Fensterbank. Darauf steht ein Vogelkäfig. Sabines Kanarienvogel, Caruso, wohnt darin und singt pausenlos.

Verbs with Fixed Prepositions

Many German verbs require the use of fixed prepositions; these combinations are usually different from their English equivalents. Some examples are:

Angst haben vor (+ *dat.*)	to be afraid of
sich ärgern über (+ *acc.*)	to be annoyed about
aufhören mit	to stop (*doing something*)
bitten um	to ask for, request
denken an (+ *acc.*)	to think of
fragen nach	to ask about
sich freuen auf (+ *acc.*)	to look forward to
sich freuen über (+ *acc.*)	to be happy about
sich interessieren für	to be interested in
warten auf (+ *acc.*)	to wait for

Verbs with Fixed Prepositions. Suggestion: Ask students for any other verbs with special prepositions that they might remember. Stress the importance of the correct use of prepositions when speaking idiomatically.

Übung 1 Kontraste

Sabine und ihr Freund Jürgen haben nicht viel gemein (*in common*). Ergänzen Sie die fehlenden Pronominaladverbien.

1. Jürgen gibt viel Geld für Unterhaltung (*entertainment*) aus.
   Sabine gibt so gut wie nichts _____ aus.
2. Jürgen interessiert sich überhaupt nicht für Fußball.
   Sabine interessiert sich leidenschaftlich (*passionately*) _____.
3. Jürgen hat Angst vor dem Staatsexamen.
   Sabine hat auch ein wenig Angst _____.
4. Sabine freut sich immer über kleine Geschenke.
   Jürgen freut sich nie _____.
5. Sabine denkt immer an alle Geburtstage.
   Jürgen denkt nie _____.
6. Sabine hat mit dem Rauchen aufgehört.
   Jürgen will einfach nicht _____ aufhören.
7. Jürgen kommt immer pünktlich zur Vorlesung.
   Sabine kommt nie pünktlich _____.
8. Jürgen ärgert sich über die laute Musik nebenan.
   Sabine ärgert sich überhaupt nicht _____.
9. Sabine freut sich auf das Ende des Studiums.
   Jürgen freut sich überhaupt nicht _____.

No. 7. Note: Remind students that location takes a special *da*-compound.

Übung 2 Beschreibungen und Situationen

Setzen Sie ein passendes Pronominaladverb in jede Lücke ein.

1. In meinem Zimmer steht ein Sofa. _____ steht eine Stehlampe. _____ steht ein kleiner Tisch. _____ liegt ein Pantoffel.
2. Gestern sind wir ins Kino gegangen. _____ sind wir eine Pizza essen gegangen, und _____ haben wir noch ein Bier getrunken.

3. Im Sommer mache ich eine Reise nach Spanien. Ich freue mich schon _____.
4. Letztes Jahr hat Robert in Göttingen studiert und viel Spaß gehabt. Er denkt noch oft _____.
5. Gestern kam endlich ein Brief von Jürgen. Melanie hat sich sehr _____ gefreut. Sie hat lange _____ gewartet.
6. Morgen hat Thomas eine große Prüfung. Er hat Angst _____. Er muss schon um acht Uhr im Prüfungsraum sein. Er ärgert sich _____, weil er nämlich ein Morgenmuffel (*a grouch in the morning*) ist.

Übung 3 Eine Umfrage im Deutschkurs 

Stellen Sie einander die folgenden Fragen in kleinen Gruppen oder im Plenum.

BEISPIEL: Wie viele Leute haben Angst vor Prüfungen? →
Sechs Leute haben Angst davor.

1. Wie viele Leute interessieren sich für Yoga? für Meditation?
2. Wer hat Angst vor Prüfungen?
3. Wer denkt (oft, nie, manchmal) an das Leben nach dem Studium?
4. Wie viele Leute sind für oder gegen eine nationale Krankenversicherung (*health insurance*)? Wer soll für die Versicherung zahlen? Arbeitgeber? Arbeitnehmer? der Staat?
5. Wer freut sich auf das Ende des Studiums? des Semesters?
6. Wer ärgert sich, wenn man in seiner Nähe raucht?

Asking About Things and Ideas: *wo*-Compounds°

°wo-Komposita

There are two ways to formulate questions with prepositions when asking about things or ideas. One way is to use a preposition with the interrogative pronoun **was.**

An was denkst du?	*What are you thinking of?*
Für was interessiert er sich?	*What is he interested in?*
Auf was warten Sie?	*What are you waiting for?*

Another way is to combine the interrogative pronoun **wo** with a preposition to form a **wo**-compound. **Wo** becomes **wor**- when the preposition begins with a vowel.

Woran denkst du?	*What are you thinking of?*
Wofür interessiert er sich?	*What is he interested in?*
Worauf warten Sie?	*What are you waiting for?*

Note that in German the preposition is never placed at the end of the sentence. All prepositions that form **da**-compounds can also form **wo**-compounds.

Übung 4 Ich möchte das gern wissen 

Formulieren Sie zuerst Fragen. Arbeiten Sie dann zusammen mit einem Partner / einer Partnerin, und beantworten Sie die Fragen abwechselnd (*taking turns*).

Wofür	freust du dich?
Womit	denkst du oft?
Woran	gibst du viel Geld aus?
Worauf	beschäftigst du dich am Wochenende?
Worüber	interessierst du dich?
Wovor	wartest du?
	hast du Angst?
	ärgerst du dich?

Subjunctive°

der Konjunktiv

Verbs may be in the indicative, the imperative, or the subjunctive mood. The indicative mood is used to express facts and to ask questions. The imperative mood is used to express commands and requests. The subjunctive mood expresses polite requests and conveys wishful thinking, conjectures, and conditions that are contrary to fact. The subjunctive is also used in indirect discourse to report what someone else said. This latter use will be presented in **Kapitel 13.**

Expressing Requests Politely

In contemporary German, the most common use of the subjunctive is for polite requests. Consider the following examples.

Ich **möchte** gern einige Reiseschecks einlösen.	*I would like to cash some traveler's checks.*
Ich **hätte** gern eine Tasse Kaffee.	*I would like a cup of coffee.*
Könntest du mir einen Gefallen tun?	*Could you do me a favor?*
Würdest du mir 50 Mark leihen?	*Would you lend me 50 marks?*
Dürfte ich mal Ihren Pass sehen?	*May I see your passport?*

The forms **möchte, hätte, könntest, würdest,** and **dürfte** are subjunctive forms of the verbs **mögen, haben, können, werden,** and **dürfen.** They are frequently used in polite requests.

Present Subjunctive* of Weak Verbs, Irregular Weak Verbs, and Modals

Present Subjunctive of Weak Verbs. Point Out: In English, "would" plus an infinitive is most often used to express nonreality, whereas German has a choice between two forms: 1. the subjunctive based on the simple past tense form, or 2. **würde** plus an infinitive. There is no difference in meaning between the two forms. More and more, the **würde** plus infinitive construction is replacing the subjunctive based on the simple past tense.

The subjunctive of regular weak verbs is identical to the simple past tense.

INFINITIVE	SIMPLE PAST	SUBJUNCTIVE
wünschen	wünschte	wünschte

Irregular weak verbs, such as **haben** and **wissen,** form the subjunctive by adding an umlaut to the simple past stem.

INFINITIVE	SIMPLE PAST	SUBJUNCTIVE
haben	hatte	h**ä**tte
wissen	wusste	w**ü**sste

Modals use the stem vowel of the infinitive in the subjunctive.

INFINITIVE	SIMPLE PAST	SUBJUNCTIVE
dürfen	durfte	d**ü**rfte
können	konnte	k**ö**nnte
mögen	mochte	m**ö**chte
müssen	musste	m**ü**sste
sollen	sollte	s**o**llte
wollen	wollte	w**o**llte

The verb endings in the subjunctive are the same as in the simple past tense.

haben SUBJUNCTIVE			
ich	hätte	wir	hätte**n**
du	hätte**st**	ihr	hätte**t**
er / sie / es	hätte	sie	hätte**n**
Sie hätte**n**			

*The forms of the subjunctive described here are also known as Subjunctive II, because they are derived from the simple past tense, the second principal part of the verb.

Übung 5 Wünsche im Restaurant

Formulieren Sie die Wünsche noch einmal mit **hätte gern** oder **möchte gern.**

BEISPIEL: Hans will ein Bier. →
Hans hätte gern ein Bier.
oder Hans möchte gern ein Bier.

1. Wir wollen die Speisekarte.
2. Ich will eine Tasse Kaffee.
3. Mein Freund will ein Bier.
4. Und was wollen Sie?
5. Willst du ein Stück Kuchen?
6. Wollen Sie sonst noch etwas?
7. Nein, wir wollen die Rechnung.

Present Subjunctive of Strong Verbs

The subjunctive of strong verbs is formed by adding an **e** to the simple past stem. If the stem vowel is **a, o,** or **u,** it takes an umlaut.

INFINITIVE	SIMPLE PAST	SUBJUNCTIVE
sein	war	w**ä**r**e**
fahren	fuhr	f**ü**hr**e**
fliegen	flog	fl**ö**g**e**
gehen	ging	ging**e**
werden	wurde	w**ü**rd**e**

sein SUBJUNCTIVE			
ich	wäre	wir	wäre**n**
du	wäre**st**	ihr	wäre**t**
er / sie / es	wäre	sie	wäre**n**
Sie wäre**n**			

As with the subjunctive of the weak verbs, the verb endings are the same as those used in the simple past tense.

The Use of *würde* with an Infinitive

In spoken German, the present subjunctive has been largely replaced by the construction **würde** plus infinitive. Like English *would,* the **würde** form can be used with almost any infinitive to express polite requests or wishes, or to give advice.

Würdest du mir **helfen?**	*Would you help me?*
Ich **würde** gerne **mitfahren.**	*I would like to come along.*
Ich **würde** nicht so viel **trinken.**	*I wouldn't drink so much.*

Verbs that are generally not used with **würde** include **sein, haben, wissen,** and the modals.

Übung 6 Etwas höflicher, bitte!

Drücken Sie die folgenden Wünsche höflicher aus.

BEISPIEL: Leih mir bitte 50 Mark! →
Würdest du mir bitte 50 Mark leihen?
oder Könntest du mir bitte 50 Mark leihen?

1. Gib mir bitte mein Geld zurück!
2. Können Sie mir 100 Mark wechseln (*change*)?
3. Darf ich mal Ihren Führerschein sehen?
4. Unterschreiben (*sign*) Sie hier, bitte!
5. Kannst du mir bitte das Postamt (*post office*) zeigen?
6. Geben Sie mir Reiseschecks für 500 Mark.
7. Ich will mit Kreditkarte bezahlen.
8. Könnt ihr mir 100 Mark bis zum Monatsende leihen?
9. Tu mir bitte einen Gefallen (*favor*)!

Übung 6. Note: Because subjunctive forms to express politeness are commonly used in German, use this exercise to elicit as many variations of individual sentences from students as possible. Rephrase imperatives with **würde** or **könnte** plus an infinitive; questions requesting something, with **würde** or **könnte;** rephrase sentences with **will,** using **möchte (gern). Suggestion:** One student requests something of another, who in turn says *Etwas höflicher bitte: Würdest du bitte . . .*, etc. **Suggestion:** Have students make up additional requests in the imperative. Ask individual students to rephrase the requests more politely.

Übung 7 Würden Sie das machen?

Sagen Sie, ob Sie die folgenden Dinge machen würden.

BEISPIEL: einem Fremden auf der Straße Geld geben →
S1: Würdest du einem Fremden auf der Straße Geld geben?
S2: Ja, ich würde einem Fremden Geld geben.
oder Ich würde ihm kein Geld geben.

1. einem Freund / einer Freundin dein Auto leihen
2. einem Freund / einer Freundin die Miete bezahlen
3. für sehr schlechtes Essen im Restaurant bezahlen
4. mehr ausgeben, als du verdienst
5. eine Stunde vor dem Kino auf einen Freund / eine Freundin warten
6. allein in Urlaub fahren
7. nachts allein im Park spazieren gehen

Expressing Wishes, Hypothetical Situations, or Preferences

Wishes introduced by the conjunction **wenn** usually include the particles **doch, doch nur,** or simply **nur.**

Wenn ich **doch nur** wüsste, wo meine Autoschlüssel sind.	*If I only knew where my car keys are.*
Wenn der Bus **doch** endlich **käme.**	*If only the bus would finally come.*

Ich wünschte or **ich wollte** (*I wish*) are fixed expressions in the subjunctive. They are always followed by a verb in the subjunctive or **würde** + infinitive.

Ich wollte, die Geschäfte in Deutschland **wären** länger geöffnet.	*I wish (that) the stores in Germany were open longer.*
Frau Schiff **wünschte,** sie **könnte** auch abends einkaufen.	*Ms. Schiff wishes she could go shopping in the evenings, too.*

Suggestion: The expression **an seiner/ihrer Stelle** allows students to practice the subjunctive without having to formulate a complex conditional clause with **wenn.** Create short sentences with weak verbs, e.g., *sparen, kaufen, reisen, studieren, sagen, warten, mit Kreditkarte bezahlen, bar bezahlen.* Say *Hans spart nicht.* The student response is *An seiner Stelle würde ich sparen.* Have another student give the English meaning: "(If I were) in his place, I would save money." Other cues: *Er kauft ein Motorrad. Er reist allein. Er kauft auf Kredit. Er wartet stundenlang auf seine Freundin.*

The expression **an deiner Stelle** (*if I were you / in your place*) is always used with a verb in the subjunctive. The possessive adjective changes depending on the person in question.

An deiner Stelle würde ich alles bar bezahlen.	*If I were you, I would pay cash for everything.*
An seiner Stelle würde ich nicht mit Kreditkarte bezahlen.	*If I were in his place, I would not pay with a credit card.*

Übung 8 Was sind die Tatsachen hier?

Übung 8. Follow-up: Have students state their own wishes and then give the facts.

Beschreiben Sie die Tatsachen. Benutzen Sie dabei den *Indikativ.*

BEISPIEL: Ich wünschte, ich könnte dir 50 Mark leihen. →
Ich habe aber kein Geld. Ich kann dir nichts leihen.

1. Ich wünschte, ich hätte eine Kreditkarte.
2. Wenn die Miete doch nicht so hoch wäre.
3. Ich wünschte, ich könnte genug Geld für eine Weltreise sparen.
4. Wenn Klaus doch nicht so viel fürs Telefon ausgeben würde.
5. Ich wünschte, ich könnte in München eine Wohnung finden.
6. Mein Freund hätte gern einen BMW.
7. Ich wünschte, mein Freund würde nicht so schnell fahren.
8. Ich wünschte, das Semester wäre zu Ende.
9. Ich wüsste gern, wo es preiswerte Bücher gibt.
10. Meine Freunde wünschten, sie hätten mehr Freizeit.

Übung 9 Wenn doch nur . . .

Was wünscht Helga sich?

BEISPIEL: Helgas Katze ist weg. →
Wenn die Katze doch wieder da wäre!

1. Helga kann ihre Schlüssel nicht finden.
2. Sie hat keine Zeit, sie zu suchen.
3. Sie weiß nicht, wo sie sind.
4. Ihr Freund kommt erst spät nach Hause.
5. Sie ist ganz allein.
6. Sie kann nicht zu Hause bleiben.
7. Sie muss um drei zu einer Vorlesung gehen.

Übung 10 Wer wünscht sich was?

Drücken Sie aus, was sich diese Leute wünschen. Benutzen Sie dabei Konjunktivformen.

BEISPIEL: Gerhard hat keine Zeit. Was wünscht er sich? →
Er wünschte sich, er hätte mehr Zeit.

1. Frau Schmidt fährt viel zu schnell auf der Autobahn. Was wünscht sich Herr Schmidt?
2. Herr Schmidt kann nicht Auto fahren. Was wünscht sich Frau Schmidt?
3. Es gibt nichts Interessantes im Fernsehen. Was wünsche ich mir?
4. Im Kino läuft kein guter Film. Was wünscht sich Max?
5. Die Gäste bleiben viel zu lange, es ist schon nach Mitternacht. Was wünscht sich der Gastgeber?
6. Morgen fliegt mein Freund nach Tahiti. Ich muss leider zu Hause bleiben. Was wünsche ich mir?
7. Alex und Tanja besuchen Madrid, aber sie können leider kein Spanisch. Was wünschen sie sich?
8. Wir wissen nicht, wie man viel Geld verdienen kann. Was wünschen wir uns?
9. Petra weiß nicht, wo sie eine gute Arbeitsstelle finden kann. Was wünscht sie sich?
10. Die Studiengebühren sind zu hoch. Was wünschen die Studenten sich?

Übung 11. Suggestion: Have students focus on the situations in the drawings, asking them to describe the scenes. Then have them express what they would do if they found themselves in one of those situations. Encourage them to use the verbs given with the exercise, but also to go beyond them.

Übung 11 Heikle Situationen

Beschreiben Sie die Situation auf jedem Bild. Suchen Sie einen passenden Ausdruck aus der Liste, und sagen Sie, was Sie an seiner oder ihrer Stelle tun würden.

BEISPIEL: An ihrer Stelle würde ich weggehen.

1.

2.

3.

1. weggehen (ging weg); „Guten Tag" sagen; freundlich sein; nichts sagen; böse sein; nicht mit ihm reden (*speak*); freundlich lächeln; ?
2. eine Reparaturwerkstatt anrufen; sich ins Auto setzen und warten, bis der Regen aufhört; Hilfe anbieten; um Hilfe bitten; zu Fuß weitergehen; den Reifen wechseln (*change the tire*); ?
3. nicht länger warten; allein ins Kino gehen; ungeduldig (*impatient*) sein; bei . . . anrufen; ?

Talking About Contrary-to-Fact Conditions

Compare the following sentences:

Wenn ich Geld **brauche, gehe** ich zur Bank.	*When I need money, I go to the bank.*
Wenn ich Geld **hätte, würde** ich mir einen neuen Wagen kaufen.	*If I had money, I would buy a new car.*

The first example states a condition of fact; therefore, the indicative mood is used. The second example states a condition that is contrary to fact. The implication is that the speaker does not have enough money to buy a new car. Therefore the subjunctive is used, in German as well as in English.

Analyse

Die Schnecke in diesem Cartoon singt ein bekanntes deutsches Volkslied (*folk song*).

- What would the snail like to be?
- What verbs express the snail's wishful thinking? How do these forms differ from the standard subjunctive forms? What could be the reasons for this?

Übung 12. Suggestion: Have one student ask another *Was würden Sie (würdest du) machen, wenn Sie (du) Zeit hätten (hättest)?* The second student answers with a complete sentence: *Wenn ich Zeit hätte, würde ich eine Reise machen.*

1. Unglückliche . . . *unhappy conditions*
2. *little bird*
3. *little wings*
4. *lame*

Follow-up: Half the class writes **wenn**-clauses, the other half result-clauses only. Call on students to combine clauses; the attempt might produce some odd and amusing combinations!

Realia. *Wenn ich ein Vöglein wär:* This cartoon is from a book by Eva Haue, *Vielleicht sind wir doch zu verschieden.*

Übung 12 Was würden Sie machen, wenn . . . ?

Sagen Sie, was Sie machen würden, wenn alles anders wäre.

BEISPIEL: Wenn ich Talent hätte, würde ich Opernsängerin.

Wenn ich Zeit hätte,
Geld
Talent
mehr Freizeit
weniger Stress im Leben
Präsident/Präsidentin wäre,
?

ein berühmter / eine berühmte _____ (z.B. Sänger/Sängerin)
interessante Leute kennen lernen
öfter ins Kino gehen
eine Insel im Pazifik kaufen
jeden Tag die Zeitung lesen
?

Übung 13 Rat geben 

Stellen Sie sich vor, ein Freund / eine Freundin hat ein Problem. Was raten Sie?

BEISPIEL: S1: Ich bin total pleite. Was soll ich nun machen?
S2: An deiner Stelle würde ich mir eine Arbeit suchen.

MÖGLICHE PROBLEME

kann keine Wohnung/Arbeit finden
zahlt zu viel Miete
langweilt sich (*is bored*)
hat Probleme mit Mitbewohnern, Freundin, Eltern
kann nicht schlafen
hat kein Geld, will aber gern um die Welt reisen
weiß nicht, was er/sie nach dem Studium machen soll
gibt zu viel für Unterhaltung aus
spart nicht genug

The Past Subjunctive°

°der Konjunktiv der Vergangenheit

The past subjunctive is used to express wishes, hypotheses, and conjectures concerning events in the past.

Wenn ich in der Lotterie **gewonnen hätte, wäre** ich überglücklich **gewesen.** — *If I had won the lottery, I would have been ecstatic.*

The hypothesis (*If I had . . .*) speculates about an event in the past: The speaker did not win the lottery. Both English and German require the past subjunctive in this case.

The past subjunctive forms are derived from the past perfect tense. Use the subjunctive form **hätte** or **wäre** plus the past participle of the main verb.

INFINITIVE	PAST PERFECT	PAST SUBJUNCTIVE
kaufen	ich hatte gekauft	ich hätte gekauft (*I had bought / would have bought*)
sein	ich war gewesen	ich wäre gewesen (*I had been / would have been*)

Ich wünschte, ich **hätte** den neuen Porsche nicht **gekauft.** — *I wish I had not bought the new Porsche.*
Ein gebrauchter Wagen **wäre** billiger **gewesen.** — *A used car would have been cheaper.*

Use **hätte** or **wäre** according to the same rules that determine the use of **haben** or **sein** in the perfect tense: Intransitive verbs that indicate a change of location (**gehen, fahren**) or a change of condition (**werden**), as well as **bleiben** and **sein,** take **wäre** (**sein**); all others take **hätte** (**haben**). The **würde**-form is not used in the past subjunctive.

A clause stating a hypothetical situation usually begins with the conjunction **wenn.** As in English, the conjunction can be omitted, in which case the conjugated verb is placed at the beginning of the sentence.

Hätten wir nur gewusst, dass Ute hier ist, so wären wir sofort vorbeigekommen.	*Had we only known that Ute was here, we would have come right over.*

Analyse

Schauen Sie sich den Cartoon an.

- Find the verb forms in the past subjunctive and give their infinitives.
- What variation from the standard form do you see?
- What is the woman speculating about?
- What stereotype does the cartoon allude to? Formulate a conclusion to the hypothesis **"Wenn ich als Blondine geboren wäre . . ."**
- What is the reality of her life?

Analyse. Suggestion: Have students first describe the cartoon in German. Ask *Finden Sie diese Situation typisch? Komisch?*

Realia. This drawing is from a book by Eva Haue, *Vielleicht sind wir doch zu verschieden.*

Übung 14 Andreas ist total pleite 

Wie ist das passiert? Sie sehen hier Andreas' Ausgaben für letzte Woche. Schauen Sie sich die Liste an. Was hätten Sie anders gemacht? Wofür hat er Ihrer Meinung nach zu viel Geld ausgegeben? Machen Sie ein paar Vorschläge, was Sie anders gemacht hätten.

Übung 14. Suggestion: Have students work in pairs. Ask each pair to come up with at least five things they would have done differently. Have several students briefly report what they would have done differently. **Follow-up:** Have students indicate what they would do differently.

	AUSGABEN
Geburtstagsgeschenk, Buch und Blumen für Freundin	65,00 DM
drei Sporthemden	120,00
Karte für „Phantom der Oper"	80,00
zweimal im Kino	22,00
Briefmarken	6,50
zweimal mit Freunden in der Kneipe	25,00
Bücher für Biologie und Computerwissenschaften	125,00
Benzin fürs Auto	90,00
Zigaretten	48,00
dreimal zum Essen ausgegangen	59,00
Spende für Amnesty International	25,00
Telefon	120,00

REDEMITTEL

An seiner Stelle hätte ich nicht so viel für . . . ausgegeben.
Das wäre wirklich nicht nötig gewesen.
Braucht er wirklich . . . ? Ich hätte . . .
Zweimal . . . ? Einmal wäre genug gewesen.

Units of Measurement: Fractions and Percentages

Fractions are derived from ordinal numbers. They are formed by adding the neuter suffix **el** to the stem of the ordinal number. They are considered (neuter) nouns and therefore capitalized.

1/3 ein Drittel   1/4 ein Viertel   1/5 ein Fünftel

Note, however:

1/2 die Hälfte

Die Hälfte aller Studenten muss nebenbei arbeiten.	*Half of all students has to work on the side.*
Ein Viertel meines Einkommens ist für Miete.	*One quarter of my income goes for rent.*
Ein Drittel aller Studenten hat wenig Geld.	*A third of all students has little money.*

Units of Measurement. Note: Fractions and percentages lend themselves to the review of the genitive case.
Suggestion: Ask a number of questions such as *Wie viel Geld geben Sie für Bücher (Miete, Essen, Telefon, Freizeit) aus?* For quick responses, ask students to guess; e.g., *Ich gebe ungefähr die Hälfte (ein Drittel, ein Viertel, mehr/weniger als ein Viertel) meines Geldes für Miete aus.* The answers can also be given in percentages, asking for rough estimates: *Ich gebe ungefähr 50 Prozent meines Geldes für Miete aus.*

Percentages are expressed by cardinal numbers followed by the word **Prozent.**

Drei Prozent aller Leute **sind** reich.	*Three percent of all people are rich.*

Übung 15 Welche Tage bringen Umsatz?

Sehen Sie sich die Statistik an, und kommentieren Sie.

BEISPIEL: Montag bringt nur dreizehn Komma sieben Prozent des Umsatzes.

Einzelhandel:[1]

Welche Tage bringen Umsatz?[2]

Vom Umsatz 1992 entfielen auf:

DIE WELT

Tag	Prozent
Montag	13,7
Dienstag	13,0
Mittwoch	13,0
Donnerstag	18,7
Freitag	15,5
Samstag	26,1

Angaben in Prozent

Der Samstag ist noch immer der Haupteinkaufstag[3] in Deutschland: Auf ihn entfallen[4] mehr als ein Viertel aller Einzelhandels-Umsätze (26,1 Prozent). Der Donnerstag rückt mit 18,7 Prozent auf Platz zwei der Umsatzstatistik vor,[5] seit die Händler ihre Läden an diesem Tag länger öffnen dürfen. QUELLE: BAG

1. *retail*
2. *sales*
3. *main shopping day*
4. *occur*
5. rückt vor *is moving up*

Realia. This chart appeared in the newspaper *Die Welt.*

Sprache im Kontext

Zuschauen

Vorschau

Sehen Sie sich die Werbung an, und überlegen Sie sich, wofür das eine Werbung sein könnte. Beschreiben Sie dann die Szene zusammen mit einem Partner / einer Partnerin.

- Wie viele Personen kommen in dieser Szene vor?
- Wie viele Etagen hat das Haus?
- Was macht die Familie gerade?

Arbeit mit dem Videotext

A. Sehen Sie sich die Werbung noch einmal an. Beschreiben Sie in 8 bis 10 Sätzen, was passiert ist.

NÜTZLICHE AUSDRÜCKE

die Abrissbirne *demolition ball*
abreißen, riss ab, abgerissen *to demolish*
der Bauarbeiter *construction worker*
der Kran *crane*
der Kranführer *crane operator*
zerstören *to destroy*

B. Was passiert jetzt? Schreiben Sie die Geschichte in Dialogform weiter. Die Personen sind der Bauarbeiter, die Frau, das Kind, der Mann.

Lesen

Zum Thema

Fragen zum Thema Geld. Beantworten Sie die folgenden Fragen erst selber, und interviewen Sie dann einige Personen im Kurs.

1. Haben Sie als Kind Taschengeld erhalten? Wie viel? Wie oft und wann?
2. Was war Ihr erster bezahlter Job? Was haben Sie mit dem Geld gemacht?
3. Können Sie gut sparen, oder geben Sie Ihr Geld impulsiv aus?

Auf den ersten Blick

A. Überlegen Sie sich, was Sie in den folgenden Situationen machen würden.

1. Sie sind im Restaurant und gerade mit dem Essen fertig. Da bemerken Sie, dass Sie weder Geld noch Kreditkarten bei sich haben. Was würden Sie machen?
2. Sie fahren durch Europa. Gewöhnlich übernachten Sie in Jugendherbergen, aber an einem Ort gibt es nur Hotels. Dafür haben Sie aber nicht genug Geld. Was würden Sie machen?

B. Lesen Sie die ersten zehn Zeilen der Geschichte „Fahrkarte bitte", und beantworten Sie die folgenden Fragen.

1. Wer sind die Hauptpersonen?
2. Wo findet die Geschichte statt („Kiel" allein genügt *[is sufficient]* nicht als Antwort)?
3. Zu welcher Tageszeit beginnt die Erzählung?
4. Was ist das Hauptproblem oder der Konflikt?

Auf den ersten Blick B: Have students write three questions about the rest of the story. As they read the story, they should try to find the answers to their questions.

Fahrkarte bitte

von Helga M. Novak

Kiel sieht neu aus. Es ist dunkel. Ich gehe zum Hafen. Mein Schiff ist nicht da. Es fährt morgen. Es kommt morgen vormittag an und fährt um dreizehn Uhr wieder ab. Ich sehe ein Hotel. Im Eingang steht ein junger Mann. Er trägt einen weinroten Rollkragenpullover.°

Ich sage, haben Sie ein Einzelzimmer?

Er sagt, ja.

Ich sage, ich habe nur eine Handtasche bei mir, mein ganzes Gepäck ist auf dem Bahnhof in Schließfächern.°

Er sagt, Zimmer einundvierzig. Wollen Sie gleich bezahlen? Ich sage, ach nein, ich bezahle morgen.

Ich schlafe gut. Ich wache auf. Es regnet in Strömen.° Ich gehe hinunter. Der junge Mann hat eine geschwollene Lippe.

Ich sage, darf ich mal telefonieren?

Er sagt, naja.

Ich rufe an.

Ich sage, du, ja, hier bin ich, heute noch, um eins, ja, ich komme gleich, doch ich muß, ich habe kein Geld, mein Hotel, ach fein, ich gebe es dir zurück, sofort, schön.

Der junge Mann steht neben mir. Er hat zugehört.

Ich sage, jetzt hole ich Geld. Dann bezahle ich.

Er sagt, zuerst bezahlen.

Ich sage, ich habe kein Geld, meine Freundin.

Er sagt, das kann ich mir nicht leisten.

Ich sage, aber ich muß nachher weiter.

Er sagt, da könnte ja jeder kommen.°

Ich sage, meine Freundin kann nicht aus dem Geschäft weg.

Er lacht.

Ich sage, ich bin gleich wieder da.

Er sagt, so sehen Sie aus.°

Ich sage, lassen Sie mich doch gehen. Was haben Sie denn von mir?

Er sagt, ich will Sie ja gar nicht.

Ich sage, manch einer wäre froh.°

Er sagt, den zeigen° Sie mir mal.

Ich sage, Sie kennen mich noch nicht.

Er sagt, abwarten und Tee trinken.°

Es kommen neue Gäste.

Er sagt, gehen Sie solange° in die Gaststube.

Er kommt nach.

Ich sage, mein Schiff geht um eins.

Er sagt, zeigen Sie mir bitte Ihre Fahrkarte.

Er verschließt° sie in einer Kassette.°

Ich sitze in der Gaststube und schreibe einen Brief.

turtleneck sweater

lockers

Es . . . *It's pouring*

da . . . *anyone could say that*

idiom: so . . . *I bet you are* (sarcastic)

manch . . . *many a man would be glad*

show

idiom: abwarten . . . *let's wait and see*

for the time being

locks / box

Liebe Charlotte, seit einer Woche bin ich im „Weißen Ahornblatt“ Serviererin. Nähe Hafen. Wenn Du hier vorbeikommst, sieh doch zu mir herein. Sonst geht es mir glänzend. Deine Maria.

Zum Text

1. Wer erzählt die Geschichte, ein Mann oder eine Frau? Welchen Beweis (*evidence*) können Sie dafür bringen?
2. Suchen Sie nach Wörtern und Äußerungen, die weitere Informationen über die Hauptpersonen geben. Was können Sie aus diesen Details schließen (*conclude*)? Es steht z. B. im Text, dass der junge Mann „eine geschwollene Lippe“ hat.
3. Wann erfahren die Leser, dass eine der Hauptpersonen ein großes Problem hat? Wie würden Sie in dieser Situation handeln (*act*)? Welche Rolle spielt die Fahrkarte?
4. Sie hören nur eine Seite des Telefongesprächs. Was könnte die Person am anderen Ende sagen?
5. Sie sind Detektiv / Detektivin. Lesen Sie die Geschichte ein zweites Mal. Glauben Sie dieser Frau? Wenn nicht, was für Beweise haben Sie, dass sie lügt?
6. Die Geschichte endet mit einem Brief. Was sagt uns der Brief über die Erzählerin? Ist Charlotte eventuell (*possibly*) dieselbe Person, mit der die Erzählerin am Telefon gesprochen hat? Welchen Beweis haben Sie dafür oder dagegen?

Sprechen und Schreiben

Aktivität 1 Ein kleines Theaterstück

Führen Sie die Geschichte „Fahrkarte bitte“ als kleines Theaterstück auf. Teilen Sie die Geschichte in verschiedene Dialoge auf (z.B. Ankunft der Erzählerin, Gespräch am nächsten Morgen).

Aktivität 2 Wie könnte die Geschichte weitergehen?

Ein Monat ist vergangen. Was ist aus der Frau geworden? Schreiben Sie eine Fortsetzung (*continuation*) der Geschichte. Was macht die Frau jetzt? Ist sie noch in Kiel? Ist sie abgereist? Hat sie Geld? Ist sie glücklich?

Sprechen und Schreiben. Aktivität 2: Students can do this in groups and perform the continuation or read their stories aloud to the rest of the class.

Sprechen und Schreiben. Additional Activity: Assign students the task of playing Charlotte and returning Maria's letter.

Geldangelegenheiten	**Money Matters**
die **Ausgabe, -n**	expense
die **Einnahme, -n**	income
das **Prozent**	percent
fünf Prozent	five percent
das **Sparen**	saving
das **Sparkonto,** *pl.* **Sparkonten**	savings account

Ausgaben	**Expenses**
das **Benzin**	gasoline
der **Bleistift, -e**	pencil
die **Computerdiskette, -n**	computer diskette
die **Ernährung**	food, diet
das **Heft, -e**	notebook
der **Kugelschreiber, -**	ballpoint pen
der **Müll**	garbage
die **Nebenkosten**	utilities; extra costs
das **Papier, -e**	paper
die **Reparatur, -en**	repair
der **Strom**	electricity
die **Studiengebühren** (*pl.*)	tuition, fees
die **Versicherung, -en**	insurance

Das Haus	**The House**
das **Dach, ¨er**	roof
das **Dachgeschoss, -e***	top floor
die **Diele, -n**	front hall
der **Eingang, ¨e**	entrance
die **Etage, -n**	floor, level
der **Flur, -e**	hallway
die **Frühstücksnische, -n**	breakfast nook
die **Garderobe, -n**	wardrobe; closet
das **Gästezimmer, -**	guest room
der **Keller, -**	basement
der **Teppichboden, ¨**	carpeting
die **Treppe, -n**	stair

Haushaltsgeräte	**Household Appliances**
der **Kühlschrank, ¨e**	refrigerator
der **Mikrowellenherd, -e**	microwave oven
die **Spülmaschine, -n**	dishwasher

Brüche	**Fractions**
die **Hälfte, -n**	half
das **Drittel, -**	third
das **Viertel, -**	quarter
das **Fünftel, -**	fifth

Sonstige Substantive	**Other Nouns**
die **Angst, ¨e**	fear
Angst haben vor (+ *dat.*)	to be afraid of
das **Bauernhaus, ¨er**	farmhouse
der **Durchschnitt**	average
im Durchschnitt	on average
der **Gruß, ¨e**	greeting
viele Grüße	many greetings
der **Hund, -e**	dog
die **Katze, -n**	cat
der **Neubau**	new building (postwar building)
der/das **Quadratmeter**	square meter
das **Quartal, -e**	(academic) quarter
das **Tier, -e**	animal
die **Umgebung, -en**	area, neighborhood
die **Zeichnung, -en**	drawing

Verben	**Verbs**
sich ärgern über (+ *acc.*)	to be annoyed about
aus•geben (gibt aus), gab aus, ausgegeben	to spend (*money*)
bauen	to build
betragen (beträgt), betrug, betragen	to amount to

*See Appendix E for alternate spelling.

bitten um, bat, gebeten	to ask for, request
denken an (+ *acc.*), **dachte, gedacht**	to think about, of
ein•richten	to furnish
ein•ziehen in (+ *acc.*), **zog ein, ist eingezogen**	to move in
fragen nach	to ask about
sich freuen über (+ *acc.*)	to be glad about
mieten	to rent (*from someone*)
vergleichen, verglich, verglichen	to compare
vermieten	to rent out

Adjektive und Adverbien — Adjectives and Adverbs

ab	from
ab 1. Juni (ab erstem Juni)	from June 1st on
bald	soon
ca. = circa	circa, approximately
deswegen	because of that
durchschnittlich	on average
eigen	own
ganz	complete(ly), total(ly)
monatlich	monthly
oben	above; upstairs
nach oben	above; upstairs (*directional*)
pleite	broke
spätestens	at the latest
übrig	left over
unten	below; downstairs
nach unten	below; downstairs (*directional*)

Sonstige — Other

an deiner Stelle	if I were you, if I were in your place

Lernziele

Use this checklist to verify that you can now . . .

- ☐ talk about money matters, such as your household budget and the types of monthly expenses you have.
- ☐ describe features of typical apartments and rooms and some kinds of appliances found in a typical household.
- ☐ understand German rental ads.
- ☐ talk and ask about things and ideas using **da-** and **wo-**compounds.
- ☐ make polite requests.
- ☐ express unrealizable wishes.
- ☐ describe preferences.
- ☐ talk about hypothetical situations and contrary-to-fact conditions.
- ☐ use **würde** + infinitive to talk about hypothetical situations or to give advice.
- ☐ use the conjunction **wenn** to describe conditions of fact, with the indicative, and contrary-to-fact conditions, with the subjunctive.
- ☐ give amounts in fractions and percentages.
- ☐ make inferences from textual clues.

- ☐ use the conjunction **wenn** to describe conditions of fact, with the indicative, and contrary-to-fact conditions, with the subjunctive.
- ☐ give amounts in fractions and percentages.
- ☐ make inferences from textual clues.

Viertes Zwischenspiel

Begegnung mit der Kunst der Gegenwart

Was ist Kunst? Das Wort „Kunst" kommt von „können". Ein Künstler oder eine Künstlerin ist ein „Könner"; jemand, der etwas „kann", z.B. malen, zeichnen, formen, komponieren, schreiben. Was erwarten Sie als Kunstbetrachter[1] von einem Kunstwerk? Soll es z.B. „schön" sein, provozieren, zum Nachdenken anregen[2] oder die Realität darstellen[3]?

Die Beispiele moderner und zeitgenössischer[4] deutscher Kunst auf diesen Seiten zeigen Kunst im Kontext von alltäglichen Dingen und ungewöhnlichen Medien. Viele Leute bewundern[5] diese Werke, andere nennen sie Werke von „Dilettanten und hochgemuten[6] Nichtskönnern". (S. 7, Faust / de Vries, „Hunger nach Bildern") Was meinen Sie?

Tisch mit Aggregat, 1958/87, Joseph Beuys

„Flaschenpost," 1990, Rolf Glasmeier

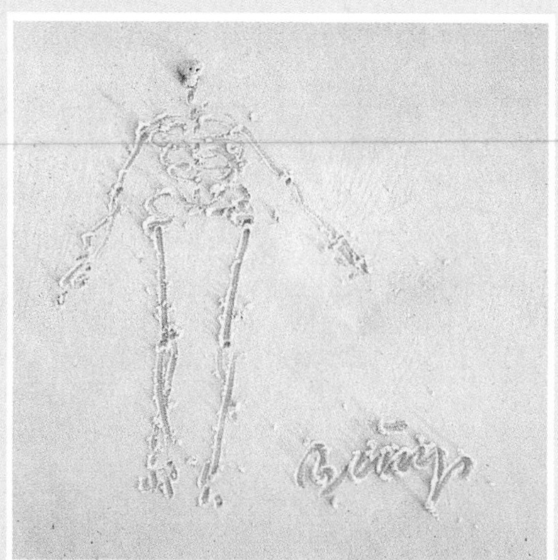

Sandzeichnung, 1975, Joseph Beuys

Aktivität 1 Kunstbewertung

A. Was halten Sie von diesen Kunstgebilden? Wie würden Sie sie charakterisieren?

BEISPIEL: Ich finde die „Flaschenpost" sehr witzig.

- ❑ aggressiv
- ❑ hässlich
- ❑ humorvoll
- ❑ komplex
- ❑ radikal
- ❑ schön
- ❑ verrückt
- ❑ kitschig
- ❑ witzig
- ❑ provozierend
- ❑ dilettantisch
- ❑ komisch
- ❑ originell
- ❑ faszinierend
- ❑ spektakulär
- ❑ kindisch
- ❑ phantasievoll
- ❑ kreativ
- ❑ tief[7]
- ❑ ?

[1]*viewer of art* [2]*incite* [3]*represent* [4]*contemporary* [5]*admire* [6]*arrogant* [7]*profound*

B. Besprechen Sie die folgenden Fragen im Plenum.

1. Welches dieser Kunstwerke gefällt Ihnen besonders gut? Wenn Ihnen keins davon gefällt, warum nicht?
2. Erinnert Sie das eine oder andere dieser Kunstwerke an etwas, was Sie schon einmal, vielleicht in einem Museum, gesehen haben? Sind Ihnen die Namen der Künstler bekannt? Wenn ja, welche Namen?
3. Wer ist Ihr Lieblingskünstler / Ihre Lieblingskünstlerin?
4. Was für Kunstwerke oder Reproduktionen von Kunstwerken haben Sie in Ihrem Zimmer oder in Ihrer Wohnung?
5. Wenn Sie eins dieser Kunstwerke erwerben[1] könnten, welches würden Sie wählen, und warum?

„Der Leser", 1981, Georg Jiři Dokoupil

claus bremer

informieren
informiere
informier
informie
inform
infor
info
inf
in
i

haltungen
altungen
ltungen
tungen
ungen
ngen
gen
en
n

nicht nur
nicht nur
nicht nur
nicht nur
nicht nur
nicht nur
nicht nur
nicht nur
nicht nur
nicht nur
nicht nu
nicht n
nicht
nich
nic
ni
n

provozieren
provozieren
provozieren
provozieren
provozieren
provozieren
provozieren
provozieren
provozieren
provozieren
provozieren
rovozieren
ovozieren
vozieren
ozieren
zieren
ieren
eren
ren
en
n

Konkrete Poesie

Hier sind zwei Beispiele konkreter Poesie. Charakteristisch für sie ist der visuelle Aspekt. Das Visuelle kann z.B. ein Piktogramm sein oder eine Figur, die mit Buchstaben und Wörtern gefüllt ist. Was halten Sie von Reinhard Döhls und Claus Bremers konkreter Poesie?

reinhard döhl

pfelApfelApfelApf
pfelApfelApfelApfelApfe
felApfelApfelApfelApfelAp
ApfelApfelApfelApfelApfelAp
pfelApfelApfelApfelApfelApfe
lApfelApfelApfelApfelApfelAp
pfelApfelApfelApfelApfelApfe
ApfelApfelApfelWurmApfelA
elApfelApfelApfelApfelApfe
felApfelApfelApfelApfelAr
ApfelApfelApfelApfel
lApfelApfelApfelA
lApfelApfelA

Aktivität 2 Sie sind dran[2]

A. Schreiben Sie jetzt Ihr eigenes konkretes Gedicht.

B. Schreiben Sie ein Gedicht im Fünfzeilenformat:

Erste Zeile:	ein Substantiv
Zweite Zeile:	zwei Adjektive
Dritte Zeile:	drei Verben im Infinitiv
Vierte Zeile:	ein Satz, eine Frage oder ein Ausdruck
Fünfte Zeile:	Wiederholung der ersten Zeile, oder ein anderes Substantiv

[1]*acquire* [2]Sie . . . *Now it's your turn*

Kapitel 13

Medien und Technik

Das aktuelle Sportstudio: eine beliebte Sportsendung im Fernsehen

Kapitel 13. Suggestion: Ask students to name any German newspapers or magazines they know, other than those pictured. Is there a German language newspaper in your area of the United States? If so, bring in a copy to show to your students. Bring in copies of any newspapers and magazines you have from Germany, Austria, or Switzerland.

Alles klar?

A. Hier sehen Sie Werbungen verschiedener deutscher Zeitungen für preiswerte Studenten-Abonnements (Abos). Welche Zeitung(en)

- liest man wahrscheinlich in ganz Deutschland?
- liest man wahrscheinlich in München?
- spezialisiert sich auf Wirtschaft und Finanzen?
- erscheint wöchentlich? täglich?

Realia. These are cards used to order student subscriptions through the *Studentenpresse*.

B. Sie hören vier kurze Berichte aus dem Radio. Welche Schlagzeile passt zu welchem Bericht? Schreiben Sie die passende Zahl (1–4) vor die Schlagzeile.

__3__ Kluges (*smart*) Köpfchen vorm Mittagessen
__4__ Spender (*donor*) der Woche
__2__ Unbekanntes Dorf im Iran entdeckt
__1__ Autodieb (*car thief*) auf Surfbrett gefangen

Wörter im Kontext

Thema 1

Medien

Was gibt's denn im Fernsehen?

THOMAS: Was gibt's denn heute im Fernsehen?

BARBARA: Nach der **Tagesschau** kommt **im ersten Programm** um 21.00 Uhr eine **Sendung** mit Placido Domingo.

THOMAS: Oper? Das ist mir heute zu anstrengend. Was gibt es denn im zweiten Programm?

BARBARA: „Die Lindenstraße."

THOMAS: Ach, dieses Melodrama. Auch nichts **Gescheites.**

BARBARA: Aber „Die Lindenstraße" ist doch immer recht gut und spannend. Was möchtest du denn **eigentlich** sehen?

THOMAS: Na, vielleicht einen **aktuellen Dokumentarfilm** oder Sport.

BARBARA: „Der Sportpalast" kommt später um 23.50 Uhr. Ich möchte mir mal einen guten **Spielfilm ansehen.**

THOMAS: Hier ist das Filmprogramm für heute Abend. **Such** dir was **aus!**

Hier klicken

Weiteres zum Thema Medien finden Sie bei ***Deutsch: Na klar!*** im World-Wide-Web unter www.mhhe.com/german.

Realia. This program guide is from *TVneu* in Hamburg.

22.15 VOX **Die letzte Schlacht**
★★★ Kriegsfilm, USA 1977. Mit Burt Lancaster, Craig Wasson. (Siehe rechts) **▶100 Min.**

22.20 RTL 2 **Man nennt mich Halleluja**
★★ Western, Ital. 1971. Mit George Hilton, Charles Southwood, Agata Flori. **▶120 Min.**

22.40 3sat **Calender**
★★★ Road Movie, Kanada 1992. Von und mit Atom Egoyan; Arsinée Khanjian. **▶71 Min.**

22.45 ORB 3 **Das Bildnis des Dorian Gray**
★★★★ Melodram, USA 1945. Mit George Sanders, Hurd Hatfield, Donna Reed. **▶105 Min.**

23.00 IA **Operation Poker – Die Ballermann-Story** Agentenfilm, Ital./Frkr. 1966. Mit Roger Browne, Andrew Scott. **▶90 Min.**
★★★

23.05 SAT.1 **Pudelnackt in Oberbayern**
★★ Sexkomödie, Dtl. 1968. Mit Beppo Brem, Christine Schubert. (Wh. morgen) **▶90 Min.**

23.10 ARTE **Der letzte Schrei**
★★★ Satire, Dtl. 1974. Mit Delphine Seyrig, Peter Hall, Barry Foster, Ellen Umlauf, Udo Kier. Regie: Robert Van Ackeren. **▶92 Min.**

23.20 PRO 7 **Mad Max**
★★★★ Action, Austral. 1978. Mit Mel Gibson, Joanne Samuel, Tim Bums. Regie: George Miller. (Siehe rechts; Wh. morgen) **▶105 Min.**

23.20 ORF 1 **Ein Bulle aus Granit**
★★★ Krimi, USA 1988. Mit Robert Conrad, Ed O'Neill, Anthony LaPaglia. **▶90 Min.**

23.20 Schweiz **Das Mädchen Irma La Douce**
★★★★ Komödie, USA 1962. Mit Jack Lemmon, Shirley MacLaine. **▶135 Min.**

23.40 Kabelkanal **Supergrass – Unser Mann bei Scotland Yard** Krimikomödie, Engl. 1985. Von und mit Peter Richardson. **▶100 Min.**
★★★

23.55 ARD **Liebe ist mein Geschäft**
★★★ Komödie, USA 1988. **▶93 Min.**

0.20 RTL 2 **Der Mann, der Venedig hieß**
★★ Krimi, Dtl./Ital. 1979. Mit Maurizio Merli, Jutta Speidel, Arthur Brauss. **▶90 Min.**

0.35 SAT.1 **Das Netz**
★★★ Krimi, Dtl. 1975. Mit Mel Ferrer, Klaus Kinski, Heinz Bennent. (Wh. um 3.40) **▶110 Min.**

0.40 ZDF **Ein Satansweib**
★★★★ Gangsterfilm, USA 1951. Mit Robert Mitchum, Jane Russell. (Siehe rechts) **▶96 Min.**

1.00 RTL **Jung, frech, frei**
★ Sexfilm, Ital. 1974. Mit Robert Wood, Karin Well, Greta Vaillant. **▶95 Min.**

1.40 ARD **Mord à la mode**
★★★ Krimi, USA 1975. Mit Jim Hutton, David Wayne, Ray Milland, Kim Hunter. **▶93 Min.**

2.10 PRO 7 **Teuflische Signale**
★★★★ Psychothriller, USA/Engl. 1982. Mit Kathryn Harrold. (Wh. vom 16.3.) **▶95 Min.**

2.35 RTL **Tuxedo Warrior**
★★★ Action, Engl. 1982. Mit John Wymann, Carol Royle, Holly Palance. **95 Min.**

3.00 Kabelkanal **Adel verpflichtet**
★★★★ Krimikomödie. (Wh. von 17.25 Uhr) **▶100 Min.**

3.40 SAT.1 **Das Netz**
★★★ Krimi, Dtl. 1975. (Wh. von 0.35 Uhr) **▶110 Min.**

4.40 Kabelkanal **Der Kongreß tanzt**
★★★ Komödie. (Wh. von 19.15 Uhr) **▶105 Min.**

BARBARA: Wie wäre es mit „Das Bildnis des Dorian Gray"?

THOMAS: So ein alter Schinken (*old hat*)! Außerdem auch ein Melodrama.

BARBARA: **Na und?** Das ist auf jeden Fall ein guter, alter Klassiker.
THOMAS: Um 22.15 Uhr läuft „Die letzte Schlacht" mit Burt Lancaster.
BARBARA: Das ist mal wieder so ein Kriegsfilm. So was habe ich gründlich satt.
THOMAS: Also, „Dorian Gray" dann. **Wovon handelt** er übrigens? . . .

Lesegewohnheiten

Fragen Sie jemanden im Kurs nach seinen/ihren Lesegewohnheiten. Sie möchten unter anderem wissen,

- ob er/sie regelmäßig Zeitung liest. Wenn ja, welche?
- ob er/sie regelmäßig **Zeitschriften** liest. Wenn ja, welche?
- wie viel Zeit er/sie mit dem Zeitunglesen verbringt.
- was er/sie zuerst in der Zeitung liest: **Politik, Wirtschaft, Feuilleton,** Sport, **Leitartikel, Lokalnachrichten, Ratgeber, Leserbriefe,** den **Fortsetzungsroman, Kleinanzeigen,** Wetterbericht, **Rätsel, Horoskop, Werbungen,** Comics.
- was er/sie immer ganz genau liest, oder was er/sie nur **überfliegt,** oder wovon er/sie nur die **Schlagzeilen** liest.
- wann er/sie gewöhnlich Zeitung liest.
- ob er/sie ein **Abonnement** für eine Zeitung hat. Wenn ja, für welche Zeitung? Wenn nein, welche Zeitung würde er/sie gern **abonnieren?**

Realia. This channel guide is from *Stern-TV-Magazin.*

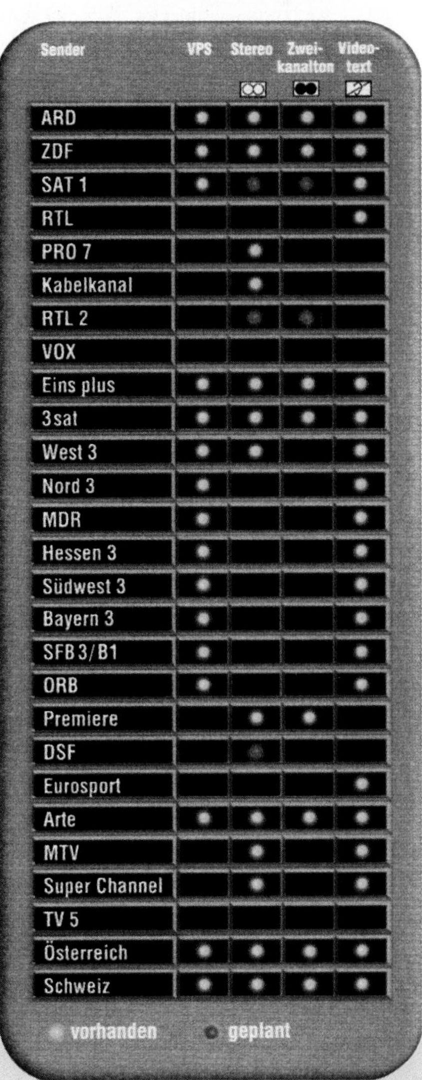

Sender	VPS	Stereo	Zwei-kanalton	Video-text
ARD	●	●	●	●
ZDF	●	●	●	●
SAT 1	●	○	○	●
RTL				●
PRO 7		●		
Kabelkanal		●		
RTL 2		○	○	
VOX				
Eins plus	●	●	●	●
3sat	●	●	●	●
West 3	●	●		●
Nord 3	●			●
MDR	●			●
Hessen 3	●			●
Südwest 3	●			●
Bayern 3	●			●
SFB 3/B1	●			●
ORB	●			●
Premiere		●	●	
DSF		○		
Eurosport				●
Arte	●	●	●	●
MTV		●		●
Super Channel		●		●
TV 5				
Österreich	●	●	●	●
Schweiz	●	●	●	●

● vorhanden ○ geplant

Lange Zeit gab es in Deutschland nur drei Programme. Die ARD (Arbeitsgemeinschaft der Rundfunkanstalten Deutschlands)—auch „Erstes Programm" genannt—und das ZDF (Zweites Deutsches Fernsehen) senden auch heute noch das erste und zweite Programm. Das „Dritte Programm" besteht aus regionalen Sendern aus ganz Deutschland. In diesen drei Programmen werden die meisten Sendungen nicht durch Werbung unterbrochen. Alle Werbespots werden blockweise zu einem bestimmten Zeitpunkt gezeigt. Jeder Haushalt muss für Radio und Fernsehen eine Gebühr, die sogenannte Rundfunkgebühr, bezahlen.

Heutzutage gibt es in deutschsprachigen Ländern eine Vielfalt an Fernsehprogrammen. Kabelfernsehen und Satellitenprogramme, z.B. Nickelodeon, NBC Super-Channel und CNN, sind sehr beliebt und zeigen viele Sendungen im amerikanischen Stil. Für diese Programme muss man zusätzliche Gebühren bezahlen.

Aktivität 1 Das Fernsehprogramm

Suchen Sie im Fernsehprogramm eine Sendung, die zu jeder der folgenden Kategorien passt.

BEISPIEL: Sport →
Um 23 Uhr gibt es die Sportschau im ARD.

1. Sport
2. Nachrichten
3. Spielfilm
4. Geschichte/Dokumentarfilm
5. Kindersendung
6. Unterhaltungssendung, z.B. Spiele und Quizsendungen

Aktivität 1. Suggestion: Ask your students if they recognize any of the TV shows listed.

Suggestion: Show a German TV program to your class. *Deutsche Welle* now broadcasts on cable stations throughout the United States.

Realia. This program guide is taken from *TVneu* in Hamburg.

FR 18.3.

ab **20** Uhr · ab **22** Uhr

ARD

18.50 Tagesschau-Telegramm
18.55 Die Dinos (RB: 18.25)
Puppenserie. 21.: Virenparty
19.25 Herzblatt
Flirtshow mit Rainhard Fendrich
19.57 Heute abend im Ersten
20.00 Tagesschau
20.15 Der Tod und die Lady
US-Psychothriller von 1993
Mit Tim Matheson, Tracy Pollan
Sie ist schön, klug und sexy. Roger glaubt, in Elaine die Frau seiner Träume gefunden zu haben. Als er mitbekommt, daß seine Angebetete unter falschem Namen lebt, ist er ihr bereits verfallen. Mit fatalen Folgen. **89 Min.**

Psychothriller

Roger (Tim Matheson) ist verrückt nach der raffinierten Betrügerin Elaine (Tracy Pollan)

21.44 Tagesthemen-Telegramm
21.45 Harald & Eddi Extra Sketche
Mit Harald Juhnke & Eddi Arent
22.10 Ausgezeichnet
Adolf-Grimme-Preis 1994
22.30 Tagesthemen / Bericht aus Bonn
23.00 Sportschau
Mit **Fußball**-Bundesliga: Leipzig – Köln / Duisburg – Hamburg
23.25 Völker hört das Finale
Ausschnitte aus dem Programm des Berliner Kabarett-Theaters „Distel"
23.55 Liebe ist mein Geschäft
US-Filmkomödie von 1988
Mit Barry Bostwick, Polly Bergen
Heiratsschwindler Larry hält sich für ein echtes Glückskind. Bis sich einige seiner Opfer kennenlernen . . . **93 Min.**
1.30 Tagesschau
1.40 Mord à la mode
US-Krimi von 1975. Mit Jim Hutton, David Wayne, Ray Milland
Der Vater von Krimiautor Ellery ist Polizist und soll den Mord an einer Modeschöpferin aufklären. Ellery wird neugierig, stürzt sich mit Feuereifer auf den verworrenen Fall. **93 Min.**
3.15 Z.E.N. Bis 3.20 Uhr

ZDF

Anschl.: **Guten Abend** (VPS 18.50)
19.00 heute / 19.20 Wetter
19.25 Der Nelkenkönig
11tlg. Serie. 8.: Im goldenen Käfig
Bebel will den Nelkenkönig endgültig entthronen. Er kauft heimlich einen ungedeckten Scheck von ihm auf.
20.15 Ein Fall für zwei
Krimiserie. Tod eines Künstlers

Krimiserie

Haben der erfolglose Künstler Gussmann (Günther Maria Halmer, Mitte) und dessen Tochter Paloma (Tina Ruland) etwas mit dem Mord an Hagen zu tun? Matula (Claus Theo Gärtner) fühlt ihnen auf den Zahn

21.15 Die Söldner Allahs
Reportage von Christian Sterley aus dem zerbombten Afghanistan. Dort tobt ein erbarmungsloser, „heiliger" Krieg der Fundamentalisten gegen die herrschenden Machthaber.
21.45 heute-journal
22.15 aspekte
Kulturmagazin
22.45 Die Sport-Reportage
Eishockey: Play-offs, Halbfinale
23.00 Alles im Griff
Unheimliche TV-Komödie von 1990
Mit Ralf Richter, Tana Schanzara, Werner Kreindl, Hans Korte
Buch, Regie: Joachim Roering
Ernstes Thema, satirisch aufbereitet: Bolle, Fahrer eines Chemie-Lasters, erfährt durch Zufall, daß seine Frau ihn verlassen will. Völlig verstört rast er mit 25 000 Litern giftiger Brühe im Tank nach Hause. Zu spät – seine Frau hat das Weite gesucht. Bolle hinterher. Eine Irrfahrt, die zur Katastrophe werden kann, beginnt. **97 Min.**
0.35 heute
0.40 Ein Satansweib
US-Gangsterfilm von 1951
Mit Robert Mitchum, Jane Russell, Vincent Price **96 Min.**
Sendeschluß: 2.20 Uhr

SAT.1

19.00 Newsmagazin
19.19 täglich ran – Sport
Mit Johannes B. Kerner
19.30 Glücksrad Gewinnshow aus Berlin. Mit Peter Bond
20.15 Kein Baby an Bord
US-Filmkomödie von 1990
Mit Gene Wilder, Christine Lahti
Regie: Leonard Nimoy
Zwischen Duffy und Meg war es Liebe auf den ersten Blick. Zum vollkommenen Familienglück fehlt beiden nur noch das ersehnte Baby. Doch gerade damit hapert es. Meg fühlt sich als Versagerin, die Ehe zerbricht. Nach Jahren treffen sie sich wieder, gereift und mit der Erkenntnis, daß ihre Liebe stärker ist als der Wunsch nach einem eigenen Kind. **120 Min.**

Komödie

Noch sind Duffy (Gene Wilder) und seine Meg (Christine Lathi) ein glückliches Paar

22.15 ran – Fußball-Bundesliga
Erste Bundesliga, 26. Spieltag
VfB Leipzig – 1. FC Köln
MSV Duisburg – Hamburger SV
Zweite Bundesliga, 24. Spieltag
Anschließend: **TopNEWS**
23.05 Pudelnackt in Oberbayern
Dt. Sexkomödie von 1968. Mit Beppo Brem, Christine Schubert **90 Min.**
0.35 Das Netz Dt. Kriminalfilm 1975
Mit Mel Ferrer, Heinz Bennent, Klaus Kinski, Elke Sommer
Der Journalist Bossi überredet den alternden Schriftsteller und Mörder Morelli, seine Memoiren zu schreiben. Als Gegenleistung verspricht er, Morelli vor der Polizei zu schützen. Doch der Deal verläuft anders. **110 Min.**
2.25 Raumschiff Enterprise
US-Serie (Wh. von 16.00 Uhr)
3.15 Vorsicht Kamera (Wh. vom Di.)
3.40 Das Netz (Wh. von 0.35 Uhr)
Anschließend: **Vorschau**
5.30 ran (Wh. von 22.15 Uhr)

RTL

oder **Familienbande** Comedyserie
18.30 Achtzehn30 Das Telefon-Thema
18.45 RTL aktuell Nachrichten
19.10 Explosiv – Das Magazin
19.40 Gute Zeiten, schlechte Zeiten
Dt. Familienserie 1994. 455. Folge
20.15 Die Heimatmelodie
Mit Gerda und Peter Steiner
Musik: Tom Astor, Rolf und seine Freunde, Marianne & Michael
Sketchpartnerin: Barbara Schöne
21.15 Zum Stanglwirt Komödienserie
„Über alls wachst mal Gras"
Christa verläßt Stefan. Die Frauen im Dorf überlegen, wie sie ihre fitneßbesessenen Männer zur Räson bringen.

Komödienserie

Opa Stangl (Peter Steiner sen., l.) und Martl (Anton Feichtner) rätseln, was die Frauen sich nun schon wieder ausgedacht haben

21.45 Cheese Comedy & Anarchie
Live-Show mit Hape Kerkeling
22.15 Wie bitte?!
Die Show, die sich einmischt
Moderation: Geert Müller-Gerbes
23.15 Gottschalk
Late Night Show mit Thomas Gottschalk und prominenten Gästen
0.00 RTL Nacht-Journal
Nachrichtenmagazin
Moderation: Heiner Bremer
0.30 Programm nach Ansage
1.00 Jung, frech, frei
Ital. Sexfilm von 1974
Die unschuldige Monika wirbelt die Männerwelt eines ganzen Dorfes gehörig durcheinander . . . **95 Min.**
2.35 Tuxedo Warrior
Engl. Actionfilm von 1982
Nach einem Bankbetrug flieht Wiley mit seiner Frau Lisa nach Afrika. Dort treffen sie auf Lisas ehemaligen Liebhaber Cliff, der in eine Diamantenschmuggelaffäre verstrickt ist. **95 Min.**
4.10 American Gladiators Action-show mit Joe Kutowski (zwei Folgen)
5.45 Zeichentrickfilm

Aktivität 2 Hin und her: Wie informieren und unterhalten sie sich?

Wie informieren sich diese Personen? Was lesen sie zur Unterhaltung? Stellen Sie Fragen an Ihren Partner / Ihre Partnerin.

BEISPIEL: S1: Wie informiert sich _____?
oder Wie unterhält sich _____?
S2: Er/Sie sieht/liest _____.

PERSON	FERNSEHSHOWS	ZEITUNGEN UND ZEITSCHRIFTEN
Martin	Talkshows und Dokumentarfilme	*die Zeit* und *die TAZ*
Stephanie	klassische Spielfilme und Komödien	*der Spiegel*
Patrick	Quizsendungen wie „Der Preis ist heiß", die Tagesschau	*die Frankfurter Allgemeine* und *Stern*
Kristin	Sportsendungen, Krimi-Serien wie „Mord ist ihr Hobby"	*das Handelsblatt, die Welt* und *Brigitte*
Mein Partner / Meine Partnerin		

Aktivität 3 Das sehe ich gern!

Was ist Ihre Lieblingssendung im Fernsehen? Warum? Was finden Sie nicht besonders gut im Fernsehen? Geben Sie Beispiele.

BEISPIEL: Ich mag Serien, zum Beispiel „Beverly Hills 90210". Die finde ich spannend. Aber Quizsendungen finde ich schrecklich langweilig.

Krimis	gewöhnlich	aktuell
Nachrichten	immer	aufregend
Dokumentarfilme	meistens	ermüdend
Quizsendungen	schrecklich	unterhaltsam
Talkshows	sehr	langweilig
Sport		komisch
Serien		spannend
Musik		oberflächlich
?		schlecht

Realia. Note: The TV channels listed are received via satellite. The TV program guide is from *TVneu.* The radio program guide comes from *TV Tip.*

22.05 –22.30 ORF 1 **Golden Girls** amerik. Comedy
22.50 –23.15 Kabel **M.A.S.H.** „Soll und Nichthaben", US-Comedy

17.25 –18.30 ARDreg. **Heidi und Erni** „Die Neue am Kiosk", Fam.-Serie

17.45 –18.45 RTL **Melrose Place** „Überfälle", US-Serie

18.00 –18.50 ZDF **Die fliegenden Ärzte** ● „Familiengeheimnisse"

19.05 –19.30 Kabel **Roseanne** WH v. 11.25 US-Comedy
19.15 –20.15 RTL **Beverly Hills, 90210** „Schmutziger Vorteil", US-Serie

Aktivität 4 Eine Sendung auswählen

Besprechen Sie mit einem Partner / einer Partnerin, was Sie heute Abend sehen möchten. Wählen Sie eine Sendung aus dem Fernsehprogramm in **Aktivität 1** aus.

S1	S2
1. Was gibt es heute Abend im Fernsehen?	**2.** Um _____ gibt es _____ .
3. Was ist denn das?	**4a.** Das ist eine Sendung über _____. **4b.** Keine Ahnung, klingt aber interessant.
5. Wer spielt mit?	**6.** Hier steht _____.
7. Wie lange _____?	**8a.** _____ Stunden/Minuten **8b.** Von _____ Uhr bis _____ Uhr.
9. Was gibt es sonst noch?	**10a.** Magst du _____? **10b.** Wie wäre es mit _____?
11a. Ja, das finde ich _____. **11b.** Nein, ich sehe lieber _____. **11c.** Ich lese heute Abend lieber _____.	**12.** Na gut.

Thema 2

Ein Blick in den deutschen Haushalt

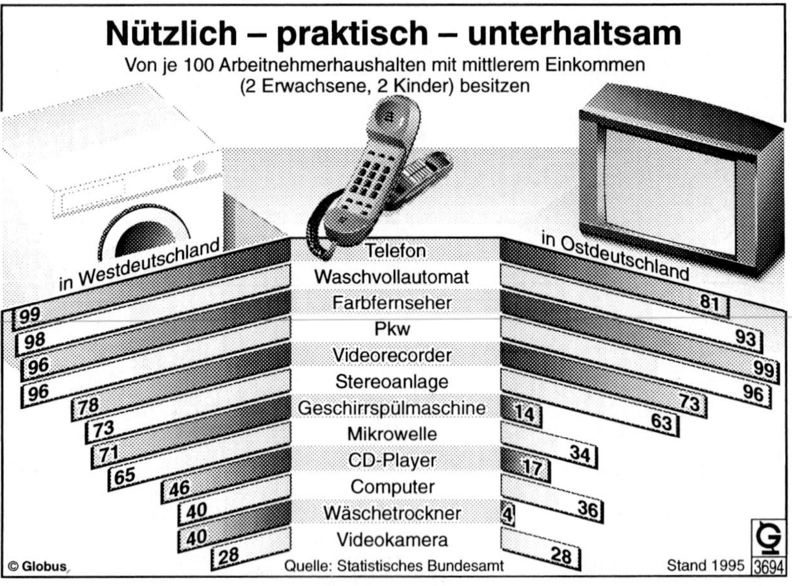

Realia. This information is from the *Globus Kartendienst*.

Der deutsche Haushalt

Schauen Sie sich das Schaubild auf der vorigen Seite an, und beantworten Sie die Fragen.

- Welche **Geräte,** die Sie im **Haushalt** für nötig halten, sehen Sie nicht auf dem Schaubild?
- Welche Geräte gibt es in deutschen Arbeitszimmern/Schlafzimmern?
- Welche Geräte hat man in den letzten fünfzig Jahren **erfunden**?
- Welche sind **Erfindungen** der letzten zwanzig Jahre?

Realia. The **Elektrogeräte** chart is from a brochure called *Wieviel Steckdosen brauchen Sie wirklich?* by Kaiser GmbH & Co.

Geräte

- Welche Geräte besitzen Sie?
- Welche sind für Sie **unbedingt** notwendig?
- **Auf** welche könnten Sie **verzichten?**

Neue Wörter

- ☐ der **Anrufbeantworter**
- ☐ der **Arbeitnehmer /** die **Arbeitnehmerin**
- ☐ der **Blick**
- ☐ der **Drucker**
- ☐ die **Geschirrspülmaschine**
- ☐ der **Staubsauger**
- ☐ der **Wäschetrockner**

Elektrogeräte . . .

...im Arbeitszimmer		...im Schlafzimmer
Wechselsprechanlage	Uhr	Wechselsprechanlage
Haustelefon	Aquarium (3-5 Dosen)	Haustelefon
Telefon	Leseleuchte	Telefon
Anrufbeantworter	Deckenleuchte	Antenne
Telefax-Gerät	Staubsauger	Fernsehgerät
Antenne		Videogerät
Fernsehgerät		Radio
Videogerät		Radiowecker
Radio		Nachttischleuchten (2 Dosen)
Tuner		Möbelbeleuchtung
CD-Player		Wand/Deckenleuchte
Plattenspieler		Stehlampe
Cassettendeck		Notlicht
Lautsprecher-Boxen (2-4 Dosen)		Solarium
Kopierer		Frisier/Schminktisch
Rechenmaschine		Alarmanlage
Computer		Staubsauger
Monitor	**Bedarf für Dauerbetrieb**	
Drucker	**Bedarf für gelegentlichen Einsatz**	
Schreibmaschine	**Anzahl der Lichtschalter und Dimmer**	

Aktivität 5 Wozu sind sie nützlich?

Was passt zusammen?

GERÄTE

1. _____ Farbfernseher
2. _____ Videogerät
3. _____ Mikrowelle
4. _____ Wäschetrockner
5. _____ Heimcomputer
6. _____ Anrufbeantworter
7. _____ Faxgerät
8. _____ Staubsauger
9. _____ Radiowecker
10. _____ Handy

DAMIT KANN MAN

a. schnell Essen zubereiten
b. die Wohnung sauber machen
c. Wäsche trocknen
d. morgens rechtzeitig aufwachen
e. telefonieren, wenn man unterwegs ist
f. schriftliche Nachrichten per Telefon senden
g. sich über Geschehnisse in der Welt informieren
h. Texte verarbeiten
i. Nachrichten hinterlassen
j. Filme und Sendungen aufnehmen

Analyse

Schauen Sie sich das Schaubild an, und beant-worten Sie dann die folgenden Fragen.

- Wie viele Patentanmeldungen gibt es insgesamt für jedes Land?
- Nennen Sie mindestens zwei Erfindungen aus Ihrem Land.

Realia. This graphic is from the *Globus Kartendienst.*

Aktivität 6 Hin und her: Technische Erfindungen durch die Jahrhunderte

Sie möchten erfahren, welche Person was und wann erfunden hat. Stellen Sie Ihrem Partner / Ihrer Partnerin Fragen.

Aktivität 6: The lack of female inventors in this activity represents a gap in recorded history. If you know of female inventors, you may wish to expand this activity.

BEISPIELE: S1: Wer hat _____ erfunden?
S2: _____.
S1: Wann hat er es erfunden?
S2: (Im Jahre) _____.

oder: S1: Was hat _____ erfunden?
S2: Er hat _____ erfunden.
S1: In welchem Jahr?
S2: (Im Jahre) _____.

PERSON	ERFINDUNG	DATUM
Johannes von Gutenberg	Buchdruck mit beweglichen Lettern (*movable type*)	um 1450
Daniel Gabriel Fahrenheit	Quecksilberthermometer	1716/18
Karl von Drais	Fahrrad (Draisine)	1817
Werner von Siemens	Dynamomaschine (*generator*)	1846
Gottlieb Daimler	Motorrad	1885
Rudolf Diesel	Dieselmotor	1893
Wilhelm Conrad Röntgen	Röntgenstrahlen (*X-rays*)	1895
Walter Bruch	„PAL“ (Farbfernsehen)	1960/63

Aktivität 7 Haben Sie Erfindergeist?

Sind Sie erfinderisch? Haben Sie Erfindergeist? Was möchten Sie gern erfinden?

BEISPIEL: Ein Hustenbonbon, das wie Schokolade schmeckt.

BEREICHE

1. Medizin
2. Technik
3. Verkehr
4. Haushalt
5. Tiere
6. Stadtplanung
7. Umwelt

Grammatik im Kontext

The Verbs *brauchen* and *scheinen*

Brauchen and **scheinen. Note:** These verbs are similar to modal verbs, except of course that the dependent infinitive is preceded by **zu.** Students need to actively master only the present tense and be able to recognize other tenses in reading. **Point Out:** Even though **brauchen . . . zu** is used instead of **müssen** when a sentence contains **nicht** or **kein, müssen** can be used in a sentence with a negative, whenever **müssen** is stressed *(Ich muss nicht arbeiten; aber ich will).* Make sure you point out the meaning "to not have to."

The verbs **brauchen** (*to need*) and **scheinen** (*to seem*) are often used with a dependent infinitive preceded by **zu. Brauchen** is used instead of the modal **müssen** when the sentence has a negative meaning.

Heute muss ich arbeiten, aber morgen **brauche** ich nicht **zu arbeiten.**	*Today I have to work, but tomorrow I don't have to work.*
Ich **brauche** keinen neuen Computer **zu kaufen:** der alte ist noch gut genug.	*I don't have to buy a new computer; the old one is still good enough.*
Das Faxgerät **scheint** kaputt **zu sein.**	*The fax machine seems to be broken.*

Übung 1 Nichts scheint zu klappen°

° *go right*

Was scheint hier los zu sein? Folgen Sie dem Beispiel.

BEISPIEL: Das Telefon klingelt nicht. (Es ist kaputt.) →
Es scheint kaputt zu sein.

1. Der Computer funktioniert mal wieder nicht. (Er ist kaputt.)
2. Hast du meine Nachricht nicht bekommen? Ich habe nämlich eine Nachricht auf deinem Anrufbeantworter hinterlassen. (Er funktioniert nicht.)
3. Meine Uhr ist stehen geblieben. (Sie braucht eine neue Batterie.)
4. Bei Firma Bauer meldet sich (*answers*) niemand am Apparat. (Niemand ist im Büro.)
5. Drei von meinen Kollegen sind heute nicht zur Arbeit gekommen. (Sie sind alle krank.)
6. Meine Waschmaschine ist kaputt, und der Handwerker, der sie reparieren sollte, ist nicht gekommen. (Er hat es vergessen.)

Übung 2 Nein, heute nicht

Fragen Sie einen Partner / eine Partnerin: Was musst du heute noch machen, was brauchst du nicht zu machen?

BEISPIEL: S1: Musst du heute arbeiten?
S2: Nein, heute brauche ich nicht zu arbeiten.

1. mit deinem Professor oder deiner Professorin reden
2. deinen Freund oder deine Freundin besuchen
3. das Auto / die Wäsche waschen
4. deinen Anrufbeantworter abhören (*to listen to*)
5. einkaufen
6. den Computer benutzen
7. ein Fax schicken
8. Rechnungen bezahlen
9. ein Geschenk für jemanden kaufen
10. die Wohnung sauber machen

Infinitive Clauses with *zu*°

°der Infinitivsatz

Infinitives may function as complements of verbs, adjectives, or nouns; that is, without them the sentence would be incomplete. When used this way, the infinitive is always preceded by **zu.**

Familie Baier hat sich entschlossen, einen Computer **zu kaufen.**	*The Baiers have decided to buy a computer.*
Es macht mir Spaß, E-Mail aus der ganzen Welt **zu bekommen.**	*I enjoy receiving e-mail from all over the world.*
Es ist leicht, einen Brief per E-Mail **zu schicken.**	*It is easy to send a letter via e-mail.*

Note that the infinitive with **zu** is always the last element of the sentence. With separable-prefix verbs **zu** is placed between the prefix and the verb.

Ich habe versucht, dich gestern **anzurufen.**	*I tried to call you yesterday.*
Du hattest versprochen **vorbeizukommen.**	*You had promised to come by.*

A comma sets off an infinitive clause that includes more than just the infinitive with **zu.** No comma is used otherwise.

1. bei . . . *reading it* 2. Macht . . . *Doesn't look bad* 3. *most renowned* 4. *discount* 5. Dem . . . *For the sake of a broader perspective.*

Übung 3 Meiner Meinung nach . . .

Sagen Sie, wie Sie das alles finden.

BEISPIEL: eine Semesterarbeit von zwanzig Seiten schreiben →
Es macht mir (keinen) Spaß, eine Semesterarbeit von zwanzig Seiten zu schreiben.

Es macht mir (keinen) Spaß	stundenlang am Computer sitzen
Ich finde es anstrengend	mit Freunden in die Kneipe gehen
langweilig	Computerspiele spielen
wichtig	Gewichte heben
schwierig	sich Kriegsfilme, Sportsendungen, usw. ansehen
aufregend	Deutsch lernen
Es nervt mich	umziehen
	den Anrufbeantworter abhören
	tanzen gehen
	ins Museum gehen
	über Politik und Wirtschaft in der Zeitung lesen
	den Hund spazierenführen
	per E-Mail korrespondieren
	?

Spaß machen. Note: Students previously learned *Lesen macht Spaß; Schwimmen macht Spaß.* When the infinitive is at the beginning of the sentence, it is the subject (the "-ing" form in English). As a verbal complement, the infinitive is used with **zu** and placed at the end of the sentence: *Es macht Spaß, im Garten zu arbeiten.* The infinitive clause generally contains more than just the infinitive with **zu.** Otherwise you would simply say *Essen macht Spaß.*

Übung 4 Aus dem Kalender

Schauen Sie sich die Stichwörter aus Cornelias Kalender an. Was hat sie vor? Was darf sie nicht vergessen?

NÜTZLICHE AUSDRÜCKE

sich für einen Kurs anmelden (*to register for a course*)
etwas besprechen (*to talk about something*)
sich treffen mit (*to meet [someone]*)
sich einen Job suchen (*to look for a job*)

BEISPIEL: Sonntag hat sie vor, mit Klaus ins Kino zu gehen.

Sonntag	19.30 mit Klaus ins Kino
Montag	Videogerät zur Reparatur bringen Reise nach Spanien buchen
Dienstag	14.30 Prof. Hauser: Seminararbeit besprechen 18.00 Anmeldung für Kurs: Bauchtanz für Anfänger
Mittwoch	Job für den Sommer suchen
Donnerstag	nicht vergessen: Mutter anrufen, Geburtstag!
Freitag	Seminararbeit fertig schreiben 20.00 Vera—Café Kadenz
Samstag	14.00 Tennis mit Klaus 20.30 Spielfilm im Fernsehen ansehen

Übung 5 Gute Vorsätze° für die Zukunft

°*intentions*

A. Sie fangen einen neuen Lebensabschnitt an. Was haben Sie beschlossen (*decided*), in Zukunft zu machen oder nicht mehr zu machen? Was haben Sie versprochen? Schreiben Sie mindestens drei Dinge auf.

BEISPIELE: Ich habe beschlossen, weniger Geld für CDs auszugeben.

Ich habe versprochen, meine Eltern regelmäßig anzurufen.

B. Tauschen Sie Ihre Vorsätze mit einem Partner / einer Partnerin aus. Haben Sie gemeinsame Vorsätze? Wenn ja, welche?

Indirect Discourse°

°die indirekte Rede

Indirect Discourse. Note: The grammar introduces only a limited number of forms and verbs for active knowledge because the indirect discourse subjunctive is used less and less in spoken German. It is still quite common in writing, however, especially in newspapers. In direct discourse, superscript opening quotes are used in most typewritten and computer-generated documents.
Suggestion: Review the more common forms of the Subjunctive II. These are also used for indirect discourse whenever there is no special indirect discourse form available.

When you report what another person has said, you can quote that person verbatim, using direct discourse. In writing, this is indicated by the use of quotation marks.

DIRECT DISCOURSE

Der Autofahrer behauptete: „Ich habe den Radfahrer nicht gesehen."	*The automobile driver claimed, "I did not see the bicyclist."*

Note that in German, opening quotation marks are placed just below the line.

Another way of reporting what someone said uses indirect discourse—a style commonly found in newspapers. In this case, German often uses subjunctive verb forms, especially the indirect discourse subjunctive. These subjunctive forms differ from those you learned in **Kapitel 12.**

INDIRECT DISCOURSE

Der Autofahrer behauptete, er **habe** den Radfahrer nicht **gesehen.**	*The driver claimed he had not seen the bicyclist.*

In using the indirect discourse subjunctive, a speaker or writer signals that the information reported does not necessarily reflect the speaker's own knowledge or views. The indirect discourse subjunctive establishes distance between the reporter and the topic. This is useful when you want to be objective or neutral.

With the exception of the verb **sein,** the indirect discourse subjunctive, or subjunctive I, is commonly used only in the third-person singular form. For other verb forms, German speakers increasingly tend to use the more common subjunctive II instead of the indirect discourse subjunctive.

The Indirect Discourse Subjunctive: Present Tense

The present tense of the indirect discourse subjunctive (subjunctive I) is used to express present and future time. It is formed from the stem of the infinitive.

sein			
Singular		*Plural*	
ich	sei	wir	seien
du	sei(e)st	ihr	sei(e)t
er / sie / es	sei	sie	seien
Sie seien			

All other verbs add **e** to the stem of the infinitive to form the third-person singular. Use subjunctive II for all but the third-person singular.

haben	**können**	**wissen**
er / sie / es } habe	er / sie / es } könne	er / sie / es } wisse

INFINITIVE	INDIRECT DISCOURSE SUBJUNCTIVE		SUBJUNCTIVE II	
bringen	er/sie/es	bringe	ich	brächte
fahren		fahre		führe
sehen		sehe		sähe
tun		tue		täte
werden		werde		würde

Im Fernsehen wurde berichtet, das Land **sei** in einer großen Krise. Niemand **wisse,** wie es weitergehen soll. Niemand **habe** eine Lösung.

It was reported on TV (that) the country was in a deep crisis. Nobody knows how it ought to continue. Nobody had a solution.

1. *close down*

Übung 6 Das stand in der Zeitung

Berichten Sie in indirekter Rede, was Sie in der Zeitung gelesen haben.

BEISPIEL: In der Zeitung stand, dass der Mensch am schnellsten vor dem Mittagessen denke.

1. Der Mensch denkt am schnellsten vor dem Mittagessen.
2. Man soll also schwierige Probleme zwischen 11 and 12 Uhr lösen.
3. Die Sinne funktionieren dagegen besser in der Dämmerung *(dusk)*.
4. Das Abendessen schmeckt deshalb besser als das Frühstück.
5. Wir sind deshalb abends für Theater, Musik und auch für die Liebe am empfänglichsten (*most receptive*).
6. Für den Sport ist der Spätnachmittag ideal.
7. Nachmittags ist das Reaktionsvermögen auf dem Höhepunkt.
8. Man ermüdet spätnachmittags nicht so schnell.

Übung 7 Immer diese Ausreden°

excuses

Sie hören drei Dialoge. Machen Sie sich zuerst Notizen. Erzählen Sie dann mit Hilfe Ihrer Notizen, was das Problem ist und was für Ausreden die Personen in den Dialogen haben.

BEISPIEL: Peter hat gesagt, er könne nicht mit ins Kino . . .

SPRECHER/IN	PROBLEM	AUSREDE
1. Peter	Verabredung fürs Kino	Wagen kaputt; hat Arbeit
2. Jens	Seminararbeit nicht fertig	Mutter krank
3. Ursula	50 Mark Schulden	Scheck kommt morgen

The Indirect Discourse Subjunctive: Past Tense

The past tense of the indirect discourse subjunctive is formed with either **sei** or **habe** and the past participle of the main verb.

INFINITIVE	INDIRECT DISCOURSE SUBJUNCTIVE		SUBJUNCTIVE II	
haben		habe gehabt		hätte gehabt
sein		sei gewesen		wäre gewesen
fahren	er/sie/es	sei gefahren	ich	wäre gefahren
sehen		habe gesehen		hätte gesehen
wissen		habe gewusst		hätte gewusst

Der Autofahrer behauptete, der Radfahrer **sei** bei Rot **gefahren.** Er **habe** ihn nicht rechtzeitig **gesehen.**

The driver claimed that the bicyclist had run a red light. He did not see him in time.

Übung 8 Ungewöhnliches° aus den Nachrichten

unusual happenings

Schreiben Sie die folgenden Sätze in indirekter Rede der Vergangenheit um. Benutzen Sie dabei Konjunktiv I oder Konjunktiv II.

Heute habe ich im Radio gehört:

1. Im Südwesten Irans hat man ein unbekanntes Dorf entdeckt.
2. Ein Mann im Gorillakostüm hat in den Straßen von Dallas 50-Dollar Scheine an Fußgänger verteilt.
3. Im Jahre 1875 haben die Leute noch 65 Stunden pro Woche gearbeitet. Im Jahre 1988 haben die meisten nur noch 39 Stunden pro Woche gearbeitet.
4. Bei einer Verkehrskontrolle in Cocoa Beach ist ein Autodieb ins Meer gesprungen. Er ist immer weiter raus geschwommen. Ein Polizist in voller Uniform hat sich auf ein Surfbrett geschwungen und hat den Dieb nach zehn Minuten eingeholt.

5. Gestern ist auf einem Spielplatz in Russland ein UFO gelandet. Die Leute, die aus dem UFO gestiegen sind, sind sehr freundlich gewesen. Nach kurzer Zeit sind sie wieder abgeflogen.

Übung 9 Ein kurzes Nachrichtenprogramm  

Übung 9. Suggestion: Encourage students to be imaginative in creating their news item. (The incident mentioned in the example actually happened in France and was reported in a German newspaper.)

Schreiben Sie ein kurzes Nachrichtenprogramm. Lesen Sie es in der Klasse vor. Die Zuhörer machen sich Notizen und berichten, was sie gehört haben.

BEISPIEL: Jeff hat berichtet, gestern Abend sei bei einer Geburtstagsfeier in einem Restaurant ein Geburtstagskuchen explodiert. Der Kellner habe zu viel Cognac über den Kuchen gegossen. Die Gäste und der Kellner seien, Gott sei Dank, unverletzt gewesen.

1. *coffee grounds*

Realia. Many people like to get the latest news from their daily paper. In Germany, too, one can subscribe to daily newspapers. This is, for example, a postcard that readers can use to subscribe to the *Volkszeitung.*

Infinitive Clauses with *um . . . zu* and *ohne . . . zu*

German uses many different ways to explain the reasons for an action. You have already learned a number of them. Compare the following sentences.

1. Stefan spart *für einen neuen* CD-Spieler. (*prepositional phrase:* **für einen neuen CD-Spieler.**)
2. Stefan will einen neuen CD-Spieler kaufen. *Deswegen* muss er jetzt sparen. (*adverb:* **deswegen** *therefore*)
3. Stefan spart. Er will *nämlich* einen neuen CD-Spieler kaufen. (*adverb:* **nämlich** [*no English equivalent*])
4. Stefan spart, *denn* er will einen neuen CD-Spieler kaufen. (*coordinating conjunction:* **denn**)
5. Stefan spart, *weil* er einen neuen CD-Spieler kaufen will. (*subordinating conjunction:* **weil**)

Yet another way to explain one's reasons for an action is with an infinitive clause with **um . . . zu.**

Um . . . zu. Point Out: The implied subject in an **um . . . zu** clause is always the same as in the introductory clause.

Stefan spart, **um** einen neuen CD-Spieler **zu kaufen.**	*Stefan is saving money to buy a new CD player.*
Familie Huber spart seit Jahren, **um** ein Haus **zu bauen.**	*The Hubers have been saving for years in order to build a house.*

Realia. This ad for DuPont advertises the type of research the company is engaged in.

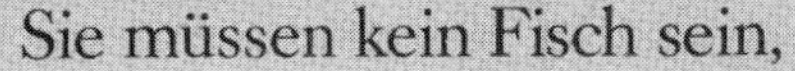

1. *sea water*

To express that you do one thing without doing another, use **ohne . . . zu.**

Hubers wollen ein Haus bauen, **ohne** große Schulden **zu machen.**	*The Hubers want to build a house without going into heavy debt.*
Er ist an mir vorbeigegangen, **ohne** mich **zu erkennen.**	*He passed by me without recognizing me.*

Note the comma before **um** and **ohne.**

Übung 10 Was sind die Gründe° dafür?

° *reasons*

Geben Sie die Gründe an. Benutzen Sie dabei **um . . . zu, weil, nämlich, denn** oder **deswegen.**

BEISPIEL: Ich muss sparen. Ich möchte mir ein Videogerät anschaffen. →
Ich spare, **um** mir ein Videogerät **anzuschaffen.**
oder: Ich will mir ein Videogerät anschaffen. **Deswegen** muss ich sparen.

1. Barbara macht den Fernseher an. Sie will die Nachrichten sehen.
2. Thomas setzt sich in den Sessel. Er will die Tageszeitung lesen.
3. Barbara möchte später einen Film im Fernsehen sehen. Sie schaut sich das Filmprogramm an.
4. Thomas programmiert den Videorecorder. Er möchte die Fußballweltmeisterschaften im Fernsehen aufnehmen.
5. Stephanie füllt ein Formular aus. Sie muss ihr Radio und ihren Fernseher anmelden. (Sonst macht sie sich als Schwarzhörerin strafbar!)
6. Oliver überfliegt die Anzeigen in der Zeitung. Er will sich einen neuen Computer anschaffen.

Im Computer-Lab

Übung 11 Daran hat niemand gedacht!

Kombinieren Sie Sätze aus beiden Spalten mit Hilfe von **ohne . . . zu.**

BEISPIEL: Oliver hat den gebrauchten Computer gekauft. . . . hat ihn aber vorher nicht überprüft. →
Oliver hat den gebrauchten Computer gekauft, ohne ihn vorher zu überprüfen.

1. Erika hat das Videogerät gekauft.
2. Herr Wunderlich hat eine Wohnung gemietet.
3. Fritz ist nach den Nachrichten ins Bett gegangen.
4. Patrick hat beim Fußballspiel wie hypnotisiert vor dem Fernseher gesessen.
5. Jemand hat eine Nachricht auf meinem Anrufbeantworter hinterlassen.
6. Susan ist von der Party nach Hause gegangen.

a. . . . hat aber seinen Namen nicht genannt.
b. . . . hat sich aber nicht von den Gastgebern verabschiedet.
c. . . . hat aber nicht nach den Nebenkosten gefragt.
d. . . . hat aber das Telefon nicht gehört.
e. . . . hat aber den Fernseher nicht abgestellt.
f. . . . hat aber nicht nach dem Preis gefragt.

Sprache im Kontext

Zuschauen

Vorschau

ARD/ZDF

Sehen Sie sich die Werbung ohne Ton an. Am Ende der Werbung liest man: „Bei ARD und ZDF sitzt man in der ersten Reihe.“ Was könnte das bedeuten?

Arbeit mit dem Videotext

Sehen Sie sich die Werbung mit Ton an, und beantworten Sie folgende Fragen.

1. Was machen die beiden Frauen?
2. Was besprechen die Frauen?
3. Wohin fällt die Zigarette der einen Frau? Warum?
4. Beschreiben Sie die beiden Frauen.
5. Sehen Sie gern fern? Warum oder warum nicht?
6. Welche Fernsehsender sehen Sie am liebsten? Warum?
7. Welchen Eindruck bekommen Sie von ARD und ZDF durch die Werbung?
8. „Bei ARD und ZDF sitzt man in der ersten Reihe.“ Was ist Ihre Meinung dazu?

Lesen

Zum Thema

1. Wie oft sehen Sie fern?
    - überhaupt nicht
    - 1–5 Stunden pro Woche
    - 5–10 Stunden pro Woche
    - 10–20 Stunden pro Woche
    - über 20 Stunden pro Woche
2. Was für Sendungen gefallen Ihnen?
    - Dramen
    - Komödien
    - Spielfilme
    - Krimis
    - Dokumentarfilme
    - Zeichentrickfilme
    - Nachrichten
    - Sportsendungen

3. Was würden Sie machen, wenn Ihr Fernseher kaputt wäre?
4. Falls Sie keinen Fernseher haben, wie verbringen Sie Ihre Freizeit?

Auf den ersten Blick

1. Suchen Sie Wörter aus dem Text, die
   a. für Fernseher stehen,
   b. etwas mit sehen zu tun haben.
2. Schauen Sie sich den Titel an, und lesen Sie die ersten zwei Sätze. Der Text ist
   a. ein Interview.
   b. ein Dialog.
   c. ein Artikel.
3. Überfliegen Sie den Text in etwa dreißig Sekunden. Dieser Text handelt von
   a. einem Ehepaar, dem ein Abend ohne Fernsehen bevorsteht.
   b. einem Ehepaar, das seinen kaputten Fernseher wegwerfen will.
   c. einem Ehepaar, das seinen Fernseher zur Reparatur bringt.

Auf den ersten Blick. Note: The reading is by Loriot, which is the pen name of one of the best-known contemporary German humorists. Loriot, a Berliner born in 1923, is a master at demonstrating the comic absurdity in everyday life. **Note for #1:** Students need to look at the first eleven lines of the story to find the answers. Other words mentioned for *Fernseher* are *das Fernsehgerät, das Gerät, der Apparat,* and *der (blöde) Kasten* (colloquial).

Fernsehabend

Fernsehabend. Suggestion: Depending upon your students' acting talent, this humorous reading could be performed in class

Loriot, *Loriots Dramatische* Werke

Ein Ehepaar sitzt vor dem Fernsehgerät. Obwohl die Bildröhre° ausgefallen° ist und die Mattscheibe° dunkel bleibt, starrt das Ehepaar zur gewohnten° Stunde in die gewohnte Richtung.

tube / broken
screen / usual

SIE: Wieso geht der Fernseher denn grade heute kaputt?
ER: Die bauen die Geräte absichtlich so, daß sie schnell kaputtgehen. . . *(Pause)*
SIE: Ich muß nicht unbedingt fernsehen. . .
ER: Ich auch nicht. . . nicht nur, weil heute der Apparat kaputt ist. . . ich meine sowieso°. . . ich sehe sowieso nicht gern Fernsehen. . .

in any case

SIE: Es ist ja auch wirklich nichts im Fernsehen, was man gern sehen möchte. . . *(Pause)*
ER: Heute brauchen wir Gott sei Dank überhaupt nicht erst in den blöden Kasten° zu gucken. . .

in. . . *at the stupid box*

SIE: Nee. . . *(Pause)*. . . Es sieht aber so aus, als ob° du hinguckst. . . .

als. . . *as if*

ER: Ich?
SIE: Ja. . .
ER: Nein. . . ich sehe nur ganz allgemein in diese Richtung. . . aber du guckst hin. . . Du guckst da immer hin!
SIE: Ich! Ich gucke da hin? Wie kommst du denn darauf?°
ER: Es sieht so aus. . .°

Wie. . . *What makes you think that?*
Es. . . *That's what it looks like.*

SIE: Das *kann* gar nicht so aussehen. . . ich gucke nämlich vorbei. . . ich gucke *absichtlich* vorbei. . . und wenn du ein kleines bißchen mehr auf mich achten würdest, hättest du bemerken° können, daß ich absichtlich vorbeigucke, aber du interessierst dich ja überhaupt nicht für mich. . .

ER: *(fällt ihr ins Wort°)* Jaaa. . . jaaa. . . jaaa. . . jaaa. . .

notice
fällt. . . *interrupts*

SIE: Wir können doch einfach mal ganz woandershin gucken. . .

ER: Woanders?. . .Wohin denn?

SIE: Zur Seite. . . oder nach hinten. . .

ER: Nach hinten? Ich soll nach hinten sehen?. . . Nur weil der Fernseher kaputt ist, soll ich nach hinten sehen? Ich laß mir doch von einem Fernsehgerät nicht vorschreiben,° wo ich hinsehen soll!

Ich. . . *I won't let a TV dictate to me*

(Pause)

SIE: Was wäre denn heute für ein Programm gewesen?

ER: Eine Unterhaltungssendung. . .

SIE Ach. . .

ER: Es ist schon eine Un-ver-schämtheit,° was einem so Abend für Abend im Fernsehen geboten wird!° Ich weiß gar nicht, warum man sich das überhaupt noch ansieht!. . . Lesen könnte man statt dessen,° Kartenspielen oder ins Kino gehen. . . oder ins Theater. . . statt dessen sitzt man da und glotzt° auf dieses blöde Fernsehprogramm!

outrage
geboten. . . *is offered*
statt. . . *instead*
stares, watches (coll.)

SIE: Heute ist der Apparat ja nu kaputt. . .

ER: Gott sei Dank!

SIE: Ja. . .

ER: Da kann man sich wenigstens mal unterhalten. . .

SIE: Oder früh ins Bett gehen. . .

ER: Ich gehe nach den Spätnachrichten der Tagesschau ins Bett. . .

SIE: Aber der Fernseher ist doch kaputt!

ER: *(energisch)* Ich lasse mir von einem kaputten Fernseher nicht vorschreiben, wann ich ins Bett zu gehen habe!

Zum Text

Richtig oder falsch? Wenn falsch, verbessern Sie die Aussagen.

1. _____ Der Fernseher ist kaputt. Aber es ist kein Problem, denn die zwei Leute haben einen zweiten Apparat im Schlafzimmer.

2. _____ Der Mann behauptet, dass er sowieso nicht gern fernsieht.

3. _____ Die zwei bleiben aber vor dem Fernseher sitzen und starren ihn einfach an.

4. _____ Die Frau schlägt eine Alternative zum Fernsehen vor.

5. _____ Der Mann meint, er darf hinschauen, wohin er will, auch wenn er den dunklen Fernseher anschaut.

6. _____ An diesem Abend gibt es Sport im Fernsehen.

7. _____ Der Mann behauptet, dass es normalerweise ausgezeichnete Sendungen im Fernsehen gibt.

8. _____ Die zwei unterhalten sich und gehen dann früh ins Bett.

Sprechen und Schreiben

Aktivität 1 Theater spielen

Wie stellen Sie sich die Kurzszene in „Fernsehabend“ vor? Üben Sie die Szene mit einer Partnerin / einem Partner ein, um sie vor der Klasse vorzuführen.

Aktivität 2 Wie geht das Leben weiter?

Wie stellen Sie sich das Leben des Ehepaars vor? Schreiben Sie einen kurzen Dialog zwischen dem Ehepaar am nächsten Tag am Frühstückstisch.

Wortschatz

Geräte	Appliances
der **Anrufbeantworter, -**	answering machine
der **Drucker, -**	printer
die **Geschirrspülmaschine, -n**	dishwasher
der **Staubsauger, -**	vacuum cleaner
der **Wäschetrockner, -**	dryer

In der Zeitung	In the Newspaper
das **Abo(nnement), -s**	subscription
das **Feuilleton**	part of a newspaper containing articles on literature, culture, and science
der **Fortsetzungsroman, -e**	serial novel
das **Horoskop, -e**	horoscope
die **Kleinanzeige, -n**	classified ad
der **Leitartikel, -**	leading article; editorial
der **Leserbrief, -e**	letter to the editor
die **Lokalnachrichten** (*pl.*)	local news
die **Politik**	politics
der **Ratgeber, -**	advice columnist
das **Rätsel, -**	riddle; puzzle
die **Schlagzeile, -n**	headline
die **Wirtschaft**	economy

Im Fernsehen	On Television
der **Bericht, -e**	report
der **Dokumentarfilm, -e**	documentary
das **Programm, -e**	station, channel
im ersten Programm	on channel 1
die **Sendung, -en**	broadcast, show
der **Spielfilm, -e**	feature film
die **Tagesschau**	daily TV news
die **Werbung, -en**	advertisement; commercial

Sonstige Substantive	Other Nouns
der **Arbeitnehmer, -**	employee
der **Blick, -e**	look, glance
der **Erfinder, -** / die **Erfinderin, -nen**	inventor
die **Erfindung, -en**	invention
das **Gerät, -e**	appliance, device
der **Haushalt, -e**	household; budget
die **Zeitschrift, -en**	magazine

Verben	Verbs
abonnieren	to subscribe to
sich etwas an•sehen (sieht an), sah an, angesehen	to look at, watch

auf•nehmen (auf Video) (nimmt auf), nahm auf, aufgenommen	to record (on video)
sich etwas aus•suchen	to choose something for oneself
erfinden, erfand, erfunden	to invent
handeln (von)	to deal with, be about
überfliegen, überflog, überflogen	to skim
verzichten (auf)	to do without

Adjektive und Adverbien / Adjectives and Adverbs

aktuell	current(ly), topical
aufregend	exciting
eigentlich	actually, really
ermüdend	tiring
gescheit	intelligent, sensible
gleichzeitig	simultaneous(ly)
oberflächlich	superficial(ly)
unbedingt	absolute(ly)
unterhaltsam	entertaining

Sonstige Ausdrücke / Other Expressions

auf alle Fälle	in any case
na und?	so what?

Lernziele

Use this checklist to verify that you can now . . .

- ☐ talk about the mass media and various types of television and radio shows, films, newspapers, and magazines.
- ☐ express your own preferences with regard to television and radio shows as well as newspapers and magazines.
- ☐ use **brauchen** and **scheinen** and other verbal expressions with **zu** + infinitive.
- ☐ report what you have heard or read using indirect discourse (Subjunctive I and II).
- ☐ expand sentences with **um . . . zu** and **ohne . . . zu** clauses.

Kapitel 14

Die öffentliche Meinung

Umweltprobleme gehen uns alle an.°

gehen . . . *concern*

Kapitel 14. Suggestion: Introduce the chapter by brainstorming with the class about the problems of the world. What are the problems in your community? In your state? Are students involved in helping out with those problems?

Alles klar?

Ob es Politik, Wirtschaft oder Umwelt ist—Deutsche sind im Durchschnitt relativ gut informiert und äußern gern ihre Meinung zu Problemen aus verschiedenen Lebensbereichen.

A. Schauen Sie sich die Umfrage an. Welches Problem passt zu den folgenden Beschreibungen?

1. **Arbeitslosigkeit**
2. **Fremdenhaß**
3. **Steuererhöhungen**
4. **Politiker**
5. **Geldmangel**
6. **Umwelt**
7. **Gewalt**

Alles klar. Have students do **A** and **B** either for homework or as an in-class activity.

A. Discuss with students the historical contexts for some of the problems, such as an influx of refugees to Germany after the dissolution of Eastern Europe, Germany's open-door policy toward political refugees and the continuing high costs of unification.

B. Discuss the results of the survey students carry out themselves and ask them to compare the problems in Germany to those they find in their own surroundings.

1. __1__ zu wenig Arbeitsplätze
2. __5__ nicht genug Geld
3. __2__ zu wenig Verständnis für Fremde im Land
4. __7__ zu hohe Kriminalität
5. __3__ zu hohe Steuern
6. __4__ zu viele Skandale in der Politik
7. __6__ Naturzerstörung

B. Machen Sie eine Umfrage im Unterricht oder auf Ihrem Campus. Was sind die drängendsten Probleme in Ihrer Umgebung?

C. Sie hören jetzt eine Beschreibung von vier verschiedenen Seminaren über Probleme in der Welt. Welche Themen behandeln diese Seminare? Schreiben Sie die entsprechende Nummer vor jedes Thema.

__2__ Kriminalität/Gewalt
__3__ Umweltverschmutzung
__4__ Menschenrechte
__1__ Medizin/Umwelt

Thema 1

Globale Probleme

A. Was sind Ihrer Meinung nach die drei größten Probleme in der Welt, in Ihrem Staat und in Ihrer Heimatstadt?

	WELT	STAAT	STADT
AIDS und andere sexuell übertragbare **Krankheiten**	□	□	□
Arbeitslosigkeit	□	□	□
Armut	□	□	□
Ausländerfeindlichkeit	□	□	□
Drogensucht	□	□	□
Gewalttätigkeit	□	□	□
Hunger	□	□	□
Korruption in der **Regierung**	□	□	□
Krieg	□	□	□
Obdachlosigkeit	□	□	□
Rassismus	□	□	□
Rechtsextremismus	□	□	□
Umweltverschmutzung	□	□	□
Verletzung der **Menschenrechte**	□	□	□
?	□	□	□

B. Was kann man gegen diese Probleme tun? Suchen Sie aus der Liste auf der nächsten Seite passende Ausdrücke, um Ihre Meinung auszudrücken.

BEISPIEL: In meiner Heimatstadt ist Obdachlosigkeit ein großes Problem. Man sollte mehr Sozialbauwohnungen bauen.

- **an Demonstrationen teilnehmen**
- mehr **Fußgängerzonen** einrichten
- mehr Geld für **Forschung** ausgeben
- Alternativenergie entwickeln
- Giftstoffe (*toxics*) **vermindern** oder **verbieten**
- Hilfsorganisationen mit Geld **unterstützen**
- Informationen über die **Gefahren** von **Alkohol** und **Drogen verbreiten**
- Kinder besser **erziehen**
- mehr **Gefängnisse** bauen
- **Recyclingprogramme einführen**
- Safer Sex praktizieren
- Sozialbauwohnungen bauen
- Stressfaktoren (z.B. **Lärm**) reduzieren
- Umschulungsprogramme **fördern**
- Arbeitsplätze **schaffen**
- verantwortungsbewusste **Politiker/ Politikerinnen wählen**
- **sich** politisch **engagieren**
- **öffentliche Verkehrsmittel** fördern
- Umwelt **schützen**
- ?

Die Kunst der Diskussion

*Neun **Bürger** und **Bürgerinnen** diskutieren über das Thema Obdachlosigkeit in ihrer Stadt.*

Suggestion: Focus on the expressions used to express an opinion. Use them in other contexts, e.g., *Ich bin der Meinung, man sollte mehr Recycling-programme beginnen.* Then go back to B above and have students do the exercise again incorporating these expressions.

FRAU MAYER: **Ich bin der Meinung,** dass Obdachlosigkeit ein viel größeres Problem ist, als wir allgemein glauben.

HERR SACHS: Das **halte** ich **für übertrieben.** Das ist nur in Großstädten ein Problem, aber nicht hier bei uns in Kleinlichterhagen.

FRAU BECKER: Im Park an der Hauptstraße schlafen aber regelmäßig Leute auf den Bänken, und am Bahnhof sitzen auch welche, die nicht wissen wohin. Und . . .

HERR GRÜNKRAUT: Ja, und die sind so **schmutzig,** lassen überall ihren Dreck. **Außerdem** sind die meisten drogensüchtig. Es ist ein Skandal, dass unsere **Regierung** bis jetzt keine **Lösung** gefunden hat. Wofür zahlen wir eigentlich unsere **Steuern?**

HERR SPITZ: **So ein Quatsch!**

FRAU RAST: **Meiner Meinung nach** hat die Regierung gute **Fortschritte** gemacht.

FRAU HOFFMANN: **Ich finde,** man sollte unbedingt Unterkunft für die **Obdachlosen** in unserer Stadt finden. Meines Erachtens (*in my view*) sollte man sie in Privatzimmern unterbringen.

FRAU NIKOLAI: Ich hoffe, Sie haben ein Zimmer frei! **Ich bin** nämlich total **dagegen. Ich bin dafür,** dass mehr Sozialbauwohnungen gebaut werden.

HERR SPITZ: **So ein Unsinn!**

FRAU LIESCHE: **Ich bedaure,** dass wir alle ohne Konzept um das Thema herum reden. Ich schlage vor, dass wir eine konkrete Strategie **entwickeln.** Nur so kann das Problem gelöst werden.

FRAU HOFFMANN: Was wohl die Obdachlosen über unsere Diskussion sagen würden!!!

HERR SPITZ: Das ist mir egal!

Aktivität 1 Hin und her: Probleme und Lösungen

Stellen Sie Ihrem Partner / Ihrer Partnerin Fragen zu den folgenden Problemen, um herauszufinden, welche möglichen Lösungen es gibt.

BEISPIEL: S1: Was kann man gegen Krieg tun?
S2: Man kann an Antikriegsdemonstrationen teilnehmen.

PROBLEME	MÖGLICHE LÖSUNGEN
Inflation	die Schulden der Regierung kontrollieren
Drogensucht	Informationen über die Gefahren von Drogen verbreiten
Umweltverschmutzung	alternative Energiequellen entwickeln
Verletzung der Menschenrechte	Organisationen wie Amnesty International unterstützen
Obdachlosigkeit	neue Wohnungen bauen
Arbeitslosigkeit	Arbeiter umschulen

Aktivität 2 Probleme in der Stadt

Vier Leute sprechen über Probleme in ihrer Stadt und wie man sie lösen könnte. Setzen Sie die passende Nummer (1–4) vor das Problem, über das der Sprecher / die Sprecherin redet, und markieren Sie auch die Lösung, die er/sie vorschlägt.

SPRECHER	PROBLEM	LÖSUNG	
2	Atomkraft (*nuclear power*)	**a.** Solarenergie	**b.** Windenergie
4	Giftstoffe in Nahrungsmitteln	**a.** strenge Staatskontrolle	**b.** keine Pestizide
1	Verkehr	**a.** Tempolimit	**b.** Wagen am Stadtrand parken
3	Lärm	**a.** weniger Flugzeuge	**b.** Autos verbieten

Aktivität 3 Um welche Probleme geht es hier?

A. Buttons—so heißen sie auch auf Deutsch—oder Aufkleber (*stickers*) sind eine beliebte Form, die Meinung zu äußern. Schauen Sie sich die Sprüche (*sayings*) auf den Buttons an, und stellen Sie fest, wofür oder wogegen sie sind. Schreiben Sie dann die passenden Zahlen in die Liste.

1. stop kernenergie
2. FRIEDEN SCHAFFEN OHNE WAFFEN · NIE WIEDER KRIEG
3. GREENPEACE RETTET DIE ROBBEN
4. UMWELT SCHÜTZEN RAD BENÜTZEN
5. ATOMKRAFT? NEIN DANKE
6. FAHRRÄDER stinken nicht
7. Ich bin Nichtraucher, und Sie? AOK[1]
8. eine FRAU ohne MANN ist wie ein Fisch ohne Fahrrad
9. Haltet Berlin sauber eßt täglich eine Taube[2]
10. Nichtstun ist besser als für nichts arbeiten..
11. Gift im Essen? Nein Danke
12. Energie sparen ja bitte
13. Stell Dir vor: es ist Krieg, und keiner geht hin.

Realia. The pictures of buttons were found on a calendar distributed by the Goethe Institut.

1. AOK = Allgemeine Ortskrankenkasse *name of a health insurance company* 2. *pigeon*

_____ fürs Faulenzen
_____ gegen Energieverschwendung
_____ für den Feminismus
_____ für die Sauberkeit (*cleanliness*) der Stadt
_____ gegen Autoabgase (*emissions*)
_____ für den Tierschutz
_____ gegen Rauchen
_____ für den Frieden gegen Krieg
_____ für höhere Gehälter
_____ gegen Giftstoffe in Nahrungsmitteln
_____ gegen Rassismus
_____ gegen Kernenergie

Aktivität 3.A. Follow-up: Which of these buttons would students wear?

B. Wählen Sie ein Problem aus **Thema 1,** und entwerfen Sie einen Spruch für einen Aufkleber. Lesen Sie der Klasse Ihre Sprüche vor.

Aktivität 4 Nehmen Sie Stellung!

In Vierergruppen, äußern Sie sich zu einigen Problemen im **Thema 1.** Benutzen Sie dabei die Redemittel im **Thema 1.** Jemand nennt das Gesprächsthema, die anderen sagen ihre Meinung.

BEISPIEL: S1: Verkehrsbelästigung
S2: Ich bin der Meinung, man sollte Autos in der Innenstadt verbieten.
S3: Meiner Meinung nach sollte man mehr Fußgängerzonen bauen.
S4: Ich finde es schade, dass Leute immer ihren Wagen benutzen. Sie sollten öfter zu Fuß gehen.

Thema 2

Umwelt

Was kann man für die Umwelt tun?

Die Zeitschrift „Natur" fragte ihre Leser „Bei welchen dieser Punkte auf der Liste glauben Sie, dass Sie mehr für die Umwelt tun könnten?" Hier sind die Antworten.

Realia. This article is from *Natur* magazine.

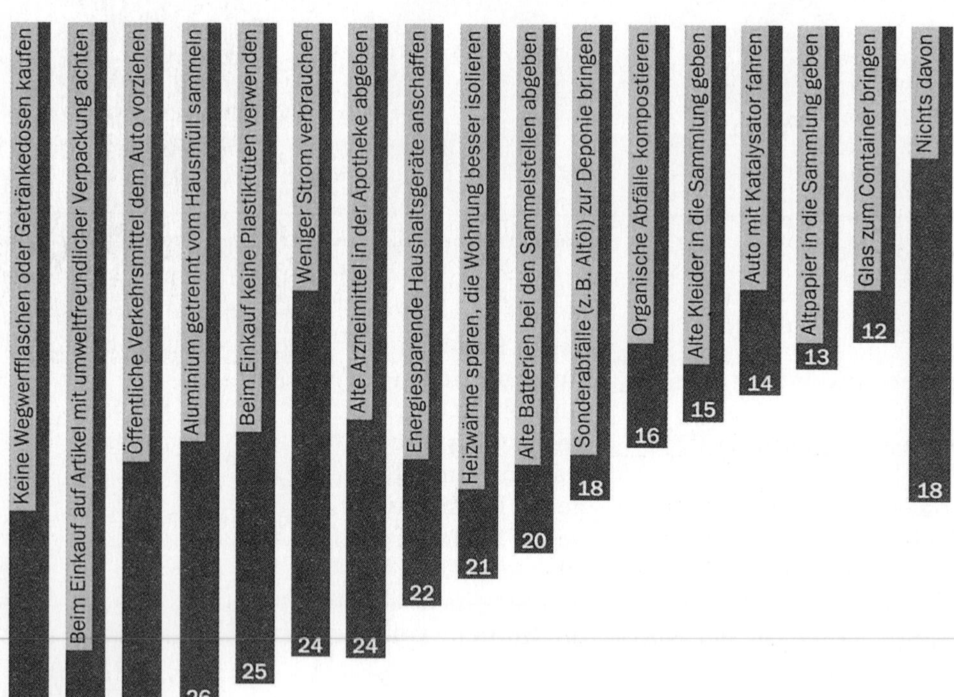

Was tun Sie persönlich für die Umwelt?

Neue Wörter

- □ der **Abfall**
- □ die **Dose**
- □ die **Plastiktüte**
- □ **anschaffen**
- □ **verbrauchen**
- □ **getrennt (trennen)**
- □ die **Sammelstelle**
- □ die **Verpackung**
- □ die **Wegwerfflasche**
- □ **verwenden**
- □ **vorziehen**
- □ **umweltfreundlich**

Viele Menschen leben heutzutage viel umweltbewusster als früher. Sie sind daran interessiert, wie man die Umwelt schützen kann und wie man selbst mithelfen kann, umweltfreundlicher zu leben. Dieses Umweltbewusstsein zeigt sich auch in der modernen Sprache. So gebraucht man oft **alt** als Präfix, wenn man von Dingen spricht, die zur Deponie, zu Sammelstellen oder zur Wiederverwertung gebracht werden; z.B. **Altbatterien, Altöl, Altpapier, Altglas** und **Altkleidung.**

Recycling in Offenbach

Aktivität 5 Langsamer, bitte! 

Sie hören zuerst ein Gespräch zwischen Andreas, einem deutschen Autofahrer, und Jennifer, seinem Gast aus den USA. Hören Sie zuerst den Dialog, und lesen Sie die Sätze unten. Bringen Sie dann die Sätze in die richtige Reihenfolge.

__3__ Bei uns ist die Höchstgeschwindigkeit (*speed limit*) 105 km pro Stunde.
__6__ Wahrscheinlich eine Baustelle (*construction area*) in der Nähe.
__7__ Also doch ein Tempolimit. Gott sei Dank. Bei 100 km pro Stunde fühle ich mich direkt wie zu Hause.
__2__ Keine Angst. Der Wagen schafft das spielend.
__4__ Dann kann man gleich zu Fuß gehen.
__5__ Schau mal. Dort ist ein Schild. Höchstgeschwindigkeit 100 km pro Stunde.
__1__ Fliegen wir eigentlich oder fahren wir?

Kulturtipp. Note: The cameras use infrared light to take pictures after dark, so it is not safe to speed at any time.

In allen Ländern Europas außer in der Bundesrepublik gibt es eine Höchstgeschwindigkeit auf der Autobahn. In Deutschland ist die Richtgeschwindigkeit (*suggested speed*) 130 km pro Stunde auf der Autobahn. Natürlich gibt es streckenweise (*for certain stretches*) Geschwindigkeitsbegrenzungen, zum Beispiel an Baustellen. Über der Autobahn sind manchmal Kameras angebracht, die einen Wagen, der zu schnell fährt, filmen. Man bekommt dann einen Strafzettel (*ticket*) mit dem Bild des Wagens und dem Nummernschild ins Haus geschickt. Niemand kann dann sagen: Das war jemand anders.

Tempogrenzen in Europa
... auf Autobahnen

Norwegen, Rumänien, Türkei	90
Dänemark, Griechenland	100
Polen, Schweden*	110
Großbritannien	112
Belgien, Bulgarien, Finnland, Luxemburg, Niederlande, Portugal, Schweiz, Spanien, Ungarn	120
Frankreich, Italien,** Österreich	130
Deutschland (Richtgeschwindigkeit: 130 km/h)	

*90 km/h vom 20.6. bis 20.8.
**110 km/h an Wochenenden, Feiertagen, in der Ferienzeit

Aktivität 6 Ein Natur-Quiz

Wie gut kennen Sie Ihre Umwelt? Beantworten Sie die Fragen, und vergleichen Sie dann Ihre Antworten mit denen eines Partners / einer Partnerin.

Suggestion: Have students compare statistics between the United States and Germany where appropriate.

1. Was ist am sparsamsten im Energieverbrauch?
   a. das Motorrad **b.** das Auto **c.** das Fahrrad **d.** die Bahn
2. In welchem Jahr und wo wurden erstmals Mülleimer (*garbage cans*) benutzt?
   a. 1213 in Rom **b.** 1473 in Amsterdam
   c. 1621 in Hamburg **d.** 1872 in Chicago
3. Wann und wo wurde die Konservendose erfunden?
   a. 1746 in Norwegen **b.** 1810 in England
   c. 1899 in Deutschland **d.** 1902 in der Schweiz
4. Wie viel Geld kostet die Umweltzerstörung in Deutschland jedes Jahr?
   a. 750 Millionen Mark **b.** 13,7 Milliarden Mark
   c. 475 Milliarden Mark **d.** 130 Milliarden Mark
5. Wie viel Papier wird in Deutschland pro Jahr verbraucht?
   a. 15 Millionen Tonnen **b.** 40 Millionen Tonnen
   c. 250 Millionen Tonnen **d.** 300 Millionen Tonnen
6. Wer ist der größte Müllproduzent?
   a. die Verpackungsindustrie **b.** die Autoindustrie
   c. die Bauindustrie **d.** die Elektronikbranche

Weiteres zum Thema Umwelt finden Sie bei ***Deutsch: Na klar!*** im World-Wide-Web unter www.mhhe.com/german.

Analyse

Seit über zwanzig Jahren wächst das Umweltbewusstsein der Deutschen. Daher werden Berufe im Umweltbereich immer beliebter. Hier sind drei neue Berufe.

Realia. These personal descriptions appeared in *Natur.*

Holger Urban, 43, ist Raumplaner in einer süddeutschen Großstadt: „Mir macht die abwechslungsreiche Arbeit Freude. Vor allem, weil ich den ökologischen Stadtumbau als eine äußerst spannende Sache erlebe."

Dr. Ralph Hantschel, 34, zählt zu den ersten Studienabgängern der Geoökologie: „Die Ausbildung in Bayreuth war intensiv und gut." Heute sucht er Wege zu einer umweltverträglichen Landwirtschaft und ist beim Forschungszentrum für Umwelt und Gesundheit (GSF) tätig.

Siegfried Müller vom Amt für Abfallwirtschaft der Stadt München: „Es macht Spaß. Aber die Verwaltungswege erscheinen mir mitunter zu lang." Der 32jährige studierte Physik. Er arbeitet in der Entsorgungsplanung.

- Holger Urban. Raumplaner. Wo arbeitet er? Warum macht ihm die Arbeit Spaß?
- Dr. Ralph Hantschel. Geoökologe. Wo hat er studiert? Wo arbeitet er jetzt?
- Siegfried Müller. Entsorger (*waste management engineer*). Was hat er studiert? Wo arbeitet er jetzt?

Gibt es diese oder ähnliche (*similar*) Berufe in Ihrem Land? Wer befasst sich mit dem Folgenden? Schreiben Sie R (für Raumplaner/Raumplanerin), G (für Geoökologe/Geoökologin) oder E (für Entsorger/Entsorgerin).

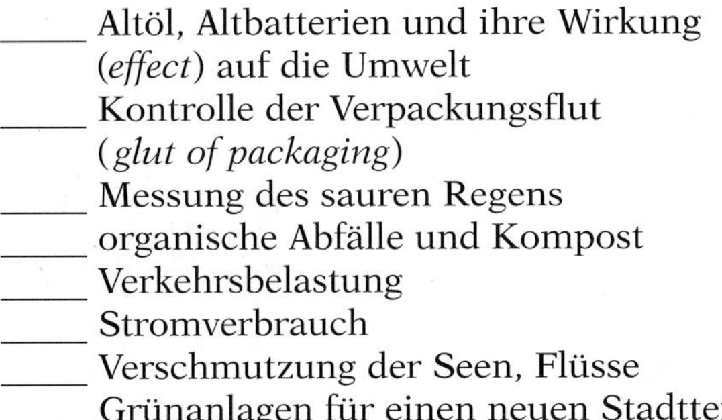

_____ Altöl, Altbatterien und ihre Wirkung (*effect*) auf die Umwelt
_____ Kontrolle der Verpackungsflut (*glut of packaging*)
_____ Messung des sauren Regens
_____ organische Abfälle und Kompost
_____ Verkehrsbelastung
_____ Stromverbrauch
_____ Verschmutzung der Seen, Flüsse
_____ Grünanlagen für einen neuen Stadtteil

Grammatik im Kontext

The Passive Voice°

das Passiv

So far you have learned to express sentences in German in the active voice. In the active voice, the subject of a sentence performs the action expressed by the verb. The person or thing performing the action is called the agent. In the passive voice, the subject is acted upon by an agent that is not always named, because it is either understood, unimportant, or unknown. Compare the following sentences.

The Passive Voice. Note: It is important for students to learn to recognize a passive voice sentence in reading; however, active mastery—integrating passive voice sentences freely in conversation—should not be expected at this level. Students should merely be able to produce simple sentences in the passive voice.

ACTIVE VOICE

Viele Leute lesen täglich eine Zeitung.	*Many people read a newspaper daily.*
Welche Zeitung lesen die Deutschen am häufigsten?	*Which paper do Germans read most often?*

PASSIVE VOICE

In Deutschland werden viele Zeitungen verkauft.	*Many newspapers are sold in Germany.*
Welche Zeitung wird am häufigsten gelesen?	*Which newspaper is read most often?*

The active voice emphasizes the subject that carries out an activity; in the passive voice the emphasis shifts to the activity itself. For this reason, the passive voice tends to be more impersonal. It is commonly used in newspapers, scientific writing, and descriptions of procedures and activities.

Formation of the Passive Voice

Formation of the Passive Voice. Suggestion: Review the conjugation of **werden.** To practice the passive with all personal forms, use *ich werde gefragt* or *ich werde eingeladen.*

The passive voice is formed with the auxiliary verb **werden** and the past participle of the main verb. (English uses *to be* and the past participle.)

The passive voice has the same tenses as the active voice. Although it can be used in all personal forms, the passive occurs most frequently in the third-person singular or plural.

Following are the commonly used tenses of the passive.

PRESENT

Die Zeitung **wird verkauft.**	*The newspaper is (being) sold.*
Die Zeitungen **werden verkauft.**	*The newspapers are (being) sold.*

SIMPLE PAST

Die Zeitung **wurde verkauft.**	*The newspaper was (being) sold.*
Die Zeitungen **wurden verkauft.**	*The newspapers were (being) sold.*

PRESENT PERFECT

Die Zeitung **ist verkauft worden.**	*The newspaper has been sold.*
Die Zeitungen **sind verkauft worden.**	*The newspapers have been sold.*

PAST PERFECT

Die Zeitung **war verkauft worden.**	*The newspaper had been sold.*
Die Zeitungen **waren verkauft worden.**	*The newspapers had been sold.*

Note that in the perfect tenses, the past participle **geworden** is shortened to **worden.** The presence of **worden** in any sentence is a clear signal that the sentence is in the passive voice.

You now know three ways in which the verb **werden** can function.

1. **werden** as independent verb (*to become*)
2. **werden** + infinitive (future tense)
3. **werden** + past participle (passive voice)

Analyse. Suggestion: Review the various functions of **werden** first; for example, *Hans wird Arzt. Was möchten Sie werden? Wir werden drei Wochen Ferien machen.* Then have students work in pairs to do the **Analyse.** When checking their answers, ask students to describe a possible context for each caption or headline.

Analyse

Read the headlines and captions and determine

- how the verb **werden** is used in each case (independent verb, future tense, passive)
- the position of the past participle in
  - **a.** a main clause in the passive voice
  - **b.** a dependent clause in the passive voice

In jeder Minute werden 21 Hektar[1] Regenwald vernichtet[2]

Schon in wenigen Jahren wird es die „Grünen Lungen[3] der Erde" nicht mehr geben

KULTURSTADT

Weimar im Blickpunkt: Die deutsche Klassiker-metropole wird 1999 Kulturstadt Europas

GREENPEACE

Wie konnten Sie es zulassen[4], daß unsere Erde[5] in so kurzer Zeit vergiftet[6] wurde?

1. 1 Hektar = *2.47 acres* 2. *destroyed* 3. *lungs* 4. *allow* 5. *earth* 6. *poisoned*

Realia. *Muß unser Dorf so häßlich werden?* is from a pamphlet published by the *Deutches Nationalkomitee für Denkmalschutz* in Bonn, which seeks to preserve the integrity and beauty of older buildings and monuments.

Expressing the Agent

As already noted, the agent causing the action in a passive voice sentence is often not stated. However, when it is stated, the agent is expressed with the preposition **von** (+ *dat.*).

In einer Stunde werden 1,5 Millionen Briefe **von Deutschen** geschrieben.	*In one hour 1.5 million letters are written by Germans.*

When the action is caused by an impersonal force, the preposition **durch** (+ *acc.*) is used.

Die Umwelt wird **durch Luftverschmutzung** zerstört.	*The environment is being destroyed by air pollution.*

Sentences in the passive voice that state the agent can also be expressed in the active voice. There is no difference in meaning, only in emphasis.

PASSIVE: In einer Stunde werden **1,5 Millionen Briefe** (*SUBJECT*) **von Deutschen** (*PREPOSITIONAL OBJECT (AGENT)*) geschrieben.

ACTIVE: **Die Deutschen** (*SUBJECT (AGENT)*) schreiben in einer Stunde **1,5 Millionen Briefe.** (*DIRECT OBJECT*)

Note that the subject in the passive voice sentence becomes the direct object in the active voice sentence, and the subject in the active voice sentence becomes the prepositional object (**von**) in the passive voice sentence.

Übung 1 Was passiert alles in 60 Minuten in Deutschland?

A. Bilden Sie Sätze im Passiv Präsens.

BEISPIEL: 1,5 Millionen Briefe werden geschrieben.

1. 1,5 Millionen Briefe	gegessen
2. Mehr als eine Million Liter Bier	verletzt
3. 77 Kinder	gekauft
4. 458 Autos	getrunken
5. 404 Fernsehgeräte	geschrieben
6. Über eine Million Zeitungen	geboren
7. 38 Menschen / in Unfällen auf der Straße	hergestellt
8. 721 Tonnen Fleisch	produziert

B. Drücken Sie die Sätze aus Teil A im Passiv Perfekt aus.

BEISPIEL: In einer Stunde sind 77 Kinder geboren worden.

Realia. This ad appeared in *Natur.*

Dr. Bouhon's bio öl
zur natürlichen Hautpflege
Mit Vitamin E

Ihrer Haut[1] zuliebe[2] wurde auf jede Chemie verzichtet[3]

1. *skin* 2. *for the sake of* 3. auf . . . *done without*

Übung 2 Achtung, Uhren umstellen!

Lesen Sie folgende Nachricht über die Sommerzeit.

Achtung,[1] Uhren umstellen[2]: Die Sommerzeit beginnt

BM/dpa Hamburg, 26. März

Der Osterhase[3] bringt in diesem Jahr auch die Sommerzeit: In der Nacht zum Sonntag um 2 Uhr werden die Uhren auf 3 Uhr vorgestellt[4]; die Nacht wird um eine Stunde verkürzt.[5] Die Sommerzeit endet am 24. September – traditionsgemäß wieder eine Sonntag-Nacht.

Die Sommerzeit war in der Bundesrepublik Deutschland – nach 30 Jahren Unterbrechung[6] – erstmals 1980 wieder eingeführt[7] worden. Das eigentliche[8] Ziel, Energie einzusparen, wurde jedoch nicht erreicht.[9] Dafür genießen[10] viele ihre Freizeit an den langen hellen Abenden.

Realia. This article appeared in the *Berliner Morgenpost.*

1. *attention*
2. *change*
3. *Easter Bunny*
4. *set ahead*
5. *shortened*
6. *interruption*
7. *introduced*
8. *real*
9. *reached*
10. *enjoy*

1. Identifizieren Sie alle Sätze im Passiv.
2. Was sind die Tatsachen?
- **a.** Die Uhren . . .
- **b.** Die Nacht . . .
- **c.** Die Sommerzeit . . .
- **d.** Das Ziel . . .

Expressing a General Activity

Sometimes a sentence in the passive voice expresses a general activity without stating a subject at all. In such cases, the "impersonal" **es** is generally understood to be the subject and therefore the conjugated verb always appears in the third-person singular. This grammatical feature has no equivalent in English.

Hier wird gerudert.	*People are rowing here.*
Hier wird gestreikt.	*There is a strike going on here. (On strike!)*

Realia. Suggestion: Give students several minutes to figure out who sits where.

Realia. This puzzle appeared in *Hörzu.*

Übung 3 Was ist hier los?

Beschreiben Sie, was die Leute auf diesen Bildern machen. Gebrauchen Sie die Verben:

debattieren	feiern	reden
demonstrieren	lachen	tanzen
diskutieren	Musik machen	trinken
essen		

BEISPIEL: Bild 1: Da wird gefeiert und . . .

1.

2.

3.

Übung 4 Eins nach dem andern!

Was kommt gewöhnlich zuerst?

BEISPIEL: Kuchen essen / Kuchen backen →
Zuerst wird der Kuchen gebacken, dann wird er gegessen.

1. duschen / aufstehen
2. Haare trocknen / Haare waschen
3. Zeitung lesen / Kaffee machen
4. Zähne putzen / frühstücken
5. im Supermarkt einkaufen / Wohnung aufräumen
6. Dosen zum Recyclingcontainer bringen / Dosen sammeln
7. Freund/Freundin anrufen / stundenlang diskutieren

Übung 5 Hin und her: Zwei umweltbewusste Städte 

In zwei Städten, Neustadt und Altstadt, wird für eine bessere Umwelt gesorgt.

BEISPIEL: S1: Was ist zuerst in Neustadt gemacht worden?
S2: Zuerst sind naturnahe Gärten angelegt worden.

	NEUSTADT	ALTSTADT
zuerst	naturnahe Gärten anlegen	Autos aus der Innenstadt verbannen
dann	Kinderspielplätze verbessern	neue Siedlungen am Stadtrand bauen
danach	Park im Zentrum säubern	Bürger über Umweltschutz informieren
schließlich	keine Wegwerfartikel in Geschäften verkaufen	neue, moderne Busse kaufen
zuletzt	nach Alternativenergie suchen	ein großes Umweltfest in der Innenstadt feiern

The Passive with Modal Verbs

Modal verbs used with a passive infinitive convey something that should, must, or can be done. Only the present tense, the simple past tense, and the present subjunctive of modals are commonly used in the passive.

Die Umwelt **muss geschützt werden.**	*The environment must be protected.*
Die Natur **darf** nicht **zerstört werden.**	*Nature must not be destroyed.*
Recyclingprogramme **sollen gefördert werden.**	*Recycling programs should be promoted.*

The passive infinitive consists of the past participle of the main verb and **werden.**

ACTIVE INFINITIVE
schützen (*to protect*)
zerstören (*to destroy*)
förden (*to promote*)

PASSIVE INFINITIVE
geschützt werden (*to be protected*)
zerstört werden (*to be destroyed*)
gefördert werden (*to be promoted*)

Übung 6 Aus Liebe zur Umwelt

Was kann und muss gemacht werden? Bilden Sie Sätze mit Modalverben und dem Passiv Infinitiv.

BEISPIEL: die Umwelt schonen / müssen → Die Umwelt muss geschont werden.

1. alle Menschen über Umweltschutz informieren / müssen
2. mehr Energie sparen / sollen
3. Recyclingprogramme fördern / sollen
4. Altglas sammeln / können
5. Abfälle wie Plastiktüten und Einwegflaschen vermeiden / müssen
6. Altbatterien nicht in den Müll werfen / dürfen
7. Wegwerfprodukte (wie z.B. Einmal-Rasierer, Einmal-Fotoapparate) nicht kaufen / sollen
8. Verpackung (wie die Mehrweg-Eierbox) wieder ins Geschäft bringen / können
9. Wälder und Flüsse schützen / müssen
10. Alternativenergie entwickeln / müssen
11. Luftverschmutzung vermindern / müssen

Kulturtipp

Beispiele für Gefahrensymbole

Gifte

Leicht entzündlich

Ätzend

Gesundheitsschädlich

In einigen Orten Deutschlands können alte Medikamente in die Apotheke zurückgebracht werden, damit sie nicht in den Abfall geworfen werden und als Giftstoffe die Umwelt gefährden. Andere potentiell gefährliche Substanzen wie alte Batterien und Farben werden von „Umweltbussen" abgeholt.

Übung 7 Was ist das Problem damit?

Übung 7. Suggestion: Go over both columns to make sure students understand the vocabulary. This will probably bring up the questions of what one can bring back to a pharmacy and what an **Umweltbus** is.

Was soll, kann oder darf damit (nicht) gemacht werden?

BEISPIEL: Digitaluhren können nicht repariert werden.

1. Billiguhren (Digitaluhren)	vom Umweltbus abholen
2. Einmal-Fotoapparate	in fast alle Apotheken zurückbringen
3. alte Batterien	nur für einen Film gebrauchen
4. Einwegflaschen	nicht in den Müll werfen
5. alte Medikamente	nicht wiederfüllen (wiedergefüllt)
6. Giftstoffe	nicht reparieren

man as an Alternative to the Passive

Generally, the passive voice is used whenever the agent of an action is unknown. One alternative to the passive is to use the pronoun **man** in the active voice.

PASSIVE VOICE	ACTIVE-VOICE ALTERNATIVE
Die Gefahr ist nicht erkannt worden. *The danger was not recognized.*	**Man hat** die Gefahr nicht **erkannt.** *People (One) did not recognize the danger.*
Die Zerstörung der Altstadt ist verhindert worden. *The destruction of the old city was prevented.*	**Man hat** die Zerstörung der Altstadt **verhindert.** *People (One) prevented the destruction of the old city.*

Note: Alternative publications often use *frau/man* in place of only *man.*

Übung 8 Was kann man für die Umwelt tun?

Bilden Sie neue Sätze mit **man.**

BEISPIEL: Wegwerfprodukte sollen vermieden werden. →
Man soll Wegwerfprodukte vermeiden.

1. Umweltschutz muss gelebt werden; er kann nicht befohlen werden.
2. Die Umwelt darf nicht weiter zerstört werden.
3. Altpapier und Glas sollten zum Recycling gebracht werden.
4. In Göttingen ist Geld für den Umweltschutz gesammelt worden.
5. Mehr Recycling-Container sind aufgestellt worden.
6. Chemikalien im Haushalt sollen vermieden werden.
7. Batterien sollen nicht in den Hausmüll geworfen werden.
8. Der Wald muss besonders geschützt werden.

Übung 9 Lebensqualität

Übung 9. **Suggestion:** Use this exercise to review other possible passive voice substitutes (*Man soll . . .* , etc.). **Suggestion:** Also review modals with a passive infinitive (*Plastiktüten sollen vermieden werden,* etc.).

Was kann man tun, um die Lebensqualität zu verbessern? Bilden Sie Sätze mit **man.**

BEISPIEL: alte Zeitungen →
Man kann alte Zeitungen zum Recycling bringen.

A. Für die Umwelt

Plastiktüten	bauen
Windenergie	fördern
Kinderspielplätze	vermeiden
Solarautos	sammeln
Altpapier	entwickeln
öffentliche Verkehrsmittel	schützen
Wälder	benutzen

B. Für die Gesellschaft

Hilfsorganisationen	verbieten
Arbeitslosigkeit	unterstützen
Programme für Alkoholiker	entwickeln
Arbeitsplätze	wählen
verantwortungsbewusste Politiker	vermindern
Rauchen in öffentlichen Gebäuden	schaffen

The Present Participle°

°das Partizip Präsens

The present participle (ending in *ing* in English) is used in a more limited way in German than it is in English. In German it functions primarily as an adjective or an adverb. As an attributive adjective (preceding a noun), the participle takes appropriate adjective endings.

The present participle of a German verb is formed by adding **d** to the infinitive.

INFINITIVE	PRESENT PARTICIPLE
kommen	kommend (*coming*)
steigen	steigend (*climbing, increasing*)

PRESENT PARTICIPLE AS ADJECTIVE

im **kommenden** Sommer	*in the coming (next) summer*
die **steigende** Arbeitslosigkeit	*increasing unemployment*

PRESENT PARTICIPLE AS ADVERB

Jennifer spricht **fließend** Deutsch.	*Jennifer speaks German fluently* (*lit. flowingly*).

No ending is added to the present participle when it is used as an adverb. (German adverbs never take endings.)

Übung 10 In der Zeitung

Worüber liest man fast täglich? Bilden Sie Sätze mit dem Partizip Präsens.

BEISPIEL: Man liest täglich über den wachsenden Verkehr.

1. die Menschen	steigen
2. die Preise	flüchten (*to flee*)
3. die Bürger	streiken
4. die Studenten	wachsen (*to grow*)
5. der Verkehr	protestieren
6. das Problem	sterben
7. der Wald	demonstrieren
8. die Arbeiter	

Sprache im Kontext

Zuschauen

Vorschau

A. Sehen Sie sich den Cartoon ein- oder zweimal ohne Unterbrechung an. Worum geht es in diesem Cartoon? Kreuzen Sie an, was passt.

	JA	VIELLEICHT	NEIN
1. Liebe im Fitnesscenter	☐	☐	☐
2. Fitnessprogramme für Kranke	☐	☐	☐
3. Siggi Sorglos: Weltmeister im Gewichteheben	☐	☐	☐
4. Gewichteheben ist gut für Frauen.	☐	☐	☐
5. Probleme mit Müllbergen	☐	☐	☐
6. Flaschen sind umweltfreundlicher als Kartons.	☐	☐	☐
7. Beim Trainieren soll man viel trinken.	☐	☐	☐
8. Schützt die Umwelt! Vermindert den Müll!	☐	☐	☐

B. Machen Sie eine kleine Umfrage in der Klasse. Wer hat wofür gestimmt? Welches Thema hat die meisten Stimmen bekommen? Warum?

Arbeit mit dem Videotext

Lesen Sie die folgenden Fragen, bevor Sie sich den Cartoon noch ein- oder zweimal ansehen. Beantworten Sie dann die Fragen.

1. In dem Cartoon sagt ein Sprecher: „Wo viel geschwitzt (*sweated*) wird, wird auch viel getrunken." Was soll das hier bedeuten? Wie kann man dies auch anders sagen (im Aktiv)?
2. Siggi Sorglos versucht zweimal, mit Fräulein Müller Wachtendonk ins Gespräch zu kommen. Was ist seine Strategie? Hat er Erfolg damit?
3. Was is das Problem mit Getränkekartons für Saft und Milch, wie Siggi Sorglos sie Fräulein Müller Wachtendonk anbietet? Wie kann das Problem gelöst werden?
4. Wie hat Siggi Sorglos schließlich Erfolg mit Fräulein Müller Wachtendonk?
5. Was ist die eigentliche Bedeutung dieses Cartoon? Was ist Ihre Meinung zu diesem Aufruf, die Umwelt zu schützen, indem man weniger Müll schafft? Ist das möglich? praktisch? Ist es utopisch oder eine absolute Notwendigkeit?
6. Kommen Sie nun auf die Themenliste in der Vorschau zurück. Welches Thema passt am besten?

Lesen

Zum Thema

Die Boulevard- und Skandalpresse. In vielen Ländern gibt es Boulevardzeitungen, die von den jüngsten Sensationen und Skandalen berichten. Auch in Fernsehmagazinen (*magazine-style TV program*) wird oft von sensationellen und skandalösen Ereignissen berichtet.

Zum Thema. Suggestion: If possible, bring in a variety of German-language newspapers. Have students skim them and draw conclusions about the newspapers from a cursory examination.

Machen Sie eine Umfrage im Kurs.

1. Wer liest regelmäßig Boulevardzeitungen? Welche? Warum?
2. Wer sieht regelmäßig Fernsehmagazine? Welche? Warum?

Auf den ersten Blick

1. Lesen Sie den Text, eine Ballade von Reinhard Mai, kurz durch. Wovon handelt die Ballade? Wer sind die Hauptfiguren? Wo spielt sich das Ereignis ab? Wann findet es statt?
2. Suchen Sie Wörter im Text, die Sie mit „gehen" ersetzen (*replace*) können. Was für Gefühle drücken diese Wörter aus?

Was in der Zeitung steht

von Reinhard Mai

Wie jeden Morgen war er pünktlich dran, seine
Kollegen sahen ihn fragend an, „Sag' mal,
hast du noch nicht gesehen, was in der
Zeitung steht?"
Er schloß die Türe hinter sich,
hängte Hut und Mantel in den Schrank fein säuberlich,° *neatly*
setzte sich, „da wollen wir erst mal sehen,
was in der Zeitung steht."

Und da stand es fett auf Seite zwei
„Finanzskandal", sein Bild dabei
und die Schlagzeile „Wie lang das wohl so weitergeht?"
Er las den Text,
und ihm war sofort klar,
eine Verwechslung,° nein, da war kein Wort' von wahr, *mistake, mix-up*
aber wie kann so etwas verlogen° sein, *fabricated*
was in der Zeitung steht?

Er starrte° auf das Blatt, *stared*
das vor ihm lag,
es traf ihn wie ein heimtückischer° Schlag, *malicious*
wie ist das möglich, daß so etwas in der Zeitung steht?
Das Zimmer ringsherum begann sich zu drehen,° sich . . . *to turn*
die Zeilen konnte er nur noch verschwommen° sehen. *blurredly*
Wie wehrt man sich° nur gegen das, wehrt . . . *does one defend oneself*
was in der Zeitung steht?

Die Kollegen sagten, „stell dich einfach stur",° „stell . . . *be stolid*
er taumelte° zu seinem Chef über den Flur, *staggered*
„aber selbstverständlich,
daß jeder hier zu Ihnen steht,
ich glaube, das Beste ist, Sie spannen erst mal aus,
ein paar Tage Urlaub, bleiben Sie zu Haus,
Sie wissen ja, die Leute glauben gleich alles,
nur weil es in der Zeitung steht."

Er holte Hut und Mantel, wankte° aus dem Raum, *swayed*
nein, das war wirklich kalt, das war kein böser Traum,
wer denkt sich sowas aus, wie das,
was in der Zeitung steht?
Er rief den Fahrstuhl,° stieg ein und gleich wieder aus, *elevator*
nein, er ging doch wohl besser durch das Treppenhaus.° *stairwell*
Da würde ihn keiner sehen, der wüßte,
was in der Zeitung steht.

Er würde durch die Tiefgarage gehen, er war zu Fuß.
Der Pförtner° würde ihn nicht sehen, *custodian*
der wußte immer ganz genau,
was in der Zeitung steht.
Er stolperte° die Wagenauffahrt° rauf, *stumbled / driveway*
sah den Rücken des Pförtners,
das Tor war auf,
das klebt wie Pech° an dir, *tar*
das wirst du nie mehr los,
was in der Zeitung steht,
was in der Zeitung steht,
was in der Zeitung steht,
was in der Zeitung steht.

Er eilte° zur U-Bahnstation, *hurried*
jetzt wüßten es die Nachbarn schon,
jetzt war es im ganzen Ort herum,
was in der Zeitung steht.
Solange die Kinder in der Schule waren,
solange würden sie es vielleicht nicht erfahren,° *find out*
aber irgendwer hat ihnen längst erzählt,
was in der Zeitung steht.

Er wich den Leuten auf dem Bahnsteig aus,° wich . . . aus *avoided*
ihm schien, die Blicke, alle richteten sich nur auf ihn,
der Mann im Kiosk da, der wußte Wort für Wort,
was in der Zeitung steht.
Wie eine Welle war es, die über ihm zusammenschlug,
wie die Erlösung° kam der Vorortszug, *deliverance*
du wirst nie mehr ganz frei, das hängt dir ewig an,
was in der Zeitung steht.

„Was wollen Sie eigentlich?“ fragte der Redakteur,° *editor*
„Verantwortung, Mann, wenn ich das schon hör’,
die Leute müssen halt nicht gleich alles glauben,
nur weil es in der Zeitung steht.“
„Na, schön, so eine Verwechslung kann schon mal passieren,
da kannst du noch so sorgfältig° recherchieren.° *carefully / research*
Mann, was glauben Sie, was Tag für Tag für ein Unfug° *nonsense*
in der Zeitung steht?“

„Ja“, sagte der Chef vom Dienst, „das ist wirklich zu dumm,
aber ehrlich,° man bringt sich doch nicht gleich um,° *honestly /* bringt . . . *one doesn't kill oneself*
nur weil mal aus Versehen° aus . . . *by mistake*
was in der Zeitung steht.“
Die Gegendarstellung° erschien am Abend schon, *retraction, corrected version*
fünf Zeilen mit dem Bedauern der Redaktion,
aber Hand aufs Herz, wer liest, was so klein
in der Zeitung steht?

Zum Text

1. Lesen Sie die folgenden Sätze, und setzen Sie sie in die richtige Reihenfolge.
   a. Am Bahnsteig meinte er, dass alle die Zeitung schon gelesen hätten.
   b. Es war ganz klein gedruckt.
   c. Der Chef fand, dass sein Selbstmord (*suicide*) übertrieben war.
   d. Er erfuhr (*found out*), was in der Zeitung stand.
   e. Er verließ das Gebäude durch die Parkgarage, um die Leute zu vermeiden.
   f. Ein Mann ging ins Büro zur Arbeit.
   g. Er sah sein Bild neben der Schlagzeile „Finanzskandal".
   h. Er ging zu seinem Chef.
   i. Er warf sich vor den Zug.
   j. In der Zeitung stand, dass der Bericht ein Irrtum (*mistake*) gewesen sei.
   k. Sein Chef meinte, es sei besser, wenn er ein paar Tage zu Hause bliebe.
   l. Der Redakteur meinte, dass er keine Verantwortung trüge.
2. Wie reagieren die Personen in der Ballade auf den Artikel in der Zeitung?
3. Wie steht der Liedermacher zu der Presse?
4. „Was in der Zeitung steht" ist eine Ballade. Schlagen Sie das Wort „Ballade" in einem Wörterbuch (*Duden* oder *Wahrig*) nach. Was sind die Merkmale einer Ballade? Was sind Beispiele dafür im Text der Ballade?

Sprechen und Schreiben

Aktivität 1 Informieren Sie sich!

Was finden Sie über die deutschsprachigen Länder in den hiesigen (*local*) Zeitungen oder Zeitschriften? Gehen Sie in die Bibliothek. Suchen Sie sich mehrere Zeitungen oder Zeitschriften aus. Schauen Sie nach, was in den letzten zwei Monaten über die deutschsprachigen Länder berichtet wurde. Welche Themen über die deutschsprachigen Länder kommen vor? Warum sind diese Themen wichtig? Wählen Sie ein Thema und geben Sie einen kurzen Bericht in der Klasse.

Aktivität 2 Reporter

Schreiben Sie einen kurzen Artikel über den Vorfall (*incident*) in der Ballade von R. Mai. Nehmen Sie dazu Stellung. Benutzen Sie dabei indirekte Rede.

Wortschatz

Weltweite Probleme	World Problems
die **Arbeitslosigkeit**	unemployment
die **Armut**	poverty
der **Ausländer, -** / die **Ausländerin, -nen**	foreigner
die **Ausländerfeindlichkeit**	xenophobia, hatred directed toward foreigners
die **Drogensucht**	drug addiction
der/die **Drogensüchtige, -n**	drug addict
die **Gewalttätigkeit, -en**	(act of) violence
der **Hunger**	hunger, famine
die **Korruption**	corruption
die **Krankheit, -en**	illness
der **Krieg, -e**	war
das **Menschenrecht, -e**	human right (*usu. plural*)
der/die **Obdachlose, -n**	homeless person
die **Obdachlosigkeit**	homelessness
der **Rassismus**	racism
der **Rechtsextremismus**	right-wing extremism
die **Umweltverschmutzung**	environmental pollution
die **Verletzung, -en**	injury, violation

Umwelt	Environment
der **Abfall, ¨-e**	waste, garbage, trash, litter
die **Dose, -n**	(tin or aluminum) can
die **Flasche, -n**	bottle
die **Wegwerfflasche, -n**	throw-away bottle
die **Fußgängerzone, -n**	pedestrian zone, mall
der **Lärm**	noise
die **Plastiktüte, -n**	plastic bag
die **Sammelstelle, -n**	recycling center
das **Verkehrsmittel, -**	means of transportation
die **Verpackung, -en**	packaging

Sonstige Substantive	Other Nouns
der **Alkohol**	alcohol
der **Bürger, -** / die **Bürgerin, -nen**	citizen
die **Demonstration, -en**	demonstration
die **Droge, -n**	drug
die **Forschung**	research
der **Fortschritt, -e**	progress
Fortschritte machen	to make progress
die **Gefahr, -en**	danger
das **Gefängnis, -se**	prison
die **Lösung, -en**	solution
die **Meinung, -en**	opinion
ich bin der Meinung . . .	I'm of the opinion . . .
meiner Meinung nach . . .	in my opinion . . .
der **Politiker, -** / die **Politikerin, -nen**	politician
die **Regierung, -en**	government
die **Steuer, -n**	tax

Verben	Verbs
sich etwas an•schaffen	to purchase
bedauern	to regret
ein•führen	to introduce
sich engagieren	to get involved
entwickeln	to develop
erziehen, erzog, erzogen	to raise, bring up
fördern	to promote
halten (für) (hält), hielt, gehalten	to hold; to consider, think
schaffen, schuf, geschaffen	to create
schützen	to protect
teil•nehmen an (+ *dat.*) **(nimmt teil), nahm teil, teilgenommen**	to participate (in)
trennen	to separate
unterstützen	to support
verbieten, verbot, verboten	prohibit, forbid
verbrauchen	to consume
verbreiten	to spread, disseminate
vermeiden, vermied, vermieden	to avoid
vermindern	to reduce
verwenden	to use, apply
vor•ziehen, zog vor, vorgezogen	to prefer
wählen	to elect; to choose

Adjektive und Adverbien	Adjectives and Adverbs
möglich	possible, possibly
öffentlich	public
sauber	clean
schmutzig	dirty
streng	strict(ly)
übertrieben	exaggerated(ly)
umweltfreundlich	environmentally friendly

Andere Ausdrücke	Other Expressions
außerdem	besides
Ich bin dafür.	I'm in favor of it.
Ich bin dagegen.	I'm against it.
Ich finde . . .	I think . . .
So ein Quatsch!	Baloney!
So ein Unsinn!	Nonsense!

Lernziele

Use this checklist to verify that you can now . . .

- ☐ give your opinion about various problems in the world and possible solutions.
- ☐ give your opinion about the environment and what people can do to protect it.
- ☐ use the passive voice in simple sentences.
- ☐ create sentences using **man.**
- ☐ use the present participle as an attributive adjective or as an adverb.

Übergang

Gestern und heute

Der verhüllte Reichstag in Berlin

Übergang. This chapter is called *Übergang* because it is considered a capstone for first-year German and a transition to second-year German. Begin the chapter by discussing a particular event from German history. Ask students which events from the recent past will become important milestones in history.

Kleine Chronik deutscher Geschichte von 1939–1991

1. September 1939 — Der Zweite Weltkrieg beginnt mit der Invasion Polens durch deutsche Truppen.

9. Mai 1945 — Um null Uhr eins endet der Zweite Weltkrieg in Europa offiziell mit der Kapitulation der Deutschen Wehrmacht.° Durch diesen Krieg verloren insgesamt 55 Millionen Menschen ihr Leben.

armed forces

Das zerbombte Reichstagsgebäude, Berlin 1945

Trümmerfrauen bei der Arbeit

5. Juni 1945 — Die vier Alliierten (die Vereinigten Staaten, die Sowjetunion, Großbritannien und Frankreich) übernehmen die oberste Regierungsgewalt in Deutschland. Deutschland wird in vier Besatzungszonen° aufgeteilt. Berlin, die ehemalige Hauptstadt, wird separat in vier Besatzungszonen aufgeteilt.

occupation zones

5. Juni 1947 — Der Marshallplan wird für Deutschland die Grundlage° für das kommende Wirtschaftswunder.°

foundation

economic miracle

Kleine Chronik. Suggestion: If it is available, show the film *Triumph des Willens* by filmmaker Leni Riefenstahl, which documents Hitler's effect on the German people, as shown in the annual ritual of the *Parteitag* in Nürnberg. **Suggestion:** Assign the *Kleine Chronik* reading as homework. Discuss and elaborate on dates and events the following day, bringing in additional pictures and slides.

Menschenschlangen stehen 1946 nach Lebensmitteln an.

Die „Luftbrücke“: Ein „Rosinenbomber“ kurz vor der Landung in Berlin

20. Juni 1948	Es gibt neues Geld: die Deutsche Mark. Jeder Bürger der Westzonen und West-Berlins bekommt zu Anfang 40 Mark.
24. Juni 1948	Beginn der Berliner Blockade. Die Sowjetunion blockiert alle Wege nach West-Berlin außer den Luftwegen. Elf Monate lang werden die Berliner durch die „Luftbrücke“ versorgt.
23. Mai 1949	Gründung der Bundesrepublik Deutschland (BRD).

7. Oktober 1949	Gründung der Deutschen Demokratischen Republik (DDR).	
17. Juni 1953	Volksaufstand° in Ost-Berlin und der DDR gegen das kommunistische Regime.	*popular uprising*
13. August 1961	Bau der Mauer° in Berlin.	*wall*
26. Juni 1963	Besuch Präsident John F. Kennedys in Berlin. Seine Erklärung der Solidarität mit Berlinern endet mit den oft zitierten Worten: „Ich bin ein Berliner."	
9. November 1989	Die Grenzen zwischen der DDR und der BRD werden geöffnet. Die Mauer zwischen Ost- und West-Berlin hat genau 10 315 Tage gehalten.	
18. März 1990	Erste freie, demokratische Wahl in der Deutschen Demokratischen Republik seit ihrer Gründung.	
3. Oktober 1990	Tag der offiziellen deutschen Einigung. Fünf neue Bundesländer (Brandenburg, Mecklenburg-Vorpommern, Sachsen, Sachsen-Anhalt und Thüringen) treten der Bundesrepublik bei.°	treten . . . bei *join*
20. Juni 1991	Der deutsche Bundestag wählt Berlin zum Regierungssitz° des vereinigten Deutschlands.	*seat of government*

Kulturtipp

Die Kaiser-Wilhelm-Gedächtniskirche liegt am Kudamm (Kurfürstendamm), dem großen Einkaufsboulevard Berlins. Die Kirche lag am Ende des Zweiten Weltkriegs in Trümmern (*ruins*). Man baute eine neue, moderne Kirche auf, ließ aber die schwarze Ruine des Turms als Mahnmal (*memorial*) an die dunklen Jahre des Krieges stehen.

Die Kaiser-Wilhelm-Gedächtniskirche in Berlin

Aktivität 1 Aus der deutschen Geschichte

Weiteres zum Thema Geschichte finden Sie bei ***Deutsch: Na klar!*** im World-Wide-Web unter www.mhhe.com/german.

Ordnen Sie zuerst die Daten und die Satzteile einander zu. Welches Bild passt zu welchem Satz?

Am 9. Mai 1945	wurde die Grenze zwischen Ost- und West-Berlin durch den Bau der Mauer geschlossen.
Am 17. Juni 1953	feierte ganz Deutschland die Öffnung der Grenze zwischen Ost- und West-Berlin und zwischen der DDR und der BRD.
Am 13. August 1961	als der Zweite Weltkrieg in Europa endete, lag ganz Deutschland in Trümmern.
Am 9. November 1989	gab es in der DDR einen Aufstand gegen das kommunistische Regime.

1.

2.

3.

4.

Aktivität 2 Faktum oder nicht?

Stimmt das oder stimmt es nicht? Korrigieren Sie die falschen Aussagen.

	DAS STIMMT	DAS STIMMT NICHT
1. Der Zweite Weltkrieg begann mit der Invasion der Sowjetunion durch deutsche Truppen im September 1939.	☐	☐
2. Der Zweite Weltkrieg kostete 55 Millionen Menschen das Leben.	☐	☐
3. Deutschland wurde nach dem Zweiten Weltkrieg in vier Besatzungszonen geteilt.	☐	☐
4. Berlin gehörte ganz zur russischen Besatzungszone.	☐	☐
5. Die BRD und die DDR wurden 1945 gegründet.	☐	☐
6. Der Marshallplan spielte eine wichtige Rolle beim Wiederaufbau Europas.	☐	☐
7. Im Juni 1948 blockierte die Sowjetunion alle Transportwege nach Berlin.	☐	☐
8. Im Jahre 1953 rebellierten die Deutschen in Ost und West gegen die kommunistische Regierung.	☐	☐
9. Im Jahre 1991 wurden die DDR und die BRD vereinigt.	☐	☐

Aktivität 3 Ein kleines Quiz

Bilden Sie mehrere Gruppen. Machen Sie mit Hilfe der kleinen Chronik deutscher Geschichte ein Quiz. Das Format bleibt jeder Gruppe überlassen. Es könnte z.B. in Form einer Quizshow sein: Wer bin ich?; es könnte eine Serie von Fragen sein, die Sie gemeinsam entwickeln; oder es könnte ein Wortratespiel sein. Die anderen im Kurs übernehmen die Rolle der Teilnehmer (*participants*).

Aktivität 3. Suggestion: Assign the creation of the quiz to each group for homework. Brainstorm some ideas with students, and do the quiz in class the next day.

Aktivität 4 Berliner Geschichte

Die folgenden spontanen Reaktionen von Menschen aus Ost und West nach dem „Fall" der Mauer am 9. November 1989 dokumentieren, wie der „kleine Mann" und die „kleine Frau" auf den Straßen Berlins den historischen Moment empfanden.

Wer hat das vielleicht gesagt, jemand aus dem Westen oder aus dem Osten? Gibt es Argumente für beides? Begründen Sie Ihre Antwort!

Große Freude nach der Öffnung der Grenzen: Eine Westberlinerin begrüßt eine DDR-Bürgerin.

BEISPIEL: Nummer eins war vielleicht jemand aus dem Osten. Diese Person war noch nie am Kudamm gewesen. Deswegen will er oder sie zuerst dahin gehen.

1. Erst mal Ku'damm.
2. Bloß mal den Fuß auf die andere Seite setzen, mal gucken, wie es hier ist.
3. Das ist der Tag, auf den wir so lang warten mussten, ich kann es nicht fassen.
4. *Ich glaube, morgen gehen im KaDeWe[1] die Bananen aus.*
5. **Auf den Tag hab ich 28 Jahre lang gewartet. Ich will nur mal sehen, ob meine Straße auch im Westen weitergeht.**
6. Wir saßen alle schon in Schlafanzügen vor dem Fernseher, als die Nachricht durchkam. Dann ging alles ruck zuck.[2]
7. *„Diese Nacht werde ich mein Leben lang nicht vergessen —jetzt weiß ich, dass wir alle zusammengehören."*
8. Ich bin der erste Japaner, der die Ostseite der Mauer berührt hat.
9. Junge Frau am Checkpoint Charlie: *„Guten Abend, ich werd' verrückt."*

1. Kaufhaus des Westens
2. ruck . . . (*coll.*) *in a flash*

Beiträge° zur deutschen Geschichte

°contributions

Wie berührt (*touches*) Geschichte unser Leben? In diesem Teil des Kapitels erleben Sie Geschichte, indem Sie persönliche Dokumente, Auszüge aus einer Autobiographie und aus einem Tagebuch und Briefe lesen. Diese persönlichen Dokumente bringen uns historische Ereignisse auf ungewöhnliche Weise näher.

Auf den ersten Blick 1

Auf den ersten Blick 1. Suggestion: Mention the different groups of people who were persecuted under Hitler: Jews, political opponents (particularly Communists), homosexuals, mentally retarded or mentally disturbed people, and other groups deemed racially inferior, such as Gypsies.

Der folgende Text, ein kurzer Ausschnitt aus der Autobiographie der Zigeunerin (*Gypsy*) Ceja Stojka, *Wir leben im Verborgenen: Erinnerungen einer Rom-Zigeunerin,* ist im Jahre 1989 erschienen. Bisher ist sehr wenig über das Schicksal (*fate*) der Zigeuner unter Hitler geschrieben worden. Ceja Stojka wurde 1933 in einem Gasthaus in der Steiermark in Österreich geboren. Während des Dritten Reiches wurde sie als Zigeunerin—sie gehörte zu der Rom Gruppe—aus rassistischen Gründen verfolgt (*persecuted*). Sie kam zusammen mit ihrer Mutter und ihren Schwestern in die Konzentrationslager Auschwitz und Ravensbrück.

Überfliegen Sie den ersten Abschnitt des Textes. Welche der folgenden Namen und Wörter stehen im Text?

- □ Auschwitz
- □ Hitler
- □ experimentieren
- □ nach Hause gehen
- □ Berlin
- □ SS-Soldaten
- □ sterilisieren
- □ Ravensbrück
- □ SS-Frauen
- □ Konzentrationslager

Die Aufseherinnen (*female guards*) in den Konzentrationslagern wurden automatisch zu Mitgliedern der SS. Daher die Bezeichnung SS-Frauen, die Ceja Stojka benutzt.

Für „arische" Frauen waren Verhütungsmittel (*birth control*), Abtreibungen (*abortions*) und Sterilisation gegen das Gesetz; aber für andere Frauen, die nicht der Norm entsprachen, gab es Zwangssterilisation (*forced sterilization*). In den Konzentrationslagern wurden Zwangssterilisationen an vielen Frauen vorgenommen, um mit neuen Methoden der Sterilisation zu experimentieren.

Kulturtipp. Note: The *SS (Schutzstaffel)* was created by Hitler in 1925 as a military organization within his party and was totally loyal to him. It became the most feared party organization during the Nazi years.

Realia. This is a **Wahlplakat** for Adolf Hitler: "Rettet die deutsche Familie. Wählt Adolf Hitler."

Wir leben im Verborgenen

von Ceja Stojka

Ja, es war nicht einfach in diesem Frauenlager Ravensbrück. Die SS-Frauen waren schlechter als jeder Satan. Eines Tages kamen zwei von ihnen und sagten zu uns: „Hört alle gut zu, was wir euch sagen. Es ist ein Schreiben aus Berlin gekommen und das sagt, alle Frauen und Kinder, die sich sterilisieren lassen, können bald nach Hause gehen." Und weiter sagten sie: „Na, ihr braucht ja keine Kinder mehr, also kommt morgen und unterschreibt,° daß ihr freiwillig dazu bereit seid. Der Oberarzt wird euch diesen Eingriff° machen. In ein paar Tagen könnt ihr dann das Lager verlassen." (Das war alles eine Lüge.° Ja, es war eine Lüge, denn wir standen alle schon auf der Liste.)

Die SS-Frauen wurden immer böser. So verging° ein Tag um den anderen. Täglich warf man Frauen in den Bunker, und sie kamen nicht mehr zurück. So ging es wochenlang.

Die Tage wurden nun schon länger und manchesmal war es nicht mehr so kalt. Ich, Mama, Kathi, Chiwe mit Burli und Rupa mußten in die Waschküche. Wir machten dort unsere Arbeit und als wir zurückkamen, sahen wir, wie zwei Häftlinge° einen Bretterwagen° vor unsere Baracke zogen. Viele Frauen waren darauf, wie Schweine lagen sie übereinander. Ganz oben lag unsere kleine liebe Resi. Sie waren sterilisiert worden, alle hatten große Schmerzen, sie konnten nicht einmal ein einziges Wort sagen. Die kleine Resi starb° gleich, auch die anderen kamen nicht mehr durch. Alle waren tot. Die SS-Frauen sagten dann zu uns: „Ihr braucht keine Angst zu haben, der Oberarzt hat ein neues Gerät bekommen, das alte hatte einen Kurzschluß,° also ein Versehen.°" Wir wußten ganz genau, daß sie uns nur besänftigen° wollten, aber wir wußten auch, daß wir ihnen nicht entkommen.° Eines Tages kamen Binz und Rabl und holten Mama, Kathi und mich ab. Sie sprachen nicht viel und sagten nur: „Marsch, Marsch". Wir gingen sehr schnell. In diesem Moment war uns alles egal. Wir kamen zu einem richtigen Haus. Es ging stockaufwärts. Die SS-Frauen machten im Vorraum dem Oberarzt ihre Meldung.° Nun warteten wir. Mama zeigte uns mit ihren blauen Augen, daß wir mutig° sein sollten, sprechen durften wir ja nicht. Die Zeit verging und es geschah nichts. Plötzlich kam der Oberarzt und sagte: „Heute ist nichts mehr, wir haben leider keinen Strom." Er schaute uns mit großen Augen an und machte seine Tür zu. Zwei SS-Frauen brachten uns wieder in das Lager zurück. Unterwegs sahen wir eine Baracke. Drinnen waren viele Frauen mit Schreibmaschinen. Das war die Schreibstube. Nun waren wir wieder in unserer Baracke. Alle fragten, was geschehen war, und alle Frauen weinten vor Freude.

Mama sagte: „*O swundo Dell gamel awer wariso de gerel amenza.*" (Der liebe Gott hat was anderes mit uns vor.)

sign
operation
lie
passed
inmates / wooden wagon
died
short circuit / accident
quiet
escape
report
brave

Zum Text 1

1. Wie wurden Ceja und ihre Familie durch die Rassenpolitik der Nazis betroffen (*affected*)?
2. Welche Erfahrungen beschreibt die Autorin?
   - Die SS-Frauen versprachen den Häftlingen, wenn sie sich freiwillig sterilisieren lassen,
     a. bekommen sie besseres Essen.
     b. brauchen sie eine Woche nicht zu arbeiten.
     c. werden sie bald freigelassen.
   - Der Sterilisationsprozess im Lager war
     a. freiwillig.
     b. ein medizinisches Experiment.
     c. eine Gesundheitsmaßnahme (*health precaution*).
   - Die Autorin erinnert sich daran, dass sie im Konzentrationslager
     a. zur Schule ging.
     b. in der Waschküche arbeitete.
     c. auf der Schreibstube arbeitete.
   - Die ersten Frauen, die sterilisiert wurden,
     a. starben an den Folgen der Sterilisation.
     b. kamen nie in die Baracken zurück.
     c. durften nach Hause gehen.
   - Die Autorin wurde nicht sterilisiert, weil
     a. der Oberarzt Mitleid (*sympathy*) mit ihr hatte.
     b. man sie in der Waschküche brauchte.
     c. es keine Elektrizität gab.

Auf den ersten Blick 2

Im Frühjahr 1947 reiste der frühere Präsident Herbert Hoover nach Deutschland und nach Österreich, um die katastrophale Ernährungssituation zu untersuchen (*investigate*). Das Resultat war die Hoover-Speisung für Schulkinder in beiden Ländern. Kinder schickten Hoover Hunderte von Briefen, um ihm für seine Hilfe zu danken. Sie lesen hier drei dieser Briefe, die jetzt in den Archiven des Hoover Instituts in Stanford, Kalifornien, gesammelt sind.

Überfliegen Sie die drei Briefe kurz.

1. Wer hat die Briefe geschrieben? (Namen und Alter)
2. Aus welchem Jahr stammen die Briefe?
3. Wie reden (*address*) die Kinder Herbert Hoover an? Wie enden ihre Briefe?

Auf den ersten Blick 2. Point Out: The letters reprinted here belong to a large collection of letters in the Hoover Institution Archives sent by German and Austrian children. The children's letters were the result of a nationwide effort to thank Hoover and the American people for their help. For many children, the *Schulspeisung* was the only regular meal of the day.

Briefe an Herbert Hoover

Heike Leopold. Note: The style, spelling (*Aberika*), and handwriting show this to be the youngest of the three writers. Heike is a refugee child who lost her home in Upper Silesia, now a part of Poland. Her keen interest in a doll with long hair, very typical for young girls of that time, reflects a child's capacity to block out the harsh realities of survival. Those realities are only hinted at by her mention of her mother frequently standing in line for bread for a long time, leaving Heike and her sister by themselves.

THE HERBERT HOOVER ARCHIVES

Eckernförde, den 26.3.47.

Lieber Onkel Hoover!

Ich habe Dich neulich im Kino gesehen und da Du so lieb und gut aussiehst, will ich Dir heute schreiben. Wir sind aus Oberschlesien hierher gekommen und haben dort unsre schönen Sachen lassen müssen.

Giebt es in Aberika schon Puppen mit langen Haaren zu kaufen? Wir sind so oft allein, weil unsre Mutti nach Brot anstehen muß. Werden bei euch alle Leute satt? Nun willst Du uns ja hier helfen in Deutschland. Viele Grüße, von Heike Leopold.

Margot Frankel

Bayreuth, den 28.5.1947.

Sehr geehrter Herr Hoover!

Wir freuten uns sehr, als uns verkündet[1] wurde, daß alle die Auslandsspeisen bekommen. Denn es wurde durch Wiegen und Messen festgestellt[2], daß viele unterernährt[3] sind. Wir sind schon immer auf die Minute gespannt[4], wenn es läutet[5] und wir unser Essen bekommen. Heute gibt es Teigwaren[6] mit Obsttunke[7]. Wenn manchmal ein Rest übrig bleibt, freuen wir uns am meisten, wenn wir es bekommen. Es gibt jetzt schon 2½ Wochen Essen. Am meisten aber freuen wir uns, wenn es am Ende der Wochen Eiscremepaste gibt. Als es das erstemal die Auslandsspeisen gab,

bekamen wir am Ende der Woche eine Tafel Schokolade. Wir mußten sie gleich anbeißen[8], damit wir nicht Schwarzhandel treiben[9]. Jeder geht jetzt gerne in die Schule.

Ich danke Ihnen nochmals dafür, für die guten Gaben[10].

Mit dankbarem Gruß
eine ergebene Schülerin
Margot Fränkel

1. *announced*
2. es . . . *it was found by weighing and measuring*
3. *malnourished*
4. *eager*
5. *the bell rings*
6. *baked goods*
7. *fruit syrup*
8. *bite into it*
9. *deal on the black market*
10. *gifts*

Frauenau, den 5. Mai 1947.

Sehr geehrter Herr Präsident Hoover!

Am Montag bekamen wir in der Schule Schokolade. Das war eine große Freude, denn wir haben schon lange keine mehr gehabt. Darum möchten wir Ihnen herzlich danken. Wir dürfen jetzt jeden Tag zur Kinderspeisung gehen. Darüber sind wir sehr froh, denn bei uns im Bayrischen Wald gibt es wenig zum Essen. Leider dürfen zur Speisung nicht alle gehen. An unserer Schule sind nämlich 650 Kinder und für 380 bekommen wir nur Speisung. Also gibt es nur zwei Möglichkeiten. Entweder dürfen die einen Kinder überhaupt nicht gehen oder wir müssen jede Woche wechseln. So bekommen wir alle nicht viel. Dennoch freuen wir uns sehr darüber und danken Ihnen von Herzen.

Im Namen der 3. Klasse
Ihre dankbare Gisela Thiemann 3. Klasse
Volksschule Frauenau Bayrischer Wald.

THE HERBERT HOOVER ARCHIVES

Zum Text 2

1. Was erfahren wir über die Folgen (*consequences*) des Krieges für die Kinder?
2. Welche Probleme erwähnen die Kinder? Wer schreibt davon, dass
   - die meisten Kinder unterernährt sind?
   - die Kinder wissen, wie man Schwarzhandel treibt?
   - die Familie aus ihrer Heimat geflüchtet (*fled*) ist?
   - sie oft allein ist, weil die Mutter nach Brot anstehen muss?
   - es nicht genug Essen für alle Kinder in der Schule gibt?

Zu guter Letzt

Berlin: Hauptstadt im Wandel

Im Juni 1991 wählte der deutsche Bundestag die Stadt Berlin zum offiziellen Regierungssitz. Mit etwa 3,4 Millionen Einwohnern ist Berlin die größte Stadt des vereinigten Deutschlands und dazu ein eigenständiger Staat der Bundesrepublik.

Von der Mauer, die von 1961 bis 1989 West-Berlin von Ost-Berlin trennte, ist kaum noch eine Spur zu sehen. Stattdessen ist Berlin jetzt ein riesiger Bauplatz: Kräne und Baustellen prägen das Stadtbild, vor allem am Potsdamer Platz und im früheren östlichen Teil. Die Stadt bereitet sich auf ihre neue Rolle als Metropole vor.

Baustellen am Brandenburger Tor

Das Wappen Berlins

Baustelle Reichstag

Aktivität 1 Berlin erleben

Stellen Sie sich vor, dass Sie Berlin besuchen wollen. Machen Sie einen Plan, was Sie unbedingt sehen und tun möchten. Wählen Sie Veranstaltungen aus dem folgenden Programm aus. Suchen Sie sich zusätzliche Informationen über Berlin im Internet, und planen Sie eine Stadtbesichtigung.

Weiteres zum Thema Berlin finden Sie bei ***Deutsch: Na klar!*** im World-Wide-Web unter www.mhhe.com/german.

BEISPIEL: Ich möchte eine Bootstour auf der Spree machen und möglicherweise einen Spaziergang durch den Tiergarten. Ich möchte auch die Baustelle am Potsdamer Platz besichtigen.

PROGRAMM BERLIN

Die Symbole der Schaustelle

- *Baustellenbesichtigungen*
- *Objektbesichtigungen*
- *Bustouren*
- *Rundgänge*
- *Radtouren*
- *Bootstouren*
- *Rundflüge*
- *Events und Veranstaltungen*

9.30, 11.00, 13.00 und 14.30
Tour 42
Spreefahrt durch den zentralen Bereich
Karten DM 20,-

10.00, 12.00, 14.00 und 16.00
Bundesministerium der Justiz
Information auf Seite 6/7
Karten DM 3,-

10.00
Tour 11
Mauerpark Prenzlauer Berg
Karten DM 15,- / 12,- (erm.)

10.00, 12.00, 14.00 und 16.00
Museumsinsel
Information auf Seite 6/7
Karten DM 3,-

10.30
Tour 1
Innenstadttour
Karten DM 29,- / 22,- (erm.)

10.30
Tour 14
Spaziergang durch den Großen Tiergarten
Karten DM 15,- / 12,- (erm.)

11.00
Tour 12
350 Jahre Unter den Linden
Karten DM 15,- / 12,- (erm.)

11.00
Tour 40
Die Großbaustelle Berlin vom Wasser aus. Altbau – Neubau – Umbau
Karten DM 20,- / 10,- (erm.)

11.00 und 15.00
Tour 18
Die Hackeschen Höfe
Karten DM 15,- / 12,- (erm.)

11.00 und 13.30
KulturKaufhaus Friedrichstr.
Information auf Seite 10/11
Karten DM 3,-

11.00
Tour 37
Mit dem Fahrrad durch Mitte
Karten DM 15,- / 12,- (erm.)

11.00
Tour 19
Neue Architektur rund um den Checkpoint Charlie
Karten DM 15,- / 12,- (erm.)

15.00 und 17.00
Jüdisches Museum
Information auf Seite 56
Karten DM 3,-

15.00
Kultur und Ökologie auf dem Gelände der UFA-Fabrik
Information auf Seite 58
Karten DM 3,-

19.30
Tour 17
Die Zukunft hat begonnen.
Vom Reichstag zum Gendarmenmarkt
Karten DM 15,- / 12,- (erm.)

Aktivität 2 Die Welt im Jahre 2050

Wie mag wohl die Welt in fünfzig oder hundert Jahren aussehen? Werden die Länder der Welt politisch zusammenwachsen oder weiter auseinander fallen? Was hat man bis dahin, zum Beispiel, zum Schutz der Umwelt getan, oder auch nicht? Gibt es neue und bessere Transportmittel, rationellere Arbeitsmethoden, schnellere Kommunikationsmöglichkeiten, neue Technologien? Dominiert eine Großmacht die Welt? Wenn ja, welche?

1. Arbeiten Sie zuerst in Gruppen, um Ideen zum Thema miteinander zu sammeln. Was sind Ihre Hoffnungen, Erwartungen, Fantasien, aber auch Ihre Ängste? Jemand in Ihrer Gruppe soll die Hauptgedanken aufschreiben und sie im Plenum vortragen.
2. Schreiben Sie einen detaillierten Bericht, wie Sie sich Ihr Leben im Jahr 2050 vorstellen: „Ein Tag in meinem Leben."

Appendix A

Einführung

Aktivität 13 Hin und her°: Wie ist die Postleitzahl?

° back and forth

This is the first of many activities in which you will exchange information with a partner. Take turns asking each other for the zip codes missing from your charts.

BEISPIEL: S1: Wie ist die Postleitzahl von Eisenach?
S2: Die Postleitzahl von Eisenach ist D-99817. Wie ist die Postleitzahl von Bitburg?
S1: Die Postleitzahl von Bitburg ist D-54634.

	Eisenach
D-54634	Bitburg
	Salzburg
CH-3800	Interlaken
	Straubing
D-06217	Merseburg
	Buxtehude
FL-9490	Vaduz

Kapitel 1

Übung 4 Hin und her: Wer sind diese Personen?

Working with a partner, take turns asking and answering questions. Use the pronouns **er, sie,** or **es** in your answers.

BEISPIEL: S1: Wie ist Herr Eichele?
S2: Er ist tolerant.

FRAGEN	ANTWORTEN
Wie ist Herr Eichele?	tolerant
Woher kommen Herr und Frau Eichele?	
Was ist Frau Eichele von Beruf?	Sozialarbeiterin
Wie heißt Frau Eichele mit Vornamen?	
Wo studiert Hans?	in Berlin
Wie heißt unser Deutschbuch?	

Kapitel 2

Aktivität 8 Hin und her: Machen sie das gern?

Find out what the following people like to do or don't like to do by asking your partner.

BEISPIEL: S1: Was macht Denise gern?
S2: Sie reist gern. Was macht Thomas nicht gern?
S1: Er fährt nicht gern Auto.

	GERN	NICHT GERN
Thomas		
Denise	reisen	kochen
Niko		
Anja	laufen	Bier trinken

Kapitel 3

Aktivität 7
Hin und her: Verwandtschaften

Ask a partner about Ulrike's family.

BEISPIEL: S1: Wie ist Axel mit Ulrike verwandt?
S2: Axel ist Ulrikes Onkel.
S1: Wie alt ist er denn?
S2: Er ist 51.

PERSON	VERWANDTSCHAFT	ALTER
Axel		
Antje	Schwägerin	29
Annette		
Hans	Bruder	30
Friedrich		

Kapitel 4

Aktivität 2 Hin und her: Zwei Stundenpläne

A. Sven und Frank sind 18 Jahre alt und gehen aufs Gymnasium (*secondary school*). Vergleichen Sie ihre Stundenpläne. Welche Kurse haben sie zusammen (*together*)?

BEISPIEL: S1: Welchen Kurs hat Sven dienstags um acht?
S2: Dienstags um acht hat Sven Informatik. Welchen Kurs hat Frank dienstags um acht?
S1: Dienstags um acht hat Frank Physik.

Zeit	Montag	Dienstag	Mittwoch	Donnerstag	Freitag	Samstag
$8 - 8^{45}$	Informatik	Physik	Kunst	Englisch	frei	Deutsch
$8^{45} - 9^{30}$	Informatik	Physik	Kunst	Englisch	frei	Deutsch
$9^{35} - 10^{20}$	Religion	Deutsch	Mathematik	Geschichte	Sozialkunde	
$10^{40} - 11^{25}$	Religion	Mathematik	Deutsch	Mathematik	Deutsch	
$11^{30} - 12^{15}$	Erdkunde	frei	Sozialkunde	Erdkunde	Geschichte	
$12^{15} - 13^{00}$	Mathematik	Englisch	Physik	Informatik	frei	
$13^{15} - 14^{00}$			Sport			
$14^{00} - 14^{45}$			Sport			

Langenscheidt ...weil Sprachen verbinden

Franks Stundenplan

B. Sven und Frank möchten Tennis spielen. Wann ist die beste Zeit? Wann haben sie beide frei?

Kapitel 5

Übung 2 Hin und her: Geschenke, Geschenke!

In der Familie Eichele gibt es viele Feste, z.B. Geburtstage, Hochzeitstage, Weihnachten. Wer kauft wem was und wann? Fragen Sie Ihren Partner/ Ihre Partnerin.

BEISPIEL: S1: Was kauft Ulrike ihrem Bruder Hans zum Geburtstag?
S2: Ulrike kauft ihrem Bruder Hans eine Jacke zum Geburtstag.

oder: S2: Wem kauft Hans ein Video zu Weihnachten?
S1: Hans kauft seiner Schwester Ulrike ein Video zu Weihnachten.

WER	WEM	WAS	ZU WELCHEM ANLASS°
Ulrike	ihr Bruder Hans	eine Jacke	zum Geburtstag
Hans	seine Schwester		zu Weihnachten
Herr Eichele	sein Sohn Wolfgang	ein Fahrrad	zum Geburtstag
Frau Eichele		drei Krawatten	zu Weihnachten
die Eichele Kinder	ihre Eltern	Konzertkarten	zum Hochzeitstag
Ulrike	ihre Kusine Annette		zum Geburtstag

°*occasion*

Kapitel 6

Übung 16 Hin und her: Warum nicht?

Fragen Sie Ihren Partner / Ihre Partnerin, warum die folgenden Leute nicht erschienen sind (*didn't show up*).

BEISPIEL: S1: Warum war Andreas gestern Vormittag nicht in der Vorlesung?
S2: Er hatte keine Lust.

PERSON	WANN	WO	WARUM
Andreas	gestern Vormittag	in der Vorlesung	keine Lust haben
Anke			arbeiten müssen
Frank	gestern Abend	auf der Party	
Yeliz			krank sein
Mario	vorgestern	im Café	
Ihr Partner / Ihre Partnerin			

Kapitel 7

Übung 9 Hin und her: Wochenende und Freizeit

Warum haben sie das gemacht? Stellen Sie Ihrem Partner/Ihrer Partnerin Fragen, um die Gründe (*reasons*) zu erfahren.

BEISPIEL: S1: Warum ist Dagmar ins Alte Land gefahren?
S2: Sie wollte auf einem Bauernhof Obst kaufen.

WER	WAS	WARUM
Dagmar	ins Alte Land fahren	auf einem Bauernhof Obst kaufen wollen
Thomas	in den Sportclub gehen	
Jürgen	zu Hause bleiben	seine Lieblingssendung im Fernsehen sehen wollen
Stefanie	Hans anrufen	
Susanne	sehr lange schlafen	die ganze Woche schwer arbeiten müssen

Kapitel 8

Aktivität 8 Hin und her: Meine Routine—deine Routine

Jeder hat eine andere Routine. Was machen diese Leute und in welcher Reihenfolge? Machen Sie es auch so?

BEISPIEL: S1: Was macht Alexander morgens?
S2: Zuerst rasiert er sich und putzt sich die Zähne. Dann kämmt er sich. Danach setzt er sich an den Tisch und frühstückt.

WER	WAS ER/SIE MORGENS MACHT
Alexander	
Elke	zuerst / sich anziehen dann / sich die Zähne putzen danach / sich kämmen
Tilo	
Kamal	zuerst / sich das Gesicht waschen dann / frühstücken danach / sich rasieren / sich anziehen
Ihr Partner / Ihre Partnerin	zuerst / ? dann / ? danach / ?
Sie	zuerst / ? dann / ? danach / ?

Aktivität 6 Hin und her: In einer fremden° Stadt

unfamiliar

Sie sind in einer fremden Stadt. Fragen Sie nach dem Weg. Benutzen Sie die Tabelle unten.

BEISPIEL: S1: Ist das Landesmuseum weit von hier?
S2: Es ist sechs Kilometer von hier, bei der Universität.
S1: Wie komme ich am besten dahin?
S2: Nehmen Sie die Buslinie 7, am Rathaus.

WOHIN?	WIE WEIT?	WO?	WIE?
Landesmuseum	6 km	bei der Universität	Buslinie 7, am Rathaus
Bahnhof			
Post	nicht weit	in der Nähe vom Bahnhof	zu Fuß
Schloss			
Opernhaus	ganz in der Nähe	rechts um die Ecke	zu Fuß, die Poststraße entlang

Übung 12 Hin und her: Was gibt es hier?

Fragen Sie einen Partner / eine Partnerin nach der fehlenden Information.

BEISPIEL: S1: Was gibt es beim Gasthof zum Bären?
S2: Warme Küche.
S1: Was gibt es sonst noch?
S2: Bayerische Spezialitäten.

WO?	WAS?	WAS SONST NOCH?
Gasthof zum Bären	Küche / warm	Spezialitäten / bayerisch
Gasthof Adlersberg		
Gasthaus Schneiderwirt	Hausmusik / originell	Gästezimmer / rustikal
Hotel Luitpold		

Kapitel 10

Aktivität 2 Hin und her: Was nehmen sie mit?

Wohin fahren diese Leute im Urlaub? Was nehmen sie mit? Ergänzen Sie die Informationen.

BEISPIEL: S1: Wohin fährt Angelika Meier in Urlaub?
S2: Sie fährt in die Türkei.
S1: Warum fährt sie in die Türkei?
S2: Weil . . .
S1: Was nimmt sie mit?
S2: Sie nimmt . . .

PERSONEN	WOHIN?	WARUM?	WAS NIMMT ER/SIE MIT?
Angelika Meier			
Peter Bayer	auf die Insel Rügen	windsurfen gehen	Sonnenschutzmittel, Badehose
Roland Metz			
Sabine Graf	nach Griechenland	eine Studienreise machen	Reiseführer, Wörterbuch, Kamera

Übung 7 Hin und her: Wie war der Urlaub?

Herr Ignaz Huber aus München war drei Wochen im Urlaub in Norddeutschland. Er war zwei Tage in Hamburg, eine Woche in Cuxhaven und nicht ganz zwei Wochen auf der Insel Sylt. Stellen Sie Ihrem Partner / Ihrer Partnerin Fragen über seinen Urlaub. Benutzen Sie den Superlativ.

BEISPIEL: S1: Wo war es am wärmsten?
S2: Am wärmsten war es in Cuxhaven.

	IN HAMBURG	IN CUXHAVEN	AUF DER INSEL SYLT
Wo war es (kalt/warm)?			
Wo hat es (häufig/wenig) geregnet?	zwei Tage	einen Tag	fünf Tage
Wo waren die Hotelpreise (günstig/teuer)?			
Wo war das Hotelpersonal (freundlich/unfreundlich)?			
Wo war der Strand (schön/unangenehm)?	kein Strand	sauber, gepflegt	zu windig

Kapitel 11

Aktivität 2 Hin und her: Wer macht was, und warum?

Ergänzen Sie die Informationen.

BEISPIEL: S1: Was macht Corinna Eichhorn?
S2: Sie ist Sozialarbeiterin.
S1: Warum macht sie das?
S2: Weil . . .

NAME	BERUF	WARUM?
Corinna Eichhorn		
Karsten Becker	Bibliothekar	sich für Bücher interessieren
Erika Lentz		
Alex Böhmer	Informatiker	mit Computern arbeiten

Aktivität 6 Hin und her: Berühmte° Personen

°*famous*

Diese berühmten Menschen, die alle einen Beruf ausübten, hatten auch andere Interessen. Ergänzen Sie die Informationen.

BEISPIEL: S1: Was war Martin Luther von Beruf?
S2: Er war Priester.
S1: Was für andere Interessen hatte er?
S2: Er interessierte sich für Literatur, Musik und die deutsche Sprache.

NAME	BERUF	INTERESSEN
Rainer Werner Fassbinder		
Bertha von Suttner	Schriftstellerin	die europäische Friedensbewegung (*peace movement*)
Marlene Dietrich	Schauspielerin	Skifahren
Käthe Kollwitz		
Martin Luther	Priester	Literatur, Musik, die deutsche Sprache
Willi Brandt		

Kapitel 12

Aktivität 6 Hin und her: Meine Wohnung—deine Wohnung

Diese Leute haben entweder eine neue Wohnung oder ein neues Haus gekauft. Wer hat was gekauft? Wie viele Stockwerke gibt es? Wie groß ist das Wohnzimmer? Wie viele WCs oder Badezimmer gibt es?

BEISPIEL: S1: Was für eine Wohnung hat Bettina Neuendorf gekauft?
S2: Eine Eigentumswohnung.
S1: Wie viele Stockwerke hat die Wohnung?
S2: Eins.
S1: Und wie viele Schlafzimmer?

PERSON	TYP	STOCKWERKE	SCHLAFZIMMER	WOHNZIMMER	WC/BAD
Bettina Neuendorf					
Uwe und Marion Baumgärtner	Haus	zwei	drei: Elternschlafzimmer, Kinderschlafzimmer, Gästezimmer	sehr groß mit Balkon 37 Quadratmeter	zwei Badezimmer: eins im Dachgeschoss und eins im Erdgeschoss
Sven Kersten					
Carola Schubärth	Haus	eins	zwei: ein Schlafzimmer ist Arbeitszimmer	klein 25 Quadratmeter	ein Bad
mein Partner / meine Partnerin					
ich					

Kapitel 13

Aktivität 2 Hin und her: Wie informieren und unterhalten sie sich?

Wie informieren sich diese Personen? Was lesen sie zur Unterhaltung? Stellen Sie Fragen an Ihren Partner / Ihre Partnerin.

BEISPIEL: S1: Wie informiert sich _____?
oder Wie unterhält sich _____?
S2: Er/Sie sieht/liest _____.

PERSON	FERNSEHSHOWS	ZEITUNGEN UND ZEITSCHRIFTEN
Martin	Talkshows und Dokumentarfilme	*die Zeit* und *die TAZ*
Stephanie	klassische Spielfilme und Komödien	*der Spiegel*
Patrick		
Kristin	Sportsendungen, Krimi-Serien wie „Mord ist ihr Hobby“	*das Handelsblatt, die Welt* und *Brigitte*
Mein Partner / Meine Partnerin		

Aktivität 6 Hin und her: Technische Erfindungen durch die Jahrhunderte

Sie möchten erfahren, welche Person was und wann erfunden hat. Stellen Sie Ihrem Partner / Ihrer Partnerin Fragen.

BEISPIELE: S1: Wer hat _____ erfunden?
S2: _____.
S1: Wann hat er es erfunden?
S2: (Im Jahre) _____.

oder: S1: Was hat _____ erfunden?
S2: Er hat _____ erfunden.
S1: In welchem Jahr?
S2: (Im Jahre) _____.

PERSON	ERFINDUNG	DATUM
Johannes von Gutenberg	Buchdruck mit beweglichen Lettern (*movable type*)	um 1450
Daniel Gabriel Fahrenheit	Quecksilberthermometer	1716/18
	Fahrrad (Draisine)	
Werner von Siemens	Dynamomaschine (*generator*)	1846
Gottlieb Daimler		
	Dieselmotor	
Wilhelm Conrad Röntgen	Röntgenstrahlen (*X-rays*)	1895
Walter Bruch	„PAL“ (Farbfernsehen)	1960/63

Kapitel 14

Aktivität 1 Hin und her: Probleme und Lösungen

Stellen Sie Ihrem Partner / Ihrer Partnerin Fragen zu den folgenden Problemen, um herauszufinden, welche möglichen Lösungen es gibt.

BEISPIEL: S1: Was kann man gegen Krieg tun?
S2: Man kann an Antikriegsdemonstrationen teilnehmen.

PROBLEME	MÖGLICHE LÖSUNGEN
Inflation	die Schulden der Regierung kontrollieren
Drogensucht	
Umweltverschmutzung	alternative Energiequellen (*energy sources*) entwickeln
Verletzung der Menschenrechte	
Obdachlosigkeit	neue Wohnungen bauen
Arbeitslosigkeit	

Übung 5 Hin und her: Zwei umweltbewusste Städte

In zwei Städten, Neustadt und Altstadt, wird für eine bessere Umwelt gesorgt.

BEISPIEL: S1: Was ist zuerst in Neustadt gemacht worden?
S2: Zuerst sind naturnahe Gärten angelegt worden.

	NEUSTADT	ALTSTADT
zuerst		Autos aus der Innenstadt verbannen
dann		neue Siedlungen am Stadtrand bauen
danach		Bürger über Umweltschutz informieren
schließlich		neue, moderne Busse kaufen
zuletzt		ein großes Umweltfest in der Innenstadt feiern

Studienfächer

Anthropologie	Anthropology
Architektur	Architecture
Astronomie	Astromony
Bauingenieurwesen	Structural Engineering
Betriebswirtschaftslehre	Business Administration
Bibliothekswissenschaft	Library Science
Biochemie	Biochemistry
Biologie	Biology
Chemie	Chemistry
Elektrotechnik	Electrical Engineering
Ernährungswissenschaft	Nutritional Science
Forstwissenschaft	Forestry
Geographie/Erdkunde	Geography
Geologie	Geology
Geophysik	Geophysics
Germanistik	German Studies
Geschichte/Geschichtswissenschaft	History
Informatik	Computer Science
Journalistik/Publizistik	Journalism
Kerntechnik/Reaktortechnik	Nuclear Engineering
Kunstgeschichte	Art History
Maschinenbau	Mechanical Engineering
Mathematik	Mathematics
Medizin	Medicine
Musik	Music
Pädagogik	Education
Pharmakologie/Pharmazie	Pharmacy
Philosophie	Philosophy
Physik	Physics
Politikwissenschaft	Political Science
Psychologie	Psychology
Rechtswissenschaft/Jura	Law
Sport	Physical Education
Sprachwissenschaft/Linguistik	Linguistics
Städtebau/Stadtplanung	Urban Planning
Statistik	Statistics
Theaterwissenschaft	Dramatic Art
Theologie	Theology
Tiermedizin	Veterinary Science
Volkswirtschaftslehre	Economics
Zahnmedizin	Dentistry

Appendix C

Berufe

der Apotheker, - / die Apothekerin, -nen — pharmacist
der Architekt, -en (-en *masc.***) / die Architektin, -nen** — architect
der Arzt, ¨e / die Ärztin, -nen — physician
der Autor, -en / die Autorin, -nen — author
der Bäcker, - / die Bäckerin, -nen — baker
der Beamte, -n (-n *masc.***) / die Beamtin, -nen** — government employee
der Bibliothekar, -e / die Bibliothekarin, -nen — librarian
der Biologe, -n (-n *masc.***) / die Biologin, -nen** — biologist
der Chemiker, - / die Chemikerin, -nen — chemist
der Chirurg, -en (-en *masc.***) / die Chirurgin, -nen** — surgeon
der Dolmetscher, - / die Dolmetscherin, -nen — interpreter
der Fernsehtechniker, - / die Fernsehtechnikerin, -nen — TV technician
der Flugbegleiter, - / die Flugbegleiterin, -nen — flight attendant
der Fotograf, -en (-en *masc.***) / die Fotografin, -nen** — photographer
der Geschäftsführer, - / die Geschäftsführerin, -nen — business manager
der Informatiker, - / die Informatikerin, -nen — computer scientist
der Ingenieur, -e / die Ingenieurin, -nen — engineer
der Journalist, -en (-en *masc.***) / die Journalistin, -nen** — journalist
der Kaufmann, (*pl.***) Kaufleute / die Kauffrau, -en** — merchant, shopkeeper
der Kellner, - / die Kellnerin, -nen — waiter / waitress / server
der Krankenpfleger, - / die Krankenschwester, -n; die Krankenpflegerin, -nen — nurse
der Künstler, - / die Künstlerin, -nen — artist
der Mathematiker, - / die Mathematikerin, -nen — mathematician
der Mechaniker, - / die Mechanikerin, -nen — mechanic
der Musiker, - / die Musikerin, -nen — musician
der Pilot, -en (-en *masc.***) / die Pilotin, -nen** — pilot
der Politiker, - / die Politikerin, -nen — politician
der Polizist, -en (-en *masc.***) / die Polizistin, -nen** — policeman/policewoman
der Professor, -en / die Professorin, -nen — professor
der Psychologe, -n (-n *masc.***) / die Psychologin, -nen** — psychologist
der Rechtsanwalt, ¨e / die Rechtsanwältin, -nen — lawyer
der Sänger, - / die Sängerin, -nen — singer
der Schaffner, - / die Schaffnerin, -nen — train conductor
der Schauspieler, - / die Schauspielerin, -nen — actor
der Schriftsteller, - / die Schriftstellerin, -nen — writer
der Sekretär, -e / die Sekretärin, -nen — secretary
der Tänzer, - / die Tänzerin, -nen — dancer
der Vertriebsrepräsentant, -en (-en *masc.***) / die Vertriebsrepräsentantin, -nen** — sales representative
der Zahnarzt, ¨e / die Zahnärztin, -nen — dentist
der Zeichner, - / Zeichnerin, -nen — draftsman/draftswoman

Appendix D

Grammar Tables

1. Personal Pronouns

	SINGULAR					PLURAL		
Nominative	ich	du / Sie	er	sie	es	wir	ihr / Sie	sie
Accusative	mich	dich / Sie	ihn	sie	es	uns	euch / Sie	sie
Dative	mir	dir / Ihnen	ihm	ihr	ihm	uns	euch / Ihnen	ihnen

2. Definite Articles

	SINGULAR			PLURAL
	Masculine	*Neuter*	*Feminine*	
Nominative	der	das	die	die
Accusative	den	das	die	die
Dative	dem	dem	der	den
Genitive	des	des	der	der

Words declined like the definite article: **jeder, dieser, welcher**

3. Indefinite Articles and the Negative Article *kein*

	SINGULAR			PLURAL
	Masculine	*Neuter*	*Feminine*	
Nominative	(k)ein	(k)ein	(k)eine	keine
Accusative	(k)einen	(k)ein	(k)eine	keine
Dative	(k)einem	(k)einem	(k)einer	keinen
Genitive	(k)eines	(k)eines	(k)einer	keiner

Words declined like the indefinite article: all possessive adjectives (**mein, dein, sein, ihr, unser, euer, Ihr**).

4. Relative and Demonstrative Pronouns

	SINGULAR			PLURAL
	Masculine	*Neuter*	*Feminine*	*Plural*
Nominative	der	das	die	die
Accusative	den	das	die	die
Dative	dem	dem	der	denen
Genitive	dessen	dessen	deren	deren

5. Principal Parts of Strong and Irregular Weak Verbs

The following is a list of the most important strong and irregular weak verbs that are used in this book. Included in this list are the modal auxiliaries. Since the principal parts of compound verbs follow the forms of the base verb, compound verbs are generally not included, except for a few high-frequency compound verbs whose base verb is not commonly used. Thus you will find **anfangen** and **einladen** listed, but not **zurückkommen** or **ausgehen.**

INFINITIVE	(3RD PERS. SG. PRESENT)	SIMPLE PAST	PAST PARTICIPLE	MEANING
anbieten		bot an	angeboten	*to offer*
anfangen	(fängt an)	fing an	angefangen	*to begin*
backen		backte	gebacken	*to bake*
beginnen		begann	begonnen	*to begin*
begreifen		begriff	begriffen	*to comprehend*
beißen		biss	gebissen	*to bite*
bitten		bat	gebeten	*to ask, beg*
bleiben		blieb	(ist) geblieben	*to stay*
bringen		brachte	gebracht	*to bring*
denken		dachte	gedacht	*to think*
dürfen	(darf)	durfte	gedurft	*to be allowed*
einladen	(lädt ein)	lud ein	eingeladen	*to invite*
empfehlen	(empfiehlt)	empfahl	empfohlen	*to recommend*
entscheiden		entschied	entschieden	*to decide*
essen	(isst)	aß	gegessen	*to eat*
fahren	(fährt)	fuhr	(ist) gefahren	*to drive*
fallen	(fällt)	fiel	(ist) gefallen	*to fall*
finden		fand	gefunden	*to find*
fliegen		flog	(ist) geflogen	*to fly*
geben	(gibt)	gab	gegeben	*to give*
gefallen	(gefällt)	gefiel	gefallen	*to like; to please*
gehen		ging	(ist) gegangen	*to go*

INFINITIVE	(3RD PERS. SG. PRESENT)	SIMPLE PAST	PAST PARTICIPLE	MEANING
genießen		genoss	genossen	*to enjoy*
geschehen	(geschieht)	geschah	ist geschehen	*to happen*
gewinnen		gewann	gewonnen	*to win*
haben	(hat)	hatte	gehabt	*to have*
halten	(hält)	hielt	gehalten	*to hold; to stop*
hängen		hing	gehangen	*to hang*
heißen		hieß	geheißen	*to be called*
helfen	(hilft)	half	geholfen	*to help*
kennen		kannte	gekannt	*to know*
kommen		kam	(ist) gekommen	*to come*
können	(kann)	konnte	gekonnt	*can; to be able*
lassen	(lässt)	ließ	gelassen	*to let; to allow*
laufen	(läuft)	lief	(ist) gelaufen	*to run*
leihen		lieh	geliehen	*to lend; to borrow*
lesen	(liest)	las	gelesen	*to read*
liegen		lag	gelegen	*to lie*
mögen	(mag)	mochte	gemocht	*to like*
müssen	(muss)	musste	gemusst	*must; to have to*
nehmen	(nimmt)	nahm	genommen	*to take*
nennen		nannte	genannt	*to name*
raten	(rät)	riet	geraten	*to advise*
reiten		ritt	(ist) geritten	*to ride*
scheinen		schien	geschienen	*to seem; to shine*
schlafen	(schläft)	schlief	geschlafen	*to sleep*
schließen		schloss	geschlossen	*to close*
schreiben		schrieb	geschrieben	*to write*
schwimmen		schwamm	(ist) geschwommen	*to swim*
sehen	(sieht)	sah	gesehen	*to see*
sein	(ist)	war	(ist) gewesen	*to be*
singen		sang	gesungen	*to sing*
sitzen		saß	gesessen	*to sit*
sollen	(soll)	sollte	gesollt	*should, ought; to be supposed*
sprechen	(spricht)	sprach	gesprochen	*to speak*
stehen		stand	gestanden	*to stand*
steigen		stieg	ist gestiegen	*to rise; to climb*
sterben	(stirbt)	starb	(ist) gestorben	*to die*
tragen	(trägt)	trug	getragen	*to carry; to wear*
treffen	(trifft)	traf	getroffen	*to meet*
trinken		trank	getrunken	*to drink*
tun		tat	getan	*to do*
umsteigen		stieg um	(ist) umgestiegen	*to change; to transfer*
vergessen	(vergisst)	vergaß	vergessen	*to forget*
vergleichen		verglich	verglichen	*to compare*
verlieren		verlor	verloren	*to lose*
wachsen	(wächst)	wuchs	(ist) gewachsen	*to grow*
waschen	(wäscht)	wusch	gewaschen	*to wash*
werden	(wird)	wurde	(ist) geworden	*to become*
wissen	(weiß)	wusste	gewusst	*to know*
wollen	(will)	wollte	gewollt	*to want*
ziehen		zog	(ist/hat) gezogen	*to move; to pull*

6. Conjugation of Verbs

In the charts that follow, the pronoun **Sie** (*you*) is listed with the third-person plural **sie** (*they*).

Present Tense

Auxiliary Verbs

	sein	**haben**	**werden**
ich	bin	habe	werde
du	bist	hast	wirst
er/sie/es	ist	hat	wird
wir	sind	haben	werden
ihr	seid	habt	werdet
sie/Sie	sind	haben	werden

Regular Verbs, Verbs with Vowel Change, Irregular Verbs

	REGULAR		VOWEL CHANGE		IRREGULAR
	fragen	**finden**	**geben**	**fahren**	**wissen**
ich	frage	finde	gebe	fahre	weiß
du	fragst	findest	gibst	fährst	weißt
er/sie/es	fragt	findet	gibt	fährt	weiß
wir	fragen	finden	geben	fahren	wissen
ihr	fragt	findet	gebt	fahrt	wisst
sie/Sie	fragen	finden	geben	fahren	wissen

Simple Past Tense

Auxiliary Verbs

	sein	**haben**	**werden**
ich	war	hatte	wurde
du	warst	hattest	wurdest
er/sie/es	war	hatte	wurde
wir	waren	hatten	wurden
ihr	wart	hattet	wurdet
sie/Sie	waren	hatten	wurden

Weak, Strong, and Irregular Weak Verbs

	WEAK	STRONG		IRREGULAR WEAK
	fragen	**geben**	**fahren**	**wissen**
ich	fragte	gab	fuhr	wusste
du	fragtest	gabst	fuhrst	wusstest
er/sie/es	fragte	gab	fuhr	wusste
wir	fragten	gaben	fuhren	wussten
ihr	fragtet	gabt	fuhrt	wusstet
sie/Sie	fragten	gaben	fuhren	wussten

Present Perfect Tense

	sein		**haben**		**geben**		**fahren**	
ich	bin	gewesen	habe	gehabt	habe	gegeben	bin	gefahren
du	bist		hast		hast		bist	
er/sie/es	ist		hat		hat		ist	
wir	sind		haben		haben		sind	
ihr	seid		habt		habt		seid	
sie/Sie	sind		haben		haben		sind	

Past Perfect Tense

	sein		**haben**		**geben**		**fahren**	
ich	war	gewesen	hatte	gehabt	hatte	gegeben	war	gefahren
du	warst		hattest		hattest		warst	
er/sie/es	war		hatte		hatte		war	
wir	waren		hatten		hatten		waren	
ihr	wart		hattet		hattet		wart	
sie/Sie	waren		hatten		hatten		waren	

Future Tense

	geben	
ich	werde	geben
du	wirst	
er/sie/es	wird	
wir	werden	
ihr	werdet	
sie/Sie	werden	

Subjunctive

Present Tense: Subjunctive I (Indirect Discourse Subjunctive)

	sein	haben	werden	fahren	wissen
ich	sei	—	—	—	wisse
du	sei(e)st	habest	—	—	—
er/sie/es	sei	habe	werde	fahre	wisse
wir	seien	—	—	—	—
ihr	sei(e)t	habet	—	—	—
sie/Sie	seien	—	—	—	—

For those forms left blank, the subjunctive II forms are preferred in indirect discourse.

Present Tense: Subjunctive II

	fragen	sein	haben	werden	fahren	wissen
ich	fragte	wäre	hätte	würde	führe	wüsste
du	fragtest	wär(e)st	hättest	würdest	führ(e)st	wüsstest
er/sie/es	fragte	wäre	hätte	würde	führe	wüsste
wir	fragten	wären	hätten	würden	führen	wüssten
ihr	fragtet	wär(e)t	hättet	würdet	führ(e)t	wüsstet
sie/Sie	fragten	wären	hätten	würden	führen	wüssten

Past Tense: Subjunctive I (Indirect Discourse)

	fahren		wissen	
ich	sei		—	
du	sei(e)st		habest	
er/sie/es	sei	gefahren	habe	gewusst
wir	seien		—	
ihr	sei(e)t		habet	
sie/Sie	sei(e)n		—	

Past Tense: Subjunctive II

	sein		geben		fahren	
ich	wäre		hätte		wäre	
du	wär(e)st		hättest		wär(e)st	
er/sie/es	wäre	gewesen	hätte	gegeben	wäre	gefahren
wir	wären		hätten		wären	
ihr	wär(e)t		hättet		wär(e)t	
sie/Sie	wären		hätten		wären	

Passive Voice

einladen			
	Present	*Simple Past*	*Present Perfect*
ich	werde	wurde	bin
du	wirst	wurdest	bist
er/sie/es	wird	wurde	ist
wir	werden	wurden	sind
ihr	werdet	wurdet	seid
sie/Sie	werden	wurden	sind
	} eingeladen	} eingeladen	} eingeladen worden

Imperative

	sein	**geben**	**fahren**	**arbeiten**
Familiar Singular	sei	gib	fahr	arbeite
Familiar Plural	seid	gebt	fahrt	arbeitet
Formal	seien Sie	geben Sie	fahren Sie	arbeiten Sie

Alternate Spelling and Capitalization

With the German spelling reform, some words now have an alternate old spelling along with a new one. The vocabulary lists at the end of each chapter in this text present the new spelling. Listed here are words appearing in the end of chapter vocabulary lists that are affected by the spelling reform, along with their traditional alternate spellings. This list is not a complete list of words affected by the spelling reform.

NEW	ALTERNATE
Abschluss (¨e)	Abschluß (Abschlüsse)
Anschluss (¨e)	Anschluß (Anschlüsse)
auf Deutsch	auf deutsch
Dachgeschoss (-e)	Dachgeschoß (Dachgeschosse)
dass	daß
Erdgeschoss (-e)	Erdgeschoß (Erdgeschosse)
essen (isst), aß, gegessen	essen (ißt), aß, gegessen
Esszimmer (-)	Eßzimmer (-)
Fass (¨er)	Faß (Fässer)
Fitness	Fitneß
Fluss (¨e)	Fluß (Flüsse)
heute Abend / . . . Mittag /. . . Morgen / . . . Nachmittag / . . . Vormittag	heute abend / . . . mittag / . . . morgen / . . . nachmittag / . . . vormittag
Imbiss (-e)	Imbiß (Imbisse)
lassen (lässt), ließ, gelassen	lassen (läßt), ließ, gelassen
Lass uns doch . . .	Laß uns doch . . .
morgen Abend / . . . Mittag / . . . Nachmittag / . . . Vormittag	morgen abend / . . . mittag / . . . nachmittag / vormittag
müssen (muss), musste, gemusst	müssen (muß), mußte, gemußt
passen (passt), gepasst	passen (paßt), gepaßt
Rad fahren (fährt Rad), fuhr Rad, ist Rad gefahren	radfahren (fährt Rad), fuhr Rad, ist radgefahren
Reisepass (¨e)	Reisepaß (Reisepässe)
Samstagabend / -mittag / -morgen / -nachmittag / -vormittag	Samstag abend / . . . mittag / . . . morgen / . . . nachmittag / . . . vormittag
spazieren gehen (geht spazieren), ging spazieren, ist spazieren gegangen	spazierengehen (geht spazieren), ging spazieren, ist spazierengegangen
Stress	Streß
vergessen (vergisst), vergaß, vergessen	vergessen (vergißt), vergaß, vergessen
wie viel	wieviel

Vocabulary

German–English

This vocabulary contains the German words as used in various contexts in this text, with the following exceptions: (1) compound words whose meaning can be easily guessed from their component parts; (2) most identical or very close cognates that are not part of the active vocabulary. (Frequently used cognates are, however, included so students can verify their gender.)

Active vocabulary in the end-of-chapter *Wortschatz* lists is indicated by the number of the chapter in which it first appears. The letter E refers to the introductory chapter, *Einführung*.

The following abbreviations are used:

acc.	accusative
adj.	adjective
coll.	colloquial
coord. conj.	coordinating conjunction
dat.	dative
decl. adj.	declined adjective
form.	formal
gen.	genitive
indef. pron.	indefinite pronoun
inform.	informal
-(e)n *masc.*	masculine noun ending in **-n** or **-en** in all cases but the nominative singular
pl.	plural
sg.	singular
subord. conj.	subordinating conjunction

A

das A und O (alpha and omega) essence
ab (+ *dat.*) as of; **ab (1. Juni)** from (June 1st) on (12)
ab und zu now and then (8)
abbestellen (bestellt ab) to cancel
abbiegen (biegt ab), bog ab, ist abgebogen to make a turn (9); **nach rechts abbiegen** to make a right-hand turn
abbrechen (bricht ab), brach ab, abgebrochen to break off
der Abend (-e) evening; **am Abend** at night, in the evening; **guten Abend** good evening (E); **heute Abend** tonight (4); **jeden Abend** every night; **morgen Abend** tomorrow evening; tomorrow night (4); **Samstagabend** Saturday evening; Saturday night (4)
das Abendessen (-) dinner, supper (5); **zum Abendessen** for dinner, supper
das Abendkleid (-er) evening gown
abends (in the) evenings (4); **eines Abends** one evening
das Abenteuer (-) adventure
der Abenteuerfilm (-e) adventure film
abenteuerlich adventurous
aber (*coord. conj.*) but, however (2)
abfahren (fährt ab), fuhr ab, ist abgefahren to depart, leave (10)
die Abfahrt (-en) departure (10)
der Abfall (⸚e) garbage (14)
der Abfallstoff (-e) waste product
die Abfallwirtschaft waste management
abfliegen (fliegt ab), flog ab, ist abgeflogen to depart, leave (by plane)
abfüttern (füttert ab) to feed
die Abgase (*pl.*) exhaust fumes
abgasfrei free of exhaust fumes
abgeben (gibt ab), gab ab, abgegeben to hand in, turn in (8)
abgelegen in a remote area
der/die Abgeordnete (*decl. adj.*) (political) representative
abgesehen davon aside from that
abgucken (guckt ab) to copy
abhängig sein von (+ *dat.*) to be dependent on
abholen (holt ab) to pick up (4)
das Abi = Abitur
das Abitur examination at the end of secondary school (Gymnasium) (11)
der Abiturient (-en *masc.*) **/ die Abiturientin (-nen)** graduate of the Gymnasium, person who has passed the Abitur
der Ablauf duration
ablaufen (läuft ab), lief ab, ist abgelaufen to expire
ablenken (lenkt ab) to distract
abliefern (liefert ab) to hand in, deliver
ablösen (löst ab) to replace
(sich) abmelden (meldet ab) to check out (of a hotel)
abnehmen (nimmt ab), nahm ab, abgenommen to lose weight
das Abo(nnement) (-s) subscription (13)
abonnieren to subscribe (13)
die Abrechnung (-en) final account
abreisen (reist ab), ist abgereist to leave (on a trip) (9)
der Absatz (⸚e) paragraph
abschaffen (schafft ab) to abolish
abschicken (schickt ab) to send off, mail
der Abschied (-e) farewell; **zum Abschied** when saying good-bye
abschließend in closing
der Abschluss (⸚e) completion (of studies or training), degree (11)
der Abschnitt (-e) paragraph, section
absolut absolute(ly)
absolvieren: eine Lehre absolvieren to complete an apprenticeship

(sich) abspielen (spielt ab) to take place
abstammen von (+ *dat.*) **(stammt ab)** to be descended from
absteigen (steigt ab), stieg ab, ist abgestiegen to dismount, get off
abstellen (stellt ab) to turn off
das Abteil (-e) compartment (10)
abtreiben (treibt ab), trieb ab, abgetrieben to have an abortion
die Abtreibung (-en) abortion
abwandern (wandert ab), ist abgewandert to migrate, move to another country
abwarten (wartet ab) to wait; **abwarten und Tee trinken** wait and see
abwechselnd taking turns
die Abwechslung (-en) diversion; change
abwechslungsreich diverse (11)
abweisen (weist ab), wies ab, abgewiesen to reject
(sich) abzeichnen (zeichnet ab) to become evident
ach oh; **Ach so!** I see! **ach wo** not at all
Achsel zuckend shrugging (one's) shoulders
acht eight (E); **um acht Uhr** at eight o'clock
achtbar respectable
achte eighth (3)
achten auf (+ *acc.*) to pay attention to (8)
Achtung! attention! (10)
achtzehn eighteen (E)
achtzig eighty (E)
der Adel nobility
das Adjektiv (-e) adjective
die Adjektivendung (-en) adjective ending
die Adresse (-n) address (E)
das Adverb (-ien) adverb
das Aerobic aerobics (7); **Aerobic machen** to do aerobics (7)
(das) Afrika Africa
AG = Aktiengesellschaft
der Agentenfilm (-e) spy movie
die Agrarreform (-en) agricultural reform
die Agressivität agression
ähnlich similar
Ähnliches (something) similar
die Ähnlichkeit (-en) similarity
Ahnung: Keine Ahnung! (I have) no idea!
das Ahornblatt (¨er) maple leaf
Ah so! (*coll.*) (*also:* **Ach so!**) Oh, I get it!
der Akkusativ accusative case
der Akteur (-e) performer
die Aktie (-n) share (of stocks)
die Aktiengesellschaft (-en) corporation
der Aktienwert (-e) share value
die Aktion (-en) (political) action
aktiv active(ly) (10); **sportlich aktiv** engaged in sports
die Aktivität (-en) activity
aktuell current (13)
der Alarm (air raid) warning; **Es ist Alarm.** There is an air raid.
die Alarmanlage (-n) alarm system
der Albaner (-) / die Albanerin (-nen) Albanian (person)
(das) Albanien Albania
albern silly
der Alkohol alcohol (14)
Alkoholeinfluss: unter Alkoholeinfluss under the influence of alcohol
alkoholfrei alcohol free (6)
der Alkoholiker (-) / die Alkoholikerin (-nen) alcoholic
der Alkoholismus alcoholism
all- all; **vor allem** above all
alle (*pl.*) all (5); **aller** of all
allein alone
allein stehend single, unattached
aller- (+ *superlative*) absolutely the most (+ *adj.*)
allerdings however; to be sure (10)
alles everything (10); **alles Gute** best wishes (3); **alles klar** everything (is) all right (E); **Das ist alles.** That is all. (5)
allgemein general; **im allgemeinen** in general
die Alliierten (*pl.*) the Allies, the Allied Forces
allmählich gradually
der Alltag everyday routine; workday
der Allwetterzoo (-s) all-weather zoo
allzu too (*emphatic*)
die Alpen (*pl.*) the Alps
das Alpenvorland foothills of the Alps
das Alphabet (-e) alphabet
alphabetisch alphabetical(ly)
als when; as; than (10); **als Kind** as a child
also thus; so; therefore; well
alt old (1); used
die Altbatterie (-n) used-up battery
der Altbau (Altbauten) old building (built before World War II)
die Altbauwohnung (-en) apartment in pre–World War II building
das Alter (-) age
alternativ alternative(ly)
der Alternativurlaub (-e) unusual vacation trip
das Altglas used glass
die Altkleider (*pl.*) used clothing
das Altöl used oil
das Altpapier used paper
die Altstadt old part of town
die Alufolie aluminum foil
das Aluminium aluminum
am = an dem; am 18. (achtzehnten) September on September 18 (3)
(das) Amerika America
der Amerikaner (-) / die Amerikanerin (-nen) American (*person*) (1)
amerikanisch American
die Ampel (-n) traffic light (9)
das Amt (¨er) bureau, agency
amüsant entertaining
an (+ *acc./dat.*) at; near (6); up to; to
die Analyse (-n) analysis
anbeißen (beißt an), biss an, angebissen to take a bite (out of)
anbieten (bietet an), bot an, angeboten to offer
anbringen (bringt an), brachte an, angebracht to install
andere different, other; **der, die, das andere** the other one; **alles andere** everything else; **unter anderem** among other things; **ein Tag um den anderen** day after day; **(et)was anderes** something else; **am anderen Morgen** the next morning; **eins nach dem anderen** one thing at a time
der/die/das andere (*decl. adj.*) other, different
(sich) ändern to change
anders different(ly) in another way; **jemand/niemand anders** somebody/nobody else
anderswo somewhere/anywhere else
die Änderung (-en) change
anderweitig elsewhere
anerkannt recognized, acknowledged
der Anfang (¨e) beginning, start; **am Anfang** in the beginning
anfangen (fängt an), fing an, angefangen to begin, start (4)
der Anfänger (-) / die Anfängerin (-nen) beginner
anfassen (fasst an) to touch
anfordern (fordert an) to request; to write away for
die Angabe (-n) statement, information; **persönliche Angaben** personal information
angeben (gibt an), gab an, angegeben to state
das Angebot (-e) offer; selection, item (10)
angehaucht: französisch angehaucht (*coll.*) with a slight French tinge
angehören (gehört an) to be a member of
angeln to fish (7)
angenehm pleasant (7)
der/die Angestellte (*decl. adj.*) employee (9)

angrenzend adjacent
die Angst (⸚e) fear (12); **keine Angst** don't be afraid; **Angst haben** (**vor** + *dat.*) to be afraid of (12)
ängstlich afraid
Anhalter: per Anhalter hitchhiking
anhand (+ *gen.*) based on
(sich) anhören (hört an) to listen to
ankommen (kommt an), kam an, ist angekommen to arrive (9); **Es kommt darauf an.** It depends.
ankreuzen (kreuzt an) to mark; to check off
die Ankündigung (-en) announcement
die Ankunft (⸚e) arrival (10)
der Anlass (⸚e) occasion
anmachen (macht an) to turn on (lights, etc.)
das Anmeldeformular (-e) registration form (9)
(sich) anmelden (meldet an) to register (9)
die Anmeldung (-en) registration
annehmen (nimmt an), nahm an, angenommen to accept
anno: pro anno per year, annual(ly)
anonym anonymous(ly)
anprobieren (probiert an) to try on (5)
der Anrufbeantworter (-) answering machine (13)
anrufen (ruft an), rief an, angerufen to call (on the phone) (4); **Ruf mal an!** Call sometime.
der Anrufer (-) / die Anruferin (-nen) caller
anrühren (rührt an) to touch
ans = an das
ansatzweise: nicht einmal ansatzweise not even in the beginning stages, not in the least
anschaffen: (sich) etwas anschaffen (schafft an) to acquire something (14)
anschauen (schaut an) to look at
anschließend afterward
der Anschluss (⸚e) connection (10); **gleich Anschluss haben** to make a direct connection
(sich) anschnallen (schnallt an) to fasten (one's) seatbelt
sich (+ *dat.*) **etwas ansehen (sieht an), sah an, angesehen** to watch, look at (13); **Ich sehe mir das an.** I'm watching that.
das Ansehen (-) prestige (11)
ansprechen (spricht an), sprach an, angesprochen to talk to somebody
(an)statt (+ *gen.*) instead of
anstehen (steht an), stand an, angestanden to stand in line
anstellen (stellt an) to turn on (radio, etc.)
der Anstieg (-e) increase
sich anstrengen (strengt an) to exert oneself (8)
anstrengend strenuous (8)
der Anteil (-e) share
die Antenne (-n) antenna
die Antwort (-en) answer
antworten to answer
der Anwalt (⸚e) / die Anwältin (-nen) attorney
die Anzahl amount; number
das Anzeichen (-) sign
die Anzeige (-n) (newspaper) advertisement
die Anzeigenannahme (-n) classified ad department
das Anzeigenblatt (⸚er) classified ad paper
(sich) anziehen (zieht an), zog an, angezogen to get dressed (8)
der Anzug (⸚e) suit (5)
der Apfel (⸚) apple (5)
der Apfelsaft apple juice (5)
die Apfelsahne (whipped) cream mixed with grated apples
der Apfelstrudel (-) apple pastry
die Apotheke (-n) pharmacy (5)
der Apparat (-e) machine, set, appliance (9); **sich am Apparat melden** to answer the telephone
das Appartement (-s) one-room apartment
die Appendizitis appendicitis
der Appetit appetite
die Aprikose (-n) apricot (5)
(der) April April (3)
das Aquarium aquarium
das Äquivalent (-e) equivalent
die Arbeit (-en) work; job (8)
arbeiten to work (1)
der Arbeiter (-) / die Arbeiterin (-nen) worker
die Arbeiterpartei (-en) workers' party
der Arbeitgeber (-) / die Arbeitgeberin (-nen) employer (11)
der Arbeitnehmer (-) / die Arbeitnehmerin (-nen) employee (13)
das Arbeitsamt (⸚er) employment (development) office (11)
das Arbeitsklima working atmosphere
arbeitslos unemployed
die Arbeitslosigkeit unemployment (14)
die Arbeitsmöglichkeit (-en) job opportunity
der Arbeitsplatz (⸚e) place of work (11)
die Arbeitsstelle (-n) work place
der Arbeitstag (-e) workday
die Arbeitsvermittlung (-en) employment agency (11)
die Arbeitswelt world of work
die Arbeitszeit (-en) working hours
das Arbeitszimmer (-) workroom, study (2)
der Arbeitszwang work obligation, pressure to work
der Architekt (-en *masc.*) **/ die Architektin (-nen)** architect (11)
die Architektur (-en) architecture
das Archiv (-e) archives
(das) Argentinien Argentina
argentinisch (*adj.*) Argentinian
der Ärger annoyance, trouble
sich ärgern (über + *acc.*) to be annoyed about (12)
das Argument (-e) argument
der Arm (-e) arm (8)
arm poor
das Armband (⸚er) bracelet
die Armbanduhr (-en) wristwatch
die Armen (*pl.*) poor people
die Armut poverty (14)
arrangieren to arrange
die Art (-en) kind, type; manner
der Artikel (-) article
das Arzneimittel (-) medication
der Arzt (⸚e) / die Ärztin (-nen) physician, doctor (11)
(das) Aschenbrödel Cinderella
das Aspirin aspirin
die Assoziation (-en) association
assoziieren to associate
das Assoziogramm (-e) associogram
die Astronomie astronomy
astronomisch astronomical(ly)
das Asyl (-e) asylum
der Äther ether
die Atmosphäre atmosphere
die Atomenergie nuclear energy
die Atomkraft nuclear power
das Atomkraftwerk (-e) nuclear power plant
die Atomwaffe (-n) nuclear weapon
die Atomwaffenfreiheit freedom from nuclear weapons
attraktiv attractive(ly)
ätzend biting, horrible; caustic
auch also, too
auf (+ *acc./dat.*) on, upon; on top of (6); **auf Wiederhören** good-bye (*on the phone*); **auf Wiedersehen** good-bye (E); **auf alle Fälle** in any case (13)
aufbauen (baut auf) to build up, rebuild
aufbewahren (bewahrt auf) to store
aufbleiben (bleibt auf), blieb auf, ist aufgeblieben to stay up
aufblicken (blickt auf) to look up
der Aufenthalt (-e) stay; layover (9)
die Aufenthaltszeit (-en) length of layover
auffordern (fordert auf): zum Tanzen auffordern to ask (somebody) to dance
die Aufforderung (-en) request

aufführen (führt auf) to perform
die Aufführung (-en) performance
die Aufgabe (-n) task (11); exercise
aufgeben (gibt auf), gab auf, aufgegeben to give up
aufgeschlossen outgoing
aufgeschnitten sliced
aufgrund (+ *gen.*) based on; because of
(sich) aufhalten (hält auf), hielt auf, aufgehalten to stay
die Aufheiterung (-en) clearing (of weather)
aufhören (mit + ***dat.*****) (hört auf)** to quit, stop (doing something) (4)
der Aufkleber (-) sticker
aufmachen (macht auf) to open
die Aufnahme (-n) accommodation
aufnehmen (nimmt auf), nahm auf, aufgenommen to record (video, etc.) (13)
aufräumen (räumt auf) to straighten up (a room) (4)
aufregend exciting (13)
die Aufregung (-en) excitement
der Aufsatz (¨e) essay
aufsaugen (saugt auf) to absorb
der Aufschnitt cold cuts (5)
aufschreiben (schreibt auf), schrieb auf, aufgeschrieben to write down
der Aufseher (-) / die Aufseherin (-nen) guard, overseer
der Aufstand (¨e) rebellion, uprising
aufstehen (steht auf), stand auf, ist aufgestanden to get up (4)
aufsteigen (steigt auf), stieg auf, ist aufgestiegen to advance
aufstellen (stellt auf) to set up, put up
der Aufstieg (-e) advancement
die Aufstiegsmöglichkeit (-en) opportunity for advancement
aufstützen: ist aufgestützt is propped up
auftauchen (taucht auf), ist aufgetaucht to appear
aufteilen (teilt auf) to divide
auftreten (tritt auf), trat auf, ist aufgetreten to present oneself, appear
aufwachen (wacht auf), ist aufgewacht to wake up (4)
die Aufzeichnung (-en) drawing
der Aufzug (¨e) elevator (9)
das Auge (-n) eye (8)
der Augenblick (-e) moment, instant; **im Augenblick** at the moment
der Augenzeuge (-n) / die Augenzeugin (-nen) eye witness
(der) August August (3)
aus (+ *dat.*) out of; from (5); **aus (Baumwolle)** made of (cotton); **aus dem Effeff** inside out; **aus Liebe** out of love
ausbauen (baut aus) to add on (to a building)
ausbessern (bessert aus) to repair
die Ausbildung (-en) education; schooling, training (11)
der Ausbildungsplatz (¨e) training position
die Ausbildungsstelle (-n) training position
ausbrechen (aus + ***dat.*****) (bricht aus), brach aus, ist ausgebrochen** to break out (of, from)
die Ausdehnung (-en) dimension
sich etwas ausdenken (denkt aus), dachte aus, ausgedacht to think up something
der Ausdruck (¨e) expression
ausdrücken (drückt aus) to express
auseinander fallen (fällt auseinander), fiel auseinander, ist auseinander gefallen to drift apart
die Auseinandersetzung (-en) altercation, argument
die Ausfahrt (-en) exit; off-ramp
ausfallen (fällt aus), fiel aus, ist ausgefallen to be canceled; to stop operating
der Ausflug (¨e) excursion
ausfüllen (füllt aus) to fill out (9)
die Ausgabe (-n) expense (12)
der Ausgangspunkt (-e) starting point
ausgeben (gibt aus), gab aus, ausgegeben to spend (12)
ausgehen (geht aus), ging aus, ist ausgegangen to go out (4); **Die Bananen gehen aus.** There are almost no more bananas.
ausgerechnet of all things
ausgeschildert marked by signs
ausgestattet furnished
ausgewählt select, chosen
ausgezeichnet excellent, great (E)
ausgleiten (gleitet aus), glitt aus, ist ausgeglitten to slip and fall
aushalten (hält aus), hielt aus, ausgehalten to endure
auskommen (kommt aus), kam aus, ist ausgekommen; to make ends meet, to get by with (money)
die Auskunft (¨e) information (10)
das Ausland foreign country (11); **im Ausland** abroad (11)
der Ausländer (-) / die Ausländerin (-nen) foreigner (14)
die Ausländerfeindlichkeit xenophobia (14)
ausländisch foreign
die Auslandsspeise (-n) foreign food
der Auslandssurlaub (-e) vacation abroad
auslassen (lässt aus), ließ aus, ausgelassen to leave out
die Ausnahme (-n) exception
auspacken (packt aus) to unpack
ausprobieren (probiert aus) to try out
die Ausrede (-n) excuse
ausrichten (richtet aus) to give a message
ausrotten (rottet aus) to eradicate
sich ausruhen (ruht aus) to rest up; to recuperate
die Aussage (-n) statement
aussagefähig capable of testifying
ausschauen (schaut aus) to look, appear
ausscheiden (scheidet aus), schied aus, ist ausgeschieden to be out of the game
ausschenken (schenkt aus) to pour, serve (beverage)
ausschließlich exclusively
der Ausschnitt (-e) excerpt, section
aussehen (sieht aus), sah aus, ausgesehen to look, appear; **gut aussehend** good-looking
außen outside; **nach außen hin** to the outside
der Außenminister (-) Secretary of State
außer (+ *dat.*) except for, besides
äußer- outer; **im äußeren Kreis** in the outer circle
außerdem besides, in addition (14)
außergewöhnlich extraordinary; extraordinarily
außerhalb (+ *gen.*) outside of (9); away from
die Äußerlichkeit (-en) formality
sich äußern to express oneself; **die Meinung äußern** to voice an opinion
äußerst extremely
die Äußerung (-en) statement
die Aussicht (-en) view; prospect
ausspannen (spannt aus) to rest, relax
aussteigen (steigt aus), stieg aus, ist ausgestiegen to get out of (a vehicle)
die Ausstellung (-en) exhibition
(sich) etwas aussuchen (sucht aus) to select something (for oneself) (13)
der Austausch (-e) exchange
austauschen (tauscht aus) to exchange
der Austauschschüler (-) / die Austauschschülerin (-nen) exchange student
der Austauschstudent (-en ***masc.*****) / die Austauschstudentin (-nen)** exchange student
(das) Australien Australia
austricksen (trickst aus) (*coll.*) to play a trick on
ausüben (übt aus) to practice
der Ausverkauf (¨e) sale
die Auswahl (-en) choice; selection

auswählen (wählt aus) to choose, select
auswandern (wandert aus), ist ausgewandert to emigrate
auswechseln (wechselt aus) to change
ausweichen (weicht aus), wich aus, ist ausgewichen to avoid, evade
der Ausweis (-e) ID card (10)
die Auszeichnung (-en) distinction
ausziehen (zieht aus), zog aus, ist ausgezogen to move out; **sich ausziehen** to get undressed (8)
der/die Auszubildende *(decl. adj.)* *(abbr.* **Azubi [-s])** trainee, apprentice (13)
der Auszug (¨-e) excerpt, extract
authentisch authentic
das Auto (-s) car, automobile (2); **Auto fahren** to drive a car (2)
die Autoabgase *(pl.)* exhaust fumes
die Autobahn (-en) freeway (10)
die Autobahnbrücke (-n) freeway overpass
die Autobahnzubringerstraße (-n) road leading to the freeway
die Autobiografie (-n) autobiography
der (Auto)bus (-se) bus
der Autodieb (-e) car thief
der Autofahrer (-) / die Autofahrerin (-nen) (automobile) driver
die Autoindustrie (-n) automobile industry
der Automat (-en *masc.***)** vending machine; **der Geldautomat** automatic teller
automatisch automatic
der Automechaniker (-) / die Automechanikerin (-nen) car mechanic
das Automobil (-e) automobile, car
das Automobilwerk (-e) automobile factory
der Autor (-en *masc.***) / die Autorin (-nen)** author
das Autoradio (-s) car radio
autoritär authoritarian
die Autoschlange (-n) long line of cars
der Autoschlüssel (-) car key
Autostop: per Autostop reisen to hitchhike (10)
das Autotelefon (-e) car telephone
das Autozubehör car accessories
Azubi = der / die Auszubildende

B

das Baby (-s) baby
der Bach (¨-e) creek, stream
backen (bäckt), backte, gebacken to bake
der Bäcker (-) / die Bäckerin (-nen) baker
die Bäckerei (-en) bakery
der Backstein (-e) brick
die Backwaren *(pl.)* baked goods (5)
das Bad (¨-er) bath; bathroom (2); spa
der Badeanzug (¨-e) bathing suit (5)
die Badehose (-n) bathing trunks
der Bademantel (¨-) bathrobe (5)
die Bademoden *(pl.)* beachwear
(das) Baden-Württemberg *one of the German states*
die Badesachen *(pl.)* beach wear; beach accessories
das Badezimmer (-) bathroom (2)
BAföG *abbreviation for German financial aid system for students*
die Baguette (-n) French bread
die Bahn (-en) train; railway (10); **mit der Bahn** by train; **die S-Bahn (-en)** light-rail line (9); **die U-Bahn (-en)** subway
der Bahnhof (¨-e) railroad station (10)
der Bahnsteig (-e) (train) platform (10)
das Bahnticket (-s) train ticket
bald soon (12); **bis bald** see you later; **möglichst bald** as soon as possible (12)
der Baldrian valerian
der Balkon (-e) balcony (2)
der Ball (¨-e) ball; **der Fußball** soccer
der Ballast ballast
das Ballett (-e) ballet (4)
die Banane (-n) banana (5)
das Band (¨-er) tape; ribbon; **vom Band laufen** to be mass-produced
die Band (-s) (musical) band
die Bande (-n) gang
der Bandscheibenschaden slipped (vertebral) disc
die Bank (-en) bank (9)
die Bankkarte (-n) bank card
der Bankschalter (-) bank window
der Banktresor (-e) bank vault
bar in cash (9); **bar jeder Vernunft** devoid of any sense
die Bar (-s) bar
das Bargeld cash (10)
der Baron (-e) baron *(nobility title)*
der Bart (¨-e) beard
(das) Baseball baseball
basteln to tinker; to build (as a hobby)
die Batterie (-n) battery
der Bau (Bauten) construction; building
der Bauch (¨-e) belly, abdomen, stomach (8)
die Bauchschmerzen *(pl.)* belly ache
der Bauchtanz (¨-e) belly dance
bauen to build (12)
der Bauer (-n *masc.***) / die Bäuerin (-nen)** farmer
das Bauernbrot (-e) farmer's bread
das Bauernfrühstück dish consisting of fried potatoes, bacon, and scrambled eggs
das Bauernhaus (¨-er) farmhouse (12)
der Bauernhof (¨-e) farm
der Bauernsalat (-e) farmer's salad
die Bauindustrie (-n) construction industry
der Baum (¨-e) tree
die Baumwolle cotton; **aus Baumwolle** made of cotton
die Baustelle (-n) construction site
bayerisch *(adj.)* Bavarian
(das) Bayern Bavaria
beachten to notice; to observe, pay attention to; **Beachtung schenken** to pay attention to
der Beamte *(decl. adj.)* **/ -die Beamtin (-nen)** agent; civil employee
beantragen to apply for
beantworten to answer
der Becher (-) beaker; container
der Bedarf demand, need; **bei Bedarf** as needed
das Bedauern regret
bedauern to regret (14)
bedeckt overcast (7)
bedenken, bedachte, bedacht to consider, think about
bedeuten to mean, signify
bedeutend important, distinguished
die Bedeutung (-en) meaning, significance
bedienen to serve
die Bedienung service (6)
das Bedienungsgeld service charge
die Bedingung (-en) condition
bedingungslos unconditional
bedroht sein to be threatened
bedrücken to depress
das Bedürfnis (-se) need, desire
sich beeilen to hurry (up) (8)
beeindruckt impressed
beeinflussen to influence
beenden to complete, finish, end
befahren *(adj.)* traveled on
sich befassen mit (+ *dat.*) to occupy oneself with
befehlen (befiehlt), befahl, befohlen to order
das Befinden well-being
sich befinden, befand, befunden to be located; to be
die Begebenheit (-en) event
begehen, beging, begangen to commit
begeistert von enthusiastic about
beginnen, begann, begonnen to begin, start (10)
begleiten to accompany
begreifen, begriff, begriffen to understand, comprehend
begründen to substantiate

begrünt overgrown with greenery
begrüßen to greet, welcome
die Begrüßung (-en) greeting
behaglich comfortable
behandeln to treat
behaupten to assert, claim
behausen to live in
sich behelfen (behilft), behalf, beholfen to make do
beherzigen to bear in mind
behindern to handicap, hinder
die Behörde (-n) regulatory authority, agency
bei (+ *dat.*) near; at; at the place of; with (5)
beibehalten (behält bei), behielt bei, beibehalten to maintain, keep up
beibringen (bringt bei), brachte bei, beigebracht to teach
beide (*pl.*) both
beifügen (fügt bei) to add; to enclose
beige beige (5)
die Beilage (-n) side dish (6)
beim = bei dem
das Bein (-e) leg (8)
das Beispiel (-e) example, model: **zum Beispiel** (*abbr.* **z.B.**) for example
beispielsweise for example
beißen, biss, gebissen to bite
der Beitrag (¨-e) contribution
beitragen (trägt bei), trug bei, beigetragen to contribute
beitreten (+ *dat.*) **(tritt bei), trat bei, ist beigetreten** to join
bekannt acquainted; known; **bekannt werden** to become acquainted
der/die Bekannte (*decl. adj.*) acquaintance
bekannt geben (gibt bekannt), gab bekannt, bekannt gegeben to announce, report
sich beklagen to complain
die Bekleidung clothing, attire
bekommen, bekam, bekommen to receive, get (6); **Was bekommen Sie?** What will you have? (6)
belasten to burden
beleben to enliven
belegen: ein Seminar belegen to register for a seminar
die Beleuchtung (-en) lighting; illumination
(das) Belgien Belgium (E)
belgisch (*adj.*) Belgian
der Belichtungsmesser (-) exposure meter
beliebt popular
belohnen to reward
die Belohnung (-en) reward
bemerken to observe; to notice
die Bemerkung (-en) remark, comment
bemühen to bother
sich benehmen (benimmt), benahm, benommen to behave
benutzbar usable
benutzen to use
das Benzin gasoline (12)
der Benzinverbrauch gasoline consumption
beobachten to observe
bequem comfortable; easy (2)
beraten (berät), beriet, beraten to advise, counsel
die Beratung (-en) consultation
der Bereich (-e) area, field
bereit sein to be willing
bereiten to prepare
bereithalten (hält bereit), hielt bereit, bereitgehalten to hold in store
bereits already
bereuen to regret
der Berg (-e) mountain (7)
bergsteigen gehen (geht), ging, ist gegangen to go mountain climbing
der Bericht (-e) report (13)
berichten to report, narrate
die Berichterstattung detailed reporting
Berliner (*adj.*) from/of Berlin
der Berliner (-) / die Berlinerin (-nen) person from Berlin
(das) Berlinerisch Berlin dialect
berücksichtigen to consider
der Beruf (-e) profession, occupation; **von Beruf** by profession (1)
beruflich on business; professional
der Berufsberater (-) / die Berufsberaterin (-nen) job counselor (11)
die Berufsberatung job counseling
berufsbildende Schule (-n) trade school
das Berufsleben professional life (11)
die Berufsschule (-n) vocational school
der/die Berufstätige (*decl. adj.*) working person
die Berufswahl (-en) career choice
der Berufswunsch (¨-e) career goal
berühmt famous (11)
berühren to touch
besänftigen to appease, placate
die Besatzung (-en) (military) occupation
die Besatzungszone (-n) occupied zone
sich beschäftigen (mit) (+ *dat.*) to occupy oneself (with); to spend time (with) (11)
die Beschäftigung (-en) activity
Bescheid: Bescheid geben/sagen (gibt/sagt Bescheid) to inform; to notify
beschließen, beschloss, beschlossen to decide
beschreiben, beschrieb, beschrieben to describe
die Beschreibung (-en) description
die Beschwerde (-n) complaint
sich beschweren über (+ *acc.*) to lodge a complaint, complain about (9)
beseitigen to remove
der Besen (-) broom
der Besenstiel (-e) broomstick
besetzen to occupy
besetzt occupied, taken (6); **Hier ist besetzt.** This place is taken. (6)
besichtigen to view, see
die Besiedlung (-en) settlement
besitzen, besaß, besessen to own, possess (11)
die Besonderheit (-en) special feature
besonders especially, particularly (8); special; **etwas Besonderes** something special; **nicht besonders (gut)** not particularly (well) (E)
besorgen to purchase, procure, get
besprechen (bespricht), besprach, besprochen to discuss, talk about
die Besprechung (-en) conference
besser better (10)
die Besserung: Gute Besserung! Get well soon!
besserwissend (*adj.*) in a know-all fashion
best-: am besten (the) best
der Bestandteil (-e) part
bestätigen to confirm, verify
bestechen (besticht), bestach, bestochen to bribe
das Besteck (-e) silverware
bestehen, bestand, bestanden to pass (an exam); **bestehen aus** (+ *dat.*) to consist of
bestellen to order; to reserve (6)
die Bestellung (-en) order; reservation
bestimmen to determine, decide
bestimmt certainly, to be sure, for certain (2)
bestrafen to punish
bestreichen, bestrich, bestrichen to spread on
der Besuch (-e) visit; visitor; **zu Besuch haben** to have (somebody) as a visitor; **zu Besuch sein** to visit; **zu Besuch kommen** to come for a visit
besuchen to visit (1)
der Besucher (-) / die Besucherin (-nen) visitor, guest
betäubt stunned; anesthetized
beteiligt sein (an + *dat.*) to participate (in)
das Beton concrete
betonen to stress, emphasize
die Betonung (-en) emphasis
die Betonwüste (-n) concrete jungle
betragen (beträgt), betrug, betragen to amount to, come to (12); **die Miete beträgt** the rent comes to

betreffen (betrifft), betraf, betroffen to concern
betreffend regarding
betreten (betritt), betrat, betreten to walk into
der Betrieb (-e) enterprise, business
die Betriebsabteilung (-en) department of a business
die Betriebswirtschaft business management
das Bett (-en) bed (2)
die Bettkarte (-n) ticket, voucher for a bed (in a train)
der Bettler (-) / die Bettlerin (-nen) beggar
das Betttuch (¨er) bed sheet
die Bettwaren (*pl.*) bedding
die Bettwäsche linens
beugen to bend
die Bevölkerung population
die Bevölkerungsexplosion population explosion
die Bevölkerungzahl population
der Bevölkerungszuwachs population increase
bevor (*subord. conj.*) before (10)
bevorzugt werden to be given priority
bewegen to move, move about
beweglich movable
die Bewegung (-en) exercise, movement
der Beweis (-e) proof, evidence
sich bewerben um (+ *acc.*) **(bewirbt), bewarb, beworben** to apply for (11)
der Bewerber (-) / die Bewerberin (-nen) applicant
die Bewerbung (-en) application (11)
das Bewerbungsformular (-e) application form (11)
bewerten to evaluate
bewohnen to reside in; to occupy
der Bewohner (-) / die Bewohnerin (-nen) resident, tenant
bewölkt cloudy, overcast (7)
die Bewölkungszunahme increasing cloudiness
bezahlbar payable; affordable
bezahlen to pay (9); **bar bezahlen** to pay in cash
die Bezeichnung (-en) label, term
bezeugen: Interesse bezeugen to show an interest
sich beziehen auf (+ *acc.*) to refer to
die Beziehung (-en) relationship; connection
beziehungsweise (bzw.) respectively, or
der Bezirk (-e) district, area
bezweifeln to doubt
die Bibliothek (-en) library
der Bibliothekar (-e) / die Bibliothekarin (-nen) librarian (11)

das Bier beer (5); **Bier vom Fass** beer on tap (6)
der Biergarten (¨) beer garden (restaurant) (6)
der Bierkeller (-) *type of restaurant where beer is served*
der Bierkrug (¨e) beer stein
bieten, bot, geboten to offer, present
der Bikini(-s) two-piece bathing suit
die Bilanz (-en) financial balance, "bottom line"
das Bild (-er) picture
bilden to form
das Bildnis (-se) picture, image
das Bildsymbol (-e) pictogram
die Bildungswissenschaft (-en) science/field of education
das Billiard (-s) billiard
billig cheap(ly); inexpensive(ly) (2)
die Billiguhr (-en) cheap watch
binden, band, gebunden to tie
das Biobrot (-e) organic bread
biographisch biographical(ly)
der Bioladen (¨) natural foods store (5)
die Biologie biology
der Biologielaborant (-en *masc.*) **/ die Biologielaborantin (-nen)** laboratory assistant
der Biologielehrer (-) / die Biologielehrerin (-nen) biology teacher
der Biologietechnologe (-n *masc.*) **/ die Biologietechnologin (-nen)** biotechnician
bis (+ *acc.*) until (6); up to; as far as; **bis bald** see you later; **bis (um) fünf Uhr** till five o'clock (6)
bisher so far, up to now
bisherig previous
ein bisschen a little (bit); somewhat
die Bistrobaguette (-n) special French bread
bitte please; you are welcome; here you are (E); **bitte schön** please (E); **bitte sehr** please (E); **Bitte sehr?** May I help you? (*in a store*)
bitten um (+ *acc.*)**, bat, gebeten** to ask for, request (12)
bitter bitter(ly)
bizarr bizarre
blasen (bläst), blies, geblasen to blow
das Blatt (¨er) sheet (of paper); leaf
blättern to leaf through
der Blattsalat (-e) green lettuce
blau blue (5); **in Blau** in blue
bleiben, blieb, ist geblieben to stay, remain (1); **stehen bleiben (bleibt stehen)** to stop walking; to stand still
der Bleistift (-e) pencil (12)
der Blick (-e) look; glance (13); **auf den ersten Blick** at first sight

der Blickpunkt (-e) focal point
der Blinddarm (¨e) appendix
die Blinddarmreizung (-en) appendix irritation
blitzen to flash (7); **Es blitzt.** There is lightning. (7)
das Blitzgerät (-e) (photographic) flash unit
die Blockade (-n) blockade
blockieren to block; to blockade
blöd(e) (*coll.*) dumb, silly
blond blond
die Blondine (-n) blond woman
bloß merely; only; **bloß mal** only just; just once
blühen to blossom
die Blume (-n) flower
der Blumenkohl cauliflower (5)
die Bluse (-n) blouse (5)
die Blutorange (-n) blood orange
der BMW (-s) (Bayerische Motor Werke) BMW automobile
die Bockwurst (¨e) *type of German hot dog*
der Boden (¨) floor of a room, ground; attic
der Bodenbelag (¨e) floor covering
der Bodenozon ground ozone
der Bodenozonwert (-e) level of ground ozone
der Bodenschatz (¨e) ore
der Bodensee Lake Constance
das Bodybuilding body-building (7); **Bodybuilding machen** to do body-building (7)
das Bogenschießen archery
die Bombe (-n) bomb
das Boot (-e) boat (1)
der Bootsverleih (-e) boat rental agency
Bord: an Bord on board
die Börse (-n) stock exchange
böse angry (angrily), mad; mean; bad; **böse sein auf** (+ *acc.*) to be mad (at somebody)
(das) Bosnien Bosnia
botanisch botanical(ly)
die Boutique (-n) boutique store
die Bouzouki (-s) bouzouki (*Greek string instrument*)
das Bowlingcenter bowling center
die Boxen (*pl.*) stereo speakers
die Boxershorts (*pl.*) boxer shorts
boykottieren to boycott
die Branche (-n) type of business
(das) Brandenburg *one of the German states*
das Brandenburger Tor Brandenburg Gate (*in Berlin*)
(das) Brasilien Brazil
der Braten (-) roast
die Bratkartoffeln (*pl.*) fried potatoes (6)

die Bratwurst (¨-e) *special type of sausage*
brauchen to need (2)
brauen to brew
die Brauerei (-en) brewery
das Brauhaus (¨-er) brewery
braun brown (5)
BRD = Bundesrepublik Deutschland
brechen (bricht), brach, gebrochen to break
die Breite (-n) latitude
der Breitensport (-s) popular sport
die Bremse (-n) brake
bremsen to put on the brakes, brake
(das) Breslau *city in former German province of Silesia, now Wrocław, Poland*
das Brett (-er) board
das Brevier (-e) breviary
die Brezel (-n) pretzel (6)
der Brief (-e) letter
der Briefkasten (¨-) mailbox
die Briefmarke (-n) postage stamp
der Briefträger (-) / die Briefträgerin (-nen) mail carrier
die Brigade (-n) team of workers (in a factory)
die Brille (-n) eyeglasses (5)
bringen, brachte, gebracht to bring; to take (7); **es zu etwas bringen** to be successful (in life)
der Brockhaus *name of German encyclopedia*
der Brokkoli (-) broccoli (5)
die Broschüre (-n) brochure, pamphlet
das Brot (-e) bread (5); **das Butterbrot (-e)** sandwich
das Brötchen (-) bread roll (5)
der Bruch (¨-e) fraction
brüchig brittle
die Brücke (-n) bridge
der Bruder (¨-) brother (3)
brüllen to yell; to roar
die Brust (¨-e) breast, chest (8)
das Buch (¨-er) book
der Buchdruck printing
buchen to book a trip, make a reservation (10)
das Bücherregal (-e) bookshelf (2)
der Bücherschrank (¨-e) bookcase
die Buchhandlung (-en) book store
das Büchlein (-) small book
der Buchmarkt (¨-e) book market
der Buchstabe (-n *masc.***)** letter of the alphabet
buchstabieren to spell; **Buchstabieren Sie!** Spell (it).
die Buchstabiertafel (-n) spelling chart
die Bucht (-en) bay
die Buchung (-en) reservation
die Bude (-n) (*coll.*) room (*slang term used by students*)
das Budget (-s) budget
die Bühne (-n) stage
das Bühnenbild (-er) stage decoration
der Bulle (-n *masc.***)** bull; (*derogatory*) policeman
bummeln to stroll
der Bund (-e) club; federation
das Bundesausbildungsförderungsgesetz (BAföG) *German law for the financial assistance of students*
der Bundesbürger (-) / die Bundesbürgerin (-nen) (German) citizen
der Bundeskanzler (-) (German or Austrian) chancellor
das Bundesland (¨-er) German state
der Bundespräsident (-en *masc.***)** German president
die Bundesrepublik Deutschland (BRD) German Federal Republic (E)
der Bundestag Federal German parliament
die Bundeswehr Federal German armed forces
der Bunker (-) bunker
bunt colorful
die Burg (-en) fortress, castle
der Bürger (-) / die Bürgerin (-nen) citizen (14)
die Bürgerinitiative (-n) grass-roots movement
der Bürgermeister (-) mayor
das Büro (-s) (11)
die Büroarbeit (-en) office work
die Bürokauffrau (-en) (female) administrator
der Bürokaufmann (¨-er) (male) administrator
bürokratisch bureaucratical(ly)
der Bus (-se) bus (10)
die Busfahrt (-en) bus ride; bus trip
die Bushaltestelle (-n) bus stop
die Buslinie (-n) bus line (10)
die Busreise (-n) bus trip
die Butter butter (5)
das Buttergemüse (-) buttered vegetable
der Butterkäse butter cheese
die Butterspätzle (*pl.*) buttered pasta dish
bzw. = beziehungsweise

C

ca = circa, zirka (12)
das Café (-s) café (6)
campen to go camping
das Camping camping
der Campingplatz (¨-e) campground
die Campingtour (-en) camping tour
der Campus (-) (school) campus
der Cartoon (-s) cartoon
die CD-Platte (-n) CD record
der CD-Spieler (-) CD player (2)
Celsius centigrade
der Champignon (-s) mushroom (6)
die Chance (-n) chance
das Chaos chaos
der Charakter (-e) character, personality
die Checkliste (-n) checklist
der Chef (-s) / die Chefin (-nen) boss, employer (11)
die Chemie chemistry
der Chemielaborant (-en *masc.***) / die Chemielaborantin (-nen)** chemical technician
die Chemikalie (-n) chemical substance
der Chemiker (-) / die Chemikerin (-nen) chemist (11)
die Chiffre (-n) code (number)
chinesisch (*adj.*) Chinese
der Chirurg (-en *masc.***) / die Chirurgin (-nen)** surgeon
der Chor (¨-e) choir, chorus; **im Chor** in a chorus
die Christianisierung christianization
christlich (*adj.*) Christian
die Chronik (-en) chronicle
der Chronobiologe (-n *masc.***) / die Chronobiologin (-nen)** chronobiologist
die Chronologie (-n) chronology
chronologisch chronological
circa = zirka about (12)
der Clown (-s) / die Clownin (-nen) clown
cm = Centimeter
die Cola (-s) cola (5)
der Computer (-) computer (2)
die Computerdiskette (-n) computer floppy disk (12)
das Computerspiel (-e) computer game (1)
der Computertisch (-e) computer table
die Computerwissenschaft (-en) computer science
der Container (-) recycling bin
der Containerstellplatz (¨-e) recycling center
die Cordhose (-n) corduroy pants
die Coronarsklerose (-n) coronary sclerosis, hardening of the arteries
die Couch (-en) couch
der Couchtisch (-e) coffee table (2)
der Cousin (-s) male cousin
die Cousine = Kusine female cousin (3)

D

d.h. = (das heißt) (8)
da there (2); since; **da drüben** over there (6)
dabei with that; in that context; **dabei sein** to be part of
das Dach (¨-er) roof (12)
das Dachgeschoss (-e) floor right below the roof (often with slanted walls) (12)
die Dachwohnung (-en) attic apartment

der Dackel (-) dachshund
dadurch for that reason; through that; because of
dafür for that; instead of that; **Ich bin dafür.** I am for it. (14)
dagegen against it (14); on the other hand; **Ich bin dagegen.** I'm against it. (14)
daher from there; for that reason, therefore
dahin there (to that place) (9); **bis dahin** until then; **Wie komme ich am besten dahin?** What's the best way to get there? (9)
dahinter behind that
daliegen (liegt da), lag da, dagelegen to lie there
damals formerly; (back) then, at that time
die Dame (-n) lady
der Damenhut (⸚e) ladies' hat
die Damenkonfektion (-en) ladies' wear
der Damenschuh (-e) ladies' shoe
die Damenwäsche lingerie
damit (*subord. conj.*) so that; with that
die Dämmerung dawn; dusk; twilight
der Dampf (⸚e) steam; **Dampf machen** (+ *dat.*) to make things uncomfortable (for somebody)
danach after that; afterward
der Däne (-n *masc.*) **/ die Dänin (-nen)** Dane, Danish person
daneben next to that
(das) Dänemark Denmark (E)
der Dank thanks; **vielen Dank** many thanks (6); **Gott sei Dank** thank God
dank (+ *gen.*) thanks to
dankbar grateful
danke thanks (E); **danke schön** (many) thanks (E); **danke sehr** thanks very much (E); **danke, es geht** O.K., thanks; **danke, gut** fine, thanks (E)
danken (+ *dat.*) to thank (5); **nichts zu danken** don't mention it, not at all (8)
dann then
(das) Danzig *German name for the town of Gdansk*
daran on that, at that, to that
darauf on that, for that; **bald darauf** soon after that
daraus from that
darin in that, in there
die Darmgegend (-en) intestinal area
die Darmgeschichten (*pl.*) intestinal troubles
darstellen (stellt dar) to portray, depict
darüber about that; above that; **darüber hinaus** moreover
darum therefore
darunter under, among (them)
das that, this
dass (*subord. conj.*) that (8)
dasselbe the same
der Dativ dative case
die Dativpräposition (-en) preposition governing the dative case
das Dativpronomen (-) pronoun in the dative case
das Dativverb (-en) verb requiring a dative object
das Datum (Daten) date (3); **Welches Datum ist heute/morgen?** What is today's/tomorrow's date? (3)
der Dauerbetrieb regular use
dauern to last; to take time (7)
dauernd constant(ly); all the time
die Dauerwelle (-n) permanent wave
der Daumen (-) thumb; **die Daumen drücken** to keep one's fingers crossed
davon of that, about that, on that; **abgesehen davon** apart from that
davor before that
dazu to that, for that
dazuverdienen (verdient dazu) to earn on the side
DB = Deutsche Bundesbahn
DDR = Deutsche Demokratische Republik
debattieren to debate
die Decke (-n) ceiling; blanket
decken to cover; **den Tisch decken** to set the table
die Deckenleuchte (-n) ceiling light
definieren to define
deftig hearty, solid
(sich) dehnen to stretch
dein your (*inform. sg.*) (3)
die Dekoration (-en) decoration
der Dekostoff (-e) decorator fabric
die Delikatesse (-n) delicacy
demnächst soon
die Demokratie (-n) democracy
demokratisch democratic(ally)
die Demonstration (-en) demonstration (14)
demonstrieren to demonstrate
denken, dachte, gedacht to think; **denken an** (+ *acc.*) to think of (12)
denkwürdig memorable
denn (*coord. conj.*) for, because (7); then; (*used in questions to express interest*) (1)
dennoch however; in spite of
die Deponie (-n) garbage dump
deportieren to deport
deprimiert depressed (8)
der, die, das the; that one
derjenige, diejenige, dasjenige the one (who)
derselbe the same
deshalb therefore, for that reason (8)
das Design (-s) design
der Designer (-) / die Designerin (-nen) designer
das Dessin (-s) pattern
desto: je . . . desto . . . the . . . the . . .
deswegen because of that (12)
das Detail (-s) detail
detailliert detailed
der Detektivroman (-e) detective story
deuten auf (+ *acc.*) to point to, refer to
deutlich clear, understandable
deutsch German; **Deutsch** German language (1); **auf Deutsch** in German
der/die Deutsche (*decl. adj.*) German person
die Deutsche Demokratische Republik (DDR) German Democratic Republic (GDR)
die Deutsche Mark (DM) German mark
die Deutschklasse (-n) German class
der Deutschklub (-s) German club
der Deutschkurs (-e) German course
(das) Deutschland Germany (E)
der Deutschlehrer (-) / die Deutschlehrerin (-nen) German teacher
der/die Deutschlernende (*decl. adj.*) German learner
deutschsprachig German speaking
der Deutschunterricht German class
die Devisen (*pl.*) foreign currency
die Deviseneinfuhr (-en) importation of foreign currency
(der) Dezember December (3)
die Dialektik dialectics
der Dialog (-e) dialogue
die Diät (-en) diet
dich you *(acc. inform. sg.)*
der Dichter (-) / die Dichterin (-nen) poet
dichtmachen (macht dicht) to close
dick fat, plump; thick; **dick machen** to be fattening; **dick werden** to gain weight; **(ein) dickes Küsschen** (a) big kiss
der Dieb (-e) thief
der Diebstahl (⸚e) theft
die Diele (-n) entranceway, hallway (12)
(der) Dienstag Tuesday (3)
dienstags on Tuesdays (4)
dieselbe the same
der Dieselmotor (-en) diesel engine
dieser, diese, dies(es) this (5)
diesmal this time
digital digital
die Digitaluhr (-en) digital watch
das Dilemma (-s) dilemma
der Dill dill (*herb*)
der Dimmer (-) (*light switch*) dimmer
das Ding (-e) thing, object
Dipl. = Diplom (*academic degree*)
der Diplomat (-en *masc.*) **/ die Diplomatin (-nen)** diplomat

der Dirigent (-en *masc.***) / die Dirigentin (-nen)** musical conductor
das Dirndlkleid (-er) *traditional dress worn mostly in Southern Germany and Austria*
die Disko (-s) disco bar (4); **in die Disko gehen** to go to a disco (4)
die Diskriminierung (-en) discrimination
die Diskussion (-en) discussion
diskutieren to have a discussion; to debate (1)
die Disziplin discipline
DM = die Deutsche Mark
doch yes (1); yes, of course; after all (4)
der Doktor (-en) physician; person holding doctorate; **Herr/Frau Doktor** *formal way of addressing individual with medical or doctoral degree*
das Dokument (-e) document
der Dokumentarfilm (-e) documentary film (13)
dokumentieren to document; to certify
der Dollarschein (-e) dollar bill
der Dolmetscher (-) / die Dolmetscherin (-nen) interpreter (11)
das Dolmetscherinstitut (-e) college for interpreters
der Dom (-e) cathedral; dome
die Donau Danube (*river*)
donnern to thunder; **Es donnert.** It is thundering. (7)
(der) Donnerstag Thursday (3)
donnerstags on Thursdays (4)
doof (*coll.*) dumb, stupid
doppelt double; twice
das Doppelzimmer (-) double room (9)
das Dorf (¨er) village (12)
der Dorfkrug (¨e) village inn
dort there
dorthin (to) there
die Dose (-n) can; jar (14)
Dr. = Doktor
das Drachenfliegen hang gliding
der Draht (¨e) wire
das Drama (Dramen) drama
dramatisch dramatic(ally)
dran sein to have (one's) turn
sich drängen to crowd
das Drängendste (*decl. adj.*) the most urgent (matter)
drastisch drastically
(sich) drauflegen (legt drauf) to lie down on top of
draußen outside (7)
drehen to turn
drei three (E)
dreihundert three hundred (E)
das Dreikornbrot three-grain bread
dreimal three times (7)
dreißig thirty (E)
dreitausend three thousand (E)
dreizehn thirteen (E)
dreizehnte thirteenth (3)
drin (= darin) (*coll.*) inside
dringend urgent (2)
drinnen inside (7)
dritte third (3); **zu dritt** as a group of three
ein Drittel a third (12)
die Droge (-n) drug; medicine (14)
drogenabhängig addicted to drugs
der/die Drogenabhängige (*decl. adj.*) drug addict
der Drogenhandel (-) drug trade
der Drogenkonsum drug consumption
die Drogensucht drug addiction (14)
der/die Drogensüchtige (*decl. adj.*) drug addict (14)
die Drogerie (-n) drugstore (5)
drüben, da drüben over there, on the other side (6)
drücken: die Daumen drücken to keep one's fingers crossed
der Drucker (-) printer (13)
du you (*inform. sg.*) (1)
düdeln to toot
dumm dumb, stupid
die Düne (-n) dune
dunkel dark (2)
dunkelblau dark blue
dunkellila dark purple
dunkelrot dark red
dünn thin; slender, skinny
durch (+ *acc.*) through; by (3)
das Durcheinander upheaval, commotion
durchaus by all means
durchfahren (fährt durch), fuhr durch, ist durchgefahren to travel without having to transfer
durchführen (führt durch) to carry out (an order)
durchkommen (kommt durch), kam durch, ist durchgekommen to get through
durchlesen (liest durch), las durch, durchgelesen to read through, peruse
durchs = durch das (3)
der Durchschnitt (-e) average; cross section (12); **im Durchschnitt** on the average (12)
durchschnittlich on the average (12)
durchziehen (zieht durch), zog durch, durchgezogen to pull through
dürfen (darf), durfte, gedurft to be allowed to; may (4)
der Durst thirst; **Durst haben** to be thirsty (2)
die Dusche (-n) shower (9)
(sich) duschen to take a shower (8)
die Duschmilk shower lotion
das Dutzend (-e) dozen
dynamisch dynamic
die Dynamomaschine (-n) generator

E

eben just; simply
ebenfalls also
ebenso just like, the same as
ebensolch- similar
echt genuine(ly), real(ly)
die Ecke (-n) corner
Effeff: aus dem Effeff inside out
die EG = Europäische Gemeinschaft
egal: Das ist mir egal. I don't care. (5)
der Egoist (-en *masc.***)** egotist
ehemalig former
das Ehepaar (-e) married couple
eher rather, sooner
ehest- soonest
die Ehre honor
der Ehrgeiz ambition
ehrlich honest
das Ei (-er) egg (5)
die Eierbox (-en) egg container
die Eieruhr (-en) egg timer
eigen own (12)
die Eigenschaft (-en) character trait; characteristic
eigentlich actually (13)
die Eigentumswohnung (-en) condominium
die Eignung (-en) ability
eilen to hurry
der Eilzug (¨e) local train
der Eimer (-) bucket
ein, eine a(n); one
einander one another
die Einbahnstraße (-n) one-way street
einbiegen (biegt ein), bog ein, ist eingebogen to turn, make a turn (9)
der Einblick (-e) insight
der Einbrecher (-) / die Einbrecherin (-nen) burglar
der Einbruch (¨e) burglary
eindeutig obvious(ly)
der Eindruck (¨e) impression
einer one (of several)
einerseits on the one hand
einfach simple; simply; one-way (ticket) (10); **ganz einfach** quite simple
das Einfamilienhaus (¨er) single-family house
einfügen (fügt ein) to insert
der Einfluss (¨e) influence
einführen (führt ein) to introduce (14)
die Einführung (-en) introduction
der Eingang (¨e) entrance (12); entranceway
eingenäht sewn in
eingerichtet furnished; equipped
eingeschlossen included
eingesperrt caged in

der Eingriff (-e) (*medicine*) small operation
einhalten (hält ein), hielt ein, eingehalten to adhere to
einheimisch local
der/die Einheimische (*decl. adj.*) native person
die Einheit unity; union
einholen (holt ein) to catch up with
einige (*pl.*) several, some
einiges several things
die Einigung (-en) unification
einjährig (*adj.*) one-year
der Einkauf (¨e) purchase
einkaufen (kauft ein); einkaufen gehen to shop, go shopping (4)
der Einkaufsboulevard (-s) shopping street
der Einkaufstag (-e) day for shopping
die Einkaufstasche (-n) shopping bag
das Einkaufszentrum (Einkaufszentren) shopping center
der Einkaufszettel (-) shopping list
der Einkauftipp (-s) shopping suggestion
das Einkommen (-) income (11)
einladen (lädt ein), lud ein, eingeladen to invite (4)
einladend inviting
die Einladung (-en) invitation
der Einlass (¨e) admission; **um Einlass bitten** to request admission
einlassen (lässt ein), ließ ein, eingelassen to let (somebody) in, admit
einlösen (löst ein) Reiseschecks einlösen to cash travelers' checks
einmal once (7)
einmalig unique
die Einnahme (-n) income (12)
einnehmen (nimmt ein), nahm ein, eingenommen to take (medicine); to seize (a city)
einrichten (richtet ein) to furnish (12), equip
die Einrichtung (-en) furnishings
eins (*numeral*) one (E)
einsam lonely
einsammeln (sammelt ein) to gather, collect
der Einsatz (¨e) operation, use
einschicken (schickt ein) to send in; to forward
einschlafen (schläft ein), schlief ein, ist eingeschlafen to fall asleep (4)
die Einsendung: bei Einsendung upon mailing in
der Einspänner (-) one-horse carriage
einsparen (spart ein) to save
einsperren (sperrt ein) to lock in
einsteigen (steigt ein), stieg ein, ist eingestiegen to board (a train) (10)
der Einsteiger (-) / die Einsteigerin (-nen) beginner, newcomer
die Einstellung (-en) attitude
einstig- former
einstmals formerly
eintreten (tritt ein), trat ein, ist eingetreten to enter
der Eintritt (-e) price of admission
der Eintrittspreis (-e) price of admission
einverstanden: einverstanden sein to be in agreement; to agree, approve; **Ich bin damit einverstanden.** I agree with that.
die Einwegflasche (-n) non-returnable bottle
der Einwohner (-) / die Einwohnerin (-nen) resident, inhabitant
einzahlen (zahlt ein) to pay in; to deposit
der Einzelhandel retail trade
der Einzelhandelskaufmann (¨er) / die Einzelhandelskauffrau (-en) retail merchant
der Einzelhandelsumsatz (¨e) retail trade
einzeln scattered; **jeder einzelne** every single one
der Einzelunterricht one-on-one instruction
der Einzelurlaub (-e) vacation alone
das Einzelzimmer (-) single room (9)
einziehen (zieht ein), zog ein, ist eingezogen to move in (12)
einzig only, sole; **nicht ein einziges Wort** not a single word
das Eis ice cream (5); ice
der Eisbär (-en *masc.*) polar bear
der Eisbecher (-) dish of ice cream with toppings (6)
das Eiscafé (-s) ice cream parlor
die Eiscreme ice cream
das Eishockey ice hockey
der Eiskaffee (-s) iced coffee mixed with ice cream and topped by whipped cream
der Eissalat (-e) iceberg lettuce
der Eisschrank (¨e) refrigerator
das Eisstadion (Eisstadien) ice skating rink (7)
das Ekg = Elektrokardiogramm
die Elbe *German river flowing into the North Sea*
der Elefant (-en *masc.*) elephant
elegant elegant(ly)
elektrisch electrical
die Elektrizität electricity
die Elektroabteilung (-en) electrical department
der Elektroinstallateur (-e) / die Elektroinstallateurin (-nen) electrician
das Elektrokardiogramm (-e) electrocardiogram
das Elektronenmikroskop (-e) electron microscope
die Elektronikbranche (-n) (field of) electronics
der Elektroniker (-) / die Elektronikerin (-nen) electronic engineer
das Element (-e) item, element
elementar basic, easy
das Elend misery, need
elf eleven (E)
elfte eleventh (3)
der Ell(en)bogen (-) elbow (8)
(das) Elsass Alsace
die Eltern (*pl.*) parents (3)
das Elternschlafzimmer (-) master bedroom
der Elternteil (-e) parent
die Emanzipation (-en) emancipation
die Emission (-en) emission
der Emmentaler Käse (-) Emmental cheese
der Empfang (¨e) reception
der Empfänger (-) / die Empfängerin (-nen) recipient
empfehlen (empfiehlt), empfahl, empfohlen to recommend (5)
empfehlenswert recommendable
die Empfehlung (-en) recommendation
empfinden, empfand, empfunden to feel, consider
empfindlich sensitive
das Ende (-) end; **am Ende** in the end; **zu Ende sein** to be over
enden to end
endgültig final; finally; once and for all
endlich finally, at last
die Endung (-en) ending
die Energie energy
energieeffizient energy-efficient(ly)
Energie sparend energy-saving
die Energieverschwendung waste of energy
eng narrow, tight
engagiert involved, concerned
(das) England England
der Engländer (-) / die Engländerin (-nen) English person
englisch English; **auf Englisch** in English
das Englisch English language
der Englischlehrer (-) / die Englischlehrerin (-nen) English teacher
der Englischunterricht English instruction
der Enkel (-) / die Enkelin (-nen) grandson, granddaughter (3)
das Enkelkind (-er) grandchild
entdecken to discover

entfallen (entfällt), entfiel, ist entfallen auf (+ *acc.*) to be allotted to
entfernen to remove; **entfernt von** away from
entgegenlaufen (läuft entgegen), lief entgegen, ist entgegengelaufen (+ *dat.*) to run toward (somebody)
enthalten (enthält), enthielt, enthalten to contain, include; **im Preis enthalten** included in the price (9)
enthusiastisch enthusiastic(ally)
entkoffeiniert decaffeinated
entkommen, entkam, ist entkommen to get away
entlang (+ *acc.*) along; alongside; **die Straße entlang** along the street
entlanggehen (geht entlang), ging entlang, ist entlanggegangen to walk alongside (9)
entlaufen (entläuft), entlief, ist entlaufen to run away
entnehmen (entnimmt), entnahm, entnommen to gather (from)
entnervt unnerved
(sich) entscheiden, entschied, entschieden to decide
entscheidend decisive
die Entscheidung (-en) decision; **eine Entscheidung treffen** to make a decision
sich entschließen, entschloss, entschlossen to decide, make up one's mind
entschuldigen to excuse (6); **sich entschuldigen** to apologize; **Entschuldigen Sie bitte.** Excuse me, please. (6)
die Entschuldigung (-en) apology, excuse; **Entschuldigung** pardon me
sich entsinnen, entsann, entsonnen to remember
der Entsorger (-) / die Entsorgerin (-nen) (toxic) waste disposal worker
die Entsorgung (-en) (toxic) waste disposal
die Entsorgungsplanung waste disposal planning
sich entspannen to relax, take a rest (8)
die Entspannung relaxation
entsprechen (+ *dat.*) **(entspricht), entsprach, entsprochen** to correspond to; to comply with; to come up to
entsprechend appropriately
entstehen, entstand, ist entstanden to originate; to come about, happen
die Entstehung origin; creation
enttäuscht disappointed
entweder . . . oder either . . . or (8)
entwerfen (entwirft), entwarf, entworfen to design, develop
entwickeln to develop (14)
die Entwicklung (-en) development (11)
das Entwicklungsland (¨-er) developing country
entziehen, entzog, entzogen to take away
entzündlich flammable
die Enzyklopädie (-n) encyclopedia
epidemisch epidemic(ally)
er he; it (1)
Erachten: meines Erachtens in my view
erbauen to build
der Erbe (-n *masc.***) / die Erbin (-nen)** heir
erben to inherit
die Erdbeere (-n) strawberry (5)
die Erde Earth
das Erdgeschoss (-e) ground floor (9)
die Erdkunde geography
sich ereignen to happen
das Ereignis (-se) event
erfahren (erfährt), erfuhr, erfahren to find out; to experience; to learn
die Erfahrung (-en) experience
erfinden, erfand, erfunden to invent (13)
der Erfinder (-) / die Erfinderin (-nen) inventor (13)
der Erfindergeist inventiveness
erfinderisch inventive
die Erfindung (-en) invention (13)
der Erfolg (-e) success (11); **Erfolg haben** to be successful
erfolgreich successful
der Erfolgszwang pressure to succeed
erfordern to demand, require
erfragen to inquire
das Erfrischungstuch (¨-er) towelette
erfüllen to fulfill
ergänzen to complete, add
sich ergeben (ergibt), ergab, ergeben to be the result, to surrender
ergeben (*adj.*) devoted
erhalten (erhält), erhielt, erhalten to get, receive
die Erhebung (-en) elevation
erhöhen to increase; to heighten
sich erholen to recuperate; to rest (8)
die Erholung rest and recuperation
der Erholungspreis (-e) vacation price
sich erinnern an (+ *acc.*) to remember
die Erinnerung (-en) memory; remembrance
sich erkälten to catch a cold (8)
die Erkältung (-en) cold (8)
erkennen, erkannte, erkannt to recognize
erklären to explain
die Erklärung (-en) explanation
erklingen, erklang, ist erklungen to sound
sich erkundigen to seek information, inquire
erlauben to allow, permit (9); **erlaubt** permitted
erleben to experience (10)
das Erlebnis (-se) experience, event
die Erlösung (-en) rescue, salvation
ermöglichen to make possible, enable
ermüdend tiring (13)
die Ernährung food, nutrition (12)
die Ernährungsaktion (-en) "operation nutrition"
das Ernährungsbewusstsein consciousness about nutrition
die Ernährungssituation (-en) food situation
erneuern to renew
ernst serious(ly) (1)
erntefrisch just harvested
erobern to conquer
die Eroberung (-en) conquest
eröffnen to open up
erraten (errät), erriet, erraten to guess
erreichbar mit able to be reached by, reachable via
erreichen to reach
erscheinen, erschien, ist erschienen to appear, come out
ersetzen to replace
ersparen to save
erst only, not until
erstaunt amazed
erste first (3); **erster Klasse** first-class (10); **zum ersten Mal** for the first time
erstklassig first class, excellent
erstmals (*adv.*) for the first time
ertönen to sound (off)
erträglich bearable
der/die Erwachsene (*decl. adj.*) adult, grownup
erwähnen to mention
erwarten to expect; to wait for
die Erwartung (-en) expectation
erweitern to expand
erwerben (erwirbt), erwarb, erworben to acquire, buy
erwünscht desired; desirable
erzählen to tell, narrate
der Erzähler (-) / die Erzählerin (-nen) narrator
die Erzählung (-en) story, narration
erzeugen to produce
erziehen, erzog, erzogen to bring up
die Erziehung upbringing, education
es it (1)
der Espresso (-s) espresso (coffee)
die Espressomaschine (-n) espresso machine
essbar edible

essen (isst), aß, gegessen to eat (2)
das Essen (-) food; meal; eating (1); **zum Essen** for dinner; **Essen und Trinken** food and drinks
die Essgewohnheit (-en) eating habits
der Essig vinegar
der Esstisch (-e) dining room table
das Esszimmer (-) dining room
die Etage (-n) floor, story (12)
etwa approximately, about
etwas something; anything; a little bit (2); **etwas anderes** something different
euch you (*acc. inform. pl.*) (3)
euer your (*inform. pl.*) (3)
euphorisch euphoric, enthusiastic
die Eurokarte (-n) European bank card
(das) Europa Europe
europäisch (*adj.*) European
der Euroscheck (-s) *type of personal check used in Europe*
eventuell perhaps
evtl. = eventuell
ewig eternal(ly), constant(ly)
das Examen (-) examination
die Ex-DDR former East Germany
die Existenz (-en) livelihood
das Experiment (-e) experiment
experimentieren to experiment (11)
der Experte (-n *masc.***) / die Expertin (-nen)** expert
explodieren to explode
exzentrisch eccentric

F

fabelhaft fabulous, great
die Fabrik (-en) factory
das Fabrikat (-e) product
das Fach (¨-er) subject (in school); **das Hauptfach** major subject; **das Lieblingsfach** favorite subject; **das Nebenfach** minor subject
die Fachakademie (-n) professional school (*university level*)
die Fachbuchhandlung (-en) textbook store
das Fachgeschäft (-e) specialty store
die Fachhochschule (-n) technical college
die Fachoberschule (-n) trade school
die Fachrichtung (-en) specific field of studies
die Fachschule (-n) technical school
die Fahne (-n) flag
fahren (fährt), fuhr, ist gefahren to drive; to ride; to travel; to go (2); **Auto fahren** to drive a car (2); **Motorrad fahren** to ride a motorcycle (2)
der Fahrer (-) / die Fahrerin (-nen) driver
die Fahrkarte (-n) ticket (10)
der Fahrkartenschalter (-) ticket window (10)
der Fahrplan (¨-e) schedule (10)
der Fahrpreis (-e) fare
das Fahrrad (¨-er) bicycle (10)
die Fahrradhose (-n) bicycle pants
die Fahrradtour (-en) bicycle tour
der Fahrschein (-e) ticket
der Fahrstuhl (¨-e) elevator
die Fahrt (-en) trip; drive, ride (10)
die Fahrtkosten (*pl.*) traveling expenses
die Fahrtstrecke (-n) travel distance
die Fakten facts
der Fall (¨-e) case
fallen (fällt), fiel, ist gefallen to fall (7); to decline (value of money)
fallen lassen (lässt fallen), ließ fallen, fallen gelassen to drop (something)
falsch false, wrong, incorrect
fälschungssicher counterfeitproof
die Familie (-n) family (3)
die Familienchronik (-en) family chronicle
das Familienfest (-e) family celebration (3)
das Familienleben family life
das Familienmitglied (-er) family member
der Familienname (-n *masc.***)** family name, last name
der Familienpass (¨-e) pass for the entire family
der Familienstammbaum (¨-e) family tree
der Familienstand marital status
die Familienvorstellung (-en) family performance
der Fan (-s) fan, admirer
fangen (fängt), fing, gefangen to catch
die Fantasiewohnung (-en) fantasy apartment
fantastisch fantastic
die Farbe (-n) color (5)
der Farbfernsehapparat (-e) color TV set
das Farbfernsehen color TV
farbig colored
der Fasching Mardi Gras (*southern Germany*) (3)
das Fass (¨-er) barrel, vat; **Bier vom Fass** beer on tap (6)
fassen to comprehend, grasp; **sich an den Kopf fassen** to take hold of one's head in disbelief; **Fuß fassen** to become acclimatized; **Ich kann es nicht fassen.** I can't comprehend it.
fast almost (8)
faszinieren to fascinate
faszinierend fascinating
fatal very serious(ly), fatal(ly)
faul lazy (1)
faulenzen to be lazy, not do anything (7)
das Faxgerät (-e) fax machine
FC = Fußballclub
(der) Februar February (3)
fehlen to be missing (10); to lack; to need; **Was fehlt Ihnen?** What's wrong? (8)
fehlend missing
der Feierabend (-e) end of workday; **am Feierabend** after work
feiern to celebrate (3)
der Feiertag (-e) holiday
fein fine, delicate; all right; **fein säuberlich** nice(ly) and neat(ly)
das Fenster (-) window (2)
die Fensterbank (¨-e) windowsill
die Ferien (*pl.*) vacation (10)
die Ferienreise (-n) vacation trip
der Ferientraum (¨-e) dream vacation
die Ferienwohnung (-en) vacation apartment
das Fernglas (¨-er) binoculars
der Fernsehapparat (-e) television set
fernsehen (sieht fern), sah fern, ferngesehen to watch TV (4)
das Fernsehen television; TV watching
der Fernseher (-) television set (2)
das Fernsehgerät (-e) television set
die Fernsehnachrichten (*pl.*) television news
das Fernsehprogramm (-e) TV program, schedule
der Fernsehtechniker (-) / die Fernsehtechnikerin (-nen) television technician
fertig finished, done; ready
das Fest (-e) festival; party, feast
fest firm; permanent (11)
sich festlegen (legt fest) to commit oneself
feststellen (stellt fest) to establish, determine
die Fete (-n) (*coll.*) party
fett fat; greasy
das Fett (-e) fat
fettarm low-fat
fett gedruckt bold-face
das Feuer (-) fire
das Feuerwerk (-e) fireworks
das Feuilleton (-s) cultural section of a newspaper (13)
das Fieber fever (8)
die Figur (-en) figure
die Filialdirektion head of a branch office
die Filiale (-n) branch office
der Film (-e) film, movie (4); roll of film
der Filmabend (-e) evening of film showing
das Filmprogramm (-e) movie program
der Filmregisseur (-e) / die Filmregisseurin (-nen) movie director

der Filmschauspieler (-) / die Filmschauspielerin (-nen) movie actor/actress
der Filmstar (-e) movie star
der Filter (-) filter
der Finanzbeamte (*decl. adj.*) **/ die Finanzbeamtin (-nen)** tax official
die Finanzen (*pl.*) finance(s)
finanziell financial(ly) (11)
finanzieren to finance
der Finanzskandal (-e) financial scandal
die Finanzzeitung (-en) financial newspaper
finden, fand, gefunden to find; to think, mean (1); **Wie finden Sie Berlin?** What do you think of Berlin?
der Finderlohn (¨-e) finder's reward
der Finger (-) finger (8)
das Fingerknipsen snapping of one's fingers
die Firma (Firmen) firm, company (11)
der Fisch (-e) fish
das Fischen fishing
das Fischerdorf (¨-er) fishing village
die Fischerei (-en) fishery
der Fischfang fishing
die Fischverarbeitung fish processing
fit fit, in shape (8); **sich fit halten** to keep in shape (8)
die Fitness fitness (8)
der Fitnessberater (-) / die Fitnessberaterin (-nen) fitness consultant, personal trainer
das Fitnesscenter (-) fitness center (7)
die Fitnessgewohnheiten (*pl.*) fitness habits
die Fitnessroutine (-n) fitness routine
das Fitnessstudio (-s) fitness studio
flach flat; even
die Fläche (-n) surface; area
das Fläschchen (-) little bottle
die Flasche (-n) bottle (14)
der Fleck (-e) spot
die Fledermaus (¨-e) bat
das Fleisch meat (5)
die Fleischabteilung (-en) meat department
die Fleischwaren (*pl.*) meats
fleißig diligent, hard-working (1)
die Flexibilität flexibility
fliegen, flog, ist geflogen to fly (7)
fließen, floss, ist geflossen to flow, run
fließend running; fluent(ly)
der Flohmarkt (¨-e) flea market
(das) Florenz Florence (Italy)
die Flöte (-n) flute
flott quick, snappy
die Flotte (-n) fleet
flüchten (ist geflüchtet) to flee, escape
der Flüchtling (-e) refugee, fugitive
der Flug (¨-e) flight
der Flugbegleiter (-) / die Flugbegleiterin (-nen) flight attendant (10)
das Flugblatt (¨-er) flyer
die Fluggesellschaft (-en) airline company
der Flughafen (¨-) airport (10)
der Flugingenieur (-e) / die Flugingenieurin (-nen) flight engineer
das Flüglein (-) small wing
die Flugreise (-n) airplane trip
der Flugschein (-e) airplane ticket (10)
das Flugzeug (-e) airplane (10)
der Flugzeugbau airplane construction
der Flugzeuglärm airplane noise
der Flur (-e) hallway (12); **für den ganzen Flur** for the entire floor
der Fluss (¨-e) river (7)
flüstern to whisper
die Folge (-n) consequence, result
folgen (+ *dat.*) to follow; **daraus folgt** the result of that is
folgend following
folglich consequently
fordern to demand
fördern to promote (14)
die Forelle (-n) trout
die Form (-en) form, shape
das Format (-e) format
formulieren to form, formulate
forschen to do research
die Forschung (-en) research (14)
das Forschungszentrum (Forschungszentren) research center
fortschreitend advancing, progressive(ly)
der Fortschritt (-e) progress (14); **Fortschritte machen** to make progress (14)
die Fortsetzung (-en) continuation
der Fortsetzungsroman (-e) serialized novel (*usually in a newspaper*) (13)
das Foto (-s) photograph (2)
das Fotoalbum (Fotoalben) photo album
die Fotoannahme (-n) photo processing place
der Fotoapparat (-e) camera
der Fotodesigner (-) / die Fotodesignerin (-nen) photographic designer
der Fotograf (-en *masc.*) **/ die Fotografin (-nen)** photographer (11)
das Fotografieren taking photographs
fotografieren to photograph
die Fotosammlung (-en) collection of photographs
die Frage (-n) question (E); **eine Frage stellen** to ask a question; **Das kommt nicht in Frage.** That is out of the question.
der Fragebogen (-) questionnaire
fragen to ask (1); **nach dem Weg fragen** to ask directions (9); **fragen nach** to ask about (12)
fragend inquisitive(ly)
das Fragewort (¨-er) interrogative pronoun (1)
(das) Frankreich France (E)
die Frankreichreise (-n) trip to/through France
der Franzose (-n *masc.*) **/ die Französin (-nen)** French man/woman
französisch (*adj.*) French
die Frau (-en) Mrs., Ms.; woman (E); wife (3)
das Frauenlager (-) women's camp
das Fräulein (-) Miss; unmarried woman, young lady (E)
frech naughty; risqué
frei free (14); vacant, available, unoccupied (2); **Ist hier noch frei?** Is this seat taken? (6); **im Freien** outdoors (11)
das Freibad (¨-er) outdoor swimming pool (7)
freihaben (hat frei) to be off work
die Freiheit freedom, liberty
freilassen (lässt frei), ließ frei, freigelassen to release, set free
(der) Freitag Friday (3)
freitags Fridays (4)
freiwillig voluntary
die Freizeit leisure time
die Freizeitaktivität (-en) leisure activity
die Freizeitpläne (*pl.*) plans for leisure time
der Freizeitservice leisure-time planning agency
der Freizeitspaß (¨-e) leisure-time fun
Freizeitzwecke: nur für Freizeitzwecke not for business use
fremd strange; unknown; foreign
der/die Fremde (*decl. adj.*) stranger
der Fremdenführer (-) / die Fremdenführerin (-nen) tour guide
das Fremdenverkehrsamt (¨-er) tourist information center
die Fremdsprache (-n) foreign language
das Fremdwort (¨-er) foreign word
die Freude (-n) joy; **vor Freude** with joy; **Freude haben an** (+ *dat.*) to enjoy; **Freude machen** (+ *dat.*) to give pleasure, enjoy
freuen: es freut mich pleased to meet you (E)
sich freuen auf (+ *acc.*) to look forward to (11); **sich freuen über** (+ *acc.*) to be happy about (12)
der Freund (-e) friend (1); boyfriend; **die Freundin (-nen)** girlfriend (1)

freundlich friendly, pleasant (1)
freundschaftlich friendly
der Friede (*also:* **der Frieden) (-n** *masc.*) peace
die Friedensbewegung (-en) peace movement
der Friedenssaal (Friedenssäle) peace-treaty hall
die Friedfertigkeit serenity
der Friedhof (¨e) cemetery
friedlich peaceful
frieren, fror, gefroren to freeze; **Ich friere.** I am cold.
das Frisbee (-s) frisbee
frisch fresh(ly) (5)
der Friseursalon (-s) beauty parlor
der Frisiertisch (-e) dresser
froh glad, happy
fröhlich cheerful (1)
der Fronteinsatz (¨e) front-line duty
die Frottierware (-n) towels
die Frucht (¨e) fruit
der Fruchtsaft (¨e) fruit juice
früh early (4); **morgen früh** tomorrow morning
früher formerly; earlier; once (7)
das Frühjahr (-e) spring (7)
die Frühkartoffel (-n) new potato
der Frühling (-e) spring (7)
frühmorgens early in the morning
der Frühnebel (-) early morning fog
die Frührenaissance Early Renaissance
das Frühstück (-e) breakfast (5); **zum Frühstück** for breakfast
frühstücken to have breakfast (4)
das Frühstücksbuffet (-s) breakfast buffet
die Frühstücksnische (-n) breakfast nook (12)
der Frühstücksraum (¨e) breakfast room (9)
das Frühstückstablett (-e) breakfast tray
der Frühstückstisch (-e) breakfast table
(sich) fühlen to feel (8); **Ich fühle mich nicht wohl.** I am not feeling well.
führen to lead, guide, conduct; to carry (merchandise); **Gespräche führen** to hold conversations; **Tagebuch führen** to keep a diary.
der Führer leader (*here:* Adolf Hitler)
der Führerschein (-e) driver's license (10)
der Führungstag (-e) day with planned guided tour
der Fund (-e) find, finding
fünf five (E)
fünfmal five times
fünfte fifth (3)
ein Fünftel a fifth (12)
fünfzehn fifteen (E)
fünfzig fifty (E)
funktionieren to function, work (9)
für (+ *acc.*) for (3); **was für** what kind of
fürchterlich horrible
fürs = für das
der Fürst (-en *masc.*) prince
der Fuß (¨e) foot (8); **zu Fuß** on foot (9); **zu Fuß gehen** to go on foot, to walk (8)
der Fußball (¨e) soccer, soccer ball (7); **Fußball spielen** to play soccer (7)
der Fußballclub (-s) soccer club
der Fußballfan (-s) soccer fan
der Fußballplatz (¨e) soccer field
das Fußballspiel (-e) soccer game
der Fußgänger (-) / die Fußgängerin (-nen) pedestrian
die Fußgängerzone (-n) pedestrian zone (14)
das Futonbett (-en) futon bed
füttern to feed
das Futur future tense

G

die Gabel (-n) fork (6)
der Gang (¨e) course
die Gangschaltung (-en) gear shift
der Gangsterfilm (-e) gangster movie
ganz very, completely; entire (12); fairly, rather; **ganz in der Nähe von** very close to; **den ganzen Tag** all day long
gar even; **gar kein** not any; **gar nicht** not at all; **gar nichts** nothing
die Garage (-n) garage (2)
garantieren to guarantee
die Garderobe (-n) check room; wardrobe closet (12)
die Gardine (-n) curtain, drape
das Gardinenkomplet (-s) set of curtains
gären to ferment
der Garten (¨) garden; yard (2)
das Gartenlokal (-e) garden restaurant
die Gartenmöbel (*pl.*) garden furniture
die Gasmaske (-n) gas mask
der Gast (¨e) guest (1)
das Gästezimmer (-) guest room (12)
die Gastfamilie (-n) host family
gastfreundlich hospitable
der Gastgeber (-) / die Gastgeberin (-nen) host/hostess
das Gasthaus (¨er) restaurant; inn
der Gasthof (¨e) hotel; restaurant, inn
die Gastronomie gastronomy
die Gaststätte (-n) restaurant (6)
die Gaststube (-n) (hotel) dining room, lounge
die Gastversorgung guest service
geachtet respected
geb. = geboren(e)
das Gebäude (-) building
geben (gibt), gab, gegeben to give (2); **Bescheid geben** to inform, let someone know (5); **sich Mühe geben** to try hard; **Rat geben** to advise; **es gibt** there is, there are (3); **Es gibt Regen.** It is going to rain. (3)
das Gebiet (-e) area, region, district
gebietsweise in some areas
geblümt flowery
geboren born; **geboren werden** to be born; **geborene** née (*maiden name*)
der Gebrauch use
gebrauchen to use
gebraucht used
die Gebühr (-en) fee; **die Studiengebühren** (*pl.*) study fees, tuition (12)
das Geburtsdatum date of birth (1)
der Geburtsort (-e) place of birth (1)
die Geburtsstätte (-n) place of birth
der Geburtstag (-e) birthday (3); **Herzlichen Glückwunsch zum Geburtstag!** Happy Birthday! (3); **Wann hast du Geburtstag?** When is your birthday? (3)
die Geburtstagsfeier (-n) birthday celebration
die Geburtstagsfete (-n) (*coll.*) birthday party
der Geburtstagsgruß (¨e) birthday wish
der Geburtstagskuchen (-) birthday cake
die Geburtstagstorte (-n) birthday cake
die Gedächtniskirche *famous church in Berlin*
gedämpft dimmed (*light*); steamed (*milk*)
das Gedicht (-e) poem
gedruckt printed; **klein gedruckt** printed in small letters
die Geduld patience
geehrt: sehr geehrter/geehrte (+ *proper name*) *formal letter address form*
geeignet sein to be suitable; appropriate (9)
die Gefahr (-en) danger (14)
gefährden to endanger
das Gefahrensymbol (-e) danger symbol
gefährlich dangerous (10)
gefallen (+ *dat.*) **(gefällt), gefiel, gefallen** to like (5); **Das gefällt mir.** I like that. (5)
der Gefallen (-) favor, **einen Gefallen tun** to do a favor
das Gefängnis (-se) jail (14)
gefasst sein auf (+ *acc.*) to be prepared for

gefroren frozen (5)
das Gefühl (-e) feeling; emotion
gefühllos insensitive
gefühlvoll sentimental; emotional
gefüttert lined
gegebenenfalls if necessary
gegen (+ *acc.*) against (3); around (+ *time*) (6); **gegen fünf Uhr** around five o'clock (6)
die Gegend (-en) area, region
die Gegendarstellung (-en) opposing view
der Gegensatz (⸚e) contrast
die Gegenseite (-n) opposing side
gegenseitig mutual(ly)
das Gegenteil (-e) opposite; **im Gegenteil** on the contrary
gegenüber von (+ *dat.*) across from (9)
gegenüberliegend opposite
das Gehalt (⸚er) salary (11)
gehen, ging, ist gegangen to go, walk (1); **zu Fuß gehen** to walk (8); **Wie geht's?** How are you? (E); **Wie geht es Ihnen?** (*form.*) How are you? (E); **Das geht.** That's all right, sure. (9)
die Gehirnoperation (-en) brain surgery
gehoben upper, elevated
das Gehör: (sich) Gehör verschaffen to make (oneself) be heard
gehorchen (+ *dat.*) to obey
gehören (+ *dat.*) to belong; to be part of (5)
die Geige (-n) violin
die Geisteswissenschaften (*pl.*) (academic field of) humanities
gelangweilt bored
gelaunt: schlecht gelaunt sein to be in a bad mood
gelb yellow (5)
das Geld (-er) money (1)
die Geldangelegenheit (-n) money matter
die Geldausgabe (-n) expenditure
der Geldautomat (-en *masc.*) automatic teller
der Geldschein (*also:* **der Schein) (-e)** bank note, paper money
gelegen situated, located
die Gelegenheit (-en) opportunity; occasion (11)
gelegentlich occasionally
der/die Geliebte (*decl. adj.*) beloved
gelingen, gelang, ist gelungen to succeed; **es gelingt mir** I am succeeding
gelten (+ *dat.*) **(gilt), galt, gegolten** to be valid; **gelten als** to be considered as
die Geltungsdauer period of validity; expiration date
das Gemälde (-) painting
die Gemeinde (-n) community
die Gemeindeverwaltung (-en) community administration
gemeinsam together; in common
der Gemeinschaftswaschraum (⸚e) communal washroom
gemeint für meant for
gemietet (*adj.*) rented
gemischt mixed
das Gemüse (-) vegetable (5)
die Gemüseabteilung (-en) produce department
der Gemüsegarten (⸚) vegetable garden
die Gemüsesorte (-n) type of vegetable
der Gemüsestand (⸚e) vegetable stand (5)
gemustert printed (*fabric*)
gemütlich cozy, comfortable, leisurely (4)
genau exact; precisely
genauso exactly like; just as
die Generation (-en) generation
genervt (*coll.*) annoyed, irritated
das Genie (-s) genius
genießen, genoss, genossen to enjoy, savor, relish
der Genießer (-) / die Genießerin (-nen) connoisseur
der Genitiv (-e) genitive case
genug enough, sufficient
genügen to suffice
das Genus (grammatical) gender
das Genussmittel (-) alcohol, tobacco, etc.; luxury articles
geöffnet open (6)
die Geographie geography
die Geographiestunde (-n) geography lesson
geographisch geographical(ly)
der Geoökologe (-n *masc.*) **/ die Geoökologin (-nen)** geo-ecologist
die Geoökologie (field of)
das Gepäck luggage (9)
die Gepäckaufbewahrung baggage checkroom (10)
gepflegt well groomed
geplant planned
geprägt characterized (by)
gepunktet polka-dotted
gerade just, just now; exactly (2); straight, erect; **Warum gerade Sie?** Why you of all people?
geradeaus straight ahead (9)
das Gerät (-e) apparatus; device; equipment (13); **das Fernesehgerät** TV set
geräuchert smoked
das Gerede talk
geregelt regulated; regular(ly)
das Gericht (-e) (*food*) dish (6)
gern (lieber, liebst-) gladly (2); **gern haben** to like (2); **ich hätte gern** I would like to have; **gern** (+ *verb*) to like to do something
gesagt: kurz gesagt in a few words
gesamt total
gesamtdeutsch *referring to unified Germany*
die Gesamtleitung overall direction
die Gesamtschule (-n) German secondary school (*grades 6 to 12*)
der Gesang (⸚e) song; singing
das Geschäft (-e) store, shop; business (5)
der Geschäftsbrief (-e) business letter
die Geschäftsfrau (-en) businesswoman (11)
die Geschäftsleute (*pl.*) business people (11)
der Geschäftsmann (Geschäftsleute) businessman (11)
geschehen (geschieht), geschah, ist geschehen to happen
gescheit intelligent, bright (13); **nichts Gescheites** nothing sensible
das Geschenk (-e) present, gift (3)
der Geschenkartikel (-) gift item
die Geschenkboutique (-n) gift shop
die Geschichte (-n) story; history
die Geschirrspülmaschine (-n) dishwasher (13)
geschlossen closed (6)
die Geschmackssache matter of taste
geschmückt decorated
das Geschnetzelte (*decl. adj.*) *special regional meat dish*
geschützt protected
geschweige denn . . . let alone . . .
die Geschwindigkeit (-en) speed
die Geschwindigkeitsbegrenzung (-en) speed limit
die Geschwister (*pl.*) brothers and sisters, siblings (3)
geschwollen swollen
gesegnet blessed
die Gesellschaft (-en) company; party
gesellschaftlich social
das Gesetz (-e) law
das Gesicht (-er) face (8)
das Gespenst (-er) ghost
gesponsert sponsored
das Gespräch (-e) conversation
der Gesprächspartner (-) / die Gesprächspartnerin (-nen) conversation partner
der Gesprächsraum (⸚e) discussion room
die Gesprächssituation (-en) conversational setting
das Gesprächsthema (Gesprächsthemen) conversational topic
gestaltet created, designed
gestern yesterday (7)
die Gestik gesticulation
gestreift striped (5)
gestresst (*adj.*) under stress

gesucht/gefunden lost/found
gesund healthy (8)
die Gesundheit health (8)
gesundheitlich health related
die Gesundheitsmaßnahme (-n) health provisions
gesundheitsschädlich unhealthy
das Gesundheitswesen health-care system
geteilt divided
das Getränk (-e) beverage, drink (5)
die Getränkedose (-n) beverage can
der Getränkeladen (⁼) beverage store (5)
getrennt separate (6); **zusammen oder getrennt?** together or separate (checks)?
gewählt selected, choice
die Gewalt violence
gewaltig enormous
die Gewalttat (-en) act of violence
die Gewalttätigkeit (-en) (act of) violence (14)
das Gewehr (-e) rifle
gewerblich commercial(ly)
die Gewerkschaft (-en) (labor) union
das Gewicht (-e) weight
gewinnen, gewann, gewonnen to win
die Gewinnung (-en) reclamation
gewiss certain(ly)
das Gewitter (-) thunderstorm (7)
gewöhnlich usual(ly) (4)
gewohnt an (+ *acc.*) accustomed to
das Gewürz (-e) spice
gewürzt spiced; spicy
gibt: es gibt there is, there are (3)
das Gift (-e) poison
die Giftreaktion (-en) toxic reaction
der Giftstoff (-e) toxic substance
gilt: Nichts gilt mehr. Nothing is valid anymore.
der Gips plaster; plaster cast
die Gitarre (-n) guitar
glänzend shiny; excellent
das Glas (⁼er) glass
glatt smooth
glauben to believe (5)
gleich right away, immediately (8); same; **gleich da drüben** right over there
die Gleichberechtigung equality (11)
das Gleiche (*decl. adj.*) the same
gleichfalls likewise (E)
gleichzeitig simultaneous(ly) (13)
das Gleis (-e) track, platform (10)
das Gleitschirmfliegen hang gliding
der Gletscher (-) glacier
das Glöckchen (-) little bell
das Glockenspiel (-e) chimes, glockenspiel
das Glück fortune, luck; happiness; **Glück haben** to be lucky; **Glück wünschen** to congratulate; **viel Glück** much luck (1, 3), lots of luck
glücklich happy
das Glücksrad (⁼er) wheel of fortune
der Glückwunsch (⁼e) congratulations; **Herzlichen Glückwunsch zum Geburtstag!** Happy Birthday! (3)
GmbH = Gesellschaft mit beschränkter Haftung corporation
das Gold gold
der Goldfisch (-e) goldfish
die Goldmedaille (-n) gold medal
(das) Golf golf
der Golfplatz (⁼e) golf course
das Golfspielen playing golf
der Gönner (-) / die Gönnerin (-nen) patron
das Gorillakostüm (-e) gorilla costume
gotisch gothic
der Gott (⁼er) god; **Gott sei Dank** thank God; **grüß Gott** hello (*in southern Germany and Austria*)
der Goudakäse (-) Gouda cheese
Gr. = Größe
der Grad (-e) degree (7); **20 Grad Celsius** 20 degrees centigrade
die Grafik (-en) drawing
das Gramm gram
die Grammatik (-en) grammar; grammar book
der Granit granite
gratulieren (+ *dat.*) to congratulate (3)
grau gray (5)
graugetigert with gray stripes
greifen, griff, gegriffen to seize
das Greifensymbol (-e) griffin symbol
die Grenze (-n) border; limit
der Grieche (-n *masc.*) **/ die Griechin (-nen)** Greek (person)
(das) Griechenland Greece
griechisch (*adj.*) Greek
der Grill (-s) grill, barbecue (6)
grillen to barbecue, grill
grillfertig ready to be grilled
die Grillparty (-s) barbecue party, cookout
die Grillscheibe (-n) slice of barbecue meat
die Grippe flu (8)
groß big; tall (1)
(das) Großbritannien Great Britain
die Größe (-n) size (5)
die Großeltern (*pl.*) grandparents (3)
größenwahnsinnig (*adj.*) megalomanic
die Großmutter (⁼) grandmother (3)
der Großonkel (-) great-uncle
der Großraumwagen (-) rail car without compartments
die Großstadt (⁼e) metropolis, large city
die Großtante (-n) great-aunt
der Großvater (⁼) grandfather (3)
grün green (5); **ins Grüne fahren** to go on an outing (to where it is green)
die Grünanlage (-n) public gardens, park
der Grund (⁼e) reason; ground
die Grundausstattung (-en) basic furnishings
gründen to found
der Gründer (-) / die Gründerin (-nen) founder
das Grundgesetz (-e) (German) constitution
die Grundlage (-n) basis, foundation
der Grundlagenvertrag (⁼e) agreement about basic principles
grundlegend basic, fundamental
das Grundrecht (-e) fundamental right
der Grundriss (-e) outline; layout; blueprint
die Grundschule (-n) elementary school (11)
das Grundstudium (Grundstudien) basic study program
die Gründung (-en) founding, establishment
die Gruppe (-n) group; team
der Gruß (⁼e) greeting; regards (12); **grüß dich** hello (*among friends and family members*) (E); **grüß Gott** hello, good day (*in Austria, southern Germany*); **herzliche Grüße** kind regards (12); **viele grüße** best wishes (12)
(sich) grüßen to say hello (to one another) (E)
die Grütze: Rote Grütze dessert made of red berries
gucken to look at, glance
die Gulaschsuppe (-n) spicy meat soup
gültig valid
der Gummistiefel (-) rubber boot
günstig favorable, advantageous (9)
die Gurke (-n) cucumber; pickle (5)
der Gürtel (-) belt (5)
gut (besser, best) good; well (10); **Es geht mir gut.** I am fine; **Alles Gute!** Best wishes (3); **guten Abend** good evening (E); **guten Morgen** good morning (E); **guten Tag** hello, good day (E); **gute Nacht** good night (E); **mach's gut** so long (E); **na gut** well, O.K. (E); **danke, gut** fine, thanks (E)
das Gutachten (-) reference letter (11)
gut bezahlt well-paid
der Güterzug (⁼e) freight train
gutnachbarlich neighborly
das Gymnasium (Gymnasien) secondary school (11)

H

das Haar (-e) hair (8); **Mir stehen die Haare zu Berge.** My hair is standing on end.

das Haarshampoo (-s) shampoo
das Haarspitzenfluid (-s) hair conditioner
haben (hat), hatte, gehabt (2); **Durst haben** to be thirsty (2); **gern haben** to like (*a person or thing*); **Hunger haben** to be hungry; **Lust haben** to feel like doing something (2); **Recht haben** to be correct (2); **Zeit haben** to have time (2)
der Hackbraten (-) meatloaf
der Hafen (¨) harbor, port (9)
das Hafentor (-e) harbor gate
der Häftling (-e) prisoner
der Hagel hail (7)
das Hähnchen (-) chicken (5)
häkeln to crochet
der Haken (-) hook
halb half; **halb zwei** one thirty (4)
die Halbgeschwister (*pl.*) half-brothers and -sisters
halbieren to divide in half
die Halbpension accommodation with two meals per day included
die Hälfte (-n) half; fifty percent (12)
der Halfter (-) (horse) harness
das Hallenbad (¨er) indoor swimming pool (7)
hallo hello (E)
die Halogenlampe (-n) halogen lamp
der Hals (¨e) neck; throat (8)
das Halsband (¨er) (animal) collar
die Halsschmerzen (*pl.*) sore throat (8)
halt (*particle*) just
Halt! Stop!
halten (hält), hielt, gehalten to hold, keep; stop; **halten für** to consider (14); **halten von** to think of; **sich fit halten (hält sich fit)** to keep fit (8); **gerade halten** to keep straight
die Haltestelle (-n) (bus or streetcar) stop (10); **die Bushaltestelle** bus stop
die Haltung (-en) posture
die Hand (¨e) hand (8)
die Handarbeit (-en) handicraft; needlework
handeln to act; **handeln von** to be about, deal with (13); **es handelt sich um** it is about; **Wovon handelt es?** What is it about?;
das Handgepäck carry-on luggage (10)
die Handlung (-en) plot
die Handschrift (-en) handwriting
handschriftlich handwritten
der Handschuh (-e) glove (10)
die Handtasche (-n) handbag
das Handtuch (¨er) towel
das Handy (-s) cellular telephone (2)
hängen, hing, gehangen to hang (6); **es hängt davon ab . . .** it depends (on) . . .
die Hansestadt (¨e) *town belonging to the old "Hanse" trade league*
harmlos harmless
die Harpune (-n) harpoon
hart hard
das Häschen (-) little rabbit (*term of endearment*)
hässlich ugly
hauen to beat
häufig frequently, often; **am häufigsten** most often; most widely
der Hauptbahnhof (¨e) main railroad station
der Haupteinkaufstag (-e) main shopping day
das Hauptfach (¨er) major subject
die Hauptfigur (-en) main character; protagonist
das Hauptgebäude (-) main building
das Hauptgericht (-e) main dish; entrée (6)
die Hauptidee (-n) main idea
die Hauptindustrie (-n) chief industry
der Hauptkonflikt (-e) main conflict
die Hauptmahlzeit (-en) main meal of the day
das Hauptproblem (-e) main problem
hauptsächlich mainly, mostly
die Hauptsaison (-s) high season
der Hauptschulabschluss (¨e) high school diploma
die Hauptschule (-n) junior high school (*grades 5–9/10*)
die Hauptstadt (¨e) capital
die Hauptstraße (-n) main street
das Hauptthema (Hauptthemen) main topic
das Haus (¨er) house; home (2); **nach Hause** home (indicating going home) (5); **zu Hause** at home (5)
die Hausarbeiten (*pl.*) homework, housework
die Hausaufgaben (*pl.*) homework
der Hausbewohner (-) / die Hausbewohnerin (-nen) tenant
die Hausfrau (-en) homemaker, housewife; **nach Hausfrauenart** according to a special recipe, homestyle
hausgebeizt home-pickled
der Haushalt (-e) household; budget (13)
das Haushaltsgeld (-er) household money
das Haushaltsgerät (-e) household appliance
die Haushaltswaren (*pl.*) household utensils
häuslich domestic
der Hausmann (¨er) house husband
der Hausmüll house trash
die Hausmusik music performed at home
die Hausnummer (-n) street address (number) (E)
der Hausschuh (-e) slipper (5)
das Haustelefon (-e) house telephone
das Haustier (-e) pet
die Haustür (-en) front door
die Haut skin
die Hautcreme (-s) skin cream
Hbf. = Hauptbahnhof
heben, hob, gehoben to lift; **Gewichte heben** to lift weights
das Heft (-e) notebook (12)
die Heide heath; **Lüneburger Heide** *area in North Germany*
das Heilbad (¨er) spa
das Heim (-e) home
die Heimat homeland, home town
die Heimatkunde local history
der Heimatort (-e) home town
die Heimatstadt (¨e) home town
der Heimcomputer (-) home computer
heimlich secret
heimtückisch treacherous
der Heimwerker (-) / die Heimwerkerin (-nen) hobbyist
heiraten to marry, get married (3)
heiß hot (7)
heißen, hieß, geheißen to be called (1)
der Heißluftballon (-s) hot-air balloon (10)
heiter pleasant, fair (7)
die Heizung (-en) heating
die Heizungsfirma (Heizungsfirmen) heating company
das Hektar (-e) hectare (= 2.471 acres)
hektisch hectic(ly)
helfen (+ *dat.*) **(hilft), half, geholfen** (5)
hell light; bright (2)
hellblau light blue
der Hellseher (-) / die Hellseherin (-nen) clairvoyant (person)
hellwach wide awake
das Hemd (-en) shirt (5)
her this way; here; **hin und her** back and forth; **um . . . her** all around
heran to, onto; **sich heranwagen (wagt heran)** to dare to come close
herauf up; upstairs
herausbringen (bringt heraus), brachte heraus, herausgebracht to publish
herausfinden (findet heraus), fand heraus, herausgefunden to find out
die Herausforderung (-en) challenge
herausgehen (geht heraus), ging heraus, ist herausgegangen to go outside
herb (*wine*) dry
der Herbst autumn, fall (7)
hereinkommen (kommt herein), kam herein, ist hereingekommen to come inside

hereinsehen (sieht herein), sah herein, hereingesehen to look in (on somebody)
herkommen (kommt her), kam her, ist hergekommen to come here
der Herr (-en, -n *masc.***)** Mr. (E); gentleman (2)
die Herrenabteilung (-en) men's department
die Herrenartikel (*pl.*) men's accessories
das Herrenhemd (-en) men's shirt
die Herrenkonfektion men's ready-to-wear clothing
der Herrenschuh (-e) men's shoe
herrlich wonderful, magnificent
die Herrschaften (*pl.*) ladies and gentlemen
herrschen to rule
herstellen (stellt her) to manufacture (11)
herum around; **um . . . herum** all around
herumgammeln (*coll.*) **(gammelt herum)** to fool around, be lazy
herumsuchen (sucht herum) to search all over
herunter (runter) down; downstairs
heruntergezogen (*adj.*) hanging
das Herz (-ens, -en) heart; **Hand auf's Herz** scout's honor; **von Herzen** from the bottom of my heart
herzhaft hearty; strong
herzlich cordial; heartfelt (E); **Herzlichen Glückwunsch zum Geburtstag!** Happy birthday! (3); **herzliche Grüße** kind regards; **herzlich willkommen** welcome (E)
(das) Hessen *German state*
hetzen to hurry; to chase; to agitate
heute today (1); **heute Abend** tonight (1); **heute Morgen** this morning (4); **heute Mittag** this noon (4); **heute Vormittag** today before noon (4); **heute Nachmittag** this afternoon (4)
heutig today's
heutzutage nowadays
hier here (1)
hierher (to) here
hierher kommen (kommt hierher), kam hierher, ist hierher gekommen to come here
hiesig local
das Hifi-Regal (-e) entertainment center
die Hilfe help, assistance; **um Hilfe bitten** to ask for help
der Hilferuf (-e) call for help
die Himbeere (-n) raspberry
der Himmel (-) sky; heaven (7); **in den Himmel loben** to praise to high heavens
himmelblau sky blue
hin (to) there; **vor sich hin** to oneself; **nach außen hin** to the outside; **hin und her** back and forth; **hin und zurück** roundtrip (10)
hinaufgehen (geht hinauf), ging hinauf, ist hinaufgegangen to go upstairs
hinaus (to) outside; **darüber hinaus** beyond that
hinausgehen (geht hinaus), ging hinaus, ist hinausgegangen to go outside
hinauskommen (kommt hinaus), kam hinaus, ist hinausgekommen to come out; to get out
hinauslaufen (läuft hinaus), lief hinaus, ist hinausgelaufen to run outside
das Hindernis (-se) impediment
hineinschauen (schaut hinein) to look in; to drop by
hingehen (geht hin), ging hin, ist hingegangen to go there
hingehören (gehört hin) to belong (somewhere)
hinkommen (kommt hin), kam hin, ist hingekommen to get there
sich hinlegen (legt sich hin) to lie down (8)
sich hinsetzen (setzt sich hin) to sit down (8)
hinten in the back
hinter (+ *acc./dat.*) behind (6)
der Hintergrund (¨e) background
die Hintergrundinformation (-en) background information
hinterher afterward
der Hinterhof (¨e) courtyard behind apartment building
hinterlassen (hinterlässt), hinterließ, hinterlassen to leave behind
hinuntergehen (geht hinunter), ging hinunter, ist hinuntergegangen to go downstairs
der Hinweis (-e) tip, clue
hinzufügen (fügt hinzu) to add
hissen to hoist (a flag)
historisch historic(al)
das Hobby (-s) hobby (7)
der Hobbyarchäologe (-n *masc.***) / die Hobbyarchäologin (-nen)** amateur archeologist
hoch (hoh-) (höher, höchst) high(ly); tall (2)
hochaktuell extremely popular
das Hochhaus (¨er) high-rise building
der Hochleistungssportler (-) / die Hochleistungssportlerin (-nen) high-powered athlete
hoch qualifiziert highly qualified
die Hochschule (-n) university, college
die Hochschulreife college qualification
höchstens at most (8)
die Höchstgeschwindigkeit (-en) maximum speed, speed limit
die Höchstgrenze (-n) maximum limit
die Höchsttemperatur (-en) highest temperature, daily high
die Hochzeit (-en) wedding (3)
die Hochzeitsfeier (-n) wedding celebration
der Hochzeitstag (-e) wedding day; anniversary
hochziehen (zieht hoch), zog hoch, hochgezogen to pull up
der Hof (¨e) farm
hoffen auf (+ *acc.*) to hope for (10)
hoffentlich I hope; hopefully (6)
die Hoffnung (-en) hope
die Hoffnungslosigkeit hopelessness
höflich courteous, polite
der Höhepunkt (-e) climax; highlight
höher higher
holen to get, fetch
(das) Holland Holland, the Netherlands
holländisch Dutch
die Hölle hell
der Höllenlärm hellish noise
der Holzhammer (-) sledge-hammer, mallet
der Holzpantoffel (-n) wooden shoe, clog
der Honig honey
die Honigmelone (-n) honeydew melon
(das) Hoppelpoppel *dish made of fried potatoes and eggs*
hören to listen to, hear (2)
der Hörer (-) / die Hörerin (-nen) listener
das Horoskop (-e) horoscope (13)
der Horrorfilm (-e) horror film
die Hose (-n) pants, trousers, slacks (5)
das Hosenbein (-e) pant leg
die Hosentasche (-n) pants pocket
das Hotel (-s) hotel (9); **im Hotel** at the hotel
die Hotelfachfrau (-en) hotel businesswoman
die Hotelpension (-en) hotel with meal plan
das Hotelpersonal hotel employees
der Hotelpreis (-e) hotel charges
das Hotelzimmer (-) hotel room
hübsch pretty (1)
die Hühnerbrust chicken breast (6)
die Hühnersuppe (-n) chicken soup
der Humor humor
humorvoll humorous; full of humor
der Hund (-e) dog (12)
das Hundehotel (-s) dog kennel
(ein)hundert one hundred (E); **Hunderte von . . .** hundreds of . . .

hundertste hundredth (3)
hundsmiserabel (*coll.*) sick as a dog (8)
der Hunger hunger (14); **Hunger haben** to be hungry (2)
hungernd starving
die Hungersnot (¨e) famine
hungrig hungry
hurra hurrah
der Husten (-) cough (8)
husten to cough
der Hut (¨e) hat (5)
die Hüttenschuhe (*pl.*) slipper socks
die Hüttentür (-en) cottage door
hypnotisieren to hypnotize

I

ich I (1)
ideal ideal(ly)
die Idee (-n) idea
identifizieren to identify
das Idyll (-e) idyllic setting
idyllisch idyllic, idyllical(ly)
ihm (to/for) him/it (5)
ihn him, it (3)
ihnen (to/for) them (5)
Ihnen (to/for) you (*form.*) (5)
Ihr (*form.*) your (3)
ihr (*inform. pl.*) you (1); her; its; their (3); (to/for) her/it (5)
illegal illegal(ly)
die Illusion (-en) illusion
die Illustrierte (-n) illustrated magazine
im = in dem; im Januar in January (3)
der Imbiss (-e) fast-food, fast-food stand (6)
immer always; ever (3)
der Immobilienmakler (-) real estate agent
der Imperativ (-e) imperative form
der Imperativsatz (¨e) imperative clause
das Imperfekt (-e) imperfect tense, simple past
impliziert implied
in (+ *acc./dat.*) in, into; inside (6); **in zwei Tagen** in two days (6)
incl. = inkl.
indem by (+ *gerund*)
der Indianer (-) / die Indianerin (-nen) American Indian (person)
(das) Indien India
der Indikativ indicative voice
indirekt indirect(ly)
die Individualität individuality
(das) Indonesien Indonesia
die Industrialisierung industrialization
die Industrie (-n) industry
die Industriekauffrau (-en) industrial businesswoman
der Industriekaufmann (¨er) industrial businessman
industriell industrial
die Industriereform (-en) industrial reform
die Industrieregion (-en) industrial area
der Infinitiv (-e) infinitive verb form
die Inflation (-en) inflation
die Informatik computer science
der Informatiker (-) / die Informatikerin (-nen) computer scientist (11)
die Information (-en) information
sich informieren to inform oneself (8)
der Ingenieur (-e) / die Ingenieurin (-nen) engineer (11)
das Ingenieurbüro (-s) engineering office
der Inhaber (-) / die Inhaberin (-nen) proprietor
der Inhalt content(s)
inkl. = inklusive
inklusive inclusive; included
innen inside
die Innenstadt (¨e) downtown (9)
inner-: im inneren Kreis in the inside circle
die Innereien (*pl.*) inner organs
innerhalb within; inside of (9)
innovativ innovative
insbesondere in particular
das Insekt (-en) insect
die Insel (-n) island
insgesamt altogether (10)
inspirieren to inspire
der Installateur (-e) / die Installateurin (-nen) installer, technician
das Institut (-e) institute
das Instrument (-e) instrument
intellektuell intellectual(ly)
intelligent intelligent(ly)
intensiv intense
die Interaktion (-en) interaction
Intercity *referring to fast intercity trains*
interessant interesting (1); **nichts Interessantes** nothing interesting
das Interesse (-n) interest (1)
sich interessieren für (+ *acc.*) to be interested in (8)
international international
internieren to intern
die Interpretation (-en) interpretation
interpretieren to interpret
Interregio *referring to fast trains between regions*
das Interrogativpronomen (-) interrogative pronoun
das Interview (-s) interview
interviewen to interview
intravenös intravenous(ly)
die Invasion (-en) invasion
investieren to invest
involvieren to get involved
inzwischen in the meantime, meanwhile
(der) Iran Iran
irgend any at all; some; **irgendetwas** anything at all; something; **irgendjemand** anybody at all; **irgendwann** anytime at all; **irgendwer** somebody; **irgendwo** somewhere
(das) Irland Ireland
der Irrtum (¨er) error
das Isartal valley of the Isar River
isolieren to isolate
(das) Israel Israel
ital. = italienisch
(das) Italien Italy (E)
der Italiener (-) / die Italienerin (-nen) Italian (*person*)
italienisch (*adj.*) Italian

J

ja yes (E)
die Jacke (-n) jacket (5)
das Jahr (-e) year (1); **nächstes Jahr** next year (1); **einmal im Jahr** once a year; **mit 10 Jahren** at age 10; **die 90er Jahre** the nineties
die Jahresausgaben (*pl.*) annual expenditures
die Jahreszeit (-en) season (7)
das Jahrhundert (-e) century
die Jahrhundertwende (-n) turn of the century
der/die 12-Jährige (*decl. adj.*) twelve-year old (person)
jährlich annual
die Jahrtausendwende (-n) turn of the millenium
der Jammer suffering, sadness
(der) Januar January (3)
(das) Japan Japan
der Japaner (-) / die Japanerin (-nen) Japanese person
japanisch (*adj.*) Japanese
jawohl yes, of course
(der) Jazz jazz
der Jazzkeller (-) jazz bar
je ever, always; **je** (+ *comparative*) **desto/umso** (+ *comparative*) the (+ *comparative*) the (+ *comparative*); **je nachdem** depending on
die Jeans (*pl.*) jeans (5)
der Jeansrock (¨e) denim skirt
jedenfalls in any case
jeder, jede, jedes each, every (5); everybody; **jeden Tag** every day (7)
jedesmal every time
jedoch however, but
jemand somebody, someone (9)
jetzig current
jetzt now, immediately (1)
jeweils in each case; individually; each time

Jh. = Jahrhundert
der Job (-s) (temporary) job
jobben to work at a temporary job
joggen to jog (7)
das Jogging jogging
der Jogginganzug (¨e) jogging suit
der Joghurt (-e) yogurt (5)
der Journalist (-en *masc.***) / die Journalistin (-nen)** journalist (11)
Judo machen to do judo
die Jugend youth, young people
das Jugendgästehaus (¨er) (type of) youth hostel
die Jugendgruppe (-n) youth group
die Jugendherberge (-n) youth hostel (9)
der/die Jugendliche (*decl. adj.*) young person; teenager (10)
die Jugendreise (-n) trip for young people
der Jugendstil Art Nouveau (*artistic style*)
(das) Jugoslawien Yugoslavia
(der) Juli July (3)
jung young (10); **jungverheiratet** newly wed
der Junge (-n *masc.***)** boy
jungverheiratet newly wed
(der) Juni June (3)
der Juniorpass (¨e) student pass
die Jura law
der Juwelier (-e) jeweler's store

K

das Kabarett (-e) cabaret
das Kabel-TV cable TV
das Kabelfernsehen cable television
der Kabelkanal (¨e) cable (TV) channel
das Kabrio (-s) convertible automobile
die Kachelplatte (-n) tile
der Käfer (-) bug, beetle
der Kaffee coffee
das Kaffeegetränk (-e) coffee drink
das Kaffeehaus (¨er) café
die Kaffeehausküche coffeehouse cuisine
die Kaffeekanne (-n) coffee pot
die Kaffeemaschine (-n) electric coffeemaker
die Kaffeemenge (-n) amount of coffee
der Kaffeesatz coffee grounds
die Kaffeesorte (-n) type of coffee
Kaiser: die Kaiser-Wilhelm Gedächtniskirche *famous church in Berlin*
der Kaiserschmarren (-) *pancake-like Austrian dessert*
die Kalbsleberwurst (¨e) veal liverwurst
der Kalender (-) calendar (3)
(das) Kalifornien California
kalkulieren to calculate
kalt cold (7)
kaltherzig coldhearted
die Kamera (-s) camera (10)
der Kamillentee camomile tea
der Kamin (-e) fireplace
sich kämmen to comb one's hair (8)
der Kampf (¨e) battle, fight
kämpfen to fight, struggle
(das) Kanada Canada
der Kanarienvogel (¨) canary
die Kanarischen Inseln (*pl.*) Canary Islands
das Kaninchen (-) rabbit
die Kaninchenbox (-en) rabbit hutch
Kännchen: ein Kännchen Kaffee a pot of coffee
das Kanufahren canoeing
das Kapitel (-) chapter
die Kapitulation (-en) capitulation
kapitulieren to capitulate
kaputt broken (9)
(das) Karate machen to do karate
die Karibik the Caribbean
kariert checkered, plaid (5)
karitativ charitable
die Karotte (-n) carrot (5)
der Karottensaft carrot juice
die Karriere (-n) career (11); **Karriere machen** to be successful in a career
die Karriereberatung (-en) career counseling
die Karrierechance (-n) career opportunity
die Karte (-n) card; ticket (6); **Karten spielen** to play cards
der Kartenvorverkauf (¨e) advance ticket sale
die Kartoffel (-n) potato (5)
die Kartoffelchips (*pl.*) potato chips
der Kartoffelpuffer (-) potato pancake
das Kartoffelpüree mashed potatoes
der Kartoffelsalat potato salad
der Käse cheese (5)
die Käseabteilung (-en) cheese department
der Käsekuchen (-) cheese cake (6)
die Käsesauce (-n) cheese sauce
der Käseteller (-) cheese platter
die Kasse (-n) cash register; cashier (5); **vorne an der Kasse** up front at the cash register
der Kassenarzt (¨e) / die Kassenärztin (-nen) physician accepting health insurance patients
die Kassette (-n) cash box; cassette
der Kassettenrecorder (-) tape recorder
der Kasten (¨) box
der Kasus (grammatical) case
der Katalog (-e) catalogue
der Katalysator (-en) catalytic converter
katastrophal catastrophic
die Katastrophe (-n) catastrophe
der Kater (-) male cat
die Kathedrale (-n) cathedral
die Katze (-n) cat (12)
das Katzenhotel (-s) cat kennel
kaufen to buy (2)
die Kauffrau (-en) businesswoman (11)
das Kaufhaus (¨er) department store (2)
die Kaufkraft (¨e) purchasing power
der Kaufmann (Kaufleute) businessman; merchant (11)
kaufmännisch (*adj.*) business; businesslike
kaum hardly; barely (8); no sooner
der Kaviar caviar
kegeln to bowl
das Keglerheim (-e) clubhouse for bowlers
die Kehle (-n) throat
kein no, not a, not any (2); **noch kein** no . . . yet; **kein . . . mehr** no more . . . (11)
keiner nobody
der Keks (-e) cookie (5)
der Keller (-) cellar, basement (12)
der Kellner (-) / die Kellnerin (-nen) waiter, server; waitress, server (6)
kennen, kannte, gekannt to know, be acquainted with (3)
kennen lernen (lernt kennen) to meet; to get to know (7)
die Keramik ceramics, pottery
die Kernenergie nuclear energy
die Kettengeschichte (-n) chain story
die Kettenreaktion (-en) chain reaction
der Kibbuz (-im) kibbutz
der Kick (-s) flair
das Kilo = Kilogramm kilogram
der Kilometer (-) kilometer
das Kind (-er) child (1); **als Kind** as a child
der Kinderbrief (-e) child's letter
die Kinderermäßigung (-en) reduced price for children
die Kinderfreunde children's friends
kinderfreundlich friendly to/comfortable for children
der Kindergarten (¨) nursery school
die Kinderhilfe children's aid
die Kinderkonfektion (-en) children's wear
die Kinderkrippe (-n) childcare center
das Kinderschlafzimmer (-) children's bedroom
der Kinderschutzbund (¨e) association for the protection of children
der Kinderspaß (¨e) fun for children
die Kinderspeisung meals provided for children
die Kinderspielecke (-n) children's play corner

der Kinderspielplatz (⸚e) children's playground
das Kinderzimmer (-) children's room
die Kindheit childhood
das Kinn (-e) chin (8)
das Kino (-s) movie house; movie theater (4); **ins Kino** to the movies; **ins Kino gehen** to go to the movies (4)
das Kinoprogramm (-e) movie program
der Kiosk (-e) kiosk
die Kirche (-n) church (9)
der Kirchhof (⸚e) cemetery
kirchlich religious
der Kirchturm (⸚e) church steeple
die Kirschblüte (-n) blossoming of the cherry trees
die Kirsche (-n) cherry
die Kiwi (-s) kiwi fruit
die Klagemauer Wailing Wall
die Klammer (-n) parenthesis
die Klamotten (*pl.*) (*slang*) clothes
klappen: nichts klappt nothing is working out
klappern to rattle
der Klapptisch (-e) folding table
klar clear; of course; **Na klar!** But of course!; You bet!; **Alles klar?** Everything clear?
der Klarlack clear lacquer
die Klasse (-n) class; classroom; **erster Klasse** first-class
der Klassenkamerad (-en *masc.*) **/ die Klassenkameradin (-nen)** classmate
der Klassenlehrer (-) / die Klassenlehrerin (-nen) main teacher
das Klassenzimmer (-) classroom
der Klassiker (-) / die Klassikerin (-nen) classical writer
klassisch classical (4)
die Klausur (-en) written exam
das Klavier (-e) piano; **Klavier spielen** to play the piano
die Klaviermusik piano music
das Klavierspielen piano playing
der Klavierunterricht piano instruction
kleben to glue; to stick
das Kleid (-er) dress (5)
das Kleidchen (-) child's dress
die Kleiderfrage (-n) clothes problem
der Kleiderschrank (⸚e) clothes closet (2)
der Kleiderständer (-) clothes rack
die Kleidung clothing
das Kleidungsstück (-e) garment, piece of clothing (5)
klein small, little (2)
die Kleinanzeige (-n) classified ad (13)
das Kleingerät (-e) small appliance
das Kleinhirn (-e) cerebellum
Kleinigkeit: eine Kleinigkeit essen to have a bite to eat
das Kleinkind (-er) small child, toddler
die Kleinkinderbetreuung child care
die Kleinstadt (⸚e) small city; town
der Klempner (-) / die Klempnerin (-nen) plumber
klettern to climb
der Klient (-en *masc.*) **/ die Klientin (-nen)** client
das Klima climate (10)
die Klimaanlage (-n) air conditioning
klingeln to ring
klingen, klang, geklungen to sound, ring (8); **Das klingt nicht gut.** That doesn't sound good.
die Klinik (-en) hospital
klopfen to knock
der Klub (-s) club
klug smart, intelligent
km = Kilometer
knabbern to nibble
das Knäckebrot crisp bread
knacken to crack
knackig crisp
die Knackwurst (⸚e) *special German sausage*
knallen to slam
knallig flashy, gaudy
knapp just about
die Kneipe (-n) pub (6)
das Knie (-) knee (8)
der Knoblauch garlic
die Knoblauchbutter garlic butter
die Kobra (-s) cobra (snake)
der Koch (⸚e) / die Köchin (-nen) cook, chef
das Kochbuch (⸚er) cookbook
das Kochen cooking (1)
kochen to cook (1); boil
das Kochgeschirr (-e) mess kit
der Kochlöffel (-) cooking spoon
die Kochnische (-n) kitchen nook
der Koffer (-) suitcase (9)
das Kofferpacken packing the suitcase
das Kofferradio (-s) portable radio
der Kofferschlüssel (-) suitcase key
die Kohle (*slang*) money
das Kokain cocaine
der Kollege (-n *masc.*) **/ die Kollegin (-nen)** colleague, coworker
(das) Köln Cologne
der Kolonialwarenladen (⸚) grocery store
kombinieren to combine
der Komfort (-s) comfort
komfortabel comfortable
komisch strange, funny
kommen, kam, ist gekommen to come (1); **Woher kommst du?** Where do you come from? (E); **der kommende Sommer** next summer
die Kommode (-n) dresser (2)
die Kommunikation (-en) communication
das Kommunikationssystem communication system
das Kommunikationswesen communications
kommunistisch communist
die Komödie (-n) comedy (4)
die Kompanie (-n) (military) company
die Komparativform (-en) comparative form (of adjective)
kompetent competent
komplett complete(ly)
kompliziert complicated
der Komponist (-en *masc.*) **/ die Komponistin (-nen)** composer
der Kompost (-e) compost
kompostierbar compostable
kompostieren to compost
das Kompott (-e) compote, stewed fruit
die Konditorei (-en) café, pastry shop (5)
die Konfektion ready-made clothing
der Konferenzraum (⸚e) conference room
der Konflikt (-e) conflict
der Kongress (-e) congress, convention
die Konjunktion (-en) conjunction
die Konjunktivform (-en) subjunctive form
konkret concrete(ly)
der Konkurrent (-en *masc.*) **/ die Konkurrentin (-nen)** competitor
können (kann), konnte, gekonnt to be able to, can; to know how (4)
konsequent consequent(ly)
konservativ conservative(ly) (1)
die Konservendose (-n) can
(das) Konstanz Constance (*town in southern Germany*)
konstruieren to build, construct
der Konstrukteur (-e) / die Konstrukteurin (-nen) technical designer
das Konsulat (-e) consulate
der Konsum consumption
der Konsument (-en *masc.*) **/ die Konsumentin (-nen)** consumer
der Konsumentenkredit (-e) consumer credit
die Konsumexplosion (-en) consumption explosion
der Konsumzwang pressure to buy
der Kontakt (-e) contact (11)
der Kontext (-e) context
kontinuierlich continual(ly)
das Konto (Konten) bank account
der Kontrast (-e) contrast
kontrollieren to inspect, keep under control
konventionell conventional(ly)
die Konversation (-en) conversation
die Konzentration concentration

das Konzentrationslager (-) concentration camp
sich konzentrieren (auf + *acc.***)** to concentrate (on)
das Konzept (-e) concept
das Konzert (-e) concert (4); **ins Konzert gehen** to go to a concert (4)
die Konzertveranstaltung (-en) concert performance
koordinierend coordinating
der Kopf (¨-e) head (8); **pro Kopf** per head; per capita
die Kopfbedeckung (-en) headgear
Köpfchen: kluges Köpfchen clever little person
das Kopfkissen (-) pillow
der Kopfsalat (-e) lettuce
die Kopfschmerzen (*pl.*) headache (8)
der Kopierer (-) copying machine
die Koproduktion (-en) coproduction
das Korn (¨-er) grain
der Körper (-) body
das Körpergewicht (-e) (body) weight
die Körpergröße (-n) (body) height
die Körperpflege personal grooming
der Körperteil (-e) body part
korrespondieren to correspond
korrigieren to correct
die Korruption (-en) corruption (14)
die Kosmetik cosmetics
kosmopolitisch cosmopolitan
kosten to cost (2)
die Kosten (*pl.*) expense
kostengünstig reasonably priced
kostenlos free of charge
köstlich delicious
das Kostüm (-e) women's suit
der Krabbencocktail (-s) shrimp cocktail
der Krach loud noise; quarrel; **mit Ach und Krach** with great difficulty
der Kraftfahrzeugmechaniker (-) / die Kraftfahrzeugmechanikerin (-nen) automobile mechanic
kräftig strong
(das) Krakau Cracow (*city in Poland*)
krank sick, ill (8)
das Krankenhaus (¨-er) hospital
die Krankenkasse health insurance company (8)
der Krankenpfleger (-) / die Krankenpflegerin (-nen) nurse (8)
die Krankenschwester (-n) female nurse (8)
die Krankenversicherung (-en) health insurance
die Krankheit (-en) sickness, disease, ailment (14)
das Kraut (*short for* **Sauerkraut**) sauerkraut
der Kräutertee (-s) herbal tea (5)
die Kräutervinaigrette (-n) herbal salad dressing
der Krautsalat (-e) coleslaw
die Krawatte (-n) tie (5)
kreativ creative(ly)
die Kreativität creativity
der Krebs cancer
die Kreditkarte (-n) credit card (9)
der Kreis (-e) circle
kreisen to circle
der Kreislauf (¨-e) cycle
die Kreislaufbeschwerden (*pl.*) circulatory problems
die Kreuzung (-en) intersection (9)
das Kreuzworträtsel (-) crossword (1)
der Krieg (-e) war (14)
kriegen to receive, get
der Kriegsfilm (-e) war movie
die Kriegsgewalt (-en) violence of war
der Krimi (-s) detective story/show (4)
die Krimikomödie (-n) detective comedy
die Kriminalität criminality
die Krise (-n) crisis
die Kriterien (*pl.*) criteria
die Kritik (-en) critique, review; criticism
der Kritiker (-) / die Kritikerin (-nen) critic
kritisch critical (1)
die Krücke (-n) crutch
der Krug (¨-e) jug, pitcher
sich krümmen to bend over, double up (with pain)
die Küche (-n) kitchen (2); cuisine, food (6)
der Kuchen (-) cake (5)
der Küchenchef (-s) chief cook
das Küchenrezept (-e) recipe
der Küchentisch (-e) kitchen table
die Kuckucksuhr (-en) cuckoo clock
der Kudamm = Kurfürstendamm
der Kugelschreiber (-) ballpoint pen (12)
die Kuh (¨-e) cow
kühl cool (7)
der Kühlschrank (¨-e) refrigerator (12)
kulinarisch culinary
die Kultur (-en) culture
der Kulturamtsleiter (-) / die Kulturamtsleiterin (-nen) head of the Department of Culture
der Kulturbummel (-) stroll through the cultural sights
kulturell cultured; cultural
die Kulturnotiz (-en) cultural comment
die Kulturstadt (¨-e) city of culture
die Kulturstätte (-n) place of culture
das Kulturzentrum (Kulturzentren) cultural center
sich kümmern um (+ *acc.***)** to take care of, look after
der Kunde (-n *masc.***) / die Kundin (-nen)** customer (2)
der Kundenberater (-) / die Kundenberaterin (-nen) customer service representative
der Kundendienst customer service
die Kundenkarte (-n) store credit card
künftig future; in the future
die Kunst art
die Kunstgeschichte art history
die Kunsthalle (-n) museum, exhibition hall
der Künstler (-) / die Künstlerin (-nen) artist (11)
künstlerisch artistic (11)
das Kunstmuseum (Kunstmuseen) art museum
die Kunstseide rayon
die Kur (-en) health cure, treatment (at a spa)
das Kuramt (¨-er) resort administration
der Kurfürstendamm *name of famous shopping street in Berlin*
der Kurgast (¨-e) spa guest
das Kurhaus (¨-er) hotel and center for all spa activities
der Kurort (-e) health spa, resort
der Kurs (-e) (*also:* **Kursus**) course; exchange rate
die Kursivschrift italic type
das Kursprogramm (-e) course program
kurz for a short time; short, brief (10); **vor kurzem** recently
der Kurzdialog (-e) short dialogue
kürzlich recently (11)
der Kurzschluss (¨-e) electrical short circuit
die Kurzwaren (*pl.*) notions
die Kusine (-n) female cousin (3)
Küsschen: ein dickes Küsschen a big kiss
die Küste (-n) coast
die Küstenlänge (-n) coastal span

L

das Labor (-s) laboratory
der Laborant (-en *masc.***) / die Laborantin (-nen)** laboratory technician
die Laborarbeit (-en) lab work
lächeln to smile
lächelnd smiling
lachen to laugh
lächerlich ridiculous
der Lachs (-e) salmon
der Lackregenmantel (¨-) shiny plastic raincoat
der Laden (¨-) store, shop (5)
die Lage (-n) location (9); situation
das Lager (-) camp

die Lagerzeit (-en) storage time
lagig: 2-lagig double-layered, 2-ply
die Lampe (-n) lamp (2)
das Lampenstudio (-s) lamp store
das Land (¨-er) country; nation, land (1); **auf dem Land** in the country
landen, hat/ist gelandet to land
die Landeshauptstadt (¨-e) state capital
das Landesmuseum (Landesmuseen) regional museum
die Landflucht (-en) massive migration from the country
die Landkarte (-n) map
der Landkreis (-e) (rural) district
das Landleben country life
die Landschaft (-en) scenery; landscape; nature
die Landstraße (-n) country road; highway
die Landwirtschaft agriculture
lang long (10); **jahrelang** for years and years
lange (*temporal*) long; **wie lange** (for) how long (1); **noch lange** still a long time
lang gestreckt stretched-out
langsam slow (10); **langsamer, bitte.** slower, please. (E)
längst- the longest; **längst nicht mehr** not for the longest time
(sich) langweilen to bore; to be bored
langweilig boring (1)
die Lappalie (-n) mere trifle
der Lärm noise (14)
die Lasagna (Lasagne) lasagna
lassen (lässt), ließ, gelassen to leave; to let (6); to have something done; **Lass uns . . .** Let's . . . (6) **Was lässt sich machen?** What can be done?
(das) Latein Latin language
(das) Lateinamerika Latin America
lateinisch (*adj.*) Latin
der Lattenrost (-e) slatted mattress platform
Lauf: im Laufe der Zeit in the course of time
laufen (läuft), lief, ist gelaufen to run, walk (2); **Der Film läuft im . . .** The film is playing at . . .
laut loud(ly); according to
läuten: es läutet the bell is ringing
der Lautsprecher (-) loudspeaker, public address system
die Lautsprecherbox (-en) (stereo) loudspeaker
lauwarm lukewarm
das Lazarett (-e) military hospital
das Leben life (11)
leben to live
der/die Lebende (*decl. adj.*) living (person)
der Lebensabschnitt (-e) period of (one's) life
lebensbedrohend life-threatening
die Lebensdaten (*pl.*) biographical dates
die Lebensfreude zest for life
lebensgefährlich life-threatening
die Lebensgewohnheiten (*pl.*) personal life-style
der Lebensinhalt purpose in life
das Lebensjahr: seit seinem zweiten Lebensjahr since he was two years old
der Lebenslauf (¨-e) resume (11); **handschriftlicher Lebenslauf** handwritten resume; **tabellarischer Lebenslauf** resume in outline form
die Lebensmittel (*pl.*) food, groceries (5)
das Lebensmittelgeschäft (-e) grocery store
die Lebensmittelhilfe humanitarian aid
die Lebensqualität quality of life
der Lebensraum (¨-e) habitat (of animals)
der Lebensstandard (-e) standard of living
der Lebensunterhalt livelihood
der Lebensweg (-e) (course of) life
die Leber (-n) liver
der Leberkäs(e) *type of Bavarian meatloaf* (6)
der Leberknöd(e)l (-) liver dumpling
die Leberwurst liverwurst
der Lebkuchen (-) gingerbread
lecker tasty, delicious
das Leder leather
die Lederbekleidung leatherwear
die Lederhose (-n) leather pants (*mostly worn in southern Germany*)
die Lederjacke (-n) leather jacket
die Ledernadel (-n) leathercraft needle
die Ledersandalen (*pl.*) leather sandals
die Lederwaren (*pl.*) leather goods
ledig unmarried, single
legen to lay, place (6)
sich (hin)legen (legt sich hin) to lie down (8)
legendär legendary
das Lehrbuch (¨-er) textbook
die Lehre (-n) apprenticeship
der Lehrer (-) / die Lehrerin (-nen) teacher (E)
der Lehrling (-e) apprentice, trainee
die Leibesübungen (*pl.*) physical education; gymnastics
leicht easy; light
das Leid sorrow, grief; **Das tut mir Leid.** I am sorry. (9)
leiden, litt, gelitten to suffer
leidenschaftlich passionate(ly)
leider unfortunately
leihen, lieh, geliehen to lend; **leihen von** (+ *dat.*) to borrow (5); **Ich leihe mir Geld.** I borrow money; **Ich leihe ihm Geld.** I lend him money.
das Leinen linen
das Leintuch (¨-er) (bed) sheet
die Leinwand (¨-e) movie screen; canvas
leise quiet(ly); softly
sich (+ *dat.*) etwas leisten to afford; **Das kann ich mir nicht leisten.** I can't afford that.
die Leistung (-en) accomplishment; **soziale Leistungen** social benefits
der Leitartikel (-) lead editorial (13)
die Leitung direction
die Lektüre (-n) reading (material)
lernen to learn (1); **Ich lerne Deutsch.** I'm learning German.
die Lernmittel (*pl.*) school supplies
das Lernziel (-e) educational goal
das Leseexemplar (-e) book copy
die Lesegewohnheiten (*pl.*) reading habits
die Leseleuchte (-n) reading lamp
lesen (liest), las, gelesen to read (2)
der Leser (-) / die Leserin (-nen) reader
der Leserbrief (-e) letter to the editor (13)
die Leserschaft readers
der Leserservice readers' service
letzt- last; **zum letzten Mal** for the last time
der Leuchtturm (¨-e) lighthouse
die Leute (*pl.*) people
das Lexikon (Lexika) dictionary, encyclopedia
das Licht (-er) light; lamp
der Lichtschalter (-) light switch
lieb dear
die Liebe love; **alles Liebe** all my love (*at end of letter*)
lieben to love
lieber (+ *verb*) rather; preferably (4); **ich möchte lieber** I would prefer, I would rather (4)
der Liebesfilm (-e) romantic movie
lieblich (*wine*) aromatic
das Lieblingsauto (-s) favorite car
die Lieblingsbeschäftigung (-en) favorite activity
das Lieblingsbuch (¨-er) favorite book
das Lieblingscafé (-s) favorite café
das Lieblingsfach (¨-er) favorite subject (in school)
die Lieblingsfarbe (-n) favorite color
das Lieblingsgetränk (-e) favorite drink
der Lieblingskomponist (-en *masc.*) / die Lieblingskomponistin (-nen) favorite composer

das Lieblingslokal (-e) favorite eating place
das Lieblingsrestaurant (-s) favorite restaurant
die Lieblingssendung (-en) favorite (TV) program
der Lieblingssport favorite sport
das Lieblingsthema (Lieblingsthemen) favorite topic
der/die/das Liebste (*decl. adj.*) dearest; best
am liebsten (+ *verb*) the best; the most (4); **möchte am liebsten** would like to (do) most (4)
(das) Liechtenstein (principality of) Liechtenstein (E)
das Lied (-er) song
der Liedermacher (-) / die Liedermacherin (-nen) (folk) songwriter
liefern to supply; to deliver
die Liegekarte (-n) ticket for sleeping compartment
liegen, lag, gelegen to lie; to be located (6)
liegen bleiben (bleibt liegen), blieb liegen, ist liegen geblieben to stay down
die Liegewiese (-n) lawn for sunning oneself
der Lift (-e) elevator
lila purple, violet (5)
die Limonade (-n) lemonade; any fruit-flavored soda, soft drink
das Linguistikseminar (-e) linguistics seminar
die Linie (-n) line; **in erster Linie** first and foremost
der Linienflug (¨e) regularly scheduled flight
links left (9); **nach links** to the left (9)
die Lippe (-n) lip
die Liste (-n) list
der Liter (-) liter
literarisch literary
das Literatenkaffeehaus (¨er) café frequented by intellectuals
die Literatur literature
loben to praise (11)
locker loose(ly); relaxed
der Löffel (-) spoon (6)
logisch logical
der Lohn (¨e) wage
sich lohnen to be worthwhile
das Lokal (-e) restaurant (6)
die Lokalnachrichten (*pl.*) local news (13)
der Lokalpatriotismus regional patriotism
los loose; off; **dann los!** let's go!; **Was ist denn los?** What's the matter? (2)
lösen to solve (a problem)
losgehen (geht los), ging los, ist losgegangen to start; to be off
loslegen (legt los) (*coll.*) to start
die Lösung (-en) solution (14)
loswerden (wird los), wurde los, ist losgeworden (*coll.*) to get rid of
losziehen (zieht los), zog los, ist losgezogen (*coll.*) to take off, leave
die Lotterie (-n) lottery
das Lotto (-s) number-drawing, lottery
die Lücke (-n) gap, hole
der Lückentext (-e) text with blanks to be filled in
die Luft air (8)
die Luftbrücke "air bridge" (5); 1949 Berlin airlift
die Luftpumpe (-n) bicycle pump
der Lüftungsbau ventilation system construction
die Luftverschmutzung air pollution
der Luftweg (-e) via air
die Lüge (-n) lie
die Lüneburger Heide Luneburg Heath (*sandy area in northern Germany*)
Lust haben to feel like doing something (2)
lustig cheerful; fun (1)
(das) Luxemburg Luxembourg (E)
der Luxusartikel (-) luxury article
die Luxusjacht (-en) luxury yacht
(das) Luzern Lucerne (Switzerland)

M

machen to make, do (1); **Kreuzworträtsel machen** to do crossword puzzles (1); **sich Sorgen machen** to worry; **mach's gut** so long (E); **Was macht . . . ?** How is . . . ?; **Das macht zusammen . . .** That comes to . . .; **eine Reise machen** to take a trip; **Urlaub machen** to go on vacation; **Das macht dick.** That is fattening; **Das macht nichts.** That doesn't matter (8); **Das macht Spaß.** That is fun.
mächtig powerful; tremendous, strenuous
das Mädchen (-) girl
der Magen (¨) stomach
die Magenbeschwerden (*pl.*) stomach troubles
die Magenvergiftung (-en) food poisoning
der Magerquark low-fat farmer's cheese
das Mahl (-e) meal
die Mahlzeit (-en) meal
das Mahnmal (¨er) memorial
(der) Mai May (3)
das Make-up makeup (5)
mal = einmal once; just; **erstmal** first of all; **Ruf mal an!** Call sometime! (*softening particle*) (4); **Moment mal** just a moment
das Mal (-e) time(s); **ein zweites Mal** a second time
malen to paint (7)
die Mama (-s) mom, mommy
man (*indef. pron.*) one; you; they; people (4)
der Managementberater (-) / die Managementberaterin (-nen) management consultant
mancher, manche, manches some; **manch ein** many a
manches Mal many a time
manchmal sometimes (8)
der Mangel (¨) lack, deficiency
der Mann (¨er) man (1); husband (3)
das Männlein (-) little man
männlich masculine
die Mannschaft (-en) team; league
die Mansarde (-n) room under the roof of a building; garret
der Mantel (¨) (over)coat (5)
die Mantelgröße (-n) coat size
das Märchen (-) fairy tale
marineblau navy blue
marinieren to marinate
die Mark mark (*German money*) (2); **die Deutsche Mark** German mark
die Marke (-n) brand (name)
markieren to mark
der Markt (¨e) (open air) market, market place
der Marktplatz (¨e) market square
die Marmelade (-n) jam
der Mars Mars
marschieren to march; **marsch!** march!
der Marshallplan Marshall Plan (*American recovery program for Europe after World War II*)
(der) März March (3)
das Marzipan sweet almond paste for candy and cakes
die Maschine (-n) machine
der Maschinenbau mechanical engineering
der Maskenball (¨e) masked ball
das Maskulinum (Maskulina) masculine noun
die Maß Bier a mug of beer (*about one liter*)
die Massage (-n) massage
mäßig moderate
massiv (*coll.*) total(ly)
maßlos endless(ly), immeasurably
das Material (-ien) material, fabric
materialistisch materialistic
(die) Mathe = (*coll.*) **Mathematik**
die Mathematik mathematics
der Matjeshering (-e) young, slightly salted herring
die Matratze (-n) mattress

die Matura = das Abitur (*in Austria and Switzerland*)
die Mauer (-n) wall
die Maueröffnung (-en) opening of the (Berlin) wall
die Maus (¨e) mouse (*term of endearment*)
maximal (*adj.*) maximum
der Mechaniker (-) / die Mechanikerin (-nen) mechanic (11)
(das) Mecklenburg-Vorpommern *one of the German states*
die Medien (*pl.*) media
das Medikament (-e) medicine (pills, etc.), medication
der Meditationsurlaub (-e) meditating vacation; retreat
meditieren to meditate
die Medizin (field of) medicine; **Medizin studieren** to go to medical school
medizinisch medical
das Meer (-e) sea; ocean (7); **am Meer** at the seaside
das Meerwasser sea water
mehr more (10); **kein . . . mehr** no . . . more . . . ; **nicht mehr** not anymore; **nie mehr** never again
das Mehrbettzimmer (-) room with several beds
mehrere (*pl.*) several
die Mehrheit majority
mehrmals often, several times, on several occasions
mehrtägig lasting for several days
die Mehrwegbox (-en) recyclable box
die Mehrwertsteuer (-n) value-added tax; national sales tax
die Mehrzahl majority (14); plural
die Meile (-n) mile
mein my (3)
meinen to mean; to observe
die Meinung (-en) opinion (14); **meiner Meinung nach** in my opinion (14); **ich bin der Meinung** I'm of the opinion (14)
die Meinungsforschung (-en) public opinion research
meist mostly
der, die, das Meiste the most (10); **am meisten** (the) most
meistens mostly (8)
die Meisterhand: von Meisterhand zugeschnitten custom-cut by the hand of a master
die Melange (-n) coffee with milk
sich (am Telefon) melden to answer the phone; **Niemand meldet sich.** No one is answering (the phone).
die Meldung (-en) message
die Mensa (-s) student cafeteria (2)
der Mensch (-en *masc.*) human being, person (2)
die Menschenrechte (*pl.*) human rights (14)
menschlich human
die Mentalität (-en) mentality
das Menü (-s) set meal, menu
merken to notice, observe
merkwürdig strange; remarkable
das Mesolithikum Mesolithic Age
messbar measurable
das Messer (-) knife (6)
das Metall (-e) metal
der Meteorologe (-en *masc.*) / die Meteorologin (-nen) meteorologist
der/das Meter (-) meter
die Methode (-n) method
der Metzger (-) butcher
die Metzgerei (-en) butcher shop (5)
der Metzgermeister (-) / die Metzgermeisterin (-nen) master butcher
(das) Mexiko Mexico
mich me (*acc.*) (3)
die Miederwaren (*pl.*) intimate apparel
das Mietangebot (-e) for-rent ad
die Miete (-n) rent (2); **die Miete beträgt** the rent comes to
mieten to rent (12)
der Mieter (-) / die Mieterin (-nen) tenant, renter
das Mietgesuch (-e) rental want ad
die Mietkosten (*pl.*) rental expenses
das Mietshaus (¨er) apartment building
der Mietwagen (-) rental car
der Mikrowellenherd (-e) microwave oven (12)
die Milch milk (5)
der Milchkaffee coffee with milk
das Milchprodukt (-e) dairy product
mild mild
das Militär army
militärisch military
die Milliarde (-n) billion
der Milliliter (-) one thousandth of a liter
die Million (-en) million
der Millionär (-e) / die Millionärin (-nen) millionaire
die Milz spleen
die Mimik mimicry
mindestens at least (8)
die Mindestmietdauer minimum rental time
die Mineralölbranche (-n) mineral oil business
das Mineralwasser mineral water (5)
die Minibar (-s) minibar
das Minigolf miniature golf (game)
der Minister (-) / die Ministerin (-nen) (political) minister
das Ministerium (Ministerien) ministry; government department
die Minute (-n) minute (4)
Mio = Million
mir (to/for) me (5)
mischen to mix, blend
die Mischform (-en) mixed form
das Mischgewebe (-) blended fabric
miserabel miserable
mit (+ *dat.*) with (5)
der Mitarbeiter (-) / die Mitarbeiterin (-nen) coworker (11)
der Mitbegründer (-) / die Mitbegründerin (-nen) co-founder
der Mitbewohner (-) / die Mitbewohnerin (-nen) roommate (2)
mitbringen (bringt mit), brachte mit, mitgebracht to bring/take along
miteinander together
miterziehen (erzieht mit), erzog mit, miterzogen to co-educate
mitfahren (fährt mit), fuhr mit, ist mitgefahren to ride/drive/come along, share the ride
die Mitfahrgelegenheit (-en) ride-sharing opportunity
die Mitfahrzentrale (-n) ride-sharing center
mitgehen (geht mit), ging mit, ist mitgegangen to come along; to join
das Mitglied (-er) member
mitkommen (kommt mit), kam mit, ist mitgekommen to come along (4, 7R)
mitkriegen: sie hat gar nichts mitgekriegt (*coll.*) she didn't understand a thing
das Mitleid compassion, pity
mitmachen (macht mit) to participate
der Mitmensch (-en *masc.*) fellow human being
mitnehmen (nimmt mit), nahm mit, mitgenommen to take along (4); **zum Mitnehmen** to take out (*food*) (6)
mitsamt together with, including
der Mitschüler (-) / die Mitschülerin (-nen) classmate
der Mitstudent (-en *masc.*) / die Mitstudentin (-nen) fellow student
der Mittag (-e) noon; **mittags** at noon (4); **heute Mittag** today at noon (4); **morgen Mittag** tomorrow noon (4); **Samstagmittag** Saturday noon (4)
das Mittagessen midday meal, lunch (5)
mittags at noon (4)
die Mittagszeit (-en) noontime
die Mitte (-n) middle, center (9); **in der Mitte** in the center (9)
mitteilen (teilt mit) to convey, tell
das Mittelalter Middle Ages
mittelalterlich medieval
die Mittelklasse (-n) middle class
das Mittelmeer Mediterranean Sea
der Mittelpunkt (-e) center
der Mittelwesten (USA) Midwest
mitten in the midst

mittler-: die mittlere Reife high school diploma (*not sufficient for university studies*)
(der) Mittwoch Wednesday (3)
mittwochs Wednesdays (4)
mitunter sometimes
mitverantwortlich also responsible
der/die Mitwirkende (*decl. adj.*) performer
ml = Milliliter
die Möbel (*pl.*) furniture
die Möbelbeleuchtung (-en) furniture illumination
möbl. = möbliert
möbliert furnished (2)
möchte: ich möchte I would like (4)
das Modalpartikel (-n) flavoring particle
das Modalverb (-en) modal verb
die Mode (-n) fashion
das Modell (-e) example, model
das Modellbeispiel (-e) model example
der Modeunsinn fashion craze
die Modewaren (*pl.*) fashion articles
modisch fashionable (5)
mögen (mag), mochte, gemocht to like (4); **Ich möchte** I would like (4)
möglich possible (14)
die Möglichkeit (-en) opportunity; possibility (10)
möglichst as . . . as possible (11); **möglichst viel(e)** as much (many) as possible (11); **möglichst bald** as soon as possible
der Mohnkuchen (-) poppy-seed cake
die Möhre (-n) carrot
der Moment (-e) moment; **Moment (mal)** just a moment
der Monat (-e) month (3)
monatlich monthly (12)
das Monatsende (-n) end of the month
der Mönch (-e) monk
(der) Montag Monday (3)
montags Mondays (4)
das Moped (-s) motor scooter
der Mord (-e) murder
der Morgen (-) morning; **guten Morgen** good morning (E); **am Morgen** in the morning
morgen tomorrow (3); **morgen früh** tomorrow morning (4); **morgen Vormittag** tomorrow morning (4); **heute Morgen** this morning (4); **morgen Mittag** tomorrow noon (4); **morgen Nachmittag** tomorrow afternoon (4); **morgen Abend** tomorrow evening; tomorrow night (4); **Samstagmorgen** Saturday morning (4)
die Morgengymnastik morning exercise
der Morgenmuffel (-) morning grouch
die Morgenroutine (-n) morning routine
morgens in the morning(s) (4)
die Mosel Moselle River
das Motel (-s) motel
das Motorrad (¨-er) motorcycle (2); **Motorrad fahren** to ride a motorcycle (2)
das Mountainbike (-s) mountain bike
(das) Mountainbiking mountain biking
müde tired (8)
die Mühe: sich Mühe geben to do one's best; **Mühe haben** to have trouble
der Müll trash, garbage (12)
der Mülleimer (-) garbage can
die Müllhalde (-n) garbage dump
der Müllproduzent (-en *masc.*) waste producer
(das) München Munich
Münchner Weißwurst (¨-e) Bavarian veal sausage
der Mund (¨-er) mouth
mündlich oral, verbal
die Münze (-n) coin (7)
der Münzfernsprecher (-) coin-operated public telephone
das Museum (Museen) museum (9)
das Musical (-s) musical
die Musik music (4)
musikalisch (*adj.*) musical
der Musikant (-en *masc.*) / die Musikantin (-nen) music maker; musician
der Musiker (-) / die Musikerin (-nen) (professional) musician (11)
das Musikfest (-e) music festival
die Musikindustrie (-n) music industry
die Musikschule (-n) music school
der Musikstudent (-en *masc.*) / die Musikstudentin (-nen) music student
musizieren to play an instrument
der Muskel (-n) muscle (8)
das Müsli *type of granola cereal* (5)
müssen (muss), musste, gemusst to have to, must (4)
das Muster (-) model; sample; example; pattern; **nach . . . Muster** patterned after . . .; **nach dem folgenden Muster** according to the following model
mutig brave
die Mutter (¨) mother (3)
mütterlicherseits on the mother's side
der Muttertag (-e) Mother's Day (3)
die Mutti (-s) mommy, mom
die Mütze (-n) cap (5)
Mwst. = Mehrwertsteuer

N

na well; so; **na, dann mach's gut** well, see you later; **na gut** all right then; **Na klar!** But of course!; You bet! (14); **na und?** so what? (13)
nach (+ *dat.*) to (*place name*) (5); after (6); **meiner Meinung nach** in my opinion; **nach links/rechts** to the left/right (8); **nach Hause** home (*indicating going home*) (5); **fünf nach zwei** five after two (4)
der Nachbar (-n *masc.*) / die Nachbarin (-nen) neighbor
die Nachbarwohnung (-en) apartment next door
nachdem (*subord. conj.*) after (10)
nachdenken über (+ *acc.*) **(denkt nach), dachte nach, nachgedacht** to think about, ponder (11)
die Nacherzählung (-en) retelling
die Nachfrage (-n) demand
nachgießen (gießt nach), goss nach, nachgegossen to add liquid
nachher afterward
nachkommen (kommt nach), kam nach, ist nachgekommen to follow, come later
der Nachmittag (-e) afternoon (4); **heute Nachmittag** this afternoon (4); **morgen Nachmittag** tomorrow afternoon (4); **Samstagnachmittag** Saturday afternoon (4)
nachmittags in the afternoon (4)
der Nachname (-ns, -n) family name (1)
die Nachricht (-en) message; **die Nachrichten** (*pl.*) news
das Nachrichtenprogramm (-e) news broadcast
der Nachrichtensprecher (-) / die Nachrichtensprecherin (-nen) anchor person
das Nachschlagewerk (-e) reference book
die Nachspeise (-n) dessert (6)
nächst- next, following; closest, nearest (10); **nächstes Jahr** next year (1)
die Nacht (¨-e) night; **gute Nacht** good night (E)
der Nachteil (-e) disadvantage
der Nachtisch (-e) dessert (6)
das Nachtlager (-) place to sleep; night's lodging; bed
nachts at night (4)
der Nachttisch (-e) nightstand
die Nachttischleuchte (-n) bedside lamp
nah (näher, nächst-) close by, near (10)
die Nähe vicinity; **in der Nähe** nearby, in the vicinity (9); **ganz in der Nähe von** very close to; **nähere Umgebung** close vicinity
die Naherholung (-en) vacation close by
der Nähkasten (¨) sewing box
die Nahrung nutrition; food

das Nahrungsmittel (-) food
das Nähzeug sewing utensils
naiv naive
der Name (-ns, -n) name (E); **im Namen** (+ *gen.*) on behalf of
namens called by; the name of
nämlich namely, that is to say (3)
nanu? now what?
die Narbe (-n) scar
narkotisieren to anesthetize
die Nase (-n) nose (8)
die Nasenlänge (-n) nose length
der Nasenring (-e) nose ring
national national(ly)
die Nationalität (-en) nationality
die Nationalsozialisten (Nazis) (*pl.*) members of the German National Socialist Party (1933–1945)
die Natur nature (10)
das Naturbett (-en) health bed
die Naturfaser (-n) natural fiber
das Naturheilmittel (-) non-medical remedy
der Naturkostladen (¨) health food store
die Naturkraft (¨e) organic energy
natürlich natural(ly); of course (3)
naturnah (*adj.*) close to nature
die Naturoase (-n) place with undisturbed nature
der Naturpark (-s) nature park
der Naturschützer (-) / die Naturschützerin (-nen) nature preservationist
der Naturschutzverband (¨e) nature preservation organization
die Naturwissenschaft (-en) natural science
naturwissenschaftlich scientifical(ly) (11)
der Nazi (-s) (*abbreviation for*) member of the German National Socialist Party (1933–1945)
das Neandertal *valley near Düsseldorf*
der Nebel (-) fog (7)
neben (+ *acc./dat.*) next to, beside (6)
nebenan next door
nebenbei on the side
das Nebenfach (¨er) minor subject (at school)
das Nebeninteresse (-n) hobby
der Nebenjob (-s) second job
die Nebenkosten (*pl.*) incidental expenses (12)
die Nebensache (-n) something of secondary importance
die Nebensaison (-s) off-season
der Nebentisch (-e) next table
neblig foggy (7)
nee (*coll.*) **= nein**
der Neffe (-n *masc.***)** nephew (3)
negativ negative(ly)
nehmen (nimmt), nahm, genommen to take (2); **Platz nehmen** to take a seat
neidisch envious
die Neigung (-en) tendency
nein no (E)
nennen, nannte, genannt to name
nennenswert worth mentioning
die Nerven (*pl.*) nerves
nerven (*coll.*) to get on one's nerves, irritate; **Das nervt mich.** That gets on my nerves.
nervös nervous (1)
die Nervosität nervousness
nett nice, pleasant (1)
das Netz (-e) net
neu new (5); **nichts Neues** nothing new
der Neubau (Neubauten) new building (*built after World War II*)
die Neubauwohnung (-en) apartment in a new building
neugierig curious, nosy
(das) Neuguinea New Guinea
das Neujahr New Year's Day (3)
neulich the other day
neun nine (E)
neunte ninth (3)
neunzehn nineteen (E)
neunzig ninety (E)
(das) Neuseeland New Zealand
neutral (*adj.*) neutral
der Neuwagen (-) new car
die Neuzeit modern time (*from ca.* A.D. *1500 to the present*)
die Nibelungen: der Ring der Nibelungen *opera by Richard Wagner*
nicht not (1); **nicht mehr** no longer (11); **noch nicht** not yet; **nicht wahr?** isn't that so?
die Nichte (-n) niece (3)
der Nichtraucher (-) / die Nichtraucherin (-nen) nonsmoker (10)
nichts nothing (2); **gar nichts** nothing at all; **nichts mehr** nothing (any)more; **nichts zu danken** don't mention it (8)
nie never (8)
der Niedergang decline and fall
die Niederlande (*pl.*) the Netherlands, Holland (E)
die Niederlassung (-en) branch office
der Niederschlag (¨e) precipitation
niedlich cute
niedrig low (2)
niemand nobody
die Niere (-n) kidney
noch still; yet (2); else; another; **noch nicht** not yet; **noch etwas** something else; **noch einmal** once more (E); **sonst noch** otherwise
nochmals once again
die Nockerln (*pl.*) Austrian dumplings
das Nomen (-) noun
der Nominativ (-e) nominative case
(das) Norddeutschland northern Germany
der Norden north; **im Norden** (in the) north
nördlich (von) north (of)
der Nordpol north pole
(das) Nordrhein-Westfalen *one of the German states*
die Nordsee North Sea
die Norm (-en) norm
normal normal(ly)
normalerweise normally
(das) Norwegen Norway
nostalgisch nostalgic
die Note (-n) grade (on a report card)
notieren to write down
nötig necessary
die Notiz (-en) note; **sich Notizen machen** to take notes
das Notlicht (-er) emergency light
notwendig necessary
(der) November November (3)
Nr. = Nummer
das Nudelgericht (-e) pasta dish
die Nudeln (*pl.*) noodles
nuklear nuclear
die Nuklearmacht (¨e) nuclear power
null zero (E)
nummerieren to number
die Nummer (-n) number (E)
nun now (1)
nur only (2)
(das) Nürnberg (city of) Nuremberg
die Nuss (¨e) nut
nützen to make use of
nützlich useful

O

ob (*subord. conj.*) if, whether (or not) (8)
obdachlos homeless
der/die Obdachlose (*decl. adj.*) homeless person (14)
die Obdachlosigkeit homelessness (14)
oben at the top; above; upstairs (12); **da oben** up there; **nach oben** above (12)
der Ober (-) waiter (6); **Herr Ober!** Waiter!
ober upper (12); outer
der Oberarzt (¨e) / die Oberärztin (-nen) chief physician
(das) Oberbayern Upper Bavaria
die Oberbekleidung (-en) outer wear
oberflächlich superficial (13)
(das) Oberschlesien Upper Silesia
das Obst fruit (5)
der Obst- und Gemüsestand (¨e) fruit and vegetable stand (5)
die Obstsorte (-n) type of fruit

die Obsttorte (-n) fruit torte
die Obsttunke (-n) fruit sauce
obwohl (*subord. conj.*) although, even though
oder (*coord. conj.*) or (7)
die Ofenkartoffel (-n) baked potato
offen open
öffentlich public(ly)
offiziell official(ly)
öffnen to open (1)
die Öffnung (-en) opening
die Öffnungszeiten (*pl.*) business hours
oft often (3)
öfter frequently
oh je! oh, dear!
ohne (+ *acc.*) without (3)
das Ohr (-en) ear (8)
der Ohrring (-e) earring
der Ökoarchitekt (-en *masc.***) / die Ökoarchitektin (-nen)** environmental architect
die Ökolebensmittel health foods
ökologisch ecological(ly)
der Ökonom (-en *masc.***) / die Ökonomin (-nen)** economist
das Oktett (-e) octet
(der) Oktober October (3)
der Ölberg Mount of Olives
die Olive (-n) olive (6)
der Ölprinz (-en *masc.***) / die Ölprinzessin (-nen)** oil prince/oil princess
die Olympischen Spiele (*pl.*) Olympic Games
die Oma (-s) grandma (3)
die Omi (-s) grandma
der Onkel (-) uncle (3)
der Opa (-s) grandpa (3)
der Opel (-) (*automobile*) Opel
die Oper (-n) opera (4); **in die Oper gehen** to go to the opera (4)
die Operation (-en) operation, surgery
die Operette (-n) operetta
das Opernhaus (¨er) opera house
der Opernsänger (-) / die Opernsängerin (-nen) opera singer
die Optik (-en) optical shop
die Orange (-n) orange (5)
orange (*adj.*) (color of) orange (5)
der Orangensaft orange juice (5)
das Orchester (-) orchestra
ordentlich neat
die Ordinalzahl (-en) ordinal number
ordnen to put in order
die Ordnung order; **geht in Ordnung** that's all right, sure; **in Ordnung bringen** to clean up; **in Ordnung sein** to function properly
die Organisation (-en) organization
organisch organic
organisieren to organize
die Orientierung (-en) orientation
die Orientierungsstufe (-n) *level in German school system*
der Orientteppich (-e) oriental rug
original original(ly)
originell inventive, unique
der Ort (-e) place; locality
örtlich local(ly)
die Ortschaft (-en) town
der Ortsteil (-e) section of town
(das) Ostberlin East Berlin
der Ostberliner (-) / die Ostberlinerin (-nen) person from East Berlin
der/die Ostdeutsche (*decl. adj.*) East German (person)
(das) Ostdeutschland East Germany
der Osten east
der Osterhase (-n *masc.***)** Easter bunny
(das) Ostern Easter (3)
(das) Österreich Austria (E)
österreichisch Austrian
östlich (von) east (of)
die Ostsee Baltic Sea
die Ostseite (-n) east side
der Ozean (-e) ocean
der Ozon (-e) ozone
das Ozonloch (¨er) ozone hole
das Ozonproblem (-e) ozone problem
die Ozonschicht (-en) ozone layer

P

das Paar (-e) pair
ein paar a few, a couple of; **ein paarmal** a few times
packen to pack
die Packung (-en) package; box
das Paket (-e) package
die Pantomime (-n) pantomime, gesturing
der Papa (-s) daddy
der Papagei (-en) parrot
das Papier (-e) paper (12); **ein Blatt Papier** a sheet of paper
das Papiergeld (-er) paper money
die Papierlaterne (-n) paper lantern
die Paprika (-s) / Paprikaschote (-n) bell pepper (6)
die Parfümerie (-n) cosmetics store
der Park (-s) park
der Parka (-s) parka
die Parkanlage (-n) public park grounds
parken to park
das Parkett main floor of a theater, orchestra seat section
die Parkgarage (-n) parking garage
das Parkhaus (¨er) high-rise parking garage
der Parkplatz (¨e) parking lot (9)
das Parkproblem (-e) parking problem
das Parkverbot: hier ist Parkverbot no parking here
das Parlament (-e) parliament
das Partizip (-ien) participle
der Partner (-) / die Partnerin (-nen) partner
die Party (-s) party (3)
das Partymenü (-s) party menu
der Pass (¨e) pass; passport
der Passagier (-e) / die Passagierin (-nen) passenger (10)
der Passagierkai (-s) boardwalk
der Passant (-en *masc.***) / die Passantin (-nen)** passer-by (9)
passen (+ *dat.*) to match, fit (5); **Das passt mir.** That fits (me).
passend matching, suitable
passieren, ist passiert to happen (7)
das Passiv passive voice
der Patient (-en *masc.***) / die Patientin (-nen)** patient
die Pauke (-n) kettle drum
das Pauschalangebot (-e) package tour offer
die Pauschalreise (-n) package tour
die Pause (-n) pause, break
pausenlos continuous, without a break
der Pazifik Pacific Ocean
das Pech pitch; bad luck; **So ein Pech!** What a shame! (What bad luck!) (8)
der Pelz (-e) fur
pendeln to commute; to go back and forth
die Pension (-en) small family-run hotel (9)
sich pensionieren lassen to retire
per via; by way of; **per Anhalter** hitchhiking
das Perfekt present perfect tense
perfekt (*adj.*) perfect
die Periode (-n) period, time
perplex amazed, confused
die Person (-en) person; **pro Person** per person (10)
der Personalausweis (-e) personal ID card
der Personalchef (-s) / die Personalchefin (-nen) head of personnel
das Personalpronomen (-) personal pronoun
der Personenkraftwagen (-) automobile
persönlich personal
die Persönlichkeit (-en) personality
die Perspektive (-n) perspective
das Pestizid (-e) pesticide
der Pfad (-e) path; **der Trimm-Pfad (-e)** parcourse, jogging path
die Pfanne (-n) frying pan (6)
der Pfarrer (-) / die Pfarrerin (-nen) minister
der Pfeffer pepper (5)
der Pfeifton (¨e) (electronic) beep
die Pfeilspitze (-n) arrowhead
der Pfennig (-e) penny (*German monetary unit*)

das Pferd (-e) horse; **zu Pferde** on horseback
das Pferderennen (-) horse race
Pfiff: mit Pfiff with style, class
der Pfirsich (-e) peach
die Pflanze (-n) plant
pflanzen to plant
die Pflanzenart (-en) type of plant
das Pflanzenschutzmittel (-) pesticide
die Pflanzensorte (-n) plant species
der Pförtner (-) / die Pförtnerin (-nen) doorkeeper
das Pfund (-e) pound
das Phantom (-e) phantom
die Pharmaziebranche (-n) pharmaceutical business
die Philologie philology
die Philosophie philosophy
philosophisch philosophical
die Physik physics
der Physiker (-) / die Physikerin (-nen) physicist (11)
das Picknick (-s) picnic
picknicken to have a picnic
der Picknickkorb (¨-e) picnic basket
der Picknickplatz (¨-e) picnic area
der Pilot (-en *masc.***) / die Pilotin (-nen)** pilot (10)
die Pilsbar (-s) beer bar
das Pilsener (-) pilsner beer (6)
die Pistole (-n) pistol, revolver
die Pizza (-s) pizza
der Pkw = Personenkraftwagen
die Plakette (-n) button, sticker
der Plan (¨-e) plan
planen to plan (3)
das Plastik plastic
das Plastikgeld plastic money
das Plastikrechteck (-e) plastic square
die Plastiktüte (-n) plastic bag (14)
die Platte (-n) record; platter
der Plattenspieler (-) record player
der Platz (¨-e) place; seat (6); **Platz nehmen** to take a seat; **Da ist kein Platz.** There is no room.
die Platzkarte (-n) reserved-seat ticket (10)
die Platzreservierung (-en) seat reservation
plaudern to chat
pleite (*coll.*) broke, out of money (12)
das Plenum: im Plenum all together
plötzlich suddenly; unexpected
der Plural (-e) plural form
der Pluspunkt (-e) plus point
das Plusquamperfekt past perfect tense
die Poesie poetry
(das) Polen Poland (E)
die Politik politics (13)
der Politiker (-) / die Politikerin (-nen) politician (14)
politisch political
die Politologie political science
die Polizei police (9)
der Polizist (-en *masc.***) /die Polizistin (-nen)** police officer
die Pommes frites (*pl.*) French fries (6)
die Popeline (-) poplin
populär popular
der Porsche (-) (*automobile*) Porsche
das Portemonnaie (-s) wallet; coin purse
die Portion (-en) portion; order of
(das) Portugal Portugal
das Porzellan china
die Posaune (-n) trombone; trumpet
positiv positive(ly)
das Possessivpronomen (-) possessive adjective
die Post postal system; post office (9); mail; **bei der Post Karriere machen** to have a career in the postal service
das Postamt (¨-er) post office
das Poster (-) poster (2)
das Postfach (¨-er) post office box
das Postgiroamt (¨-er) post office bank
die Postkarte (-n) postcard
die Postleitzahl (-en) zip code (E); **Wie ist die Postleitzahl von . . . ?** What is the zip code of . . . ?
postwendend by return mail
potenziell potential(ly)
das Präfix (-e) prefix
prägen to shape
das Praktikum (Praktika) internship
praktisch practical (1)
die Präposition (-en) preposition
das Präsens present tense
präsentieren to present
der Präsident (-en *masc.***) / die Präsidentin (-nen)** president
die Praxis (Praxen) practice; professional practice
der Preis (-e) price; **im Preis enthalten** included in the price (9)
preisgeben (gibt preis), gab preis, preisgegeben to reveal
preiswert inexpensive, a bargain (2)
die Premiere (-n) premiere
die Presse press (*newspapers, etc.*)
das Prestige prestige (11)
der Preuße (-n *masc.***) / die Preußin (-nen)** Prussian (person)
der Priester (-) / die Priesterin (-nen) priest
prima excellent, great (E)
privat private; **privat wohnen** to have a room in somebody's house or apartment
das Privatleben personal life
das Privatzimmer (-) private room
pro per; **pro Kopf** per head; **pro Person** per person (10)
das Problem (-e) problem (2); **ein Problem lösen** to solve a problem
problemlos without any problem
das Produkt (-e) product
die Produktion (-en) production
produzieren to produce
der Professor (-en) / die Professorin (-nen) professor (1)
der/die Profi (-s) professional (person)
das Programm (-e) program; (TV) channel (13); **im ersten Programm** on channel 1 (13)
progressiv progressive
das Projekt (-e) project
die Promenade (-n) place for strolling
promenieren to stroll
die Prominenz prominent people, socialites
das Pronomen (-) pronoun
das Pronominaladverb (-ien) pronominal adverb
propagiert publicly advocated
prophezeien to predict
der Prospekt (-e) brochure
protestieren to protest
provisorisch temporary, temporarily
provozierend provoking
die Prozedur (-en) procedure
das Prozent (-e) percent (12)
prüfen to test
die Prüfung (-en) test, exam
der Prüfungsraum (¨-e) examination room
der Psychologe (-n *masc.***) / die Psychologin (-nen)** psychologist (11)
die Psychologie psychology
der Psychothriller (-) psycho-thriller (movie)
das Publikum public; audience
der Pudding (-e) pudding
der Pudel (-) poodle
pudelnackt stark naked
der Pullover (-) sweater, pullover (5)
der Puls (-e) pulse
Pump: auf Pump (*coll.*) on credit
der Punkt (-e) point; period
pünktlich punctual, on time
die Puppe (-n) doll
die Puppenstube (-n) dollhouse
pusten to blow
putzen to polish, clean (8); **sich die Zähne putzen** to clean, brush one's teeth (8)

Q

qm = Quadratmeter
das Quadrat (-e) square
der/das Quadratmeter (-) square meter (12)
die Qualifikation (-en) qualification
qualifizieren to qualify
die Qualität (-en) quality

der Quark curd cheese
das Quartal (-e) (academic) quarter (12)
der Quatsch (*coll.*) nonsense (14); **so ein Quatsch** baloney (14)
quatschen (*coll.*) to talk, chat
das Quecksilber mercury, quicksilver
die Quelle (-n) source; spring
quer durch across
das Quiz (-) quiz
der Quizmaster (-) quizmaster
die Quizsendung (-en) quiz program
die Quizshow (-s) quiz show

R

das Racket (-s) (tennis) racket
das Rad (¨-er) wheel; bicycle
das Radabzeichen (-) bike emblem
die Radbekleidung (-en) biking clothes
Rad fahren (fährt Rad), fuhr Rad, ist Rad gefahren to ride a bicycle (7)
der Radfahrer (-) / die Radfahrerin (-nen) cyclist
das Radio (-s) radio (2); **im Radio** on the radio
die Radiosendung (-en) radio broadcast
der Radiotechniker (-) / die Radiotechnikerin (-nen) radio technician
der Radiowecker (-) clock radio
der Radius (Radien) radius
die Radreise (-n) bike trip
die Radtour (-en) bicycle tour
die Radtourfahrt (-en) bicycle trip
der Radweg (-e) bike path
raffiniert smart; sophisticated
der Rahm cream
die Rakete (-n) rocket
der Rand (¨-er) edge; **am Rande** at the edge, outskirts
der Rang balcony, circle (*in the theater*); **der erste Rang** mezzanine; **der dritte Rang** upper balcony
rar rare
das Rascheln rustling
die Raserei rushing around, driving too fast
die Rasiercreme (-s) shaving cream (5)
sich rasieren to shave (8)
das Rasierzeug shaving kit
die Rassenpolitik politics of racism
der Rassismus racism (14)
rassistisch racist
der Rastplatz (¨-e) rest area
der Rat advice (8)
raten (rät), riet, geraten to guess; to advise
der Ratgeber (-) advisor; advice column (13)
das Rathaus (¨-er) city hall
der Ratschlag (¨-e) advice
das Rätsel (-) puzzle, riddle (13)
der Ratskeller (-) (cellar) restaurant near town hall
die Räuberhöhle (-n) thieves' den
der Rauch smoke
das Rauchen smoking
rauchen to smoke
der Rauchtisch (-e) coffee table
rauf = herauf
der Raum (¨-e) room; space; **der Abstellraum** storage room
der Raumplaner (-) / die Raumplanerin (-nen) interior decorator
raus = heraus, hinaus; er muss raus he has got to go; **rein und raus** in and out
rausgehen (geht raus), ging raus, ist rausgegangen to go outside
rauskommen (kommt raus), kam raus, ist rausgekommen to come outside; to get out
rausschwimmen (schwimmt raus), schwamm raus, ist rausgeschwommen to swim out into the sea/lake
reagieren auf (+ *acc.*) to react to
die Reaktion (-en) reaction
real real, genuine
der Realschulabschluss (¨-e) diploma attained at the end of the Realschule
die Realschule (-n) *secondary school with a commercially oriented curriculum*
der Rebell (-en *masc.*) rebel
rebellieren to rebel
das Rebland (¨-er) wine country
die Rechenmaschine (-n) calculator
recherchieren to investigate, research
rechnen (mit + *dat.*) to count (on), expect
die Rechnung (-en) bill (6)
recht right (2); quite (2); **auf der rechten Seite** on the right-hand side; **nicht so recht** not quite; **Das ist mir recht.** That's fine with me.
das Recht (-e) right; law; **Recht haben** to be correct (2)
rechtfertigen to justify
rechtlich legal(ly)
rechts on the right (9); **nach rechts** to the right (9)
der Rechtsanwalt (¨-e) / die Rechtsanwältin (-nen) attorney, lawyer (11)
rechtsextrem (*adj.*) on the extreme political right
der Rechtsextremismus rightwing extremism (14)
der/die Rechtsradikale (*decl. adj.*) radical (person) on the political right
rechtzeitig in time
das Recycling recycling
recyclingfähig recyclable
der Recyclingingenieur (-e) / die Recyclingingenieurin (-nen) recycling engineer
das Recyclingprogramm (-e) recycling program
der Redakteur (-e) / die Redakteurin (-nen) chief editor
die Rede (-n) speech
das Redemittel (-) speech
reden to talk about (4); **reden über** (+ *acc.*) to talk about; **um das Thema herumreden** to beat around the bush
reduzieren to reduce
das Reflexivpronomen (-) reflexive pronoun
das Reflexivverb (-en) reflexive verb
die Reformkost health food
das Regal (-e) shelf (2)
die Regel (-n) rule
regelmäßig regularly (8)
der Regen rain (7); **Es gibt Regen.** It is going to rain.
die Regenbekleidung (-en) rainwear
der Regenmantel (¨-) raincoat
der Regenschauer (-) rain shower (7)
der Regenschirm (-e) umbrella (7)
der Regenwald (¨-er) rain forest
die Regie (-n) (film) direction
die Regierung (-en) government (14)
die Regierungsgewalt (-en) government power
das Regime (-) regime
die Region (-en) region, area
regional regional(ly)
der Regisseur (-e) / die Regisseurin (-nen) (film) director
regnen to rain; **Es regnet.** It's raining. (7)
regnerisch rainy (7)
das Reich (-e) empire; realm
reich rich
reichen to reach; to suffice; to hand; **Das reicht.** That's enough.
reichhaltig abundant, plentiful
die Reichskanzlei (-en) (former) German Chancellery
die Reife: mittlere Reife diploma attained at the end of the Realschule
der Reifen (-) tire
die Reihe (-n) row
die Reihenfolge sequence; order
das Reihenhaus (¨-er) town house (12)
sich reimen to rhyme
rein = herein; rein und raus in and out
die Reinigung (-en) dry cleaning
reinkommen (kommt rein), kam rein, ist reingekommen to come in, enter
der Reis rice (6)
die Reise (-n) trip, journey (10)
die Reiseapotheke (-n) portable first-aid kit

die Reiseberatung (-en) travel consultation
der Reisebericht (-e) travel report
das Reisebüro (-s) travel agency (10)
der/die Reisebüroangestellte (*decl. adj.*) travel agency employee
die Reisebürokauffrau (-en) / der Reisebürokaufmann (⸚er) licensed travel agent
der Reisebüroleiter (-) / die Reisebüroleiterin (-nen) travel agency manager
die Reisecheckliste (-n) travel checklist
der Reisefilm (-e) travel film
der Reiseführer (-) travel guide (10)
das Reisegepäck luggage
der Reiseleiter (-) / die Reiseleiterin (-nen) tour guide.
die Reiselektüre vacation reading material
der Reisemantel (⸚) travel coat
die Reisemöglichkeit (-en) travel opportunity
reisen, ist gereist to travel (1); **das Reisen** traveling
der/die Reisende (*decl. adj.*) traveler
der Reisepass (⸚e) passport (9)
das Reisepersonal travel staff
der Reiseprospekt (-e) travel brochure (10)
der Reiseproviant food for a trip
der Reisescheck (-s) traveler's check (9)
die Reiseverbindung (-en) travel connection
die Reisevorbereitungen (*pl.*) travel preparations
die Reisewettervorhersage (-n) traveler's weather forecast
reiten, ritt, ist geritten to ride on horseback (7)
die Reitschule (-n) riding school
die Reklame (-n) advertising
der Rekord (-e) record
relativ relative(ly)
das Relativpronomen (-) relative pronoun
der Relativsatz (⸚e) relative clause
die Religion (-en) religion
die Remouladensauce (-n) dressing made of mayonnaise and herbs
die Renaissance Renaissance (period)
der Rennfahrer (-) / die Rennfahrerin (-nen) race driver
renovieren to renovate
die Renovierungskosten (*pl.*) remodeling costs
rentabel profitable
die Rente (-n) pension
das Rentiergeweih (-e) reindeer antlers
der Rentner (-) / die Rentnerin (-nen) retired person
die Reparatur (-en) repair (12)
die Reparaturwerkstatt (⸚e) repair shop
reparieren to repair (9)
der Reporter (-) / die Reporterin (-nen) reporter
der Repräsentant (-en *masc.***) / die Repräsentantin (-nen)** representative
repräsentieren to represent
die Republik (-en) republic
reservieren to book, reserve (7)
die Reservierung (-en) reservation
die Residenzstadt (⸚e) government capital
der Rest (-e) remainder
das Restaurant (-s) restaurant (6)
restaurieren to restore
das Resultat (-e) result
retten to save, rescue
das Rezept (-e) recipe
die Rezeption reception desk (9)
die Rezession (-en) recession
der Rhein Rhine (River)
das Rheinland *area along the river Rhine*
(die) Rheinland-Pfalz *one of the German states*
sich richten an (+ *acc.*) to address; **sich richten auf** (+ *acc.*) to be directed at
richtig correct, right (1)
die Richtung (-en) direction; **in Richtung** in the direction of
der Riese (-n *masc.***)** giant
das Rieseneisbein (-e) gigantic pork hock
riesig enormous, gigantic
der Rinderbraten (-) beef roast (5)
die Rinderroulade (-n) beef roulade
das Rindfleisch beef (5)
der Ring (-e) ring
ringen, rang, gerungen to wrestle
ringsum all around
der Ritter (-) knight
das Roastbeef roast beef
der Rock (⸚e) skirt (5)
die Rockband (-s) rock band
die Rockgruppe (-n) rock group
das Rockkonzert (-e) rock concert
die Rockmusik rock music
roh raw
die Rohmilch raw milk
die Rolle (-n) role
rollen to roll
das Rollenspiel (-e) role play
der Rollkragen (-) turtleneck
der Rollkragenpullover (-) turtleneck sweater
der Rollschuh: Rollschuh laufen roller-skating
der Roman (-e) novel
die Romanfortsetzung (-en) continuation of novel
romantisch romantic (1)
die Röntgenstrahlen (*pl.*) X-rays
das Rostbratwürstl (-) grilled sausage
rot red (5)
(das) Rotkäppchen Little Red Riding Hood
der Rotwein (-e) red wine
die Routine (-n) routine
das Rübenkraut sugar-beet syrup
rüber = herüber
die Rubrik (-en) category; column
der Rücken (-) back (8)
rücken (+ *dir. obj.*) to move (*something*)
die Rückenschmerzen (*pl.*) backache
die Rückfahrt (-en) return trip
der Rucksack (⸚e) backpack (5)
der Rückstrahler (-) rear reflector
rückwärts backward
rudern, ist gerudert to row
der Ruf (-e) call, shout
rufen, rief, gerufen to call (out)
die Ruhe rest, calm (8); **in Ruhe** in peace and quiet, at one's leisure; **in Ruhe lassen** to leave alone
der Ruhetag (-e) day when restaurant is closed (6)
ruhig quiet, calm (1)
das Rührei (-er) scrambled egg
(sich) rühren to stir
die Ruine (-n) ruin
(das) Rumänien Rumania
das Rumpsteak (-s) steak
rund round; around
der Rundfunk radio; broadcasting
die Rundfunkanstalt (-en) broadcasting corporation
rundum all around
der Russe (-n *masc.***) / die Russin (-nen)** Russian (person)
russisch (*adj.*) Russian
(das) Russland Russia
rustikal rustic
die Rüstung (-en) armament
das Rüstzeug equipment

S

die Sache (-n) thing, object; event; **in Sache** concerning; **mit 200 Sachen** (*coll.*) driving at 200 km an hour
(das) Sachsen *one of the German states*
(das) Sachsen-Anhalt *one of the German states*
die Sackgasse (-n) dead end
die Safari (-s) safari
der Saft (⸚e) juice (5)
saftig juicy
sagen to say, tell (1); **sag mal, . . .** say, . . . ; tell me, . . . (1); **Wie sagt man . . . auf Deutsch?** How does one say . . . in German? (E)
die Sahne cream (6)
das Sahneeis ice cream

die Sahnehaube (-n) (whipped) cream topping
die Saison (-s) season
der/das Sakko (-s) man's jacket, coat (5)
der Salat (-e) salad; lettuce (6); **der Kartoffelsalat** potato salad
die Salatbar (-s) salad bar
der Salatkranz (¨-e) bed of lettuce
die Salatplatte (-n) mixed salad dish
das Salz salt (5)
sammeln to collect (7)
die Sammelstelle (-n) recycling center (14)
der Sammler (-) / die Sammlerin (-nen) collector
die Sammlung (-en) collection
(der) Samstag Saturday (3); **samstags** Saturdays (4); **Samstagmorgen** Saturday morning (4); **Samstagvormittag** Saturday before noon (4); **Samstagmittag** Saturday noon (4); **Samstagabend** Saturday evening; Saturday night (4)
sämtlich total, all
die Sandale (-n) sandal
der Sänger (-) / die Sängerin (-nen) singer
die Sanierung (-en) renovation
der Satan (-e) devil
das Satansweib (-er) devilish woman
das Satellitenprogramm (-e) satellite program
die Satire (-n) satire
satt full, having had enough to eat; **satt werden** to get enough to eat
der Sattel (¨-) saddle
der Satz (¨-e) sentence
die Satzklammer (-n) sentence bracket
der Satzteil (-e) part of a sentence, clause
sauber clean
(sich) sauber halten (hält sauber), hielt sauber, sauber gehalten to keep (oneself) clean (15)
die Sauberkeit cleanliness
säuberlich neatly
sauber machen (macht sauber) to clean house
das Sauerfleisch marinated meat
das Sauerkraut sauerkraut, pickled cabbage (6)
säuerlich sour-tasting
der Sauerregen (-) acid rain
die Sauna (-s) sauna (9)
die S-Bahn (-en) light-rail inner city train
(das) Schach chess (7); **Schach spielen** to play chess (7)
die Schachtel (-n) box
schade too bad
schaden to harm
der Schaden (¨-) damage; **ohne Schaden** without being hurt
schädlich harmful
das Schäfchen (-) lamb
schaffen, schuf, geschaffen to create (14)
schaffen, schaffte, geschafft to accomplish, succeed; **Wir schaffen es nicht.** We're not going to make it.
der Schaffner (-) / die Schaffnerin (-nen) conductor (10)
der Schal (-s) shawl, scarf (5)
die Schale (-n) bowl
die Schande disgrace
scharf sharp
die Schärfe (-n) sharpness
der Schatz: mein Schatz my darling
das Schaubild (-er) diagram
die Schaubühne (-n) theater
schauen to look; **Schau mal!** Look! (2)
der Schauer (-) (rain) shower (8)
das Schaufenster (-) store window
der Schauspieler (-) / die Schauspielerin (-nen) actor, actress (11)
der Scheck (-s) check
die Scheckkarte (-n) bank card
die Scheibe (-n) slice
scheiden, schied, ist geschieden to divorce
der Schein (-e) bank note, paper money
scheinbar apparently
scheinen, schien, geschienen to shine; to appear, seem; **Die Sonne scheint.** The sun is shining.
schenken to give (a gift) (5)
scheußlich horrible
schick stylish
schicken to send (5)
das Schicksal (-e) fate
schieben, schob, geschoben to push
schießen, schoss, geschossen to shoot
das Schiff (-e) ship (10)
die Schiffsfahrt (-en) boat trip
die Schiffsreise (-n) voyage
das Schild (-er) sign, road sign
der Schilling (-e) *Austrian monetary unit*
schimpfen to scold
der Schinken (-) ham (5)
der Schirm (-e) umbrella
die Schlacht (-en) battle
der Schlaf sleep
der Schlafanzug (¨-e) pajama
schlafen (schläft), schlief, geschlafen to sleep (2); **schlafen gehen** to go to bed
das Schlafmittel (-) sleeping pills
der Schlafraum (¨-e) sleeping room
der Schlafsack (¨-e) sleeping bag
die Schlaftablette (-n) sleeping pill
das Schlafzimmer (-) bedroom
der Schlag (¨-e) blow
schlagartig sudden(ly)
der Schlägel (-) drumstick; mallet
schlagen (schlägt), schlug, geschlagen to beat
der Schlager (-) hit song; hit
das Schlagobers whipped cream topping
die Schlagzeile (-n) headline (13)
das Schlagzeug (-e) (set of) drums; percussion instruments
die Schlämmkreide fine chalk
schlank slender
schlapp without energy, rundown, listless; worn out (8)
schlecht bad (E); **schlecht erreichbar** hard to reach; **Mir ist schlecht.** I feel sick to my stomach. (8)
schleifen, schliff, geschliffen to sharpen
schleppen to drag, lug
(das) Schleswig-Holstein *one of the German states*
schließen, schloss, geschlossen to close; **schließen aus** (+ *dat.*) to conclude (from)
das Schließfach (¨-er) locker
schließlich finally, in the end
schlimm bad
das Schlimme (*decl. adj.*) the bad thing
der Schlips (-e) tie (5)
der Schlittschuh (-e) ice skate (7)
Schlittschuh laufen (läuft), lief, ist gelaufen to ice-skate (7)
das Schloss (¨-er) castle; palace
der Schlossgarten (¨-) palace garden
der Schluckauf hiccup
schlucken to swallow (8)
der Schlüssel (-) key (9)
schmecken to taste; **Das schmeckt (mir) gut.** That tastes good (to me). (5)
schmelzen (schmilzt), schmolz, ist geschmolzen to melt; to thaw
der Schmerz (-en) pain, ache (8); **vor Schmerz schreien** to cry out with pain
(sich) schminken to put on makeup (8)
der Schminktisch (-e) makeup table
der Schmuck jewelry
der Schmutz dirt
die Schmutzarbeit (-en) menial work
schmutzig dirty (14)
die Schnecke (-n) snail
der Schnee snow (7)
die Schneekette (-n) snow chain
der Schneemann (¨-er) snowman
schneiden, schnitt, geschnitten to cut
schneien to snow (7); **Es schneit.** It is snowing. (7)
schnell quick; fast (10)

der Schnittkäse sliced cheese
das Schnitzel (-) cutlet (5)
der Schnupfen cold; sniffle (8)
schnurlos cordless
der Schnurrbart (¨-e) mustache
die Schokolade chocolate
die Schokoladentorte (-n) chocolate torte
der Schokoriegel (-) chocolate bar
schon already; yet; ever (2)
schön beautiful (2); **bitte schön** please (E); **danke schön** (many) thanks (E); **schön warm** nice and warm
schonen to protect
die Schönheit (-en) beauty
der Schonkaffee low-acid decaffeinated coffee
schöpfen to scoop; to draw (from a well)
der Schornsteinfeger (-) chimney sweep
der Schrank (¨-e) cupboard; closet; wardrobe
schrecklich horrible
der Schrei (-e) scream; **der letzte Schrei** the latest fashion
schreiben, schrieb, geschrieben to write (2)
die Schreibmaschine (-n) typewriter
die Schreibstube (-n) office; writing room
der Schreibtisch (-e) desk (2)
die Schreibwaren (*pl.*) stationery goods
schreien, schrie, geschrien to scream
schriftlich in writing
der Schriftsteller (-) / die Schriftstellerin (-nen) writer, author
der Schritt (-e) step (11)
die Schublade (-n) drawer
der Schuh (-e) shoe (5)
das Schuhgeschäft (-e) shoe store
die Schuhgröße (-n) shoe size
der Schuhkauf (¨-e) shoe purchase
das Schuhwerk footwear
der Schulabgänger (-) / die Schulabgängerin (-nen) school graduate
die Schularbeiten (*pl.*) homework
die Schuld guilt; blame
die Schulden (*pl.*) debts; **Schulden machen** to go into debt
schuldig guilty
die Schule (-n) school; **Schule machen** to set an example
der Schüler (-) / die Schülerin (-nen) pupil, student in primary or secondary school
das Schulessen (-) school lunch
die Schulferien (*pl.*) school vacation, holidays
der Schulfreund (-e) / die Schulfreundin (-nen) school friend
das Schuljahr (-e) school year; **im zehnten Schuljahr** in tenth grade
das Schulkind (-er) pupil
der Schulort (-e) town in which one attends school
die Schulsachen (*pl.*) school supplies
die Schulspeisung meal provided at school
die Schulter (-n) shoulder (8)
das Schultergelenk (-e) shoulder joint
die Schulterpartie (-n) shoulder area
der Schultyp (-en *masc.***)** type of school
die Schüssel (-n) bowl
der Schutz (-e) protection
schützen to protect
schwach weak
die Schwäche (-n) weakness
schwachsinnig (*coll.*) crazy
der Schwager (¨-) brother-in-law (3)
die Schwägerin (-nen) sister-in-law (3)
schwanger pregnant
schwarz black (5)
das Schwarzbrot black bread
schwarzhaarig dark-haired
der Schwarzhandel black market
der Schwarzwald Black Forest
die Schwarzwälder Kirschtorte (-n) Black Forest cake
der Schwarzweißfilm (-e) black-and-white film
(das) Schweden Sweden
das Schwefeldioxyd (-e) sulfur dioxide
das Schwein (-e) pig; **kein Schwein** (*coll.*) nobody
der Schweinebraten (-) pork roast (6)
das Schweinefleisch pork (5)
das Schweinegulasch pork goulash
das Schweineschnitzel (-) pork cutlet
die Schweineschulter (-n) pork shoulder
die Schweinshaxe (-n) pork knuckle
das Schweinskotelett (-s) pork cutlet
der Schweiß perspiration
die Schweiz Switzerland (E)
der Schweizer Käse Swiss cheese
schwer heavy; difficult; **schwer arbeiten** to work hard
der Schwerpunkt (-e) focus, emphasis
die Schwester (-n) sister (3)
die Schwiegermutter (¨-) mother-in-law (3)
der Schwiegervater (¨-) father-in-law (3)
schwierig difficult
die Schwierigkeit (-en) difficulty
das Schwimmbad (¨-er) swimming pool (7)
schwimmen, schwamm, ist geschwommen to swim (2)
die Schwimmflosse (-n) flipper
die Schwimmhalle (-n) indoor pool (9)
die Schwimmstufe (-n) swimming level
schwitzen to sweat
schwül muggy (7)
der Schwung: voll Schwung full of zest
sechs six (E)
sechste sixth (3)
sechzehn sixteen (E)
sechzig sixty (E)
die sechziger Jahre the sixties
der See (-n) lake (7); **auf dem See** on the lake; **die See** ocean
der Seekanal (¨-e) sea channel
das Segelflugzeug (-e) glider
der Segelkurs (-e) sailing course (10)
segeln to sail (7)
sehen (sieht), sah, gesehen to see (2)
sehenswert worth seeing
sehenswürdig remarkable
die Sehenswürdigkeit (-en) (tourist) attraction
sehr very (1)
die Seide silk
die Seidenblume (-n) silk flower
die Seidenbluse (-n) silk blouse
das Seil (-e) rope
sein (ist), war, ist gewesen to be (1)
sein his, its (3)
seit (+ *dat.*) since; for (5); **seit wann** since when (6); **seit zwei Jahren** for two years (6)
seitdem since then
die Seite (-n) side; page
der Sekretär (-e) / die Sekretärin (-nen) secretary
der Sekt champagne
die Sekunde (-n) second (4)
selb- (*adj.*) same; **derselbe, dieselbe, dasselbe** the same
selber self; **selber machen** to do (*something*) oneself
selbst self
selbständig independent(ly) (11)
die Selbstbedienung self-service
das Selbstbewusstsein self-confidence
selten seldom(ly), rare(ly) (2)
das Semester (-) semester (1)
das Seminar (-e) seminar (2)
die Seminararbeit (-en) paper written for a seminar
die Semmel (-n) bread roll (*southern Germany and Austria*)
senden, sandte, gesandt to send
die Sendung (-en) TV or radio program (13)
der Senf mustard (6)
(der) September September (3)
die Serie (-n) series
servieren to serve
die Serviette (-n) napkin
der Sessel (-) armchair, easy chair (2)
setzen to set, put (6); **sich (hin)setzen** to sit down (8)
das Shampoo (-s) shampoo

sicher safe(ly) (10)
die Sicherheit security
die Sicherheitskraft (¨e) security force
sicherlich certainly
sichern to secure
sichtbar visible
Sie (*form.*) you (1)
sie she; it; they (1); her, it; them (*acc.*) (3)
sieben seven (E)
sieb(en)te seventh (3)
siebzehn seventeen (E)
siebzig seventy (E)
die Siedlung (-en) housing development
das Signal (-e) signal
signalisieren to signal, indicate
das Silber silver
das Silbergeld silver pieces of money
die Silbermünze (-n) silver coin
silbern silver(y)
(das) Silvester (-) New Year's Eve (3)
singen, sang, gesungen to sing
sinken, sank, ist gesunken to sink; to drop
der Sinn (-e) sense; meaning; feeling; **Sinn für Humor** sense of humor
sinnlos senseless
die Situation (-en) situation
der Sitz (-e) seat
sitzen, saß, gesessen to sit (6)
sitzen bleiben (bleibt sitzen), blieb sitzen, ist sitzen geblieben to be left behind; to fail a class
die Sitzgruppe (-n) living room set
der Sitzplatz (¨e) seat
die Sitzung (-en) session
(das) Sizilien Sicily
das Skalpell (-e) scalpel
das Skeetschießen skeet shooting
skeptisch skeptical
der Sketch (-e) sketch
Ski fahren (fährt), fuhr, ist gefahren to ski
die Skihose (-n) ski pants
Ski laufen (läuft), lief, gelaufen to ski
der Skiläufer (-) / die Skiläuferin (-nen) skier
der Skipass (¨e) lift pass
die Skulptur (-en) sculpture
der Slawenfürst (-en *masc.***)** Slavic prince
slawisch Slavic
(die) Slowakei Slovakia
(das) Slowenien Slovenia (E)
so so; like that (2); **so . . . wie** as . . . as (10)
sobald (*subord. conj.*) as soon as
die Socke (-n) sock (5)
das Sofa (-s) sofa, couch (2)
sofort immediately (9)
sogar even (8)
sogenannt so-called
der Sohn (¨e) son (3)
solange (*subord. conj.*) as long as
das Solarauto (-s) solar automobile
die Solarenergie (-n) solar energy
das Solarium (Solarien) solarium
das Solarmobil (-e) solar car
solch ein- such a
der Soldat (-en *masc.***) / die Soldatin (-nen)** soldier
die Solidarität solidarity
solide solid, sound
sollen (soll), sollte, gesollt shall; to be supposed to; ought; should (4); said to be
der Sommer (-) summer (7)
der Sommergarten (¨) summer garden
das Sommerstipendium (Sommerstipendien) summer scholarship
der Sommertag (-e) summer day
die Sommerzeit (-en) daylight savings time
der Sonderabfall (¨e) radioactive waste
die Sonderaktion (-en) special (sales) offer
das Sonderangebot (-e) special offer (at a store)
sonderbar strange
sondern but rather (7)
der Sonderpreis (-e) special price
(der) Sonnabend Saturday (3)
sonnabends Saturdays (4)
die Sonne (-n) sun (7); **Die Sonne scheint.** The sun is shining. (7)
die Sonnenblume (-n) sunflower
die Sonnenbrille (-n) sun glasses
die Sonnenenergie (-n) solar energy
der Sonnenschein sunshine (7)
das Sonnenschutzmittel (-) suntan lotion, sunblock (10)
sonnig sunny (7)
(der) Sonntag Sunday (3)
sonntags Sundays (4)
sonst (noch) otherwise; else; other than that; **Sonst noch was?** Anything else? (10)
sonstig other, additional (10)
Sonstiges other items, miscellaneous
die Sorge (-n) worry; **sich Sorgen machen** to worry
sorgenfrei carefree
sorgfältig careful
die Sorte (-n) kind; variety
das Souvenir (-s) souvenir
der Souvenirverkauf (¨e) souvenir sale
so viel so much
so viele (*pl.*) so many
so was something like that
so weit: Endlich ist es so weit. It's finally happening.
sowie as; as well as; like
sowieso anyway
die Sowjets (*pl.*) Soviets
die Sowjetunion Soviet Union
sowohl . . . als auch . . . . . . as well as . . .
sozial social
der Sozialarbeiter (-) / die Sozialarbeiterin (-nen) social worker
der Sozialismus socialism
die Sozialkunde social science
die Sozialwissenschaften (*pl.*) social sciences
die Soziologie sociology
die Spalte (-n) (printed) column
das Spanferkel (-) roasted suckling pig
(das) Spanien Spain
spanisch (*adj.*) Spanish
spannend exciting, suspenseful (4)
das Sparen saving (12)
sparen to save
der Spargel (-) asparagus
die Sparkasse (-n) savings bank
das Sparkonto (Sparkonten) savings account (12)
der Sparpreis (-e) discount price (10)
das Sparschweinchen (-) piggy bank
der Spartopf (¨e) cookie jar for savings
der Spaß fun; **Spaß machen** to joke; **Das macht mir Spaß.** That's fun. I enjoy that. (1). **Viel Spaß!** Have fun! (1)
spät late (4)
spätestens at the latest (12)
spazieren to go for a walk, stroll
spazieren führen (führt spazieren) to take for a walk
spazieren gehen (geht spazieren), ging spazieren, ist spazieren gegangen to go for a walk
der Spaziergang (¨e) walk, stroll
der Speck bacon
der Speditionskaufmann (Speditionskaufleute) / die Speditionskauffrau (-en) forwarding agent
speichern to store
die Speise (-n) meal
die Speiseauswahl (-en) food selection
die Speisekarte (-n) menu (6)
speisen to eat; to dine
der Speisewagen (-) dining car
die Speisung (-en) food distribution
spektakulär spectacular
die Spekulation (-en) speculation
spekulieren to speculate; to gamble
die Spende (-n) donation, contribution
spenden to donate
das Spendenkonto (Spendenkonten) account for donations
der Spender (-) / die Spenderin (-nen) donor
die Spezialausrüstung (-en) special clothing
das Spezialgericht (-e) (*food*) specialty

sich spezialisieren auf (+ *acc.*) to specialize in
die Spezialität (-en) specialty
spezifisch specific
der Spiegel (-) mirror
das Spiegelei (-er) fried egg (6)
das Spiel (-e) play; game
die Spielecke (-n) play corner
spielen to play (1); **Computerspiele spielen** to play computer games (1); **Karten spielen** to play cards (1)
spielend (*adv.*) without effort, easily
der Spieler (-) / die Spielerin (-nen) player
der Spielfilm (-e) feature film (13)
der Spielplatz (¨-e) playground
das Spielzeug (-e) toy, toys
der Spinat spinach
die Spinne (-n) spider
der Spiritus (-se) spirit, alcohol
die Spitze (-n) tip; (pointed) top
das Spitzenprodukt (-e) top product
spontan spontaneous
der Sport sports (7)
Sport treiben, trieb, getrieben to engage in sports (7)
die Sportanlage (-n) sports grounds
die Sportart (-en) type of sport
der Sportartikel (-) sports equipment
die Sportbekleidung (-en) sporting clothes
das Sportcamp (-s) sports camp
die Sporthalle (-n) gymnasium (7)
das Sporthemd (-en) sportshirt
der Sportlehrer (-) / die Sportlehrerin (-nen) gym teacher
sportlich athletic; casual; **sportlich aktiv** active in sports (10)
die Sportnachrichten (*pl.*) sports news
der Sportplatz (¨-e) athletic field, stadium (7)
die Sportschau (-s) sports show
der Sportschuh (-e) athletic shoe
die Sportsendung (-en) sports program
das Sporttreiben playing sports
der Sportwagen (-) sports car
das Sportzentrum (Sportzentren) athletic center
die Sprache (-n) language; **die Fremdsprache** foreign language
der Sprachkurs (-e) language course
das Sprachlabor (-s) language lab
sprechen (spricht), sprach, gesprochen to speak (2)
der Sprecher (-) / die Sprecherin (-nen) speaker
die Sprechstunde (-n) office hour (8)
der Springbrunnen (-) fountain
springen, sprang, ist gesprungen to jump
spritzen to spray
der Spruch (¨-e) saying; message
der Sprudel (-) carbonated water, soft drink
die Spülmaschine (-n) dishwasher (12)
das Squash squash (game)
der Staat (-en) state, nation
staatlich by the government
der Staatsbesuch (-e) state visit
das Staatsexamen (-) state examination
die Staatsgewalt (-en) government power
die Staatskontrolle (-n) government control
die Staatsprüfung (-en) examination administered by a national board
stabil stable; solid
der Stacheldraht barbed wire
das Stadion (Stadien) stadium (7)
die Stadt (¨-e) city; town (E)
das Stadtarchiv (-e) city archives
das Stadtbad (¨-er) municipal bath
der Stadtbewohner (-) / die Stadtbewohnerin (-nen) city dweller
das Stadtbild (-er) urban picture
das Städtchen (-) little town
stadteinwärts toward the center of town
die Stadtführung (-en) city tour
der Stadtgraben (-) town moat
das Stadtkino (-s) city movie theater
das Stadtklima urban climate
das Stadtleben (-) city life
die Stadtmitte (-n) town center
der Stadtpark (-s) city park
der Stadtplan (¨-e) city street map
die Stadtplanung urban planning
der Stadtrand (¨-er) edge of town
der Stadtrundgang (¨-e) city tour
der Stadtteil (-e) city district
das Stadttheater (-) municipal theater
das Stadttor (-e) city gate
der Stadtumbau (-ten) town reconstruction
die Stadtverwaltung (-en) city administration
der Stadtwall (¨-e) town wall
das Stadtzentrum (Stadtzentren) town center
stagnieren to stagnate
der Stamm (¨-e) stem
der Stammbaum (¨-e) family tree
stammen aus (+ *dat.*) to come from; to originate
der Stammgast (¨-e) regular guest
der Stammtisch (-e) permanently reserved table
das Standesamt (¨-er) hall of records
ständig always; permanent
der Standort (-e) position
die Standuhr (-en) grandfather clock
der Star (-s) (film, etc.) star
stark strong (10)
starr rigid
starren to stare
der Start (-s) start
starten to start
die Starthilfe (-n) starting assistance
der Startpunkt (-e) starting point
die Statistik (-en) statistics
statistisch statistical(ly)
(an)statt (+ *gen.*) instead of
stattdessen instead of (that)
stattfinden (findet statt), fand statt, stattgefunden to take place
der Stau (-s) traffic jam
der Staubsauger (-) vacuum cleaner (13)
staunen to be amazed
der Stausee (-n) artificially created lake behind a dam
das Steak (-s) steak (5)
stecken to put into; to put (*inside*); to be (*inside*) (6); **seine Hände in die Hosentasche stecken** to put one's hands in one's pocket
stecken bleiben (bleibt stecken), blieb stecken, ist stecken geblieben to be stuck
stehen, stand, gestanden to stand (5); to look good; **Das steht dir gut.** That looks good on you. (5); **(im Text) stehen** to say (in the text)
stehen bleiben (bleibt stehen), blieb stehen, ist stehen geblieben to stop (running)
die Stehlampe (-n) floor lamp
stehlen (stiehlt), stahl, gestohlen to steal
der Stehplatz (¨-e) standing room
die Steiermark *one of the Austrian states*
steigen, stieg, ist gestiegen to climb, go up, rise
steigend increasing
steigern to increase
der Stein (-e) stone
die Steinzeit Stone Age
die Stelle (-n) place, position (11); **an seiner Stelle** in his place; **auf der Stelle** right away, immediately; on the spot; **an erster Stelle** in first place; **eine feste Stelle** permanent position
stellen to place, put (upright) (6); **eine Frage stellen** to ask a question
das Stellenangebot (-e) job offer (11)
die Stellenanzeige (-n) want ad
der Stellenmarkt (¨-e) job market
die Stellensuche job search
die Stellung (-en) position; **Stellung nehmen zu** (+ *dat.*) to state one's opinion on
die Steppdecke (-n) comforter
sterben (stirbt), starb, ist gestorben to die
die Stereoanlage (-n) stereo system (2)

die Sterilisation (-en) sterilization
sterilisieren to sterilize
der Stern (-e) star
stetig regularly
das Steuer (-) steering wheel
die Steuer (-n) tax (14)
die Steuerberatung (-en) tax consultant
die Steuereinnahme (-n) tax revenue
die Steueroase (-n) tax-free country
das Stichwort (⸚er) key word, cue
sticken to embroider
der Stiefel (-) boot (5)
der Stil (-e) style
die Stimme (-n) voice; vote
stimmen to be correct; **(Das) stimmt.** That's correct.
stinken, stank, gestunken to smell bad
das Stipendium (Stipendien) scholarship
der Stock floor, story (9); **im ersten Stock** on the second floor
stockaufwärts up to the next floor
das Stockwerk (-e) = Stock (9)
der Stoff (-e) fabric
der Stoffbezug (⸚e) fabric cover
stöhnen to moan, sigh
der Stollen (-) (type of) fruit cake
stolpern, ist gestolpert to stumble
stolz proud; **stolz sein auf** (+ *acc.*) to be proud of
stören to bother, disturb
stoßen (stößt), stieß, gestoßen to push
der Strand (⸚e) beach (9)
die Straße (-n) street (E); **die Straße entlang** along the street; **auf der Straße** in the street
die Straßenbahn (-en) streetcar
der Straßenverkehr street traffic
die Strategie (-n) strategy
die Strecke (-n) stretch of the road; route
(sich) strecken to stretch (8)
streckenlang for stretches on end
der Streifen (-) strip
das Streifendesign (-s) stripe pattern
streiken to go on strike
streng strict (14)
der Stress stress (8)
der Stressfaktor (-en) stress factor
stressfrei stress-free
stricken to knit
die Strickwaren (*pl.*) knitwear
der Strohhut (⸚e) straw hat
der Strom electricity (12); **Es regnet in Strömen.** It is pouring rain.
der Stromverbrauch electricity consumption
der Strumpf (⸚e) stocking (5)
die Strumpfboutique (-n) hosiery store
das Stübchen (-) / das Stuberl (-n) small room (*used in restaurant names*)
die Stube (-n) room
das Stück (-e) piece; (theater) play (4); **pro Stück** each, per piece
der Student (-en *masc.***) / die Studentin (-nen)** student (1)
das Studentenabonnement (-s) student subscription
der Studentenalltag (-e) student's daily routine
das Studentenbudget (-s) student budget
das Studentenheim (-e) dormitory
die Studentenkneipe (-n) student pub
das Studentenleben (-) student life
das Studentenwohnheim (-e) dormitory (2)
die Studentenzeitung (-en) student newspaper
das Studentenzimmer (-) student's room
der Studienabgänger (-) graduate
die Studienbedingung (-en) university requirement
die Studiendauer length of study program
das Studienfach (⸚er) academic subject
die Studiengebühren (*pl.*) study fees, tuition (12)
das Studienjahr (-e) academic year
der Studienplatz (⸚e) place at a university
die Studienreise (-n) study trip
studieren to study (a subject at a university) (1)
das Studio (-s) studio
das Studium (Studien) course of studies
der Stuhl (⸚e) chair (2)
die Stunde (-n) hour (4)
stundenlang for hours
der Stundenplan (⸚e) hourly class schedule
stur stubborn, obstinate
das Substantiv (-e) noun
die Substanz (-en) substance
die Suche search; **auf der Suche nach** searching for
suchen to look for (2)
(das) Südamerika South America
süddeutsch southern German
(das) Süddeutschland southern Germany
der Süden south; **im Süden** (in the) south
südlich von (+ *dat.*) to the south of
die Südseite (-n) south side
südwestlich (*adj.*) southwest
der Südwesten southwest
die Summe (-n) sum, amount
die Superlativform (-en) superlative form
der Supermarkt (⸚e) supermarket (5)
die Supermarktanzeige (-n) supermarket ad
die Suppe (-n) soup (6)
das Surfbrett (-er) surfboard
surfen to surf
süß sweet; **etwas Süßes** something sweet
die Süßigkeiten (*pl.*) sweets
die Süßwaren (*pl.*) sweets
das Sweatshirt (-s) sweatshirt
(das) Sylt *German island in the North Sea*
das Symbol (-e) symbol
sympathisch likable, pleasant, nice (1)
das Symptom (-e) symptom
synkron synchronous(ly)
die Synthetik (-en) synthetic material
die Szene (-n) scene

T

der Tabak tobacco
die Tabakpflanze (-n) tobacco plant
der Tabaksamen (-) tobacco seed
tabellarisch in tabular form
die Tabelle (-n) table; index
das Tablett (-s) tray
die Tablette (-n) pill
die Tafel (-n) chalkboard; **die Tafel Schokolade** chocolate bar
der Tag (-e) day (2); **guten Tag** hello, good day (E); **eines Tages** one of these days; **jeden Tag** every day (7)
das Tagebuch (⸚er) diary; **Tagebuch führen** to keep a diary
die Tagebucheintragung (-en) diary entry
der Tagesablauf daily routine
die Tageshälfte (-n) half of the day
die Tageshöchsttemperatur (-en) maximum temperature during the day
das Tagesprogramm (-e) daily program
die Tagesschau *German television news program* (13)
die Tagestemperatur (-en) temperature during the day
die Tageszeit (-en) time of day
die Tageszeitung (-en) daily newspaper
täglich daily (6)
tagsüber during the day
das Tagungshotel (-s) convention hotel
das Talent (-e) talent
der Taler (-) old German coin
die Talkshow (-s) talk show
tanken to get gasoline
die Tankstelle (-n) gas station (9)
die Tante (-n) aunt (3)
der Tanz (⸚e) dance (1)

das Tanzen dancing; **jemanden zum Tanzen auffordern** to ask someone to dance
tanzen to dance (1)
die Tasche (-n) bag, handbag (5); pocket
das Taschenbuch (¨er) paperback book
das Taschengeld allowance
die Taschenuhr (-en) pocket watch
die Tasse (-n) cup (4); **eine Tasse Kaffee** a cup of coffee (4)
tätig sein to be active; to work
die Tätigkeit (-en) activity; occupation (11)
der Tätigkeitsbereich (-e) field of activity
die Tatsache (-n) fact
tatsächlich in fact; actual
die Taube (-n) pigeon
tauchen to dive (7)
die Taucherausrüstung (-en) diving equipment
taumeln, ist getaumelt to sway, stagger
tauschen to exchange; to swap
tausend thousand (E)
tausendste thousandth (3)
das Taxi (-s) taxicab (10)
der Taxifahrer (-) / die Taxifahrerin (-nen) taxi driver (10)
das Team (-s) team
die Technik technical engineering; technology (11)
der Technikberater (-) / die Technikberaterin (-nen) technical advisor
technisch technical; mechanical
das/der Techno techno
der Teddy = Teddybär
der Teddybär (-en *masc.***)** teddy bear
der Tee tea (5)
der Teener (-) teenager
die Teigwaren (*pl.*) pasta
(sich) teilen to share; to divide
teilhaben (hat teil), hatte teil, teilgehabt to have a share in
teilnehmen (an + *dat.***) (nimmt teil), nahm teil, teilgenommen** to participate (14)
der Teilnehmer (-) / die Teilnehmerin (-nen) participant
die Teilung (-en) division
teilweise partly
das Telefaxgerät (-e) fax machine
das Telefon (-e) telephone (2)
der Telefonanruf (-e) telephone call (9)
das Telefonbuch (¨er) telephone directory
das Telefongespräch (-e) telephone call, conversation
telefonieren to telephone
telefonisch over the telephone
die Telefonkarte (-n) telephone card (*for use in public telephones instead of coins*)
die Telefonnummer (-n) telephone number (E); **Wie ist Ihre Telefonnummer?** What is your telephone number?
die Telefonrechnung (-en) telephone bill
das Telegramm (-e) telegram
der Teller (-) plate (6)
das Temperament (-e) temperament
die Temperatur (-en) temperature (7)
das Tempo (-s) speed
das Tempolimit (-s) speed limit
(das) Tennis tennis (7); **Tennis spielen** to play tennis (7); **(das) Tennisspielen** playing tennis (7)
die Tennisanlage (-n) tennis courts (7)
der Tennisplatz (¨e) tennis court (7)
der Tennisschuh (-e) tennis shoe (5)
die Tennissocke (-n) tennis sock
das Tennistraining tennis practice
der Teppich (-e) carpet, rug (2)
der Teppichboden (¨) wall-to-wall carpet (12)
der Termin (-e) appointment (8)
die Terrakotta (Terrakotten) terracotta
die Terrasse (-n) terrace (2)
der Terror terror
der Terrorismus terrorism
der Terrorist (-en *masc.***) / die Terroristin (-nen)** terrorist
das Testergebnis (-se) test result
teuer expensive (2)
teuflisch devilish
der Text (-e) text
der Textausschnitt (-e) (text) excerpt
das Theater (-) theater (4); **ins Theater gehen** to go to the theater (4)
die Theaterkarte (-n) theater ticket
das Theaterstück (-e) play (4)
das Thema (Themen) theme; topic
die Theorie (-n) theory
das Thermalbad (¨er) thermal bath
der Thermalbrunnen (-) thermal spring
die Thermalkur (-en) thermal cure
das Thermometer (-) thermometer
der Thunfisch (-e) tuna fish
(das) Thüringen *one of the German states*
der Tick (-s) tic, twitching
das Ticket (-s) ticket (10)
tief low; deep; **tief schlafen** to be in a deep sleep
die Tiefgarage (-n) underground garage
tiefgekühlt frozen
das Tier (-e) animal (12)
der Tierarzt (¨e) / die Tierärztin (-nen) veterinarian
der Tiger (-) tiger
der Tipp (-s) hint, piece of advice
tippen to type
der Tiroler Hut Tyrolean hat
der Tisch (-e) table (2); **den Tisch decken** to set the table
das Tischchen (-) little table
die Tischreservierung (-en) table reservation
(das) Tischtennis table tennis
die Tischwäsche table linen
der Titel (-) title
der Toast (-e) toast
die Tochter (¨) daughter (3)
der Tod death
tödlich deathly; to death
die Toilette (-n) toilet (9)
der Toilettenartikel (*pl.*) toiletries
das Toilettenpapier toilet paper (5)
die Toilettensachen (*pl.*) toiletries
toll (*coll.*) great
die Tomate (-n) tomato (6)
der Ton (¨e) sound
die Tonne (-n) ton
das Tor (-e) gate; (*soccer*) goal
der Tornister (-) field pack
die Torte (-n) torte, pie, cake
tot dead
total total(ly)
die Tour (-en) tour
das Tourenprogramm (-e) tour program
der Tourismus tourism
der Tourist (-en *masc.***) / die Touristin (-nen)** tourist
die Touristeninformation (-en) tourist information
das Tourrad (¨er) touring bike
die Tracht (-en) traditional costume
die Tradition (-en) tradition
traditionell traditional
traditionsgemäß traditionally
tragen (trägt), trug, getragen to wear; to carry (5); **die Verantwortung tragen** to be responsible
die Tragik tragedy
die Tragödie (-n) tragedy (4)
trainieren to train; to practice
das Training training, practice
der Trainingsanzug (¨e) jogging suit
trampen, ist getrampt to hitchhike
die Transportbranche (-n) transportation business
das Transportmittel (-) means of transportation
der Transportweg (-e) transport road
trauen to trust
der Traum (¨e) dream
träumen (von + *dat.***)** to dream (of)
traumhaft: traumhaft schön unbelievably beautiful
traurig sad (1)
die Traurigkeit sadness
(sich) treffen (mit + *dat.***) (trifft), traf, getroffen** to meet (8)
der Treffpunkt (-e) meeting place

treiben, trieb, getrieben: Sport treiben to engage in sports (7); **Schwarzhandel treiben** to trade on the black market
trennbar separable
sich trennen to separate (14)
die Trennung (-en) separation
die Treppe (-n) staircase (12)
das Treppenhaus (¨er) stairwell
treten (tritt), trat, ist getreten to step (on)
die Tretmühle (-n) daily grind
treu loyal, faithful (1)
der Trimm-Pfad (-e) par course, jogging path (7)
sich trimmen to exercise in order to lose weight
trinken, trank, getrunken to drink (2)
die Trinkkur (-en) mineral-water drinking cure
trocken dry
die Trompete (-n) trumpet
trompeten to play the trumpet
der Tropfen (-) drop
trotz (+ *gen.*) in spite of (9)
trotzdem nevertheless
die Trümmer (*pl.*) rubble, ruins
die Truppen (*pl.*) troops
der Truthahn (¨e) turkey (5)
das Truthahnschnitzel (-) turkey cutlet
(das) Tschechien Czechia (E)
(das) Tschernobyl Chernobyl
Tschüs (*coll.*) so long (E)
das T-Shirt (-s) T-shirt (5)
das Tuch (¨er) scarf; piece of cloth
die Tüchtigkeit efficiency
der/die Tumorkranke (*decl. adj.*) person suffering from a tumor
tun, tat, getan to do, make (8); **Was tun?** What can be done?; **viel zu tun haben** to be busy; **weh tun** (*dat.*) **(tut weh)** to hurt (8); **Tut mir Leid.** I am sorry.
der Tuner (-) (radio) tuner
der Tunnel (-) tunnel
die Tür (-en) door (2); **die Türen knallen** to slam the doors
der Türke (-n *masc.*) **/ die Türkin (-nen)** Turk, Turkish person
die Türkei Turkey
türkisch Turkish
der Turm (¨e) tower
turnen to do gymnastics (7)
die Turnhalle (-n) gymnasium (7)
die Turnschuhe (*pl.*) gym shoes; sneakers
der Typ (-en) type
typisch typical

U

die U-Bahn (-en) subway
die U-Bahnstation (-en) subway station
übel nauseated; **Mir ist übel.** I feel nauseated.
üben to practice
über (+ *acc./dat.*) over, above (6); about
überall everywhere
überarbeitet overhauled; overworked
überblicken to overlook, have a good view of
die Überdachung (-en) roof cover
übereinander one on top of the other
überfliegen, überflog, überflogen to quickly read, skim (13)
überfordert asked too much; overtaxed
überfüllt overcrowded
überglücklich overjoyed
überhaupt at all; **überhaupt nicht** not at all
überheblich arrogant
überholen to pass (a vehicle)
überlassen (überlässt), überließ, überlassen to leave to
sich (*dat.*) **etwas überlegen** to think about something; **Ich will es mir überlegen.** I want to think about it.
die Überlegung (-en) consideration
der Übermut exuberance
übernachten to stay overnight (10)
die Übernachtung (-en) overnight stay (9)
die Übernachtungskosten (*pl.*) lodging expenses
übernehmen (übernimmt), übernahm, übernommen to take over
überprüfen to double-check
überqueren to cross (a street)
überraschen to surprise
überreden to talk into, persuade
die Überredungskunst (¨e) persuasiveness, ability to persuade
überregional national (for a newspaper)
überschwemmt flooded
der Übersetzer (-) / die Übersetzerin (-nen) translator, interpreter
übertragen (überträgt), übertrug, übertragen to transfer
die Übertragung (-en) (live) show; broadcast
übertreiben, übertrieb, übertrieben to exaggerate
übertrieben exaggerated (14)
übertrumpfen to outdo
überwiegend predominant(ly)
überzeugen to convince
das Übliche (*decl. adj.*) the usual (thing)
übrig left over (12)
übrigens by the way, furthermore (9)
die Übung (-en) exercise
das Ufer (-) bank (of a body of water)
das Ufo (-s) UFO (flying saucer)
die Uhr (-en) clock, watch (2); **Wie viel Uhr ist es?** What time is it? (4); **Die Uhr geht nicht.** The clock isn't working.
der Uhrmacher (-) / die Uhrmacherin (-nen) watchmaker
die Uhrzeit (-en) time of day (4)
die Ukraine Ukraine
ultramodern extremely modern
um (+ *acc.*) around; about (3); at; **um sieben Uhr** at seven o'clock (4); **um wie viel Uhr?** at what time (4); **um . . . herum** all around; **um . . . zu** in order to
umarmen to embrace, hug
der Umfang size
umfassen to include, consist of
die Umfrage (-n) poll, survey
umgebaut remodeled
die Umgebung (-en) surroundings, vicinity (12); **nähere Umgebung** close vicinity
umgehen mit (geht um), ging um, ist umgegangen to deal with, treat (11)
umgekehrt the other way around
umgestalten (gestaltet um) to remodel
das Umland (¨er) surrounding countryside
der Umlaut (-e) mark indicating change of vowel sound
die Umleitung (-en) detour
ums = um das
umsatteln (sattelt um) to change, switch
der Umsatz (¨e) sales, turnover
die Umsatzstatistik (-en) sales statistic(s)
die Umschulung (-en) vocational retraining
der Umstand (¨e) condition
umsteigen (steigt um), stieg um, ist umgestiegen to change (trains), transfer (10)
umstellen (stellt um) to reset
die Umwälzung (-en) upheaval
die Umwelt environment
die Umweltbelastung (-en) environmental pollution
umweltbewusst conscious of the environment
die Umweltbranche (-n) environmental business
der Umweltbus (-se) ecological bus
umweltfreundlich environmentally friendly (14)
umweltschädlich environmentally harmful, polluting
der Umweltschutz environmental protection
die Umweltverschmutzung environmental pollution (14)
umweltverträglich environmentally safe
umziehen (zieht um), zog um, ist umgezogen to move (residence)

der Umzug (¨e) move
unabhängig independent (11)
unbedingt by all means; absolutely, really (13)
unbegrenzt unlimited
unbehandelt untreated
unbekannt unknown
unbemerkt unnoticed
unbeschadet unharmed
unbestimmt uncertain
unbewohnt vacant
und and (E)
und so weiter and so on (etc.)
unentschieden: Das Spiel ist unentschieden. The game ends in a tie.
unerlaubt forbidden, not permitted
unerträglich unbearable
unerwartet unexpected
der Unfall (¨e) accident
der Unfug nonsense
(das) Ungarn Hungary (E)
ungeduldig impatient
ungefähr approximately (9)
ungeheuer immense(ly)
ungehindert unobstructed
ungemütlich uncomfortable
ungenügend insufficient
ungern (+ *verb*) to dislike . . . (2)
ungestört undisturbed(ly)
ungesund unhealthy
ungewöhnlich unusual
das Ungeziefer vermin, bugs
ungezwungen casual, relaxed
unglaublich unbelievable
das Unglück (-e) accident
unheimlich terrific
unhöflich impolite
die Uni = Universität
die Unibibliothek (-en) university library
die Uniform (-en) uniform
die Universität (-en) university, college (1)
der Universitätsprofessor (-en) / die Universitätsprofessorin (-nen) university professor
die Universitätsstadt (¨e) university town
unkompliziert uncomplicated
unkonventionell unconventional
die Unkosten (*pl.*) expenses
unkritisch uncritical (1)
unlogisch illogical
unmittelbar direct(ly)
unmöglich impossible
unnötig unnecessary
die Unordnung disorder, mess
unpersönlich impersonal
unregelmäßig irregular
die Unruhe unrest
uns us (*acc.*) (3); (*dat.*) (5)
unser our (3)
unsicher insecure
der Unsinn nonsense (14); **So ein Unsinn!** Nonsense! (14)
unteilbar indivisible
unten downstairs, below, at the bottom (12)
unten erwähnt mentioned below
unter (+ *acc./dat.*) under, below; among, between (6); **unter anderem** among other things; **unter uns** between (the two of) us
unterbrechen (unterbricht), unterbrach, unterbrochen to interrupt
die Unterbrechung (-en) interruption
unterernährt malnourished
untergehen (geht unter), ging unter, ist untergegangen to go down; (*sun*) to set
die Untergrundbahn (-en) subway
der Unterhalt upkeep, support
(sich) unterhalten (unterhält), unterhielt, unterhalten to have a conversation; to entertain
unterhaltsam entertaining (13)
die Unterhaltung (-en) conversation; entertainment
die Unterkunft (¨e) accommodation (9)
die Unterkunftsmöglichkeit (-en) accommodations
die Unterlagen (*pl.*) documents (11)
die Untermiete sublet (11); **zur Untermiete wohnen** to rent a room
das Unternehmen (-) business, enterprise
unternehmen (unternimmt), unternahm, unternommen to undertake (10); **eine Reise unternehmen** to take a trip
die Unternehmensberatung business consultant
das Unterrichtsfach (¨er) subject of instruction
der Unterrichtstag (-e) day of school
unterschätzen to underestimate
der Unterschied (-e) difference
unterschreiben, unterschrieb, unterschrieben to sign
die Unterschrift (-en) signature (9)
unterstreichen, unterstrich, unterstrichen to underline
unterstützen to support (14)
untersuchen to examine
untertags during the day
der Untertitel (-) subtitle
die Unterwäsche (*pl.*) underwear
unterwegs on the road
die Unterwürfigkeit servility
unterzeichnen to sign
untrennbar inseparable
unübersehbar incalculable
unverletzt unharmed
unverschämt impertinent
unwichtig unimportant
unwohnlich not livable; uncomfortable
unzumutbar unacceptable
der Urenkel (-) / die Urenkelin (-nen) great-grandson; great-granddaughter
die Urgroßeltern (*pl.*) great-grandparents
die Urgroßmutter (¨) great-grandmother
der Urgroßvater (¨) great-grandfather
der Urlaub (-e) vacation (10); **Urlaub machen** to go on vacation (8)
das Urlaubshotel (-s) resort hotel
die Urlaubspläne (*pl.*) vacation plans
die Urlaubstipps (*pl.*) vacation advice
die Ursache (-n) cause
ursprünglich original(ly)
die USA (*pl.*) the United States; **aus den USA** from the United States
usw. = und so weiter and so on

V

der Valentinstag (-e) Valentine's Day (3)
der Vampir (-e) vampire
das Vanilleeis vanilla ice cream
die Vanillesauce (-n) vanilla sauce
der Vater (¨) father (3)
väterlicherseits on the father's side
Vati Daddy
der Vegetarier (-) / die Vegetarierin (-nen) vegetarian (*person*)
vegetarisch vegetarian (6)
(das) Venedig Venice (Italy)
die Verabredung (-en) date; appointment
verabschieden: ein Gesetz verabschieden to pass a law
verändern to change
die Veränderung (-en) change
veranstalten to put on (an event)
die Veranstaltung (-en) event
verantwortlich responsible
die Verantwortung (-en) responsibility
verarbeiten to process
das Verb (-en) verb
verbessern to correct; to improve
die Verbesserung (-en) improvement; correction
verbieten, verbot, verboten to prohibit (14); **Rauchen verboten** no smoking
verbinden, verband, verbunden to connect
die Verbindung (-en) connection
verborgen: im Verborgenen leben to live in isolation
der Verbrauch consumption
verbrauchen to consume (14)
der Verbraucher (-) /die Verbraucherin (-nen) consumer
verbreiten to spread; to disseminate (14)

verbringen, verbrachte, verbracht to spend (7); **Zeit verbringen** to spend time
verbunden connected
verdanken (+ *dat.*) to be indebted to
verdienen to earn (11); **Geld verdienen** to make money (11); **es sich** (*dat.*) **verdient haben** to deserve it
der Verdruss dissatisfaction
der Verein (-e) club
die Vereinbarung: nach Vereinbarung by appointment
vereinfachen to simplify
vereinigt united; **die Vereinigten Staaten** (*pl.*) United States
die Vereinigung (-en) unification
vereint: vereintes Europa united Europe
die Verfassung (-en) constitution
verfolgen to follow; to persecute
verfügen über (+ *acc.*) to control
Verfügung: zur Verfügung stehen to be available, be at one's disposal
die Vergangenheit past
vergehen, verging, ist vergangen to pass; **Ein Monat ist vergangen.** A month has passed. **Die Zeit vergeht wie im Flug.** Time flies by.
vergessen (vergisst), vergaß, vergessen to forget (10)
vergiften to poison
die Vergiftung (-en) poisoning
der Vergleich (-e) comparison
vergleichen, verglich, verglichen to compare (12)
das Vergnügen (-) pleasure
vergnüglich amusing
die Vergnügung (-en) amusement, entertainment
sich verhalten (verhält), verhielt, verhalten to act, behave
das Verhältnis (-se) condition; relationship, affair
sich verhaspeln to get muddled (speaking)
verheiratet married
verhindern to prevent
verhüten to prevent
das Verhütungsmittel (-) contraceptive
verkaufen to sell
der Verkäufer (-) / die Verkäuferin (-nen) salesperson (2)
das Verkaufsgebiet (-e) sales region
das Verkaufstalent (-e) salesmanship
das Verkaufstraining sales training
der Verkehr traffic
das Verkehrsamt (¨er) tourist office
die Verkehrsbelästigung (-en) traffic disturbance
der Verkehrsknotenpunkt (-e) traffic junction
die Verkehrskontrolle (-n) vehicle checkpoint
der Verkehrsminister (-) / die Verkehrsministerin (-nen) transportation minister
das Verkehrsmittel (-) vehicle, means of transportation (14)
die Verkehrsplanung traffic planning
verkehrsreich heavily traveled (*street*)
das Verkehrsschild (-er) traffic sign
das Verkehrssystem (-e) traffic system
das Verkehrswesen (-) transportation system
verkehrt the other way around; **Kaffee verkehrt** more milk than coffee
verkleidet dressed up
das Verknoten wringing (of hands)
verkraften to handle, cope with
verkrüppelt crippled
die Verkündigung (-en) announcement
verkürzen to shorten
der Verlag (-e) publishing house
verlangen to demand
verlängern to lengthen
verlassen (verlässt), verließ, verlassen to leave
verlässlich reliable
verlegen to relocate
der Verleger (-) / die Verlegerin (-nen) publisher
die Verlegung (-en) relocation
verleihen: Farbe verleihen to give color
sich verletzen to injure oneself (8)
die Verletzung (-en) violation; injury (14)
sich verlieben in (+ *acc.*) to fall in love with
verlieren, verlor, verloren to lose
sich verloben (mit + *dat.*) to get engaged (to)
verlogen sein to be full of lies
der Verlust (-e) loss
sich vermehren to multiply
vermeiden, vermied, vermieden to avoid (14)
vermieten to rent (out) (12); **zu vermieten** for rent
der Vermieter (-) / die Vermieterin (-nen) landlord, landlady
vermindern to decrease, lessen (14)
vermitteln to arrange; to mediate
das Vermögen (-) capital
vermuten to assume
vernichten to destroy
die Vernunft: bar jeder Vernunft totally senseless
verordnen to prescribe
die Verpackung (-en) packaging, wrapping (14)
die Verpackungsflut (-en) excess use of packaging
die Verpackungsindustrie (-n) packaging industry
sich verpflichten to commit oneself; **Adel verpflichtet** nobility has a responsibility, noblesse oblige
verraten (verrät), verriet, verraten to betray
verräterisch treacherous
verreisen, ist verreist to go on a trip; **verreist sein** to be on a trip
verringern to reduce
verrückt crazy, mad (8)
der Versandkatalog (-e) mail-order catalogue
versäumen to miss
verschaffen: (sich) Gehör verschaffen to make (oneself) heard
verschieden different
verschliessen, verschloss, verschlossen to lock up
verschmutzen to pollute
die Verschmutzung (-en) pollution
verschoben (*adj.*) postponed
verschreiben, verschrieb, verschrieben to prescribe (8)
verschrotten to scrap
verschuldet in debt
verschwenden to waste
das Versehen (-) mishap; **aus Versehen** by accident
die Versicherung (-en) insurance (12)
der Versicherungsfachmann (¨er) / die Versicherungsfachfrau (-en) insurance expert
der Versicherungskaufmann (Versicherungskaufleute) / die Versicherungskauffrau (-en) insurance sales agent
die Version (-en) version
versorgen to supply (with)
verspätet delayed
die Verspätung (-en) delay
versprechen (verspricht), versprach, versprochen to promise
versprühen to spray around
der Verstand reason
verständlich understandable; understandably
das Verständnis (-se) understanding
verstehen, verstand, verstanden to understand (E); **sich verstehen mit** to get along with
versteigern to auction off
verstopfen to clog up
verstoßen: gegen das Gesetz verstoßen to do something illegal
versuchen to try (8)
verteidigen to defend
verteilen to distribute
vertonen to set to music

der Vertrag (¨e) contract; lease; **einen Vertrag schließen** to sign a contract
vertrauensvoll trusting
der Vertreter (-) / die Vertreterin (-nen) sales representative
der/die Vertriebene (*decl. adj.*) refugee
der Vertriebsrepräsentant (-en *masc.*) **/ die Vertriebsrepräsentantin (-nen)** marketing representative
verunsichert insecure
verursachen to cause
vervollkommnen to make perfect
vervollständigen to complete
die Verwaltung (-en) administration
der Verwaltungsweg (-e) administrative route
das Verwaltungszentrum (Verwaltungszentren) administrative center
die Verwandlung (-en) transformation
verwandt related
der/die Verwandte (*decl. adj.*) relative
die Verwechslung (-en) mistake, confusion
verwenden to use (14)
verwirklichen to make real
verwirrt confused
der/die Verwundete (*decl. adj.*) injured person
verzehren to consume
verzeichnet sein to be marked/listed
das Verzeichnis (-se) list, index
verzichten (auf + *acc.*) to do without (13)
verziert decorated
der Vetter (-n) male cousin (3)
das Video (-s) video(tape) (2)
das Videogerät (-e) VCR
die Videokamera (-s) video camera
der Videorecorder (-) video recorder (2)
das Videospiel (-e) video game
das Vieh cattle; animals
viel (mehr, meist-) much (1); **Viel Glück!** Much luck! (1); **Vielen Dank!** Many thanks! (6); **Viel Spaß!** Have fun! (1)
viele (*pl.*) many (1); **wie viele** how many
die Vielfalt diversity
vielleicht perhaps (2)
vielmehr rather
vier four (E); **zu viert** with four people
das Viermächteabkommen (-) four-power pact
viermal four times
viertägig (*adj.*) four-day (10)
vierte fourth (3)
das Viertel (-) quarter (12); **Es ist Viertel nach/vor zwei.** It is a quarter after/to two. (4)
vierzehn fourteen (E)
vierzig forty (E)
die Villa (Villen) villa
vis-à-vis across from
das Visum (Visen) visa
das Vitamin (-e) vitamin
die Vitamintablette (-n) vitamin pill
der Vogel (¨) bird
der Vogelkäfig (-e) bird cage
der Vogelschutz bird preservation
das Vöglein (-) little bird
die Vokabeln (*pl.*) vocabulary
die Vokabelsuche vocabulary search
die Vokabelübung (-en) vocabulary exercise
die Vokaländerung (-en) vowel change
das Volk (¨er) nation; people
der Volksaufstand (¨e) people's revolt
das Volksfest (-e) public festival; fair
die Volksfeststimmung (-en) party mood
das Volkslied (-er) folk song
die Volksschule elementary school
der Volkssport national sport
die Volkswirtschaft economics
voll full; crowded (6); **in voller Uniform** dressed in full uniform
vollenden to achieve, complete
völlig total(ly)
das Vollkornbrot (-e) whole-grain bread
die Vollkornnudeln (*pl.*) whole-grain pasta
die Vollmilch whole milk
die Vollpension accommodation and three meals per day included
vollständig complete
voll tanken (tankt voll) to get gasoline, fill up
vollwert full nutritional value
vom = von dem
von (+ *dat.*) from; by (5); of; out of; **von . . . bis** from . . . to (6)
vor (+ *acc./dat.*) before (4); in front of; ago (6); **vor allem** above all; **vor kurzem** recently; **vor sich hin** to oneself; **vor Florida** off the coast of Florida; **fünf vor zwei** five to/of two (4); **vor zwei Tagen** two days ago (6)
vorankommen (kommt voran), kam voran, ist vorangekommen to get ahead
die Voraufführung (-en) preview performance
voraus; im voraus in advance; **voraus sein** to be ahead
die Voraussetzung (-en) prerequisite
vorbei past, gone, over (9); **vorbei sein** to be gone
vorbeifahren (fährt vorbei), fuhr vorbei, ist vorbeigefahren to drive past
vorbeigehen (geht vorbei), ging vorbei, ist vorbeigegangen to pass by
vorbeikommen (kommt vorbei), kam vorbei, ist vorbeigekommen to drop in, come by (4)
vorbeimarschieren (marschiert vorbei) to march past
vorbereiten (bereitet vor) to prepare (11)
die Vorderseite (-n) front side
der Vorfall (¨e) incident
vorgebeugt bent forward
vorgestern day before yesterday
vorhaben (hat vor) to plan, have plans (4)
vorhanden sein to exist
vorher before that; before
die Vorhersage (-n) forecast
vorig previous, last
vorkommen (kommt vor), kam vor, ist vorgekommen to occur
die Vorlesung (-en) (university) lecture
vorletzt-: die vorletzte Woche week before last
vorliegend at hand
der Vormittag (-e) morning; **morgen Vormittag** tomorrow morning (4); **heute Vormittag** today before noon (4); **Samstagvormittag** Saturday before noon (4)
vormittags in the morning(s) (4)
vorn in the front; **nach vorne** toward the front
der Vorname (-ns, -n) first, given name (1)
vorne in front (6); **ganz vorne** way in front
vornehmen (nimmt vor), nahm vor, vorgenommen to plan, carry out
der Vorort (-e) suburb
der Vorortszug (¨e) commuter train
der Vorraum (¨e) front hall
der Vorsatz (¨e) resolution
die Vorschau (-en) preview
der Vorschlag (¨e) suggestion
vorschlagen (schlägt vor), schlug vor, vorgeschlagen to suggest (10)
vorsetzen (setzt vor) to place in front
vorsichtig careful, cautious
der/die Vorsitzende (*decl. adj.*) chairperson
die Vorspeise (-n) appetizer (6)
die Vorstadt (¨e) suburb
sich (*dat.*) **etwas vorstellen (stellt vor)** to imagine (11); **sich** (*acc.*) **vorstellen** to introduce oneself (11); **die Uhr vorstellen** to set the clock forward; **Stell dir vor!** Just imagine!
die Vorstellung (-en) performance; introduction; concept
das Vorstellungsgespräch (-e) job interview (11)
der Vorteil (-e) advantage
der Vorverkauf (¨e) advance sale
die Vorverkaufsstelle (-n) advance sales agency
vorwärts forward

vorwärts kommen (kommt vorwärts), kam vorwärts, ist vorwärts gekommen to get ahead
vorweisen (weist vor), wies vor, vorgewiesen to show, present
das Vorwort (-e) preface
vorziehen (zieht vor), zog vor, vorgezogen to prefer (14)
vorzüglich excellent
der VW (-s) (*automobile*) Volkswagen

W

wach werden (wird wach) to wake up
wachsen (wächst), wuchs, ist gewachsen to grow
wachsend increasing, growing
die Waffe (-n) weapon
der Waffenexport (-e) arms export
der Wagen (-) car (10)
die Wagenauffahrt (-en) driveway
der Waggon (-s) (train) car
die Wahl (-en) election
wählen to vote, elect; to choose (14)
wahlweise optional
der Wahnsinn madness
wahr true; **nicht wahr?** isn't it true?
während (+ *gen.*) during; while (9)
die Wahrheit truth
wahrscheinlich probably (11)
die Währung (-en) currency
die Währungsreform (-en) *1948 introduction of new German currency*
die Währungsunion (-en) *equalization of East- and West-German monetary systems*
der Wald (¨er) forest (7)
der Waldweg (-e) forest trail
die Walküre *opera by Richard Wagner*
der Walzer (-) waltz
die Wand (¨e) wall (2); **die vier Wände** (*fig.*) one's home
die Wanderfahrt (-en) field trip
die Wanderkarte (-n) trail map
das Wandermagazin (-e) magazine for hikers
wandern, ist gewandert to hike (1)
die Wanderreise (-n) walking tour
die Wanderschuhe (*pl.*) hiking shoes
der Wanderstock (¨e) hiking stick
die Wandertour (-en) hiking tour
die Wanderung (-en) hike; walking tour
der Wanderweg (-e) hiking trail (10)
wanken, ist gewankt to stagger, sway
wann when (1); **seit wann** since when
das Wappen (-) coat of arms
das Wappentier (-e) heraldic animal
wäre: Wie wäre es mit . . . ? How about . . . ?
die Ware (-n) goods, product
warm warm (7); heated; **schön warm** nice and warm (7); **warme Küche** hot food
die Wärme warmth
warmherzig warm-hearted
(das) Warschau Warsaw (Poland)
warten auf (+ *acc.*) to wait for (6)
warum why (1)
was what (1); **was für** what kind of (11)
das Waschbecken (-) sink
die Wäsche underwear; linens; **Wäsche waschen** to do one's laundry
die Wäschegarnitur (-en) lingerie ensemble
(sich) waschen (wäscht), wusch, gewaschen to wash (oneself) (8); **Ich wasche mir die Hände.** I am washing my hands.
der Wäschetrockner (-) clothes dryer (13)
das Wäschewaschen doing laundry
die Waschküche (-n) laundry room
die Waschmaschine (-n) washing machine
das Waschmittel (-) laundry detergent
der Waschraum (¨e) washroom
der Waschvollautomat (-en *masc.***)** washing machine
das Wasser water (5)
die Wassermusik water music
das Wasserskifahren waterskiing
die Watte absorbent cotton
das WC toilet (9)
der Wechsel (-) change
der Wechselkurs (-e) exchange rate
wechseln to change, exchange; **Geld wechseln** to exchange money
der Wecker (-) alarm clock (2)
das Weckglas (¨er) preserving jar
weg away, off
der Weg (-e) path, way; road; **nach dem Weg fragen** to ask directions (9)
wegbleiben (bleibt weg), blieb weg, ist weggeblieben to stay away
wegen (+ *gen.*) because of (9)
weggehen (geht weg), ging weg, ist weggegangen to leave
wegnehmen (nimmt weg), nahm weg, weggenommen to take away
wegwerfen (wirft weg), warf weg, weggeworfen to throw away
die Wegwerfflasche (-n) nonreturnable bottle (14)
das Wegwerfprodukt (-e) disposable product
der Wehrdienst military service
sich wehren to defend oneself
(sich *dat.***) weh tun (tut weh), tat weh, weh getan** to hurt (oneself) (8)
weiblich feminine
weich soft
der Weichkäse (-) soft (young) cheese
(das) Weihnachten Christmas (3)
der Weihnachtsbaum (¨e) Christmas tree (3)
das Weihnachtsgeschenk (-e) Christmas present
weil (*subord. conj.*) because (8)
die Weile while, span of time (11); **eine Weile lang** for a while
weilen: unter den Lebenden weilen to be alive
der Wein (-e) wine (6); **eine Flasche Wein** a bottle of wine
weinen to cry
die Weinflasche (-n) wine bottle
die Weintraube (-n) grape (5)
die Weise (-n) manner, way
weisen, wies, gewiesen to point
weiß white (5)
das Weißbier (-e) wheat beer
das Weißbierglas (¨er) *special glass used for* **Weißbier**
der Weißwein (-e) white wine
die Weißwurst (¨e) Bavarian veal sausage (6)
weit far (9); **weit von hier** far from here; **ganz schön weit** pretty far
weitaus by far
weiter further, farther; (+ *verb*) to continue to . . .
weiter bestehen (besteht weiter), bestand weiter, weiter bestanden to continue to exist
weiterentwickeln (entwickelt weiter) to develop further
weitergehen (geht weiter), ging weiter, ist weitergegangen to continue walking
weitermachen (macht weiter) to continue
welcher, welche, welches which (5)
der Wellensittich (-e) parakeet
die Welt world, earth
weltbekannt world famous
der Welthunger world hunger
die Welthungerorganisation (-en) world hunger organization
die Weltkonferenz (-en) world conference
der Weltkrieg (-e) world war
die Weltreise (-n) trip around the world
weltweit throughout the world, global
wem (to/for) whom (5)
wen whom (*acc.*) (2)
wenig little (8); **zu wenig** too little
wenige (*pl.*) few, a few
weniger less
wenigstens at least
wenn (*subord. conj.*) when; if; whenever (8)
wer who (1)
die Werbeagentur (-en) advertising agency
das Werbeplakat (-e) advertising poster
der Werbetext (-e) advertising copy
der Werbespruch (¨e) advertising slogan

die Werbung (-en) commercial (13)
werden (wird), wurde, ist geworden to become (3); **leiser werdend** becoming more and more quiet
werfen (wirft), warf, geworfen to throw
das Werk (-e) work, opus
die Werkstatt (¨-en) workshop
das Werkzeug (-e) tool
der Wert (-e) value
das Wertpapier (-e) bond, stock
die Wertvorstellung (-en) concept of values
wesentlich essential(ly)
wessen whose
(das) Westberlin West Berlin
westberliner (*adj.*) (from) West Berlin
westdeutsch (*adj.*) West German
der Westen west (9); **im Westen** (in the) west; **nach Westen** to the west
die Western Musik Western music
(das) Westfalen Westphalia
westfälisch Westphalian
die Westküste (-n) west coast
westlich western, from the west
westlich von (+ *dat.*) to the west of
die Westmächte (*pl.*) Western powers (France, Great Britain, USA)
(das) Westpommern West Pomerania (*former German province*)
die Westzone (-n) western zone (*parts of Germany that later became the Federal Republic*)
der Wettbewerb (-e) contest
wetten to bet
das Wetter weather (7)
der Wetterbericht (-e) weather report (7)
der Wetterdienst weather service
der Wetterexperte (-n *masc.***) / die Wetterexpertin (-nen)** weather expert
der Wetterhahn (¨-e) weathercock
die Wetterlage (-n) weather condition
die Wettervorhersage (-n) weather forecast
Whg. = Wohnung
wichtig important (3)
wie how (1); **Wie geht's?** How are you? (*inform.*) (E); **Wie geht es dir?** How are you? (*inform.*) (E); **Wie geht es Ihnen?** How are you? (E); **Wie bitte?** How's that, please? (E); **wie lange** how long (1); **wie viel** how much (1), **wie viele** how many (1); **Wie viel Uhr ist es?; Wie spät ist es?** What time is it? (4) **wie wäre es mit . . .** how about . . . (10)
wieder again; back; **schon wieder** yet again (*emphatic*) (2)
der Wiederaufbau reconstruction
wieder aufbauen (baut wieder auf) to rebuild
wieder finden (findet wieder), fand wieder, wieder gefunden to find again, rediscover
wieder hochkommen (kommt wieder hoch), kam wieder hoch, ist wieder hochgekommen to come back up
wiederholen to repeat; to review (E)
die Wiederholung (-en) review; **zur Wiederholung** as a review
Wiederhören: auf Wiederhören good-bye (*only on the phone*) (9)
wiederkommen (kommt wieder), kam wieder, ist wiedergekommen to come back
Wiedersehen: auf Wiedersehen good-bye (E)
wiederum again
wieder verwenden (verwendet wieder) to reuse
wieder verwerten (verwertet wieder) to recycle
(das) Wien Vienna
das Wiener Schnitzel (-) veal cutlet (6)
die Wiese (-n) meadow
wieso why
wildfremd: wildfremde Leute total strangers
das Wildgehege (-) game preserve
wild lebend wild, free
der Wildwestfilm (-e) Western (movie)
willkommen (*adj.*) welcome (E); **herzlich willkommen** welcome (E)
der Wind (-e) wind (7)
die Windenergie wind energy
windig windy (7)
das Windsurfen windsurfing
(das) Windsurfing machen to do windsurfing (7)
der Winter (-) winter (7)
der Wintermantel (¨) winter coat
wir we (1)
wirken to have an effect
wirklich really (1)
die Wirklichkeit reality; **in Wirklichkeit** in fact, actually
die Wirkung (-en) effect
die Wirtschaft economy (13)
wirtschaftlich economic
die Wirtschaftswissenschaft (-en) economics
das Wirtschaftswunder (-) economic miracle
die Wirtschaftszeitung (-en) business magazine
das Wirtshaus (¨-er) eating place, inn
das Wissen knowledge
wissen (weiß), wusste, gewusst to know (a fact) (3); **Ich weiß es nicht.** I don't know. (E)
die Wissenschaft (-en) science
der Wissenschaftler (-) / die Wissenschaftlerin (-nen) scientist
wissenschaftlich scientific(ally), scholarly
die Witterung (-en) weather
der Witterungshinweis (-e) weather advisory
die Witwe (-n) widow
der Witz (-e) joke
wo where (1)
woanders elsewhere
wobei whereby
die Woche (-n) week (7); **einmal die Woche** once a week (7)
das Wochenende (-n) weekend (7); **am Wochenende** on the weekend
wochenlang for weeks
der Wochentag (-e) day of the week (3)
die Wochenzeitung (-en) weekly newspaper
wodurch through what; by what
wofür for what; why
wogegen against what
woher from where (1); **Woher sind Sie?** Where are you from?
wohin where (to) (5); **Wohin gehst du?** Where are you going?
wohinter behind what
wohl well; probably (11)
sich wohl fühlen (fühlt wohl) to feel well
wohl geachtet respected
der Wohlstand affluence
wohnbar livable
der Wohnbereich (-e) living space
wohnen to live, reside (1)
die Wohngemeinschaft (-en) (*abbr.* **WG**) group of people sharing living quarters (2)
das Wohnheim (-e) (student) dormitory
der Wohnort (-e) place of residence (1)
das Wohnumfeld (-er) living environment
die Wohnung (-en) apartment (2)
das Wohnungsangebot (-e) for-rent ad
der Wohnungsschlüssel (-) house key
die Wohnungssuche apartment search
der Wohnungstyp (-en) type of apartment
der Wohnwagen (-) camper, trailer
das Wohnzimmer (-) living room (2)
die Wolke (-n) cloud (7)
das Wolkenband (¨-er) cloud bank
wolkenlos without clouds (7)
wolkig cloudy (7)
die Wolle wool
wollen (will), wollte, gewollt to want (to) (4)
die Wollqualität (-en) wool quality
womit with what
wonach after what; according to what
woneben next to what
woran on what; about what
worauf on what; for what

woraus from what; of what
worin in what
das Wort (¨er) word
das Wortelement (-e) word element
das Wörterbuch (¨er) dictionary
das Wortratespiel (-e) word-guessing game
der Wortschatz vocabulary
die Wortschatzübung (-en) vocabulary exercise
der Wortteil (-e) part of word
worüber about what
worum about what; around what
worunter under what
wovon of what
wovor before what; in front of what; of what
wozu for what; why
wozwischen between what
wuchern to grow abundantly
wund (*adj.*) sore
das Wunder (-) miracle; **kein Wunder** no wonder
wunderbar wonderful
das Wunderkind (-er) child prodigy
der Wunsch (¨e) wish
wünschen to wish (3)
würden: Würden Sie bitte . . . ? Would you please . . . ? (9)
der Wurmfortsatz (¨e) (*anatomy*) appendix
die Wurst (¨e) sausage (5)
das Würstchen (-) small sausage; hot dog
der Wurstsalat (-e) salad made of strips of cold cuts
würzen to season

Z

zaghaft timid(ly)
die Zahl (-en) number; amount; **die Postleitzahl** zip code (E)
zahlen to pay (5); **Zahlen, bitte!** Check, please! (6); **bar zahlen** to pay in cash
zählen to count
das Zahlenlotto (-s) number lottery
zahm tame
der Zahn (¨e) tooth
der Zahnarzt (¨e) / die Zahnärztin (-nen) dentist (11)
die Zahnpasta (Zahnpasten) toothpaste (5)
die Zahnschmerzen (*pl.*) toothache
zappeln to jerk
zart tender (5)
zärtlich affectionate
der Zauberer (-) / die Zauberin (-nen) magician
zaubern to do magic
(das) ZDF *German television station*
die Zehe (-n) toe (8)
zehn ten (E)
der Zehner (-) ten-mark bill
der Zehnmarkschein (-e) ten-mark bill
zehnte tenth (3)
zehntreichst- tenth richest
das Zeichen (-) sign
zeichnen to draw, sketch (7)
der Zeichner (-) / die Zeichnerin (-nen) draftsman/draftswoman
die Zeichnung (-en) drawing (12)
zeigen to show (5)
die Zeile (-n) line
die Zeit (-en) time (2); **die ganze Zeit** all the time; **eine Zeit lang** for a while; **mit der Zeit** as time goes by; **um diese Zeit** at this time; **zur Zeit** now; **Die Zeit vergeht wie im Flug.** Time flies by. (10)
die Zeitansage (-n) time recording
das Zeitbudget (-s) time budget
die Zeitform (-en) time expression
der Zeitpunkt (-e) moment; time
die Zeitschrift (-en) periodical; magazine (13)
die Zeitung (-en) newspaper (1)
das Zeitunglesen reading newspapers
der Zeitungsleser (-) / die Zeitungsleserin (-nen) newspaper reader
zeitweise temporary; temporarily
das Zelt (-e) tent (10)
die Zensur (-en) grade (on a report card)
der Zentimeter (-) centimeter
zentral central(ly) (2)
die Zentralheizung (-en) central heating
das Zentralnervensystem (-e) central nervous system
das Zentrum (Zentren) center; **im Zentrum** in the center of town
zerbrochen broken
zerschlagen shattered
zerstören to destroy
die Zerstörung (-en) destruction
der Zettel (-) piece of paper
das Zettelchen (-) small piece of paper
der Zeuge (-n *masc.*) **/ die Zeugin (-nen)** witness
das Zeugnis (-se) report card (11)
ziehen, zog, ist/hat gezogen to pull; to move (somewhere)
das Ziel (-e) aim, goal, target; destination
die Zielstrebigkeit determination
ziemlich rather (6)
die Zigarette (-n) cigarette
der Zigeuner (-) / die Zigeunerin (-nen) gypsy
das Zimmer (-) room (2); **Dreizimmerwohnung** three-room apartment
die Zimmerbestellung (-en) room reservation
der Zimmergenosse (-n *masc.*) **/ die Zimmergenossin (-nen)** roommate
der Zimmerkollege (-n *masc.*) **/ die Zimmerkollegin (-nen)** roommate
die Zimmerpflanze (-n) indoor plant (2)
die Zimmervermittlung (-en) room rental agency
zirka about, approximately
zitieren to quote
die Zitrone (-n) lemon
der Zivildienst community service (*as an alternative to military conscription*)
die Zivilisation (-en) civilization
der Zivilist (-en *masc.*) **/ die Zivilistin (-nen)** civilian
zögern to hesitate
zögernd hesitant(ly)
der Zoll customs
die Zone (-n) zone; **die Fußgängerzone (-n)** pedestrian zone
der Zoo (-s) zoo
das Zoogelände (-) zoo grounds
zu (+ *dat.*) to (5); too; **zu Hause** at home (5)
das Zubehör accessories
zubereiten (bereitet zu) to prepare
zubetonieren (betoniert zu) to fill in with concrete
die Zucchini (*pl.*) zucchini
zucken: mit den Achseln zucken to shrug one's shoulders
der Zucker sugar (5)
zuckerkrank diabetic
zueinander to one another
zuerst (erst) at first, first (9)
zufrieden content, satisfied
der Zug (¨e) train (10); **mit dem Zug** by train
der Zugang (¨e) access
zugeben (gibt zu), gab zu, zugegeben to admit
zugeschneit covered with snow, snowed in
zügig fast
zugreifen (greift zu), griff zu, zugegriffen to grab
die Zugreise (-n) train trip
das Zugrestaurant (-s) train restaurant
die Zugspitze *name of Germany's highest mountain*
zu Hause home
das Zuhause home
zuhören (hört zu) to listen
die Zukunft future
zulassen (lässt zu), ließ zu, zugelassen to allow
zuletzt last, last time, finally
zum (= zu dem); zum Geburtstag for (your) birthday (3)
die Zunge (-n) tongue

zumachen (macht zu) to close
zumindest at least
zunächst first; for the time being
zunehmen (nimmt zu), nahm zu, zugenommen to increase, gain
zur = zu der
zurechtmachen (macht zurecht) to prepare
(jemandem) zureden (redet zu) to encourage
zurück back; **hin und zurück** roundtrip
zurückbringen (bringt zurück), brachte zurück, zurückgebracht to return (something)
zurückgeben (gibt zurück), gab zurück, zurückgegeben to give back
zurückhaltend reserved
zurückkommen (kommt zurück), kam zurück, ist zurückgekommen to come back, return (4)
zurückrufen (ruft zurück), rief zurück, zurückgerufen to call back
zurücktreten (tritt zurück), trat zurück, ist zurückgetreten to resign
zurückzahlen (zahlt zurück) to pay back
zurückziehen (zieht zurück), zog zurück, ist zurückgezogen to move back
zusagen: Es sagt mir nicht zu. I don't like it.
zusammen together (5); **Das macht zusammen . . .** That comes to . . . (6); **zusammen oder getrennt** together or separate (checks)
die Zusammenarbeit team work
zusammenfassen (fasst zusammen) to summarize
die Zusammenfassung (-en) summary
zusammengehören (gehört zusammen) to belong together
zusammengesetzt compounded
der Zusammenhang (¨e) connection
zusammenhängen (hängt zusammen), hing zusammen, zusammengehangen to be connected
zusammenkrampfen: Mein Herz krampft sich zusammen. It breaks my heart.
zusammenleben (lebt zusammen) to live together
zusammenpassen (passt zusammen) to match
zusammenschlagen (schlägt zusammen), schlug zusammen, ist zusammengeschlagen *here:* to engulf (of a wave)
sich zusammenschließen zu (+ *dat.*) **(schließt zusammen), schloss zusammen, zusammengeschlossen** to form a group
zusammenschrauben (schraubt zusammen) to assemble with screws
die Zusammensetzung (-en) combination
zusammenstellen (stellt zusammen) to put together
der Zusammenstoß (¨e) clash
zusammenwachsen (wächst zusammen), wuchs zusammen, ist zusammengewachsen to grow together
zusammenwohnen (wohnt zusammen) to live together
zusätzlich additional
der Zuschlag (¨e) surcharge (10)
zuschneiden (schneidet zu), schnitt zu, zugeschnitten to custom-cut
Zuschr. = Zuschriften
die Zuschrift (-en) letter; reply
(jemandem) zusprechen (spricht zu), sprach zu, zugesprochen to comfort; to give friendly advice
der Zustand (¨e) condition
zutreffen (trifft zu), traf zu, zugetroffen to be correct
das Zutreffende (*decl. adj.*) the correct (answer)
zuverlässig reliable
die Zuversicht confidence
zu viel too much
zu wenig too little, not enough
der Zwang pressure, stress
die Zwangssterilisation (-nen) forced sterilization
zwanzig twenty (E)
der Zwanziger (-) twenty-mark bill
zwar however; admittedly; **und zwar** that is to say
zwei two (E); **zu zweit** two of (us, them)
der Zweifel (-) doubt
zweifelnd doubtful
zweihundert two hundred (E)
zweimal twice (7)
zweitausend two thousand (E)
zweite second (3); **zweiter Klasse** second-class (10)
die Zwiebel (-n) onion (6)
die Zwiebelringe (*pl.*) onion rings
die Zwillinge (*pl.*) twins
zwischen (+ *acc./dat.*) between (6); **zwischen zwei und drei Uhr** between two and three o'clock (6)
zwischendurch in between
zwölf twelve (E)
zwölfte twelfth (3)
zypriotisch (*adj.*) Cyprian (from Cyprus)

English–German

This list contains all the words from the end-of-chapter vocabulary sections.

A

able: to be able to, can können (kann), konnte, gekonnt (4)
about über (+ *acc.*); (+ *time*) gegen; ungefähr (9); **to be about** handeln von (+ *dat.*)
above über (+ *acc./dat.*) (6); (nach) oben (12)
abroad im Ausland (11)
absolutely unbedingt (13)
academic quarter das Quartal (-e) (12)
accommodation die Unterkunft (¨-e) (9)
account das Konto (Konten); **savings account** das Sparkonto; **on account of** wegen (+ *gen.*) (9)
accusative case der Akkusativ (4)
acquainted: to be acquainted with (to know) kennen, kannte, gekannt; **to get acquainted (with)** bekannt werden mit (E)
across from gegenüber (+ *dat.*) (9)
act of violence die Gewalttätigkeit (-en) (14)
active(ly) aktiv (10)
actor/actress der Schauspieler (-)/die Schauspielerin (-nen) (11)
actually eigentlich (13)
ad: classified ad die Kleinanzeige (-n) (13)
addict: drug addict der/die Drogensüchtige (*decl. adj.*) (14)
address die Addresse (-n); **street address** die Hausnummer (-n); **What's the address?** Wie ist die Adresse? (E)
adjective das Adjektiv (-e) (2)
adverb das Adverb (-ien) (2)
advertisement (*commercial*) die Werbung (-en) (13)
advice der Rat (8)
advice columnist der Ratgeber (-) (13)
aerobics das Aerobic; **to do aerobics** Aerobic machen (7)
afraid: to be afraid (of) Angst haben (vor + *dat.*); (hat Angst) (12)
after nach (+ *dat.*) (6); **a quarter after two** ein Viertel nach zwei (4); nachdem (*subord. conj.*) (10)
afternoon der Nachmittag (-e); **this afternoon** heute Nachmittag; **Sunday afternoon** Sonntagnachmittag; **tomorrow afternoon** morgen Nachmittag (4)
afternoons: in the afternoon nachmittags (4)
again wieder (2)
against gegen (+ *acc.*) (3) **against it** dagegen (14)
ago vor (+ *dat.*); **two days ago** vor zwei Tagen (6)
ahead: straight ahead (immer) geradeaus (9)
air die Luft (8)
airplane das Flugzeug (-e) (10)
airplane ticket der Flugschein (-e) (10)
airport der Flughafen (¨) (10)
alarm clock der Wecker (-) (2)
alcohol der Alkohol (14)
all alle (*pl*) (5); **All the best!** Alles Gute! **all right** in Ordnung
allowed: to be allowed to dürfen (darf), durfte, gedurft (4)
almost fast (8)
along entlang (+ *acc./dat.*); **to bring along** mitbringen (bringt mit), brachte mit, mitgebracht; **to come along** mitkommen (kommt mit), kam mit, ist mitgekommen; **to take along** mitnehmen (nimmt mit), nahm mit, mitgenommen (4)
already schon (2)
also auch (8)
altogether insgesamt (10)
aluminum can die Dose (-n) (14)
always immer (3)
American (*person*) der Amerikaner (-) /die Amerikanerin (-nen) (1)
among unter (+ *acc./dat*) (5)
to amount to betragen (beträgt), betrug, betragen (12)
and und (*coord. conj.*) (E)
animal das Tier (-e) (12)
annoyed: to be annoyed about sich ärgern über (+ *acc.*) (12)
to answer antworten (3)
answering machine der Anrufbeantworter (-) (13)
any: not any . . . yet noch kein . . . ; **in any case** auf alle Fälle (13)
anything etwas; **anything else?** sonst noch etwas? (6)
apartment die Wohnung (-en) (2)
appetizer die Vorspeise (-n) (6)
apple der Apfel (¨) (5)
apple juice Apfelsaft (5)
appliance der Apparat (-e), das Gerät (-e) (9); **household appliance** das Haushaltsgerät (-e) (12)
application die Bewerbung (-en) (11)
application form das Bewerbungsformular (-e) (11)
to apply verwenden; **to apply (for)** sich bewerben (um + *acc.*) (bewirbt), bewarb, beworben (11)
appointment der Termin (-e) (8)
approximately circa (12); ungefähr (9)
April (der) April (3)
architect der Architekt (-en *masc.*)/die Architektin (-nen) (11)
are: there are/there is es gibt (4)
area der Bereich (-e); die Umgebung (-en) (12)
arena: sports arena das Stadion (Stadien) (7)
arm der Arm (-e) (8)
armchair der Sessel (-) (2)
around um (+ *acc.*); (*spatial*) um . . . herum; (+ *time*) gegen (3); **to lie around** faulenzen (7)
arrival die Ankunft (¨-e) (10)
to arrive ankommen (kommt an), kam an, ist angekommen (9)
article der Artikel (-); **leading (newspaper) article** der Leitartikel (13); **article of clothing** das Kleidungsstück (-e) (5)
artist der Künstler (-)/die Künstlerin (-nen) (11)
as als; wie; **as far as** bis (zu); **as soon as possible** möglichst bald (9)
to ask fragen (1); **to ask for** bitten um (+ *acc.*) (bittet), bat, gebeten (12); **to ask about** fragen nach (+ *dat.*) (12); **to ask directions** nach dem Weg fragen (9)
assignment die Arbeit (-en) (8)
at an, auf (+ *acc./dat.*) (6); bei (+ *dat.*) (5); **at least** wenigstens; **at most** höchstens (8); **at night** abends (4); **at noon** mittags (4); **At what time?** Um wie viel Uhr? (3); **at two** um zwei
athletic sportlich (10)
athletic field der Sportplatz (¨-e) (7)
to attempt versuchen (8)
attention: to pay attention achten auf (+ *acc.*) (8) **Attention!** Achtung! (10)
attorney der Rechtsanwalt (¨-e) / die Rechtsanwältin (-nen) (11)
August (der) August (3)
aunt die Tante (-n) (3)
Austria (das) Österreich (E)
autumn der Herbst (7)

available frei; **Is this seat available?** Ist dieser Platz frei? (6)
average der Durchschnitt (-e); **on average** im Durchschnitt, durchschnittlich (12)
to avoid vermeiden, vermied, vermieden (14)

B

back zurück; **to come back** zurückkommen (kommt zurück), kam zurück, ist zurückgekommen (4); **in back of** hinter (+ *acc./dat.*) (6)
back der Rücken (-) (8)
backpack der Rucksack (¨e) (5)
bad(ly) böse; schlecht (E); **What bad luck!** So ein Pech! (8)
bag die Tüte (-n); **plastic bag** die Plastiktüte (14)
baggage das Gepäck (9)
baggage check die Gepäckaufbewahrung (10)
baked goods die Backwaren (*pl.*) (5)
bakery die Bäckerei (-en) (5)
balcony der Balkon (-s) (2)
ballet das Ballett (-e) (4)
ballpoint pen der Kugelschreiber (-) (12)
Baloney! (So ein) Quatsch! (14)
banana die Banane (-n) (5)
bank die Bank (-en) (9)
bar die Kneipe (-n), das Lokal (-e) (6)
barbecue der Grill (-s) (6)
bargain: to be a bargain preiswert sein (2)
basement der Keller (-) (12)
bathing suit der Badeanzug (¨e) (5)
bathroom das Badezimmer (-); das WC (-s) (2)
Bavarian meatloaf der Leberkäs (6)
to be sein (ist), war, ist gewesen (1)
to be able to können (kann), konnte, gekonnt (4)
to be about handeln von (+ *dat.*) (13)
to be acquainted with kennen, kannte, gekannt (E)
to be afraid Angst haben (hat Angst) (12)
to be allowed dürfen (darf), durfte, gedurft (4)
to be annoyed (about) sich ärgern (über + *acc.*) (12)
to be called heißen, hieß, geheißen (E)
to be correct Recht haben (2)
to be glad (about) sich freuen (über + *acc.*) (12)
to be hungry Hunger haben (hat Hunger) (2)
to be interested in sich interessieren für (+ *acc.*) (11)
to be lazy faulenzen (7)
to be located liegen, lag, gelegen (6)
to be missing fehlen (10)
to be permitted to dürfen (darf), durfte, gedurft (4)
to be right Recht haben (hat Recht) (2)
to be supposed to sollen (soll), sollte, gesollt (4)
to be thirsty Durst haben (hat Durst) (2)
beach der Strand (¨e) (9)
beautiful schön (2)
because denn (*coord. conj.*) (7); weil (*subord. conj.*) (8)
because of wegen (+ *gen.*) (9); **because of that** deswegen (12)
to become werden (wird), wurde, ist geworden (3)
bed das Bett (-en) (2)
bed-and-breakfast inn die Pension (-en) (9)
beef das Rindfleisch (5)
beer das Bier (-e) (5); **draft beer** Bier vom Fass; **pilsner beer** das Pilsner (6)
beer garden der Biergarten (¨) (6)
before vor (+ *acc./dat.*) (6); **before noon** am Vormittag (4)
to begin anfangen (fängt an), fing an, angefangen (4)
behind hinter (+ *acc./dat.*) (6)
beige beige (5)
Belgium (das) Belgien (F)
to believe glauben(+ *dat.*); glauben an (*acc.*) (5)
bell pepper die Paprikaschote (-n) (6)
belly der Bauch (¨e) (8)
to belong gehören (+ *dat.*) (5)
below unten; nach unten (12); unter (+ *acc./dat.*) (6)
belt der Gürtel (-) (5)
beside neben (+ *acc./dat.*) (6)
besides außerdem (14)
best best-; **All the best!** Alles Gute! (7)
better besser (7)
between zwischen (+ *acc./dat.*) (6)
beverage das Getränk (-e) (5)
beverage (liquor) store der Getränkeladen (¨) (5)
bicycle das Fahrrad (¨er) (10)
to bicycle Rad fahren (fährt Rad), fuhr Rad, ist Rad gefahren (7)
big groß (10)
bill die Rechnung (-en) (9)
birthdate das Geburtsdatum (Geburtsdaten) (1)
birthday der Geburtstag (-e); **When is your birthday?** Wann hast du Geburtstag? **Happy birthday!** Herzlichen Glückwunsch zum Geburtstag! (3)
birthplace der Geburtsort (-e) (1)
black schwarz (5)
blouse die Bluse (-n) (5)
blue blau (5)
to board (*train, etc.*) einsteigen (steigt ein), stieg ein, ist eingestiegen (10)
body der Körper (-); **parts of the body** die Körperteile (*pl.*) (8)
body-building das Bodybuilding (7); **to do body-building** Bodybuilding machen (7)
book das Buch (¨er) (1); **notebook** das Heft (-e) (12)
to book buchen (10)
bookcase das Bücherregal (-e); der Bücherschrank (¨e) (2)
bookshelf das Bücherregal (-e) (2)
boot der Stiefel (-) (5)
boring langweilig (5)
to borrow (from) leihen (von + *dat.*) (5)
bottle die Flasche (-n); **nonreturnable bottle** die Wegwerfflasche (14)
bread das Brot (-e) (5)
breakfast das Frühstück (-e); **to eat breakfast** frühstücken (5)
breakfast nook die Frühstücksnische (-n) (12)
breakfast room Frühstücksraum (¨e) (9)
breast die Brust (¨e) (8)
bright hell; (*weather*) heiter (2)
to bring bringen, brachte, gebracht (7)
to bring up (children) erziehen, erzog, erzogen (14)
broadcast die Sendung (-en) (13)
broccoli der Brokkoli (-) (5)
brochure der Prospekt (-e); **travel brochure** der Reiseprospekt (10)
broke (*coll.*) pleite (12)
broken kaputt (9)
brother der Bruder (¨) (3)
brother-in-law der Schwager (¨) (3)
brown braun (5)
to brush (one's teeth) sich (die Zähne) putzen (8)
budget das Budget (-s); der Haushalt (-e) (13)
to build bauen (12)
bus der Bus (-se) (10)
bus line die Buslinie (-n) (10)
bus stop die Haltestelle (-n) (10)
businessman der Geschäftsmann (Geschäftsleute) (11)
businesswoman die Geschäftsfrau (-en) (11)
but aber (*coord. conj.*) (2); **but rather** sondern (*coord. conj.*) (7)
butcher shop die Metzgerei (-en) (5)
butter die Butter (5)
to buy kaufen (2)
by von (+ *dat.*); **to come by** vorbeikommen (kommt vorbei), kam vorbei, ist vorbeigekommen (4)
by the way übrigens (9)

C

café das Café (-s) (6)
cafeteria: student cafeteria die Mensa (Mensen) (1)

cake der Kuchen (-) (5); **cheese cake** der Käsekuchen (6)
calendar der Kalender (-) (3)
call: telephone call der Telefonanruf (-e) (12)
to call up anrufen (ruft an), rief an, angerufen (4)
called: to be called heißen, hieß, geheißen (E)
camera die Kamera (-s) (10)
can die Dose (-n) (14)
can, to be able to können (kann), konnte, gekonnt (4)
cap die Mütze (-n) (5)
car der Wagen (-) (10); das Auto (-s) (2); **to drive a car** Auto fahren (fährt Auto), fuhr, ist gefahren (2)
card die Karte (-n); **playing cards** Karten spielen (7); **identification card** der Ausweis (-e) (10); der Personalausweis (-e); **report card** das Zeugnis (-se) (11)
care: take care, so long mach's gut; **I don't care.** Das ist mir egal. (5)
to care for, like mögen (mag), mochte, gemocht (4)
carpet der Teppich (-e) (2)
carpeting der Teppichboden (¨) (12)
carrot die Karotte (-n) (5)
to carry tragen (trägt), trug, getragen (5)
carry-on luggage das Handgepäck (10)
case: in any case auf alle Fälle (13)
cash das Bargeld; **in cash** bar (9)
cash register die Kasse (-n) (5)
cat die Katze (-n) (12)
to catch a cold sich erkälten (8)
cauliflower der Blumenkohl (5)
CD player der CD-Spieler (-) (2)
to celebrate feiern (3)
cellular telephone das Handy (-s) (2)
center die Mitte; **center of town** die Innenstadt **in the center (of the city)** in der Mitte (der Stadt) (9); **recycling center** die Sammelstelle (-n) (14)
cereal das Müsli (5)
certain(ly) bestimmt (2)
chair der Stuhl (¨e); **armchair** der Sessel (-) (2)
channel (*TV*) das Programm (-e); **on Channel 1** im ersten Programm (13)
characteristics die Eigenschaften (*pl.*) (1)
cheap(ly) billig (2)
check der Scheck (-s); **Check, please.** Zahlen, bitte! (6); **traveler's check** der Reisescheck (-s) (9)
to check in (*hotel*) sich anmelden (meldet an) (9)
to check out (*of hotel*) sich abmelden (meldet ab) (9)
checkout stand die Kasse (-n) (5)
cheerful fröhlich (1)
cheese der Käse (5); **cheese cake** der Käsekuchen (-) (6)
chemist der Chemiker (-)/die Chemikerin (-nen) (11)
chess das Schach; **to play chess** Schach spielen (7)
chest die Brust (8)
chicken das Hähnchen (-) (5)
chicken breast die Hühnerbrust (¨e) (6)
child das Kind (-er) (1)
chin das Kinn (-e) (8)
to choose wählen (14); **to choose something for oneself** sich etwas aussuchen (sucht aus) (13)
Christmas Weihnachten; **Christmas tree** der Weihnachtsbaum (¨e) (3)
church die Kirche (-n) (9)
cinema das Kino (-s) (4)
circa zirka, circa (12)
citizen der Bürger (-)/die Bürgerin (-nen) (14)
city die Stadt (¨e) (E); **in the city** in der Stadt; **inner city** die Innenstadt (9)
class die Klasse (-n); **first-class** erster Klasse (6)
classified ad die Kleinanzeige (-n) (13)
clean sauber (14)
to clean (one's teeth) sich (die Zähne) putzen (8); **to clean up** aufräumen (räumt auf) (4)
cleaner: vacuum cleaner der Staubsauger (-) (13)
clock die Uhr (-en); **alarm clock** der Wecker (-) (2); **five o'clock** fünf Uhr
closed geschlossen; **day a business is closed** der Ruhetag (-e) (6)
clothes closet der Kleiderschrank (¨e) (2)
clothing die Kleidung; **article of clothing** das Kleidungsstück (-e) (5)
cloud die Wolke (-n) (7)
cloudless wolkenlos (7)
cloudy wolkig (7)
coat der Mantel (¨); **sports coat** das Sakko (-s) (5)
coffee table der Couchtisch (-e) (2)
cola die Cola (-s) (5)
cold (*adj.*) kalt (10)
cold die Erkältung (-en); **to catch a cold** sich erkälten; **head cold** der Schnupfen (8)
cold cuts der Aufschnitt (5)
to collect sammeln (7)
color die Farbe (-n) (5)
columnist: advice columnist der Ratgeber (-) (13)
to comb (one's hair) sich (das Haar) kämmen (8)
to come kommen, kam, ist gekommen (1)
to come along mitkommen (kommt mit), kam mit, ist mitgekommen (4)
to come back zurückkommen (kommt zurück), kam zurück, ist zurückgekommen (4)
to come by vorbeikommen (kommt vorbei), kam vorbei, ist vorbeigekommen (4)
comedy die Komödie (-n) (4)
commercial die Werbung (-en) (13)
comparative die Komparativform (-en) (7)
to compare vergleichen, verglich, verglichen (12)
compartment das Abteil (-e) (10)
to complain sich beschweren (9)
complete(ly) ganz (12)
completion (*of training or school*) der Abschluss (¨e) (11)
computer der Computer (-) (2)
computer diskette die Computerdiskette (-n) (12)
computer scientist der Informatiker (-)/die Informatikerin (-nen) (11)
concert das Konzert (-e) (4)
conductor (*bus/train*) der Schaffner (-)/die Schaffnerin (-nen) (10)
congestion: nasal congestion der Schnupfen (8)
to congratulate gratulieren (+ *dat.*) (3)
conjunction die Konjunktion (-en) (8)
connection der Anschluss (¨e) (10)
conservative konservativ (1)
to consider sich überlegen; halten für (+ *acc.*) (hält), hielt, gehalten (14)
to consume verbrauchen (14)
contact der Kontakt (-e) (11)
to cook kochen (1)
cookie der Keks (-e) (5)
cool kühl (7)
corruption die Korruption (14)
to cost kosten (2)
costs die Kosten (*pl.*) (12)
cough, coughing der Husten (8)
counselor der Berater (-)/die Beraterin (-nen); **employment counselor** der Berufsberater (-)/die Berufsberaterin (-nen) (11)
country das Land (¨er); **foreign country** das Ausland (14)
course (*food*) der Gang (¨e) (6); **sailing course** der Segelkurs (-e) (10)
of course natürlich, allerdings (3)
cousin (*female*) die Kusine (-n); (*male*) der Vetter (-n), der Cousin (-s) (3)
coworker der Mitarbeiter (-)/die Mitarbeiterin (-nen) (11)
cozy, cozily gemütlich (4)
crazy verrückt (8)
cream die Sahne (6); **ice cream** das Eis (5)
to create schaffen, schuf, geschaffen (14)

credit card die Kreditkarte (-n) (9)
crossword puzzle das Kreuzworträtsel (-) (1)
crowded voll (6)
cucumber die Gurke (-n) (5)
cuisine die Küche (6)
cup die Tasse (-n); **a cup of coffee** eine Tasse Kaffee (4)
current aktuell (13)
customer der Kunde (-n *masc.*)/die Kundin (-nen) (2)
cutlet das Schnitzel (-) (5); **breaded veal cutlet** das Wiener Schnitzel (6)
Czechia (das) Tschechien (E)

D

daily täglich (6)
dairy product das Milchprodukt (-e) (5)
to dance tanzen (1)
dangerous gefährlich (10)
dark dunkel (2)
date of birth das Geburtsdatum (Geburtsdaten) (1)
dative case der Dativ (5)
daughter die Tochter (¨) (3)
day der Tag (-e) (2); **every day** jeden Tag (7); **good day** guten Tag (E); **day a business is closed** der Ruhetag (6); **four-day** (*adj.*) viertägig (10)
day of the week der Wochentag (-e) (3)
to deal with umgehen mit (+ *dat.*) (geht um), ging um, ist umgegangen (11); handeln von (+ *dat.*) (13)
December (der) Dezember (3)
definite(ly) bestimmt (2)
degree (*school*) der Abschluss (¨e) (11)
demonstration die Demonstration (-en) (14)
Denmark (das) Dänemark (E)
dentist der Zahnarzt (¨e)/die Zahnärztin (-nen) (11)
to depart abreisen (reist ab), ist abgereist (10); abfahren (fährt ab), fuhr ab, ist abgefahren (9)
department store das Kaufhaus (¨er) (2)
departure die Abfahrt (-en) (10)
depressed deprimiert (8)
to deserve verdienen (11)
desire die Lust; **to feel like (doing something)** Lust haben (2)
desk der Schreibtisch (-e) (2)
dessert die Nachspeise (-n); der Nachtisch (-e) (6)
detective (*film or book*) der Krimi (-s) (3)
to develop entwickeln (14)
development die Entwicklung (-en) (11)
dining room das Essimmer (-) (2)
directions: to ask for directions nach dem Weg fragen (9)
dirty schmutzig (14)
disco die Disko (-s); **to go to a disco** in die Disko gehen (4)
discount price der Sparpreis (-e) (10)
to discuss diskutieren über (+ *acc.*) (1)
dish (*food*) das Gericht (-e); **main dish** das Hauptgericht; **side dish** die Beilage (-n); **dish of ice cream** der Eisbecher (-) (6)
dishwasher die Geschirrspülmaschine (-n) (12)
diskette (*computer*) die Diskette (-n) (12)
disloyal untreu (1)
to disseminate verbreiten (14)
to dive tauchen, ist getaucht (7)
to do tun, tat, getan (8); machen; **What do you do for a living?** Was sind Sie von Beruf? (1); **to do gymnastics** turnen; **to do sports** Sport treiben, trieb, getrieben (7); **to do without** verzichten (auf + *acc.*) (13); **to do crossword puzzles** Kreuzworträtsel machen (1)
dock der Hafen (¨) (9)
doctor der Arzt (¨e)/die Ärztin (-nen) (8)
document die Unterlage (-n) (11)
documentary (film) der Dokumentarfilm (-e) (13)
dog der Hund (-e) (12); **sick as a dog** hundsmiserabel (8)
door die Tür (-en) (2)
dormitory das Studenten(wohn)heim (-e) (2)
downstairs unten; nach unten (12)
downtown die Innenstadt (9)
draft beer das Bier vom Fass (6)
drama das Theaterstück (-e) (3)
to draw zeichnen (7)
drawing die Zeichnung (12)
dress das Kleid (-er) (5)
dressed: to get dressed sich anziehen (zieht an), zog an, angezogen (8)
dresser die Kommode (-n) (2)
drink das Getränk (-e) (5)
to drink trinken, trank, getrunken (2)
to drive fahren (fährt), fuhr, ist gefahren; **to drive a car** Auto fahren (2)
driver's license der Führerschein (-e) (10)
drug addict der/die Drogensüchtige (*decl. adj.*) (14)
drug addiction die Drogensucht (14)
dryer der Wäschetrockner (-) (13)
during während (+ *gen.*) (9)

E

each jeder, jede, jedes (5)
ear das Ohr (-en) (8)
early früh (4); **earlier** früher (7)
to earn verdienen (11)
Easter (das) Ostern (3)
to eat essen (isst), aß, gegessen (2); **to eat breakfast** frühstücken (4)
economy die Wirtschaft (13)
editor: letter to the editor der Leserbrief (-e) (13)
editorial der Leitartikel (-) (13)
egg das Ei (-er) (5); **fried egg** das Spiegelei (6)
eight acht (E)
eighteen achtzehn (E)
eighty achtzig (E)
elbow der Ell(en)bogen (-) (8)
to elect wählen (14)
electricity der Strom (12)
elevator der Lift (-e) (9)
eleven elf (E)
else: Anything else? Sonst noch etwas? (6)
employee der Arbeitnehmer (-)/die Arbeitnehmerin (-nen) (13)
employer der Arbeitgeber (-)/die Arbeitgeberin (-nen) (11)
employment counselor der Berufsberater (-)/die Berufsberaterin (-nen) (11)
employment office das Arbeitsamt (¨er) (11)
engineer der Ingenieur (-e)/die Ingenieurin (-nen) (11)
entertaining unterhaltsam (13)
environment die Umwelt (14)
environmental pollution die Umweltverschmutzung (14)
environmentally friendly umweltfreundlich (14)
equality die Gleichberechtigung (11)
especially besonders (8)
evaluation (*from a former employer*) das Zeugnis (-se) (11)
even sogar (8)
evening der Abend (-e); **good evening** guten Abend (E); **this evening** heute Abend (4); **in the evening, evenings** abends; **tomorrow evening** morgen Abend; **Saturday evening** Samstagabend (4)
evening meal das Abendessen (5)
every jeder, jede, jedes; **every day** jeden Tag (5)
everything alles (10)
exactly gerade (2)
exaggerated übertrieben (14)
examination at the end of secondary school das Abitur (-e) (11)
excellent ausgezeichnet (E)
except for außer (+ *dat.*) (5)
exciting aufregend (13)
to excuse entschuldigen; **Excuse me.** Entschuldigung. Entschuldigen Sie! (6)
to exert oneself sich anstrengen (strengt an) (8)
expense die Ausgabe (-n) (12)
expensive teuer (2)

to experience erleben (10)
eye das Auge (-n) (8)

F

face das Gesicht (-er) (8)
fair (*weather*) heiter (7)
fall (*autumn*) der Herbst (7)
to fall fallen (fällt), fiel, ist gefallen (7)
to fall asleep einschlafen (schläft ein), schlief ein, ist eingeschlafen (4)
familiar: to be familiar with, to know kennen, kannte, gekannt (3)
family die Familie (-n) (3)
family gathering das Familienfest (-e) (3)
family name der Nachname (-n *masc.*) (1)
family tree der Stammbaum (¨e) (3)
famine der Welthunger (14)
far weit; **as far as** bis zu (+ *dat.*) (9)
farmhouse das Bauernhaus (¨er) (12)
fashionable modisch (5)
fast schnell (10)
fast-food stand der Imbissstand (¨e) (6)
father der Vater (¨) (3)
favor: I'm in favor of it. Ich bin dafür. (14)
fear die Angst (¨e); **to be afraid** Angst haben (12)
feature film der Spielfilm (-e) (13)
February der Februar (3)
to feel (sich) fühlen (8); **to feel like doing** Lust haben (2)
fees (*university*) die Studiengebühren (*pl.*) (12)
female cousin die Kusine (-n) (3)
fever das Fieber (8)
few wenige (*pl.*) (8)
fifteen fünfzehn (E)
fifth das Fünftel (12)
fifty fünfzig (E)
to fill out ausfüllen (füllt aus) (9)
film der Film (-e) (4)
financial finanziell (11)
to find finden, fand, gefunden (1)
fine (sehr) gut; **fine, thanks** danke, gut (E)
finger der Finger (-) (8)
firm (*adj.*) fest (11)
first erst (3); **at first** zuerst (9)
first name der Vorname (-n *masc.*) (1)
to fish angeln (7)
fit fit; **to keep fit** sich fir halten (hält fit), hielt fit, fit gehalten (8)
to fit passen (+ *dat.*) (5)
fitness die Fitness (8)
fitness center das Fitnesscenter (-) (7)
five fünf (E)
to flash blitzen (7)
flight attendant der Flugbegleiter (-)/die Flugbegleiterin (-nen) (10)
floor der Stock, das Stockwerk (-e), die Etage (-n) (9); **ground floor** das Erdgeschoss (-e) (9)
flu die Grippe (8)
to fly fliegen, flog, ist geflogen (7)
fog der Nebel (7)
food(s) die Lebensmittel (*pl.*) (5); die Speise (-n) (6); das Essen (1); die Küche (6); (*nutrition*) die Ernährung (12); **organic foods store** der Bioladen (¨) (5)
foot der Fuß (¨e); **to go on foot** zu Fuß gehen, ging, ist gegangen (8)
for denn (*coord. conj.*); (*time*) seit (+ *dat.*) (5); für (3)
foreign country/countries das Ausland (11)
forest der Wald (¨er) (7)
to forget vergessen (vergisst), vergaß, vergessen (10)
fork die Gabel (-n) (6)
form das Formular (-e); **registration form** das Anmeldeformular; **application form** das Bewerbungsformular (-e) (11)
forty vierzig (E)
forward: to look forward to sich freuen auf (+ *acc.*) (11)
four vier (E)
four-day (*adj.*) viertägig (10)
fourteen vierzehn (E)
France (das) Frankreich (E)
free frei (6)
free time die Freizeit (2)
French fries die Pommes frites (*pl.*) (6)
fresh frisch (5)
Friday (der) Freitag; **Fridays, on Friday(s)** freitags (3)
fried egg das Spiegelei (-er) (6)
fried potatoes die Bratkartoffeln (*pl.*) (6)
friend der Freund (-e)/die Freundin (-nen) (1)
friendly freundlich (1)
from aus (+ *dat.*), von (+ *dat.*) (5); ab (+ *dat.*); **from (June 1)** ab (1. Juni) (12); **I'm from . . .** Ich komme aus . . . (E); **from where** woher (1); **across from** gegenüber (+ *dat.*); **from . . . to** von . . . bis; **from two to three** von zwei bis drei (6)
in front of vor (+ *acc./dat.*) (6)
front hall die Diele (-n) (12)
frozen gefroren (5)
fruit das Obst (5)
fruit and vegetable stand der Obst- und Gemüsestand (¨e) (5)
full voll (6)
fun der Spaß; **That's fun.** Das macht (mir) Spaß. **Have fun!** Viel Spaß! (1)
to function funktionieren (11)
to furnish einrichten (richtet ein) (12)
furnished möbliert (2)

G

game das Spiel (-e); **computer game** das Computerspiel (1)
garage die Garage (-n) (2)
garbage der Müll, der Abfall (¨e) (12)
garden der Garten (¨) (2); **beer garden** der Biergarten (¨) (6)
gasoline das Benzin (12)
gas station die Tankstelle (-n) (9)
genitive case der Genitiv (9)
gentleman der Herr (-en, -n *masc.*) (2)
German deutsch; (*language*) (das) Deutsch (1); **How does one say . . . in German?** Wie sagt man . . . auf Deutsch? (E)
German mark die Deutsche Mark (DM) (2)
Germany Deutschland (E)
to get (receive) bekommen, bekam, bekommen (6); **(turn)** werden (wird), wurde, ist geworden
to get acquainted (with) bekannt werden (mit + *dat.*) (wird bekannt) wurde, ist geworden (E)
to get dressed sich anziehen (zieht an), zog an, angezogen (8)
to get into (*a vehicle*) einsteigen (steigt ein), stieg ein, ist eingestiegen (10)
to get undressed sich ausziehen (zieht aus), zog aus, ausgezogen (8)
to get up aufstehen (steht auf), stand auf, ist aufgestanden (4)
to get well sich erholen; **Get Well!** Gute Besserung! (8)
to give geben (gibt), gab, gegeben (2); **to give** (*as a gift*) schenken (5)
given name der Vorname (-n *masc.*) (1)
glad: to be glad about sich freuen über (+ *acc.*) (12)
gladly gern (10)
glance der Blick (-e) (13)
glasses (eyeglasses) die Brille (-n) (5)
glove der Handschuh (-e) (10)
to go gehen, ging, ist gegangen (1); **to go to the movies** ins Kino gehen; **to go for a walk** spazieren gehen (geht spazieren); **to go out** ausgehen (geht aus) (4); **to go on foot** zu Fuß gehen; **to go on vacation** Urlaub machen (8); **food "to go"** zum Mitnehmen (6)
good gut, sehr gut; **good day** guten Tag; **good evening** guten Abend; **good night** gute Nacht (E); **Good luck!** Viel Glück! (1); **good morning** guten Morgen; **good-bye** auf Wiedersehen (E); **good-bye** (*telephone*) auf Wiederhören! (9)

goods: baked goods die Backwaren (*pl.*) (5)
granddaughter die Enkelin (-nen) (3)
grandfather der Großvater (¨) (3)
grandma die Oma (-s) (3)
grandmother die Großmutter (¨) (3)
grandpa der Opa (-s) (3)
grandparents die Großeltern (*pl.*) (3)
grandson der Enkel (-) (3)
granola (cereal) das Müsli (5)
grape die Weintraube (-n) (5)
gray grau (5)
green grün (5)
greeting die Begrüßung (-en), der Gruß (¨e) (12); **many (kind) regards** viele Grüße (12)
grill der Grill (-s) (6)
guest der Gast (¨e) (12)
guest room das Gästezimmer (-) (12)
guide: travel guide der Reiseführer (-) (10)
gym das Fitnesscenter (-) (7)
gymnasium die Turnhalle (-n) (7)
gymnastics: to do gymnastics turnen (7)

H

hail der Hagel (7)
hair das Haar (-e) (8)
half halb; die Hälfte (-n) (12); **half past one** halb zwei (4)
hall: front hall die Diele (-n) (12)
hallway der Flur (-e) (12)
ham der Schinken (-) (5)
hand die Hand (¨e) (8)
handbag die Tasche (-n) (5)
to hand in abgeben (gibt ab), gab ab, abgegeben (8)
handsome hübsch, gut aussehend (7)
to hang (something) hängen; **to be hanging** hängen, hing, gehangen (6)
to happen passieren, ist passiert (7)
happiness das Glück; **Much happiness!** Viel Glück! (3)
happy glücklich; **Happy birthday!** Herzlichen Glückwunsch zum Geburtstag! (3)
harbor der Hafen (¨) (9)
hat der Hut (¨e) (5)
hatred of foreigners die Ausländerfeindlichkeit (14)
to have haben (hat), hatte, gehabt (2); **I have a question.** Ich habe eine Frage. **Have fun!** Viel Spaß! (1)
to have time Zeit haben (2)
to have to (must) müssen (muss), musste, gemusst (4)
he er (1)
head der Kopf (¨e) (8)
headache die Kopfschmerzen (*pl.*) (8)
head cold der Schnupfen (8)
headline die Schlagzeile (-n) (13)
health die Gesundheit (8)
healthy gesund (8)
to hear hören (2)
heavy (*weather*) stark (7)
hello grüß dich (*inform.*) (E); guten Tag (E); hallo (E)
to help helfen (+ *dat.*) (hilft), half, geholfen
her ihr; sie (3)
here hier (1)
hi grüß dich (*inform.*) (E)
high hoch (hoh-) (2)
highway die Autobahn (-en) (10)
to hike wandern, ist gewandert (1)
hiking trail der Wanderweg (-e) (10)
him ihn (3); ihm (5)
his sein (3)
hobby das Hobby (-s) (2)
to hold halten (hält), hielt, gehalten (14)
holiday der Feiertag (-e) (13)
home: (to) home nach Hause; **(at) home** zu Hause (5)
homelessness die Obdachlosigkeit (14)
homeless person der/die Obdachlose (*decl. adj.*) (14)
to hope hoffen (10); **I hope** hoffentlich (6)
horoscope das Horoskop (-e) (13)
horseback: to ride horseback reiten, ritt, ist geritten (7)
hostel: youth hostel die Jugendherberge (-n) (9)
hot heiß (7)
hot-air balloon der Heißluftballon (-s) (10)
hotel das Hotel (-s); **at the hotel** im Hotel (9)
hour die Stunde (-n) (4); **office hour** die Sprechstunde (8)
house das Haus (¨er) (2)
household der Haushalt (-e) (13)
household appliance das Haushaltsgerät (-e) (12)
houseplant Zimmerpflanze (-n) (2)
housing: shared housing die Wohngemeinschaft (-en) (WG) (2)
how wie (1); **how long** wie lange; **how much** wie viel; **how many** wie viele (1); **How are you?** (*inform.*) Wie geht's? Wie geht es dir?; (*form.*) Wie geht es Ihnen? (E); **How do you say . . . in German?** Wie sagt man . . . auf Deutsch?; (E)
however aber (2)
human being der Mensch (-en *masc.*) (2)
human right das Menschenrecht (-e) (14)
humid schwül (7)
Hungary (das) Ungarn (E)
hunger der Hunger; **world hunger** der Welthunger (14)
hungry: to be hungry Hunger haben (2)
to hurry up sich beeilen (8)
to hurt weh tun (tut weh), tat weh, weh getan (8)
husband der Mann (¨er) (3)

I

I ich; **I am** ich bin (E); **I'm from . . .** ich komme aus . . . (E); **I'm sorry.** Das tut mir leid. (9) **I don't know.** Das weiß ich nicht. (E) **I don't care.** Das ist mir egal. (5)
ice das Eis (5)
ice cream das Eis (5); **dish of ice cream** der Eisbecher (-) (6)
ice skate der Schlittschuh (-e) (7)
to ice-skate Schlittschuh laufen (läuft), lief, ist gelaufen (7)
ice-skating rink das Eisstadion (Eisstadien) (7)
identification card (ID) der Ausweis (-e), Personalausweis (-e) (10)
if wenn (*subord. conj.*) (8); **if I were you** an deiner Stelle (12)
ill krank (8)
illness die Krankheit (-en) (14)
to imagine sich (*dat.*) vorstellen (11)
immediately sofort (8)
important wichtig (3)
in in (+ *acc./dat.*) (6); **in the morning(s)** morgens (4); **in shape** fit (8); **in spite of** trotz (+ *gen.*) (9); **in German** auf Deutsch (E)
included in the price im Preis enthalten (9)
income das Einkommen (-) (12)
independent selbständig, unabhängig (11)
indoor swimming pool die Schwimmhalle (-n) (9)
industrious fleißig (1)
inexpensive preiswert (2)
to inform (oneself) sich informieren (8)
information die Auskunft (¨e); die Information (-en) (10)
to injure oneself sich verletzen (8)
inner city die Innenstadt (¨e) (9)
inside drinnen (7)
insurance die Versicherung (-en) (12)
intelligent gescheit (13)
interest das Interesse (-n) (1)
to be interested in sich interessieren für (+ *acc.*) (8)
interesting interessant (1)
interpreter der Dolmetscher (-)/die Dolmetscherin (-nen) (11)
interrogative das Fragewort (¨er) (1)
intersection die Kreuzung (-en) (9)
to introduce einführen (führt ein) (11)
to invent erfinden, erfand, erfunden (13)

invention die Erfindung (-en) (13)
inventor der Erfinder (-)/die Erfinderin (-nen) (13)
to invite einladen (lädt ein), lud ein, eingeladen (14)
irregular unregelmäßig (7)
is: there is/there are es gibt (3)
it es, er, sie (1); ihn, sie, es (3); ihm, ihr (5)
Italy (das) Italien (E)
its sein; ihr (3)

J

jacket die Jacke (-n); **sports jacket** das Sakko (-s) (5)
January der Januar; **in January** im Januar (3)
jeans die Jeans (*pl.*) (5)
job die Stelle (-n); der Arbeitsplatz (⸚e) (11)
job interview das Vorstellungsgespräch (-e) (11)
job offer das Stellenangebot (-e) (11)
jogging path der Trimm-Pfad (-e) (7)
journalist der Journalist (-en *masc.*)/die Journalistin (-nen) (11)
juice der Saft (⸚e) (5)
juicy saftig (5)
July der Juli (3)
June der Juni (3)
just gerade; knapp (2); **in just ten minutes** in knapp zehn Minuten

K

keep on going straight immer geradeaus gehen (9)
key der Schlüssel (-) (9)
kitchen die Küche (-n) (2)
knee das Knie (-) (8)
knife das Messer (-) (6)
to know (be acquainted with) kennen, kannte, gekannt (3); **to know something as a fact** wissen (weiß), wusste, gewusst (3); **I don't know.** Das weiß ich nicht. (E)

L

lake der See (-n) (7)
lamp die Lampe (-n) (2)
large groß (7)
to last dauern (7)
late spät; **at the latest** spätestens (12)
to lay (something) down legen (6)
lazy faul; **to be lazy** faulenzen (7)
leading editorial der Leitartikel (-) (13)
to learn lernen (1)
least: at least wenigstens; mindestens (8)
left links; **to the left** nach links (9)
left over übrig (12)
leg das Bein (-e) (8)
leisure time die Freizeit (7)
to lend leihen (5)
to let lassen (lässt), ließ, gelassen; **Let's . . .** Lass uns doch . . . (6)
letter der Brief (-e) (13)
letter to the editor der Leserbrief (-e) (13)
lettuce der Salat (-e) (6)
level (in a building) die Etage (-n); der Stock; das Stockwerk (-e) (9)
librarian der Bibliothekar (-e)/die Bibliothekarin (-nen) (11)
to lie liegen, lag, gelegen (6); **to lie around** faulenzen (7)
Liechtenstein (principality of) (das) Liechtenstein (E)
to lie down sich hinlegen (legt sich hin) (8)
life das Leben (11)
light (*adj.*) hell (2)
light: traffic light die Ampel (-n) (9)
lightning: There's lightning. Es blitzt. (7)
likable sympathisch (1)
to like gern haben (hat gern) (2); mögen (mag), mochte, gemocht (4); **(be pleasing to)** gefallen (*dat.*) (5); **(to do) something** gern (+ *verb*) (2); **would like to** möchte (n) (4); **What do you like to do?** Was macht dir Spaß? (4)
likewise gleichfalls (E)
line die Linie (-n); **bus line** die Buslinie (10)
litter der Abfall (⸚e) (14)
little klein; wenig; **a little** etwas (+ *adj./noun*) (8)
to live leben; **(reside)** wohnen (1)
living room das Wohnzimmer (-) (2)
loaf of bread das Brot (-e) (5)
local news die Lokalnachrichten (*pl.*) (13)
to be located liegen, lag, gelegen (6)
location die Lage (-n) (9)
long lang(e) (10); **how long** wie lange (1); **so long** mach's gut, tschüs (E)
look der Blick (-e) (13)
to look at sich etwas ansehen (sieht an) (13); **to look good** (*on a person*) stehen (+ *dat.*) (5)
to look for suchen (2)
to look forward to sich freuen auf (+ *acc.*) (11)
to lose verlieren, verlor, verloren (7)
a lot viel(e) (1)
lotion: suntan lotion das Sonnenschutzmittel (-) (10)
low niedrig (2)
loyal treu (1)
luck: Good luck! Viel Glück! (1); **What bad luck!** So ein Pech! (8)
luggage das Gepäck (9); **carry-on luggage** das Handgepäck (10)
lunch das Mittagessen (-) (5)
Luxembourg (das) Luxemburg (E)

M

machine: answering machine der Anrufbeantworter (-) (12)
magazine die Zeitschrift (-en) (13)
main dish das Hauptgericht (-e) (6)
to make machen (1); tun, tat, getan (8)
makeup das Make-up (5)
male cousin der Vetter (-n) (3)
mall die Fußgängerzone (-n) (14)
man der Mann (⸚er) (1)
to manufacture herstellen (stellt her) (11)
many viele (*pl.*); **how many** wie viele (1)
March (der) März (3)
Mardi Gras der Karneval (*Rhineland*), der Fasching (*southern Germany*) (3)
mark (German mark) die Mark, DM (Deutsche Mark) (2)
to marry heiraten (3)
matter: What's the matter? Was ist (denn) los? Was fehlt Ihnen? (2); **That doesn't matter.** Das macht nichts. Das ist mir egal. (8)
May (der) Mai (3)
may, to be permitted to dürfen (darf), durfte, gedurft (4)
maybe vielleicht (2)
meadow die Wiese (-n) (7)
meal das Essen; **evening meal** das Abendessen; **midday meal** das Mittagessen (5)
to mean bedeuten; **What does . . . mean?** Was bedeutet . . . ? (E)
means: by means of mit (+ *dat.*) (5)
meat das Fleisch (5)
meatloaf (*Bavarian style***)** der Leberkäs (6)
meats die Fleischwaren (*pl.*) (5)
mechanic der Mechaniker (-) / die Mechanikerin (-nen) (11)
medicine das Medikament (-e) (5)
to meet (sich) treffen (trifft), traf, getroffen (8); **Pleased to meet you.** Freut mich. (E)
mention: Don't mention it. Nichts zu danken. (8)
menu die Speisekarte (-n) (6)
microwave oven der Mikrowellenherd (-e) (12)
milk die Milch (5)
mineral water das Mineralwasser (5)
minute die Minute (-n) (4)
Miss . . . Fräulein . . . (E)
missing: to be missing fehlen (10)
modal verb das Modalverb (-en) (4)
Monday (der) Montag (3); **on Monday** am Montag; **Mondays** montags (4)
money das Geld (1); **to earn money** Geld verdienen (11)
month der Monat (-e) (3); **once a month** einmal im Monat (7)

monthly monatlich (12)
more mehr (10); **once more** noch einmal (7)
morning: good morning guten Morgen; **this morning** heute Morgen; **tomorrow morning** morgen früh; **in the morning, mornings** morgens; **Saturday morning** Samstagmorgen (4)
most meist-; **at most** höchstens (8)
mother die Mutter (¨) (3)
Mother's Day der Muttertag (-e) (3)
motorcycle das Motorrad (¨er); **to ride a motorcycle** Motorrad fahren (fährt Motorrad), fuhr, ist Motorrad gefahren (2)
mountain der Berg (-e) (7)
to move in einziehen (zieht ein), zog ein, ist eingezogen (12)
movie der Film (-e); **watching movies** Filme sehen (9)
movie theater das Kino (-s); **to go to the movies** ins Kino gehen (4)
Mr. . . . Herr . . . (E)
Mrs. . . . Frau . . . (E)
Ms. . . . Frau . . . (E)
much viel (10); **how much** wie viel (1)
muggy schwül (7)
muscle der Muskel (-n) (8)
museum das Museum (Museen) (9)
mushroom der Champignon (-s) (6)
music die Musik (4); **listening to music** Musik anhören
must, to have to müssen (muss), musste, gemusst (4)
mustard Senf (6)
my mein (3)
mystery (*film or book*) der Krimi (-s) (9)

N

name der Name (-ns, -n); **What's your name?** (*form.*) Wie ist Ihr Name? Wie heißen Sie?; (*inform.*) Wie heißt du?; **My name is . . .** Mein Name ist . . . (E); **family name (surname)** der Nachname; **first name (given name)** der Vorname (1); **Under what name?** Auf welchen Namen? (9)
to be named heißen, hieß, geheißen (E)
namely nämlich (3)
napkin die Serviette (-n) (6)
nasal congestion der Schnupfen (8)
natural foods store der Bioladen (¨) (5)
natural(ly) natürlich (3)
nature die Natur (10)
near bei (+ *dat.*) (5); in der Nähe (von + *dat.*) (9)
necessary nötig (5)
neck der Hals (¨e) (8)
necktie die Krawatte (-n) (5)
to need brauchen; **What size do you need?** Welche Größe brauchen Sie? (5)
neighborhood die Umgebung (-en) (12)
nephew der Neffe (-n *masc.*) (3)
Netherlands (die) Niederlande (*pl.*) (E)
never nie (8)
new neu (5)
New Year's Day das Neujahr (3)
New Year's Eve (der) Silvester (3)
news die Nachrichten (*pl.*); **local news** die Lokalnachrichten; **daily TV news** die Tagesschau (13)
newspaper die Zeitung (-en) (1); **reading the newspaper** Zeitung lesen (liest Zeitung), las, gelesen
newspaper cultural section das Feuilleton (-s) (13)
next nächst- (10); **next to** neben (6)
nice nett, schön (1)
niece die Nichte (-n) (3)
night die Nacht (¨e); **at night** nachts, abends (4); **good night** gute Nacht (E)
nightstand der Nachttisch (-e) (2)
nine neun (E)
nineteen neunzehn (E)
ninety neunzig (E)
no nein (E); **no (not any)** kein; **no longer** nicht mehr; **no more** nicht mehr; **no . . . yet** noch kein (2)
nonalcoholic alkoholfrei (6)
none kein (2)
nonreturnable bottle die Wegwerfflasche (-n) (14)
noon der Mittag; **at noon** mittags; **before noon** am Vormittag; **tomorrow noon** morgen Mittag; **afternoon** der Nachmittag; **today before noon** heute Vormittag; **today at noon** heute Mittag; **Saturday before noon** Samstagvormittag (4)
nose die Nase (-n) (8)
not nicht; **not any** kein; **not yet** noch nicht (2)
nothing nichts (2)
to notify Bescheid sagen (sagt Bescheid) (10)
noun das Substantiv (-e) (1)
novel der Roman (-e); **serial novel** der Fortsetzungsroman (13)
November der November (3)
now nun (1); **now and then** ab und zu (8)
number die Nummer (-n), die Zahl (-en) (E); **telephone number** die Telefonnummer (E)
nurse der Krankenpfleger (-) / die Krankenpflegerin (-nen)

O

occasionally ab und zu (8)
occupied besetzt (6)
to occupy oneself (with) sich beschäftigen (mit + *dat.*) (11)
ocean das Meer (7)
o'clock: It's one o'clock. Es ist eins. Es ist ein Uhr. (4)
October (der) Oktober (3)
of (+ *time*) vor; **five of two** fünf vor zwei (4); **made of** aus (+ *dat.*); **out of** aus (+ *dat.*); von (+ *dat.*) (5); **of course** allerdings; natürlich (13)
offer das Angebot (-e) (10); **job offer** das Stellenangebot (11)
office das Büro (-s); **employment office** das Arbeitsamt (¨er) (11); **office hour** die Sprechstunde (-n) (8)
often oft (3)
O.K.: I'm feeling O.K. Es geht. (E)
old alt (10)
olive die Olive (-n) (6)
on an (+ *acc./dat.*); **on (top of)** auf (+ *acc./dat.*) (6); **on Monday** am Montag (4); **on television** im Fernsehen (13)
once einmal; früher (7); **once more** noch einmal
one eins (E); (*indef. pron.*) man (4)
oneself sich (8)
one-way ticket einfach (10)
onion die Zwiebel (-n) (6)
only nur (2)
open geöffnet (6)
opera die Oper (-n) (4)
opinion die Meinung (-en); **in my opinion** meiner Meinung nach (14)
opportunity die Gelegenheit (-en) (11)
or oder (*coord. conj.*) (8)
orange (*color*) orange (5)
order die Ordnung; **in order** in Ordnung (14)
to order bestellen (6)
other ander-, sonstig (10)
ought to sollen (soll), sollte, gesollt (4)
our unser (3)
outdoors im Freien (11)
out of aus (+ *dat.*) (5)
outside draußen (7); **outside of** außerhalb (+ *gen.*) (9)
oven: microwave oven der Mikrowellenherd (-e) (12)
over über (+ *acc./dat.*); **over there** da drüben (6); **left over** übrig (12)
overcast bedeckt; bewölkt (7)
overnight stay die Übernachtung (-en) (9)
own eigen (12)
to own besitzen, besaß, besessen (11)

P

packaging die Verpackung (-en) (14)
pain der Schmerz (-en) (8)
to paint malen (7)
pair of eyeglasses die Brille (-n) (5)
pan die Pfanne (-n) (6)
pants die Hose (-n) (5)

paper das Papier (-e) (12); **toilet paper** das Toilettenpapier (5)
Pardon? Wie bitte? (E)
parents die Eltern (*pl.*) (3)
parking (space) der Parkplatz (¨e) (9)
part der Teil (-e); **parts of the body** die Körperteile (*pl.*) (8)
to participate teilnehmen an (+ *dat.*) (nimmt teil), nahm teil, teilgenommen (14)
particular(ly) besonders (8); **not particularly well** nicht so gut (E)
party die Party (-s) (3)
passenger der Passagier (-e)/die Passagierin (-nen) (10)
passer-by der Passant (-en *masc.*) (9)
passport der Reisepass (¨e) (9)
past: half past one halb zwei (4)
pastry shop die Konditorei (-en) (5)
patio die Terrasse (-n) (2)
to pay zahlen (5); bezahlen (9); **Check, please!** Zahlen, bitte! (6)
to pay attention (to) achten (auf + *acc.*) (8)
pedestrian zone die Fußgängerzone (-n) (14)
pen: ballpoint pen der Kugelschreiber (-) (12)
pencil der Bleistift (-e) (12)
people (*indef. pron.*) man (4)
pepper der Pfeffer (5); **bell pepper** die Paprikaschote (-n) (6)
percent das Prozent (-e) (12)
perhaps vielleicht (2)
to permit erlauben (9)
to be permitted to dürfen (darf), durfte, gedurft (4)
person die Person (-en); der Mensch (-en *masc.*) (2); **per person** pro Person (10)
pharmacy die Apotheke (-n) (5)
photograph das Foto (-s) (2)
photographer der Fotograf (-en *masc.*)/die Fotografin (-nen) (11)
physician der Arzt (¨e)/die Ärztin (-nen) (8)
physicist der Physiker (-)/die Physikerin (-nen) (11)
to pick up (*from a place*) abholen (holt ab) (4)
pilot der Pilot (-en *masc.*)/die Pilotin (-nen) (10)
pilsner beer das Pilsner (-) (6)
place der Platz (¨e); **This place is taken.** Hier ist besetzt. (6); **place of residence** der Wohnort (-e) (1); **if I were in your place** an deiner Stelle (12)
to place (*in a standing position*) stellen (6)
plaid kariert (5)
to plan planen; vorhaben (hat vor), hatte vor, vorgehabt (3); **plan to do (something)** (etwas) vorhaben (4)
plane ticket der Flugschein (-e) (10)
plant: house plant die Zimmerpflanze (-n) (2)
plastic bag die Plastiktüte (-n) (14)
plate der Teller (-) (6)
platform (*train*) der Bahnsteig (-e) (10)
play (*theater*) das Theaterstück (-e) (4)
to play spielen; **to play computer games** Computerspiele spielen; **to play cards** Karten spielen (1)
player: CD player der CD-Spieler (-) (2)
pleasant angenehm (7)
please bitte, bitte schön, bitte sehr (E)
pleased to meet you freut mich (E)
to be pleasing to gefallen (+ *dat.*) (gefällt), gefiel, gefallen (5)
Poland (das) Polen (E)
police, police station die Polizei (9)
politician der Politiker (-)/die Politikerin (-nen) (14)
politics die Politik (13)
pollution: environmental pollution die Umweltverschmutzung (14)
pool: swimming pool das Schwimmbad (¨er) (7); **indoor swimming pool** die Schwimmhalle (-n) (9)
poor(ly) schlecht (E)
pork das Schweinefleisch (5); **pork roast** der Schweinebraten (-) (6)
position (*job*) der Arbeitsplatz (¨e), die Tätigkeit (-en); die Stelle (-n) (11)
possibility die Möglichkeit (-en) (10)
possible möglich (14); **as soon as possible** möglichst bald (11)
poster das Poster (-) (2)
post office die Post (Postämter) (9)
potato die Kartoffel (-n) (5); **fried potatoes** die Bratkartoffeln (6)
poverty die Armut (14)
practical praktisch (1)
to prefer (to do something) lieber (+ *verb*) (4); vorziehen (zieht vor), zog vor, vorgezogen (14)
to prepare (for) sich vorbereiten (auf + *acc.*) (bereitet vor) (11)
preposition die Präposition (-en) (5)
to prescribe verschreiben, verschrieb, verschrieben (8)
present das Geschenk (-e) (3)
prestige das Ansehen, das Prestige (11)
pretty hübsch (1)
pretzel die Brezel (-n) (6)
price der Preis (-e) (9); **discount price** der Sparpreis (10); **reasonable in price** günstig; **included in the price** im Preis enthalten (9)
primary school die Grundschule (-) (11)
printer der Drucker (-) (13)
prison das Gefängnis (-se) (14)
probably wahrscheinlich, wohl (11)
problem das Problem (-e) (2)
to produce herstellen (stellt her) (11)
product das Produkt (-e); **dairy products** die Milchprodukte (*pl.*) (5)
profession der Beruf (-e) (1); **What do you do for a living?** Was sind Sie von Beruf? (1)
professional life das Berufsleben (11)
professor der Professor (-en)/die Professorin (-nen) (1)
program das Programm (-e) (13)
progress der Fortschritt (-e); **to make progress** Fortschritte machen (14)
to promote fördern (14)
pronoun das Pronomen (-) (1)
to propose vorschlagen (schlägt vor), schlug vor, vorgeschlagen (10)
psychologist der Psychologe (-n *masc.*)/die Psychologin (-nen) (11)
pub die Kneipe (-n), das Lokal (-e), das Wirtshaus (¨er) (6)
pullover sweater der Pullover (-) (5)
punctual(ly) pünktlich (10)
to purchase (something) sich (etwas) anschaffen (schafft an) (14)
purple lila (5)
to put (*in a lying position*) legen; (*in a standing position*) stellen (6)
puzzle das Rätsel (-) (13); **crossword puzzle** das Kreuzworträtsel (1)

Q

quarter (*academic*) das Quartal (-e) (12)
quarter das Viertel; **a quarter to two** Viertel vor zwei (12)
question die Frage (-n); **I have a question.** Ich habe eine Frage. (E)
question word das Fragewort (¨er) (6)
quick(ly) schnell (10)
quiet ruhig (1)
quite recht (2)

R

racism der Rassismus (14)
radio das Radio (-s) (2)
railway die Bahn (-en) (10)
rain der Regen (7)
to rain regnen; **It's raining.** Es regnet. (7)
rain shower der Regenschauer (-) (7)
rainy regnerisch (7)
to raise (*a child*) erziehen, erzog, erzogen (14)
rare(ly) selten (2)
rather ziemlich, lieber; **would rather** möchte lieber (4)
to read lesen (liest), las, gelesen (2); **reading books/the newspaper** Bücher/Zeitung lesen
really wirklich (1)

reasonable in price günstig (9)
to receive bekommen, bekam, bekommen (6)
reception der Empfang (¨e); **reception desk** die Rezeption (9)
to recommend empfehlen (empfiehlt), empfahl, empfohlen (5)
to record (on video) aufnehmen (nimmt auf), nahm auf, aufgenommen (13)
recorder: video recorder der Videorecorder (-) (2)
to recover sich erholen (8)
recycling das Recycling; **recycling center** die Sammelstelle (-n) (14)
red rot (5)
to reduce vermindern (14)
refrigerator der Kühlschrank (¨e) (12)
register: cash register die Kasse (-n) (5)
registration form das Anmeldeformular (-e) (9)
to regret bedauern (14)
regular(ly) regelmäßig (8)
to relax sich entspannen (8)
to remain bleiben, blieb, ist geblieben (10)
rent die Miete (-n) (2)
to rent (*from someone*) mieten; **to rent out** vermieten (12)
repair die Reparatur (-en) (12)
to repair reparieren (9)
to repeat wiederholen; **Please repeat.** Wiederholen Sie, bitte. (E)
report der Bericht (-e) (13)
report card das Zeugnis (-se) (11)
to request bitten um (+ *acc.*), bat, gebeten (12)
research die Forschung (-en) (14)
to reserve reservieren (7)
residence: place of residence der Wohnort (-e) (1)
restaurant das Restaurant (-s), das Lokal (-e), die Gaststätte (-n) (6)
restroom die Toilette (-n) (9)
rice der Reis (6)
riddle das Rätsel (-) (13)
to ride fahren (fährt), fuhr, ist gefahren; **to ride a motorcycle** Motorrad fahren (2); **ride (on horseback)** reiten, ritt, ist geritten (7)
right recht; **to be right** Recht haben (2); **all right** in Ordnung; **(to the) right** rechts (9)
right das Recht; **human right** das Menschenrecht (14)
river der Fluss (¨e) (7)
roast: pork roast der Schweinebraten (-) (6)
roll das Brötchen (-) (5)
romantic romantisch (1)
roof das Dach (¨er) (12)
room das Zimmer (-); **bathroom** das Badezimmer (2); **bedroom** das Schlafzimmer; **breakfast room** der Frühstücksraum (¨e); **room with two beds** das Doppelzimmer; **room with one bed** das Einzelzimmer, das Einbettzimmer (9)
roommate der Mitbewohner (-)/die Mitbewohnerin (-nen) (2)
round-trip (*adj.*) hin und zurück (10)
rug der Teppich (-e) (2)
to run laufen (läuft), lief, ist gelaufen (2)

S

sad traurig (7)
safe sicher (10)
to sail segeln (7)
sailing course der Segelkurs (-e) (10)
salad der Salat (-e) (6)
sales person der Verkäufer (-)/die Verkäuferin (-nen) (2)
salt das Salz (5)
Saturday (der) Samstag, Sonnabend (3)
sauerkraut das Sauerkraut (6)
sauna die Sauna (-s) (9)
sausage die Wurst (¨e) (5); **Bavarian veal sausage** die Weißwurst (6)
to save sparen (12)
saving (das) Sparen; **savings account** das Sparkonto (Sparkonten) (12)
to say sagen (1); **How do you say . . . in German?** Wie sagt man . . . auf Deutsch? (E)
saying good-bye beim Abschied (E)
scarcely kaum (8)
scarf der Schal (-s) (5)
schedule (train) der Fahrplan (¨e) (10)
school: secondary school das Gymnasium (Gymnasien) (11)
scientific wissenschaftlich (13)
season die Jahreszeit (-en) (7)
seat der Platz (¨e) (6)
seat reservation die Platzkarte (-n) (10)
second die Sekunde (-n) (4)
to see sehen (sieht), sah, gesehen (2)
semester das Semester (-) (1)
to send schicken (5)
separate getrennt (6)
to separate trennen (14)
September (der) September (3)
serial novel der Fortsetzungsroman (-e) (13)
serious ernst (1)
service die Bedienung (-en) (6)
to set (*put in a sitting position*) setzen (6)
seven sieben (E)
seventeen siebzehn (E)
seventy siebzig (E)
shame: What a shame! So ein Pech! (8)
shampoo das Shampoo (-s) (5)
shape: in shape fit; **to keep in shape** sich fir halten (hält), hielt, gehalten (8)
shared housing die Wohngemeinschaft (-en) (2)
to shave sich rasieren (8)
shaving cream die Rasiercreme (-s) (5)
she sie (1)
shelf das Regal (-e) (2)
shirt das Hemd (-en) (5)
shoe der Schuh (-e); **tennis shoe** der Tennisschuh (5)
to shop einkaufen (kauft ein); **to go shopping** einkaufen gehen (geht), ging, ist gegangen (4)
short kurz; (*person*) klein (10)
shoulder die Schulter (-n) (8)
show die Show; (*TV*) die Sendung (-en) (13)
to show zeigen (5)
shower die Dusche (-n) (9)
to shower (sich) duschen (8)
siblings die Geschwister (*pl.*) (3)
sick krank; **sick as a dog** hundsmiserabel (8)
side dish die Beilage (-n) (6)
signature die Unterschrift (-en) (9)
simple einfach (10)
simultaneous(ly) gleichzeitig (13)
since seit (+ *dat.*) (5); da (*subord. conj.*)
sister die Schwester (-n) (3)
sister-in-law die Schwägerin (-nen) (3)
to sit sitzen, saß, gesessen (6)
to sit down sich (hin)setzen (setzt sich hin) (8)
six sechs (E)
sixteen sechzehn (E)
sixty sechzig (E)
size die Größe (-n) (5)
skate: ice skate der Schlittschuh (-e); **to skate: to ice skate** Schlittschuh laufen (läuft) lief, ist gelaufen (7)
skating rink (*ice*) das Eisstadion (Eisstadien) (7)
to sketch zeichnen (7)
to skim überfliegen, überflog, überflogen (13)
skirt der Rock (¨e) (5)
sky der Himmel (7)
to sleep schlafen (schläft), schlief, geschlafen (2)
slipper der Hausschuh (-e) (5)
Slovakia (die) Slowakei (E)
Slovenia (das) Slowenien (E)
slow(ly) langsam (10); **A bit slower, please.** Etwas langsamer, bitte. (E)
small klein (2)
to smoke rauchen (8)
snow der Schnee (7)
to snow schneien; **It's snowing.** Es schneit. (7)
so so (2); **so long** mach's gut, tschüs (E)
soccer der Fußball; **to play soccer** Fußball spielen (7)

sock die Socke (-n) (5)
sofa das Sofa (-s) (2)
solution die Lösung (-en) (14)
something etwas (2)
sometimes manchmal (8)
somewhat ziemlich (6)
son der Sohn (¨e) (3)
soon bald (12)
sooner eher (13)
sore throat die Halsschmerzen (*pl.*) (8)
sorry: I'm sorry. Das tut mir leid. (9)
to sound klingen, klang, geklungen (8)
soup die Suppe (-n) (6)
to speak sprechen (2)
to spend (*money*) ausgeben (gibt aus), gab aus, ausgegeben (12); (*time*) verbringen (8)
spite: in spite of trotz (+ *gen.*) (9)
spoon der Löffel (-) (6)
sport der Sport (Sportarten); **to do sports** Sport treiben, trieb, getrieben (7)
sports arena die Sporthalle (-n) (7)
sports coat das Sakko (-s) (5)
to spread verbreiten (14)
spring das Frühjahr, der Frühling (7)
stable (*adj.*) fest (11)
stadium das Stadion (Stadien) (7)
stairway die Treppe (-n) (12)
to stand stehen, stand, gestanden (6)
to stand up aufstehen (steht auf), stand auf, ist aufgestanden (4)
to stand up (*put in a standing position*) stellen (6)
station: train station der Bahnhof (¨e) (10); **television station (channel)** das Programm (-e) (13)
stay der Aufenthalt (-e); **overnight stay** die Übernachtung (-en) (9)
to stay bleiben, blieb, ist geblieben; **to stay overnight** übernachten (10)
to stay up aufbleiben (bleibt auf), blieb auf, ist aufgeblieben
steak das Steak (-s) (5)
stereo die Stereoanlage (-n) (2)
still noch (2); **still none/no** noch kein
stocking der Strumpf (¨e) (5)
stomach der Brauch (¨e) (8)
stop (*e.g. bus*) die Haltestelle (-n) (10)
to stop (doing something) aufhören (hört auf) (4)
store das Geschäft (-e); der Laden (¨) (5)
story (*level*) der Stock, das Stockwerk (-e), die Etage (-n) (9)
straight ahead (immer) geradeaus (9)
to straighten up aufräumen (räumt auf) (4)
strawberry die Erdbeere (-n) (5)
street die Straße (-n) (E)
street address die Hausnummer (-n) (E)
strenuous anstrengend (8)
stress der Stress (8)
to stretch sich strecken (8)
striped gestreift (5)
strong stark (10)
student der Student (-en *masc.*)/die Studentin (-nen) (1)
student cafeteria die Mensa (Mensen) (2)
to study studieren; lernen (1)
to subscribe to abonnieren (13)
subscription das Abonnement (-s) (13)
success der Erfolg (-e) (11)
sugar der Zucker (5)
to suggest vorschlagen (schlägt vor), schlug vor, vorgeschlagen (10)
suit der Anzug (¨e); **bathing suit** der Badeanzug (¨e) (5)
suitable geeignet (9)
suitcase der Koffer (-) (9)
summer der Sommer (7)
sun die Sonne (7); **The sun is shining.** Die Sonne scheint. (7)
sunblock das Sonnenschutzmittel (-) (10)
Sunday (der) Sonntag (3)
sunny sonnig (7)
sunshine der Sonnenschein (7)
suntan lotion das Sonnenschutzmittel (-) (10)
superficial(ly) oberflächlich (13)
superlative die Superlativform (-en) (7)
supermarket der Supermarkt (¨e) (5)
to support unterstützen (14)
to be supposed to sollen (soll), sollte, gesollt (4)
surcharge der Zuschlag (¨e) (10)
surname der Nachname (-n *masc.*) (1)
to be suspended hängen, hing, gehangen (6)
suspenseful spannend (4)
to swallow schlucken (5)
sweater der Pullover (-) (5)
to swim schwimmen, schwamm, ist geschwommen (2)
swimming pool das Schwimmbad (¨er); **indoor swimming pool** die Schwimmhalle (-n) (7)
Switzerland die Schweiz (E)

T

table der Tisch (-e); **coffee table** der Couchtisch (2)
to take nehmen (nimmt), nahm, genommen (2); dauern (7); **take-out (food)** zum Mitnehmen (6); **to take along** mitnehmen (nimmt mit), nahm mit, mitgenommen (4)
tall groß (1)
tape (*video*) das Video (-s) (2)
task die Aufgabe (-n) (11)
to taste (good) schmecken (+ *dat.*); **That tastes good (to me).** Das schmeckt (mir). (5)
tax die Steuer (-n) (14)
taxi das Taxi (-s) (10)
taxi driver der Taxifahrer (-)/die Taxifahrerin (-nen) (10)
tea der Tee (-s) (5)
teacher der Lehrer (-)/die Lehrerin (-nen) (E)
technique die Technik (-en) (11)
technology die Technologie (-en) (11)
telephone das Telefon (-e) (2)
telephone call der Telefonanruf (-e) (9)
telephone number die Telefonnummer (-n) (E)
television (TV) das Fernsehen; **on television** im Fernsehen; **to watch television** fernsehen (sieht fern), sah fern, ferngesehen (13)
television set der Fernseher (-) (2)
television station (channel) das Programm (-e) (13)
to tell sagen; **tell me** sag mal (1)
temperature die Temperatur (-en) (7)
ten zehn (E)
tender zart (5)
tennis das Tennis; **to play tennis** Tennis spielen (7)
tennis court der Tennisplatz (¨e) (7)
tennis shoe der Tennisschuh (-e) (5)
tent das Zelt (-e) (10)
terrace die Terrasse (-n) (2)
terrible scheußlich (7)
to thank: thank you, thanks danke; **thank you very much** danke schön, danke sehr; **fine, thanks** danke, gut (E); **Many thanks!** Vielen Dank! (6); **No thanks necessary.** Nichts zu danken. (8)
that (*subord. conj.*) dass (8)
the der, die, das (E)
theater das Theater (-); **movie theater** das Kino (-s) (4)
their ihr (3)
then dann (1); **now and then** ab und zu (8)
there da (2); **over there** da drüben (6); **there is/there are** es gibt (3)
therefore deshalb (8)
they sie; man (*indef. pron.*) (1)
to think (about/of) denken (an + *acc.*), dachte, gedacht; nachdenken (über + *acc.*) (denkt nach), dachte nach, nachgedacht (11)
to think (of), consider finden, fand, gefunden; halten für (+ *acc.*) (hält), hielt, gehalten; **I think it is a pity.** Ich finde es schade. (12)
third das Drittel (-) (12)
to be thirsty Durst haben (2)
thirteen dreizehn (E)

thirty dreißig (E)
this dieser, diese, dies(es); das (5); **this is** das ist (E); **this evening** heute Abend (4)
three drei (E)
three times dreimal (7)
throat der Hals (¨e); **sore throat** die Halsschmerzen (*pl.*) (8)
through durch (+ *acc.*) (3)
to thunder donnern; **It's thundering.** Es donnert. (7)
thunderstorm das Gewitter (-) (7)
Thursday (der) Donnerstag (3)
ticket das Ticket (-s), die Fahrkarte (-n); **airplane ticket** der Flugschein (-e); **one-way** (*ticket*) einfach (10)
ticket window der Fahrkartenschalter (-) (10)
till bis; **till five o'clock** bis fünf Uhr (6)
time die Zeit, die Uhrzeit (-en) (2); **free time** die Freizeit; **to have time** Zeit haben (2); **What time is it?** Wie spät ist es? **At what time?** Um wie viel Uhr? (4)
time of day die Tageszeit (-en) (2)
tin can die Dose (-n) (14)
tired müde (8)
tiring anstrengend, ermüdend (8)
to an (+ *acc./dat.*) (6); zu (+ *dat.*); nach (+ *dat.*); **(to) home** nach Hause; **to the theater** ins Theater (5)
today heute (1)
toe die Zehe (-n) (8)
together gemeinsam, zusammen (6)
toilet das WC (-s) (9)
toilet paper das Toilettenpapier (5)
toiletries die Toilettenartikel (*pl.*) (5)
toiletries and sundries store die Drogerie (-n) (5)
tomato die Tomate (-n) (6)
tomorrow morgen (3); **tomorrow afternoon** morgen Nachmittag; **tomorrow morning** morgen früh (4)
tonight heute Abend (4)
toothpaste die Zahnpasta (5)
topical aktuell (13)
total: The total is . . . Das macht zusammen . . . (6)
town die Stadt (¨e) (E)
track (*train*) das Gleis (-e) (10)
tradition die Tradition (-en) (3)
traffic light die Ampel (-n) (9)
tragedy die Tragödie (-n) (4)
trail: hiking trail der Wanderweg (-e) (10)
train die Bahn (-en), der Zug (¨e) (10)
train platform der Bahnsteig (-e) (10)
train station der Bahnhof (¨e) (10)
training das Training; **sales training** das Verkaufstraining (11)
transcript (*school*) das Zeugnis (-se) (11)
to transfer umsteigen (steigt um), stieg um, ist umgestiegen (10)
trash der Abfall (¨e) (14)
to travel reisen, ist gereist (1)
travel agency das Reisebüro (-s) (10)
travel brochure der Reiseprospekt (-e) (10)
traveler's check der Reisescheck (-s) (9)
travel guide (*person*) der Reiseleiter (-)/die Reiseleiterin (-nen); (*book*) der Reiseführer (-) (10)
tree der Baum (¨e); **family tree** der Stammbaum (3)
trip die Fahrt (-en) (10)
trousers die Hose (-n) (5)
to try probieren, versuchen (8); **to try on** anprobieren (probiert an) (5)
T-shirt das T-Shirt (-s) (5)
Tuesday (der) Dienstag (3)
tuition die Studiengebühren (*pl.*) (12)
turkey der Truthahn (¨e) (5)
to turn in abgeben (gibt ab), gab ab, abgegeben (8)
to turn into einbiegen in (+ *acc.*) (9)
TV (television) das Fernsehen (2)
twelve zwölf (E)
twenty zwanzig (E)
twice zweimal (7)
two zwei (E)
type die Art (-en), die Sorte (-n); **types of fruit** die Obstsorten (*pl.*) (5)

U

umbrella der Regenschirm (-e) (7)
uncle der Onkel (-) (3)
under unter (+ *acc./dat.*); (6) **Under what name?** Auf welchen Namen? (9)
to undertake unternehmen (unternimmt), unternahm, unternommen (10)
undressed: to get undressed sich ausziehen (zieht sich aus), zog sich aus, hat sich ausgezogen (8)
university die Universität (-en) (1)
upstairs oben; nach oben (12)
urgent dringend (2)
to use verwenden (14)
usually gewöhnlich (4)
utilities Nebenkosten (12)

V

vacation: to go on vacation Urlaub machen (8)
vacuum cleaner der Staubsauger (-) (13)
Valentine's Day der Valentinstag (-e) (3)
varied abwechslungsreich (12)
veal cutlet das Wiener Schnitzel (-) (6)
veal sausage (*Bavarian*) die Weißwurst (¨e) (6)
vegetable das Gemüse; **type of vegetable** die Gemüsesorte (-n); **fruit and vegetable stand** der Obst- und Gemüsestand (¨e) (5)
vegetarian vegetarisch (6)
verb das Verb (-en) (1); **modal verb** das Modalverb (5)
very sehr; **very well** sehr gut (E)
vicinity die Nähe (9)
video(tape) das Video (-s) (2)
video recorder (VCR) der Videorecorder (-) (2)
view: in my view meines Erachtens (14)
violence, act of violence die Gewalttätigkeit (-en) (14)
to visit besuchen (1)

W

to wait (for) warten (auf + *acc.*) (6)
waiter der Kellner (-); der Ober (-) (6)
waitress die Kellnerin (-nen) (6)
to wake up aufwachen (wacht auf), ist aufgewacht (4)
walk: to go for a walk spazieren gehen (geht), ging spazieren, ist spazieren gegangen (8)
to walk zu Fuß gehen, ging, ist gegangen (8); **to walk along** entlanggehen (geht entlang), ging entlang, ist entlanggegangen (9)
wall die Wand (¨e) (2)
to want wollen (will), wollte, gewollt (4)
war der Krieg (-e) (14)
warm warm (7)
to wash oneself sich waschen (wäscht), wusch, gewaschen (8)
waste der Abfall (¨e) (14)
to watch achten auf (*acc.*) (8); sich (etwas) ansehen (sieht an), sah an, angesehen (13); **to watch television** fernsehen (sieht fern), sah fern, ferngesehen (4); **Watch out!** Achtung! (10)
water das Wasser; **mineral water** das Mineralwasser (5)
way der Weg (-e) (9); **along the way** unterwegs; **by the way** übrigens (9)
we wir (1)
weak schlapp (8)
wear tragen (trägt), trug, getragen (5)
weather das Wetter (7)
weather report der Wetterbericht (-e) (7)
wedding die Hochzeit (-en) (3)
Wednesday (der) Mittwoch (3)
week die Woche (-n); **once a week** einmal die Woche (7)
weekend das Wochenende (-n) (7)
weight training das Bodybuilding (7)
welcome: (a hearty) welcome herzlich willkommen; **you're welcome** bitte (E)
well gut; wohl; **not so well** nicht so gut; **very well** sehr gut (E); **to get well** sich erholen (8)

what was (1); **What is your name?** (*form.*) Wie ist Ihr Name? / Wie heißen Sie? (*inform.*) Wie heißt du? (E); **what kind of (a)** was für (ein) (11); **What does . . . mean?** Was bedeutet . . . ? (E); **So what?** na und? (13)
when als (*subord. conj.*); wann (1); wenn (*subord. conj.*) (8); **When is your birthday?** Wann hast du Geburtstag? (3)
where wo; **from where** woher (1); **(to) where** wohin (5); **Where are you from?** (*form.*) Woher kommen Sie? (*inform.*) Woher kommst du? (E)
whether ob (*subord. conj.*) (8)
which welcher, welche, welches (5)
whipped cream die Sahne (6)
white weiß (5)
who wer (1)
whom wen (*acc.*) (2); wem (*dat.*) (5)
why warum (1)
wife die Frau (-en) (3)
wind der Wind (7)
window das Fenster (-) (2); **ticket window** der Fahrkartenschalter (-) (10)
windy windig (7)
wine der Wein (-e) (6)
winter (der) Winter (7)
to wish wünschen (3)
with mit (+ *dat.*); bei (+ *dat.*) (5)
without ohne (3); **to do without** verzichten (13)
woman die Frau (-en) (1)
wonderful fabelhaft (E)
word das Wort (¨er); **question word** das Fragewort (¨er) (1)
work die Arbeit (8)
to work arbeiten (1); funktionieren (9)
workroom das Arbeitszimmer (-) (2)
world hunger der Welthunger (14)
would: would like (to) möchte; **would rather** möchte lieber; **would like best** möchte am liebsten (4); **Would you please . . . ?** Würden Sie bitte . . . ? (9)
to write schreiben, schrieb, geschrieben (2)

X

xenophobia die Ausländerfeindlichkeit (14)

Y

year das Jahr (-e); **next year** nächstes Jahr (1); **once a year** einmal im Jahr (7)
yellow gelb (5)
yes ja (E); doch (1)
yesterday gestern (7)
yet noch (2); **no . . . yet** noch kein; **not any . . . yet** noch kein (11); **not yet** noch nicht
yogurt der Joghurt (5)
you du (*inform. sg.*); ihr (*inform. pl.*); Sie (*form sg./pl.*) (1); dich (*acc. inform. sg.*); euch (*acc./dat. inform. pl.*); Sie (*acc. form.*) (3); dir (*dat. inform. sg.*); Ihnen (*dat. form.*) (5)
young jung (10)
your dein (*inform. sg.*); euer (*inform. pl.*); Ihr (*form sg./pl.*) (3)
youth der/die Jugendliche (*decl. adj.*) (10)
youth hostel die Jugendherberge (-n) (9)

Z

zero null (E)
zip code die Postleitzahl (-en) (E)

Index

The Index is followed by a list of major topics ("Culture") appearing in the **Kulturtipp** boxes along with other pertinent cultural topics, and a list of vocabulary items grouped by category ("Vocabulary"). References to reading strategies are incorporated in the Index under *reading strategies*. *Note*: *KT* = **Kulturtipp** ; *ST* = **Sprachtipp**; *N* = footnote.

Y

Z

Culture

Vocabulary

Photographs: *1* © Ulrike Welsch; *2* © Ulrike Welsch *(top)*; *2* © Beryl Goldberg *(bottom)*; *3* © Ulrike Welsch; *22* © Ulrike Welsch; *23* © Kevin Galvin *(left)*; *23* © Ulrike Welsch *(right)*; *25* © Owen Frank/Stock Boston; *31* © Peter Menzel Photography; *50* © Ulrike Welsch; *59* © Joseph Guido Giannetti/Stock Boston *(left)*; *59* © Tony Stone Images *(right)*; *78* © Ulrike Welsch; *86* © McGraw-Hill, Inc.; *95* © Bob Krist/Corbis; *96* © Archiv fur Kunst und Geschichte, Berlin; *104* © Archiv fur Kunst und Geschichte, Berlin *(top left)*; *104* © Archiv fur Kunst und Geschichte, Berlin *(middle)*; *104* © Archiv fur Kunst und Geschichte, Berlin *(right)*; *104* © Archiv fur Kunst und Geschichte, Berlin *(bottom)*; *105* © Bilderdienst Suddeutscher Verlag, Munchen *(top)*; *105* © Archiv fur Kunst und Geschichte, Berlin *(bottom)*; *106* © Ulrike Welsch; *118* © Zefa/Damm; *132* Courtesy Miguel Guglielminpietro; *138* © Ulrike Welsch; *170* © Ulrike Welsch; *173* Courtesy Miguel Guglielminpietro; *174* © Kevin Galvin/Stock Boston; *177* © Daniel Aubry; *195* © Topham/The Image Works; *200* © Helga Lade/Peter Arnold, Inc. *(left)*; *200* © Rudy Muller/Envision *(right)*; *200* © Hugh Rogers/Monkmeyer; *202* © Ulrike Welsch; *208* © Julie Marcotte/Stock Boston *(top left)*; *208* © Reichmann/Monkmeyer *(top right)*; *208* © Fridmar Dann/Leo de Wys, Inc. *(bottom left)*; *208* © David Ulmer/Stock Boston *(bottom right)*; *223* © Bettmann Archive; *226* © Peter Menzel Photography; *228* © Michael P. Gadomski/Photo Researchers *(top)*; *228* © Helga Lade/Peter Arnold, Inc. *(bottom); 229* © Tony Stone Images; *237* © Ulrike Welsch; *250* © Richard Elliott/Tony Stone Images; *278* © Helga Lade/Peter Arnold, Inc. *(left)*; *278* © Helga Lade/Peter Arnold, Inc. *(top right)*; *278* © Zefa/Waldkirch *(bottom right)*; *280* © McGraw-Hill, Inc.; *284* © Ulrike Welsch; *297* © McGraw-Hill, Inc.; *314* © Stephen L. Newton; *326* © Helga Lade/Peter Arnold, Inc.; *344* © Ulrike Welsch; *346* © Owen Franken; *376* © 1995 Artists Rights Society, NY/Bild-Kunst, Bonn/© AKG London *(top)*; *376* © 1995 Artists Rights Society, NY/Bil-Kunst, Bonn *(middle)*; *376* © 1995 Artists Rights Society, NY/Bild-Kunst, Bonn/© AKG London *(bottom)*; *378* © Keystone Pressedi/The Image Works; *396* © Ulrike Welsch; *402* © Zefa/Hrdlicka; *409* © Ulrike Welsch; *428* © R. Bossu/Sygma; *429* © Topham/The Image Works *(left)*; *429* © UPI/Bettman Archive *(right)*; *430* © Keystone Pressedi/The Image Works *(top)*; *430* © Bettmann Archive *(bottom)*; *431* © Dallas and John Heaton/Stock Boston; *432* © Reuters/Bettmann Archive *(top left)*; *432* © UPI/Bettmann Archive *(top right)*; *432* © UPI/Bettmann Archive *(bottom left)*; *432* © Topham/he Image Works *(bottom right)*; *433* © Michael Schwarz/The Image Works.

Realia: *4* Beate and Klaus Stetten; *6* © Eva Heller. From *Vielleicht sind wir eben zu verschieden (bottom right); 9 © Funk Uhr (bottom right); 11 © Berliner Morgenpost (right); 12* Volkswagen AG *(bottom); 17* Reprinted with permission of Peter Falk, star of *Colombo (C)*; *38* Epson Deutschland *(right); 40* From *Huhnstage von Peter Gaymann* © Fakelträger Verlag 1984; *42* From *Huhnstage von Peter Gaymann* © Fakelsträger Verlag 1984; *43* Reprinted with permission of Galerie in der Töpferstube; *58* © Goldmann Verlag; *64* Reprinted with permission of Werner Buchi/*Brückenbauer*; *68* Reprinted with permission of Wolfgang Horsch; *82* Koelbl/Stern; *83* Courtesy of DM-Heerlen *(top); 93* Reprinted with permission of Deutsche Welthungerhilfe *(top right); 99 Die Ganze Woche*; *111* Reprinted with permission of Langenscheidt-Verlag, Berlin and Munich; *114 PM*, Gruner + Jahr AG; *117* ICC Berlin *(top left); 123* © Droemer Knauer Verlag, Munich; *124* Reprinted permission of Christine Sielung, Düsseldorf *(top); 124* Beate Heinen, Kunstverlag, D 56653 Maria Laach, Nr. 2705 *(bottom right); 132* © Express Newspaper Ltd./Distr. Bulls; *171* Reprinted with permission of Offenbach-Stuben; *184* Deutsche Telekom; *190* Detlef Kersten/Cartoon-Caricature-Contor, Munich; *203* © Globus Infografik GmbH; *205* Jugendamt und Sport- und Bäderamt, Göttingen; *210* BZ/Image Presseservice Gensler GmbH; *214* Reprinted with permission of Kalkberg GmbH, Bad Segeberg; *219* Reprinted with permission of Fremdenverkehrsverein Altes Land e.V., D-21635 Jork; *222 Focus* 24/97; *232* Reprinted with permission of René Fehr, Brückenbauer; *239 Rheinische Post*, Düsseldorf; *240* Reprinted with permission of Wolfgang Horsch; *240* © Tribune Media Services. All Rights Reserved. Reprinted with permission. © Associated Newspaper Ltd./Distr. Bulls *(top); 241* Reprinted with permission of Uli Stein; *257* Warnemünde-Prospekt 1992/Kuramt; *294* ADAC Hessen-Thüringen, Schumannstraße 4-6, D-60325; *308 Sports—Die Sportzeitschrift*, Jahr-Verlag GmbH; *315* © Globus Infografik GmbH; *318* From *Berufswahl—Trips, Trends, Tests*, Commerzbank, Frankfurt am Main; *326 Tatsachen über Deutschland* © Societäts-Verlag, Frankfurt; *328* Erich Rauschenbach, Cartoon-Caricature-Contor Munich; *331* Konica Business Machines International; *332* © Handelsblatt GmbH, Düsseldorf *(right); 347* © Globus Infografik GmbH; *366* © Eva Heller. From *Vielleicht sind wir eben zu verschieden*; *367* Reprinted with permission of Wolfgang Horsch; *368* Eva Heller. From *Vielleicht sind wir eben zu verschieden*; *370* Reprinted with permission of *Die Welt*; *377* "Der Leser", by Jiri Georg Dokoupil. Reprinted with permission *(left); 377* Illustration by Claus Bremer from *Konkrete Poesie* (Ditzingen: Philipp Reclam Jun. Verlag, 1976) *(top right); 377* Illustration by Reinhard Dohl from *Konkrete Poesie* (Ditzingen: Philipp Reclam Jun. Verlag, 1976) *(middle right); 379 Süddeutsche Zeitung, Frankfurter Rundschau, Die Zeit,* and *Die Tageszeitung*; *380 TV Neu*; *381 Stern-TV-Magazin*; *382 TV Neu*; *384* © Globus Infografik GmbH; *385* © Kaiser GmbH; *386* © Globus Infografik GmbH; *389 Neue Zürcher Zeitung; 392* Detlev Kersten © Lappan Verlag; *394 Volkszeitung*; *403 TV Hören & Sehen*; *408 Natur*, Ringier Verlag; *410 Natur*, Ringier Verlag; *411 Natur*, Ringier Verlag; *413* Reprinted with permission of Greenpeace Germany *(top left); 415* © *Berliner Morgenpost (top); 415* © ALI Press Agency *(bottom)*; *437–439* Herbert Hoover Collection, Memorabilia, Hoover Institution Archives; *440* Reprinted with permission of Andreas Muhs (top); *440* Reprinted with permission of Reimer Wulf *(bottom); 441*Partner für Berlin—Gesellschaft für Haupstadt-Marketing GmbH.

Readings: *133* "Immer das gleiche" © Christine Wuttke; *164 TV Media*; *195* "Kaffeehäuser" reprinted with permission of Fremdenverkehrsverband für Wien; *223* From *Gesammelte Werke* by Bertolt Brecht © Suhrkamp Verlag, Frankfurt am Main, 1967; *246* Text: *Focus*, illustrations: reprinted with permission of Reinhardt Wendlinger; *273* "Die Gitarre des Herrn Hatunoglu" by Heinrich Hannover from *Als der Clown die Grippe hatte* (rotf. 669). Copyright © 1992 by Rowohlt Taschenbuch Verlag, Reinbek; *309* From *Outdoor*, 4/97, Rotpunkt Verlag; *340 Für Sie*; *372* "Fahrkarte bitte" by Helga M. Novak from *Palisaden* © 1980 Luchterhand Literaturverlag; *398* "Fernsehabend," Loriots Dramatische Werke. All rights reserved, © 1981 by Diogenes Verlag AG Zürich; *423* "Was in der Zeitung steht" by Reinhard Mai, *Alle meine Lieder*, Maikäfer Musik Verlagsgesellschaft, Berlin; *436* From *Wir leben im Verborgenen* by Ceja Stojka, reprinted with permission of Picus Verlag.

About the Authors

Robert Di Donato is Associate Professor of German and Chair of the German, Russian, and East Asian Languages Department at Miami University in Oxford, Ohio. He received his Ph.D. from the Ohio State University. He has written articles about foreign language methodology and has given numerous keynote speeches, workshops, and presentations, both in the United States and abroad, about foreign language methods and teacher education. He has been a consultant for a number of college-level textbooks on foreign language pedagogy.

Monica D. Clyde is a native of Düsseldorf. She received her Ph.D. in German Literature from the University of California at Berkeley. She has taught German language and literature at Mills College, Cañada College, the Defense Language Institute, and the College of San Mateo. She is currently Director of Faculty Development and Scholarship at Saint Mary's College of California. She has coauthored ***Texte und Kontexte*** and was a contributor to ***Mosaik: Deutsche Kultur und Literatur,*** Third Edition, both intermediate college-level German textbooks.

Jacqueline Vansant received her Ph.D. from the University of Texas at Austin. She has taught at Hamilton College and Miami University in Oxford, Ohio, and currently teaches at the University of Michigan-Dearborn, where she also heads the German section of the Department of Humanities. She is the main author of ***Blickwechsel,*** an intermediate German reader. Her particular interest in language pedagogy lies in reading and reading strategies. In addition, she has written widely on contemporary Austrian literature and culture.

Listening Comprehension Scripts

Einführung

Hallo! Guten Tag! Herzlich willkommen!

Im Tennisklub in Offenbach

TENNIS-TRAINER: Guten Tag! Herzlich willkommen! Mein Name ist Pohle, Norbert Pohle. Und wie ist Ihr Name?
SABINE: Sabine Zimmermann.
TENNIS-TRAINER: Und Sie? Wie heißen Sie?
ANTONIO: Ich heiße Antonio Coletti.
ARI: Und ich bin Ari Pappas.

Auf einem Studentenball in Bonn

PETER: Grüß dich. Ich heiße Peter Sedlmeier.
KATARINA: Mein Name ist Katarina Steinmetz.
PETER: Woher kommst du?
KATARINA: Aus Dresden. Und du?
PETER: Aus Rosenheim.

Ein Treffen in Berlin

HERR GROTE: Frau Kühne, das ist Herr Michels aus Berlin. Frau Kühne kommt aus Potsdam.
HERR MICHELS: Freut mich.
FRAU KÜHNE: Gleichfalls.

Aktivität 8 Wie geht's?

Dialog 1

URSEL: 'n Abend, Thomas.
THOMAS: 'n Abend, Ursel.
URSEL: Na, wie geht's?
THOMAS: Ach, nicht besonders gut. Und dir?
URSEL: Danke, gut.

Dialog 2

FRAU ENGELHARDT: Grüß Gott, Herr Kümmerli.
HERR KÜMMERLI: Grüß Gott, Frau Engelhardt.
FRAU ENGELHARDT: Wie geht es Ihnen?
HERR KÜMMERLI: Danke, gut. Und wie geht es Ihnen?
FRAU ENGELHARDT: Danke, auch gut.
HERR KÜMMERLI: Na, dann, auf Wiedersehen.
FRAU ENGELHARDT: Auf Wiedersehen, Herr Kümmerli.

Dialog 3

NINA: Grüß dich, Dieter.
DIETER: Nina. Wie geht's?
NINA: Ach, es geht nicht besonders gut und nicht besonders schlecht. Und dir?
DIETER: Ausgezeichnet.
NINA: Na, dann mach's gut!
DIETER: Tschüs.

Aktivität 10 Wichtige Telefonnummern

Fernsehprogramme	1 15 03
Kinoprogramme	1 15 11
Küchenrezepte	11 67
Sportnachrichten	11 63
Theater und Konzertveranstaltungen	1 15 17
Verbraucher- und Einkauftipps	1 16 06
Wettervorhersage	38 53
Zahlenlotto	11 62
Zeitansage	1 19 94

Aktivität 12 Die Adresse und Telefonnummer, bitte!

1. A: Wie ist die Adresse von Professor Hauser, bitte?
B: Moment mal. Gartenstraße 19.
A: Und die Postleitzahl?
B: 82067 Ebenhausen/Isartal.
A: Und wie ist die Telefonnummer?
B: 41 34 76.
A: Vielen Dank.
B: Bitte schön.

2. A: Bitte schön, die Adresse von Margas Fitnessstudio?
B: Bautzner Straße 15.
A: Wissen Sie übrigens die Postleitzahl?
B: Jawohl. 01093 Dresden.
A: Und die Telefonnummer?
B: Die Telefonnummer ist 20 86 73.
A: Danke sehr. Wiederhören!
B: Wiederhören!

3. A: Könnten Sie mir bitte die Adresse von Autohaus Becker sagen?
B: Freilich. Das wäre Landstuhler Straße 54.
A: Haben Sie die Postleitzahl?
B: Ja. Die ist 66482 Zweibrücken-Ixheim.
A: Und die Telefonnummer?
B: 1 88 42.
A: Vielen Dank. Wiederhören!
B: Wiederhören!

Aktivität 17 Sie verstehen schon etwas Deutsch!

1. Der neue Opel Astra: Komfort, Sicherheit und Technik. Das neue Auto für die 90er Jahre.
2. Im Neuen Theater Hamburg spielt heute Abend um 20.00 Uhr „Das Phantom der Oper" von Andrew Lloyd Webber.
3. Lillehammer, Norwegen, Olympische Spiele. Die Deutschen gewinnen 9 Goldmedaillen.

4. Café-Restaurant Schönberger sucht einen Koch oder eine Köchin mit klassischer Ausbildung.
5. Bei Kinderfreude haben wir Freude an Kindern. Unsere Kinderkrippe ist kinderfreundlich, sauber, modern und sicher.

Kapitel 1

Alles klar?

B. **1.** Grüß Gott. Mein Name ist Nikolaus Euba. Ich bin Student und komme aus München.
2. Guten Tag. Mein Name ist Marco Berger. Ich bin Journalist und komme aus Köln.
3. Guten Tag. Ich heiße Andrea Rubik. Ich bin Sportlehrerin. Ich komme aus Wien.
4. Mein Name ist Marion Hintze. Ich bin Architektin und komme aus Leipzig.
5. Guten Tag. Ich heiße Zafir Brückner. Ich bin Physiker und komme aus Zürich.

Wörter im Kontext

Aktivität 1 Eine neue Studentin

BEAMTER: Ihr Name, bitte?
JULIE: Julie Harrison.
BEAMTER: Buchstabieren Sie das bitte!
JULIE: Vorname: J-u-l-i-e
Nachname: H-a-r-r-i-s-o-n
BEAMTER: Beruf?
JULIE: Studentin.
BEAMTER: Und woher kommen Sie?
JULIE: Aus den USA, Cincinnati.
BEAMTER: Ihr Pass, bitte.
JULIE: Hier, bitte.
BEAMTER: Ihre Adresse hier in Berlin?
JULIE: Brandenburgerstraße 37.
BEAMTER: Geburtsdatum?
JULIE: Vierter April 1980.
BEAMTER: Danke, jetzt brauche ich nur noch Ihre Unterschrift.

Thema 2: Sich erkundigen

„Glücksrad Fortuna"

QUIZMASTER: Guten Abend, meine Damen und Herren. Willkommen im Studio bei Glücksrad Fortuna. Mein Name ist Dieter Sielinsky. Wer gewinnt heute Abend—und was? Das ist die große Frage! Und nun zu unserem ersten Kandidaten. Wie ist Ihr Name, bitte?
KANDIDAT: Lentz, Gertraud Lentz.
QUIZMASTER: Woher kommen Sie, Frau Lentz?
KANDIDAT: Aus München.
QUIZMASTER: Frau Lentz, was sind Sie von Beruf?
KANDIDAT: Ich bin Hausfrau.
QUIZMASTER: Haben Sie Hobbys, Frau Lentz?
KANDIDAT: Ja, natürlich! Lesen, Reisen, Kochen, Wandern, und ich mache gern Kreuzworträtsel.
QUIZMASTER: Wie finden Sie Berlin?
KANDIDAT: Sehr interessant, wirklich faszinierend.
QUIZMASTER: So, danke sehr, Frau Lentz.
KANDIDAT: Bitte schön.
QUIZMASTER: Na dann, viel Spaß und viel Glück.

Ein Gespräch an der Uni

HELMUT: Grüß Gott! Helmut Sachs.
JULIE: Guten Tag! Ich heiße Julie Harrison.
HELMUT: Woher kommst du, Julie?
JULIE: Ich komme aus Cincinnati.
HELMUT: Cincinnati, wo ist denn das?
JULIE: In den USA, im Mittelwesten, im Bundesstaat Ohio.
HELMUT: Sag mal, was machst du jetzt hier?
JULIE: Ich lerne Deutsch am Sprachinstitut. Und du?
HELMUT: Ich studiere Physik an der T. U.
JULIE: Was ist die T. U. denn?
HELMUT: Die Technische Universität. Und wie lange bleibst du hier in München?
JULIE: Zwei Semester. Nächstes Jahr bin ich wieder in Ohio.
HELMUT: Ach so.

Aktivität 8 Kurzdialoge

1. A: Wie heißt du?
B: Ich heiße Dieter.
2. A: Woher kommen Sie?
B: Ich studiere hier.
3. A: Was machen Sie hier?
B: Wir besuchen Freunde.
4. A: Wie heißen Sie?
B: Mein Name ist Lentz.
5. A: Hallo. Grüß dich, Helmut!
B: Auf Wiedersehen.
6. A: Woher kommst du?
B: Aus Berlin.
7. A: Wie finden Sie Berlin?
B: Ich komme aus den USA.
8. A: Wo ist denn das?
B: Das ist in den USA.
9. A: Auf Wiedersehen, Frau Keller.
B: Guten Tag!
10. A: Was studieren Sie?
B: Englisch.

Grammatik im Kontext

Übung 1 Was hören Sie?

1. Wie bitte, wie ist der Name?
2. Die Frau kommt aus Amerika.
3. Wie heißt das Land?
4. Wie ist die Adresse von McDonald's?
5. Woher kommt der Student?
6. Die Studentin lernt Deutsch in Erfurt.
7. Was macht das Mädchen in Berlin?
8. Wo wohnt der Professor?

Übung 16 Das Studentenleben

A. Karin Renner kommt ursprünglich aus Dresden. Familie Renner wohnt immer noch da. Jetzt wohnt Karin aber in Göttingen. Sie studiert da nämlich Informatik. Sie ist sehr gut in Mathematik. Karin wohnt in einem Studentenwohnheim am Rosenbachweg. Das Wohnheim ist sehr groß und modern, aber auch unpersönlich. Karin arbeitet viel für ihre Kurse.

Sie ist auch sportlich sehr aktiv. Sie geht regelmäßig schwimmen. Sie geht auch oft ins Café. Sie findet das Café Kadenz besonders nett. Sie trifft da oft ein paar Freunde, und dann diskutieren sie über ihre Kurse, die Arbeit, die Politik und natürlich die Professoren.

Kapitel 2

Alles klar?

B. **1.** INGRID: Was suchst du in der Zeitung?
KIRSTEN: Eine Wohnung. Ich brauche eine Dreizimmerwohnung.
INGRID: Warum so groß?
KIRSTEN: Für mich und Angelika.

2. GERD: Suchst du eine neue Wohnung?
JOCHEN: Ja. Die alte ist zu klein. Ich suche eine Zweizimmerwohnung mit Küche und Bad.

3. GABI: Suchst du im Moment ein Zimmer?
ANJA: Ja. Bei einer Familie.
GABI: Ein Appartement ist besser. Es ist privater.

Wörter im Kontext

Thema 1: Auf Wohnungssuche

STEFAN: Tag, Ulla! Wie geht's?
ULLA: Ach, nicht besonders.
STEFAN: Was ist denn los?
ULLA: Ich suche dringend eine Wohnung oder ein Zimmer. Wohnungen sind aber alle so teuer.
STEFAN: Ist denn nichts frei im Studentenheim?
ULLA: Hier in Freiburg? Bestimmt nicht!
STEFAN: Hier ist die Zeitung von heute. Vielleicht gibt es doch etwas. Ah, hier, Wohnungsanzeigen. Da, schau mal: schönes, möbliertes Zimmer.
ULLA: Wie hoch ist die Miete?
STEFAN: Nur 200 Mark.
ULLA: Das ist recht preiswert. Wo ist das Zimmer?
STEFAN: In Zußdorf.
ULLA: In Zußdorf?! Kommt nicht in Frage! Das ist viel zu weit weg.
STEFAN: Na, da hast du Recht. Preiswert ist es, aber Zußdorf ist nicht gerade zentral gelegen.

Aktivität 1 Wir brauchen eine Wohnung oder ein Zimmer

1. Fotodesigner, 22, sucht preiswertes Zimmer in junger Wohngemeinschaft, möglichst zentral zum ersten Juli.
2. Freundlicher Schauspieler aus Hamburg sucht Zimmer in Wohngemeinschaft vom ersten Mai bis ersten August in München.
3. Architekturstudentin, 25, sucht zum ersten oder fünfzehnten Mai ruhiges Zimmer bis 400 Mark inklusive, in Wohngemeinschaft.
4. Freundlicher, junger 37-jähriger Englischlehrer sucht 1 Zimmer in Wohngemeinschaft, um mit euch Deutsch zu sprechen und es besser zu lernen.
5. Musiker, 24, sucht Zimmer oder Raum in Wohngemeinschaft zum ersten Juni oder etwas früher. Zahle bis 500 Mark inklusive.

Aktivität 4 Ulla hat jetzt endlich ein Zimmer.

KARIN: Tag, Ulla. Wie geht's dir denn?
ULLA: Tag, Karin. Es geht mir prima. Ich habe jetzt endlich ein Zimmer.
KARIN: Wo denn?
ULLA: Schillerstraße 13.
KARIN: Toll, in zentraler Lage. Ist das Zimmer möbliert?
ULLA: Ja. Es hat ein Bett, einen Schreibtisch, einen Stuhl, einen Tisch und einen Sessel. Ich brauche nur noch eine Lampe für den Schreibtisch und ein Bücherregal.
KARIN: Wie hoch ist die Miete?
ULLA: Nur 200 Mark.
KARIN: Hast du Telefon?
ULLA: Nein, noch nicht.

Aktivität 6 Ein Gespräch im Kaufhaus

VERKÄUFER: Bitte sehr?
ULLA: Ich suche eine Lampe für meinen Schreibtisch.
VERKÄUFER: Hier haben wir Lampen.
ULLA: Was kostet die Lampe hier?
VERKÄUFER: 350 Mark. Die ist aus Italien.
ULLA: Die ist sehr schön, aber zu teuer.
VERKÄUFER: Hier ist eine Lampe für 50 Mark, sehr preiswert und modern. Ein Sonderangebot.
ULLA: Gut, die nehme ich. Und wo finde ich hier Bücherregale?
VERKÄUFER: Tut mir leid. Wir führen keine Bücherregale.

Grammatik im Kontext

Übung 2 Neu in Göttingen

STEFAN: Hallo, Birgit. Komm bitte rein.
BIRGIT: Tag Stefan. Also das ist deine neue Wohnung. Du hast wirklich Glück. Ich suche nämlich immer noch eine Wohnung.
STEFAN: Komm, ich zeige dir die Wohnung erst mal. Hier ist das Wohnzimmer mit Kochnische. Und hier ist das Bad.
BIRGIT: Na, das Zimmer ist ja ein bisschen klein. Wo schläfst du denn?
STEFAN: Ich brauche noch ein paar Möbel, ein Bett zum Beispiel. Im Moment schlafe ich auf dem Boden im Schlafsack.
BIRGIT: Kauf doch so ein japanisches Futon-Bett. Das ist ganz praktisch. Tagsüber ist es eine Couch, und dann kannst du es ausziehen, und es ist ein Bett.
STEFAN: Gute Idee. Bitte, setz dich doch. Leider habe ich nur einen Stuhl im Moment.
BIRGIT: Nein, danke, ich sitze gern auf dem Boden.
STEFAN: Morgen kaufe ich einen Schreibtisch und ein Bücherregal. Möchtest du einen Kaffee?
BIRGIT: Gern. Komm, ich helfe.

STEFAN: Ach, da fällt mir gerade ein: Ich habe Kaffee, aber ich brauche noch eine Kaffeemaschine. Gehen wir doch ins Café. Kennst du das Café Kadenz? Das ist mein Lieblingscafé.
BIRGIT: Na, gut.

Übung 7 Immer diese Ausreden!

1. KALLE: Grüß dich, Reinhard! Heute Abend spielt ein toller Film im Kino. Kommst du mit?
   REINHARD: Tut mir leid, es geht wirklich nicht. Ich habe nur noch eine Mark.
2. ALEXANDRA: Morgen gehen wir in die Disko. Kommst du mit, Erika?
   ERIKA: In die Disko? Wer geht denn sonst noch mit?
   ALEXANDRA: Nur Peter und ich. Helmut kommt doch sicher mit, nicht?
   ERIKA: Helmut ist nicht da. Und allein habe ich keine Lust.
3. FRAU WEISS: Frau Becker, haben Sie jetzt Zeit für eine Tasse Kaffee?
   FRAU BECKER: Tut mir wirklich leid, aber ich trinke keinen Kaffee. Kaffee trinken macht mich zu nervös.
4. FRANK: Hallo Jens! Servus Ulla! Kommt ihr heute abend zur Party? Wir haben Pizza und Bier.
   JENS: Hmmm, wir möchten gerne, aber wir müssen leider morgen unsere Examen schreiben. Ich habe noch viel Arbeit und brauche die Zeit heute Abend zum Lernen.
5. LYDIA: Peter, hast du Lust, mit ins Museum zu gehen?
   PETER: Ins Museum? Heute? Ach, ich bin kein Museumsfan. Ins Museum gehen macht mir überhaupt keinen Spaß. Ich bin eher Fußballfan.

Kapitel 3

Alles klar?

B. Hallo! Ich bin Ulrike Eichele aus Koblenz. Auf dem Foto siehst du meine Familie vorm Standesamt in Koblenz. Mein Bruder Hans hat geheiratet. Eigentlich habe ich zwei Brüder, beide viel älter als ich. Wolfgang ist 25 und studiert Theologie in Berlin. Er reist sehr gern. Bei ihm ist immer was los. Der große Bruder Hans ist 30, ist Rechtsanwalt und wohnt in Mainz mit seiner Frau. Er ist sehr nett und immer für alle da. Mein Vater ist auch Rechtsanwalt. Meine Mutter macht viel mit Asylbewerbern und lernt zur Zeit Russisch. Meine Eltern sind ziemlich tolerant und nerven nicht so viel. Ich bin 17 und bin nächstes Jahr bei meiner Kusine in den USA.

Wörter im Kontext

Aktivität 6 Eine Einladung zum Geburtstag

TOM: Tom McKay.
HEIKE: Hallo, Tom? Hier ist Heike.
TOM: Tag, Heike.
HEIKE: Du, Tom, ich mache eine kleine Party zu Hause. Ich habe nämlich Geburtstag. Ich möchte dich einladen.
TOM: Vielen Dank für die Einladung. Ich komme gern. Wann ist die Party denn?
HEIKE: Am Samstag.
TOM: Schön. Wer kommt sonst noch?
HEIKE: Du kennst doch die Gabi? Die kommt auch. Und vielleicht Jürgen. Sonst sind nur meine Eltern und Geschwister da.
TOM: Also gut, bis Samstag dann.
HEIKE: Mach's gut. Tschüs.

Grammatik im Kontext

Übung 1 Herzlichen Glückwunsch!

Guten Morgen, liebe Hörerinnen und Hörer. Willkommen zu unserem Programm: Von Haus zu Haus. Unsere Hörer senden Glückwünsche zum Geburtstag. Außerdem ist heute ein ganz besonderer Tag: Valentinstag.

1. Unsere liebe Mutter, Frau Sibille Heinemann aus Krefeld, ist heute achtzig. Herzlichen Glückwunsch senden dir deine Kinder.
2. Unser Opa, der beste Opa der Welt, wird heute sechzig. Es gratulieren deine Enkel Kai, Inge, Uwe, Sandra und Claudia aus Würzburg.
3. Hallo, Uwe! Endlich ist es so weit. Du bist achtzehn. Alles Gute wünscht dir deine Freundin Elke.
4. Hurra, unser Vater wird heute vierzig Jahre. Er ist der beste. Wir wünschen dir noch viele schöne Jahre. Alles Liebe zum Geburtstag, deine Söhne Helmut, Friedrich und Klaus-Daniel.
5. Unsere Tochter Hannelore wird heute einundzwanzig. Wir wünschen dir alles Liebe und Gute, deine Eltern.
6. Liebe Eltern, zum Valentinstag liebe Grüße aus Dresden, eure Kinder Wolfgang und Martina.
7. Für meine Kinder Steffi und Sebastian in Weimar alles Liebe, viel Spaß und alles Gute zum Valentinstag, eure Mutter.
8. Liebe Gabi, zum Valentinstag alles Liebe und Gute, dein Tiger.

Übung 10 Die neue Mitbewohnerin

1. Wann beginnt das Semester?
2. Kennst du das Buch von Professor Seufert?
3. Wo ist die Unibibliothek?
4. Ist das Theater hier gut?
5. Wie sind die anderen Mitbewohner hier im Wohnheim?
6. Ist das Wetter hier immer so schlecht?
7. Kennst du den Professor Kreuzer?
8. Weißt du, wo das Sportzentrum ist?

Kapitel 4

Alles klar?

B. DIRK: Hier Dirk Krekel. Ich bin im Moment nicht zu Hause. Hinterlassen Sie bitte eine kurze Nachricht. Warten Sie bitte auf den Pfeifton.
ERIKA: Hallo Dirk! Hier ist Erika. Hast du Samstagnachmittag schon etwas vor? Thomas und ich machen nämlich eine kleine Fete bei uns zu Hause. Um vier gibt's Kaffee und Kuchen. Hast du Zeit? Ruf uns bitte zurück!

Wörter im Kontext

Aktivität 5 Zeitansagen

1. Die Zeit ist 17 Uhr 35.
2. Die Zeit ist 3 Uhr 6.
3. Die Zeit ist 14 Uhr 15.
4. Die Zeit ist 11 Uhr 25.
5. Die Zeit ist 19 Uhr 45.
6. Die Zeit ist 13 Uhr 40.
7. Die Zeit ist 0 Uhr 15.
8. Die Zeit ist 21 Uhr 50.

Thema 3: Kino, Musik und Theater

JAN: Ich gehe heute Abend ins Theater. Willst du mit?
ULLA: Nein, danke. Ich bin kein Theaterfan. Ich möchte lieber ins Kino.
JAN: So. Du bist ein Kinofan. Was für Filme siehst du denn gern?
ULLA: Am liebsten Horrorfilme und Psychothriller—die sind so spannend.

Aktivität 8 Zwei Einladungen

Dialog 1

PETER: Möchtest du heute Abend ins Kino?
KARLA: Leider kann ich nicht. Ich habe nämlich am Montag eine Klausur.
PETER: Eine Klausur?
KARLA: Ja, in Physik. Ich muss noch dafür arbeiten.
PETER: Na, dann wünsche ich dir viel Glück.
KARLA: Danke, ich kann es brauchen.

Dialog 2

GABI: Hallo, Hans. Hast du heute Abend Zeit? Im Olympia läuft ein toller Film, „Ich und Er".
HANS: Ich möchte schon mitgehen. Wann fängt er denn an?
GABI: Um 17 Uhr.
HANS: Das ist mir zu früh. Ich habe nämlich noch eine Vorlesung bis fünf.
GABI: So spät am Freitag noch?
HANS: Ja, leider.

Grammatik im Kontext

Übung 1 Daniels Tagesablauf

Ich wache morgens schon früh auf und stehe um fünf Uhr auf. Ich wohne zusammen mit meinem Bruder Mark in einer alten Villa in Berlin. Wir haben ein Zimmer unter dem Dach. Das kostet uns nichts. Wir beide sind nämlich so etwas wie Hausmänner für die Familie Schröder: Wir gehen für sie einkaufen, reparieren Sachen und arbeiten im Garten.

Ich habe zwei Tagesabläufe: einen für das Geld und einen für die Kunst. An drei Tagen arbeite ich im Hotel als Junge für alles. Um sieben fängt die Arbeit an. Im Hotel arbeiten Leute aus Jugoslawien, Afghanistan, Italien und Amerika. Ich arbeite gern da. So gegen drei Uhr nachmittags komme ich nach Hause zurück. Dann schlafe ich erst mal ein bis zwei Stunden. Da habe ich die Illusion, mein Tag fängt noch einmal neu an. Dann fängt nämlich mein Leben für die Kunst an. Meistens habe ich ein Projekt vor. Ich mache Skulpturen aus Metall und Plastik. Abends rufe ich manchmal ein paar Freunde an. Die kommen dann vorbei, und dann reden wir und trinken Bier bis Mitternacht. Vor ein Uhr nachts schlafe ich nie ein. Ich brauche auch nicht viel Schlaf.

Übung 9 Im Deutschen Haus

CHRIS: Ich will schlafen.
Du willst schlafen.
Er will schlafen.
Wir wollen schla . . .
JEFF: Chris, was machst du da?
CHRIS: Ich lerne deutsche Grammatik.
JEFF: Das kann ich hören.
CHRIS: Morgen haben wir einen Test über Modalverben. Ich muss unbedingt ein A bekommen.
JEFF: Musst du das denn so laut machen? Kannst du das nicht leise machen?
CHRIS: Ich kann leider nur laut Deutsch lernen.
JEFF: Ich muss aber auch arbeiten, und ich höre nur immer „Ich will schlafen". Du hypnotisierst mich. Jetzt will ich auch schon schlafen.
CHRIS: Also gut, ich gehe ins Badezimmer. Da kannst du mich nicht hören. Ich will dich nicht stören.

Übung 14 In der Sprechstunde

1. PROFESSOR: Guten Tag, Frau Lerner, bitte, kommen Sie herein!
2. PROFESSOR: Bitte, nehmen Sie Platz!
3. MARY: Herr Professor, erklären Sie mir bitte, was dieser Satz heißt!
4. PROFESSOR: Verstehen Sie das nicht?
5. MARY: Sprechen Sie etwas langsamer, bitte!
6. PROFESSOR: Gehen Sie regelmäßig jede Woche ins Sprachlabor?
7. PROFESSOR: Warten Sie einen Moment, bitte.
8. STUDENT: Hallo, Herr Professor Schwermut, kommen Sie heute Abend zu unserm Filmabend im Deutschklub?
9. PROFESSOR: Rufen Sie mich bitte später wieder an! Ich habe im Moment keine Zeit.
10. PROFESSOR: Haben Sie ein Wörterbuch zu Hause, Frau Lerner?
11. PROFESSOR: Lesen Sie jeden Tag eine Stunde Deutsch?
12. PROFESSOR: Kommen Sie nächste Woche wieder vorbei!
13. MARY: Haben Sie nächsten Mittwoch Zeit?
14. PROFESSOR: Vergessen Sie Ihre Bücher nicht! Also dann, auf Wiedersehen.
    MARY: Auf Wiedersehen.

Kapitel 5

Alles klar?

B. 1. Heute im vierten Stock. Preiswerte Kameras. Nur 299 Mark.
2. Modische italienische Herrenschuhe im zweiten Stock. Aus Leder von hoher Qualität. Nur 169 Mark.

3. In unserer Elektroabteilung im vierten Stock bieten wir Krups Kaffeemaschinen. Heute Sonderpreis 59 Mark 50.
4. Zu Hause haben Sie bestimmt Platz für einen zweiten Videorecorder. Heute im Sonderangebot für 499 Mark. Im vierten Stock.

Wörter im Kontext

Thema 2: Beim Einkaufen im Kaufhaus

VERKÄUFER: Bitte schön. Kann ich Ihnen helfen?
HERR GÖTTGES: Ich brauche ein paar neue Sporthemden.
VERKÄUFER: Welche Größe brauchen Sie?
HERR GÖTTGES: Größe 42.
VERKÄUFER: Und welche Farbe?
HERR GÖTTGES: Grün oder blau.
VERKÄUFER: Wie gefällt Ihnen dieses gestreifte Hemd in Marineblau? Sehr dezent und modisch.
HERR GÖTTGES: Ich finde, die Farbe steht mir nicht. Haben Sie das in Hellblau?
VERKÄUFER: Ja, hier ist ein Hemd in Hellblau.
HERR GÖTTGES: Ist das aus Baumwolle oder Synthetik?
VERKÄUFER: Das ist 100 Prozent Baumwolle. Möchten Sie es anprobieren?
HERR GÖTTGES: Nein, das ist nicht nötig. Größe 42 passt mir bestimmt. Wie viel kostet dieses Hemd?
VERKÄUFER: 80 Mark.
HERR GÖTTGES: Gut. Ich nehme drei Hemden.
VERKÄUFER: Alle in Hellblau?
HERR GÖTTGES: Nein, geben Sie mir bitte zwei in Blau und ein Hemd in Weiß.
VERKÄUFER: Das macht zusammen 240 Mark. Bitte zahlen Sie vorne an der Kasse!
HERR GÖTTGES: Danke schön.
VERKÄUFER: Bitte sehr.

Aktivität 5 Gespräche im Geschäft

Dialog 1

VERKÄUFER: Bitte schön, kann ich Ihnen helfen?
KUNDE: Ich brauche ein Paar Schuhe.
VERKÄUFER: Welche Größe bitte?
KUNDE: Größe 44.
VERKÄUFER: Und welche Farbe?
KUNDE: Schwarz bitte.

Dialog 2

VERKÄUFERIN: Guten Tag. Kann ich Ihnen helfen?
KUNDIN: Ich brauche eine Hose.
VERKÄUFERIN: Welche Größe, bitte?
KUNDIN: Ich glaube Größe 38. Aber ich bin nicht sicher.
VERKÄUFERIN: Und welche Farbe soll es sein?
KUNDIN: Haben Sie etwas in Blauweiß gestreift?

Dialog 3

VERKÄUFERIN: Guten Tag, kann ich Ihnen helfen?
KUNDE: Ja, ich suche ein Geschenk für meine Freundin. Eine Bluse vielleicht.
VERKÄUFERIN: Und welche Größe hat Ihre Freundin?
KUNDE: Hmm, ich weiß nicht, sie ist ziemlich klein. Ich glaube ungefähr Größe 44.
VERKÄUFERIN: Das ist aber ziemlich groß. Sie sagen, sie ist ziemlich klein?
KUNDE: Ja.
VERKÄUFERIN: Ich empfehle Ihnen Größe 38.
KUNDE: Vielen Dank. Also, Größe 38.
VERKÄUFERIN: Und welche Farbe?
KUNDE: Rot.

Dialog 4

VERKÄUFER: Bitte schön. Kann ich Ihnen helfen?
KUNDE: Ich suche einen Wintermantel.
VERKÄUFER: Und welche Größe brauchen Sie?
KUNDE: Größe 44.
VERKÄUFER: Und welche Farbe?
KUNDE: Haben Sie was in Dunkelblau?
VERKÄUFER: Ja, da bin ich ganz sicher.

Aktivität 9 Wo? Was? Wie viel?

Dialog 1

VERKÄUFERIN: Bitte schön. Was darf's sein?
KUNDE: Ich möchte gern ein Dutzend Würstchen.
VERKÄUFERIN: Sonst noch etwas?
KUNDE: Ja, ein Pfund Aufschnitt.
VERKÄUFERIN: Und sonst noch etwas?
KUNDE: Nein, danke. Das ist alles.
VERKÄUFERIN: Das macht zusammen 17 Mark 50.

Dialog 2

VERKÄUFERIN: Guten Morgen, Frau Linder.
KUNDIN: Guten Morgen. Haben Sie frische Brötchen?
VERKÄUFERIN: Ja, natürlich. Ganz frisch von heute Morgen. Wie viele möchten Sie?
KUNDIN: Sechs Brötchen, bitte, und noch ein Schwarzbrot.
VERKÄUFERIN: Sonst noch etwas?
KUNDIN: Nein, danke.
VERKÄUFERIN: Das macht zusammen 6 Mark 50.

Dialog 3

VERKÄUFERIN: Bitte schön?
KUNDIN: Haben Sie frische Tomaten?
VERKÄUFERIN: Ja, Tomaten haben wir, ganz frisch aus Holland.
KUNDIN: Wie viel kosten die denn?
VERKÄUFERIN: 10 Mark das Kilo.
KUNDIN: Das ist aber teuer. Was haben Sie denn an Obst?
VERKÄUFERIN: Erdbeeren sind sehr preiswert. Nur 1 Mark 50 für 250 Gramm.
KUNDIN: Na, dann nehme ich 1 Pfund Erdbeeren und ungefähr ein Pfund Tomaten.
VERKÄUFERIN: Das macht zusammen 8 Mark.

Grammatik im Kontext

Übung 1 Situationen im Alltag

Dialog 1

HANS: Du, Werner, ich brauche unbedingt etwas Geld. Kannst du mir ein paar Mark leihen bis morgen? Meine Mutter hat nämlich Geburtstag, und ich möchte ihr unbedingt ein paar Blumen schicken.
WERNER: Es tut mir leid, Hans, aber ich habe selber kein Geld. Schreib ihr doch einen Brief.

Dialog 2

STUDENTIN: Können Sie uns bitte sagen, wo das Café Kadenz ist?

PASSANT: Natürlich. Kommen Sie. Ich zeige es Ihnen. Es liegt in der Berliner Straße.

Dialog 3

MARIANNE: Helmut hat morgen Geburtstag. Was soll ich ihm bloss schenken? Er hat ja alles.

UTE: Schenk ihm doch eine CD.

MARIANNE: Ich glaube, ich schreibe ihm nur eine Karte.

Dialog 4

STUDENTIN: Ich stehe jeden Morgen um fünf Uhr auf und mache Yoga.

STUDENT: Und das soll ich dir glauben? Wieso kommst du denn dann immer zu spät in die Vorlesung?

STUDENTIN: Doch, ich mache das schon lange. Ich kann es dir nur empfehlen.

Dialog 5

STUDENT: Achim sagt, er lebt nur von Wasser und Brot.

STUDENTIN: Du musst ihm nicht alles glauben, was er sagt. Er geht doch fast jeden Abend aus.

Übung 8 Ein typischer Tag

Maxi wohnt seit einem Monat in Göttingen. Sie studiert da Geschichte. Sie wohnt mit drei anderen Studentinnen zusammen in einer Wohnung. Sie wohnen nicht zu weit von der Universität. Sie können zu Fuß gehen.

Maxi kommt gerade mit ihrer Freundin Inge aus dem Café Kadenz. Jetzt muss sie noch schnell einkaufen. Inge geht gleich mit. Sie braucht auch einiges. Zuerst gehen sie zum Supermarkt. Da kaufen sie aber nur ein paar Bananen. Dann kaufen sie frische Brötchen beim Bäcker direkt um die Ecke. Ach, da ist der neue Laden mit den tollen CDs! Die beiden möchten ja gerne mal schnell hineinschauen, aber es wird spät, und Maxi muss noch zur Bank. Sie gehen schnell durch die Fußgängerzone zur Bank. Maxi muss etwas Geld von der Bank holen. Es ist inzwischen fünf Uhr, und die Bank ist zu. Gott sei Dank kann sie mit der Bankkarte am Geldautomaten Geld bekommen.

Kapitel 6

Alles klar?

B. DORIS: So. Jetzt wo ich das Problem mit dem BAföG gelöst habe, hätte ich gern eine weitere Information.

REFERENTIN: Gern. Wie kann ich dir weiter helfen?

DORIS: Meine Eltern kommen am Wochenende zu Besuch, und ich möchte mit ihnen im Restaurant essen. Ich bin ja neu hier in Berlin und kenne mich nicht so gut aus.

REFERENTIN: Du hast Glück. Wir haben gerade einen Kneipenführer zusammengestellt. Aber Berlin ist eine riesige Stadt. Wo seid ihr dann am Wochenende?

DORIS: Wohl in Mitte oder Prenzlauerberg.

REFERENTIN: Wenn einer von euch vegetarisch isst, dann kann ich den Kartoffelkeller im Nikolaiviertel empfehlen. Außer Kartoffeln gibt es verschiedene Salate, und man sitzt dort sehr gemütlich

DORIS: Ich habe von einem Restaurant im Brecht Haus gehört. Warst du schon mal dort? Meine Eltern interessieren sich für Brecht.

REFERENTIN: Nein, aber Freunde von mir waren dort. Es heißt einfach „Kellerrestaurant“ und serviert österreichische Küche. Einige Gerichte sollen nach Rezepten von Helene Weigel, Brechts Frau, sein.

DORIS: Kennst du ein gutes italienisches Restaurant?

REFERENTIN: Ja. Da geht ihr am besten in die Oranienburger Straße. So weit ich weiß, heißt das Restaurant einfach „Ristorante Italiano“. Dort kann man eine sehr gute Pizza bekommen, und es ist nicht so teuer. Mir fällt auch ein neues Restaurant in der Gormann Straße ein. Es heißt „Brazil“ und bietet brasilianische Spezialitäten, vor allem Fleischgerichte—sehr beliebt unter Studenten und jungen Leuten. Es ist immer rappelvoll und für deine Eltern vielleicht ein wenig laut, aber es macht viel Spaß, dort zu essen.

DORIS: Vielen Dank. Berlin hat wirklich viele tolle Lokale. Tschüs.

REFERENTIN: Tschüs.

Wörter im Kontext

Aktivität 4 Was bestellen Norbert und Dagmar?

NORBERT: Was möchtest du essen?

DAGMAR: Ich nehme Nürnberger Rostbratwürst'l mit Kraut und Kartoffelpüree.

NORBERT: Nimmst du eine Vorspeise?

DAGMAR: Ich nehme Gulaschsuppe. Und du?

NORBERT: Auch Gulaschsuppe und Spanferkel mit Bratkartoffeln. Und was willst du trinken?

DAGMAR: Ich sehe hier alkoholfreies Bier auf der Speisekarte. Das muss ich unbedingt mal probieren.

NORBERT: Ich nehme auch Bier, aber kein alkoholfreies. Herr Ober, wir möchten bestellen.

Aktivität 7 Im Brauhaus Matz

STEFANIE: Hier ist es aber ziemlich voll. Hoffentlich finden wir noch Platz.

JENS: Da drüben ist noch etwas frei. Da sitzen nur zwei Leute am Tisch. Ich gehe mal dahin und frage.

JENS: Entschuldigen Sie bitte! Ist hier noch frei?

HERR AM TISCH: Nein, hier ist besetzt.

JENS: Entschuldigen Sie. Ist hier noch frei?

DAME AM TISCH: Ja, hier ist noch frei. Bitte sehr.

JENS: Danke schön.

Aktivität 9 Wir möchten zahlen, bitte.

Dialog 1

HERR X: Bedienung, ich möchte zahlen.

KELLNERIN: Jawohl. Drei Bier, zwei Knackwürste und Sauerkraut. Und hatten Sie auch Brot?

HERR X: Nein.

KELLNERIN: Das macht zusammen 24 Mark 50.

Dialog 2

FRAU X: Herr Ober, wir möchten zahlen.

OBER: Zwei Tassen Kaffee, ein Stück Käsekuchen und ein Stück Obsttorte. Das macht zusammen 17 Mark 45.

Dialog 3

HERR Y: Bedienung, wir möchten zahlen.

KELLNERIN: Zusammen oder getrennt?

HERR Y: Zusammen, bitte.

KELLNERIN: Dreimal Leberknödlsuppe, zweimal Schweinskotelett mit Salat und einmal zwei Münchner Weißwürste.
HERR Y: Und fünf Brezeln.
KELLNERIN: Ja, und fünf Bier und eine Portion Emmentaler Käse. Das macht zusammen 78 Mark 40.

Kapitel 7

Alles klar?

B. 1. X: Was machst du so in deiner Freizeit?
ULRIKE: Ich lese sehr sehr viel und ich tanze.
X: Wo tanzt du denn? In der Disko?
ULRIKE: Nein, nein, ich gehe einmal die Woche zum
Ballettunterricht.
X: Ach so.

2. X: Und wie verbringst du deine Freizeit?
WOLFGANG: Na, mit Fernsehen.
X: Und sonst nichts?
WOLFGANG: Ab und zu spiele ich Fußball mit ein paar Freunden. Fußball spielen macht mir Spaß.

3. X: Sag mal, Antje, was machst du so in deiner Freizeit?
ANTJE: Freizeit, kenn' ich nicht. Ich studiere und habe eine Nebenbeschäftigung. Da bleibt mir keine Freizeit.
X: Na, hör mal, das gibt's doch wohl nicht.
ANTJE: Na ja, gelegentlich gehe ich mal ins Kino. Ach ja, und ich habe übrigens einen neuen Computer. Da surfe ich schon mal im Internet. Das macht mir Spaß.

Wörter im Kontext

Aktivität 5 Pläne für einen Ausflug

VERENA: Sag mal, wie wäre es mit einem Ausflug am Wochenende?
ANTJE: Prima Idee! Ich brauche unbedingt Abwechslung. Die Arbeit geht mir im Moment auf die Nerven. Was schlägst du denn vor?
VERENA: Warst du schon mal im Neandertal?
ANTJE: Nein, noch nie. Wie weit ist das von hier?
VERENA: Nicht zu weit. Wir können mit dem Rad dahin. Man kann bequem in zwei Stunden da sein. Der Weg führt fast nur durch den Wald.
ANTJE: Soll ich Stefan auch einladen?
VERENA: Schön. Wenn er Lust hat.
ANTJE: Ich weiß, dass er gern mitkommt. Hoffentlich bleibt das Wetter schön.

Aktivität 7 Wetterberichte im Radio

Der Wetterbericht aus Zürich: Sonnig und warm. Temperaturen zwischen 20 und 25 Grad.

Und aus Wien: Wolkig. Vor allem in der zweiten Tageshälfte Neigung zu Gewittern. Höchsttemperaturen um 18 Grad.

Und nun unser Wetterbericht für Berlin: Morgens noch Schauer, dann nachmittags wolkig bis heiter. Tagestemperaturen bis zu 20 Grad.

Der Wetterbericht aus Paris: Schön mit leichtem Wind aus Südwest. Tagestemperatur: 29 Grad.

Und aus London: Morgens Nebel, später stark bewölkt und Regen. Tagestemperaturen nicht über 10 Grad.

Grammatik im Kontext

Übung 3 In meiner Kindheit

1. HERR HARTER
Was hat mir als Kind Spaß gemacht? Also, ich habe immer viel gesammelt, zum Beispiel Briefmarken, tote Insekten, Bilder mit Fußballspielern. Und dann habe ich Trompete gespielt. Ich habe dann in der Schule in unserer Band gespielt. Das hat mir immer viel Spaß gemacht.

2. FRAU BEITZ
Ich mochte Tiere immer gern, und als Kind hatte ich einen Hund. Das war der Charly. Ich habe mit meinem Hund gespielt. Ich war auch gern im Zoo und habe die Tiere gefüttert. Ja, das hat mir Spaß gemacht. Und ich habe auch gerne gemalt und gezeichnet.

3. HERR HUPPERT
Als Junge habe ich leidenschaftlich gern Cowboy gespielt. Meine Eltern haben mir immer Bücher von Karl May zum Geburtstag geschenkt. Ich bin immer noch ein großer Karl-May-Fan, und ich fahre manchmal nach Bad Segeberg zu den Karl-May-Spielen. Ich habe alle Bücher von Karl May gesammelt. Ich war auch in einem Fußballverein und habe Fußball gespielt. Das hat wirklich Spaß gemacht.

Kapitel 8

Alles klar?

B. HERR LOHMANN: Jeden Tag gehen wir ins Thermalbad. Danach bekommen wir auch eine Massage. In die Sauna gehen wir nie. Mittags essen wir gern vegetarisch. Nachmittags spielen wir manchmal Karten mit einigen anderen Kurgästen. Und natürlich gehen wir viel spazieren.
HERR KRANZLER: Ich bin allein hier. Meine Familie wohnt in Mainz. Ich spiele viel Golf, gehe auch gern wandern und schwimmen. Danach gehe ich immer in die Sauna und ins Thermalbad. Und dann mache ich eine Trinkkur. Da trinke ich jede Stunde ein Glas Wasser.
FRAU DIETMOLD: Ja, ich mache auch eine Trinkkur, und dann gehe ich ins Thermalbad und bekomme Massagen. Tischtennis macht mir viel Spaß. Ich gehe hier abends oft ins Theater. Ich spiele auch Mini-Golf, und dann tanze ich gern.

Wörter im Kontext

Thema 1: Fit und gesund

TINA: Für meine Gesundheit tue ich viel. Ich esse vegetarisch, versuche so gut es geht, den Stress in meinem Leben zu reduzieren. Zur Arbeit gehe ich meistens zu Fuß. Ich trinke viel Kräutertee und nur selten Alkohol, höchstens ab und zu ein Glas Wein zum Essen.
WALTER: Fitness ist mir sehr wichtig. Deshalb rauche ich nie und esse gesund, das heißt wenig Fleisch und viel Gemüse.

Ich treibe regelmäßig Sport, besonders an der frischen Luft. Ich möchte mich fit halten.

ANITA: Mindestens zweimal im Jahr mache ich Urlaub, denn meine Arbeit ist sehr anstrengend. Ich bin nämlich Krankenschwester. Ich achte auf meine Gesundheit und esse nur Ökolebensmittel, entweder direkt vom Bauernhof oder vom Naturkostladen. Ich mache jede Woche Yoga. Da kann ich mich richtig entspannen.

Thema 2: **Der menschliche Körper**

CHRISTOPH: Schmidt.

UTA: Hallo, Christoph? Hier ist Uta.

CHRISTOPH: Ja, grüß dich, Uta.

UTA: Nanu! Was ist denn los? Du klingst ja so deprimiert.

CHRISTOPH: Ich liege im Bett. Ich fühle mich hundsmiserabel.

UTA: Was fehlt dir denn?

CHRISTOPH: Ich habe eine Erkältung, vielleicht sogar die Grippe. Der Hals tut mir weh, ich kann kaum schlucken, mir ist schlecht. Ich habe Fieber, Halsschmerzen, Husten und Schnupfen. Ich habe auch Kopfschmerzen und bin so müde und schlapp. Und morgen muss ich eine Arbeit bei Professor Höhn abgeben.

UTA: So ein Pech. Warst du schon beim Arzt?

CHRISTOPH: Nein.

UTA: Wie lange bist du denn schon krank?

CHRISTOPH: Seit fast zwei Wochen schon.

UTA: Du bist verrückt! Geh doch gleich zum Arzt. Er kann dir sicher was verschreiben.

CHRISTOPH: Aber ich kriege bestimmt keinen Termin.

UTA: Das macht nichts. Geh einfach in die Sprechstunde.

CHRISTOPH: Na gut. Ich danke dir für den Rat.

UTA: Nichts zu danken . . . Ich wünsche dir gute Besserung!

Aktivität 4 **Im Aerobic-Kurs**

AEROBIC-LEHRERIN: Strecken Sie die Arme nach oben. Langsam den Rücken nach vorne beugen. Die Knie gerade halten. Mit den Fingern bis an die Füße reichen. Langsam wieder hoch kommen.

Drehen Sie den Kopf erst nach rechts, dann nach links, dann langsam rollen. Das ist gut für den Hals. Jetzt die Schultern bis an die Ohren hoch ziehen und langsam wieder fallen lassen. So und jetzt geht's etwas flotter. Fünf Minuten auf der Stelle laufen. Eins, zwei, eins, zwei, eins, zwei!

MANN: Morgen tun mir bestimmt alle Muskeln weh.

Aktivität 5 **Beschwerden**

Dialog 1

LENI: Ich fühle mich hundsmiserabel.

DORIS: Was fehlt dir denn?

LENI: Ich hab' 'ne Erkältung. Ich muss immer husten, habe Kopfschmerzen, und ich kann mich auf nichts konzentrieren.

DORIS: Du siehst auch wirklich müde aus. Geh doch nach Hause, und leg dich ins Bett. Gute Besserung!

LENI: Danke.

Dialog 2

DORIS: Na, geht's dir wieder besser?

LENI: Ja, ich habe mich ein paar Tage zu Hause ausgeruht. Jetzt bin ich wieder fit.

DORIS: Ich fühle mich heute überhaupt nicht gut. Ich glaube, ich werde auch krank.

LENI: Na, hoffentlich nicht. Was ist denn los?

DORIS: Also, es ist mein Bauch. Ich habe irgendetwas gegessen.

LENI: Geh lieber gleich zum Arzt. Übrigens, trink viel Kamillentee. Der ist gut gegen Bauchschmerzen.

Dialog 3

ARZT: Was fehlt Ihnen denn?

PATIENT: Ach, Herr Doktor. Ich habe überhaupt keine Energie, fühle mich immer schlapp. Und nachts kann ich nicht schlafen. Ich bin immer nervös. Ich kann mich nicht konzentrieren.

ARZT: Hmm. Wie lange haben Sie diese Symptome schon?

PATIENT: Schon seit Monaten.

ARZT: Sie brauchen Urlaub. Sie haben zu viel Stress in Ihrem Leben. Ich empfehle Ihnen eine Kur im Schwarzwald. Ich schreibe Ihnen auch ein Rezept für Schlaftabletten.

Grammatik im Kontext

Übung 7 **Beim Arzt**

HERR SCHNEIDER: Guten Tag, Herr Doktor.

ARZT: Guten Tag, Herr Schneider. Bitte, setzen Sie sich. Was fehlt Ihnen denn?

HERR SCHNEIDER: Ich fühle mich so schlapp, ich kann mich überhaupt nicht konzentrieren.

ARZT: Seit wann fühlen Sie sich schon so schlapp?

HERR SCHNEIDER: Schon seit Wochen.

ARZT: Müssen Sie sich bei der Arbeit zu sehr anstrengen?

HERR SCHNEIDER: Ja, leider ist meine Arbeit mit sehr viel Stress verbunden. Ich bin Vertreter für eine Firma und bin ständig unterwegs, Termine mit Kunden, Staus auf der Autobahn. Ich habe einfach keine Zeit, mich mal zu entspannen.

ARZT: Sie müssen sich aber einfach entspannen. Der ständige Stress ist sehr schlecht für Ihre Gesundheit. Ich empfehle Ihnen eine Kur im Schwarzwald. Da können Sie sich vom Stress erholen.

HERR SCHNEIDER: Ja, das sagt meine Frau auch. Ich habe leider keine Zeit, in Urlaub zu fahren.

ARZT: Interessieren Sie sich für Sport? Etwas Aerobic kann Ihnen nicht schaden.

HERR SCHNEIDER: Leider interessiere ich mich nicht für Sport. Aerobic ist mir zu anstrengend.

ARZT: Nun, dann verschreibe ich Ihnen ein paar Vitamintabletten. Nehmen Sie abends und morgens 125 Stück. Und kommen Sie in vier Wochen wieder.—Übrigens, seit wann haben Sie diesen Schluckauf schon?

HERR SCHNEIDER: Schluckauf? Welchen Schluckauf?

ARZT: Herr Schneider, ich muss Ihnen dringend raten, sofort auf Kur zu gehen. Sie brauchen dringend Entspannung. Sie sind mit Ihren Nerven am Ende!

Kapitel 9

Alles klar?

B. Jedes Jahr kommen rund vier Millionen Touristen in die sächsische Hauptstadt Dresden. Heute leben in der Stadt etwa 470 000 Einwohner. Dresden ist bekannt für viele Sachen. Zum Beispiel, die erste deutsche Loko-motive kommt aus Dresden. Und hier hat man Bierdeckel, Kaffeefilter und Zahnpasta entwickelt! Dresden ist aber auch eine Stadt der Musik. Heinrich Schütz hat hier die erste deutsche Oper geschrieben. Und später hat der Komponist Richard Wagner viele Jahre in Dresden verbracht. Zwei seiner Opern, „Tannhäuser" und „Der fliegende Holländer" wurden hier uraufgeführt. Den Dresdener Besucher erwartet ein großes kulturelles Angebot: Musik, Museen und Theater. Dresden gilt auch als die europäische Hauptstadt des Dixieland. Der alte Zoologische Garten in Dresden ist einer der ältesten deutschen Tiergärten—gebaut im Jahr 1861.

Wörter im Kontext

Aktivität 1 Zwei telefonische Zimmerbestellungen

Erstes Telefongespräch

REZEPTION: Hotel Mecklenheide, guten Tag.

HERR DEGENER: Guten Tag. Haben Sie noch ein Zimmer frei?

REZEPTION: Brauchen Sie ein Einzelzimmer oder ein Doppelzimmer?

HERR DEGENER: Ich hätte gern ein Doppelzimmer mit Bad für drei Nächte.

REZEPTION: Wir haben noch ein Doppelzimmer frei, aber leider ohne Bad.

HERR DEGENER: Hmmm. Na gut. Und was kostet das Zimmer?

REZEPTION: 95 Mark, mit Frühstück.

HERR DEGENER: Also gut. Ich nehme es. Übrigens, ich habe einen Hund, einen Pudel. Ich hoffe, Sie haben nichts dagegen.

REZEPTION: Oh, es tut mir schrecklich leid, aber Hunde sind leider nicht erlaubt.

HERR DEGENER: Na, dann muss ich es eben woanders versuchen. Auf Wiederhören.

REZEPTION: Auf Wiederhören.

Zweites Telefongespräch

FRAU BETZ: Jugendgästehaus Am Stadtgraben.

GABRIELE: Ich möchte ein Zimmer für August bestellen. Haben Sie noch ein Einzelzimmer?

FRAU BETZ: Wir haben überhaupt keine Einzelzimmer. Unsere Schlafräume haben jeweils zehn Betten.

GABRIELE: Hmm, zehn Betten?

FRAU BETZ: Ja, aber die Räume sind sehr gemütlich. Unser Haus ist fast 800 Jahre alt. Es liegt ganz in der Nähe der Innenstadt.

GABRIELE: Gibt es auch Bad und Dusche und WC im Haus?

FRAU BETZ: Aber natürlich. Jedes Zimmer hat einen Waschraum mit Dusche und Toilette.

GABRIELE: Eine Dusche für zehn Leute? Hm. Und was kostet die Übernachtung?

FRAU BETZ: 18 Mark pro Übernachtung, mit Frühstück.

GABRIELE: Na, das ist ja sehr günstig. Bitte reservieren Sie mir ein Bett für vier Nächte vom ersten August an.

FRAU BETZ: Gut, geht in Ordnung. Und wie ist Ihr Name?

GABRIELE: Holzschuh, Gabriele.

Thema 2: Im Hotel

Teil A:

REZEPTION: Guten Abend.

GAST: Guten Abend. Ich habe ein Zimmer für zwei Nächte bestellt.

REZEPTION: Auf welchen Namen, bitte?

GAST: Thompson.

REZEPTION: Ah, ja. Herr Thompson. Ein Einzelzimmer mit Bad. Würden Sie bitte das Anmeldeformular ausfüllen?

GAST: Möchten Sie auch meinen Reisepass sehen?

REZEPTION: Nein, das is nicht nötig. Ihr Zimmer liegt im ersten Stock, Zimmer 21. Hier ist der Schlüssel. Der Aufzug ist hier rechts.

GAST: Danke.

REZEPTION: Wir bringen Ihr Gepäck aufs Zimmer. Haben Sie nur den einen Koffer?

GAST: Ja . . . Übrigens, wann gibt es morgens Frühstück?

REZEPTION: Zwischen 7 und 10 Uhr im Frühstücksraum hier gleich links im Erdgeschoss.

GAST: Danke sehr.

REZEPTION: Bitte sehr. Ich wünsche Ihnen einen angenehmen Aufenthalt.

Teil B:

REZEPTION: Rezeption.

THOMPSON: Guten Abend. Der Fernseher in meinem Zimmer ist kaputt. Es gibt kein Bild, keinen Ton, nichts.

REZEPTION: Das tut mir leid, Herr Thompson. Ich schicke sofort jemand auf Ihr Zimmer. Wenn er den Apparat nicht gleich reparieren kann, bringen wir Ihnen einen anderen.

THOMPSON: Vielen Dank. Auf Wiederhören.

REZEPTION: Auf Wiederhören.

Teil C:

THOMPSON: Guten Morgen. Ich reise heute ab.

REZEPTION: Jawohl . . . Zwei Übernachtungen und ein Telefonanruf nach Wien. Das macht zusammen 315 Mark 60.

THOMPSON: Nehmen Sie Kreditkarten oder Reiseschecks?

REZEPTION: Sie können mit Eurokarte, Euroscheck oder in bar bezahlen.

THOMPSON: Keine Reiseschecks?

REZEPTION: Doch. Ein Reisescheck geht auch.

THOMPSON: Gut.

REZEPTION: Ich brauche nur noch Ihre Unterschrift da oben.

THOMPSON: Ach ja, natürlich.

REZEPTION: Hoffentlich hat es Ihnen bei uns gefallen.

THOMPSON: Ja, sehr.

Thema 3: Ring sum die Stadt

TOURIST: Entschuldigung, wie komme ich am besten zum Hotel Neptun?

PASSANT: Gehen Sie hier die Mühlenstraße entlang, dann biegen Sie rechts in die Richard-Wagnerstraße ein. Gehen Sie immer geradeaus. Das Hotel Neptun liegt gegenüber von der Schwimmhalle.

TOURIST: Ist es weit von hier?

PASSANT: Nein. Ungefähr 5 bis 7 Minuten zu Fuß.

Aktivität 5 Drei Touristen

Dialog 1

JULIA: Entschuldigung, wie kommt man hier zum Markt?

KATRIN: Gehen Sie immer geradeaus bis zur Ampel, dann links.

Dialog 2

ULRICH: Bitte, können Sie mir sagen, wo das Hotel Continental ist?

GISELA: Gehen Sie zwei Straßen geradeaus, dann rechts.

Dialog 3

PETER: Entschuldigung, wo ist hier eine Post?

SEPP: Tut mir leid. Ich bin Tourist und kenne die Stadt auch nicht.

Grammatik im Kontext

Übung 10 Kurze Gespräche

Dialog 1

GERD: Sag mal, seit wann hast du denn blaue Haare?

GABI: Seit letzter Woche. Gefallen sie dir?

GERD: Na ja, ich war an deine braunen Haare gewöhnt.

GABI: Ich habe ja auch blaue Augen. Die blauen Haare passen gut zu meinen blauen Augen.

GERD: Ein merkwürdiger Grund. Na ja, meine Oma hat dunkellila Haare.

Dialog 2

PASSANT: Entschuldigung, wo ist das Rathaus?

PASSANTIN: Meinen Sie das alte oder das neue?

PASSANT: Oh, es gibt zwei? Ein altes und ein neues? Ich suche das Rathaus mit dem berühmten Glockenspiel.

PASSANTIN: Also, das ist das alte Rathaus. Gehen Sie geradeaus, dann die zweite Straße links. Das Rathaus liegt auf der rechten Seite.

Kapitel 10

Alles klar?

B. Dialog 1

TONI: Wo wart ihr denn im Urlaub?

ELKE: An der Ostsee. In Warnemünde. Es war einfach herrlich! Strand, Wind und Meer!

TONI: Habt ihr dort viel unternommen?

ELKE: Wir wollten unbedingt segeln lernen—und das haben wir auch getan. Karl ist ein begeisterter Segler. Nächstes Jahr will er wieder dahin.

Dialog 2

UTE: Wo hast du denn dieses Jahr Urlaub gemacht?

BERND: In Südamerika, in Bolivien.

UTE: In Bolivien? Wie war es denn?

BERND: Fantastisch. Ich wollte ja immer schon mein Spanisch verbessern. Da habe ich mich zu einem Sprachurlaub in Bolivien entschlossen.

UTE: Hast du im Hotel gewohnt?

BERND: Nein. Ich hatte Glück. Ich habe eine Privatunterkunft bei einer Familie gefunden. Die waren alle unheimlich nett. Wir haben natürlich nur Spanisch gesprochen. Wir haben auch gemeinsam was unternommen. So habe ich viel gesehen und erlebt. Ich kann das nur empfehlen. So, ich muss jetzt gehen. Also, hasta mañana.

UTE: Tschüs.

Dialog 3

HANS: Einen Aktivurlaub habt ihr gemacht? Wieso?

JENS: Ganz einfach. Wir wollten mal was anderes machen. Da haben wir uns für einen Aktivurlaub entschieden—Wandern und Bergsteigen in den Dolomiten. Am aufregendsten war das Bergsteigen. Das war ein Erlebnis. Es hat mir unheimlich viel Spaß gemacht.

Wörter im Kontext

Thema 2: Im Reisebüro

FRAU SIEMENS: Mein Freund und ich möchten dieses Jahr mal einen Aktivurlaub machen. Wir wollen mal was anderes erleben. Können Sie etwas vorschlagen?

HERR BITTNER: Ja, gern. Wofür interessieren Sie sich denn? Es gibt so viele Möglichkeiten. Sind Sie sportlich aktiv?

FRAU SIEMENS: Nicht besonders. Manchmal spielen wir Tennis und fahren auch schon mal Rad.

HERR BITTNER: Wie wäre es mit einer Radreise durchs Elsass—oder mit einem Segelkurs an der Ostsee?

FRAU SIEMENS: Ach, ein Segelkurs ist mir zu anstrengend. Ich kann auch nicht gut schwimmen. Und eine Radreise . . . ich weiß nicht. Was können wir sonst noch unternehmen?

HERR BITTNER: Wir haben hier ein Angebot für eine viertägige Wandertour im Naturpark Solling-Vogler in der Nähe von Göttingen. Hier ist ein Reiseprospekt. Das kann ich sofort für Sie buchen.

FRAU SIEMENS: Hm, klingt gut. Ich sehe hier, die Gruppen sind relativ klein, höchstens zwölf Personen und ein Reiseleiter. Wo übernachtet man denn?

HERR BITTNER: Im Zelt natürlich!

FRAU SIEMENS: Ach, ich weiß nicht, ob mein Freund damit einverstanden ist. Er liebt die Natur zwar, aber in der Natur übernachten? Das ist etwas anderes. Wo beginnt die Wandertour?

HERR BITTNER: In Holzminden. Da treffen sich die Teilnehmer mit dem Reiseleiter. Von da aus fährt die Gruppe mit dem Bus zum Park. Die Fahrt dauert nicht lange, und unterwegs sieht man viel Grünes.

FRAU SIEMENS: Was kostet die Reise insgesamt?

HERR BITTNER: Pro Person 500 Mark.

FRAU SIEMENS: Das ist günstig. Wir werden es uns überlegen. Ich sage Ihnen in zwei Tagen Bescheid. Den Koffer packe ich noch nicht. Ich hoffe, mein Freund ist damit einverstanden.

HERR BITTNER: Ich hoffe es auch. Bis dann. Auf Wiedersehen.

FRAU SIEMENS: Auf Wiedersehen.

Aktivität 5 Pläne für einen interessanten Urlaub

Dialog 1

NICOLA: Ja, guten Tag. Ich möchte bitte Information über italienische Sprachkurse für Reisende.

ANGESTELLTE: Was halten Sie von Sizilien?

NICOLA: Das wäre nicht schlecht. Sizilien soll traumhaft schön sein.

ANGESTELLTE: Sehen Sie, hier im Reiseprospekt: „Italienisch für Anfänger"—vier Wochen lang in der Nähe von Palermo. Sie fliegen von hier aus direkt nach Palermo.

NICOLA: Das klingt fantastisch. Aber ich möchte natürlich nicht nur arbeiten, sondern auch etwas von der Gegend sehen.

ANGESTELLTE: Der Unterricht findet am Morgen statt, die Nachmittage und Wochenenden stehen Ihnen zur freien Verfügung.

Dialog 2

ANGESTELLTER: Guten Tag. Kann ich Ihnen helfen?

MARIANNE: Wir suchen Urlaubstipps für einen Alternativurlaub. Wir interessieren uns nämlich für Meditation. Können Sie etwas vorschlagen?

ANGESTELLTER: Es gibt ein paar interessante Möglichkeiten. Hier ist zum Beispiel ein Angebot auf der griechischen Insel Korfu—eine Woche Meditationsurlaub mit Workshops.

ASTRID: Hm, Korfu und Meditation? Na, was meinst du, Marianne?

MARIANNE: Ich weiß noch nicht. Ich will es mir überlegen.

Dialog 3

ANGESTELLTE: Grüß Gott, kann ich Ihnen helfen?

SABINE: Wir haben vor, Urlaub in Alaska zu machen. Haben Sie Reiseprospekte über Alaska?

ANGESTELLTE: Natürlich. Alaska ist ein sehr beliebtes Ziel. Natur, spektakuläre Berge, Gletscher, Eisbären, um nur ein paar Sehenswürdigkeiten zu nennen. Wie lange wollen Sie insgesamt bleiben?

HERBERT: Zwei bis drei Wochen.

ANGESTELLTE: Hier ist ein Angebot für eine vierzehntägige Reise. Sie fliegen zuerst nach Anchorage. Von dort aus kommen Sie mit Bus und Schiff weiter.

SABINE: Haben Sie gesagt Eisbären? Davor habe ich aber Angst.

ANGESTELLTE: Keine Sorge! Das war nur im Spaß gemeint. Sie sehen sie höchstens aus der Ferne, wenn überhaupt.

Dialog 4

SEBASTIAN: Guten Tag. Ich möchte bitte Information über eine Studienreise nach Israel. Haben Sie einen Reiseprospekt?

ANGESTELLTER: Ich kann Ihnen den Studiosus-Prospekt geben.

SEBASTIAN: Ich interessiere mich sehr für die Kulturstätten in Israel.

ANGESTELLTER: Wie wäre es mit diesem Angebot: Felsendom, Ölberg, Klagemauer, Schwimmen im Toten Meer und Aufenthalt im Kibbuz.

SEBASTIAN: Das klingt ja alles sehr interessant.

ANGESTELLTER: Wie viel Zeit haben Sie?

SEBASTIAN: Drei Wochen. Können Sie die Reise noch heute buchen?

ANGESTELLTER: Selbstverständlich.

SEBASTIAN: Danke schön.

ANGESTELLTER: Bitte sehr.

Thema 3: Eine Fahrkarte, bitte!

MICHAEL: Eine Fahrkarte nach Hamburg, bitte.

BEAMTER: Hin und zurück?

MICHAEL: Nein, einfach, zweiter Klasse, bitte.

BEAMTER: Das macht 89 Mark. Das ist übrigens der Sparpreis für Jugendliche. Haben Sie Ihren Ausweis dabei?

MICHAEL: Ja, natürlich. Wann fährt denn der nächste Zug?

BEAMTER: In dreißig Minuten. In Hannover müssen Sie dann umsteigen.

MICHAEL: Habe ich da gleich Anschluss?

BEAMTER: Sie haben achtzehn Minuten Aufenthalt. Dann können Sie mit dem ICE weiter nach Hamburg fahren. Für den ICE müssen Sie allerdings noch einen Zuschlag bezahlen und einen Platz reservieren. Möchten Sie im Großraumwagen sitzen, oder lieber in einem Abteil?

MICHAEL: Lieber in einem Abteil. Nichtraucher, bitte. Wann komme ich in Hamburg an?

BEAMTER: Um 13 Uhr 56.

MICHAEL: Danke schön.

BEAMTER: Bitte sehr.

Aktivität 8 Am Fahrkartenschalter

Dialog 1

HERR BÖLL: Zwei Fahrkarten nach Hamburg, hin und zurück, erster Klasse.

HERR STEIN: Zweimal, hin und zurück. Das macht 375 Mark.

HERR BÖLL: Hat der Zug einen Speisewagen?

HERR STEIN: Ja.

HERR BÖLL: Ich möchte auch Platzkarten.

HERR STEIN: Raucher oder Nichtraucher?

HERR BÖLL: Nichtraucher.

Dialog 2

HERR FRANK: Ich möchte gern fünf Fahrkarten, hin und zurück, nach Salzburg.

FRAU BETZ: Alles Erwachsene?

HERR FRANK: Nein, zwei Erwachsene und drei Kinder.

FRAU BETZ: Kinder fahren zum halben Preis.

HERR FRANK: Gibt es ein Restaurant im Zug?

FRAU BETZ: Ja.

Dialog 3

FRAU SACHS: Einmal einfache Fahrt nach Bonn.

FRAU BETZ: Das macht 75 Mark.

FRAU SACHS: Und wann fährt der nächste Zug?

FRAU BETZ: In fünf Minuten fährt ein Zug nach Bonn.

FRAU SACHS: Danke, da muss ich mich aber beeilen.

Grammatik im Kontext

Übung 4 Werners Reisevorbereitungen

SEBASTIAN: Sag mal, Werner. Hast du eigentlich schon gepackt?

WERNER: Ach wo. Ich hatte einfach noch keine Zeit. Ich musste bis um sieben Uhr arbeiten.

SEBASTIAN: Wann fährt denn dein Zug?

WERNER: Morgen um vierzehn Uhr fünfzig. Übrigens kannst du mir einen Koffer leihen? Mein alter ist zu klein.

SEBASTIAN: Hast du schon alles für die Reise?

WERNER: Fast alles. Ich brauche noch Film für meine Kamera.

SEBASTIAN: Welche nimmst du mit?

WERNER: Die kleine. Sie nimmt nicht so viel Platz wie die Videokamera. Ich kann sie praktisch in meine Hosentasche stecken.

SEBASTIAN: Wie lange bleibst du weg?

WERNER: Insgesamt sechs Wochen.

SEBASTIAN: So eine lange Reise?

WERNER: Ja, so lange habe ich noch nie Urlaub gemacht.

Übung 17 Münchhausens Reise

Münchhausens Reise nach Russland begann im Winter. Er reiste mit Pferd und Wagen, weil das am bequemsten war. Leider trug er nur leichte Kleidung, und er fror sehr. Da sah Münchhausen eine alte Frau im Schnee. Er gab ihr etwas zu essen und ritt weiter. Er konnte leider kein Gasthaus finden. Er war müde und stieg vom Pferd ab. Dann band er das Pferd an einen Baumast im Schnee und legte sich hin. Er schlief tief und lange. Als Münchhausen am Morgen aufwachte, fand er sich mitten auf dem Marktplatz eines Dorfes. Wo aber war sein Pferd? Er konnte es über sich hören. Er schaute in die Höhe und sah sein Pferd vom Dach des Rathauses hängen. Was war passiert? Das Dorf war in der Nacht zugeschneit gewesen. In der Sonne war der Schnee geschmolzen. Der Baumast, an den Münchhausen sein Pferd gebunden hatte, war in Wirklichkeit die Spitze des Rathauses gewesen. Nun nahm er seine Pistole und schoss nach dem Halfter des Pferdes. Das Pferd landete ohne Schaden direkt neben Münchhausen. Dann reiste er weiter.

Kapitel 11

Alles klar?

B. INTERVIEWER: Frau Sommer, wie sind Sie darauf gekommen, Tierärztin zu werden?

GABRIELE: Schon als Kind habe ich mich sehr für Tiere interessiert. Ich bin zu Hause mit Hunden, Katzen, drei Kanarienvögeln, und sogar einem Pferd aufgewachsen. Meine Familie wohnte damals nämlich am Rande der Lüneburger Heide, und da hatten wir Kinder immer ein Reitpferd. In der Schule war ich in naturwissenschaftlichen Fächern immer am besten. Ich hatte Glück, denn ich habe nach dem Abitur sofort einen Studienplatz in Erlangen bekommen. In Tiermedizin bekommt man schon eher einen Studienplatz. Ich bin jetzt im letzten Studienjahr. Mein Traum ist eine eigene Praxis in einer Kleinstadt, aber das wird noch lange dauern.

Wörter im Kontext

Aktivität 1 Drei junge Leute

INTERVIEWERIN: Tina, was möchtest du beruflich tun?

TINA: Eigentlich möchte ich gerne im Freien arbeiten, als so etwas wie Landschaftsarchitektin oder als Gärtnerin. Ich habe keine Lust, Büroarbeit zu machen. Großes Ansehen zu haben oder viel Geld zu verdienen—das ist mir nicht wichtig.

INTERVIEWERIN: Und du, Markus? Was würde dich am meisten beruflich interessieren?

MARKUS: Am liebsten würde ich in meinem Beruf viel reisen und vielleicht sogar im Ausland arbeiten. Meine Tätigkeit soll abwechslungsreich sein. Mit Menschen zu tun haben—das gefällt mir.

INTERVIEWERIN: Und du, Andrea? Wofür interessierst du dich beruflich?

ANDREA: Ich arbeite gerne mit meinen Händen und interessiere mich für technische Sachen—wie zum Beispiel Maschinen. Computer interessieren mich auch—ich würde gern mit Computern arbeiten.

Aktivität 9 Ein Gespräch unter Freunden

GÜNTHER: Wie steht's denn mit deiner Suche nach einem Ausbildungsplatz? Hast du schon was gefunden?

PETRA: Ich habe noch nichts Definitives. Gestern war ich mal wieder beim Arbeitsamt.

GÜNTHER: Na, da kannst du lange warten, bevor die was für dich finden.

PETRA: Man kann nie wissen. Vor ein paar Tagen stand eine Anzeige in der Zeitung für Ausbildungsstellen für Laboranten.

GÜNTHER: Bei welcher Firma?

PETRA: Alpha Pharma. Die suchen Bewerber.

GÜNTHER: Muss man Abitur haben?

PETRA: Für die Ausbildung als Biologielaborantin braucht man Abitur. Aber für die Ausbildung zur Chemielaborantin braucht man nur Realschulabschluss.

GÜNTHER: Ist ja super. Hast du dich schon beworben?

PETRA: Ja, ich habe gleich meine Unterlagen eingeschickt, das Übliche: Lebenslauf, Foto und Zeugnisse.

GÜNTHER: Hast du schon mal angerufen?

PETRA: Nein, noch nicht. Wenn die Firma einen will, muss man noch einen Test machen.

GÜNTHER: Weißt du irgendetwas über die Firma?

PETRA: Nur, was in der Anzeige stand. Ich muss erst mal abwarten und sehen, ob sie mich zum Test einladen.

Grammatik im Kontext

Übung 8 Ein unkonventioneller Klub

SVEN: Was liest du denn da?

ANJA: Ein Buch.

SVEN: Na, das kann ich auch sehen! Was für ein Buch ist das denn?

ANJA: Es heißt *Das literarische Oktett.*

SVEN: Was für ein merkwürdiger Titel ist das denn?

ANJA: Das ist ein Buch, das acht Studenten geschrieben haben. Sie haben einen Klub der Dichter gegründet. Der Klub nennt sich auch „das literarische Oktett."

SVEN: Was für Gedichte schreiben sie denn? Komplizierte Gedichte, die kein Mensch verstehen kann?

ANJA: Nein, sie schreiben hauptsächlich kleine, freche Geschichten. Aber es gibt auch ein paar Gedichte im Buch.

SVEN: Über was für Themen schreiben die denn?

ANJA: Na, für was für Themen interessieren sich Studenten schon? Sex, Liebe, Studentenalltag, Essen, Trinken, und so weiter. Es ist alles recht provozierend, aber auch originell und unkonventionell.

SVEN: Ich möchte es auch mal lesen.

ANJA: Gut, wenn ich fertig bin, gebe ich es dir.

Kapitel 12

Alles klar?

B. INTERVIEWER: Jens, was bedeutet dir Geld?

JENS: Geld bedeutet für mich zwei Dinge: etwas für andere damit tun, aber auch etwas für mich selbst tun. Ich habe nicht viel, denn ich bin Student, aber wenn ich genug Geld hätte, würde ich einen Teil davon für medizinische Forschung spenden. Ich bin aber auch ein bisschen Egoist und würde mir vielleicht einen neuen Wagen oder eine neue Wohnung kaufen.

INTERVIEWER: Welche Bedeutung hat Geld für dich, Lucia?

LUCIA: Ja, ich meine auch, mit Geld muss man anderen Menschen helfen, besonders den Armen. Wenn ich Geld nur für mich ausgeben würde, würde ich wahrscheinlich weiter studieren—vielleicht im Ausland. Ich musste mein Studium unterbrechen, weil ich im Moment kein Geld habe. Später aber möchte ich vielleicht mein eigenes Geschäft aufmachen.

INTERVIEWER: Und für dich, Elke?

ELKE: Wenn ich viel Geld hätte, würde ich es bestimmt investieren. Ich würde einen langen Urlaub machen, aber dann würde ich wieder arbeiten. Wichtig für mich sind die Welthungerorganisationen—denen würde ich soviel Geld wie möglich geben.

Wörter im Kontext

Aktivität 2 Andreas Dilemma

ANDREA: Sag mal, könntest du mir einen Gefallen tun?

STEFAN: Was denn?

ANDREA: Würdest du mir bis Ende der Woche 50 Mark leihen? Ich bin total pleite.

STEFAN: Fünfzig Mark? Das ist viel Geld.

ANDREA: Ich musste 150 Mark für Bücher ausgeben. Und jetzt habe ich keinen Pfennig mehr übrig. Ich warte auf Geld von meinen Eltern.

STEFAN: Hm, ich würde es dir gern leihen. Aber 50 Mark habe ich selber nicht mehr. Ich kann dir höchstens 20 Mark leihen.

ANDREA: Ich zahle es dir bis Ende des Monats bestimmt zurück.

STEFAN: Eben hast du gesagt, bis Ende der Woche.

ANDREA: Ja, ja. Das Geld von meinen Eltern kann jeden Tag kommen.

STEFAN: Na gut. Hier ist ein Zwanziger.

ANDREA: Vielen Dank.

Aktivität 4 Einnahmen und Ausgaben

Dialog 1

INTERVIEWER: Woher bekommst du monatlich Geld, Stefanie?

STEFANIE: Hauptsächlich von meinen Eltern, aber während der Semesterferien arbeite ich und verdiene mir etwas Geld zum Studium.

INTERVIEWER: Als was arbeitest du denn?

STEFANIE: Gewöhnlich als Kellnerin. Während des Semesters habe ich aber keine Zeit zum Jobben.

INTERVIEWER: Und wo wohnst du?

STEFANIE: Ich habe Glück. Ich habe nämlich ein Zimmer im Studentenwohnheim. Da kostet die Miete nur 200 Mark im Monat.

Dialog 2

INTERVIEWER: Woher bekommst du monatlich Geld, Gert?

GERT: Ich bekomme BAföG. Und in den Semesterferien arbeite ich dann. Letztes Jahr habe ich bei der Post als Briefträger gearbeitet.

INTERVIEWER: Und wo wohnst du?

GERT: Ich wohne privat bei Bekannten von meinen Eltern. Ich habe da ein Zimmer.

INTERVIEWER: Und was musst du dafür bezahlen?

GERT: Es ist sehr günstig. Nur 300 Mark pro Monat. Das Haus liegt allerdings etwas außerhalb. Ich muss jeden Tag mit der U-Bahn zur Uni fahren.

Dialog 3

INTERVIEWER: Und wie finanzierst du dein Studium, Susanne?

SUSANNE: Meine Eltern unterstützen mich. Aber ich arbeite auch während des Semesters nebenbei.

INTERVIEWER: Was machst du denn?

SUSANNE: Ich gebe Englischunterricht. Ich habe drei Schüler.

INTERVIEWER: Und wo wohnst du?

SUSANNE: Ich wohne mit drei anderen Studentinnen in einer Wohngemeinschaft. Wir teilen uns die Miete für eine Vierzimmerwohnung. Jeder bezahlt 350 Mark im Monat.

Dialog 4

INTERVIEWER: Und nun zu Martin. Woher bekommst du Geld fürs Studium?

MARTIN: Ich bekomme Geld von meinen Eltern, aber es ist nicht genug. Ich muss also nebenbei arbeiten, auch während des Semesters und in den Semesterferien.

INTERVIEWER: Und wo wohnst du?

MARTIN: Seit letztem Jahr wohne ich in der Studentenstadt. Da habe ich eine kleine Wohnung. Die kostet nur 400 Mark.

Aktivität 5 Die ideale Wohnung

Dialog 1

INTERVIEWER: Frau Heine, Sie suchen eine Wohnung. Wie stellen Sie sich Ihre ideale Wohnung vor?

FRAU HEINE: Die Wohnung muss in der Innenstadt liegen. Ich arbeite nämlich dort. Ich möchte gern einen Neubau mit Zentralheizung. Ich bin gern an der frischen Luft. Deswegen muss meine Wohnung einen Balkon haben. Ich habe keinen Wagen. Eine Garage brauche ich deshalb nicht.

Dialog 2

INTERVIEWER: Ich spreche jetzt mit Herrn und Frau Zumwald aus Hannover. Herr und Frau Zumwald, was für eine Wohnung wäre für Sie und Ihre Kinder ideal?

HERR ZUMWALD: Wir suchen ein komfortables Haus außerhalb der Stadt. Wir brauchen einen großen Garten für unsere zwei Kinder und unseren Hund. Wir möchten gern ein älteres Haus, weil Altbauten oft gemütlicher sind. Allerdings muss das Haus Zentralheizung haben. Unwichtig ist uns, ob das Haus Teppichboden hat.

Dialog 3

INTERVIEWER: Meine Herren, Sie studieren hier an der Uni?

THOMAS: Ja. Meine zwei Freunde hier und ich suchen eine komfortable Altbauwohnung in der Innenstadt. Die Mietkosten dürfen natürlich nicht zu hoch sein. Wir haben alle Fahrräder. Deswegen ist eine Garage nicht so wichtig. Eine Waschmaschine im Haus ist wichtig, aber ein Teppichboden in der Wohnung interessiert uns überhaupt nicht. Aber ohne Zentralheizung möchten wir nicht sein. Die ist sehr wichtig.

Aktivität 9 Ist die Wohnung noch frei?

FRAU KRENZ: Hier Krenz.

HERR BRUNNER: Brunner. Guten Tag. Ich rufe wegen der Anzeige in der Zeitung an. Ist die Wohnung noch frei?

FRAU KRENZ: Ja, die ist noch frei.

HERR BRUNNER: Ich hätte einige Fragen. Ist Heizung in den Nebenkosten eingeschlossen?

FRAU KRENZ: Nein, Heizung ist extra.

HERR BRUNNER: In welchem Stock liegt die Wohnung?

FRAU KRENZ: Im vierten Stock.
HERR BRUNNER: Gibt es denn einen Aufzug im Haus?
FRAU KRENZ: Aber natürlich. Sind Sie allein stehend, oder haben Sie Familie?
HERR BRUNNER: Ich bin allein stehend. Kann ich mir die Wohnung mal ansehen?
FRAU KRENZ: Ja, gerne. Wann können Sie vorbeikommen?
HERR BRUNNER: Möglichst bald. Am besten direkt nach der Arbeit.
FRAU KRENZ: Schön, wie wäre es mit morgen so um 18.00 Uhr?
HERR BRUNNER: Das ist mir recht. Übrigens, bevor ich es vergesse, wie ist die Adresse?
FRAU KRENZ: Augustinerstraße 27. Es ist ganz leicht zu finden. Das Haus steht nämlich direkt gegenüber vom Museum.
HERR BRUNNER: Vielen Dank. Bis morgen dann. Auf Wiederhören.
FRAU KRENZ: Auf Wiederhören.

Kapitel 13

Alles klar?

B. Bericht 1
Bei einer Verkehrskontrolle in Cocoa Beach sprang ein 21jähriger Autodieb ins Meer und schwamm immer weiter raus. In voller Uniform schwang sich ein Polizist auf ein Surfbrett und hatte den Mann nach 10 Minuten eingeholt und als Ballast auf das Surfbrett gehoben.

Bericht 2
Im Südwesten Irans hat man ein unbekanntes Dorf entdeckt, das bisher auf keiner Karte verzeichnet ist. Die Bewohner leben ohne jeden Kontakt mit der modernen Zivilisation.

Bericht 3
Am schnellsten denkt der Mensch vor dem Mittagessen, fanden amerikanische Chronobiologen heraus. Wer also ein schwieriges Problem lösen muss, soll sich zwischen 11 und 12 Uhr damit befassen.

Bericht 4
Ein Mann im Gorillakostüm verteilte in den Straßen von Dallas, Texas, 6000 Dollar in 50-Dollar-Scheinen an Fußgänger. In einem Interview sagte er: „Ich mache das, um die erstaunten Gesichter der Menschen zu sehen, denen ich das Geld gebe. Das macht unheimlichen Spaß." Beim Interview trug er sein Gorillakostüm, seinen Namen gab er nicht preis.

Wörter im Kontext

Thema 1: Medien

Was gibt's denn im Fernsehen?

THOMAS: Was gibt's denn heute im Fernsehen?
BARBARA: Nach der Tagesschau kommt im ersten Programm um 21.00 Uhr eine Sendung mit Placido Domingo.
THOMAS: Oper? Das ist mir heute zu anstrengend. Was gibt es denn im zweiten Programm?
BARBARA: „Die Lindenstraße."
THOMAS: Ach, dieses Melodrama. Auch nichts Gescheites.
BARBARA: Aber „Die Lindenstraße" ist doch immer recht gut und spannend. Was möchtest du denn eigentlich sehen?
THOMAS: Na, vielleicht einen aktuellen Dokumentarfilm oder Sport.
BARBARA: „Der Sportpalast" kommt später um 23 Uhr 50. Ich möchte mir mal einen guten Spielfilm ansehen.
THOMAS: Hier ist das Filmprogramm für heute Abend. Such dir was aus!
BARBARA: Wie wäre es mit „Das Bildnis des Dorian Gray"?
THOMAS: So ein alter Schinken! Außerdem auch ein Melodrama.
BARBARA: Na und? Das ist auf jeden Fall ein guter, alter Klassiker.
THOMAS: Um 22 Uhr 15 läuft „Die letzte Schlacht" mit Burt Lancaster.
BARBARA: Das ist mal wieder so ein Kriegsfilm. So was habe ich gründlich satt.
THOMAS: Also, „Dorian Gray" dann. Wovon handelt er übrigens? . . .

Grammatik im Kontext

Übung 7 Immer diese Ausreden

Dialog 1
PETER: Du, Jan, hier ist Peter.
JAN: Grüß dich, Peter.
PETER: Also, ich kann heute Abend leider nicht mit ins Kino. Ich muss noch für morgen eine Arbeit fertig schreiben und 150 Seiten Psychologie lesen. Außerdem ist mein Wagen kaputt.
JAN: Schade, aber mach dir weiter keine Sorgen. Bis demnächst dann. Tschüs.
PETER: Tschüs, bis bald.

Dialog 2
JENS: Hier Jens Hertling. Ist Herr Professor Hauser in seinem Büro?
SEKRETÄR: Nein, er hat heute keine Sprechstunde.
JENS: Würden Sie ihm bitte sagen, dass ich meine Seminararbeit heute nicht einreichen kann. Meine Mutter ist nämlich krank, und ich muss sie ins Krankenhaus bringen.
SEKRETÄR: Ich werde es ihm ausrichten. Auf Wiederhören.

Dialog 3
KARIN: Sag mal, Ursula, kannst du mir vielleicht die 50 Mark zurückzahlen, die ich dir vor drei Wochen geliehen habe?
URSULA: Oh, das tut mir leid. Ich kann dir das Geld aber heute leider noch nicht zurückzahlen. Ich erwarte morgen einen Scheck von meinen Eltern. Ich bringe dir das Geld morgen Abend.
KARIN: Schön. Bis morgen Abend dann.
URSULA: Wiedersehen.

Kapitel 14

Alles klar?

C. Seminar 1

In diesem Seminar werden verschiedene Ursachen der Vergiftung untersucht. Der Schwerpunkt liegt auf Ursachen der Magenvergiftung. Heutzutage vermehren sich allergische Reaktionen auf Nahrungsmittel sowie auf die Umwelt dramatisch. Insbesondere wird in diesem Seminar das Thema Giftreaktionen im Magen behandelt.

Seminar 2

In den letzten zehn Jahren hat die Zahl der Gewalttaten drastisch zugenommen. Im Fernsehen und in den Zeitungen wird das Thema heiß debattiert. Dieses Seminar befasst sich mit der steigenden Gewaltbereitschaft von Jugendlichen und Kindern und dem Zulauf zu rechtsextremen Gruppen.

Seminar 3

Die Umweltbelastung durch Luftverschmutzung und Lärm ist das Hauptthema dieses Seminars. Weiter wird untersucht, wie man durch Verkehrsplanung und die Entwicklung umweltfreundlicher Verkehrsmittel die Autoabgase und insgesamt die Verkehrsbelästigung in den Innenstädten reduzieren kann.

Seminar 4

Dieses Seminar behandelt als Hauptthema menschliche Grundrechte und Freiheiten und wie sie in verschiedenen Ländern interpretiert werden. Die Lektüre für das Seminar besteht hauptsächlich aus Dokumenten und Berichten von Amnesty International und von der Weltkonferenz über Menschenrechte, die in Wien stattfand.

Wörter im Kontext

Thema 1: Globale Probleme

FRAU MAYER: Ich bin der Meinung, dass Obdachlosigkeit ein viel größeres Problem ist, als wir allgemein glauben.

HERR SACHS: Das halte ich für übertrieben. Das ist nur in Großstädten ein Problem, aber nicht hier bei uns in Kleinlichterhagen.

FRAU BECKER: Im Park an der Hauptstraße schlafen aber regelmäßig Leute auf den Bänken, und am Bahnhof sitzen auch welche, die nicht wissen wohin. Und . . .

HERR GRÜNKRAUT: Ja, und die sind so schmutzig, lassen überall ihren Dreck. Außerdem sind die meisten drogensüchtig. Es ist ein Skandal, dass unsere Regierung bis jetzt keine Lösung gefunden hat. Wofür zahlen wir eigentlich unsere Steuern?

HERR SPITZ: So ein Quatsch!.

FRAU RAST: Meiner Meinung nach hat die Regierung gute Fortschritte gemacht.

FRAU HOFFMAN: Ich finde, man sollte unbedingt Unterkunft für die Obdachlosen in unserer Stadt finden. Meines Erachtens sollte man sie in Privatzimmern unterbringen.

FRAU NIKOLAI: Ich hoffe, Sie haben ein Zimmer frei! Ich bin nämlich total dagegen. Ich bin dafür, dass mehr Sozialbauwohnungen gebaut werden.

HERR SPITZ: So ein Unsinn!

FRAU LIESCHE: Ich bedaure, dass wir alle ohne Konzept um das Thema herum reden. Ich schlage vor, dass wir eine konkrete Strategie entwickeln. Nur so kann das Problem gelöst werden.

FRAU HOFFMANN: Was wohl die Obdachlosen über unsere Diskussion sagen würden!!!

HERR SPITZ: Das ist mir egal!

Aktivität 2 Probleme in der Stadt

INTERVIEWER: Was halten Sie für das größte Problem?

SPRECHER 1: Das größte Problem ist der Verkehr. Wir wohnen etwas außerhalb der Stadt. Der Verkehr in der Stadt wird jährlich immer stärker. Früher haben wir fast eine Stunde mit Fahren und im Stau auf der Landstraße verbracht. Da kam man schon genervt zur Arbeit. Seit etwa einem halben Jahr parken wir unseren Wagen am Rande der Stadt und nehmen von dort einen Bus in die Innenstadt.

SPRECHERIN 2: Der Staat investiert zu viel Geld in die Forschung von Atomenergie. Jetzt soll hier in der Nähe ein neues Atomkraftwerk gebaut werden. Aber niemand kann garantieren, dass wir nicht eines Tages ein Tschernobyl-Unglück bei uns haben. Ich finde, der Staat soll mehr Geld in die Forschung für alternative Energie stecken, zum Beispiel Windenergie. Wind haben wir doch genug hier.

SPRECHER 3: Wir wohnen in der Nähe des Flughafens. Der ständige Lärm durch die Flugzeuge, die hier landen, ist unerträglich geworden. Den ganzen Tag hören wir über unseren Dächern die Flugzeuge. Man könnte die Zahl der Flugzeuge reduzieren. Aber die Fluggesellschaften haben eine starke Lobby.

SPRECHERIN 4: Ich mache mir Sorgen um die Qualität unserer Nahrungsmittel, besonders Obst und Gemüse. Da hört man, wie immer stärkere Pestizide für Gemüse und Obst verwendet werden. Und das Fleisch ist auch voller Giftstoffe. Man sollte diese Sachen streng vom Staat kontrollieren lassen und viele Pestizide verbieten.

Aktivität 5 Langsamer, bitte!

JENNIFER: Sag mal, fliegen wir eigentlich oder fahren wir?

ANDREAS: Wieso?

JENNIFER: Wie kannst du mit 200 Sachen durch die Landschaft fahren? Mir stehen die Haare zu Berge.

ANDREAS: Keine Angst. Mein BMW schafft das spielend. Der liegt doch wie ein Brett auf der Straße.

JENNIFER: Ich bin an so ein Tempo nicht gewöhnt. Bei uns ist die Höchstgeschwindigkeit nur etwa 105 km pro Stunde.

ANDREAS: Dann kann man ja gleich zu Fuß gehen.

JENNIFER: Zu Fuß gehen würde weniger Abgase verursachen. Und bei dieser Raserei verbraucht man auch viel mehr Benzin.

ANDREAS: Das ist alles übertrieben. Und außerdem ist mein Wagen für hohe Geschwindigkeiten gebaut.

JENNIFER: Du, schau mal, da ist ein Schild über der Autobahn: Höchstgeschwindigkeit 100 km.

ANDREAS: Wahrscheinlich eine Baustelle in der Nähe.

JENNIFER: Also doch ein Tempolimit. Gott sei Dank. Bei 100 km fühle ich mich direkt wie zu Hause.